THE LIGHT OF THY COUNTENANCE

VOLUME TWO

STUDIES IN THE HISTORY

OF

CHRISTIAN THOUGHT

EDITED BY

HEIKO A. OBERMAN, Tucson, Arizona

IN COOPERATION WITH
ROBERT J. BAST, Knoxville, Tennessee
HENRY CHADWICK, Cambridge
BRIAN TIERNEY, Ithaca, New York
ARJO VANDERJAGT, Groningen

VOLUME XCVIII

STEVEN P. MARRONE

THE LIGHT OF THY COUNTENANCE

VOLUME TWO

THE LIGHT OF THY COUNTENANCE

SCIENCE AND KNOWLEDGE OF GOD IN THE THIRTEENTH CENTURY

VOLUME TWO

GOD AT THE CORE OF COGNITION

BY

STEVEN P. MARRONE

BRILL

LEIDEN · BOSTON · KÖLN

2001

This book is printed on acid-free paper.

Library of Congress Cataloging-in-Publication Data

Marrone, Steven P., 1947-
  The light of Thy countenance : science and knowledge of God in the thirteenth century / by Steven P. Marrone.
    p.   cm. — (Studies in the history of Christian thought, ISSN
  0081–8607 ; v. 98)
    Includes bibliographical references (v. 2, p.) and indexes.
    Contents: v. 1. A doctrine of divine illumination—Gods at the core of
    cognition.
    ISBN 9004119477 (set : alk. paper)
    1. Knowledge, Theory of (Religion)—History. 2. God—Knowableness—
    History of doctrines. 3. Religion and science—History. 4. Thirteenth
    century. I. Title. II. Series.
  BT50 .M28   2000
  261.5'5'09022—dc21
                                                            00–046862
                                                            CIP

Die Deutsche Bibliothek - CIP-Einheitsaufnahme

Marrone, Steven P.:
The light of thy countenance : science and knowledge of god in the
thirteenth century / by Steven P. Marrone. – Leiden ; Boston ; Köln :
Brill
      (Studies in the history of Christian thought ; Vol. 98)
      ISBN 90–04–11947–7

Vol. 2. God at the core of cognition. - 2001

ISSN   0081-8607
ISBN   90 04 11947 7 (set)

PRINTED IN THE NETHERLANDS

CONTENTS

VOLUME ONE

A DOCTRINE OF DIVINE ILLUMINATION

PART ONE

BIRTHPANGS OF A PHILOSOPHICAL DISCUSSION 1210–1245

ROBERT GROSSETESTE AND WILLIAM OF AUVERGNE

PART TWO

THE CLASSIC AUGUSTINIANS 1250–1280

BONAVENTURE, GILBERT OF TOURNAI, JOHN PECHAM AND
MATTHEW OF AQUASPARTA

VOLUME TWO

GOD AT THE CORE OF COGNITION

INTRODUCTION TO VOLUME TWO

This book has two subjects. One concerns the deepening impress of an Aristotelian and apodictic model of science on thirteenth-century Scholasticism, specifically mounting insistence on assimilating modes of explication to logical rules of argument and impatience with analysis straying far from concrete operations in the natural world. The subject here is approached obliquely by examining how such a model was accommodated in an academic arena where more than speculative concerns were at work, some of religious and devotional import potentially hostile to the aspirations of the new science. The second subject has to do with the history of an Augustinian current throughout the same hundred years. Occasion for considering this current is the emergence of a doctrine of divine illumination in the wayfarer's cognition and that doctrine's subsequent fate in the hands of ostensibly sympathetic scholastics. But the narrative subtext bears more broadly on the question of schools of scholastic thought, not just whether it is legitimate to suppose such schools existed but also how they might be characterized, assuming that they did.

The decision to develop these two themes simultaneously relies upon the conviction that an Augustinian school can be identified for the thirteenth century, one conceding the importance of the new ideal of scientific argumentation but retaining a special regard for attitudes threatened by the penetration of the apodictic model and its accompanying worldliness into all fields of thought. Yet a fundamental assumption of this book as well is that the identity of the Augustinian school, indeed of any of the "schools" often proposed for the thirteenth century, cannot be located by applying specifically doctrinal criteria. The general drift of the thirteenth century towards consensus about descriptions of mind that counted as plausible and the epistemic parameters of the problem of truth practically ensured that doctrinal differences among competing groups of intellectuals would be eroded over time. They would require reconfiguration if lines of divergence were to be preserved and extended.

Of course, the precise dimensions of the latter phenomenon, because investigated here with regard to merely the notion of intellectual illumination of the wayfarer by God, can only be approximated by extrapolation even with regard to the profile of a single school. But limited as the evidence presented may be, it suggests a general picture that is credible and could readily be tested with reference to other presumed marks of Augustinianism as well.

Volume 1 has chronicled the gradual condensation of an Augustinian core, culminating in the emergence of an authentic doctrine of divine illumination by the third quarter of the thirteenth century. The "classic" Augustinians, Bonaventure and his followers John Pecham and Matthew of Aquasparta, managed to bring together traditional themes of largely Neoplatonic inspiration into a structure of noetics and epistemology calibrated to meet contemporary expectations for science while still upholding Augustinian values about knowledge, mind and the wayfarer's relation to God. Their achievement could well serve as ideal type for the notion of divine illumination adopted by conventional historical accounts of Augustinianism in the high Middle Ages.

The theoretical construct they produced is presented above as a composite of elements serving four discrete functions, each of which followed a separate path both before and after Bonaventure and his admirers brought them together.[1] First and most emblematic was the association of divine cognitive light with a normative epistemic intervention whereby mind was enabled to separate truth from falsehood, or at least sharpen a perception of truth it had already gained. Second came Godly illumination in the mainly noetic guise of contributory source of simple concepts to mind, entailing potentially a divine element in the referential conditions of much of normal human knowledge. Third, though somewhat less centrally, there was the weaving of God's light into the explanation of how some truths could be immutable. Last was the connection between the image of divinity radiating into mind and human knowledge of God in the state of sin, a thread of analysis sometimes extending beyond death to beatitude.

Special about the classic Augustinians was not only the fact that they turned to a notion of divine illumination to account for every one of the four functions but also that they seemed to have the same process in mind whenever, for each function, they spoke about the

---

[1] Refer to the initial discussion of these functions in the introduction to Part 1, pp. 33–34.

action of God's light. In these two peculiarities lies the essence of what it means to say that for them there existed a genuine *doctrine* of divine illumination, not just a congeries of invocations of an illuminative operation throughout epistemology and noetics.

Yet the appearance of this doctrine on the academic scene shortly after mid-thirteenth century, striking sign of extraordinary developments in the tenor of university discourse, was also short-lived. Already by the 1270s even masters whose support might have been expected were finding contradictions within it and inconsistencies with the general rules of scientific exposition in line with which it had originally been advanced. In less than a decade efforts were afoot to resolve the problems. Such efforts rescued the noetic and epistemological heritage of Augustine from a surely suicidal collision with the ideals of apodictic truth. But by formally separating the functional elements the classic Augustinians had consolidated, refashioning some of them so as to engage less explicitly a mechanism of illumination arising from God, the rescue shattered the theoretical unity so recently acquired.

From the late 1270s on, the story of divine illumination therefore ceases being that of a coherent doctrine and reverts to the tale of a collection of theories related more by image and evocation than philosophical intent. And that spells the end of any potential for uncovering doctrinal continuity in a presumed Augustinian school. Still, the Augustinian current did not expire with the demise of the classic ideal of illumination. Nor did all the functional applications of the notion of God's light disappear from theory of mind cultivated by masters with a loyalty to Bonaventure's and his followers' attempt to fashion a peculiarly Augustinian brand of thought. Volume 2 takes up this narrative, once the unified doctrine of divine illumination was on its way out but while the spirit animating it was yet very much alive.

Part 3, on the third stage in illumination's thirteenth-century career, chronicles the efforts of the classic Augustinians' immediate successors to retain the religious and devotional resonances of their thinking, especially the sense of God's intimacy to mind, while taking steps to erase the residues of ontologism that criticism of the classic position had laid bare. The story revolves almost exclusively around Henry of Ghent in the 1270s and 1280s, though attention must also be given to his younger contemporary Vital du Four and the somewhat later Richard of Conington. Key is the theoretical divorce of

guaranteeing knowledge of truth from the function of providing a
source for ideas, and severance of the latter from connection to the
literal notion of God as offering intelligible illumination.

The fourth stage, told in Part 4, turns to masters responding more
to Henry than to the classic Augustinians themselves, readier than
Henry to abandon the specifics of illumination but responsive to the
same desire to stress the cognitive intimacy of God. Evident, therefore, is still a fundamental loyalty to Augustinian inspiration, but
now with no tolerance for even the slightest awkwardness entailed
by the classic doctrinal structure. From 1290 to the first years of the
fourteenth century, William of Ware and John Duns Scotus confidently
laid out a theory of knowledge and of mind with not so much as a
hint of the offending attributes of earlier illumination theory. It displayed all the while deep structural parallels with the preceding ideal's
approach to the relation between intellect and God.

As might be expected, the change in complexion of the story from
Volume 1 to Volume 2 brings with it a shift in method as well.
Examination of Augustinian attitudes towards knowledge and illumination in the decades from William of Auvergne and Robert
Grosseteste through Matthew of Aquasparta necessarily dwelt upon
synthetic efforts to integrate functions and draw relations among
them. Those were after all years when Augustinians grew to recognize the utility of presenting their ideas in systematic form, most
striking manifestation of which was the emergence of a doctrine of
divine illumination. From Henry of Ghent through Duns Scotus the
posture towards illumination was, in contrast, critical of a doctrine
already put forward. Because of this new coloration, the developmental dynamics at work in these later stages are less amenable to
description in narrative mode, more difficult to analyze in typically
linear historiographical fashion. There is, however, compensation in
the fact that the philosophical issues at play are more nuanced and
complex. Among the most prominent of these is the problem of
invention, the challenge of moving from a critique of materials at
hand to novel formulation of issues or explanations, or both at once,
productive of an acceptable resolution.

Of course, to save the notion of intellectual school in such a milieu
requires a different ideal type, or perhaps a different approach to
recognizing affiliations and similarities. Volume 2 thus covers a ter-
ritory where the alternative mode of conceiving schools advanced in

the introduction can be put to the test, because it is that mode alone which holds out promise of saving the notion of schools in such turbulent intellectual waters.[2] It is as a set of undercurrents of allegiance, and not lines of doctrinal agreement, that Augustinianism goes forth into the early fourteenth century.

---

[2] On this non-doctrinal notion of schools of thought, consult the Introduction, p. 15.

PART THREE

A PARTING OF THE WAYS 1275–1295
HENRY OF GHENT AND VITAL DU FOUR

INTRODUCTION TO PART THREE

The accomplishments of Bonaventure, John Pecham and Matthew of Aquasparta are obvious. During the three decades from 1250 to 1280 they succeeded in fabricating an integrated doctrine of divine illumination out of divergent strands of Augustinian, broadly Neoplatonic and Aristotelian inspiration present in the eclectic writings of theologians from the second quarter of the century. Partial products of a wider effort to erect a system of consciously Augustinianizing thought, the epistemology and noetics embedded in this illuminationist theory have come to be regarded as emblematic of a conservative vein in thirteenth-century Scholasticism.

Yet the classic Augustinian synthesis, impressive though it was, would not long endure. Already in the later years of Matthew of Aquasparta's magisterium it was beginning to dissolve. Bonaventure's and his followers' efforts at system-building were, after all, not unique, and the emergence of philosophical schools, a fortiori of coherent doctrines like the theory of illumination, was a phenomenon of wider scope than the history of medieval Augustinianism. If Franciscans brought the energy and discipline of their young order to bear on Neoplatonizing traditions of the Latin West and newly emergent strains of Aristotelianism, imposing system on chaos, it can be argued that Dominicans did them one better, even quicker to bring their efforts to fruition. To many minds in the decades of the 1260s and 1270s Thomas Aquinas was the systematizer par excellence, the thinker with whom "philosophy" came of age.

The appearance of competing systems of thought and the philosophically meticulous attitudes giving birth to them did much to unsettle the atmosphere at the universities, so that along with the enthusiasm of the first decades after mid-century came an increase in what can only be called intellectual anxiety. Academic politics had always been highly charged, but as philosophy became more serious business, the consequences of philosophizing grew to be regarded more soberly, at times with fear. The faculty of theology, most eminent of those at Paris, was particularly alarmed, first in the 1260s at the aggressive posture of some of those teaching in arts

and then in the 1270s even at the speculation of leading Aristotelianizers within its own ranks, Thomas among them.[1] A series of
Parisian condemnations, one in 1270 and another in 1277, echoed
by a condemnation at Oxford in 1277 and another two in 1284 and
1286, were only the most obvious signs of consternation. At Paris
in 1277 formal processes of investigation were initiated in the theology faculty probably against the now-dead Thomas and surely
against his very much alive champion, Giles of Rome, while at
Oxford in the years immediately following 1284, Archbishop Pecham –
Bonaventure's former student – engaged in what can fairly be described
as an all-out attack on Thomists in the Dominican Order.

In such an atmosphere, the integrity of any system of thought
would be put to the test. Critics abounded, ready to hammer away
at the slightest fissure in an intellectual edifice with hopes of break-
ing the whole apart. Ironically it was the Thomists, hardest hit by
their often partisan critics, who were best at keeping their system –
or, more precisely, systems – intact. The ostensibly more traditional
vision of Bonaventure, Pecham and Matthew did not survive.

Still, the short life of the classic Augustinian synthesis cannot be

---

[1] On the condemnations of the 1270s and 1280s, see, for a start, Roland Hissette,
Enquête sur les 219 articles condamnés à Paris le 7 mars 1277 (Leuven, 1977); and the
lucid introduction to Thomas by Simon Tugwell in Albert and Thomas, *Selected
Writings*, ed. Simon Tugwell (New York, 1988), pp. 226–32 and 236–44. Following
Hissette's work, there has been increasing debate about the real target and even
the exact events in 1277. Here, especially with regard to Thomas and Giles of
Rome, one must begin with Robert Wielockx's "Commentaire" to Giles of Rome's
Apologia, Aegidii Romani Opera Omnia, 3, 1, Unione Accademia Nazionale, Corpus
Philosophorum Medii Aevi, Testi e Studi, 4 (Florence, 1985), pp. 67–225; and his
"Autour du procès de Thomas d'Aquin," in *Thomas von Aquin. Werk und Wirkung im
Licht neuerer Forschungen*, ed. Albert Zimmermann, Miscellanea Mediaevalia, 19 (Berlin,
1988), pp. 413–38. Important, too, are Ludwig Hödl, "Neue Nachrichten über die
Pariser Verurteilungen der thomasischen Formlehre," *Scholastik* 39 (1964): 178–96;
John F. Wippel, "The Condemnations of 1270 and 1277 at Paris," *The Journal of
Medieval and Renaissance Studies* 7 (1977): 169–201; "Thomas Aquinas and the
Condemnation of 1277," *The Modern Schooman* 72 (1995): 233–72; and "Bishop
Stephen Tempier and Thomas Aquinas. A Separate Process Against Aquinas?"
Freiburger Zeitschrift für Philosophie und Theologie 44 (1997): 117–36; Roland Hissette,
"L'implication de Thomas d'Aquin dans les censures parisiennes de 1277," *Recherches
de Théologie et Philosophie Médiévales* 64 (1997): 3–31; and Johannes M.M.H. Thijssen,
Censure and Heresy at the University of Paris 1200–1400 (Philadelphia, 1998), especially
ch. 2, pp. 40–56. Finally, for entrée to the interesting speculations of Luca Bianchi
on the significance of 1277, see his "1277. A Turning Point in Medieval Philosophy?"
in *Was ist Philosophie im Mittelalter*, eds. Jan A. Aertsen and Andreas Speer, Akten
des X. Internationalen Kongresses für mittelalterlichen Philosophie, Miscellanea
Mediaevalia, 26 (Berlin, 1998), pp. 90–110.

attributed solely to the fierceness of external opposition. Dominican scholars sympathetic to Thomas, the most likely detractors of the Augustinians, were at first too busy defending their own doctrines to mount a full-scale attack on those of the Franciscans arrayed against them. Instead Bonaventure's, Pecham's and Matthew's creation fell largely of its own weight, among friends, with the most corrosive criticism coming from minds sympathetic to the general philosophical attitudes it promoted.

Classic Augustinian doctrines were simply too fragile for the world of late thirteenth-century thought. Bonaventure and his followers had made a heroic effort to translate what they considered the essential core of Christian speculation into the idiom of high medieval Scholasticism. They had respected the novel demands for technical precision and the Aristotelianizing call for explaining natural phenomena in terms of concrete processes in the world, all the while, in accordance with the canons of the day, striving for systematic coherence. Yet vast areas of their thought appeared to possess a unity more contrived than real, the rhetoric of tradition overlying philosophical images and analytical devices that sounded collectively discordant and seemed individually unfit to withstand scrutiny in the harsh light of the new Aristotelianizing world.[2] If an Augustinian program was to succeed – if place was to be made in high-medieval Scholasticism for a system of thought defiantly bearing witness to the spirit of the Augustinian and Neoplatonic vision as Bonaventure, Pecham and Matthew had conceived it – then the whole structure would have to be redesigned. A new plan would have to be drafted to specifications this time indisputably conforming to the requirements for technical precision and Aristotelianizing worldliness current in the schools. Nothing less was required than another Augustinian synthesis, even more relentlessly detailed, concrete and systematic – philosophical in Van Steenberghen's rigorous sense – than classical Augustinianism had been.

---

[2] Modern scholarly discussion of this issue goes back again to Gilson's seminal article from 1934, "Sur quelques difficultés," cited above, general introduction, n. 37. Patrick J. Doyle, *The Disintegration of Divine Illumination Theory in the Franciscan School, 1285–1300: Peter of Trabes, Richard of Middleton, William of Ware* (Ph.D. diss., Marquette University, 1983/Ann Arbor [University Microfilms], 1984), pp. 13–15, offers a nice statement of the problem, quoting notable passages from Gilson's article as well as from his *History of Christian Philosophy* and David Knowles's *Evolution of Medieval Thought*.

Nowhere was this clearer than with the doctrine of divine illumination. The theoretical components from which the classic doctrine had been built, dealing in turn with the divine role in humankind's knowledge of truth, the primary objects of its intellection and the origin in mind of a number of special concepts, including that of God, had always carried a danger of ontologism. How could intellect have recourse to something divine as normative standard or ultimate object or conceptual foundation without seeing divinity itself? Bringing the discrete elements together, by reinforcing the doubts each piece engendered on its own, only magnified the threat, calling for heroic effort to show how the doctrine could be defended without drawing in God as direct object of the wayfarer's mind. By the 1270s even sympathizers were concluding that the labors of Bonaventure, Pecham and Matthew were insufficient, and the revision of their work among those of Augustinian temperament had begun.

The dominant voice in the revisionist current was that of Henry of Ghent. He advanced an interpretation of knowledge and mind that, for all its debt to the classic Augustinianism of the decades preceding, was distinctly different and, along with the novel understanding of divine illumination it promoted, rapidly won the field among thinkers valuing Augustine's special emphasis on intimacy between God and intellect. For the rest of the thirteenth century and some of the fourteenth as well, his ideas were those typically associated with Augustinian thought.

What Henry did was to prolong the life of the notion of divine illumination in normal human cognition, only recently codified in a coherent doctrine by the classic Augustinians, but at the price of cleaving in two the seamless structure his immediate predecessors had so painstakingly contrived. He accomplished this in effect by drawing a clear theoretical line separating the normative action of divine illumination as guarantor of certitude from noetic matters concerning divinity's role in ideogenesis and attendant questions of reference and an objective ontological ground. With this simple maneuver he managed to retain the paradigmatic Augustinian notion that knowing truth required an infusion of light from divinity and yet, by avoiding the suggestion that such illumination implicated mind in knowing God, insulate himself from charges of ontologism. From his perspective, the set of issues regarding the cognitive object, especially in sensitive cases concerning special concepts like first intentions, had to be kept apart from discussion of illumination most typically speaking, regarded in fact as dependent on an entirely different mental process.

One might suppose this meant reverting to the eclecticism and ideological imprecision of William of Auvergne and Robert Grosseteste, where a variety of approaches to divine intervention in normal human understanding were not bound up in an integrated whole, but such was not the case. Henry was even more responsive to the systematizing and Aristotelianizing demands of late thirteenth-century Scholasticism than Bonaventure, Pecham and Matthew had been. When he split the classic doctrine of illumination in two, it was to insure that his full account of knowledge was more precise, more concrete and more coherent than anything Augustinians had come up with before.

Equally important, his success in realizing this philosophical program depended on preserving one of the most significant ideological advances the classic Augustinians had made. Besides combining the role of divine light as revealer of truth with its function in ideogenesis – the move Henry's theoretical fastidiousness led him to reject – their unified doctrine of divine illumination had contrived to absorb William's and Robert's vision of a dynamic naturally inclining mind towards God as ultimate cognitive goal, the most dramatic result of which was their theory of the wayfarer's natural knowledge of divinity in a general concept of being. To this achievement Henry remained steadfastly true, continuing to tie the ideogenic and referential conditions of mind's understanding of fundamental concepts to a sense of its inclination into God as authentic object and on this basis erecting a theory of natural knowledge of God in first intentions. Given his strict separation between the truth-giving process of divine illumination and the mechanics of God's role in generating concepts, he could in fact spin out the theory with less fear of the ontologizing pitfalls his predecessors had struggled to avoid. Confidence in mind's intimate access to God, heretofore bound either to the paradigmatic illuminationist image for knowing truth or the mystical conception of the *via contemplativa*, could thus be completely transferred to a notion of God as natural object of intellect, a philosophical figure free of the ontologist odors of much of preceding Augustinian noetics and epistemology but still redolent of the devotional tradition in which illuminationist language had flourished.

Henry's modulation of the Augustinian heritage did not in fact stop there, for his mature ideas once more reconfigured, virtually to

the point of doing away with them altogether, the theoretical boundaries he had worked to erect early in his career – particularly between
analysis of knowledge of truth and philosophical justification for knowing God in the concept of being. Yet from first to last, his pronouncements on these matters confirmed the precariousness of the
classic Augustinians' views, marking the beginnings of a new direction
in the Augustinian current of high medieval thought. His initial insistence on radically distinguishing God as light of truth from God
as object to be known thus inaugurated a third stage in the history
of the developmental processes with which this study is concerned.

The history of this third stage is largely the story of Henry's speculations alone, because for all the resonance his ideas found in scholastic debates during the decades before and after his death, few
thinkers adopted them with any inclination to reproduce authentically the intellectual vision from which they had originally sprung.
Henry more readily stimulated reaction than adherence. Yet he did
have his followers, some so slavish as to repeat him word for word
with minimal elaboration or comment, and two are worth looking
at, the few occasions when they advanced beyond him sometimes
clarifying ambiguities in his thought or confirming the interpretation
of debatable points. If there can be no certainty such glosses on
Henry's ideas accurately represent his intentions, they at least reveal
how he was understood by sympathetic minds among his contemporaries and immediate successors.

Interestingly enough, this third stage of development brings us for
a moment back out of the world of exclusively Franciscan theologians. Henry was a secular priest, canon at two wealthy sees in
Flanders and vigorous opponent of the privileges of the mendicant
orders in the acrimonious debates about them in late thirteenth-
century Paris.[3] He incepted in theology at Paris in 1276, assuming
one of the secular chairs at the university, where he taught and wrote

---

[3] Henry probably studied at the cathedral school of Tournai. By 1277 he was
archdeacon of Bruges and in 1278 or 1279 was appointed to the same office at
Tournai. On his role in the political struggle over the privileges granted the men-
dicants by Martin IV's bull of 1281, see Heinrich Finke, "Das Pariser Nationalkonzil
vom Jahre 1290," *Römische Quartalschrift* 9 (1895): 171–82; Léopold Delisle, "Das
Pariser Nationalkonzil vom Jahre 1290," *Journal des Savants* (1895): 240–44; Palémon
Glorieux, "Prélats français contre religieux mendiants. Autour de la Bulle 'Ad fruc-
tus uberes,'" *Revue d'Histoire de l'Eglise de France* 11 (1925): 309–31, 471–95; Raymond
Macken, "Ein wichtiges Ineditum zum Kampf über das Beichtprivilegium des
Bettelorden: der 'Tractatus super facto praelatorum et fratrum' des Heinrich von
Gent," FS 60 (1978): 301–310; and most importantly Ludwig Hödl's "Theologiege-

in the theology faculty almost without interruption till near his death in 1293.[4] In 1277 Bishop Tempier named him to the commission of masters appointed to scrutinize doctrines being taught at the university for their orthodoxy, the report of which most likely served as basis for Tempier's condemnation of 219 propositions that same year.[5] He was, in a word, a leading light in the conservative constellation arrayed against the reputedly extreme Aristotelianism of such as Thomas and, even more, a circle of the radicals in the Faculty of Arts.[6]

---

schichtliche Einführung" to Henry of Ghent, *Tractatus super facto praelatorum et fratrum*, ed. Ludwig Hödl and Marcel Haverals, Henrici Opera, 17 (Leuven, 1989), pp. vii–cxvii.

[4] It is possible that Henry was not at Paris during the academic year 1283–84. The critical reconstruction of his biography began with Franz Ehrle, "Beiträge zu den Biographen berühmter Scholastiker: Heinrich von Gent," *Archiv für Literatur- und Kirchengeschichte des Mittelalters* 1 (1885): 365–401, 507–8 (translated into French by J. Raskop as "Recherches critiques sur la biographie de Henri de Gand dit le Docteur Solennel," *Bulletins de la Société Historique et Littéraire de Tournai* 21, suppl. [1887]: 7–51). For scholarly progress on the subject since then, see Hippolyte Delehaye, "Nouvelles recherches sur Henri de Gand," *Messager des Sciences Historiques ou Archives des Arts et de la Bibliographie de Belgique* (1886): 328–55, 438–55, and (1887): 59–85; and "Notes sur Henri de Gand," ibid. (1888): 421–56; Alphonse Wauters, "Sur les documents apocryphes qui concerneraient Henri de Gand, le docteur solennel, et qui le rattachent à la famille Goethals," *Bulletin de la Commission Royale d'Histoire* (Brussels), 4th series, 14 (1887): 179–90; "Sur la signification du mot latin *Formator*, à propos de Henri de Gand," ibid. 16 (1889): 12–15; and "Le mot latin *Formator*, au moyen âge, avait la signification de Professeur," ibid. 16 (1889): 400–410; Napoléon De Pauw, "Note sur le vrai nom du Docteur solennel Henri de Gand," ibid. 15 (1888): 135–45; and "Dernières découvertes concernant le Docteur solennel Henri de Gand, fils de Jean le Tailleur (Formator ou de Sceppere)," ibid. 16 (1889): 27–138; Clemens Baeumker, "Jahresbericht über die abendländische Philosophie im Mittelalter. 1890," *Archiv für Geschichte der Philosophie* 5 (1892): 113–38; Maurice De Wulf, *Histoire de la philosophie en Belgique* (Brussels, 1910), pp. 80–116; Martin Grabmann, *Mittelalterliche lateinische Aristotelesübersetzungen und Aristoteleskommentare in Handschriften spanischer Bibliotheken*, Sitzungsberichte der Bayerischen Akademie der Wissenschaften, Philosophisch-philologische und historische Klasse, 1928, 5. Abhandlung (Munich, 1928), pp. 95–96; Palémon Glorieux, *La littérature quodlibétique de 1260 à 1320*, 1, 177; *Répertoire des maîtres en théologie de Paris au XIIIe siècle*, 1, 387; and *Aux origines de la Sorbonne*, I: *Robert de Sorbon* (Paris, 1966), p. 809; Jean Paulus, *Henri de Gand: Essai sur les tendances de sa métaphysique* (Paris, 1938), pp. xi–xxiii; Raymond Macken's introduction to Henry of Ghent, *Quodlibet I*, ed. Macken, Henrici Opera, 5 (Leuven, 1979), pp. vi–xii; and Robert Wielockx in his edition of Giles of Rome, *Apologia*, pp. 152, 171, and 239–40. For other works on Henry's life, consult the bibliography at the end of Raymond Macken, "Hendrik van Gent (Henricus de Gandavo), wijsgeer en theoloog," in *Nationaal biografisch woordenboek*, 8:377–95 (Brussels, 1979).

[5] See Henry's own statement in his Quodlibet 2, q. 9 (in *Quodlibet II*, ed. Robert Wielockx, Henrici Opera, 6 [Leuven, 1983], p. 67, ll. 21–24).

[6] On Henry's ongoing debate with Thomas's follower, Giles of Rome, see Edgar Hocedez, "Gilles de Rome et Henri de Gand sur la distinction réelle (1276–1287),"

All Henry had to say on the issues of illumination, human cognition and knowledge of God can be found in two massive works, his *Summa quaestionum ordinariarum* and his collected *Quodlibeta*.[7] The former is a greatly revised, most likely expanded, compilation of questions probably disputed in class while he was bachelor or master of theology; the latter simply his final redactions, polished for publication through the university bookseller, of the special open disputations he held practically every year from his first as master in 1276 up through 1291 or 1292. Although the *Summa* gives the impression of having been composed all at once, it is clear Henry wrote, or at least revised, it in sections over the course of his long career, so that the finished version progresses chronologically from beginning to end in parallel with the obviously sequential series of quodlibets.[8] It is absolutely crucial to keep this chronology of composition

---

Gregorianum 8 (1927): 358–84; and "Le premier Quodlibet d'Henri de Gand (1276)," *Gregorianum* 9 (1928): 92–117; Jean Paulus, "Les disputes d'Henri de Gand et de Gilles de Rome sur la distinction de l'essence et de l'existence," AHDLMA 13 (1940–42): 323–58; and again Wielockx, introduction to Giles of Rome, *Apologia*.

[7] The editions of Henry's works chiefly used in the present book are *Summa quaestionum ordinariarum*, 2 vols. (Paris, 1520/reprinted St. Bonaventure, N.Y., 1953); and *Quodlibeta*, 2 vols. (Paris, 1518/reprinted Leuven, 1961). Henceforth all citations of these works will be made to *Summa* and *Quod.*, followed by volume and folio numbers. A critical reedition of all Henry's writings has been begun at the De Wulf-Mansion Center of the Katholieke Universiteit Leuven – see Macken, *Bibliotheca manuscripta Henrici de Gandavo*, Henrici Opera, 1–2 [Leuven, 1979]; "Die Editionstechnik der 'Opera Omnia' des Heinrich von Gent," FS 63 [1981]: 227–39; and "Der Aufbau eines wissenschaftlichen Unternehmens: Die 'Opera Omnia' des Heinrich von Gent," FS 65 [1983]: 82–96; and Ludwig Hödl, "Literar- und Problemgeschichtliches zur neuen kritischen Edition der Opera omnia des Heinrich von Gent," *Freiburger Zeitschrift für Philosophie und Theologie* 32 (1985): 295–322; and "Der Projektband der kritischen Edition der Summa des Heinrich von Gent," *Ephemerides Theologicae Lovanienses* 64 (1988): 225–28. Quodlibets I, II, VI, VII, IX, X, XII and XIII, and *Summa*, a. 31–46, have appeared so far, references to which will henceforth be cited as Henrici Opera, followed by volume and page number.

[8] In this study Henry's works are dated generally according to the schema devised by José Gómez Caffarena, "Cronología de la 'Suma' de Enrique de Gante por relación a sus 'Quodlibetos,'" *Gregorianum* 38 (1957): 116–33. Since Henry systematically revised all his works for publication, sometimes making the revisions in several stages, no chronology for them will ever be perfect, but Gómez Caffarena's comes close to the mark, with my own work (see, for example, Marrone, *Truth and Scientific Knowledge in the Thought of Henry of Ghent* [Cambridge, Mass., 1985], pp. 117, n. 65; and 119, n. 68) and that of the editors of the Leuven edition suggesting only minor modifications. A table of the various dates proposed for the Quodlibets can be found in Macken's introduction to his edition of Henry's *Quodlibet I*, Henrici Opera, 5:xvii. For a short bibliography of studies on dating Henry's works, see Raymond Macken, "La théorie de l'illumination divine dans la philosophie d'Henri de Gand," RTAM 39 (1972): 88–89, n. 26. Recent ideas on the publication – as opposed

continually in mind, as Henry's thought was profoundly developmental, perhaps more so than that of any high-medieval thinker
besides Duns Scotus, and can be understood only if one gives due
consideration to growth and change.

First of Henry's followers to be examined is the Gascon friar, Vital
du Four, who studied theology at Paris in the late 1280s and early
1290s, where he surely heard Henry of Ghent, at least attending his
public disputations.[9] During the academic year 1295–1296, Vital was
lecturer in the Franciscan *studium generale* at Montpellier, and he is
found holding the same position in Toulouse in 1297. Sometime
afterwards but before 1307 he rose to master of theology, although it
is not clear where or exactly what year. By 1307, when he was named
provincial minister of Franciscans in Aquitaine, his career as an eccle-
siastic had taken off, propelled by the patronage of fellow country-
man, Clement V, first of the Avignonese popes. He was made cardinal
priest of St. Martin in Montibus in 1312, then cardinal bishop of
Albano in 1321, dying in 1327 a wealthy and privileged member of
the religious establishment.

Vital's literary career as a scholastic was probably finished by 1300.
Of his works important for the present study, the first Quodlibet was

to composition – of the *Summa* in one or two blocks are discussed by Hödl in the
"Introduction" to Raymond Macken's edition of Henry of Ghent, *Summa (Quaestiones
ordinariae) art. XXXI–XXXIV*, Henrici Opera, 27 (Leuven, 1991): pp. xxiv–xxviii;
Macken in his "Etude critique" in the same work, pp. xlv–lvii; and Marrone, "Henry
of Ghent in Mid-Career as Interpreter of Aristotle and Thomas Aquinas," in *Henry
of Ghent. Proceedings of the International Colloquium on the Occasion of the 700th Anniversary
of his Death (1293)*, ed. Willy Vanhamel (Leuven, 1996), pp. 208–9.

[9] On Vital's life and the dating of his works, see Ferdinand M. Delorme, "Praefatio,"
in Vital du Four, *Quodlibeta tria*, ed. Ferdinand M. Delorme, v–xxii (Rome, 1947);
Franz Pelster, "Neue Textausgaben von Werken des hl. Thomas, des Johannes
Pecham und Vitalis de Furno," *Gregorianum* 31 (1950): 284–303; and Valens Heynck,
"Zur Busslehre des Vitalis de Furno," FS 41 (1959): 163–212; and "Vitalis de
Furno," in *Lexikon für Theologie und Kirche*, 2nd ed., ed. Josef Höfer and Karl Rahner,
10:819–20 (Freiburg im Br., 1965). See also Charles-Victor Langlois, "Vidal du
Four, Frère Mineur," in *Histoire Littéraire de la France*, 36:295–305 and 647–52 (Paris,
1924 & 1927); Delorme, "L'oeuvre scolastique de maître Vital du Four d'après le
MS. 95 de Todi," *La France Franciscaine* 9 (1926): 421–71; and "Les questions brèves
'De rerum principio' du Cardinal Vital du Four," *Sophia* 10 (1942): 290–327; Ephrem
Longpré, "Pour la défense de Duns Scot," RFN 18 (1926): 32–42; Palémon Glorieux,
"Pour en finir avec le 'De rerum principio,'" AFH 31 (1938): 225–34; P. Godefroy,
"Vital du Four," in *Dictionnaire de Théologie Catholique* 15, 2:3102–3115 (Paris, 1950);
Friedrich Stegmüller, "Vitalis de Furno," in *Repertorium biblicum medii aevi*, 5:424–25
(Madrid, 1955); John E. Lynch, *The Theory of Knowledge of Vital du Four* (St. Bonaventure,
N.Y., 1972); and Alexandre-Jean Gondras, "Un commentaire avignonnais sur le
Liber de sex principiis, attribué à 'Maître Vital,'" AHDLMA 42 (1975): 183–317.

written before 1295 and surely after 1290.[10] Between 1297 and 1300 he composed Quodlibets II and III, presumably at Toulouse, as well as his most significant piece on mind and epistemology, a collection of eight *Quaestiones de cognitione.*[11] An inveterate plagiarizer, he incorporated stretches of other authors' writings into his own work so frequently and on so vast a scale as to make him exceptional even at a time when such unattributed copying was established practice. He gives the impression of being a careerist who published sufficiently to advance but never engaged deeply enough in ideas to bother with originality.

Whatever the reason, his views on knowledge and illumination are so derivative of Henry that they can be used only to shed light on the master. Indeed, most of the passages from *Quaestiones de cognitione* cited here are pastiches of quotations from Henry's works. Since there is so little of Vital himself in them, the chronology of their composition is of virtually no importance. For the record, it should be pointed out that despite his debt to Henry in epistemology and noetics, Vital was not on all matters a follower of Henry's thought. A truly catholic bricoleur, his writings are strewn with verbatim insertions drawn also from John Pecham, Matthew of Aquasparta, Roger Marston, Giles of Rome, Godfrey of Fontaines and Peter Olivi.[12]

Second of Henry's followers is the English Franciscan, Richard of Conington. No less uncritical an admirer of the Flemish master's epistemology and noetics than Vital, he is referred to by some English scholastics of the early fourteenth century as Henry's disciple.[13] By rights he belongs to the generation of Duns Scotus, for he taught at Oxford as master of theology sometime around 1305–1307, before

---

[10] Vital's Quodlibet I appears in Vital du Four, *Quodlibeta tria*, ed. Ferdinand M. Delorme, Spicilegium Pontificii Athenaei Antoniani, 5 (Rome, 1947). An early edition of Quodlibet I appeared in Ferdinand M. Delorme, "Le Quodlibet I du Cardinal Vital du Four," *La France Franciscaine* 18 (1935): 113–42.

[11] Quodlibets II and III have been edited by Delorme in *Quodlibeta tria*, cited in the previous note. Henceforth all citations of Vital's quodlibets will be made to this edition. The *Quaestiones 8 de cognitione* have also been edited by Delorme in "Le Cardinal Vital du Four. Huit questions disputées sur le problème de la connaissance," AHDLMA 2 (1927): 156–336.

[12] See Godfroy, "Vital du Four," col. 3107–3108, Delorme, "L'oeuvre scolastique de maître Vital," p. 28; and Stephen D. Dumont, "Giles of Rome and the 'De rerum principio' Attributed to Vital du Four," AFH 77 (1984): 81–109.

[13] See Franz Pelster, "Franziskanerlehrer um die Wende des 13. und zu Anfang des 14. Jahrhunderts in zwei ehemaligen Turiner Hss.," *Gregorianum* 18 (1937): 308–9.

becoming provincial minister of England in 1310.[14] Yet because his account of knowing essence, set fully in the context of Henry's metaphysics, elucidates a point never explicitly addressed in Henry's own work, he is included here in examination of the Augustinian current's third stage.

Among Richard's extant writings are a relevant question from his *Quaestiones ordinariae* and another from his *Quodlibet I*, both products of his regency at Oxford or Cambridge around 1306–1310, the Quodlibet following close upon the *Quaestiones*.[15] His early teaching was probably well known to Duns, and it would seem that his exposition of ideas drawn from Henry was in some instances expressly intended to defend them against Scotus's criticism.[16] Because most of his activity postdates the period covered in the present study, he, like Vital, will not be interrogated for evidence of further development of Henry's thought but rather used for historical corroboration of an interpretation of doctrines assigned to the master himself. It is Henry who dominates the Augustinian stage after Pecham and before Scotus, his defenders figuring as mere epigones in his presence.

---

[14] For what is known of Richard's life, see Victorin Doucet, "L'oeuvre scolastique de Richard de Conington, O.F.M.," AFH 29 (1936): 396–442; Stephen F. Brown, "Sources for Ockham's Prologue to the Sentences," FrS 26 (1966): 36–65; and the entry "Conington, Richard de," in *A Biographical Register of the University of Oxford to A.D. 1500*, ed. A.B. Emden, 1:447 (Oxford, 1957).

[15] Question 1 from the *Quaestiones ordinariae* has been edited by Doucet in "L'oeuvre scolastique," pp. 430–38; question 2 from *Quodlibet I* by Stephen F. Brown in "Richard of Conington and the Analogy of the Concept of Being," FS 48 (1966): 300–307.

[16] The editors of the Vatican edition of Duns's complete works speculated on Duns's knowledge of Conington as an expositor of Henry's ideas – see references to that edition below, Pt. 3, ch. 11, n. 81; and Pt. 4, ch. 14, n. 86.

CHAPTER NINE

TRUTH, CERTITUDE AND SCIENCE

The determination to dispel the slightest whiff of ontologism marked Henry's approach to the epistemological and noetic legacy of the classic Augustinians from the start. Key to his efforts was uncompromising fidelity to the analytical device already employed by his Augustinian predecessors, the distinction between object of knowledge (*obiectum cognitum*) and means of knowing (*ratio cognoscendi*).[1] Where the classic Augustinians had regarded this binary opposition as a tool occasionally indispensable for defending the theory of illumination from particular charges of ontologism, Henry made it into a structural principle of his noetics, intended permanently to insulate the processes of illumination from criticism at any point.[2]

At first glance the difference between the two approaches is hardly apparent. Henry agreed with the classic Augustinians that seeing God as full object of understanding was not what was entailed in any of divine illumination's manifestations in normal cognition in the world of sin, since God or a divine exemplar entered into human cognition on earth as manifest object only under the most extraordinary circumstances. Not even saving grace could fortify mind's natural powers sufficiently to allow so exalted a vision; what was required was an exceptional infusion of light almost never delivered outside of heaven.[3] A few privileged individuals had been granted the blessing before their death, perhaps no more than Moses on the mountain, Paul in rapture on the road to Damascus and Benedict in an incident reported in Gregory's account of his life.[4] For most Christians, such cognitive access to God would come only with beatitude.

Like his Augustinian predecessors, Henry insisted that where God was involved in the wayfarer's normal processes of intellection, it

---

[1] See Henry, *Summa*, a. 1, q. 2 (1:5rE); and also a. 1, q. 2 (1:6rI); and a. 24, q. 9 (1:146rV).
[2] On classic use of the opposition, see above, Part 2, ch. 5, pp. 141–42; ch. 6, p. 147; and ch. 7, pp. 186–87.
[3] Henry, *Summa*, a. 1, q. 2 (1:6vI).
[4] Ibid.

was as means of knowing.[5] There were, however, two ways such a means could take part in the cognitive act. An element extrinsic to the perceptive power might serve as means of knowing something else while at the same time being in some measure perceived.[6] For example, the reflection in a mirror brought the eyes to seize upon that of which it was an image but also offered itself as object to be seen. Henry made ample use of this model of cognitive instrumentality in accounting for God's role in the wayfarer's understanding, taking it as foundational for his version of classic Augustinian theories about natural knowledge of God. He steadfastly denied it had anything to do with divinity's role in normal, truth-seeking acts of mind.[7]

Instead, God intervened in the wayfarer's apprehension of truth as means of knowing *alone* (*ratio cognoscendi tantum*).[8] Vital faithfully echoed Henry on this score.[9] Just as, in contrast to an image in a mirror, the sensible species in the senses or intelligible species in intellect was cognitive means in no way seen or known, so God as revealer of truth brought intellect to conceive of something else without revealing himself at all.[10] Thus Henry returned to the views of John Pecham, who had also compared God's role in illumination of truth to that of sensible species in sensation and drawn a sharp distinction between acting as only means of knowing and acting as

---

[5] *Summa*, a. 1, q. 2 (1:6vI): "Si vero sciatur sincera veritas aspiciendo ad divinum exemplar ut ad rationem cognoscendi, hoc modo posuit Plato omnem veritatem cognosci aspiciendo ad exemplar aeternum. . . . Hanc igitur sententiam Platonis insecutus est Augustinus. . . ."

[6] See Henry, *Summa* (*Qq. ord.*), a. 33, q. 3, ad 4. (Henrici Opera, 27:161, ll. 8–12). In this passage Henry was not drawing the distinction so as to use it in exactly the same way it is employed here, but his words can nonetheless be taken as a legitimate and concise statement of the general point.

[7] To this degree Henry agreed with Matthew that God as mirror was not an appropriate model for understanding the normal procedure of divine illumination. See above, Pt. 2, ch. 5, n. 99; and ch. 8, n. 71.

[8] See Henry's precise language in *Summa*, a. 1, q. 2 (1:6rI); a. 2, q. 1 (1:23vB); and a. 24, q. 8, ad 2. (1:145vR).

[9] Vital, *Quaestiones de cognitione*, q. 8 (ed. Delorme, "Huit questions," p. 331).

[10] See above, n. 6, and also Henry, *Summa*, a. 1, q. 3 (1:8vA): "Quod enim non habet rationem obiecti, nullo modo potest dici esse per se and in se cognitum a nobis; utputa species sensibilis in oculo, quia potentia supra sensum, nullum potest facere sensum, neque species intelligibilis informans intellectum. Lux autem divina illustrans mentem in notitiam veritatis simpliciter vel sincere solum se habet ut ratio intelligendi, non ut obiectum visui et intellectui." In the passage cited above, n. 9, Vital reproduces in abbreviated form the very words quoted here.

means and object, too.[11] He merely rendered Pecham's thoughts more technically precise, defining a means of knowing as a formal entity somehow resident in intellect and activating its intellective potential.[12]

The innovation of Henry's approach becomes evident only when one goes beyond his choice of analytical devices, all of which were inherited, to examine the use he made of them. For in his early works, Henry insisted on interpreting the description of God's illuminative role as means alone in the strictest, most literal sense, excluding even the merest implication that divinity thereby also served as object of mind. With such uncompromising standards, he was led to segregate, as theoretically unrelated, occasions where the mechanism of divine intervention had been used to resolve the epistemological, and normative, problem of truth from those where it was applied to matters of the cognitive object and ideogenesis. The upshot was that noetic processes and functions concerning God's role as guarantor for knowledge of truth were kept absolutely separate from those accounting for the wayfarer's knowledge of God. In the interest of philosophical purity, Henry opened a cleavage straight down the middle of the doctrine of divine illumination the classic Augustinians had only recently made unified and whole.

Henry was the first among thirteenth-century Augustinians to make this fundamental division and defend it in explicit and unmitigated terms. Moreover he believed that it was true to the intention of Augustine, who, he thought, had expected his readers to discriminate between instances where God related to mind as somehow object and those where God was *ratio tantum*.[13] Since the heart of

---

[11] See above, Part 2, ch. 5, especially nn. 86 and 89. This time Henry was ignoring the warnings of Matthew, who had criticized Pecham's ideas on this point – see again above, Pt. 2, ch. 5, n. 99. In *Summa*, a. 24, q. 6, ad 3. (1:143vC), Henry used language to describe the distinction especially reminiscent of Pecham's words in the passage cited in n. 89. There is more on this distinction and Henry's elaborations on it below, Part 3, ch. 10, pp. 300–2.

[12] *Summa (Qq. ord.)*, a. 34, q. 5 (Henrici Opera, 27:205, ll. 2–4): "Ratio intelligendi in intelligentia est esse formale quo intelligibile facit intelligentiam talem in actu, quale ipsum est, cum de se, in quantum intelligentia est, non est nisi in potentia tale." It is important to be forewarned that this volume of the Leuven edition of Henry's Opera Omnia sometimes presents readings patently inferior to those of the Badius edition of the *Summa* reprinted at St. Bonaventure in 1953 (see above, introduction to Part 3, n. 7) – as, for example, in the sentences following the ones quoted just above.

[13] Henry, *Summa*, a. 1, q. 2, ad 5. (1:8rR); and a. 24, q. 8, ad opp. (1:145v–46r[S]). For more on Henry's view of the distinction, see below, Pt. 3, ch. 10, n. 7.

Augustinian illumination had always lain with the normative matter of knowledge of truth and attainment of certitude, it is hardly surprising Henry chose to privilege that particular aspect of theory of knowledge with exclusive linkage to the circumstances where God and his reasons acted as means of knowing alone. To see how he worked out the details, one must look at the vision, laid out in the first years of his magisterium and never again in just the same manner, of the wayfarer's cognition at all grades of comprehension, including those where God had no direct role. Because Henry was more sanguine than Bonaventure, Pecham or even Matthew about mind's power to act without intervention from God, his view of knowledge embraced a greater variety of types than had previously been the case.

Henry's cognitive schema revolved around his concept of truth. As he explained it most broadly, being true constituted that aspect of a thing by which it was object of intellect; indeed it could be said that truth itself was intellect's objective domain.[14] Other ways of putting this were that the precise nature (*praecisa ratio*) of truth was intelligibility, or that truth was that aspect of a thing relating it to mind (*respectus ad intellectum*).[15] In short, only what was true could be known, and whatever was known was ipso facto true. Yet there was another, more philosophically revealing notion of truth, for a thing was properly designated "true" insofar as it contained within itself that which the exemplar according to which it had been created set forth.[16] Restating Henry's formula, Vital simply said that a thing was true insofar as it represented the exemplar according to which it was made.[17]

The implications of all this were clear. Both Henry and Vital, like the classic Augustinians and even Grosseteste before, ascribed to a view of truth that applied to knowledge of simple objects, a fact differentiating them from strict Aristotelianizers and setting them in line with thinkers whose epistemology owed more to Augustine.

---

[14] Henry, *Summa*, a. 1, q. 2 (1:4vC); and also *Summa*, a. 2, q. 6 (1:27rE): ". . . . veritas rei est id quo res scitur et intelligitur, quia ipsa est proprium obiectum intellectus."

[15] Henry, *Summa* (*Qq. ord.*), a. 33, q. 2 (Henrici Opera, 27:137, ll. 41–42; and 139, l. 00–140, l. 3).

[16] Henry, *Summa*, a. 1, q. 2 (1:5rD): "[Quaelibet res potest considerari] inquantum in esse suo habet quod de ea exemplar ad quod est repraesentat. Sic convenit ei intentio veri. Intantum enim vera est quaecumque res, inquantum in se continet quod exemplar eius repraesentat."

[17] Vital, *Quaestiones de cognitione*, q. 8 (ed. Delorme, "Huit questions," p. 324).

Moreover, as with nearly all Augustinians, so for these thinkers knowing the truth of simple cognition entailed making a judgment based
on comparing object to exemplar, so that some minimally complex
procedure of mind was bound up with knowledge even at what
would appear to be its simplest stage.

Yet despite the echoes of Augustine, Henry was more generous
about the possibility of absolutely simple acts of intellect and less
demanding of the need for illuminative intervention from God than
were the classic Augustinians. Characterizing *knowledge* as the correlative in the knowing subject of the *true* object, he continued by
defining it in the most general sense possible (*scire large*) as certain
understanding (*certa notitia*), without error or deception, of a thing as
it was.[18] Thus all knowledge – *scientia* most broadly construed –
entailed a minimal degree of certitude, the question being in what
it consisted and how it was attained.

There were those, Henry noted, who maintained that, left completely to its own devices (*ex puris naturalibus*), mind had no possibility of attaining knowledge construed along these lines, no matter
how loosely. Instead, for intellect truly to know something it had to
receive a supernatural infusion of intellective light from God, the
truth-giving intervention Henry typically referred to as special divine
illumination (*specialis illustratio divina*) but at times simply divine illumination (*divina illustratio*) or the illumination commonly available
(*illustratio communis*) to mind.[19] Defenders of this position character-

---

[18] Henry, *Summa*, a. 1, q. 1 (1:1vB): "Dicendum quod scire large accepto ad
omnem notitiam certam qua cognoscitur res sicut est absque omni fallacia et deceptione." See also *Summa*, a. 6, q. 2 (1:43rL). It is interesting to note that according
to this broad definition even sensory cognition qualified as knowledge, although it
was not *scire* properly speaking – see *Summa*, a. 1, q. 2 (1:4vB–C).

[19] Henry, *Summa*, a. 1, q. 2 (1:4rB). Other references to "specialis illustratio" in
this sense appear in the same question, ad 1. and ad 2. (1:8rN & O). For "divina
illustratio" broadly see the same question, (1:7vM); for "illustratio communis," *Summa*,
a. 13, q. 5 (1:93rQ). "Special illumination" of this sort was to be distinguised from
any other illumination from God, as for instance the exceptional light of grace
wherein mind saw the divinity as full and beatific object – see above, n. 3 – although
Henry occasionally referred to such other illuminations as "special." (In *Summa*,
a. 6, q. 1 [1:42vD]; and a. 13, q. 6 [1:94rC], Henry refers to the illumination leading to truth as a "divina illustratio generalis" in order to distinguish it from an
even higher illumination – referred to as "specialis" in these passages – which he
thought brought theology to the level of a science. On Henry's "special light of
theology," see Stephen Dumont, "Theology as a Science and Duns Scotus's Distinction
between Intuitive and Abstractive Cognition," *Speculum* 64 [1989]: 585–89.) The fact
that Vital adopted Henry's standard usage with absolute consistency would indicate

ized it as faithful to Augustine, whose notion of true knowledge as dependent on judgmental recourse to a standard above mind imposed, they said, so heavy a burden on all acts worthy of the verb "to know."[20] Among their number must surely be included Bonaventure and his followers.

For all his sympathy with the Augustinian line, Henry objected that such a posture derogated from the dignity of human mind, in no uncertain language insisting to the contrary that any human being could come to knowledge without special illumination, solely on his or her own power.[21] By this he did not mean to exclude an indirect role for divinity, for God exercised on all intellection a general influence (*generalis influentia*) analogous to his function as first mover in all natural motion.[22] Yet, sometimes calling the influence "general providence," Henry apparently regarded it as simply the noetic expression of God's creative role, endowing each mind with its natural intellectual light, to which degree he endorsed John of La Rochelle's opinion that God was illuminator just by virtue of being creator.[23]

Having disposed of the most ambitious application of a theory of divine illumination, Henry was then obligated to explain exactly what he thought the wayfarer's knowledge consisted in. Here is where he laid out his scheme of cognitive levels. He chose to begin at the bottom of the ladder, and since for him knowledge formally entailed certainty, that meant starting with knowledge that was least certain.[24]

According to Henry, the most primitive grade of knowledge obtained when mind knew the true (*verum*) but not yet the truth (*veritas*).[25] Vital

---

that his readers already took such language to be technically specific – see for instance Vital, *Quaestiones de cognitione*, q. 8 (ed. Delorme, "Huit questions," pp. 311 and 324).

[20] See the first citation given above, n. 19.

[21] *Summa*, a. 1, q. 2 (1:4vB): "Absolute ergo concedere oportet quod homo per suam animam absque omni speciali divina illustratione potest aliqua scire aut cognoscere, et hoc ex puris naturalibus. Contrarium enim dicere multum derogat dignitati animae et humanae naturae." See also Henry's comments immediately after introducing the so-called Augustinian position in the same question (1:4rB).

[22] See the continuation of the passage from *Summa*, a. 1, a. 2 (1:4vB), quoted in the preceding note, and also the same question, ad 1. (1:8rN).

[23] See Henry *Summa*, a. 3, q. 5 (1:30rT). In *Summa*, a. 1, q. 7 (1:17rK), Henry divided God's general action into his role as "universale causans" (that is, creator) and as "universale movens" (conservator of his creation). For Rochelle's view, see above, Part 2, intro., n. 4.

[24] See Henry, *Summa*, a. 6, q. 2 (1:43r–v[L]).

[25] *Summa*, a. 1, q. 2 (1:4vC): "Aliud tamen est scire de creatura id quod verum est in ea, et aliud est scire eius veritatem; ut alia sit cognitio qua cognoscitur res,

adopted his words without modification.[26] At minimum their statement reaffirmed the fact that all acts of intellect were by definition
directed towards what was true, but the purpose being to mark off
one cognitive level from another, the important distinction lay between
"true" and "truth." The problem is that neither in Henry's early
works nor in Vital's at any point in his career is it exactly clear how
to draw the boundary between the two.

From the beginning Henry's language suggested two lines of attack.[27]
On the one hand, knowing the true involved grasping just that which
a thing was (*id quod res est*), while coming to truth required seizing
the formal whatness (*quid est*). From this perspective the level of
knowledge attained corresponded to something about the object,
specifically the clarity or fullness in which it was perceived. On the
other hand, in knowing the true mind worked by simple understanding (*simplex intelligentia*); getting to truth depended on compounding
and dividing (*intelligentia componente et dividente*). Here the emphasis lay
on the character of the mental act – precisely its simplicity or complexity. Again Vital echoed Henry with exactly the same phrases.[28]

Although Henry may have intended these two approaches to be
fully complementary, his early work made no attempt to bring them
together. The first set "true," pointing to less than an object's "whatness," against a "truth" residing in the profound reaches of "whatness"

---

alia qua cognoscitur veritas eius." Not all scholars have taken note of this important
distinction, although it was pointed out already in the work of Paulus, *Henri de Gand*,
p. 4; and Theophiel Nys, *De werking van het menselijk verstand volgens Hendrik van Gent*
(Leuven, 1949), p. 123.

[26] Vital, *Quaestiones de cognitione*, q. 8 (ed. Delorme, "Huit questions," pp. 322–23),
which simply took up Henry's language from the previous note, inserting it into
the author's own gloss. Martin Grabmann, *Der göttliche Grund menschlicher Wahrheitserkenntnis*, pp. 35–36, called attention to an anonymous text in MS Bibl. Vat., *Vat.
lat.* 3054, drawing exactly the same distinction, even dividing knowledge of *veritas*
as Henry would between that aided by divine light and that which was not.

[27] See Henry, *Summa*, a. 1, q. 2 (1:4vC): "Cognitione igitur intellectiva de re creata potest haberi duplex cognitio. Una qua praecise sci<tur> sive cognoscitur simplici intelligentia id quod res est. Alia qua scitur et cognoscitur intelligentia componente
et dividente veritas ipsius rei. In prima cognitione intellectus noster omnino sequitur
sensum, nec est aliquid conceptum in intellectu, quod non erat prius in sensu. Et
ideo talis intellectus inquantum huiusmodi bene potest esse verus concipiendo sive
cognoscendo rem sicuti est, quemadmodum et sensus quem sequitur, licet non concipiat vel intelligat ipsam veritatem rei certo iudicio percipiendo de ipsa quid sit,
ut quod sit verus homo vel verus color."

[28] Vital, *Quaestiones de cognitione*, q. 8 (ed. Delorme, "Huit questions," p. 323), a
discussion dependent closely on Henry's words in the passage from which the quotation in the previous note is drawn.

itself – that is, quiddity or essence – and indeed throughout his career
Henry consistently identified truth with a thing's essence or quiddity. Of course, that had been Grosseteste's position in the *Commentary
on the Posterior Analytics*, with the difference that there truth, essence
and quiddity were equated with Augustine's *id quod est*.[29] Perhaps
Henry was trying to maintain Grosseteste's early distinction in *De
veritate* between *quod est* and truth while reading the latter term in
line with the *Commentary*. Still, there is no perfect fit with either
Grosseteste's early or later views. Henry went on to explain that in
knowing "the true" mind laid hold only of what was available to
the senses, and Vital repeated his words almost verbatim, adding,
as often, his own comments and illustrations.[30] Presumably both relied
on an Aristotelianizing conviction that, since access to quiddity was
the mark of intellect, any mental act not reaching so far had to be
more or less equivalent to sensation. Henry even characterized knowledge of "the true" as an *intellectus phantasticus*.[31]

What could cognition amount to at this lower level? Once Henry
contrasted knowledge *simpliciter* with the distinct (*distinctive*) understanding obtained after further consideration, as if this were a way
to differentiate knowing the true from knowing truth.[32] In the same
vein he spoke of a confused or indeterminate knowledge of simple
terms opposed to determinate knowledge of "truth of the quiddity"
in definitiva ratione.[33] He would seem in both cases to have been moving

---

[29] See Henry, *Summa*, a. 2, q. 6 (1:27rD); and *Quodlibet* II, q. 6 (ed. Robert
Wielockx, Henrici Opera, 2), p.32. In *Summa*, a. 24, q. 8 (1:145rN), Henry used
the even more authentically Aristotelian phrase "quod quid est" as equivalent to
"truth." On Grosseteste, see above, Part 1, ch. 1, nn. 15, 20 and 21. For an interesting take on Henry's identification of knowledge of truth with knowledge of essence,
arguing, somewhat differently from what is maintained in the present work, that
his dissatisfaction with mind's grasp of essence led him even in the early articles of
the *Summa* to doubt that truth could be attained by intellect without divine assistance, see Robert Pasnau, "Henry of Ghent and the Twilight of Divine Illumination,"
The Review of Metaphysics 49 (1995): especially 66–71.

[30] On Henry, see above, n. 27, as well as *Summa*, a. 1, q. 2 (1:5rD); and *Quodlibet*
II, q. 6 (Henrici Opera, 2:32, ll. 58–60); for Vital, *Quaestiones de cognitione*, q. 8 (ed.
Delorme, "Huit questions," p. 323). The latter prudently added ("Huit questions,"
p. 324) that knowledge of the true, for all its similarity to sensation, took mind
deeper (*profundius*) than the senses could penetrate, an observation perhaps reliant
on Henry in *Summa*, a. 1, q. 2, ad opp. (1:8rS).

[31] Henry, *Summa*, a. 24, q. 8 (1:145rM–N); and also, though less clearly, a. 13,
q. 6 (1:94vD).

[32] Henry *Summa*, a. 1, q. 3 (1:8vA).

[33] Henry, *Summa*, a. 1, q. 12 (1:22rK–L), significantly contrasting the prior knowledge, *in significato nominis*, from the subsequent, *in definitiva ratione*.

towards the Aristotelian distinction between preliminary nominal knowledge and consequent understanding of quiddity in the definition, although the unambiguous exposition of such a scheme would appear only in his later works.[34] His understanding along such lines remained at best inchoate at the beginning of his career.

Significantly, Vital, while accepting much of Henry's language on this matter, was reluctant to carry the distinction so far. In question 8 of *Quaestiones de cognitione* he laid out what is essentially Henry's mature contrast between knowing "the true" as, in Vital's words, a "confusa manifestatio rei" and knowing truth in the definition.[35] Adopting almost verbatim Roger Marston's arguments in his *Quaestiones de anima*, he roundly condemned such a position, apparently much too Aristotelianizing for his taste.[36] If this is fair indication, by the late 1290s Henry's followers preferred a sanitized version of the master's thought, suppressing developments of his middle years in favor of the tenor of his earliest writings when Aristotelian themes had not yet been brought into full relief.

Henry's second approach to "true" and "truth" saw knowledge of the two as different because the former was simple, the latter semi-discursive and necessitating a procedure of compounding and dividing after which intellect made a judgment (*iudicium*) about what it had apprehended at the lower level.[37] The reference to judgment in what constituted, strictly speaking, non-propositional cognition was sure sign of Augustinian influence, for though Henry possessed an authentically Aristotelian notion of compounding and dividing as leading to truly complex cognition, that was not what he had in

---

[34] Robert Grosseteste had made an early attempt to explain this distinction in his *Comm. Post. an.* II, 2 (pp. 322–41). See also the interesting remarks of Stephen D. Dumont, "The quaestio si est and the Metaphysical Proof for the Existence of God according to Henry of Ghent and John Duns Scotus," FS 66 (1984): 342–49. Dumont's analysis of Henry's interpretation of Aristotle draws largely on writings from the middle of his career.

[35] Vital, *Quaestiones de cognitione*, q. 8 (ed. Delorme, "Huit questions," pp. 312–13.)

[36] Vital, *Quaestiones de cognitione*, q. 8 (ed. Delorme, "Huit questions," pp. 315–21). Against the Aristotelianizing view and in favor of a more strictly illuminative scheme (which is itself later rejected as too strict), Vital took up the arguments from Marston's *Quaestiones de anima*, q. 3 (in *Quaestiones disputatae*, BFS, 7 [Quaracchi, 1932], pp. 253–64, 265, 267–68). Marston's, and perforce Vital's, arguments were, it must be admitted, only incidentally directed against an emphasis on the distinction between confused and definitive knowledge, more immediately targeting the implied rejection of a normal divine illumination.

[37] See the passage quoted above in n. 27, as well as *Summa*, a. 1, q. 2 (1:5rD); and a. 24, q. 8 (1:145rN).

mind here.[38] Knowledge of truth in this instance was neither entirely complex nor entirely simple; in Henry's words it was a *cognitio discretiva* as opposed to the absolute *cognitio simplicis notitiae* of perceiving just "the true."[39] This time Vital wholeheartedly supported him, even sharpening his terminology by adding that getting to truth required the power of reasoning (*ratiocinando*).[40] But just as before, in the second approach the lower grade, knowledge of the true, remained – at this early point for Henry and always for Vital – shrouded in obscurity. All one can say is that the term by which Henry referred to this primitive form of knowledge, *simplex intelligentia*, held constant throughout his career, reminder that below truth knowledge was simple absolutely and in every sense of the word.[41]

To be honest, Henry was not much interested in knowledge of the true, his philosophical appetite aroused only at the level of knowing truth. Here he relied in his earliest work on the Augustinian instincts of his second approach, attuned to judgment and the relative simplicity or complexity of the cognitive act, putting off till later in his career capitalizing on the Aristotelianizing potential of his first line of reasoning, in which grasping the definition provided the critical difference.

To explain why complexity of procedure was necessary to get to the second level of knowledge, Henry turned to the two most general terms known by mind, "being" and "true." Although as discussion of the first stage of cognition made plain, intellect knew every object insofar as it was true, "true" was not the precise attribute

---

[38] For the Aristotelian notion, see Henry, *Summa*, a. 1, q. 5 (1:14v–15r[B]), in contrast to an Augustinian interpretation of compounding and dividing leading to simple cognition in *Summa*, a. 24, q. 8 (1:145rN), cited in the preceding note.

[39] Henry, *Summa*, a. 1, q. 3 (1:8vA). In *Summa*, a. 24, q. 9 (1:146vX), Henry defined *cognitio discretiva* as "cum animadversione notitia, qua scilicet [intellectus] cognitum unum discernit ab alio."

[40] Vital, *Quaestiones de cognitione*, q. 8 (ed. Delorme, "Huit questions," p. 324), which, except for a few additions, including *ratiocinando*, follows almost word for word Henry's *Summa*, a. 1. q. 2 (1:5rD), cited above n. 37. It must be a lapse on Vital's part that in this passage he exemplifies knowledge of the truth with a case of clearly propositional knowledge.

[41] Henry did not always use exactly the phrase, *simplex intelligentia*; approximations include: *simplex notitia* (see the first citation above in n. 39); *cognitio simplicis apprehensionis* (*Summa*, a. 1, q. 10, ad 3. [1:20vK]; and *intellectus* or *intelligentia simplicium* (see *Summa*, a. 1, q. 2 [1:5rD]; a. 24. q. 8 [1:145rN]). Raphael Braun, *Die Erkenntnislehre des Heinrich von Gent* (Fribourg, 1916), pp. 43–44, mistakenly put Henry's *simplex intelligentia* on the level of what he called knowledge of logical truth. To the contrary, *simplex intelligentia* was precisely below knowledge of truth of any sort.

mind recognized first, which was instead the absolutely fundamental "being" (ens).[42] Perceiving an object as "true" required stepping
beyond the absolute – which is to say, entirely non-relative – parameters of "being" to consider it in relation to something else.[43] The
pertinent relation was, of course, the relative orientation (respectus)
towards intellect Henry had submitted among his characterizations
of "truth," quite naturally described according to the traditional
definition of truth as an accommodation of thing and intellect (adaequatio rei et intellectus).[44] Henry more readily depicted it as a relation
to an exemplar, precisely the conformity of object to an exemplar
representing or otherwise setting it forth.[45] This conformity constituted the truth mind would have to know in order to move beyond
simplex intelligentia, and, as itself complex, it demanded a complex act
of intellect to be perceived.

Such talk brought Henry back to Grosseteste in De veritate and, as
he and Vital both confessed, the authoritative words of Anselm in
his work of the same name, thus to the heart of the Augustinian
traditions associating knowledge with divine illumination.[46] But Henry
was not yet ready to incorporate illumination into his theories; he
wanted to keep the views of the classic Augustinians a while longer
at arm's length. Instead, he turned his attention for a time to analysis of the idea of scientific cognition.

---

[42] Henry, Summa, a. 1, q. 2 (1:4vC). Vital argued almost identically in his Quaestiones
de cognitione, q. 8 (ed. Delorme, "Huit questions," p. 323).

[43] Henry, Summa, a. 1, q. 2 (1:5rD): "Quia igitur verum dicit intentionem rei in
respectu ad suum exemplar, quae non est prima sed secundaria, ens enim dicit
intentionem rei primam et absolutam, id quod est ens et verum in re bene potest
apprehendi ab intellectu absque hoc quod intentio veritatis eius ab ipso apprehen-
datur. . . . Intentio vero entis apprehenditur in re absoluta sine omni reali respectu."
Vital gave essentially the same account, though in his own words, in Quaestiones de
cognitione, q. 8 (ed. Delorme, "Huit questions," p. 324).

[44] See above, n. 15; and Henry, Summa, a. 1., q. 2 (1:7rL); a. 1, q. 3 (1:10rF);
a. 7, q. 2 (1:48vK). Vital also cited the definition of truth as adaequatio in his
Quaestiones de cognitione, q. 8 (ed. Delorme, "Huit questions," p. 330).

[45] See the quotation in n. 16, above; also slightly lower on the same page of the
Summa: "Intentio enim veritatis in re apprehendi non potest nisi apprehendendo
conformitatem eius ad suum exemplar" – a description Vital reproduces in Quaestiones
de cognitione, q. 8 (ed. Delorme, "Huit questions," p. 324). See also p. 327 of the
same question 8.

[46] See Henry, Summa, a. 1, q. 2 (1:5rE); and Vital, Quaestiones de cognitione, q. 8
(ed. Delorme, "Huit questions," p. 324). The passages Henry and Vital proffered
as from Anselm on truth and conformity correspond, approximately though not literally, to statements made in De veritate, 7 (ed. Schmitt, 1, 185–86-see above, Pt. 1,
ch. 1, n. 3); for Grosseteste, see above, Part 1, ch. 1, n. 7.

Henry respected, and always accepted, the Aristotelian definition of science in strictest terms as knowledge of apodictically proved conclusions.[47] From Grosseteste on, thirteenth-century scholastics took this as given. Yet in accordance with the Augustinian heritage Henry also entertained a notion of scientific knowledge more broadly construed, expanded so as to embrace complex knowledge of more than demonstrated conclusions – that is, principles, too – and more importantly the special sort of simple understanding upon which such complex cognition was based. He called this broad category "science properly speaking" (*proprie scire*) to contrast it with "knowledge in the broadest sense of the word" (*scire large*), which he had associated with the first and lowest degree of certainty.[48] Only slightly modifying Henry's language, Vital said that this was what it meant "truly to know" (*vere scire*).[49]

Such broad but still proper scientific cognition constituted, according to Henry, "certain knowledge of truth" (*certa veritatis notitia*), which, momentarily recalling his first approach to the true-truth dichotomy, he also designated as knowledge of the object's quiddity or *quod quid est*.[50] In short, "scientific knowledge properly speaking" and "knowledge of the truth" were, for Henry as well as for Vital, congruent categories.[51] The two thinkers agreed, however, that cognition of this kind was available to human minds in the world at two different levels, and this partition of science into two grades yielded, after the distinction between knowing the true and knowing truth, the second fundamental division in their taxonomy of human cognition, crucial

---

[47] See, from Henry's early writings, *Summa*, a. 1, q. 1, arg. 1 and ad 1. (1:1rA and 2vE); a. 1, q. 5 (1:15rB); a. 1, q. 10 (1:20rC); a. 6, q. 1, arg. 1 and ad 1. (1:42rA and 42vE); and a. 33, q. 2 (Henrici Opera, 27:147, ll. 4–7), in all of which he quotes or alludes to Aristotle's *Posterior Analytics*, including the famous passage from Book I, ch. 2 (73b10–12), that science is obtained by knowing the cause. The latter text, universally influential in the thirteenth century, was of course also important for the other Augustinians – for Grosseteste and William, see above, Part 1, ch. 1, n. 46; for Bonaventure, Part 2, ch. 5, nn. 30 and 31.

[48] Henry, *Summa*, a. 1, q. 2 (1:5rD). On *scire large*, see above, n. 18.

[49] Vital, *Quaestiones de cognitione*, q. 8 (ed. Delorme, "Huit questions," p. 324).

[50] For "certain knowledge of the truth," see Henry, *Summa*, a. 2, q. 2 (1:24rF) – *Summa*, a. 1, q. 2 (1:5vE) seems to have reserved the same phrase for a higher level of cognition – for quiddity and *quod quid est*, *Summa*, a. 2, q. 2, ad 1. (1:24rG); and a. 3, q. 4 (1:29vP). All this suited the general notion that science was only of universals – see *Summa*, a. 6, q. 1, ad 2. (1:42v–43r[F]) – and should be associated with the *scientia stricte appellata* of *Summa*, a. 6, q. 1 (1:42vB).

[51] The correspondence between science and knowledge of truth is nowhere clearer than in Henry's *Summa*, a. 2, q. 6 (1:27rD); and a. 7, q. 2 (1:48vK).

in determining their attitude toward the theory of divine illumination. For according to Henry and Vital, at only one of the two levels of science – the higher – was divine illumination in play. Science in the first instance was available to mind working solely by its natural powers.

After all, Henry's and Vital's model of knowing truth and thus attaining scientific knowledge demanded that mind go beyond seizing a simple objective content on the level of "the true" (*verum*) and compare its object critically with an exemplar. Yet there were two exemplars to consider. First was the universal intelligible species elicited from the object itself and residing as mental marker in intellect, the abstracted species of Aristotelianizing noetics; second was the ideal reason of the thing present in God's mind, describable as a kind of divine art because it contained the exemplary forms according to which all things were made.[52] Faithful follower, Vital reproduced Henry's ideas in a virtual epitome of his words.[53] From the duality of exemplars resulted the doubling of science properly speaking, so that there were, as Henry put it, two kinds of truth (*duplex veritas*) and two ways by which truth could be known (*duplex modus sciendi veritatem*).[54]

---

[52] Henry, *Summa*, a. 1, q. 2 (1:5rE): "Et est dicendum quod cum, ut dictum est iam, veritas rei non potest cognosci nisi ex cognitione conformitatis rei cognitae ad suum exemplar . . . secundum quod duplex est exemplar rei, dupliciter ad duplex exemplar veritas rei habet ab homine cognosci. Est enim secundum quod vult Plato in primo *Timaei*, duplex exemplar: quoddam factum atque elaboratum, quoddam perpetuum atque immutabile. Primum exemplar rei est species eius universalis apud animam existens, per quam acquirit notitiam omnium suppositorum eius, et est causata a re. Secundum exemplar est ars divina continens omnium rerum ideales rationes, ad quod Plato dicit deum mundum instituisse. . . ." See also *Summa*, a. 24, q. 8 (1:145vP), referring back to this passage and summarizing it. In *Summa*, a. 1, q. 7 (1:17rK), Henry called the first exemplar "abstractum et causatum a re."

[53] See Vital, *Quaestiones de cognitione*, q. 8 (ed. Delorme, "Huit questions," pp. 324–25), drawing at times verbatim from the passage quoted above, n. 52.

[54] Henry, *Summa*, a. 1, q. 2 (1:5vF). In Matthew of Aquasparta's early works appears a related notion of two truths, although not exactly the same as Henry's and not used to the same effect – see above, Part 2, ch. 5, nn. 18 and 19. Some scholars (for instance, Braun, *Die Erkenntnislehre*, pp. 43–44; Edward Dwyer, *Die Wissenschaftslehre Heinrichs von Gent* [Würzburg, 1933], p. 36; and Prospero Stella, "La prima critica di Herveus Natalis O.P. alla noetica di Enrico di Gand: Il 'De intellectu et specie' del cosiddetto 'De quatuor materiis,'" *Salesianum* 21 [1959]: 127) have distinguished Henry's two truths as "logical" and "ontological," but for the reasons given in *Truth and Scientific Knowledge*, p. 26, n. 26, I prefer not to employ this terminology.

It was this epistemic topology that allowed Henry, in contrast to the classic Augustinians, to defend a kind of scientific knowledge "ex puris naturalibus" – that is, with no greater divine intervention than the general providence God exercised over all nature. At the lower grade of science – first level of knowing truth – there was neither recourse to a divine ideal nor special illumination in the technical sense Henry assigned to that phrase. Instead intellect worked solely with objects found in the world and the mental entities it had, on its own, drawn from them. As he explained, mind came to knowledge of this completely natural sort of truth by first employing the intelligible species it had abstracted not as object to know but as means of knowing (*ratio cognoscendi*). Then, looking back on the species, it generated in itself a concept in conformity with it, thus formally knowing the truth and attaining to science of the lower sort.[55] Vital seconded Henry by simply repeating him, almost word for word.[56]

Henry's description was not free of inconsistency. He had formally characterized truth at this level as conformity between object, outside intellect, and exemplar, the intelligible species in mind, so that knowing truth called for comparing the two to see how they conformed. Yet in describing the actual mental process he spoke of fashioning a concept conforming to the species.

In his early work Henry never explained exactly where the conformity lay. Perhaps an explanation was impossible. If, as he insisted, the intelligible species served only as means of knowing, how could one ask that mind compare it, unperceived, to something else or generate something in conformity with it? His theory would seem to have been caught in the contradiction between an Augustinian noetics demanding judgment even in simple cognition and a more Aristotelianizing one taking mental entities such as species to be mere instruments for unreflective access to what lay outside mind. Not the sole late-thirteenth-century scholar to confront this dilemma, he ultimately decided it required a dramatic response, by mid-career jettisoning the notion of intelligible species altogether.[57]

---

[55] Henry, *Summa*, a. 1, q. 2 (1:5rE). Dwyer, *Die Wissenschaftslehre*, p. 11, failed to notice this first sort of science, claiming that according to Henry all science required divine illumination.

[56] Vital, *Quaestiones de cognitione*, q. 8 (ed. Delorme, "Huit questions," p. 325).

[57] See Marrone, *Truth and Scientific Knowledge*, pp. 22–23; and for the classic discussion of Henry's abandoning intelligible species, Nys, *De werking van het menselijk*

Meanwhile he simply tolerated ambiguity. He noted that the concept mind devised in knowing truth, mental marker of its new cognition, was not another intelligible species but rather, drawing from
Augustine's lexicon, a mental word (*verbum*).[58] This word was wholly
product of an act of intellect and permitted more perfect understanding of the object than did the species generated somewhat pas-
sively *ab extra* in knowing merely "the true."[59] By the terms of his
ascending scale of cognitive perfection, this meant that science at the
first level was more certain than any knowledge coming before.[60]
Where knowledge of the true, *scire large*, had been without error or
deception, the initial grasp of truth resulted in a mind not just free
from error (*notitia libera ab omni errore*) but also unplagued by doubt
(*nequaquam de ea dubitare possumus*).[61]

Such knowledge was not, however, obtained in absolute fullness
of mental vision (*in aperta veritatis visione*), wherein truth was seen
clearly (*clare*) by mind's eye.[62] As Henry explained while examining
the status of theology as a science, certainty could be reduced to
two component factors on the part of mind: security and evidence.
The former was almost exclusively a subjective matter; Henry even

verstand (in an abbreviated Latin version: *De psychologia cognitionis humanae secundum
Henricum Gandavensem* [Rome, 1949]). Braun, *Die Erkenntnislehre*, passim, remarked on
Henry's rejection of the notion of impressed species, but he was not aware that
Henry's earliest ideas supported the opposite view.

[58] For instance, Henry, *Summa*, a. 1, q. 2, ad 2. (1:8rO); a. 1, q. 5, ad 2. (1:15vF);
and most fully, *Quodlibet* 2, q. 6 (Henrici Opera, 6:32, ll. 56–66). In *Summa*, a. 1,
q. 3 (1:10rF), Henry traced his use of "verbum" back to Augustine's *De Trinitate*
IX, 7 (eds. Mountain and Glorie, 1, 303–4). Vital followed Henry, even adding the
term "verbum" to the passage cited above, n. 56, patterned on a section in Henry's
Summa that spoke merely of "concept." For more detailed description of "word" by
Vital, again dependent on Henry's ideas, see *Quaestiones de cognitione*, q. 6 (ed. Delorme,
"Huit questions," p. 294).

[59] Henry, *Summa* (*Qg. ord.*), a. 34, q. 2, ad 4. (Henrici Opera, 27:185, ll. 19–23);
and *Summa*, a. 1, q. 12, ad 4. (1:23vR). In *Summa*, a. 24, q. 8 (1:145rN), Henry
maintained, inconsistently with what he said practically everywhere else, that judgment of the word was necessary for knowledge of truth, but with Henry one can
rarely be sure what is contradiction and what simply reformulation of an old idea.

[60] For the scale of certitude, see above, n. 24.

[61] On the certainty of *scire large*, see above, n. 18; of the initial levels of knowledge of truth, Henry, *Summa*, a. 2, q. 1 (1:23vB). A more general observation on
the connection between knowing truth and certitude is referred to above, n. 50.

[62] See the passage from the *Summa* cited in the previous note. Vital commented
that "some" thinkers (among whom he must have included Henry) maintained that,
left solely to its own devices, mind came to know truth "quodam modo tenebroso
et non omnino clare" – see Vital, *Quaestiones de cognitione*, q. 8 (ed. Delorme, "Huit
questions," p. 328).

called it "certitudo adhaesionis," or what might be termed the strength
of intellectual assent. The latter pointed the subject more towards
objective conditions, registering its degree of access to the cognitive
referent.[63] By saying that the first level of knowing truth was error-
free and untainted by doubt but not entirely clear, Henry was conceding that it met the strictest subjective demands but had some way
to go so far as evidential foundations were concerned, sufficient
achievement all the same to meet the sceptical arguments of the
Academics.[64]

He went on to observe that science of this sort was what Aristotle
had aimed for, meaning that it provided the foundation for apodictic knowledge along the lines laid out at the beginning of the
Metaphysics and the end of the *Posterior Analytics*.[65] Surprisingly he
added that it was also what Augustine often had in mind when
speaking of human cognition.[66] Indeed Henry interpreted the famous
passage from *De Trinitate* about mind's eye seeing in an incorporeal
light of its own kind as referring specifically to the parameters of
this way of knowing.[67] On this point Vital seems to have differed;

---

[63] Henry, *Summa*, a. 7, q. 2 (1:49rN): "Ex parte vero scientis dupliciter contingit
scientiae certitudo: uno modo ex parte securitatis de veritate eorum que continet
haec scientia, alio modo ex parte evidentiae in notitia veritatis, quam sciens de sci-
tis ex hac scientia consequitur. . . . Et appellatur haec securitas certitudo adhaesionis, quae bene potest esse sine omni clara et evidenti notitia."

[64] Again see the passage from Henry's *Summa*, cited above, n. 61. Modern philosophers, and most scholastics in the fourteenth century, have typically asked more in
the way of evidence for even the most modest forms true knowledge. On the problem of scepticism facing scholastics, see the cogent remarks of Marilyn Adams in
her *William Ockahm* (Notre Dame, Ind., 1987), I, 551.

[65] Henry, *Summa*, a. 1, q. 2 (1:5rE). The Aristotelian passages were the classic
texts in *Metaphysics* I, 1 (981a5–6); and *Posterior Analytics* II, 19 (100a3–9) – see above,
Pt. 2, ch. 5, n. 116; and ch. 6, nn. 8 and 18, for instances where Bonaventure and
Matthew of Aquasparta cited the same texts. Vital paraphrased Henry, with refer-
ence not to Aristotle but to the "philosophi," in *Quaestiones de cognitione*, q. 8 (ed.
Delorme, "Huit questions," p. 325).

[66] Consult the passage from the *Summa* cited in the preceding note. Transcribing
into his own work these words of Henry's, Vital deleted the association with
Augustine – see also the citation in the preceding note – thus confirming his reluctance, referred to in n. 68 below, to recognize anything but a call for divine illumination in Augustine's explication of knowledge of truth.

[67] Henry, *Summa*, a. 1, q. 2, ad 3. (1:8rP). The Augustinian passage about a "lux
sui generis" comes in *De Trinitate* XII, 15 (eds. Mountain and Glorie, 1, 378). Henry
interpreted this passage inconsistently: in *Quodlibet* IX, q. 15 (ed. Raymond Macken,
Henrici Opera, 13:261, ll. 91–99), claiming Augustine was referring to the light of
God, while in *Quodlibet* XIII, q. 8 (ed. Jos Decorte, Henrici Opera, 18:50, ll. 40–44),
returning to the earlier reading, seeing the light as one of mind's natural powers.

at least he was sympathetic to Marston's criticism of those who read Augustine in such a way.[68]

Both Henry and Vital concurred, on the other hand, that scientific knowledge at this first level embraced a limited domain of knowables. Dependent on an exemplar drawn from objects in the sensible world, it could not rise above material things and whatever they implied – what Henry denominated "scibilia philosophica" – or pretend to proper understanding of the most elevated subjects, especially not perfect knowledge of God.[69] Never absolutely lucid, it did not even offer full understanding of the objects falling within its range, the reason being its reliance on those imperfect purveyors of data, the phantasms of sensible cognition. Echoing Grosseteste, perhaps, too, the occasional pessimism of William of Auvergne, Henry called Aristotle's science at bottom "phantastic knowledge of truth" (*veritatis notitia phantastica*), while Vital spoke of it more pejoratively still as cloudy (*nebulosa cognitio*).[70] Knowledge generated without Godly intervention might be able to attain certitude, but such certainty was hardly the best mind could manage, even in the world of sin.[71]

For as the doubling of the category of science implied, both theologians believed mind could go beyond what Aristotle had imagined. Above knowledge of truth constructed with regard to the worldly exemplar came truth-perception of the second sort, more perfect than any understanding available to mind working with its natural

---

[68] In *Quaestiones de cognitione*, q. 8 (ed. Delorme, "Huit questions," p. 314), Vital offered unattributed Henry's interpretation of the passage, while on p. 317 he produced, nearly verbatim, Marston's arguments against it from *Quaestiones de anima*, q. 3, ad 1. (in Marston, *Quaestiones disputatae*, BFS, 7, p. 265). Though Vital never explicitly stated his own view, by implication he agreed with Marston.

[69] Henry, *Summa*, a. 3, q. 4 (1:29vP).

[70] *Summa*, a. 1, q. 2 (1:5vG); and a. 1, q. 3 (1:9vE). This *notitia phantastica* was, of course, different from the *intellectus phantasticus* mentioned above (see n. 31) in connection with knowledge of "the true." On Robert and William, see Marrone, *New Ideas of Truth*, pp. 35–36 and 203–9; and above, Pt. 1, ch. 4, pp. 98–102. For Vital, see *Quaestiones de cognitione*, q. 8 (ed. Delorme, "Huit questions," pp. 327 and 329), and also the passage cited above, n. 62.

[71] On rare occasions the early Henry revealed some hesitation about fully accepting that mind could have knowledge of truth without a special divine intervention. As argued in Marrone, *Truth and Scientific Knowledge*, pp. 25–26, n. 42, these instances should not be seen as undermining his formal position in favor of such knowledge but rather as signs of an underlying anxiety about cutting himself loose from the classic Augustinian view. In addition to the examples cited in *Truth and Scientific Knowledge*, see also *Summa*, a. 1, q. 3 (1:10vG). As might be expected, Vital echoed Henry's ambivalence – see *Quaestiones de cognitione*, q. 8 (ed. Delorme, "Huit questions," p. 335), Vital's rewrite of the passage from Henry's *Summa*, a. 1, q. 3.

powers alone but still accessible to the wayfarer and not requiring a gift of grace. Henry called it certain or perfect science.[72] It depended, of course, on having recourse to an exemplar in the divine mind, thus entailing divine intervention beyond God's general providence.[73] Here is where Henry made room for the divine illumination of classic Augustinians, "special illumination" in his own vocabulary.[74] To his eyes this was the type of cognition consonant with Augustine's, and he thought the proper, interpretation of Plato's views about mind and knowledge, which pointed to a kind of science truer (*verior modus acquirendi scientiam*) than that accounted for by the Aristotelian formula.[75]

Surely not by accident, Henry commented that this mode of cognition was pertinent to the cognitive foundations for knowing conclusions as well as principles.[76] Indeed he specifically took aim at those who wanted to limit God's illuminating intervention in human science to knowledge of first principles and the rules of rational discourse alone.[77] From the wording of his argument it would seem almost certain the target was John Pecham, who had used the very language Henry criticized on those occasions where he defended illumination only with respect to principal cognition.[78] Again, Henry's views were carefully calibrated to be distinguishable from those of the classic Augustinians, Vital faithfully echoing him on this score.[79]

---

[72] Henry, *Summa*, a. 1, q. 2 (1:5vE) for "certa scientia;" *Summa*, a. 1, q. 4 (1:12vD) for "perfecta scientia."

[73] Henry, *Summa*, a. 1. q. 2 (1:7v–8r[M]).

[74] See above, n. 19.

[75] For Henry on Augustine, see *Summa*, a. 1, q. 1, ad 4. (1:3r–vI); and a. 1, q. 2 (1:6vI), quoted above, n. 5; for comparison to Aristotle, *Summa*, a. 1, q. 2 (1:7vL), where Henry added that he thought it likely Aristotle personally agreed with Plato but, like many in the Academy, simply hid his true ideas from the vulgar crowd of readers.

[76] Henry, *Summa*, a. 1, q. 2 (1:7rL).

[77] Henry, *Summa*, a. 1, q. 3 (1:10vG): "Unde patet quod peccant qui ponunt quod prima principia et regulae speculabilium sunt impressiones quaedam a regulis veritatis aeternae, et cum hoc non ponunt aliquam aliam impressionem fieri aut informationem in nostris conceptibus a luce aeterna quam illam solam quae fit a specie a re accepta adiutorio lucis naturalis ingenitae."

[78] See above, Pt. 2, ch. 6, especially the passages cited in nn. 42 and 43.

[79] Vital, *Quaestiones de cognitione*, q. 8 (ed. Delorme, "Huit questions," p. 336). Lynch, in his *Theory of Knowledge*, p. 191, suggests that Vital and therefore Henry had Thomas Aquinas in mind, which is possible, although their language makes Pecham the more likely candidate. Richard of Mediavilla, *In II. Sent.* 10, 2, 1, ad 3. (in *Super quatuor libros Sententiarum*, 2, 130a [Brescia, 1591/repr. Frankfurt am Main, 1963]), also spoke of human knowledge of first principles in a way that might make him Henry's and Vital's target, at least as much as Thomas, with whom Richard was on this point in essential agreement.

Since science at this higher level constituted knowledge of the second of two sorts of truth Henry recognized, he chose, drawing on Augustine, to demarcate its object by calling it "pure truth" (*sincera veritas*), a phrase employed so consistently in his early work that it can be considered a technical term in his, as well as Vital's, philosophical thesaurus.[80] Other labels for the same thing were "clear truth" and "certain truth."[81] On the scale of certitude, knowledge arriving at truth of this kind could be described as completely certain (*certa omnino notitia*), an epistemic achievement Henry thought was manifested in two ways.[82] First of all, such cognition was free from error, like knowledge of "the true," and indubitable, as with science at the first level, but also, advancing to a degree of subjective intellectual security immune to even the most obdurate scepticism, in Henry's words infallible.[83] Second, it was knowledge of truth that was fully open (*in aperta veritatis visione*), sufficiently so for it to be designated intellectually "clear."[84] For the first time Henry could point to a type of cognition that unconditionally satisfied science's objective requirements for evidence and clarity of mind.

---

[80] See, for example, Henry, *Summa*, a. 1, q. 2 (1:5vE & G, 6rH); and Vital, *Quaestiones de cognitione*, q. 8 (ed. Delorme, "Huit questions," p. 328, and 327): "sincere [cognita] veritas." In *De diversis quaestionibus 83*, q. 9, Augustine had spoken of a special *sinceritas veritatis*, a passage Henry incorrectly quoted (*Summa*, a. 1, q. 2 [1:5vE]) as referring to *sincera veritas*. About the time Henry was writing, Matthew of Aquasparta used the more authentic Augustinian form to refer to much the same thing. For citations to Augustine and Matthew, see above, Part 2, ch. 5, n. 49. As almost always with Henry, one can find exceptions. In *Summa*, a. 1, q. 1, ad 2. (1:2vF), he said that truth known without the divine exemplar might be called "pure truth," although not "absolutely" (*simpliciter*) pure. *Summa*, a. 1, q. 2 (1:5vG) noted that those who did not recognize his higher form of science simply failed to distinguish between the two kinds of truth.

[81] For "clear truth" (*liquida veritas, clara veritas*), see Henry, *Summa*, a. 1, q. 2 (1:7vM and 8rS); and a. 2, q. 1 (1:23vB); for "certain truth" (*certa veritas*), *Summa*, a. 1, q. 8 (1:18rE).

[82] Henry, *Summa*, a. 1, q. 2 (1:5vE).

[83] Ibid. It was thus the source of what could be called "infallible science" (*Summa*, a. 1, q. 3 (1:10vG). Vital repeated Henry about infallibility in *Quaestiones de cognitione*, q. 8 (ed. Delorme, "Huit questions," pp. 325–26). See above, nn. 18 and 61, on the two lower ranks of security; and n. 63, for the subjective and objective ingredients of certitude. As for the claim here about immunity to scepticism, Marilyn Adams (*William Ockham*, I, 570), quoting from Henry, *Summa*, a. 2, q. 1 (1:23vB), points out that this is not quite true, as there was still some evidential imperfection at this level of science, a concession Henry surely intended more to protect the exclusivity of the beatific vision than to allow scepticism an opening into his theory of knowledge in the world.

[84] See *Summa*, a. 2, q. 1 (1:23vB), also cited above, n. 63. In *Summa*, a. 1, q. 2 (1:5vG), Henry called it "notitia liquida" – compare references to "liquida veritas" given above, n. 81.

As always, the problem was explaining how the noetic process worked. Henry's model of truth as conformity would have mind act to compare exemplar, in this case divine ideal, with appropriate object in the created world.[85] How could he then circumvent the ontologism perennially stalking the Augustinian explanation of truth?

Henry appealed once more to the distinction between object known and means of knowing. Mind could look to divine exemplar as to an object providing means for knowing that which it exemplified or as to means alone (ratio tantum).[86] If divine exemplar was grasped as object and means, then intellect would be able to draw a comparison so sharp as to pass above science of pure truth to a higher level, the most perfect way of knowing truth, which Henry called perfect certitude.[87] Vital agreed.[88] But such cognition was impossible without an illumination more special than Henry's technical "special illumination," more elevated even than the common light of saving grace.[89] To see the divine exemplar in this way required that infusion of light so extraordinary that it had to be considered a gift of special grace, granted exclusively to the blessed and those rare earthly seers: Moses, Paul and Benedict.[90] The process amounted to seeing the divine essence face to face, and Henry associated it with what he called the "eye of contemplation" (oculus contemplationis).[91] For

---

[85] See Henry, Summa, a. 1, q. 7 (1:16vK).

[86] Henry, Summa, a. 1, q. 2 (1:6rI); and a. 24, q. 8, ad 2. and ad 3. (1:145vR–S); the first passage taken up almost verbatim by Vital, Quaestiones de cognitione, q. 8 (ed. Delorme, "Huit questions," p. 327).

[87] Henry, Summa, a. 1, q. 2 (1:6rI); and a. 2, q. 1 (1:23vB), where he said truth could be known in this way "perfecta certitudine."

[88] Vital, Quaestiones de cognitione, q. 8 (ed. Delorme, "Huit questions," p. 328).

[89] Henry, Summa, a. 1, q. 2 (1:6vI) – cited above, n. 3 – and also a. 24, q. 2 (1:138rI). Braun, in Die Erkenntnislehre, seems not to have discriminated adequately between these two types of special illumination, so that he interprets Henry as positing no divine illumination short of a gift equivalent to a special light of grace. Mieczysław Gogacz, Problem istnienia boga u Anselma z Canterbury i problem prawdy u Henryka z Gandawy (Lublin, 1961), may be making a similar interpretation, although I am not sure I have understood him correctly. See also Gogacz, "Czy według Henryka z Gandawy jest możliwe poznanie czystej prawdy bez pomocy oświecenia" ("La connaissance de la vérité pure selon Henry de Gand"), Roczniki Filozoficzne 8, n. 1 (1960): 161–71.

[90] Again, see the passage cited above, nn. 3–4, and consult Summa, a. 1, q. 3 (1:8vA and 9vE); and a. 2, q. 1 (1:23vB). Vital reproduces the second of the two passages from a. 1, q. 3 in Quaestiones de cognitione, q. 8 (ed. Delorme, "Huit questions," p. 333.)

[91] Henry, Summa, a. 1, q. 4 (1:12rD). Henry thought there was another way God presented himself to mind as both object and means of knowing, not in his essence but under a general attribute. That way will be discussed below in Part 3, ch. 10.

knowledge just of pure truth, Henry maintained and Vital agreed, the divine exemplar was grasped only as means for knowing.[92] And here, as at the first level of science, in conceiving this, its second truth, mind formed in itself a concept or word – the second word in the whole process – which served as mental marker of its new-found cognition.[93]

But did Henry's words really make sense? As with truth at the lower level, the need to reconcile an injunction against objective status for the exemplar with a call for comparison of exemplar and exemplified generated a tension, so much greater in this case given the risk of implying a vision of God. It is fair to say that Henry never entirely resolved the problem in his early work. There is no doubt, however, that he recognized the sensitivity of the issue and at least pointed in the direction of a resolution – that no literal comparison to the exemplar occurred.[94] He tried to defend his claim by maintaining, with Vital repeating him nearly verbatim, that God as illuminator in knowledge of pure truth acted in analogy to three basic elements in sensible sight: light, species of color, and object's determining shape or figure.[95] A cautionary note was necessary simply to warn the reader that God, unlike light, species or figure in sensation, would never inhere (*non inhaerendo*) in the receptive power as form in subject but rather flowed (*illabendo*) into mind, subtly making his presence felt.[96]

---

[92] See Henry, *Summa*, a. 1. q. 2 (1:6vI); a. 1, q. 3 (1:8vA) – quoted above, n. 10 – and a. 24, q. 9 (1:146rV); and Vital, *Quaestiones de cognitione*, q. 8 (ed. Delorme, "Huit questions," pp. 327–28 – drawing on Henry's *Summa*, a. 1, q. 2 – and p. 331 – reproducing the passage from a. 1, q. 3). On Vital's copying Henry, see Leo von Untervintl, "Die Intuitionslehre bei Vitalis de Furno, O. Min. (+1327)," CF 25 (1955): 228–36.

[93] Henry, *Summa*, a. 1, q. 2 (1:7rK).

[94] For full discussion, see Marrone, *Truth and Scientific Knowledge*, pp. 30–39.

[95] Henry, *Summa*, a. 1, q. 3 (1:9rB): "Ut autem ex modo illustrationis videamus quomodo ars divina . . . possit esse ratio cognoscendi . . . considerandum est in simili de visione oculi corporalis. In ipso enim ad completionem actus videndi . . . tria requiruntur ex parte obiecti quod in nobis operatur actum videnti. . . . Primum illorum quae requiruntur in visu corporali est lux illuminans organum ad acuendum. Secundum est species coloris immutans eum ad intuendum. Tertium figuratio determinans eum ad discernendum." Lower on the same page (9rC), Henry called the third element a "character figurae corporis colorati." Vital's version of the passage can be found in *Quaestiones de cognitione*, q. 8 (ed. Delorme, "Huit questions," p. 331), where he called the third element a "configuratio."

[96] Henry, *Summa*, a. 1, q. 3 (1:9rD).

By advancing the claim about inherence Henry was, of course, rejoining the classic Augustinians, most especially Pecham, in their concern to protect God's transcendence.[97] He even rationalized divinity's flowing presence as Bonaventure had by recalling that God was, of all things, most intimate to mind.[98] Vital appreciated the relevance of arguments some of the classic Augustinians had brought against the notion of divine illumination merely by means of an "influence" and, using language reminiscent of the early Matthew of Aquasparta, noted that were the illuminating force to inhere in intellect it would have to be created, not divine, thus no suitable standard for immutable truth.[99] Ironically, ideas from Matthew's early years were thereby turned against the position Matthew himself adopted later in his career.

Yet putting aside restrictions on formal inherence, the introduction of the analogy made the point that divinity's illuminative action was subject to a threefold description: working as spiritual light, as form or species, and as figure or character. At first glance each way would seem to have been coequal to the others. Only a closer look reveals that Henry, and thus also Vital, did not intend to give them all the same weight.

Acting as incorporeal light God served to purge and heal mind, sharpening it in preparation for arrival at pure truth.[100] Since only the blessed were exposed to divine light without intermediary, this shining was indirect, with God diffusing his light first on the intelligible species of things – literally, on intelligible things by means of

---

[97] Pecham had specifically warned against seeing God the illuminator as inhering in mind – see above, Part 2, ch. 5, nn. 70 and 71.

[98] See again the passage cited above, n. 96. For Bonaventure, see above, Part 2, ch. 8, n. 42.

[99] Vital, *Quaestiones de cognitione*, q. 8 (ed. Delorme, "Huit questions," p. 332): "Hanc autem impressionem seu caracterizationem non facit lux divina menti nostrae inhaerendo tamquam quaedam dispositio . . . quia . . . tunc illa impressio, cum sit creatura, esset mutabilis et per consequens non posset esse medium ad cognoscendum immobilem veritatem." Note how close the language here is to that of Matthew in the passage from his *Commentary on the Sentences* quoted above, Part 2, ch. 5, n. 73. Delorme (in the edition of Vital, p. 332, n. 5) draws attention to Marston, *Quaestiones de anima*, q. 3, ad 15. (in Marston, *Quaestiones disputatae*, pp. 268–69) as source for Vital's ideas, but though it is true Marston is making much the same point as Vital in the passage indicated by Delorme, the similarities of language are not nearly so great as between Vital and Matthew. Still, it is hard to believe Vital had actually seen a copy of Matthew's *Commentary*.

[100] Henry, *Summa*, a. 1, q. 3 (1:9vD).

their species – and through them reflectively (*obliquo aspectu*) on intellect.[101] A passage late in the *Summa* seems to suggest that this literally illuminationist characterization of God's truth-giving act should take pre-eminence among the three, for it is there claimed that by acting as light God was most properly said to lead mind to knowledge of pure truth, but immediately Henry added he was referring not to the preparatory honing described just now but rather to the divine role as art and book of reasons, terms paradigmatically associated with God's functioning in the third way, as figure or character.[102] Far from being central to Henry's thought, the description of God as vision-sharpening light was in fact a minor theme, rarely mentioned in his work.

As form or species, analogous to the species of color in sensible sight, God somehow transformed (*immutare*) or even informed (*formare*) mind so that it could see, not distinctly but after the manner of pure perception of color undetermined by shape or figure.[103] Precisely how Henry intended this simile to be taken is hard to say, but it is tempting to read it as making the divine exemplar literally

---

[101] Henry, *Summa*, a. 1, q. 3 (1:9vF). Vital copied him in *Quaestiones de cognitione*, q. 8 (ed. Delorme, "Huit questions," pp. 333–34). Some have read their description as making of God a kind of Avicennian agent intellect, a phrase Henry actually applied to the divinity later on – see Marrone, *Truth and Scientific Knowledge*, p. 31. Etienne Gilson was first to suggest there was a current of thirteenth-century thinkers holding to a notion of agent intellect qualifying them as proponents of an "augustinisme avicennisant" – see his works cited above in the general introduction, n. 4. Paulus, *Henri de Gand*, pp. 5–6; and José Gómez Caffarena, *Ser participado y ser subsistente en la metafísica de Enrique de Gante* (Rome, 1958), p. 246, agreed that Henry could be called an Avicennizing Augustinian, at least so far as his theory of illumination was concerned. Raymond Macken, "La théorie de l'illumination divine," pp. 92–93; and Faustino Prezioso, *La critica di Duns Scoto*, p. 62, both accept Henry as an Avicennizing Augustinian in his later years, Prezioso (p. 20) going so far as to claim him as a proponent of an "immediatistico-attualistico" version of divine illumination, along with William of Auvergne, Roger Bacon, Roger Marston and John Pecham. In *Quaestiones de cognitione*, q. 8 (ed. Delorme, "Huit questions," p. 329), Vital admitted God appeared to act as a kind of agent intellect.

[102] Henry, *Summa*, a. 1, q. 8 (1:18rE), where he listed the alternatives of influencing intellection by means of light or by means of species, claiming that God acted in the former and not the latter way in leading to knowledge of truth. This assertion would seem to contradict his support for what was Pecham's view – that God illuminated as a species – cited above, nn. 10 and 11, but it is likely that Henry was using neither "light" nor "species" in anything like their normal sense.

[103] Henry, *Summa*, a. 1, q. 3 (1:10rF). Vital gives the same description in his own words in *Quaestiones de cognitione*, q. 8 (ed. Delorme, "Huit questions," p. 334). On how color could not cause distinct vision without shape or figure, see Henry, *Summa*, a. 1, q. 3 (1:9rC).

a second species available to mind which it could set alongside the preceding species abstracted from created reality so as to derive a compounded understanding of pure truth. Gilson interpreted Henry's position on illumination this way in general, and one brief passage in the *Summa* referring to "double species" can be cited on his behalf.[104] Such talk would echo earlier language of John Pecham on two species leading to knowledge authenticated by God as well as intimations in others of the classic Augustinians that a dual species was at work in divine illumination, and it would surely come closest to the Anselmian prototype of comparison of two objects present to mind.[105] Yet the very passage about two species seems in fact to have been intended as analysis of God's illuminative action according to the third mode, determining figure.[106] Like the first, the second description, too, was apparently not central to Henry's thought, perhaps included only to echo Bonaventure's words about God as species in mind.[107] Henry's eventual blanket repudiation of impressed intelligible species meant that it would disappear without a trace in his later work.

Which leaves the third description of divine action, as figure or character transforming intellect and bringing it to understand pure truth distinctly.[108] God functioned in this instance like an art, store-

---

[104] Gilson, "Roger Marston: Un cas d'augustinisme avicennisant," AHDLMA 8 (1933): 41, n. 1. The passage in Henry is his *Summa*, a. 1, q. 3 (1:10rG): "Sciendum est quod duplex species et exemplar rei debet interius lucere in mente tamquam ratio et principium cognoscendi rem: una species accepta a re quae disponat mentem ad cognitionem ipsi inhaerendo; altera vero est quae est causa rei quae non disponit mentem ad cognitionem ei inhaerendo, sed ei illabendo praesentia, et maiori quam inhaerendo in ea lucendo."

[105] On Pecham, see *Quaestiones de anima*, q. 5, arg. 7 and ad 7. (18.) (ed. Spettmann, in *Quaestiones tractantes de anima*, pp. 64 and 70), where he relied upon analogy between intellect and sensory sight, claiming that just as two visual images merged as they fed into a single nerve leading to the brain, so two species representing the same object – one abstracted, the other supplied by God – could come together in the mind's eye. On Bonaventure, see Part 2, ch. 6, nn. 6, 55 and 56; for Matthew of Aquasparta, Part 2, ch. 6, nn. 119 and 120.

[106] See the context of the passage quoted above, n. 104.

[107] For Bonaventure, see above, Pt. 2, ch. 8, nn. 39, 41 and 43. This cautionary stance acts as a healthy corrective against taking too far the similarity between Henry and Pecham on illumination working along the lines of cognitive species – see above, nn. 10 and 11.

[108] The following description depends on Henry, *Summa*, a. 1, q. 3 (1:10rF). Of all classic Augustinians, Pecham came nearest to anticipating Henry on this score with his characterization of God the illuminator as exemplary and quasi-efficient form – see above, Pt. 2, ch. 5, n. 71.

house of the exemplary models by which all things had been made
and all knowledge would ultimately be certified. More concretely
put, the divine exemplar made an impression on the already knowing intellect, which impression constituted a word in which mind
seized the pure truth about that which it had previously compre-
hended only imperfectly. It all happened, as Augustine had suggested,
the way a signet ring impressed its image on wax.[109] Here lay the
key to interpreting the illuminative process, and Vital copied Henry's
rendition of it almost word for word.[110]

Henry was quick to point out that God worked on mind in this
operation in coordination with the lower exemplar drawn from the
object, an intelligible species already in intellect.[111] Knowing pure
truth was therefore continuous with earlier cognitive processes dependent on the senses, and Henry always insisted that there could be
no natural knowledge of objects outside mind that did not begin
with sensation.[112] How it happened was that the divine exemplar
spiritually present to mind acted upon the word already formed in
the business of knowing truth at the first grade of science, reshap-
ing it and making it into a second, more perfect word capable of
representing truth at the level of *sincera veritas*.[113] The new word was
more perfect precisely because refashioned in conformity with the
creative exemplar, ultimate source of truth for either thing or mind.
Today one might say the divine exemplar worked as a normative
force, bringing concepts more into line with truth. Henry's words
were that intellect began with something "material and incomplete" –
the word at the first stage based on an abstracted species – and then

---

[109] Augustine, *De Trinitate* XV, 15 (eds. Mountain and Glorie, 2, 451).

[110] Vital, *Quaestiones de cognitione*, q. 8 (ed. Delorme, "Huit questions," p. 334.).

[111] See Henry, *Summa*, a. 1, q. 3 (1:10rF); and also (1:10vG).

[112] See the combined testimony of *Summa*, a. 1, q. 10 (1:21rC); and a. 1, q. 4
(1:12vD); as well as the texts cited above, n. 111.

[113] Henry, *Summa*, a. 1, q. 3 (1:10rF): "Verbum perfectum veritatis debet esse
formata cogitatio secundum supremam et perfectam similitudinem ad ipsam rem,
quae non potest esse nisi exemplar illud aeternum. . . . [S]ic verbum quod non est
simillimum neque sincerae veritatis, sive etiam veritatis simpliciter, expressivum,
formatum a sola specie et exemplari accepto a re, . . . fiat simil<l>imum et sincerae
veritatis, et etiam veritatis, simpliciter expressivum, solum ab exemplari aeterno."
See also *Summa*, a. 1, q. 2 (1:7rL): "Necesse est igitur quod illa veritas increata in
conceptu nostro [i. e. verbo] se imprimat, et ad characterem suum conceptum nostrum transformet, et sic mentem nostram expressa veritate de re informet similitu-
dine illa quam res ipsa habet apud primam veritatem." The former passage is
essentially reproduced by Vital in his *Quaestiones de cognitione*, q. 8 (ed. Delorme,
"Huit questions," pp. 334–35).

moved on to something "formal and complete" – the word shaped
or normalized by the eternal exemplar.[114] Though the parallel is
imperfect, such language nearly enough recalls Matthew of Aquasparta
in *De cognitione* characterizing the abstracted species as formal but
incomplete cognitive element, the light God poured into mind as
formal, complete and consummating, to suggest that both scholastics were edging towards the same idea, Matthew's infused illumination approximating Henry's perfect word of truth.[115] Since Matthew's
text probably postdates Henry's, classic Augustinianism was in this
case striving to accommodate the more fastidious philosophizing of
the 1270s and 80s.

It is easy to see why Henry found his third description of illumination most attractive for conceiving the role two exemplars played
in knowledge of pure truth, for only this model laid bare a trian-
gular set of relations: of mind's word through abstracted species to
object, of object immediately to divine exemplar, and finally of mind's
word to exemplar again.[116] By these terms knowledge itself reflected
the objective truth of the referent in the world; indeed because of
its impressed relation to divine exemplar, the mental word could be
said to reproduce the object's truth in intellect.[117] If this idea strayed

---

[114] Henry, *Summa*, a. 1, q. 3 (1:10r–v[G]): "Et sunt in conceptu huius verbi duo
consideranda. . . . Est enim in eo considerare aliquid materiale et incompletum, et
aliquid formale et completum, ut illud incompletum fiat perfectum et completum.
Ex exemplari enim accepto a re habet quod materiale est in ipso et incompletam
similitudinem ad veritatem rei. . . . Ex exemplari autem aeterno recipit comple-
mentum et informationem perfectam, ut sit verbum expressae similitudinis ad rem
extra. . . ." Vital reproduces this nearly word for word in *Quaestiones de cognitione*,
q. 8 (ed. Delorme, "Huit questions," p. 335).

[115] See above, Pt. 2, ch. 6, n. 118, but also the cautions below, nn. 120 and
121, about taking Henry, like Matthew, to be talking about an "influence."

[116] Henry, *Summa*, a. 1, q. 3 (1:10rG): "Istis siquidem duabus speciebus exem-
plaribus in mente concurrentibus . . . mens concipiat verbum veritatis perfecte infor-
matae . . . ut ad modum quo prima veritas sigillavit rem veritate quam habet in
essendo, sigillet etiam mentem ipsam veritate quam habet in eam cognoscendo, ut
eadem idea veritatis qua habet res suam veritatem in se, habeat de ea veritatem
ipsa anima, ut sic sit expressa similitudo verbi ad rem ipsam, et utriusque ad eius
exemplar primum. . . ."

[117] Henry, *Summa*, a. 1, q. 3 (1:10vG): "Et cum tale verbum perfectae veritatis
formatum fuerit in anima, est ibi considerare tres veritates sibi correspondentes.
Primo veritatem exemplaris divini. Secundo veritatem rei productae ab illa. Tertio
veritatem in conceptu mentis ab utraque expressam, quae est tamquam conformitas utriusque et ex utriusque ratione concepta et menti impressa, qua mens formaliter vera nominatur." Vital reproduces this in *Quaestiones de cognitione*, q. 8 (ed.
Delorme, "Huit questions," p. 335), where comparison with Henry suggests that in
the last line on this page of Delorme's edition "res" should read "mens."

from the formal notion of knowledge of truth as mind's consideration of object's conformity to exemplar, it compensated by revealing how intellect could itself come to participate in the non-mental
exemplary relations by which creation was sustained.

Moreover, emphasizing a normative impression on intellect over
comparison of exemplar to object nicely minimized the latent ontologism of the classic illuminationist tradition. Henry practically admitted
as much at the end of the *Summa*'s article 1, question 3, validating
the inference some drew from the Augustinian model that in grasping truth one actually saw God, but only to the extent that in knowing pure truth mind possessed a word shaped by the eternal exemplar,
through which it could have a minimal understanding of the exemplary agent.[118] In support he even cited the famous passage from
Augustine's *De Trinitate* about knowing God by means of a similitude inferior to the divine nature, effective of knowledge not face to
face but rather *per speculum et in aenigmate*.[119] Camille Bérubé takes
this to mean that Henry subscribed to Gilbert of Tournai's – and by
extension the mature Matthew of Aquasparta's – notion of divine illumination by an influence from God.[120] But Henry's inferior similitude
was not an active principle like Gilbert's and Matthew's "influence";
it was rather the word, product of an act performed by God and
itself merely marker of knowledge of pure truth. Wary of ontologism, Henry found a way of accounting for illumination that in no
measure reduced the immediacy of God's intervention.[121]

---

[118] See Henry, *Summa*, a. 1, q. 3, ad 1., 5., 6. (1:10vH, K, and L), which marks
a unique concession that the process of divine illumination leading to truth might
be connected with at least one natural way of knowing God, two phenomena otherwise sharply separated in his early works.

[119] See above, Pt. 2, ch. 8, n. 15. For other classic Augustinians on this, see the
same chapter, nn. 44, 112, 136 and 137.

[120] See, for instance, Bérubé, "Henri de Gand et Mathieu d'Aquasparta," p. 145.
Prezioso, *La critica*, pp. 98–100, similarly maintained that Henry, like Matthew,
interpreted divine illumination as working through an influence of God. I have
argued elsewhere that I do not agree – see Marrone, "Matthew of Aquasparta,"
pp. 263–65.

[121] This is especially obvious in contrast to Matthew, who specifically used the
passage from Augustine about an inferior similitude to defend his vision of an active
principle of illumination *lower* than God but *above* the mind, which he identified as
the illuminative influence – see above, Pt. 2, ch. 8, nn. 136 and 138. To the degree
that Vital offers a clue as to what Henry was thinking, it is instructive to recall
(above, n. 99) his version of Henry's warning against seeing God as inhering in
mind, which reached back to Matthew's early language ruling out any attempt to
reduce the active principle of illumination to a mere influence.

Meanwhile he tackled another problem confronting the classic Augustinians: whether divine illumination occurred naturally or depended in each instance on the will of God, and at any rate what it implied about the naturalness of human intellection. With regard to the first part of the question his response paralleled Gilbert's – and William of Auvergne's – in opposition to Bonaventure.[122] Henry took every act of illumination to be voluntary on God's part and so distinguished knowledge of pure truth from the natural, thus necessary, processes of cognition below it. Since God's inscrutable choice decided who would know what with the certitude of illumined science, evil minds might occasionally be given greater access to divine reasons than good Christians.[123] Yet inherent strength of mind had at least some role to play in the process.[124] While at times Henry seems to have meant by this that God took account of the mental powers of individuals, offering divine assistance more fully to those who could make better use of it, on other occasions his implication is that God decided, voluntarily but still irrevocably, to give illumination to all minds, allowing each to make use of it according to its own capacity.[125] Vital preferred the latter view, for when he copied Henry's general assertion that God offered illumination to whomever he chose, he added his own comment that so far as pure truth was concerned divine assistance was available to everyone who wanted it.[126]

As for the naturalness of intellection of pure truth, Henry appears to have grasped the difficulty of the question even better than Matthew, who touched on it about the same time.[127] In the increasingly Aristotelianizing atmosphere of late-thirteenth-century Scholasticism, Augustinians were hard pressed to explain how illumination of any sort could bear upon mind, the Godly light being not only far above human intellect but also foreign to its nature. Henry's response was to divide the various meanings of "natural." Admitting that mind

---

[122] See above, Pt. 2, ch. 5, nn. 105–6.

[123] Henry, *Summa*, a. 1, q. 2 (1:7vM).

[124] See Henry, *Summa*, a. 1, q. 3 (1:9vE).

[125] For the first position, see *Summa*, a. 1, q. 4 (1:11vD); for the second, *Summa*, a. 1. q. 2, ad arg. (1:8vS); or the even stronger statement in *Summa*, a. 13, q. 6 (1:94vE). It is interesting to see that immediately after the passage in a. 1, q. 2, Henry noted that the evil of some might incline God to withhold all illumination from them, counter to the implications of the passage cited above, n. 123.

[126] Compare the passage cited above in n. 123 with Vital, *Quaestiones de cognitione*, q. 8 (ed. Delorme, "Huit questions," p. 330).

[127] See above, Pt. 2, ch. 5, n. 108.

did not know pure truth naturally, if this meant solely by virtue of its own natural powers (*ex puris naturalibus naturaliter*), he insisted that it nevertheless came to know it, through God's help, with all its powers intact and none of them violated (*in puris naturalibus constitutus*).[128] In other words, although the wayfarer's natural strength of intellect alone was insufficient to perceive pure truth, it was not "unnatural" for mind to have access to so much of the divine light as was necessary to raise it to such a vision.[129] Later on, when addressing the problem of knowledge by a still higher gift of grace, Henry advanced a parallel argument even more clearly.[130] Knowledge by grace was not according to mind's natural powers, in which sense it was not natural. Yet intellect was by nature ordained to be receptive of a free gift permitting knowledge higher than the natural powers could by themselves attain. Such ordination or proclivity constituted a kind of naturalness, though of a different sort from what was normally meant by the word.[131] It is uncanny how much Henry's defense anticipated criticisms Duns would level against illumination over two decades later. As always, the secular master proved himself extraordinarily aware of the philosophical hurdles to be overcome if Augustinian noetics and epistemology were to survive.

---

[128] Henry, *Summa*, a. 1, q. 2 (1:8rM).

[129] Henry, *Summa*, a. 1, q.2 (1:7vM).

[130] Henry, *Summa*, a. 3, q. 5, ad 2. (1:30rY): ". . . quod illius luminis gratiae non est susceptibilis per naturam . . . dicendum quod verum est, ita quod ex puris naturalibus illud sibi acquirat, vel quod naturaliter lumen ipsum sibi inditum habeat. Est tamen ipsius susceptibilis per naturam, quia natura de se ad hoc ordinata est, ut munere creatoris hoc recipiat. . . ."

[131] See Henry, *Summa*, a. 3, q. 4, ad 2. (1:29vR), where he explicitly talks about these two ways to use the term "natural" (*naturaliter*).

CHAPTER TEN

MIND'S OBJECT AND THE ROAD TO GOD

The distinction between object and means had permitted Henry to embrace a theory of divine illumination in knowledge of truth while at the same time avoiding charges of ontologism that might be leveled against the epistemology of the classic Augustinians. Yet did the particular way he applied the distinction not threaten the sense of intimacy between God and mind central to Augustinian intellectual traditions? After all, his uncompromising separation of object and means severed Augustine's paradigmatic image of God's irradiating truth from most matters of origin of concepts, object of knowledge and nature of its metaphysical grounding, even though it had been on the ideological terrain of the latter issues that classic Augustinians had made the greatest strides in reinforcing illuminationism's assurance of divine intimacy to mind. Indeed a mark of their accomplishment was their success in integrating earlier ideas about a dynamic sweeping mind up to God as ultimate object with those very ideogenic and referential elements of the traditional cluster of illuminationist ideas, thereby drawing out of Augustinian noetics for the first time a scholastically respectable theory of the wayfarer's natural knowledge of God. If the same elements were now to be divorced from the notion of a divine light of truth for the sake of insulating the latter from ontologizing implications, what was to prevent them from either degenerating into a fully ontologist description of the vision of God in the sinful life or collapsing into an incoherence forfeiting the remarkable achievements Bonaventure and his followers had made?

Henry had no intention of allowing his predecessors' achievements to be lost. Instead of undermining philosophical support for God's intimacy to mind, his radical division between means and object permitted him to lavish greater attention on the notion of natural knowledge of God, making it even more technically precise and concrete, thus capable of drawing still greater profit from classic Augustinians' introduction of a God-oriented cognitive dynamic into traditional Augustinian theories of mind. In fact, since from the days of Grosseteste the literal image of a light of truth was, of all facets of illuminationist discourse, most fraught with ontologist ambiguity, it would

appear that Henry simply decided he could gather together the
threads of that discourse entailing knowledge of God and, by dealing with them in theoretical isolation from the notion of divinity's
irradiating function as guarantor of truth, liberate Augustinian ideas
about object and ideogenesis from the most menacing implications
of ontologism. Meanwhile, ironically, the conventional core of illumination, increasingly linked exclusively to knowledge of truth and
relieved of the philosophical burden of explaining cognitive reference
or knowledge of God, could be yet further extracted from its own
ontologizing past. In short, cleaving the newly unified doctrine of
illumination promoted less hesitant and more explicit analysis on
either side.

This bifurcation of what had grown into a seamless whole with
the classic Augustinians – this theoretical separation of knowledge of
truth from knowledge of God – proved a watershed for Augustinianism
in the thirteenth century. Given the Aristotelianizing pressures of the
university milieu, it opened the door to rapid decline of support even
among self-styled conservatives for the notion of a normative illuminative function for God, which could henceforth be abandoned
without risk to the valued sense of divine cognitive intimacy. It likewise marked the beginnings of an Augustinian understanding of natural knowledge of divinity that would, unlike the pathbreaking efforts
of Bonaventure and his followers, be increasingly unconnected to an
image of Godly intellectual light. The structural foundations for such
an understanding constitute Henry's second fundamental contribution to illuminationism in the initial years of his magisterium, coun-
terpoint to his efforts to preserve a place for divine light in a scientific
epistemology and in the long run more enduring.

Since, in contrast to his handling of illumination in knowledge of
truth, Henry's first endeavors with regard to issues of reference, origin of concepts and cognition of God established the parameters of
a single approach to which he remained faithful throughout his
career, it is not necessary here to discriminate between the ideas of
his early and later writings. As before, discussion hinged on the distinction between means of knowing and object known, the difficulty
in this case consisting in finding a way for God to serve to some
degree as mental object without being fully and clearly perceived.[1]

---

[1] See above, Pt. 3, ch. 9, nn. 3–4; and also *Summa*, a. 3, q. 4 (1:29vP), for

Because this was an instance of divine intervention in normal human cognition, Henry's noetics required placing God technically in the role of part means for knowing other things, part object of mind.[2] A suitable account of the whole process would thus have to turn to Henry's idea of the kind of cognitive means mentioned before: an image in a mirror, seen itself but also taken as a way to know the imaged object.[3]

Of course, a full object of cognition could furnish the means to know something else, the way direct vision of the divine exemplars facilitated perfect knowledge of all exemplified creatures, but full knowledge of God was already out of the question.[4] The problem was finding proper middle ground between full object and means alone, God's illuminative role in leading to knowledge of pure truth.[5] Here the analogy to a mirror's image was by itself insufficient guide, for Henry conceived of the noetic mechanism it stood for as broad enough to embrace even so elevated a matter as God's role in the beatific vision.[6] Simply put, it was not enough that the divine element active in natural knowledge of God constitute, in contrast to truth perception, object and not only means; the very nature of the divine factor had to be different. God acted as illuminator of truth in virtue of being exemplar for all creation, an aspect of his reality specifically correlated to divine substance and thus capable of revealing him "in his own particularity."[7] If divinity were in any way exposed to mind as object and not just means by virtue of this same

Henry's comments about the impossibility of what he called "perfect knowledge of God" by natural means.

[2] To see how Henry understood this configuration, condense his comments in *Summa*, a. 24, q. 8, ad 1., ad 2., and ad opp. (1:145v[Q–S]). For Henry's general views on means of knowing and God's intervention in normal cognition, see above, Pt. 3, ch. 9, nn. 5–6.

[3] See above, Pt. 3, ch. 9, nn. 6 and 7.

[4] On exemplars functioning as both object and means, see Henry, *Summa*, a. 1, q. 2 (1:6rI); on the exclusion of full vision of God, n. 1, above.

[5] See Henry, *Summa*, a. 1, q. 3 (1:8vA); a. 24, q. 9 (1:146rV), which refers back to this passage; and on illumination of truth, Pt. 3, ch. 9, nn. 8 and 10.

[6] The beatific vision is, in fact, one of the ways Henry applied the example of a mirror's image in the passage cited in Pt. 3, ch. 9, n. 6.

[7] Henry, *Summa*, a. 1, q. 3 (1:8vA): "[Lux divina] non est ratio cognoscendi sinceram veritatem in aliis sub ratione alicuius generalis attributi dei, quale a nobis cognoscibile est in hac vita ... sed ut est ipsa divina substantia et ars increata in suo esse particulari, quae ut obiectum sine lumine gloriae in vita futura vel specialis gratiae in praesenti a mente humana videri non potest. ..." See also a. 24, q. 8 (1:145r–v[O–P]); a. 24, q. 9 (1:146rV); and the first passages cited above, n. 2.

aspect, the resultant vision would potentially be tantamount to that more correctly relegated to the resurrected life. Knowledge of God available naturally to mind working in the world had therefore necessarily to be dependent on divinity acting under some other guise.

What Henry was reaching for was the idea Bonaventure had briefly suggested decades earlier, that the foundation for all that mind perceived of God by purely natural means lay in seizing divinity as an object known only in general, or as Henry put it, by virtue of one of his general attributes (*sub ratione alicuius generalis attributi Dei*).[8] Another way of saying this was that in mind's initial efforts God was not conceived naturally by means of a proper understanding (*in speciali*) befitting a specific term like "God," applicable solely the divinity, but rather more generally (*in generali*) by means of apprehension of any of the broad properties God shared with creatures.[9] This, Henry thought, was the sort of understanding John of Damascus referred to in the famous passage dear to the classic Augustinians about knowledge of God's being naturally inserted into mind.[10] Grasped naturally in this general way, God was in fact mind's very first cognitive object, with everything else perceived in him as in the most primitive means of knowing.[11]

All this, of course, merely amplified the classic Augustinians' view that natural knowledge of God was somehow immanent in mind's cognition of "being" and other first concepts.[12] Like his predecessors, Henry defended this position by quoting Avicenna on "being" as among the initial concepts impressed on soul, adding a reference to the *Liber de causis* as well.[13] As if to prove that the idea also

---

[8] See the quotation given above, n. 7. On Bonaventure, see Pt. 2, ch. 8, n. 62.

[9] Henry, *Summa*, a. 22, q. 2 (1:130vQ).

[10] Henry, *Summa*, a. 22, q. 2 (1:130vQ): "Et solummodo de illa notitia essendi Deum generali loquitur Damascenus quando dicit illam nobis naturaliter insertam esse." See also above, n. 9; and *Summa*, a. 22, q. 6 (1:135vL). On the quotation from John and its use by the classic Augustinians, see Pt. 2, ch. 8, nn. 32, 34, 79 and 140, from which it is obvious that Henry and his predecessors did not interpret the remark from Damascene in exactly the same way.

[11] See Henry, *Summa*, a. 1, q. 2, ad 5. (1:8rR); and also a. 22, q. 6 (1:135vL), cited below, n. 33; as well as a. 24, q. 9 (1:146vX), cited in n. 34.

[12] See above, Pt. 2, ch. 8, n. 49.

[13] On the passage from Avicenna, see Henry, *Summa*, a. 22, q. 5 (1:134vD); and also a. 1, q. 12 (1:22rL); a. 3, q. 1 (1:28rB); and *Quodlibet* VI, q. 1 (ed. Gordon A. Wilson, Henrici Opera, 10:3, ll. 63–65); for Bonaventure's use of it, above, Pt. 2, ch. 8, nn. 51 and 52. On *Liber de causis*, see *Summa*, a. 1, q. 2 (1:4vC) – the text erroneously refers to the fourth proposition of *De causis* as "prima propositio" – and for Bonaventure's citation of it, Pt. 2, ch. 8, nn. 53 and 54; as well as n. 120 for a citation by Matthew.

belonged to the Christian tradition, he produced a long excerpt from Augustine's *De Trinitate* about how in knowing primary concepts like "good" which were impressed on the soul mind thereby knew God.[14]

Of these authorities, it was Avicenna, so often Henry's guide along the borderland between noetics and metaphysics, who carried the greatest weight. In a reference momentarily shifting attention away from simple to complex cognition, Henry claimed that the knowledge of God he had in mind lay behind Avicenna's assertions at the beginning of his *Metaphysics* where, on the topic of natural knowledge (*notitia naturalis et ex puris naturalibus acquisita*), it was suggested that in addition to a posteriori proofs of God's existence there was one that worked a priori.[15] Avicenna had not used the phrase "a priori" – his exact words were that this proof came "not through the testimony of the senses but rather out of universal propositions known per se" – but the implication had been plain enough for Averroes, who in his own commentary on the *Physics* criticized this apparent concession to apodictic knowledge of God's existence.[16]

Well aware of this history of controversy, Henry admitted that if Avicenna had meant that in constructing its proof mind had no recourse to sensible cognition, then Averroes's strictures were justified. For all Damascene's words about naturally inserted knowledge of God and despite the fact that such primitive cognition was achieved without analysis or investigation, it could not be considered innate.[17]

---

[14] See Henry, *Summa*, a. 22, q. 5 (1:134vD). The quotation was patched together from passages in *De Trinitate* VIII, 2 and 3 (CC, 50:271–73). As should be clear from n. 17, below, Henry took neither Avicenna's nor Augustine's reference to an impression to mean the knowledge was innate. For how both Bonaventure's and Henry's stand on knowledge of "being" and "God" entailed shifting Avicenna's authentic position in the direction of Augustine, see above, Pt. 2, ch. 8, n. 56.

[15] Henry, *Summa*, a. 22, q. 5 (1:134r–v[B]).

[16] In the passage cited above, n. 15, Henry quoted from Avicenna, *Liber de philosophia prima* I, 3 (ed. Van Riet, 1, 23–24), including the phrase: "non ex via testificationis sensibilium, sed ex via propositionum universalium intelligibilium [per se notarum]." He noted that Averroes criticized Avicenna for this in his *Commentary on the Physics* I, 5 (in *Aristotelis Opera cum Averrois commentariis*, 4 [Venice, 1562/repr. Frankfurt am Main, 1962], f. 47c).

[17] The passage from Henry's *Summa*, a. 22, q. 2 (1:130vQ), quoted above, n. 10, continues: "Et hoc ideo quia huiusmodi generalem notitiam essendi Deum homo naturaliter sine studio et investigatione primo conceptu concipit . . . sicut capit prima principia, non quia aliqua notitia nobis sit innata. . . ." Some historians have described Henry's theory of knowledge of God, as well as his view of illumination, as dependent on a kind of cognitive innatism – see, for instance, Efrem Bettoni, *Il processo astrattivo nella concezione di Enrico di Gand* (Milan, 1954), pp. 73 and 81; Paulus, *Henri de Gand*, p. 10, on what is called an "innéisme mitigé" (also below, n. 34); and Braun, *Die Erkenntnislehre*, pp. 59, 67–69, on an innate disposition. Strictly speaking,

Here Henry drew the line, rejecting at least the terminology of the otherwise sympathetic position of John Pecham, for what was at stake was natural knowledge, thus neither inborn nor revealed but necessarily derived from sensation.[18]

But Henry believed that Avicenna had not actually intended to eliminate a foundational role for the senses, pointing the way instead to a proof of God's existence drawing on them though not really arguing from the data they produced, at least not in the way an a posteriori demonstration would by inferring existence of a cause from evidence of its effects. There was, therefore, a legitimate way of proving God's existence that worked, literally speaking, "not through the testimony of the senses," so long as one realized that any such proof necessarily took its origin from sensation all the same.[19] In a remarkable passage, one Duns Scotus surely read and rejected, Henry suggested that Avicenna was thinking of a middle way between the a posteriori proof of the natural scientist and the nonempirical conviction of the theologian or believer, what he saw as the path of the philosopher, more precisely first philosopher or metaphysician.[20] This way was better than any a posteriori proof, since it was truly

---

such an interpretation cannot stand, as Dwyer realized, in *Die Wissenschaftslehre*, pp. 44–45, arguing against Braun as cited just above. On innatism in Bonaventure – whose words veer closer to it than Henry's – see above, Pt. 2, ch. 8, n. 67.

[18] See above, Pt. 2, ch. 8, n. 81.

[19] Henry, *Summa*, a. 22, q. 5 (1:134vE): "Est enim iste modus alius a via cognoscendi Deum esse testificatione sensibilium, qua esse creaturae testificatur esse Dei, secundum quod apparuit in questione praecedenti. Non tamen non est omnino iste alius modus a via cognoscendi Deum esse per creaturas, quia iste modus ortum sumit a cognitione essentiae creaturae." (The reading of the last sentence is corrupt. A more likely version might begin: Non tamen est iste modus omnino alius a. . . . "At any rate, its meaning is clear enough, for confirmation of which, see the same question, f. 135rE.) As Henry indicates, he had given numerous a posteriori proofs for God's existence in *Summa*, a. 22, q. 4 (1:132v–34r). Raymond Macken, "The Metaphysical Proof for the Existence of God in the Philosophy of Henry of Ghent," FS 68 (1986): 253–55, has argued that the last five of the proofs offered in a. 22, q. 4, were actually close to the kind of proof he was thinking of in q. 5.

[20] Henry, *Summa*, a. 22, q. 5 (1:135rF). In *Summa*, a. 24, q. 6 (1:141r–v[N]), Henry described this as the way of the metaphysician, and in a. 22, q. 5 (1:134rB), he confessed that his interpretation of Avicenna took the latter to be talking as a "pure philosopher." As I have pointed out in "Matthew of Aquasparta," p. 281, n. 141, Bérubé misreads Henry when he claims, "Henri de Gand," pp. 151–53, that he was discussing here a proof open only to the theologian working with supernatural evidence. The mistake is related to Bérubé's views on Henry's supposed innatism – see again above, Pt. 3, ch. 8, n. 67.

a priori, dependent on enough of an understanding of God's essence to reveal that in the proposition "God is," the predicate necessarily inhered in the subject.[21]

Henry's, and Avicenna's, metaphysical, a priori way of proving God's existence thus ultimately rested on a suitable explanation of God's role as simple object to mind operating with only its natural powers. When Avicenna made reference to universal propositions as the springboard for his middle way to God, Henry explained, he was thinking about the class of general propositions involving "being," "unity" and "good," primary concepts that by the end of the century would be known as transcendentals and which Henry, in technical terms, commonly called the first intentions of reality or sometimes first concepts. If Avicenna was right about an a priori proof, it was because these were not just simple concepts, even the first seized by mind; it had to be that in them intellect also perceived God himself.[22]

To appreciate how Henry thought this was so, and how, due to his strict segregation of natural knowledge of God from the paradigmatic image of a truth-revealing light, his approach contrasted with that of the classic Augustinians from whom he drew inspiration, it is necessary to review his understanding of simple cognition, beginning with the assumptions about reference upon which it was based. Henry held the proper object of intellect to be quiddity – universal quiddity, he said – and for the wayfarer working with only natural powers, that was limited to the quiddity of things perceptible

---

[21] See *Summa*, a. 22, q. 5 (1:135rE); and also (1:134vC).

[22] Henry, *Summa*, a. 22, q. 5 (1:134vD): "Hoc ut credo intellexit Avicenna, cum dixit quod possit homo scire Deum esse ex via propositionum universalium intelligibilium, non ex via testificationis sensibilium. Sunt autem propositiones illae universales de ente, uno, et bono, et primis rerum intentionibus, quae primo concipiuntur ab intellectu, in quibus potest homo percipere ens simpliciter, bonum, aut verum simpliciter. Tale autem . . . ipse Deus est." See also a. 22, q. 2 (1:130vQ), cited above, n. 9. For "first intentions" or "first intentions of reality" (*primae rerum intentiones*), see, for example, *Summa*, a. 1, q. 12, ad 1. (1:22vN); and a. 22, q. 5 (1:134vD), quoted just above; for "first concepts" (*primi conceptus*), *Summa*, a. 22, q. 2 (1:130vQ) (n. 9); and for both, *Summa*, a. 1, q. 5 (1:14vB); and a. 24, q. 6 (1:142vV). In *Summa*, a. 1, q. 5 (1:15rB), Henry called knowledge of these intentions or concepts "indivisibilium intelligentia," the phrase used by Thomas to describe all understanding of simple objects – see Thomas, *Commentarium in libros Posteriorum analyticorum*, prooemium, 5 (in Opera Omnia [Leonine ed.], I [Rome, 1882], p. 138b), quoted in Marrone, *New Ideas of Truth*, pp. 21–22, n. 21.

to the senses.[23] Yet "proper object" for him meant something like "perfect object," achieved under the best circumstances, for as indicated in the preceding chapter mind had access less conditionally to a more all-encompassing object, close to quiddity but below it: what Henry called "id quod est."[24] Since everything known under this broader rubric could be described as "true," "truth" designating the quality of a thing as object of understanding, it was therefore not precisely quiddity that mind knew in general but rather "the true."[25]

Once it was established that "true" was broadly speaking the object of intellect, Henry promptly considered other ways to denominate the same thing. "Being," "one" and "good" came immediately to mind, not by chance, of course, the very four terms Bonaventure had focused on in his *Itinerarium* when discussing mind's primary knowledge of God.[26] These were, by common consent, the most fundamental of transcendentals or first intentions, not merely the broadest characterizations of mind's general object but also, because of this, the very first concepts it seized in its efforts at cognition. Among them, moreover, obtained an order of priority. As already explained, "true" was not the attribute of the object that came first to understanding but rather "being," for although mind invariably knew what was true, it did not take stock of that quality as such without further reflection. At first it simply conceived a true thing, the most primitive characterization of which was "being" or *ens*.[27]

The argument could be taken still further with comparison to propositions, for just as all complex cognition could ultimately be pursued back to one absolutely first and best known principle (*primum et notissimum*), so it was possible to trace all simple concepts to

---

[23] See, for example, Henry, *Summa*, a. 24, q. 1 (1:137vE); a. 34, q. 2 (1:211vO and 212rR); *Quodlibet* 2, q. 6 (Henrici Opera, 6:32); *Quod.* 3, q. 15 (1:76vA); and *Quod.* 5, q. 14 (1:175vG).

[24] For the association of perfect cognition with grasping quiddity, see Henry, *Summa*, a. 1, q. 12, resp. and ad 4. (1:22vL and 23rR); and a. 2, q. 2, ad 1. (1:24rG). On knowledge of "id quod est" below quiddity, see above, Pt. 3, ch. 9, n. 27.

[25] See Pt. 3, ch. 9, nn. 14 and 15. Of course "true" as the broader category embraced the narrower "quiddity"; indeed "truth" and "quiddity" were identical – see Pt. 3, ch. 9, nn. 29 and 50; also *Summa* (*Qq. ord.*), a. 34, q. 5 (Henrici Opera, 27:203, ll. 41–44).

[26] Henry, *Summa*, a. 1, q. 2 (1:4vC–D). Vital's version of this discussion can be found in *Quaestiones de cognitione*, q. 8 (ed. Delorme, "Huit questions," p. 323). For Bonaventure, consult Pt. 2, ch. 8, n. 49, already cited above, n. 12.

[27] See above, Pt. 3, ch. 9, nn. 42 and 43; and also, in the context of knowing God, *Quodlibet* 13, q. 1 (Henrici Opera, 18:5, ll. 28–36).

one alone that was first of all.[28] On this point Henry agreed with Bonaventure, and Gilbert, too, about what Bonaventure called the resolution of all terms into one simple idea.[29] However, unlike his predecessors, he had in mind as primary object not "God's being" but rather a general notion of *ens*, more authentically Avicennian than they going so far as to call it "being as being" (*ens inquantum ens*), a phrase duly attributed to its Avicennian source.[30] Vital faithfully echoed him on this score.[31] Like the classic Augustinians, they both meant not only that this was mind's very first concept but also that all others were in some way seen in or derived from it.[32]

Only here, after having faithfully followed Avicenna to his theoretical foundations, did Henry veer off to rejoin his Augustinian predecessors in granting entry to a natural knowledge of God, in effect a cognition of divinity at the fountainhead of all that could be naturally known not only about him but also about creatures. Anyone knowing anything about creatures in a concept that could be referred as well to God, he explained, by that fact knew God himself, but the first intentions – "being" most of all – were concepts of just this sort, each applying more readily indeed to divinity than any of the other concepts by which mind knew creation. Thus in knowing "being" intellect also knew God, and since "being" was first of all concepts that it formed, it knew God among all objects absolutely first, although in a general and confused way.[33] This general knowledge of God was likewise means for knowing all other objects, just as the first intentions – again "being" most importantly – were means for understanding all ideas less fundamental than they.[34] As Richard

---

[28] Henry, *Summa* (*Qq. ord.*), a. 34, q. 3 (Henrici Opera, 27:190, ll. 31–40); and *Quodlibet* 10, q. 7 (ed. Raymond Macken, Henrici Opera, 14:171–72).

[29] See Pt. 2, ch. 8, nn. 11, 12 and 49.

[30] Henry, *Summa*, a. 1, q. 12 (1:22rL); a. 3, q. 4 (1:29rO); and a. 34, q. 3 (Henrici Opera, 27:190, ll. 38–40). The last of these texts explicitly cites Avicenna, *Liber de philosophia prima* I, 2 (ed. Van Riet, I, 12). Henry was, however, capable of using Bonaventuran language to describe the reduction of all knowledge into a simple concept of being referring properly to God, as, for instance, in *Summa*, a. 24, q. 7, ad 2. (1:144vK); and a. 24, q. 8 (1:145vP).

[31] Vital, *Quaestiones de cognitione*, q. 1 (ed. Delorme, "Huit questions," p. 172): "ens ut ens;" and *Quodlibet* 2, q. 1 (ed. Delorme, p. 42): "ens inquantum ens."

[32] See Henry, *Summa*, a. 1, q. 2 (1:4vD); a. 1, q. 12 (1:22rL); a. 2, q. 3 (1:25rM); and a. 3, q. 4 (1:29rO).

[33] Henry, *Summa*, a. 22, q. 6 (1:135vL); and also *Summa*, a. 24, q. 9 (1:146vX). The same argument, greatly abbreviated, appears later in Richard of Conington, *Quaest. ord.*, q. 1 (ed. Doucet, p. 437).

[34] Henry, *Summa*, a. 24, q. 9 (1:146vX); and also the preceding note and n. 11,

of Conington said in epitome, God was conceived in the conception of any single thing, constituting in fact the first thing conceived
of all.[35]

Critical, of course, was the fact that at issue here was general
knowledge of God (*in generali*) – in Henry's words also confused (*confuse, sub confusione, in intellectu confuso*) or universal (*in universali*) knowledge – as opposed to specific or particular understanding (*in speciali,
in particulari*).[36] By "general" as opposed to "specific" he was thinking in this instance not of the logical distinction between universal
and particular but rather the difference between knowing God in an
attribute shared with creation and knowing him plainly in his essence.[37]
It was perfectly possible to have knowledge of creatures, either general or specific, without having "specific" or "particular" knowledge
of God in the latter sense; in fact, by normal means one never knew
God "specifically" or "in particular" in this way, since that required
beatific or rapturous vision.[38] The most one could conceive naturally
about God fell under an attribute like "being," "true," or "good,"
opening equally well onto creatures and entailing only vague, though
still minimally quidditative, idea of what God was.[39] Perhaps draw-

---

above. Richard of Conington, in *Quaest. ord.*, q. 1 (ed. Doucet, p. 438), put this into
the language of causality, saying that the concept of God in mind was cause of the
concepts of all other things. In discussing Henry's theory of the primacy of knowledge of God, Paulus (*Henri de Gand*, pp. 58–63) likewise turned to the idea of cognitive causality, in doing so suggesting Henry came close to positing an innate idea
of God.

[35] Richard of Conington, *Quaest. ord.*, q. 1 (ed. Doucet, p. 434): "Hiis premissis,
dicendum ad questionem quod intellectus concipiendo intentionem creature, per
speciem creature necessario concipit actualiter et formaliter intentionem propriam
Deo, licet imperceptibiliter. Secundo, quod concipit eam prius naturaliter quam
intentionem creature."

[36] Henry, *Summa*, a. 22, q. 6, resp. and ad 1. (1:135v[L & M]). The passage
cited above, n. 9 (*Summa*, a. 22, q. 2 [1:130vQ]), makes it even clearer how this
analysis applied not only to complex knowledge of God's existence but also to the
simple cognition upon which it was based. In the same question (1:131rV), Henry
characterized the two ways – confused and particular – as "cognitio in universali
et indeterminata" and "cognitio determinata et in particulari." For the term *sub
confusione*, and the distinction *in speciali/in generali*, see again n. 9. For *in intellectu confuso*, see above, n. 33.

[37] Henry, *Summa*, a. 24, q. 9 (1:146vX); and also *Summa*, a. 24, q. 6 (1:142rP).

[38] See above, nn. 36 and 7. Henry called the rapturous or beatific knowledge of
God *in particulari* a *visio aperta* of divinity – see *Summa* a. 24, q. 6 (1:142rP); also
a. 22, q. 2 (1:131rV), cited above n. 36; and a. 22, q. 5, ad 2. (1:135vI).

[39] As the first passage cited above in note 37 shows, Henry realized God's simplicity dictated that his attributes be identical with his essence, so that knowing any
attribute in all its fullness would mean attaining specific knowledge of divinity. He

ing on Duns Scotus, Richard of Conington added in passing that
this was imperfect knowledge, with an imperfection no human understanding of divinity could escape short of supernatural aid.[40]

Henry's notion of a general, primary knowledge of God was furthermore embedded in a complicated network of cognitive levels. As he
saw it, there were three successive grades to the cognition intellect
could naturally acquire about God through an attribute: general,
more general and most general.[41] Following the ordinary progression
of cognitive processes from confused to distinct, such understanding
began with the most general or confused mode, knowing God in the
most general conception of being, which level was itself further sub-
divided into three subgrades or submodes.[42] First mind knew only a
singular but still indeterminate object, "this being" (*hoc ens*); then it
stripped away singularity, knowing "being" itself as common to many
objects (simply *ens* – that is, *ens commune*); finally it progressed to the
notion of a thoroughly independent, "subsistent being" (*ens subsistens*),
unparticipated though still not grasped with distinctness or lack of
generality. At each subgrade the referential domain included a divine
element, for knowledge of any shared attribute always pointed at
least in part to God, but only with the last was everything but divinity excluded.

For clarity's sake, Henry explained that there were two kinds of
abstraction by which a form could be intellectually separated from
instantiations (*supposita*) in the real world.[43] One was to abstract from

therefore explained, in *Summa*, a. 24, q. 6 (1:142rP), that by general knowledge the
wayfarer did not seize the divine attribute as identical to essence but rather as a
"certain universal disposition" (*quaedam dispositio universalis*) of the divinity by which
God had some resemblance (*communicare*) to creation.

[40] Richard of Conington, *Quaest. ord.*, q. 1 (ed. Doucet, p. 437). On Duns, see
below, Pt. 4, ch. 15, nn. 6, 9 and 10.

[41] Henry, *Summa*, a. 24, q. 6 (1:142vT). He called them the *modus* (or *gradus*) *generalis*, the *modus generalior*, and the *modus generalissimus* – see *Summa*, a. 24, q. 7 [1:244rF]),
for an instance actually employing the adjectival, and not the adverbial, forms of
the three key words.

[42] Henry worked out his example in *Summa*, a. 24, q. 6 (1:142v) in terms of
"good," not "being," but as he noted that his reasoning applied to any of the attributes – thus to an understanding of God in any first intention (see f. 142vS & V;
and also a. 24, q. 9 [1:146vY] – it is legitimate to substitute "being" as here in
the text. Henry surely chose "good" because he was working off a passage in
Augustine's *De Trinitate* VIII, 3 (CC, 50:273) about knowing God in "the good."
The *De Trinitate* passage followed immediately after those quoted by Henry before
and cited above, n. 14.

[43] Henry, *Summa*, a. 24, q. 6 (1:142vS).

perceived objects to a generality in which they participated, as from particular to universal; the other was to abstract from them to a sort of template absolutely untouched by them, as from particular participants to an unparticipated subsistent form serving as model for the attribute they shared. By means of the former abstraction mind worked from knowledge in particular of an attribute predicable of both divinity and creatures – for instance, "this being" – to that of the general form the particular instantiation participated in – "being" alone – thereby progressing from the first subgrade of most general natural knowledge of God to the second. By means of the latter, it moved from the same starting point to knowledge of "subsistent being," the indivisible and exemplary being of the Creator himself, thus passing on to the third subgrade. The idea was surely lifted, almost untouched, from Pecham's *Commentary on the Sentences*, where Henry's predecessor likewise attempted to explain the Augustinian notion of knowledge of God in the understanding of a generality like "good."[44] As a quick answer to the question of how mind drew knowledge of God from cognition of the world, it worked well.

After the "most general" level, with its three subdegrees, followed the two higher modes, in which mind refined its perception of the attribute, focusing increasingly on what was exclusively divine. At the "more general" (*generalior*) grade it considered its object, by now "subsistent being," no longer as something which by its exemplarity and perfection pointed back to the participating beings of creation but rather that which stood eminently above and apart from all other reality.[45] Here intellect consciously acknowledged that its object, though still viewed through a general attribute as if in a universal concept, was of a type radically different from any other being perceived, for the first time considering it under the express guise (*sub tali ratione*) of assignment to divinity alone. The consequent "general" (*generalis*) mode brought intellect even closer to particular consideration of God, with the realization that all divinity's attributes were reducible to one first and absolutely simple principle (*unum primum simplicissimum attributum*), the divine unity reflective of the fact that God, alone among all entities, was as an individual immediately and

---

[44] See above, Pt. 2, ch. 8, n. 90.
[45] Henry, *Summa*, a. 24, q. 6 (1:142v–43r[V]), where he said this was knowledge of God in an attribute, but "sub quadam praeeminentia, ut scilicet est quaedam natura excellentissima."

indivisibly his own essence.[46] At last mind was able to see that God's attributes were no different from the quiddity in which they resided, even though this "whatness" could not naturally be represented otherwise than by giving it an attribute's name – for instance, "absolutely simple being." Beyond this stage intellect could not advance without special divine assistance.

The same scheme of three modes was loosely correlated to a division Henry drew between knowing God in an attribute by means of indistinct cognition and knowing him in an attribute distinctly, the difference depending on whether the attribute registered as a quality still vaguely shared with creatures or one appropriated exclusively to God.[47] The dividing line plainly fell somewhere between the lower subgrades of "most general" knowledge of divinity and the two higher modes, "more general" and "general." More revealing was a differentiation between natural and rational knowledge of God. Citing Aristotle's *Physics* as authority, Henry called attention to a fundamental disjunction among operative principles between reason and nature – between those that might have variable effects and those that, under normal conditions, always produced the same result. In human cognition, for example, knowledge of primary principles, where mind was constrained to consent, could be described as natural, while knowledge of conclusions, where it had to deliberate on whether to assent or disagree, could be called rational.[48]

Applied to knowledge of God *ex creaturis*, the kind of knowledge at issue here, the latter distinction dictated that the initial, confused cognition of divinity in first intentions be called natural in a strict sense of the word, since immediate and involuntary, while the more

---

[46] *Summa*, a. 24, q. 6 (1:143rZ).

[47] Henry, *Summa*, a. 24, q. 3 (1:139vX); and a. 24, q. 6 (1:141vN).

[48] Henry, *Summa*, a. 1, q. 4, ad 1. (1:13rG). The same division could be described from a different perspective as between natural (or unpremeditated) and voluntary knowledge – see *Summa*, a. 1, q. 5 (1:15r[B–C]). As his source for the latter version of the dichotomy, Henry cited Averroes, *Commentarium magnum in Aristotelis De anima libros* III, 36 (ed. Crawford, p. 496) – a passage René A. Gauthier has called to our attention in "Notes sur Siger de Brabant," p. 227. In *Summa*, a. 1, q. 11 (1:21rC), Henry spoke of the involuntary, natural knowledge of such things as principles as verging on necessity, thus inevitable once the senses had been exposed to the appropriate objects outside mind. Henry realized his distinction was at work in the standard scholastic opposition between *intellectus* and *scientia* and was related to another technical duality, intellectual versus rational *modi intelligendi*. On the Aristotelian terms *intellectus* and *scientia*, see above, Pt. 1, ch. 1, n. 49; and Henry, *Summa*, a. 1, q. 4, ad 3. (1:13rI); for *intellectualis* versus *rationalis*, see *Summa*, a. 1, q. 12 (1:22vL).

reflective understanding built on these foundations be called rational.[49]
Henry even indicated precisely how his various modes of general
knowledge should be distributed. The first two subgrades of most
general knowledge, where mind was directed to creatures as well as
God, constituted natural knowledge of divinity; the third subgrade
and the two subsequent modes, more general and general, advanced
to the category of rational, with God exclusive object, known more
or less distinctly for himself.[50]

A by-product of this division between two kinds of unrevealed
knowledge of God was greater clarity about how and when God
was first object of mind. Again, Henry seems to have drawn inspiration
from John Pecham, this time his distinction between discursive and
simple cognition of God, and once more what Pecham merely suggested grew in Henry's hands into fully elaborated theory.[51] For rational
knowledge, the equivalent of Pecham's discursive cognition, divinity
was in fact not first mental object, since the reasoning intellect began
with an indiscriminate knowledge of creatures and only subsequently
progressed to conceiving whatever could be known of God's essence
from sensory data through a willful process of cogitation and reconsideration.[52] Because the resultant semi-distinct cognition was perforce
a constructed knowledge, although not constructed on the foundations of formal a posteriori argumentation but instead on the simpler basis of metaphysical analysis, it was moreover not truly immediate,
in contrast to strictly natural knowledge of God, in which not even
minimal reasoning intervened. Yet if not "natural" in either of these
ways – primary and immediate – it was still "natural" in the looser
sense of not requiring special intervention from above. Free of revelation, such cognition was, Henry readily admitted, open to what
he called the best of philosophers (*summi philosophi*), people of wisdom (*sapientes*) even outside Christian tradition, as the history of philosophy confirmed.[53]

Only with natural knowledge of God in the strict sense – equivalent to Pecham's simple cognition – could Henry reaffirm the tradi-

---

[49] Henry, *Summa*, a. 24, q. 7 (1:144rF); and also *Summa*, a. 24, q. 9 (1:146vY).
[50] Henry, *Summa*, a. 24, q. 7 (1:144r[F–G]).
[51] See above, Pt. 2, ch. 8, nn. 100–102; for a hint of the same idea already present in Bonaventure, see Pt. 2, ch. 8, n. 64.
[52] Henry, *Summa*, a. 24, q. 7 (1:144rF).
[53] See Henry, *Summa*, a. 22, q. 2 (1:131rV); a. 24, q. 3 (1:139vV); and a. 24,
q. 6 (1:143rV).

tion holding God to be first object for wayfarer's mind. At his first two subgrades of "most general" knowledge of God, where divinity was grasped in the attribute "being" as yet indiscriminately and generally conceived, God was very first thing seized by mind and means for it to know all else, thus truly first and most fundamental cognitive object.[54]

The reason for this had to do with the nature of indetermination. In line with what he had already asserted about the direction of cognitive processes, Henry reminded his reader that intellect, just like the senses, moved naturally from indeterminate to determinate, so that by nature, if not always by temporal priority, mind knew more universal and cognitively confused objects before the more particular or distinct, and it knew the same object under more universal, confused guise before knowing it in its particularity.[55] But there were two different types of indetermination. An intelligible object was indeterminate privatively if grasped without determination although it was, at another time or under different consideration, capable of being determined, while an object was indeterminate negatively if it was under no circumstances susceptible to determination, either in itself or from any point of view. Indetermination of the first sort characterized the universal notion of "being"; of the second sort, "being" as subsistent and unparticipated, thus totally beyond determination. Negative indetermination, as the greatest (*maior*) kind imaginable, was cognitively the more primitive, thus always known prior even to indetermination of the privative sort.[56]

Of course, knowledge of God at the first two subgrades of "most general" cognition was confused or indeterminate in the broad sense of looking away from any distinct or particular quality of divinity, but perhaps surprisingly Henry insisted as well that each of the two

[54] Henry, *Summa*, a. 24, a. 7 (1:144r[G–H]): "Loquendo autem de primo modo supra iam dicto intelligendi Deum quid est, scilicet naturaliter in primis intentionibus entis, que sunt ens, verum, unum, bonum, naturaliter intellectis, quod pertinet ad modum intelligendi Deum quid sit modo generalissimo in primo et secundo gradu eius, dicendum quod quid est Deus est primum comprehensibile per intellectum. . . . Absolute ergo dicendum quod in generalissimo modo intelligendi quid est Deus, quo ad primum et secundum eius gradum, quid est Deus est primum obiectum quod ab humano intellectu ex creaturis habet intelligi."

[55] Henry, *Summa*, a. 24, q. 7 (1:144rG). For the preceding formulation of the same dynamic principle in terms of confused and distinct knowledge, see above, n. 42.

[56] Henry, *Summa*, a. 24, q. 7 (1:144rH). See also a. 21, q. 2, ad 3. (1:124v–25r [P–Q]).

subgrades embraced confusion or indetermination of both of his two
different sorts. Thus at each grade mind seized "universal being" –
that is, being privatively undetermined – and also "subsistent being" –
the negatively undetermined being of God. It could therefore be concluded not only that "most general" knowledge, at both subgrades,
was, by virtue of either indeterminate object, principal or fundamental to human cognition but also that among the two objects the
one constricted to divinity's type of being came, at each subgrade,
absolutely first.[57] Because of his radical indeterminacy, God stood at
the source of all that could be understood, nothing else being conceivable unless God was known first in at least this most general
way.[58]

The delineation of natural and rational knowledge of God constituted a considerable achievement, erasing many of the ambiguities and contradictions that had plagued the classic Augustinians
when they tried to explain how humankind's primary perception of
God related to processes of reasoning.[59] With his penchant for drawing sharp theoretical boundaries, Henry had gone a long way towards
eliminating the philosophical embarrassments of his predecessors. He
did so, moreover, without recourse to the image of a light of truth,
banished from his understanding of God as first object even though
it had helped predecessors like Pecham introduce a modicum of clarity into their otherwise somewhat untidy thoughts.[60]

Still, one might question whether the deepest theoretical difficulties
had been resolved. In natural cognition of God, the first two subgrades of most general knowledge, divinity was by express stipulation the primary object. Yet Henry's initial description of the three
subgrades had presented mind as beginning with "this being," a particular object which even if known indistinctly was for the wayfarer

---

[57] *Summa*, a. 24, q. 7 (1:144rH): "Ergo cum semper intellectus noster naturaliter
prius concipit indeterminatum quam determinatum . . . intellectus noster intelligendo
bonum quodcumque in ipso naturaliter prius cointelligit bonum negatione indeterminatum, et hoc est bonum quod Deus est. Et sicut de bono, ita et de omnibus aliis
de Deo intellectis ex creaturis." Henry's argument about indetermination was succinctly summarized (without the language of negative and privative indetermination) by Richard of Conington in his *Quaest. ord.*, q. 1 (ed. Doucet, p. 437).

[58] Henry, *Summa*, a. 24, q. 7 (1:144rH): "Et sicut nihil aliud potest perfecte
cognosci nisi ipso [Deo] prius perfecte cognito, sic nec aliquid potest cognosci quan-
tumcumque imperfecte, nisi ipso prius saltem in generalissimo gradu cognito."

[59] See Pt. 2, ch. 8, nn. 64, 67–68, 93, and 95–96.

[60] See Pt. 2, ch. 8, pp. 227–29.

by necessity creaturely and not divine. And to get to the second sub-grade intellect abstracted from the initial particular object to a universal "being" in which all such particulars participated – to "participated being" as he so often called it – which would ostensibly lie exclusively within the realm of created entity as well.[61] By these terms, did it not make more sense to say that in its journey to God mind knew created objects first? The dilemma went back at least to Gilbert of Tournai, and similar difficulties had plagued the classic Augustinians.[62]

Henry evidently believed that he had a solution, which lay in distinguishing between conscious and unconscious cognition. Rational knowledge was fully conscious; natural knowledge was not. Thus, although God was naturally first object for mind, intellect did not always take note of the priority.[63] Indeed, natural knowledge being what it was – nonreflective – at the very moment mind was engaged in the first two subgrades of most general knowledge of God, it literally could not grasp the significance of what it saw.

All this would explain the apparent equivocation in Henry's language. Since conscious cognition was unambiguous and easy to picture, Henry simply fashioned his precise description of the three substages of "most general" knowledge to reflect a rational point of view. If mind consciously – that is, rationally – looked back over the steps of its cognition, it would, after all, inevitably conclude that it had known first "this being," and then a universal intention of "participated being," before coming to anything that could be identified

---

[61] For instance, Henry, *Summa*, a. 24, q. 7 (1:144rF): "Abstrahendo enim ab hoc bono singulari, et etiam a bono simpliciter universali et participato a creaturis, ipsum bonum simpliciter quod non est bonum participatum sed subsistens bonum, prius oportet intelligere bonum singulare a quo primo fit abstractio boni universalis, et deinde etiam ipsum bonum universale participatum, a quo ulterius bonum separatum non participatum per eminentiam et remotionem abstrahitur, quam illud quod ab illo abstrahitur." See the same implications in Henry's introduction of the two sorts of abstraction, cited above, n. 43.

[62] On Gilbert, see above, Pt. 2, ch. 8, p. 204.

[63] Henry, *Summa*, a. 24, q. 7, ad 1. (1:144vI), where he said mind did not discern (*non discernit*) God as first object; and ad 2.(1:144vK): "In omnibus ergo generalibus intentionibus rerum cum aliquam illarum intelligis simpliciter – ut ens, verum, bonum – primo Deum intelligis, etsi non advertis. . . ." Immediately before the latter passage, Henry implied that the difference between knowing God confusedly in natural cognition and knowing him distinctly was simply a matter of becoming mentally aware, an idea surely related to the definition for discrete knowledge in *Summa*, a. 24, q. 9 (1:146vY): "cum animadversione notitia."

with the divine. Correlating this same progression with the simulta-
neous but inverted dynamics of natural knowledge, where divine
object was first known but not consciously perceived, was a messier
affair, so Henry satisfied himself with just reminding the reader that,
despite rational appearances, a more complicated configuration of
referents was actually at work. Though such a strategy ran the risk
of confusion, Henry could argue in his own defense that by describing the first two subgrades as pointing to "this being" and "universal being" – both of which from the rational perspective implicated
solely created objects – he was not so much obscuring the reality of
a primary knowledge of God as reflecting the subjective impression
of mind. At each level God lurked below the surface; intellect, as
natural, was merely unprepared to put that fact into words.

There is, to be sure, no explicit confirmation in Henry's words
that this is what he had in mind. However, a few decades later
Richard of Conington, surely responding to Duns Scotus's critique
of the idea of God as first known but not perceived, returned to
Henry's claim about unconscious knowledge, leaving no doubt that
he read the master in precisely this manner. First he outlined a number of ways in which concepts could be conceived without at the
same time being discerned by mind.[64] Then he applied the scheme
to the general notion of being, which he said was a concept actually and formally (*actualiter et formaliter*) conceived in every act of cognition, though not fully perceived (*non percipitur*), at least not in the
initial stages.[65] Finally he turned to the simple notion of being proper
to God, a notion he surely meant to correspond to whatever mind
knew about God in Henry's first two subgrades of "most general"
knowledge, asserting that it, too, was actually and formally conceived
by mind in every cognitive act, although – and here, under pressure
from Duns, he parted ways with Henry – mind working without
revelation in the world was never able to bring it to conscious perception.[66] A clearer statement of the solution could hardly be desired.

Yet in addition to an explanation for the subjective impression,
or misimpression, of mind about its first object, a full defense of

---

[64] Richard of Conington, *Quaest. ord.*, q. 1 (ed. Doucet, p. 432).

[65] Richard of Conington, *Quaest. ord.*, q. 1 (ed. Doucet, p. 433). The Latin phrases
come from the outline of the scheme given on p. 432 of Doucet's text (n. 64,
above).

[66] See Richard of Conington, *Quaest. ord.*, q. 1, arg. 5 and ad 6. (ed. Doucet, pp.
431 and 438); and also the discussions below, nn. 87 and 93.

Henry's theory needed to offer an accounting of noetical details, and this accounting would have to satisfy two potentially conflicting demands. To sustain his vision of the real if not temporal priority of a general concept of divinity, it would have to guarantee that from the very start the wayfarer's knowledge embraced both God and creation. But to save the idea of naturalness, it would also be required to respect the rule that all human cognition in the world, short of revelation, was drawn from creatures (*ex creaturis*) and began with sensation. Finding a philosophical reckoning to serve both ends would be difficult, forcing Henry to focus on mental processes and cognitive entities as well as objective conditions and their connection to mind. Precisely what, in external reality, was grasped at the first two stages of most general knowledge, and how was it made available to intellect? Was what was known something common to God and creatures, and if not, how could two objects be seized at once? Finally, with respect to mental entities in which knowledge was made manifest, was there a common concept of divine and created being or was any such concept impossible to conceive?

These concerns were not new, but with Henry they took on an urgency never seen before, signaling a new phase in the high medieval discussion of the object of mind. Simply put, the peculiar dynamics of Henry's thought, the theoretical demands imposed by his desire to attain a systematic balance between Aristotelianizing and Augustinian perspectives, brought him face to face with the question of the univocity of the concept of being, an issue that would plague scholars in more or less the same form for a generation to come.

Like all scholastics before and after, Henry held that there was nothing really common to God and creatures, no aspect of one, substantial or accidental, that could also be found in the other. Even an attribute so general as being was not really the same in a creature and in divinity.[67] Consequently, when a universal like "being" was predicated of both God and creatures, this was not a sign of real referential unity but rather an indication of unity by name alone

---

[67] For example, Henry, *Summa*, a. 21, q. 2 (1:124rF): "Quare cum multo minus in aliquo uno reali conveniunt creator et creatura, quam duae creaturae, substantia scilicet et accidens . . . nullo modo ens potest esse aliquid commune reale Deo et creaturae. Et ideo absolute dicendum quod esse non est aliquid commune reale in quo Deus communicet cum creaturis." See also *Summa*, a. 21, q. 3, resp. and ad 2. (1:126rE and 126vI). As late as *Summa*, a. 75, q. 6, ad 3. (2:311vZ), Henry was making the same point.

(*sola nominis communitas*), so that no term, not even "being," referred univocally to absolutely everything there was. Yet Henry agreed with his contemporaries, that when the term "being" was applied to creatures and creator the usage was not purely equivocal, either. There was instead a middle ground: "being" signified God and creatures by analogy (*analogice*).[68]

Henry explained what he meant by looking at how terms were connected to the forms they signified.[69] A term was univocal if it always signified exactly the same form – for instance, "horse" or "animal." A term was purely equivocal – Henry used the technical description drawn from Boethius: "aequivocum casu" – if it signified different forms but without any determinate order or priority.[70] His example was the name "Ajax," which referred to many men of that appellation and to no one of them more readily than any other. Finally, a term was analogical if it signified different forms but in a definite order, so that it pointed to just one form principally and all others with respect to or in proportion to the first. "Being" was a term of this sort, primarily signifying the Godhead but secondarily, and always in deference to its primary significance, capable of referring to creatures, too. On occasion Henry spoke of this kind of signification as a case of attribution, a technical description again dependent on Boethius, who had listed it among the types of *aequivocatio a consilio*, accepted by scholastics as the general rubric under which analogy fell.[71] Both Vital and Richard of Conington expressed similar views while striving for even greater exactitude about the precise nature of the analogy ensconced in "being."[72]

---

[68] The passage quoted above in n. 67 continues: "Et ita si ens aut esse praedicatur de Deo et creaturis, hoc est sola nominis communitate, nulla rei, et ita non univoce per definitionem univocorum, nec tamen pure aequivoce, secundum definitionem aequivocorum casu, sed medio modo ut analogice." See also *Summa*, a. 24, q. 6 (1:142vS); and *Quodlibet* VII, qq. 1–2, ad 2. (ed. Gordon A. Wilson, Henrici Opera, 11:27–28). Richard of Conington reproduced these ideas in *Quaest. ord.*, q. 1, resp. and ad 4. (ed. Doucet, pp. 434, 436 and 438). Like his contemporaries, Henry held that "being" was not univocal, but only analogical, to the ten categories, too – see Henry, *Summa*, a. 26, q. 1 (1:157rC); *Quodlibet* 10, q. 8 (Henrici Opera, 14:202); and *Quodlibet* 13, q. 9 (Henrici Opera, 18:57–58).

[69] Henry, *Summa*, a. 21, q. 2 (1:124rI); see also *Summa*, a. 75, q. 6, ad 3. (1:313rK).

[70] See Boethius, *In Categorias Aristotelis libri quatuor* I (PL 64:166).

[71] Henry, *Summa*, a. 7, q. 3 (1:50rB). For Boethius, again consult the passage cited above, n. 70.

[72] Vital, *Quodlibet* 3, q. 5 (ed. Delorme, p. 130), noting two kinds of analogy, one by attribution of two divergent *significanda* to a third and another by attribution of

The whole scheme made metaphysical sense if one understood how some logical relations among terms arose out of the way their referents agreed in form (*convenientia in forma, communicatio in forma*).[73] To be precise, there were two kinds of formal agreement. One was for things to agree in form in respect to the same formal consideration (*secundum eandem rationem*). It was this way that objects participating in an identical universal form communicated, as white things in whiteness or men in humanity, and Henry said the word for this type of agreement was similarity (*similitudo*). Univocity presupposed correspondence of this strong sort. The other kind of formal agreement applied when things communicated in form but in respect to different considerations (*secundum aliam et aliam rationem*). Agreement of this weaker sort, called imitation, was what was generally found between cause and effect, and since God was the ultimate cause of all created being, all creatures agreed with him – imitated him – in precisely this way.[74] The analogical character of "being" rested on such imitation.

From this Henry concluded that there could be literally no single concept signifying both God and creatures, no matter how general or unspecific the concept might be. Concepts were correlated to form, even to formal consideration (*ratio*), so that one concept could never refer to two things whose form, in respect to at least one consideration, was not the same. Another way of putting it was to say that concepts were constrained by univocity. Applied to the noetics

---

one *significandum* to another, with "being" predicated by analogy of the latter sort. Richard of Conington, in *Quodlibet* 1, q. 2 (ed. Brown, pp. 300 and 302), simply used the Boethian terms, *aequivocatio a casu* and *aequivocatio a consilio*, the latter indicative of a unity of "signified intentions" that was, although not univocal, at least *secundum quid*. In *Quaest. ord.*, q. 1 (ed. Doucet, p. 436), Richard also spoke of the analogy of "being" in terms of attribution.

[73] Henry, *Summa*, a. 21, q. 2 (1:124rG): ". . . notandum quod convenientia rei ad rem maxime in forma attenditur, et hoc dupliciter, secundum quod duplex est modus communicandi aliqua in forma. Una secundum eandem rationem, quae dicitur convenientia similitudinis, et est eorum quae una forma participant secundum rem, ut albedine duo alba, et humanitate duo homines, quae facit convenientiam univocationis, qualis, ut dictum est, non est Dei et creaturae in esse. Alia vero est convenientia in forma secundum aliam et aliam rationem, quae dicitur convenientia imitationis, et est universaliter in efficientibus et factis, causis et causatis." In a similar discussion in *Summa*, a. 24, q. 6, ad 1. (1:143vA), Henry was back to describing the difference with reference solely to form, without mention of consideration (*rationes*), as above, n. 69. See also *Summa*, a. 21, q. 2, ad 2. in opp. (1:125vV); a. 21, q. 3, resp. and ad 2. (1:126rE & 126vI); and a. 26, q. 2, ad 2. (1:159vV).

[74] Henry, *Summa*, a. 21, q. 2 (1:124rH).

of knowing God, this meant that at every point in the course of
mind's investigation of being, any single concept devised by it, no
matter how general, necessarily referred either to uncreated being
or to created being but not to both.[75] Richard of Conington echoed
Henry on this score, going so far as to claim that at their most general the concepts of uncreated and created being might be said to
form a unity in a manner of speaking (*secundum quid*), not in any
real sense of the word (*simpliciter*).[76]

The problem was that Henry's language frequently implied just
the opposite. When it came to the workings of mind in the first two
subgrades of "most general" knowledge of God, he could hardly
resist the temptation to speak as if there were a single concept referring jointly to God's being and that of creatures.[77] Sometimes this

[75] Henry, *Summa*, a. 21, q. 2, ad 3. (1:124vO): "Nunquam enim potest concipi
aliquis intellectus entis simpliciter absque eo quod homo concipit aliquem intellectum Dei aut creaturae, ut concipiat aliquem unicum intellectum simplicem communem ad Deum et creaturam, alium praeter intellectum Dei aut creaturae, quia
nullus potest esse talis. Sed si aliquid concipit homo, illud est aut quod pertinet ad
esse Dei tantum, aut quod pertinet ad esse creaturae tantum. . . . Omnis ergo conceptus realis quo aliquid rei concipitur concipiendo esse simpliciter, aut est conceptus rei quae Deus est, aut quae creatura est, non alicuius communis ad utrumque."
See also *Summa*, a. 21, q. 2, ad 2. in opp. (1:125r[T–V]); and a. 21, q. 3 (1:126rE).
[76] Richard of Conington, *Quodlibet* 1, q. 2 (ed. Brown, p. 306): "Sed quod dicunt,
quod intentio entis abstracta a Deo et creatura, ab accidente et substantia[,] est
una, falsum est." Also the same question, ad 2. (p. 307): "Ad secundum dicendum
quod intellectus sistit et terminatur ad unum secundum quid quod est duo simpliciter, percipiendo tamen unitatem non dualitatem." The same view is expressed
in the language of analogy in Richard's *Quaest. ord.*, q. 1 (ed. Doucet, p. 436). On
unity *secundum quid* according to Richard, see also above, n. 72. Stephen F. Brown,
in "Avicenna and the Unity of the Concept of Being. The Interpretations of Henry
of Ghent, Duns Scotus, Gerard of Bologna and Peter Aureoli," FrS 25 (1965): 123,
renders Henry's views in terms of Conington's distinction between *secundum quid*
unity and duality *simpliciter*, but he gives no supporting citation to Henry's works,
and is surely reading Henry through Conington's eyes.
[77] For instance, Henry, *Summa*, a. 21, q. 3 (1:126rE): "Prius enim res quaecumque
nata est movere intellectum ratione qua ens est indeterminate conceptum sub
indifferentia ad duplicem determinationem praedictam, quam ratione qua Deus creator est aut creatura." See also *Summa*, a. 24, q. 9 (1:146vY). Gómez Caffarena, in
Ser participado, p. 183; and Bérubé, in "Olivi, critique," p. 86, n. 63; and "Henri
de Gand," pp. 160–61, attribute the inconsistency to Henry's having changed his
mind. They argue – Gómez Caffarena by implication and Bérubé explicitly – that
in article 24 Henry lent his support to the notion of a common concept, later abandoning the idea and inserting language in article 21 denying conceptual community. The passages cited in the present note and those that follow furnish evidence
that their contention is not justified: in both article 24 and article 21 Henry's language appears at some point to come down on each side of the question. The like-
liest explanation is that he tried to make it clear there was no common concept
but never succeeded in purging language which might give rise to the opposite

took the form of reference to a "most common being" (*ens commu-nissime dictum*).[78] Sometimes he simply talked about "being" (*ens*) as a common, although analogical cognitive entity (*commune analogum*), in the same way that Richard of Conington would speak of a common, but not univocal, concept applicable to God and creatures (*intentio communis non univoca Deo et creature*).[79] Occasionally Henry even suggested that intellect descended from the most general notion of being to more specific concepts of it by adding conceptual determinations, as if "being" were a genus.[80] He actually dared speak of one formal consideration (*ratio*) of "being" in respect to which it was common to creatures and to God and another in respect to which it was proper to creatures, thus entangling the term "being" in the very technicalities he had used before to distinguish univocity from analogy.[81]

---

view, the difficulites inherent in explaining primary knowledge of God *ex creaturis* simply proving too great to allow him absolute clarity. All this has led Stephen D. Dumont, "The Univocity of the Concept of Being in the Fourteenth Century: John Duns Scotus and William of Alnwick," MS 49 (1987): 5, n. 10, to remark how close Henry came to positing the univocity of the concept of being. Bérubé points out in "Henri de Gand," p. 161, n. 87, that both he and Robert Prentice discovered an anonymous question from the late thirteenth century that falls into the same ambivalence as Henry.

[78] See Henry, *Summa*, a. 21, q. 2 (1:124rI); and a. 26, q. 2, ad 1. (1:159rT): "...est alia ratio entis et intentio eius, scilicet quod est commune analogum creatori et creaturae, et eius quod est proprium creaturae et analogum substantiae et accidenti. Ens enim analogum creatori et creaturae est ens communissime dictum, et sub intentione simplicissima sine omni additione accepta." Much the same point is made in a. 24, q. 9 (1:146vY), where Henry speaks of an "intellectus entis simpliciter communis de Deo et creaturis."

[79] See Henry, *Summa*, a. 26, q. 2, ad 1. (1:159rT), quoted above, n. 78; a. 24, q. 6 (1:142vV): and a. 24, q. 7, ad 1. (1:144vI). The logical peculiarity of talking about an analogical concept is noted above, Pt. 2, ch. 8, nn. 12 and 59. Other texts implying a common concept of being are *Summa*, a. 21, q. 3 (1:126rD); and a. 24, q. 7, ad 2 (1:144vK). For Richard of Conington, see *Quaest. ord.*, q. 1 (ed. Doucet, p. 434).

[80] Henry, *Summa*, a. 24, q. 3 (1:138vP): "...omnis alia cognitio de re sive creati sive increati, sive substantiae sive accidentis, per additionem se habet ad istam [i. e. cognitionem primi et simplicissimi conceptus entis], sicut omnis alia intentio entis se habet per additionem ad esse, et differens est ab illa vel secundum rationem vel secundum intentionem aliquam." In *Summa*, a. 26, q. 2 (1:158vN), he made the point again with regard to the descent from created "being" to the ten categories. In *Quodlibet* 10, q. 8 (Henrici Opera, 14:196–97, ll. 25–29), Henry tried to be more technically cautious by speaking of "being" analogous to the categories as having a unity broader or logically superior to generic unity: "communitas quaedam superior quam sit communitas generis." In *Summa*, a. 74, q. 6, ad 3. (1:311r[V–Y], Henry finally got around to listing the degrees of unity various general terms or markers might have, including the greater and lesser univocity of species and genuses.

[81] Henry, *Summa*, a. 24, q. 6 (1:142rQ); a. 26, q. 2, ad 1. (1:159rT), quoted

There was an excuse for this language, or at least Henry thought he could account for it innocently enough, although his reasoning would not satisfy critics like Duns Scotus. Indeed, he felt his usage was practically unavoidable, the explanation being precisely what Matthew of Aquasparta seems to have picked up from him and employed in his own writings to resolve the same dilemma.[82] According to Henry, the unity of "being" at its most general, the unity he was thinking about when he spoke of a "most common being" and that appeared from time to time in his descriptions of the first two sub-grades of "most general" knowledge of God, reduced to the paradigmatic equivocal unity of word (*vox*) or name (*nomen*). As word – not mental concept but simply spoken or written marker – "being" was apt to refer indifferently and equally immediately to either of the two kinds of being, divine or created.[83] Just a word, therefore, and not a concept constituted the cognitive reality jointly pointing to creatures and to God. But the word "being," unlike purely equivocal terms, descended from this most common, conceptually indiscriminate signification to its two less general but proper applications, referring to either of the two primary sorts of being, without attachment of any explicit modifiers.[84] For example, both Sirius and Fido

---

above, n. 78; and *Quod.* 11, q. 3 (2:446rE). On the description of univocity according to identity of *rationes*, see above, n. 73. In *Summa*, a. 75, q. 6, ad 3. (2:311v[Y–Z]), Henry actually used the word "univocal" to describe the term "being" as signifying both created and uncreated objects, but as his immediately succeeding comments show he did not mean this in the way "univocal" was normally taken or so as to defy his usual proscription of the unity of all being in any single *ratio*. What he intended was that insofar as all things were God, because radically from God, they could be said to have his being, and thus described as "being" univocally with the creator; insofar as they were separably themselves, of course, they did not possess such being. Thus general "being" was, Henry concluded, partly univocal, partly equivocal (*partim univocum et partim aequivocum*). The same way all things "are" in virtue of God's being is explained in *Quodlibet* 9, q. 2 (Henrici Opera, 13:30, ll. 9–14).

[82] On Matthew, see above, Pt. 2, ch. 8, pp. 233–39.

[83] In *Summa*, a. 21, q. 2, ad 3 (1:124vO), just after explaining that there was no single concept signifying both divine and created being (see the quotation in n. 75, above), Henry said: "Sed utrumque eorum [i.e. esse Dei et esse creaturae] indifferenter et aeque simul quantum est ex parte vocis natum est praesentari in significato eius quod est esse." Remember also the passage quoted above, n. 68, where Henry insisted that the unity of "being" applied to both God and creature was a unity in name alone.

[84] Henry, *Summa*, a. 75, q. 6, ad 3. (2:311rY). This is a view on the use of "being" as a term that Duns would reject (see below, Pt. 4, ch. 15, pp. 521–24). Only if Duns had held to it as well as to his position on the univocity of "being" as transcendental would Allan Wolter's interpretation of him as given in *The*

were "dogs," in an equivocal application of the term, but to pick out one or the other it was necessary to speak explicitly of "dog star" or "barking dog." "Being," on the other hand, could legitimately be used precisely to designate either God or creature, the ontological reality of the referent alone sufficing to narrow the term without added qualifier.

Moreover it was not just that the word "being" was unusually elastic; there was also a psychological or subjective element involved. Some minds, not recognizing the conceptual division between God's being and created being, simply took unity of word for unity of concept and proceeded upon the assumption that "being," as embracing all reality, was truly univocal. Plato, Henry thought, provided a notorious example of a philosopher who took this route.[85] Indeed all intellects made this assumption initially, at the first two subgrades of most general knowledge of God, by not registering the distinction between divine and created being. In such primitive cognitive endeavors there was thus something approaching a common concept of being, which instead of a legitimate concept was more truly a confused mode (*modus confusus*) of understanding, a conceiving of two different objects, or concepts, as if they were one.[86] Richard of

---

Transcendentals and their Function, pp. 46–48, n. 35, be justified (see also Marrone, "The Notion of Univocity in Duns Scotus's Early Works," FrS 43 [1983]: 372–75). (Wolter maintains that Duns used "being" alone sometimes as an absolutely simple and common term, in which case it was the univocal applying to both God and creatures, and sometimes as a proper term, in which case it stood for one of the two analogous concepts, created and uncreated being.) It would appear that Richard of Conington, like Henry an opponent of univocity of "being," retained Henry's attitude toward the term's logical descent; in *Quaest. ord.*, q. 1, ad 2. and ad 3. (ed. Doucet, p. 438), he claimed that there was an unmodified term "being" proper to God (in deference to Duns he described it as absolutely simple [*simpliciter simplex*]) which was also included in another "being" that was somehow broader (if only unified in a manner of speaking – see above, nn. 72 and 76).

[85] The passage from Henry's *Summa*, a. 21, q. 2, ad 3. (1:124vO), quoted above in n. 75, making the point about the impossibility of a common concept for the being of God and creature, continues: "Videtur tamen hoc [i.e. conceptus entis communis esse ad esse Dei et esse creaturae] non potentibus distinguere multiplicitatem entis et esse creatoris ab esse creaturae, sicut nec potuit Plato ponens ens esse genus, tamquam sit nominis entis unum aliquid commune conceptum, quod non videtur subtilioribus potentibus distinguere ens et eius significata discernere, qualis erat Aristotelis." On this failure properly to distinguish the concepts of being, see also *Summa*, a. 24, q. 7, ad 1. (1:144vI); and a. 24, q. 9 (1:146vY).

[86] Henry, *Summa*, a. 24, q. 6 (1:142vV): "Et licet secundum se diversos intellectus distinctos faciunt bonum creatoris et bonum creaturae, sicut et ens de Deo et de creatura, quia tamen proximi sunt, intellectus noster concipit modo confuso utrumque ut unum." Stephen Brown, "Avicenna and the Unity of the Concept of

Conington made the point by saying that at this most general cognitive level mind simply failed to perceive the duality of concepts,
involuntarily abstracting from its two objects distinctly understood to
a kind of imperceptible distinction (*impercepta distinctio*).[87]

Mind was wrong to do this – technically speaking, Henry said it
was in error – but the mistake was nonetheless understandable.[88] As
already explained, at the first two subgrades of most general knowledge of God cognition was highly indeterminate; indeed at these
stages mind seized its dual object under the two most indeterminate
modes possible.[89] It should not be surprising that such indetermination was reflected in mind's assessment of its knowledge, preventing
it at first from deciding what sort of object it knew, whether divine,
created or both.[90] To put the argument another way, the negative
indetermination of the primary concept of God's being and the privative indetermination of the primary concept of being of creatures
were so close (*propinquae* or *proximae*) that intellect fell naturally into
taking the two concepts for one and the same, thinking of its object,
erroneously of course, as undivided.[91]

Being", pp. 122 and 148, describes this as the "apparent unity" of the concept of
being in Henry's thought.

[87] Richard of Conington, *Quodlibet* 1, q. 2 (ed. Brown, p. 306): "Alia est abstractio duarum intentionum a seipsis distincte intelligibilibus, in quantum huiusmodi,
ad sui ipsarum imperceptam distinctionem. Et quia quod a dualitate non abstrahitur oportet quod sit duo et utrumque, manifestum est quod talis abstractio non terminatur ad intentionem unam et neutram sed ad duas et utrasque, tamen sine
dualitate [dualitatis?] et utriusque perceptione. Unde dico quod concipiens ens concipit Deum et creaturam, sed non percipit nec distinguit intuitive sed convincit necessaria ratione quod ita est." See also above, n. 76. Matthew of Aquasparta adopted
the idea of a confused knowledge of two kinds of being in terms more literally
faithful to Henry's – see *Quaestiones de productione rerum*, q. 1, ad 4. (BFS, 17, 20),
partially quoted above, Pt. 2, ch. 8, n. 135.

[88] For the word "error," see below, n. 91.

[89] See above, n. 56.

[90] See Henry, *Summa*, a. 21, q. 2, ad 3. (1:124vP).

[91] Henry, *Summa*, a. 21, q. 2, ad 3. (1:125rS): "Per hunc ergo modum esse indeterminatum per abnegationem convenit Deo, et per privationem creaturae. Et quia
indeterminatio per abnegationem et per privationem propinquae sunt, quia ambae
tollunt determinationem, una tantum secundum actum, alia secundum actum simul
et potentiam, ideo non potentes distinguere inter huiusmodi diversa pro eodem con-
cipiunt esse simpliciter et esse indeterminatum, sive uno modo sive alter, sive sit
Dei sive creaturae. Natura enim est intellectus non potentis distinguere ea quae
propinqua sunt, concipere ipsa ut unum, quae tamen in rei veritate non faciunt
unum conceptum. Et ideo est error in illius conceptu." For the term "proximi,"
see the account in *Summa*, a. 24, q. 6 (1:142vV), quoted in n. 86 above. In *Summa*,
a. 24, q. 9 (1:146vY), Henry gave the same explanation, saying God's being and
created being were "prope existentia."

Henry even found a way to account for mind's error that advanced dramatically in the direction of Duns's later notion of "being" as an absolutely simple (*simpliciter simplex*) concept. As he saw it, mind's confusion, its initial inability to discern God's being from being proper to creatures, could be traced to the extreme simplicity of both primitive general concepts under which being was conceived.[92] Concepts so simple just did not furnish mind with much by which to tell them apart. Of the two, predictably enough, it was the concept of being referring to God that was simplest of all, and Richard of Conington evidently took this fact as justification for adopting Duns's very term, "simpliciter simplex." The notion of "being" proper to God that the

---

[92] Henry, *Summa*, a. 24, q. 9 (1:146vY): "Unde ista cognitio eius quod quid est de Deo . . . habetur . . . naturaliter et simplici conceptu, sicut et concipiuntur prima principia complexa et incomplexa, inter quae conceptus Dei sub ratione entis aut boni simpliciter <aut> alicuius huiusmodi intentionis generalis est, aut primo primus, quem non discernit propter eius simplicitatem ab intentionibus huiusmodi convenientibus creaturis, a quibus concipitur quod in eis convenit creatori; sicut etiam intelligendo entia particularia in quibus primo conceptu homo intelligit intentionem entis simpliciter et universalis ad omne ens creatum, non discernit illam propter eius simplicitatem ab aliis intentionibus communibus et particularibus, quamvis non sit tantae simplicitatis ut est intellectus entis simpliciter communis de Deo et creaturis, et maxime ut est intentio entis quae soli Deo convenit." See also *Quodlibet* 6, q. 1 (Henrici Opera, 10:3, ll. 63–65); and *Quodlibet* 13, q. 1 (Henrici Opera, 18:5, ll. 28–32). It is worth noting that in the passage from a. 24, q. 9 quoted here, and in *Summa*, a. 26, q. 2, ad 1. (1:159rT), quoted above, n. 78, Henry claimed that the "being" analogically common to God and creatures – for all that it was not a true concept – was also most simple (*simplicissimum*). Except for the matter of univocity, this was Duns's mature position on "being;" or perhaps one should say that including the stand on analogical community, it was precisely the position Duns seems to have advocated in his early works, where he had not yet come to posit the univocity of "being" – see Marrone, "The Notion of Univocity," pp. 368–70. In *Summa* (*Qg. ord.*), a. 34, q. 3 (Henrici Opera, 27:190, ll. 43–48), Henry observed that when descending from the analogically unified notion of being – as from the "being" applicable to the ten categories – to any more proper concept – as, for instance, to "substantial being" – the formal aspect (*ratio*) added to the original term could not be extraneous to being itself. This, too, foreshadows Duns, in this case his theory of the descent from univocal "being" by intrinsic modes.

Passages like the one from *Summa*, a. 24, q. 9, quoted in the present note, are what prompted Gómez Caffarena and Bérubé to claim that at one point Henry held to the notion of a single concept of being absolutely common to God and creatures (see above, n. 77). But a full reading of a. 24, q. 9 (1:146vY), reveals how his position there was compatible with his notion of a unity of "being" as common to creatures and God only by means of a "confused mode" of understanding, not any real unity of concept. Indeed it was in article 24–q. 6 (1:142vV) – and not in article 21, as Gómez Caffarena and Bérubé would suggest, that Henry introduced the phrase "confuso modo" to describe the way mind thought of God's being and created being as somehow one (see above, n. 86).

wayfarer acquired in this life, though always without perceiving it, was according to Richard "absolutely simple."[93]

In sum, Henry's response to the concerns about the precise noetic conditions of the wayfarer's natural knowledge of God was emphatically to reaffirm that both the concept of God's being and that of creatures were primitive to mind, present at the very beginnings of cognitive activity and both drawn somehow from sensory cognition of the world. Intellect was thus positioned at the very foundation of its knowledge here below to know both God and creatures, even if at first it did not perceive the former as legitimately and naturally its object. Logical reflection revealed, furthermore, that by simplicity and metaphysical elementarity the concept of God's being, even as confusedly known in a general attribute, held the place of absolute cognitive priority.

Somewhat unexpectedly, given his theoretical separation of the normative functions of illumination from the phenomenon of natural knowledge of God, Henry sometimes elucidated his theory of divine being as mind's first object by turning to explanatory devices which, for the classic Augustinians, had been bound up with God's literal role as light of truth. In his hands these schemes took on an altered coloration and, put to new use, assumed novel significance.

For instance, he distinguished two ways something could be designated as that out of which (*ex quo*) another object was known: formally and materially.[94] An object was known out of another formally when the latter constituted formal means of knowing it (*formalis ratio cognoscendi*), in the way knowledge of conclusions was drawn from principles or, more generally, inferred understanding derived by discursive thought from a more fundamental source. Taking "out of" in this sense, natural knowledge of God conceived most generally in an attribute like "being" was that out of which created things were known, while for rational understanding of divinity just the reverse held true, with God in the third subgrade of most general cognition and at the more general and general levels being known out of prece-

[93] See the passages from Richard's *Quaest. ord.*, q. 1 (ed. Doucet, pp. 431 and 438) cited above, nn. 66 and 84, and the discussion below, Pt. 4, ch. 15, n. 87. In *Quodlibet* 1, q. 2, ad 4. (ed. Brown, p. 307), Richard conceded to Duns that "being" was "simpliciter simplex" while insisting that this did not necessarily mean it was also univocal, yet the "being" he had in mind this time was not God's being, but rather a common being, such as the "being" shared by the ten categories.
[94] Henry, *Summa*, a. 24, q. 7, ad 1. (1:144vI).

dent cognition of creatures. An object was known out of another materially, on the other hand, when the means for knowing it were extracted (*extrahitur*) from the latter, the way intelligible species were culled from sensation. In this way God was in no way source of knowledge here below, everything mind knew by normal procedures, including natural knowledge of divinity, coming materially out of sensory perception of creatures.

The point is reminiscent of Matthew's commentary about material and completive formal causes for cognition in his sketch of the ingredients of human knowledge in question 3 of *De cognitione*.[95] In Matthew's version all knowledge came materially from sensation; formally and completively it was an influence from God that furnished the source. The difference is, of course, that Matthew was talking about knowledge of truth and conceiving of the completive formal origin as truth-revealing light, Henry was not. Otherwise the ideas of the two thinkers are so close that it is likely Matthew drew on Henry for his more elaborate but still more traditionally Augustinian scheme.

Looking at the formal origins of knowledge alone, Henry drew a further distinction, again suggestive of ideas of the classic Augustinians. Despite his initial proposal that natural knowledge of God was formally source for cognition of all else after the fashion of complex principles with respect to conclusions, he now confessed only two questions later that this was not precisely so.[96] Strictly speaking, principles constituted a proper and absolute object (*per se absolutum obiectum*) for discursive mind, thus known better and more clearly than the conclusions for which they provided the formal source, but the same was not true of God. Since divinity was naturally known only obliquely and in general, a better analogue for the way knowledge of God yielded the formal source for all else known was the action of light in sensory vision of color, where radiation was means of seeing but only in a secondary and restrained sense object seen.

Adding to the two preceding modes the even more limited manner in which God served as cognitive means in illumination of truth, one is left with three ways Henry posited for one thing to act as formal source for knowledge of another: after the manner of principles for conclusions, light for color, or a species – more exactly a

---

[95] See above, Pt. 2, ch. 6, n. 118.
[96] Henry, *Summa*, a. 24, q. 9, ad 1. (1:146v–47r[Z]).

character or figure – for that which it made known.[97] Given the comment about principles noted just above, it is clear that Henry believed
God could serve as formal source for knowledge along the lines of
syllogistic principles for conclusions in cases of beatific vision and
rapture alone.[98] His three ways of serving as formal origin thus picked
out three major ways he understood God to intervene in human
thought: as beatific object after the fashion of principles, as first thing
naturally known after that of light, and as revealer of truth after
that of character or species.

Surely more than by coincidence, Matthew, in *De fide*, laid out
precisely the same three ways to be means for knowing something
else, like Henry on first object of mind settling on light as the appropriate image for explaining God's role in the knowledge with which
he was concerned.[99] Once more, however, there is the difference
that Matthew, but not Henry, was talking about illumination and
truth. Henry's view of the latter always more closely approached
that of John Pecham, for whom God was illuminator in the manner of a mental species.[100] A second time, Henry and Matthew seem
to have converged on an analytical structure only to part ways when
applying the schema to specific noetic concerns.

Still, with these exceptions, Henry generally avoided applying to
his theory of natural knowledge of God philosophical contrivances
from the classic Augustinians not designed specifically to illustrate
the role of "being." Most notably absent from his work was the
notion of impressed similitude or species.[101] Admittedly he did quote
Augustine's *De Trinitate* on knowledge of God as ultimate good – thus
ultimate being – impressed on intellect from the start, while at times
in his Quodlibets he cited the well-worn passage from the same work
on conceiving God by means of a similitude inferior to divine essence
and residing in mind.[102] Yet none of this was intended to undermine

[97] On God's formal role in illumination, see above, Pt. 3, ch. 9, nn. 10, 103
and 108.
[98] See above, Pt. 3, ch. 9, nn. 3–4, 87 and 89–90; and also this chapter, nn.
4 and 6.
[99] See above, Pt. 2, ch. 5, n. 99.
[100] See above, Pt. 2, ch. 5, n. 91; Pt. 3, ch. 9, n. 11; and this chapter, n. 5.
[101] On this idea in Bonaventure's thought and that of his followers, see above,
Pt. 2, ch. 8, pp. 210–14, 222–25 and 234–42.
[102] On the first reference, see above, n. 14; as well as Henry's *Summa*, a. 24, q. 7,
ad 1. (1:a44vI); and a. 24, q. 8 (1:145vP). The statement about the impression of
good on the mind comes from *De Trinitate* VIII, 3 (CC 50:272). On the inferior

an uncompromising denial of innate knowledge of God.[103] Instead, the references to Augustine's more audacious formulations made simply a deferential nod to the most illustrious proponent of the tradition to which he saw himself belonging, reverently expounded so as to fit the cognitive model he had in mind. Henry was otherwise conspicuously silent about the whole Bonaventuran account of knowledge of the divinity as dependent on direct impression from God. Such language, however generously represented in the intellectual genealogy from which so much of his theory of knowledge arose, had no place in his considerably more Aristotelianized philosophical world.

The noetics of Henry's natural knowledge of God projected, in sum, a novel vision, drawing on numerous elements in the classic Augustinian synthesis but systematically eliminating any connection to the light of truth and eschewing all hint of innate understanding. His caution on these matters amounted to an insurance policy against charges of ontologism. Augustinian, even Avicennian, on the relation of mind to God, he would nonetheless do nothing to obscure the radical effects of the Fall. Yet Henry managed to leave ample room for the cherished notion of divine intimacy to intellect in the world, making sure his readers appreciated that the knowledge of God he posited as natural was, if attenuated and general, nevertheless knowledge of God in his quiddity.[104] To this extent he surpassed the zeal of predecessors like Bonaventure and Pecham, for whom knowledge of divinity in a general property like "being" could not claim quidditative status.[105] Only Matthew among classic Augustinians

---

similitude, consult Henry, *Quod.* 3, q. 1 (1:48vX); and also *Quod.* 4, q. 7 (1:95vF); and q. 8 (1:98vQ). For the use of this text by the classic Augustinians, see above, Pt. 2, ch. 8, nn. 15, 44 and 136, and to somewhat different effect, n. 112; for its use by Henry in a different context, see above, Pt. 3, ch. 9, nn. 118 and 119.

[103] See above, n. 17.

[104] Henry, *Summa*, a. 58, q. 2 (2:131vM); and perhaps slightly more tentatively, a. 24, q. 6 (1:141r–v[N]). The latter question (1:141vO) insisted that even if "most general" knowledge of God did not give access "simpliciter" to the divine "quid secundum substantiam," it did so "aliquo modo." After all, Augustine himself made clear that some quidditative knowledge of God had to be available to all mankind, even in the present life – see *Summa*, a. 24, q. 1 (1:137rC) and especially (137vE): "Absolutely igitur concedendum quod quiditas Dei et essentia ab homine est cognoscibilis, non solum in futuro . . . sed et in praesenti."

[105] See Pt. 2, ch. 8, nn. 62, 80 and 93–94. Jean Paulus, "Henri de Gand et l'argument ontologique," AHDLMA 10–11 (1935–36): 321, identified from Bonaventure to Duns Scotus a progessive movement among Franciscan theologians towards increasing the quidditative nature of the wayfarer's knowledge of God.

conceded that intellect naturally conceived God's *quid est*, and he
had benefit of Henry's prior arguments to open the way.[106] To be
sure, knowledge of God in an attribute, never rising to essential particulars, would be perception of God's quiddity only universally and
as if by accident (*in universali et secundum accidens solum*), yet it surpassed the nominal knowledge (*quid est quod dicitur per nomen*) that was
all Pecham granted to the wayfarer's mind.[107] Though Henry conceded that still at the third subgrade of "most general" knowledge
intellect's concept of divinity was only nominal, with "more general"
and "general" knowledge – the upper levels of rational cognition –
it advanced to at least something of God's essence.[108]

Equipped with so well-developed a natural theory, Henry was,
again like Matthew of Aquasparta, less interested than most of his
predecessors in exploring the dynamics of contemplation as a way
of guaranteeing God's intimacy to mind.[109] At least his early writings
display nothing remotely like the febrile dynamism of Bonaventure's
noetics, in which a near-mystical vision of God always lay within
reach, or the more sedate occupation of the later Grosseteste with
preparations for mystical transcendence. Henry demonstrated, in fact,
almost no interest in urging mind to push beyond its natural state
to the point where it might touch God. Thus while he continued
along the path begun by the classic Augustinians, like them shifting
the function of William of Auvergne's and Robert Grosseteste's vision
of a progressive sweep into a higher world of truth onto worldly and
ordinary processes, he seems to have been more fully satisfied than
any save perhaps Matthew to keep within the limits of normal intellection. Indeed, he did more than all of them, Matthew included,
to naturalize – or perhaps Aristotelianize – the notion of what normal
cognition might be. Here was a theologian who brought the Augustinian tradition down to earth. On the noetics of knowing God, only
a short step separated Henry from the even more worldly ideas of
Duns himself.

---

[106] See above, Pt. 2, ch. 8, n. 143.
[107] Henry, *Summa*, a. 24, q. 6 (1:142rQ). On natural knowledge of God as not
in his particularity, see also above, nn. 7 and 8. For Pecham's view, see Pt. 2, ch. 8,
n. 80. On nominal knowledge in general, see Pt. 3, ch. 9, n. 34.
[108] Henry, *Summa*, a. 24, q. 5 (1:140vG).
[109] On Matthew, see the comments above, Pt. 2, ch. 8, pp. 243–45.

It remains to be asked whether Henry's views on God as first object naturally known impinged on his understanding of the way to knowledge of the common principles of science. According to the broadly Aristotelianizing Scholasticism in which he had been educated, common principles were special because they were constructed out of the most general terms, his first intentions, the very elements of simple cognition in which God, conceived generally and in a confused manner, was made available to mind as its first and fundamental object. Did this mean that knowledge of such principles was somehow drawn from God?

Henry fully conceded the epistemological connection between first intentions and intellect's primary complex cognition. Combining the principles of excluded middle and noncontradiction into a single superprinciple, he called it the very first complex truth known to mind, explaining its priority as a direct result of its foundation exclusively on the concept of being, first in order of simple understanding.[110] Moreover, all further common principles followed immediately upon this most basic proposition and preceded less primitive complex truths precisely because they arose out of the other first intentions, subsequent to "being" but known before the rest of simple concepts. Among such principles he listed the assertions that the whole is greater than any of its parts and that if equals are taken from equals the remainders are equal.[111] He also realized that, philosophically speaking, first intentions established a link between knowledge of principles and his theory of God as first cognitive object. Much of his discussion of principles can be found in articles 22 and 24 of the *Summa*, two key sections devoted to investigating human knowledge of divinity.[112]

Yet when it came to explaining how mind composed common principles and knew them to be true, Henry passed up the opportunity to exploit this link, relying instead exclusively on the Aristotelianizing account of principal cognition and its place in science sweeping the universities by the second half of the thirteenth century. In a completely unexceptional paraphrase of Aristotle, he held

---

[110] Henry, *Summa*, a. 1, q. 12 (1:22rL). See also *Summa*, a. 24, q. 3 (1:138vP).
[111] See Henry, *Summa*, a. 1, q. 5 (1:14v–15r[B]).
[112] For example, see the references given above, n. 110; and below, nn. 114 and 115.

that principles were propositions knowledge of whose truth was
acquired by mind without any preceding complex cognition, while
conclusions were affirmed from knowledge of the principles upon
which they were based.[113] Among principles, furthermore, some were
more basic than others, constituting the foundations for rational
thought, and these were, in words drawn from the standard lexicon,
the first principles of science (*prima principia scientiarum*). Other names
for them included the Boethian phrase, "common concepts of the
soul" (*communes animi conceptiones*), and the more authentically Aristotelian
"dignitates" and "propositiones maximae."[114] The reason their veri-
fication did not require precedent complex cognition was that their
truth lay immediately exposed to any mind grasping the simple terms
of which they were composed, a point Henry supported by quoting
the familiar phrase from Aristotle's *Posterior Analytics* that principles
were known insofar as their terms were understood.[115]

Since the same Aristotelianizing ground had been covered by the
classic Augustinians, there is nothing remarkable about its appearance in Henry's thought. He even followed his predecessors on what
it meant for knowledge of principles to arise virtually without effort
at intellect's initial stirrings. His account in question 11 of article 1
could well have been based on Bonaventure's declaration in the
Commentary on the Sentences that principles were both received, since
the intelligible species grounding their terms were acquired through
reception, and also innate, but only to the extent that they depended
on an inborn judgmental light.[116] Henry differed merely by avoid-

---

[113] Henry, *Summa*, a. 1, q. 1, ad 5. & 6. (1:3vK); and a. 1, q. 10 (1:20rC).

[114] For "first principles of science," see Henry, *Summa*, a. 1, q. 5 (1:15rB); for
"common concepts," a. 1, q. 12 (1:22vL); a. 22, q. 2 (1:130vR); and a. 24, q. 3
(1:138vP); for "dignitates" and "propositiones maximae," a. 22, q. 2 (1:131rT). On
these terms and their origins, see above, Pt. 1, ch. 1, nn. 52 and 53; and Pt. 2,
ch. 6, n. 19.

[115] See Henry, *Summa*, a. 1, q. 5 (1:15rB); and a. 22, q. 1 (1:130rL), in both of
which Henry quoted Aristotle; as well as the related a. 22, q. 2 (1:130vR). On the
Aristotelian text and its citation by classic Augustinians, see above, Pt. 2, ch. 6, nn.
5 and 18. Henry recognized both an objective and subjective component to the
immediacy or *per se notum* quality of principles, since beyond the nature of the object
evidence was important in determining which propositions were truly first principles. Only those whose truth was immediately evident to mind working normally
in the world would qualify – see Henry, *Summa*, a. 22, q. 2 (1:130vS and 131vX).

[116] Henry, *Summa*, a. 1, q. 11 (1:21rC). For rejection of any innate knowledge
for mankind, see also *Summa*, a. 1, q. 5 (1:15rB). On Bonaventure, see above, Pt. 2,
ch. 6, n. 5; and ch. 8, n. 23. Matthew also adopted these ideas, in a manner truer
to Bonaventure's language – see Pt. 2, ch. 6, n. 20.

ing the word "innate," drawing instead on the Bonaventuran reference to natural judgment (*naturale iudicatorium*) for his own cautious
description of knowledge of principles as "naturally acquired" (*naturaliter acquisitum*). The term "natural" nicely recalled his own distinction between natural and rational aspects of the wayfarer's cognition
of God. Knowledge of first principles was natural – like the most
primitive knowledge of God – because acquired as if by nature alone
and without discursive reasoning; all other complex cognition depended
on the analytical and argumentative powers of inquiring mind, thus
on rational procedure.[117]

But Henry took such theories even farther than predecessors like
Bonaventure and Matthew along the path to divorcing knowledge
of principles from consideration of a special cognitive role for God.
As noted above, at times he rehabilitated the pure Avicennian notion
of mind's first concept as signifying "ens inquantum ens," and it is
telling that one of the occasions he did so was when considering
knowledge of principles.[118] To found principal cognition on "being"
conceived in this way deflected attention away from the involvement
of God and went hand in hand with Henry's other efforts to reduce
what he must have perceived as intrusions of the supernatural in the
noetics of the classic Augustinians. His rejection of the language of
innate knowledge and of that part of Bonaventure's description of
natural cognition of divinity invoking a mental impression had the
same effect. Indeed the one explicit place he reserved for God in
discussion of knowledge of principles had nothing to do with divinity as first object of intellect but rather with its separate function as
illuminator of truth. Twice he noted that principles were seized with
the aid of divine light, of course just insofar as pure truth was concerned.[119] In short, nothing in Henry compares to Pecham's theory

---

[117] Henry, *Summa*, a. 1, q. 4, ad 3. and ad 5. (1:13rI and 13vL); and a. 1, q. 5
(1:15rB) – see also above, n. 48. In a. 1, q. 4, ad 3. (1:13rI), he echoed the passage from Bonaventure's *Comm. in lib. II. Sent.*, d. 39, a. 1, q. 2 (cited Pt. 2, ch. 6,
n. 5; and referred to above, n. 116), that habits of principal cognition were "quodam modo . . . innati et quodam modo acquisiti." In Henry's hands, this was transformed into the statement that knowledge of principles "quodam modo est naturalis,
et quodam modo est acquisita." There could be no clearer indication how much
Henry's idea of natural knowledge rested on Bonaventure's prior notion of a cognition he called innate.

[118] See the first reference given above, n. 30.

[119] Henry, *Summa*, a. 1, q. 4, ad 5. (1:13vL); and ad 3. (1:13rI). In making his
claim, Henry could point to the prior example of Bonaventure – see above, Pt. 2,
ch. 6, nn. 6 and 7; and ch. 8, n. 26.

of first principles as impressed from above, which in turn drew upon
William of Auvergne's association of principles and God's direct
action.[120] All that remains in his thought of these powerful currents
from Augustinian tradition of the preceding decades is the unelaborated convergence at the same point in his noetics of knowledge
of principles, knowledge of "being," and knowledge of God.

---

[120] On Pecham, see above, Pt. 2, ch. 6, nn. 40–43.

CHAPTER ELEVEN

ESSENCE AND THE ONTOLOGY OF THE
MENTAL OBJECT

In the first years of his magisterium Henry had managed to refor-
mulate the classic Augustinian position on human knowledge so as
to embrace its two core elements, a theory of illumination validating Augustine's intuitions about truth and certitude and an explanation of divinity as natural cognitive object insuring God's intimacy
to mind, while steering conspicuously clear of implications of ontologism. But his efforts to preserve Augustinianism in the critical world
of high medieval Scholasticism confronted one final obstacle. For all
the subtlety of Henry's handling of concept and reference, he had
yet to accommodate his notion of primitive knowledge of God in a
general grasp of "being" by means of a plausible psychology of concept formation to an account of objective reality.

The problem went back to the two potentially conflicting demands
on his noetics.[1] Like all scholars up to his time he had maintained
there was no single concept univocally capable of representing God
and creatures, even "being" at its most general possessing only analogical unity and masquerading for two real concepts, one referring
properly to God and the other to creatures. How was he to remain
faithful to such semantic strictures while positing the primitive emergence in mind of both concepts of being out of sensation alone. It
was easy to picture the origin of the concept proper to creatures:
intellect simply distilled it from data provided by the actions of creatures themselves on the senses. But why should the concept of God's
being – referentially radically distinct and, counter to expectations,
by nature as well as logic absolutely first – be derivable from the
same source? And if it was not, since no other data were normally
available to sinful mind, how could the wayfarer know God the way
Henry said it did?

The dilemma can be framed in language drawn from Henry's own
work. In the early article 3, question 4, of the *Summa*, he confronted

---

[1] See above, Pt. 3, ch. 10, pp. 316–317.

the oppositional argument that, if, as he had said, knowledge of being at its most general lay at the foundation of thought, then the wayfarer's intellect should have absolutely unlimited access to all things, including God himself. After all, "being" at its broadest included in potency the idea of every conceivable object, so nothing should fall outside mind's purview.[2] His response was to insist that such reasoning overlooked the constraints imposed by the way mind's first concepts were generated.[3] In all natural processes, he reminded his readers, whatever arose from something prior retained the flavor of its roots. Since the wayfarer's notion of being was taken from sensory data, regardless of what was true about "being" viewed absolutely and without limitation, "being" as known by mind working naturally in the world was suitable for underpinning knowledge only of those things at least implicitly included in the domain of sensible reality. One should therefore not expect to know much about God, or any immaterial substance, in the world of sin. According to the technical terms introduced later in the *Summa* and mentioned in the preceding chapter, intellect's natural knowledge of divinity was drawn "materially out of" sensible cognition.[4] The point here was that it could never escape the limitations of such material origins.

Was this response not tacit admission of the bankruptcy of Henry's position on natural knowledge of God? Did it not invalidate his claim that mind working naturally in the world came up with a primitive concept of being proper to God capable of yielding a quidditative notion of divinity? Duns Scotus would advance something very much like this critique, couched in words reminiscent of the response from article 3 of the *Summa*, when he attacked Henry's theory of knowing God.[5] The same accusations, possibly drawn from Duns, appear

---

[2] Henry, *Summa*, a. 3, q. 4, arg. 1 (1:29rO).

[3] Henry, *Summa*, a. 3, q. 4, ad 1. (1:29vQ): ". . . sicut in naturalibus illud quod procedit ex radice semper tenet et sapit naturam radicis, nec potest naturam radicis excedere, sic prima principia naturalis cognitionis cum a sensibus et sensibilibus velut a radice trahantur . . . vim et naturam sensibilium excedere non possunt. . . . Licet ergo ratio entis simpliciter et absolute accepta sit sufficiens in potentia ratio cognoscendi quodlibet cognoscibile quod sub ratione generali entis continetur, inquantum tamen est accepta per sensum a sensibilibus limitata est ut sit in potentia principium cognoscendi solum illa ad quae potest deducere ratio naturalis adminiculo sensuum et sensibilium et non alia." The same principle of the cognitive origin setting formal limits on all subsequently known appears as well in Matthew of Aquasparta – see above, Pt. 2, ch. 8, n. 129.

[4] See above, Pt. 3, ch. 10, n. 94.

[5] See below, Pt. 4, ch. 15, n. 26; and also further on, n. 116.

as an argument Richard of Conington felt compelled to answer in defense of Henry's position in his own Quodlibet I.[6]

Of course, the general problem was not peculiar to Henry, for every theologian of the high medieval period struggled to explain how there might be natural but still meaningful discourse about God. Yet the not untypical insistence on the sensible origin of all the wayfarer's ideas placed uncommon strains on Henry's thought. Purer Aristotelianizers could simply assert that intellect devised a concept of divinity by spinning out an analogy with whatever it knew from the sensible world. Since such a concept would be neither quidditative nor, contrary to Henry's claim, a priori, but unabashedly a posteriori, no philosophical awkwardness followed from admitting that it was ultimately constrained by the inferential limitations of sensory evidence. Such thinkers were satisfied with so modest a degree of natural human knowledge of divinity. The classic Augustinians would likewise not have been much confounded by an argument about concepts savoring of their roots. Although not conceding the limitation to a posteriori natural cognition of God, neither were they committed – at least before Matthew – to its quidditative nature. But even if they had demanded so much, at their disposal lay the theoretical resources of an integrated doctrine of divine illumination. With the light of eternal truth directly active in all mind's endeavors, it was not surprising that concepts should emerge resonant with more meaning than purely sensible foundations would bear. For them, intellect was not left to cross the analogical gap between created and divine "being" on its own, since God's luminous presence was there to lead the way.[7]

But how could Henry, who despite his Augustinian sympathies had, fearing ontologism, insulated the processes of natural knowledge of God from the mechanism by which mind was illumined in knowing pure truth, justify proposing a richer natural conception of divinity than the non-quidditative, a posteriori notion allowed by Aristotelianizers? How could he agree with earlier Augustinians that sinful intellect had a fuller idea of what God was? Given his noetics

---

[6] Richard of Conington, *Quodlibet* 1, q. 2, arg. 7 (ed. Brown, p. 304).

[7] Essentially this understanding of the Augustinian position led Allan Wolter to remark that "the medieval theory of analogy" was rooted in Augustinian illuminationism (Wolter, *The Transcendentals and their Function*, pp. 32 and 40–43). See also Marrone, "Henry of Ghent and Duns Scotus on the Knowledge of Being," *Speculum* 63 (1988): 30–31.

and the suppositions of his semantics, it would seem that there was no avoiding the damning implications of his own early confession about the limited cognitive horizon of the wayfarer in the world.

There is in fact no sign that Henry sensed the least threat from his statements in article 3, question 4, about constraints on mind's primitive idea of being. Instead, he plainly regarded his response in that question as merely demonstrating the impossibility of perfect cognition of divinity or higher spiritual substances so long as mind relied on its natural capacities alone, a limitation fully compatible with his account of the wayfarer's knowledge of God in a general attribute.[8] Simply put, he intended to concede only that mind, working on its own in the world, could attain – as indeed he always believed – no particular concept of God or spiritual substances, nothing more than the general understanding implicit in the cognition of "being" and other transcendental attributes.[9] The concession left him entirely at ease insisting that it had such general knowledge, that it had it a priori, and that its understanding was at least minimally quidditative.

How could he be so confident? The answer would seem to lie in his metaphysics, specifically his theory of essence, and in the possibilities this theory opened up for the mechanics of ideogenesis and attendant views about knowledge. Admittedly Henry advanced no such claim himself, never even laying out explicitly how his metaphysics bore on problems of noetics in general or more particularly on the question of what kind of objects were available to mind. But for all his silence on the matter, his theory of essence so clearly provided an exit from the noetic dilemma he faced that one cannot but believe it played a pivotal role in his decision to support a complex of ideas about natural knowledge of God that would otherwise have stood in grave doubt. It provided the crucial, if unspoken, justification for advancing beyond the views of both Aristotelianizers and Augustinians immediately preceding him.[10]

---

[8] Henry's point is obvious from *Summa*, a. 3, q. 4 (1:29vP): that working purely naturally mind could have neither a clear knowledge of God nor one equal even to the enigmatic understanding of faith.

[9] *Summa*, a. 3, q. 3 (1:29rL), makes it clear that Henry, in that article, wanted to deny to mind working by philosophy alone cognitive access simply to the particularity of God and spiritual substances. On the impossibility of natural knowledge of God in particular, see above, Pt. 3, ch. 10, nn. 7, 36 and 37.

[10] For fuller analysis of the relevant aspects of Henry's metaphysics, see my *Truth and Scientific Knowledge*, pp. 105–30, upon which the following pages rely. For Henry's

In the late thirteenth century, after the seminal efforts of Thomas Aquinas, it was commonplace to distinguish between essence (*essentia*) and being (*ens, esse*) or existence (*existentia*). Every thinker accepted the notion that for each object these two elements had to be differentiated, and debate focused on how the separation was to be made. Despite the universality of the issue, however, Henry's views were so complicated and unusual that they must be considered a special case.

Along with his contemporaries, Henry traced the origin of the distinction to Avicenna, but more than most he saw fit to resurrect what he considered Avicenna's authentic views, beginning with discussion of "thing" or *res*, in his opinion key to the Arab philosopher's theories. In the same passage from Avicenna's *Metaphysics* he had used to defend his claim about the cognitive priority of the concept of being, "thing" was also listed as among mind's first impressions.[11] According to Henry, Avicenna in fact meant to imply that "thing" was the most fundamental concept of all, by nature very first even if not initially seized by human intellect.[12] Any object was therefore capable of being regarded absolutely in itself (*simpliciter et absolute*) as "thing" without consideration of its conditions of being, whether as being in mind, being outside it in particulars, or simply nonbeing.[13]

The reason Avicenna could attribute this special status to "thing," Henry thought, was because he believed that in the structure of the world thing (*res*) and being (*ens* in the Latin translation of Avicenna, *esse* in Henry's words) were radically different. "Thing" pointed to the essential or quidditative aspects of an object – in the Latin Avicenna also denominated "certitudo," "quidditas" and even "esse proprium" – while "being" possessed what would later be called a modal character, referring to the terms of existence.[14] Thus Avicenna's "absolute

---

own words, see especially *Summa*, a. 21, qq. 2 and 4; a. 28, q. 4; a. 34, q. 2; *Quodlibet* 1, q. 9; 3, q. 8; 5, q. 2; 7, qq. 1–2; and 10, qq. 7 and 8, works spanning the period from 1276 to 1286.

[11] See above, Pt. 3, ch. 10, n. 13; for the citation to Avicenna as well as Bonaventure's evocation of it, Pt. 2, ch. 8, nn. 51 and 52.

[12] Henry, *Summa* (*Qg. ord.*), a. 34, q. 2 (Henrici Opera, 27:174, l. 40–175, l. 55); and *Quod.* 3, q. 9 (1:60vO).

[13] Henry, *Summa* (*Qg. ord.*), a. 34, q. 2 (Henrici Opera, 27:174, ll. 46–50): "Ratio enim rei, ut dicit Avicenna . . ., ratio propria est quod nomine suo exprimat naturam et quiditatem eius cuius est simpliciter et absolute absque omni conditione esse, sive in intellectu sive extra ipsum, aut non esse." The marks in the edition, indicating direct quotation from Avicenna, have here been dropped as misleading.

[14] See above, n. 13, and also Henry, *Quod.* 3, q. 9 (1:60vO): "Hic est advertendum

thing" – that is, "thing" regarded solely in itself (*secundum se et absolute*) –
was the same as "absolute essence" (*essentia absolute*), which was essence
apart from consideration of either being or universality and particularity.[15] Here lay the basis for the commonplace separation of being
and essence. Vital merely appropriated all this by quoting Avicenna
to the same effect about the absolute consideration of "thing."[16]

As Henry saw it, there were three ways the word "thing" could
be used, and they pointed to three telescoping fields of reality.[17] First
came "imaginable thing" (*res a reor reris dicta*), covering all that was
knowable or even fanciable, excluding only that which was absolutely
nothing at all.[18] This constituted the broadest of the three fields,
ranging from concrete objects like the book one was reading to the
most fantastic – a golden mountain, the mythical chimera, or Aristotle's
goat-stag.[19] It was consequently the most tenuously real.

Second came "conceivable thing" (*res a ratitudine dicta*), corresponding
to what Avicenna meant by "absolute thing" or "absolute essence"
and what Henry variously called "essence," "nature" or "quiddity."[20]

---

quod secundum quod vult Avicenna in primo *Metaphysicae* suae, unaquaeque res in
sua natura specifica habet certitudinem propriam quae est eius quiditas qua est id
quod est et non aliud a se, sicut albedo in sua natura habet certitudinem qua est
albedo et non nigredo nec aliquid aliud. Et ob hoc convenit ei intentio qua dicitur res, quae est intentio alia circa naturam ipsam ab intentione de esse." The reference to Avicenna is to *Liber de philosophia prima sive scientia divina* I, 5 (ed. Van
Riet), I, 34–35.

[15] See Henry, *Quodlibet* 2, q. 1 (Henrici Opera, 6:4–5, ll. 30–54); and *Quodlibet* 7,
qq. 1 & 2 (ed. Gordon A. Wilson, Henrici Opera, 11:18). In both passages Henry
refers to Avicenna, *Liber de philosophia prima* V, 1 (see above, Pt. 2, ch. 7, n. 32).

[16] Vital, *Quaestiones de cognitione*, q. 6 (ed. Delorme, "Huit questions," p. 274),
which draws, sometimes verbatim, on Henry's *Quod.* 3, q. 9 (1:60vO).

[17] In *Summa*, a. 21. q. 4 (1:127rO); and a. 34, q. 2 (1:212r[R-S]), Henry spoke
of three formal aspects (*rationes*) of "thing" – in line with the language used just
above, three different ways "thing" could be considered. The essentials of his understanding of these three fields of reality can be found in *Summa*, a. 21, q. 2 (1:124vK);
a. 21, q. 4 (1:127r–v[O]); a. 28, q. 4 (1:167vV); a. 34, q. 2 (Henrici Opera,
27:174–75); *Quod.* 5, q. 2 (1:154rD); and *Quodlibet* 7, qq. 1 & 2 (Henrici Opera
11:26–28). For more extended analysis, see Marrone, *Truth and Scientific Knowledge*,
pp. 108–12; and for possible sources, Marrone, "Henry of Ghent in Mid-Career,"
pp. 206–7, n. 44.

[18] On absolutely nothing (*purum nihil*) in this sense, see *Quodlibet* 7, qq. 1 & 2
(Henrici Opera 11:26–27, ll. 49–53); also "non ens": *Quodlibet* 6, q. 3, ad 2. (Henrici
Opera 10:49–50).

[19] For goat-stag, see *Summa*, a. 24, q. 3 (1:138vO); for goat-stag and golden mountain, *Quodlibet* 7, qq. 1 & 2 (Henrici Opera, 11:27); for goat-stag and Chimera, *Quod.*
3, q. 9 (1:61vO); and *Quod.* 5, q. 2 (1:154rD). Aristotle spoke of the goat-stag in
Posterior Analytics II, 7 (92b5–8).

[20] At least once Henry anomalously called the level of "res a reor reris" that of
"res absolute" – see *Summa*, a. 21, q. 4 (1:127r–v[O]).

Here was located essence in itself, shorn of consideration of actuality or logical determinations of universality or individuality. Henry also referred to it as "being" (*ens* this time and not *esse*, which for him signified more act than object) as well as "essential" or "quidditative being" (*ens per essentiam, ens quidditativum*) and "being pure and simple" (*ens simpliciter dictum*).[21] Everything at this level also counted of course as "res a reor reris" – that is, was included in the previous, broader field – but it comprised something more, or more restricted, since it had truly essential content.

For Henry, essentiality was manifested in three basic qualities or characteristics. First, whatever was essence was a proper object of intellect; whatever was not essence was not. Thus, while anything that was "res a reor reris" could be imagined, put together piecemeal by fantasy from disparate elements drawn from mind's store of knowledge, only essence – "res a ratitudine" – could, technically speaking, be known. In Henry's words, essence was uniquely "ratum quid."[22] Second, to every essence, but only to essence, corresponded an ideal reason or exemplar (*ratio exemplaris*) in the divine mind.[23] This made sense, because essence as uniquely knowable had to be conceived by God, who apprehended all objects through his ideas. The one exception to this rule was God himself, who, though essence, was essence of a very special sort and not represented by any idea.[24] Third, and as a consequence of the preceding, essences taken together made up the realm of all possibles. Since God selected the objects he wanted to create, to bring into existence, from among his ideas, everything that was essence, but only what was essence, had the potential to appear in the actual world.[25] For this reason Henry referred to essence as creatable whatness (*creabile quid*), also that which was producible (*factibile*).[26]

---

[21] For "ens" used this way, see *Summa*, a. 21, q. 2 (1:124vK); and also a. 2, q. 6 (1:27rD); for "ens per essentiam," *Summa*, a. 28, q. 4 (1:167vV); for "ens quidditativum," *Summa* (*Qg. ord.*), a. 34, q. 2 (Henrici Opera, 27:174, ll. 42–45); for "ens simpliciter dictum," *Summa*, a. 21. q. 4 (1:127rM).

[22] Henry, *Summa* (*Qg. ord.*), a. 34. q. 2 (Henrici Opera, 27:174, ll. 42–46).

[23] Henry, *Quodlibet* 6, q. 3, ad 2. (Henrici Opera, 10:49, ll. 10–12); and *Quodlibet* 9, q. 2 (Henrici Opera, 13:34). Vital made the same point in his *Quodlibet* 3, q. 5 (ed. Delorme, p. 145).

[24] Henry, *Quod.* 5, q. 2 (1:154rD); and *Quodlibet* 7, qq. 1 & 2 (Henrici Opera, 11:27–28).

[25] Henry, *Summa*, a. 21, q. 4 (1:127rO).

[26] For "creabile quid," see Henry, *Quodlibet* 9, q. 1 (Henrici Opera, 13:8, ll. 18–20); for "factibile," *Quod.* 8, q. 9 (2:314rK). Vital referred to essences as "factibilia" in

Following essence and last of all came the narrowest field, limited
to "actually existing thing" (*res existens in actu*), or what Henry also
denominated "natural thing" (*res naturalis*) or "thing of nature" (*res
naturae*), taking the word "nature" this time in a more restrictive sense
than that which applied with "res a ratitudine."[27] Again, everything
here was found in the preceding field as well, since every existing
thing was ipso facto possible, but these were the possibles actualized
at a given moment. For all moments taken together, they constituted, in addition to God himself, everything God would ever create
or cause to be generated in the world.

Among the three fields, "res a ratitudine" or essence provided the
fulcrum for Henry's metaphysics. Ontologically everything derived
from it, "res a reor reris" by declension into merely imaginable constructs, "res existens" by elevation into actuality.[28] This is probably
what one would expect, given his essentialist ontology, heavily dependent on Avicenna, but what is most important about the centrality
of essence is that at precisely this point "being" entered into the
scheme. Following Avicenna's lead, Henry had divided thing (*res*) or
essence (*essentia*) from being – his *esse* – but he had also revealingly
called the second level of reality – essence or "res a ratitudine" –
"being" according to the substantive form of the same root: *ens*. The
reason was not just that he posited no real (*re*) separation between
essence and being (*esse*) – that is, that they were not *really* or in actuality different things.[29] It was also that for him there was a way
being was bound to essence, so that in a sense beingness or entity –
not actual entity, to be sure, but a lesser kind of being – began at
the essential level. A variant terminology he sometimes applied to
the three fields was shaped accordingly: *res* for "res a reor reris" but,
beginning with "res a ratitudine," *ens secundum essentiam*, and then
with "res in actu," *ens secundum existentiam*.[30] "Res a reor reris" alone

the passage cited above, n. 23; and in *Quaestiones de cognitione*, q. 6 (ed. Delorme,
"Huit questions," p. 273) – where he also used the term "creabile" – and q. 8 (p. 323).
[27] For "res naturalis," see *Quod.* 3, q. 9 (1:61rO); for "res naturae," *Summa* (*Qq.
ord.*), a. 34, q. 2 (Henrici Opera, 27:175, ll. 58–59).
[28] For fuller discussion, see Marrone, *Truth and Scientific Knowledge*, pp. 120–21.
[29] See Henry's arguments against Giles of Rome on the real distinction of essence
and existence in *Quodlibet* 10, q. 7 (Henrici Opera, 14, esp. pp. 151–66), as well as
those probably aimed at the same target in *Quodlibet* 1, q. 9 (Henrici Opera, 5:48–56).
Henry inveighed against the real distinction, and most likely expressly against Giles,
throughout his career.
[30] See Henry, *Summa*, a. 21, q. 4 (1:127vS), where the match between *res* and *res*

stood as in no way being, or, at most, being in only an imaginary sense (*ens secundum imaginationem*).[31]

This subtle subordination of being to essence emerged even more strikingly in Henry's metaphysics with a peculiarity that marks his understanding of the being-essence distinction as truly astonishing. In Henry's system there was not just a single "being" opposed to "essence" – the "being" signifying existence as distinguished from the quiddity to which it attached. Instead he saw two grades of being: a "being of existence" (*esse existentiae*) corresponding to the actuality of an object at his third level of "thing" but also a "being of essence" (*esse essentiae*) appropriated to essence in "thing's" second field, short of consideration of it as actualized in either mind or external world.[32] Henry said he found the distinction already in Avicenna's works, a claim Vital merely repeated in his defense of Henry's quite extra-ordinary views.[33]

Henry thought of *esse essentiae* as a sort of being that essence possessed in and of itself, an idea which, aside from historical sources, seems to have arisen out of the perceived need to find a metaphysical principle for differentiating the realm of possibles from entirely fictitious objects like goat-stag or chimera. After all, his ontology had been designed to fence off the pure or absolute nothing that was not even imaginable, the null set outside of "res a reor reris," but he believed in addition that exclusively imaginary objects included in the latter field should themselves be considered pure nothing or nonbeing to some degree, since they could never actually exist and were therefore not even potentially actual things. He sometimes called this *less*

a reor is not exact but close enough for the point made here. The same idea is reflected in similar language in Vital's *Quaestiones de cognitione*, q. 8 (ed. Delorme, "Huit questions," p. 323). See also below, n. 89.

[31] Henry, *Quod.* 8, q. 9 (2:314rK). Borrowing Henry's words, Vital, in *Quaestiones de cognitione*, q. 6 (ed. Delorme, "Huit questions," p. 277), said such "real" nonentities had only "entitas secundum imaginationem."

[32] Consult Marrone, *Truth and Scientific Knowledge*, pp. 105, 112–14. Key passages in Henry's work are: *Quodlibet* 1, q. 9 (Henrici Opera, 5:53–54); *Summa*, a. 21, q. 2 (1:124vK); a. 21, q. 4 (1:127r–v[O]); and a. 28, q. 4 (1:167vV).

[33] Henry, *Quodlibet* 1, q. 9 (Henrici Opera, 5:53, ll. 64–69), which traces the relevant passage from Avicenna to *Metaphysics* (*Liber de philosophia prima*) VI, almost surely an error for *Liber de philosophia prima* V, 1 (ed. Van Riet, p. 295). Vital, in *Quaestiones de cognitione*, q. 6 (ed. Delorme, "Huit questions," p. 273), reproduces Henry's claim down to the inaccurate citation to Avicenna. Pasquale Porro, *Enrico di Gand. La via delle proposizioni universali* (Bari, 1990), pp. 23–24, n. 15, notes that Jan Pinborg suggested Roger Bacon as inventor of the term, "esse essentiae."

empty empty set "pure nothing so far as nature or essence was concerned" (*purum nihil in natura et essentia*).[34] Essences, or real natures,
were consequently distinguishable from the imaginable nothings of
this *essentially* empty set by greater ontological density, a way of being
on a metaphysical plane somehow rarer than actuality. Since this
special being was *of* essence, indeed arose *out of* essence (*ex essentia*),
Henry saw it as itself essential, save only the fundamental Avicennian
principle that it and essence should not be regarded as entirely identical. He called it, besides "being of essence," "quidditative being"
(*esse quidditativum*) and "definitive being" (*esse definitivum*), and it constituted so much a part of thing as essence that it was no less impossible for it to be separated from (*absolvi*) essence as for essence to be
divided from itself.[35]

But of course essences considered in themselves were, as Henry
had said, indifferent to being and nonbeing, in the fuller sense of
"being" as actuality.[36] In their own way, therefore, absolute essences
were nonentities compared to actually existing things.[37] Explaining
the ontological density of the latter was the function of his second
sort of "being," "being of existence," which came closer to what
most scholastics meant when using the term and arose not so much
ex essentia as from the outside, almost accidentally to thing itself.[38]
He even dared call it an accidental being (*esse accidentale*).[39] All of
which, down to the distinction between types of nonbeing, was taken
up by Vital nearly untouched from Henry's work.[40]

---

[34] For "purum nihil" in this sense, see *Summa*, a. 24, q. 3 (1:138vO); and a. 68,
q. 5 (2:230vT); for "purum non ens," *Summa*, a. 21, q. 2 (1:124vK); *Quod.* 3, q. 9
(1:62rQ); and *Quod.* 5, q. 2 (1:154rD); for "non ens simpliciter," *Summa*, a. 30, q. 2,
ad 1. (1:179rF); for "purum nihil in natura et essentia," *Summa*, a. 21, q. 4 (1:127rO);
and for "omnino nihil per essentiam," *Summa*, a. 26, q. 1 (1:157vC). On the even
emptier kind of absolute nothing, see above, n. 18.

[35] For "esse quidditativum," see *Quod.* 5, q. 2 (1:154rD); and less properly, *Summa*
(*Qq. ord.*), a. 34, q. 2 (Henrici Opera, 27:174, l. 43); for "esse definitivum," *Quodlibet*
1, q. 9 (Henrici Opera, 5:53, ll. 72–73); and *Quod.* 3, q. 9 (1:61rO); for both, *Quod.*
7, q. 13 (Henrici Opera, 11:93–94), the latter passage revealing most plainly how
such being arose out of essence-ness itself. On its inseparability from essence, see
Summa, a. 26, q. 1 (1:157vD). As will be clear below, n. 44, Henry thought essence
could nonetheless be considered, at least by *ratio*, separately from its essential being.

[36] See above, nn. 13 and 14, and even more clearly, *Summa*, a. 28, q. 4 (1:167vV).

[37] For "non ens" this way, as opposed to the two sorts of "purum non ens," see
Quod. 3, q. 9 (1:61vP and 62rR), the latter referring also to "non esse in effectu."

[38] See *Quodlibet* 1, q. 9 (Henrici Opera, 5:54, ll. 78–86; and [ad 3.] 57, ll. 55–56);
and *Quodlibet* 2, q. 1 (Henrici Opera, 6:4, ll. 34–39).

[39] Henry, *Summa*, a. 26, q. 1 (1:157vD).

[40] See Vital, *Quaestiones de cognitione*, q. 6 (ed. Delorme, "Huit questions," pp.
273–74), which took special care to explain how existence was not truly an acci-

Strictly speaking, both types of being represented an addition to thing or essence in itself but were in the last analysis not really different from it.[41] There was thus composition in reality among the bearer of being and the two kinds of being that were borne, though not composition of different things, and Henry struggled to find an adequate description throughout his career. Clearly the combination of essence and being of existence found in actual existents was more salient, joining elements more divergent than being of essence and essence, or whatever it was within essence to which being of essence was added.[42] Henry attempted to express this variance in terms of kinds of difference – not just real (*re*) but also conceptual (*ratione*) and even a middle way, intentional (*intentione*), that he was first to champion and which provided an intellectual source for Duns's later formal distinction.[43] Yet he could never irrevocably decide how the analysis applied. Always insisting that essence and being of existence differed intentionally, consistent with the salience of their composition, he

---

dent (*res accidentis*). Vital's desire to play down Henry's description of "esse existentiae" as coming "extrinseca participatione" (see *Quodlibet* 1, q. 9 [Henrici Opera, 5:54, l. 79]) or "ab extrinseco" (*Quodlibet* 1, q. 9, ad 3. [Henrici Opera, 5:57, l. 54]), which led him to say (ed. Delorme, p. 273) that essence actually had existence "intrinsece," probably violated Henry's own intentions. Oddly enough, the text called the *Memoralia quaestionum fratris Vitalis de Furno*, n. 8 (given in Vital's *Quodlibeta tria*, ed. Delorme, p. 247), defends the real (*realiter*) difference of being (*esse*) and essence. Either Vital radically changed his mind or the attribution to Vital of the views presented in this text must be reconsidered.

[41] On Henry's opposition to real distinction between being and essence, see above, n. 29.

[42] On Henry's almost absurdly complicated attempts to explain composition at the level of absolute or pure essence, see my *Truth and Scientific Knowledge*, pp. 113–14, n. 60, adding to the references to Henry given there *Summa*, a. 28, q. 4 (1:168rV); *Quod.* 5, q. 2 (1:154r–v[D]); and *Quodlibet* 10, q. 8 (Henrici Opera, 14:202, ll. 95–98).

[43] The literature on this is vast. For a beginning, see Edgar Hocedez, "Gilles de Rome et Henri de Gand," pp. 358–84; Ludwig Hödl, "Neue Begriffe und neue Wege der Seinserkenntnis im Schul- und Einflussbereich des Heinrich von Gent," in *Die Metaphysik im Mittelalter*, ed. Paul Wilpert, Miscellanea Mediaevalia, 2 (Berlin, 1963), p. 614; John F. Wippel, *The Metaphysical Thought of Godfrey of Fontaines* (Washington, D.C., 1981), pp. 80–85; and Raymond Macken, "Les diverses applications de la distinction intentionelle chez Henri de Gand," in *Sprache und Erkenntnis im Mittelalter*, Akten des VI. internationalen Kongresses für mittelalterliche Philosophie, 29 August–3 September 1977, Miscellanea Mediaevalia, 13 (Berlin, 1981), II:769–76. Henry was not allowed to advance his theory of intentional distinction without controversy – see his *Summa*, a. 27, q. 1, ad 5. (1:161vM and 162r–v[O–P]); and an extraordinary pair of passages showing him engaged in debate with Giles of Rome, possibly following confrontation with him during the public disputations, over the rationality of positing a middle way for objects to differ: *Quodlibet* 10, q. 7 (Henrici Opera, 14:163–166); and *Quod.* 11, q. 3 (2:444v[Q–T]). Vital explained intentional difference in *Quaestiones de cognitione*, q. 6 (ed. Delorme, "Huit questions," pp. 281–82).

wavered on the matter of essence (or something within essence) and being of essence, holding early on that they differed only conceptually (*ratione*), later suggesting it was by intention, in the end hesitating to endorse an opinion, although probably leaning again towards conceptual difference.[44] Vital picked up on the first and most likely final posture, affirming an intentional distinction between essence and being of existence, merely a conceptual one between essence and being of essence.[45]

Unambiguous, however, was the fact that no matter how the composition was described, the two kinds of being attached to "thing" or its essential core in differing ways. This had to be so because being of essence was truly of or out of essence whereas being of existence fell to essence almost accidentally.[46] At times Henry even spoke of being of existence as coming to its subject *de novo*, as if in time and following upon a previous state of positive nonexistence. The ease with which he slipped into such language is not hard to comprehend in light of the fact that reception of being of existence

---

[44] See Marrone, *Truth and Scientific Knowledge*, pp. 114–19, especially nn. 65 and 66. For other treatments of the same issue, see Jean Paulus, *Henri de Gand*, p. 314; and "Les disputes d'Henri de Gand et de Gilles de Rome," p. 327; Paul Bayerschmidt, *Die Seins- und Formmetaphysik des Heinrich von Gent in ihrer Anwendung auf die Christologie*, Beiträge, 36, 3–4 (Münster, 1941), passim; John F. Wippel, "Godfrey of Fontaines and Henry of Ghent's Theory of Intentional Distinction between Essence and Existence," in *Sapientiae procerum amore. Mélanges médiévistes offertes à Dom Jean-Pierre Müller O.S.B.*, ed. Theodor W. Köhler, 289–321 (Rome, 1974), passim; and "The Relationship between Essence and Existence in Late-Thirteenth-Century Thought: Giles of Rome, Henry of Ghent, Godfrey of Fontaines, and James of Viterbo," in *Philosophies of Existence. Ancient and Medieval*, ed. Parviz Morewedge, 131–64 (New York, 1982), p. 160, n. 69; and Pasquale Porro, *Enrico di Gand*, pp. 63–64, n. 54.

[45] See Vital, *Quaestiones de cognitione*, q. 6 (ed. Delorme, "Huit questions," pp. 282 and 274). This question relies heavily on Henry's *Quodlibet* 10, q. 7, from which Vital quotes extensively, but a critical passage (in the Delorme edition, p. 281, 1st paragraph) drawn nearly verbatim from *Quodlibet* 10, q. 7 (Henrici Opera, 14:159–60, ll. 39–47) interpolates an explicit affirmation, not found in the finished text of Henry, of merely conceptual distinction between essence and being of essence. Vital went so far as to say that in actuality – as manifested in a thing already created in effect – essence did not differ from its being of existence even by intention (p. 284). Henry would never have conceded this point, and its appearance in Vital shows how in the debates over essence and existence in late-thirteenth-century Paris Henry's position was diluted among his followers, probably out of desire to avoid being seen as in any way supportive of Giles of Rome's real distinction.

[46] Henry literally described being of existence as "falling to" essence (*accidit ei*) – see *Quod.* 3, q. 9 (1:62rQ); and *Quodlibet* 10, q. 7 (Henrici Opera, 14:190, l. 61); language taken up by Vital in *Quaestiones de cognitione*, q. 6 (ed. Delorme, "Huit questions," p. 274); and *Quodlibet* 3, q. 5 (ed. Delorme, p. 145). The idea was connected to the notion of being of existence as "accidental" – see above, nn. 38 and 39.

corresponded typically to creation, an event temporally determinable for every creature.[47]

Indeed both kinds of being were God's gift, accepted by "thing," or again its essential core, "ab alio" from him who was origin of both essence and existence, even though the terms of acceptance were significantly dissimilar.[48] All essence possessed being of essence formally (*formaliter*) – that is, it received it, loosely speaking, from an ideal exemplar acting as formal cause. Put another way, essence was essence just because an exemplary form for it could be found in God. In fact, being of essence arose immediately from divine mind, constituting a quality attributable to essence less by virtue of an authentic act than by the omniscient nod of God's head (*Dei intentione*).[49] On the other hand, particular essences instantiated in actuality possessed being of existence effectively (*effective*) – that is, they received it, properly speaking, from God as creative force in the role of efficient cause. One could say that actualized essence was existent because produced by a legitimate act, and since the act was voluntary, being of existence emanated not so directly from God's ideal reasons as from divine will.[50] As before, all this was simply accepted and epitomized by Vital.[51]

---

[47] See Marrone, *Truth and Scientific Knowledge*, on Henry's difficulties clarifying the idea of creation. John Wippel has much more on the subject in *The Metaphysical Thought of Godfrey of Fontaines*. On the reception of being of existence *de novo*, see Henry, *Summa*, a. 21, q. 4 (1:127rN and 127vO), and on the connection between this fact and creation, *Quodlibet* 1, q. 9, ad 3. (Henrici Opera, 5:57, ll. 49–59).

[48] Henry, *Summa*, a. 21, q. 3 (1:126vG): "Omnis autem res quae creatura est formaliter habet esse essentiae suae ab alio ut a causa exemplari, a qua etiam effective habet suum esse existentiae . . . et hoc vel immediate ex prima creatione . . . vel mediantibus aliis causis ex rerum creatarum gubernatione." Henry used the term "formal cause" in this context in *Quodlibet* 9, q. 1, ad 2. (Henrici Opera, 13:22, ll. 71–74); "efficient cause" in *Quod*. 11, q. 3 (2:444rO); and both in *Quodlibet* 10, q. 7 (Henrici Opera, 14:151, ll. 51–56); and q. 8 (Henrici Opera, 14:201 and 202, ll. 92 and 5). Vital drew on these ideas in his *Quaestiones de cognitione*, q. 6 (ed. Delorme, "Huit questions," p. 273). In *Quod*. 8, q. 9, ad 1. (2:320rK) – quoted below, n. 53– and *Quodlibet* 10, q. 8 (Henrici Opera, 14:202, ll. 3–7), Henry referred to the granting of "esse existentiae" as "productio." While Vital accepted Henry's general views on being as a gift of God, he was always more cautious about employing the phrase *ab alio* (see above, n. 40).

[49] See Henry, *Quod*. 3, q. 9 (1:61rO). This is reflected in Henry's statement in *Quodlibet* 9, q. 1, ad 2. (Henrici Opera, 13:23, ll. 99–01), that essences were caused by God's knowledge (*scientia*).

[50] Henry, *Quodlibet* 1, q. 9 (Henrici Opera, 5:54, ll. 76–78): "Secundum esse non habet creatura ex sua essentia sed a Deo, in quantum est effectus voluntatis divinae iuxta exemplar eius in mente divina."

[51] See the passage from Vital cited above, n. 48, and also *Quaestiones de cognitione*, q. 6 (ed. Delorme, "Huit questions," p. 277).

In the end, Henry viewed both kinds of being as the participation of creaturely things in God – more precisely, in God's being –
the exact mode of which was determined by the type of causal role
God played in either case.[52] He even spoke in patently Neoplatonic
fashion of two different flowings from divinity.[53] Essence participated
in God's being formally (*formaliter*) insofar as it enjoyed being of
essence; it participated efficiently (*effective*) in the same divine being
through being of existence.[54] By extension, essence thus participated
in being of essence practically through itself, since essence itself composed each thing's formality, while participation in being of existence arose to a greater degree *ab alio*.[55] Differently put, an object's
essential core possessed being of essence by participation (*participa-
tive*) yet still essentially (*essentialiter*), which is to say by virtue of its
very essentiality (*ex sua essentia*), but being of existence came by a less
intrinsic participation (*quadam extrinseca participatione*) and so was more
aptly described as arriving from God (*ex Deo*).[56]

Most important, each participation established a relationship between
creature and God, the relation implicating God not under the mere
guise of a general attribute but more amply as divine essence manifested in an ideal reason, idea or exemplar.[57] At the foundation of

[52] Henry, *Summa*, a. 28, q. 4 (1:167vV); and *Quodlibet* 10, q. 8 (Henrici Opera,
14:201–2, ll. 87–92 and 3–5): "Esse vero est in ipsa essentia participatio quaedam
divini esse, qua ipsa essentia in se ipsa est quaedam similitudo divini esse atque
divinae essentiae.... Est autem ista participatio divini esse in essentia, esse essentiae, in quantum essentia illa exemplatum est divini esse secundum rationem causae
formalis.... Est vero dicta participatio divini esse in essentia, esse existentiae, in
quantum est similitudo producta a divino esse secundum rationem causae efficientis...."
See also *Quodlibet* 2, q. 1 (Henrici Opera, 6:4, ll. 34–41); *Quod.* 5, q. 2 (1:154rD);
and *Quodlibet* 10, q. 7 (Henrici Opera, 14:163, ll. 20–24).
[53] Henry, *Quod.* 8, q. 9, ad 1. (2:320rK): "Et secundum hoc essentiae sive formae rerum quasi dupliciter fluunt a primo: uno modo per quandam imitationem
formalem, et hoc quo ad esse essentiae . . .; alio modo per quandam productionem,
et hoc quo ad esse existentiae...."
[54] Henry *Summa*, a. 26, q. 2, ad 2. (1:159vV). In *Quodlibet* 1, q. 9 (Henrici Opera,
5:55, ll. 99–02), Henry referred to the two kinds of being as "esse participatum
formaliter" and "esse participatum effective."
[55] See the the central paragraph, Marrone, *Truth and Scientific Knowledge*, p. 121.
[56] Henry, *Quodlibet* 1, q. 9 (Henrici Opera, 5:53–54, ll. 69–80). The point relates
to the contrast between the intrinsic and extrinsic character of the two kinds of
being according to Henry as cited above, n. 40.
[57] Henry, *Quod.* 5, q. 1 (1:151vM): "Omnia enim quae sunt in creatura habent
respectum ad sapientiam divinam non ratione qua est attributum, sed ratione qua
est in ea idealis ratio cuiuscumque, quam respicit secundum esse essentiae suae ut
rationem formalem, secundum esse existentiae ut rationem effectivam quodammodo."
Henry spoke about ideas in God in *Summa*, a. 1, q. 1, ad 4. (1:3rI); a. 68, q. 5

being of essence thus lay a relation of thing to God as to its formal reason (*ratio formalis*); at that of being of existence, a relation to God as to efficient cause (*ratio effectiva*).[58] Vital, too, pointed to distinct relations by which an object was constituted either as essence or as actual existent.[59] For his part, Henry occasionally spoke in terms of comparison (*comparatio*) of each thing to divine essence.[60]

This notion that being entailed a relation to God explained how either of a thing's two beings were not really (*re*) different from essence. Since being of essence and being of existence emerged, one might say, first as God conceived of an essence and then as he produced it in the real world, they were in fact no more than the metaphysical expression of two causal processes originating in God and terminating in an identical object, the essence itself. Nothing in reality would seem to correspond to them more perfectly than the very relations the processes set up.[61] Indeed, Henry went nearly so far as to say that each being was the relation itself, or more precisely the relative orientation (*respectus*), according to which it was constituted – but not quite.[62] And to defend himself against the complaint of Giles

---

(2:231rV); *Quodlibet* 7, qq. 1 & 2 (Henrici Opera, 11:5); and *Quodlibet* 9, q. 2 (Henrici Opera, 13:36–37); and he referred to these ideas as divine exemplars in *Quodlibet* 7, qq. 1 & 2 (Henrici Opera, 11:19); and *Summa*, a. 68, q. 5 (2:230vT). Depending on which term was used for the divine correlative, essences could be called "exemplata" (as related to an exemplar) or "ideata" (as related to an idea) – for instances of the former, see *Summa*, a. 21, q. 4 (1:127vQ and 128rS); a. 28, q. 4 (1:167vV); *Quodlibet* 9, q. 1, ad 2. (Henrici Opera, 13:22, ll. 71–73); and q. 2 (Henrici Opera, 13:37, ll. 2–4); and *Quodlibet* 10, q. 8 (Henrici Opera, 14:201, ll. 90–92); for an instance of the latter, *Summa*, a. 68, q. 5 (2:230vT).

[58] See the passage quoted just above, n. 57, and also Henry, *Summa*, a. 21, q. 4 (1:128rS), the latter speaking both of a relation (*relatio*) and the relative orientation (*respectus*) established by it in the related thing. On the relation pertaining to being of essence alone, see also Henry, *Summa*, a. 21, q. 4 (1:127vO & Q); *Quod.* 5, q. 2 (1:154rD); and *Quodlibet* 9, q. 1, ad 1. (Henrici Opera, 13:8, ll. 10–14). Naturally, these relations could also be thought of as holding directly between each thing and the two different kinds of divine cause from which it drew its two sorts of being, and Henry sometimes referred to them that way – see *Quodlibet* 9, q. 1 (Henrici Opera, 13:22, ll. 71–74); *Quodlibet* 10, q. 8 (Henrici Opera, 14:201–202, ll. 87–07); and *Quod.* 11, q. 3 (2:444r–v[O–P]).

[59] Vital, *Quaestiones de cognitione*, q. 6 (ed. Delorme, "Huit questions," pp. 277, 278 and 290).

[60] Henry, *Quodlibet* 10, q. 7 (Henrici Opera, 14:151, ll. 48–51).

[61] See Henry's suggestive comments, *Quodlibet* 10, q. 7 (Henrici Opera, 14:151–52, ll. 56–59; 161–62, ll. 87–95; and 163, ll. 21–24)

[62] See the remarkable passage in Henry's *Quodlibet* 10, q. 7 (Henrici Opera, 14:160, ll. 48–58), which Vital repeated nearly word for word in his own *Quaestiones de cognitione*, q. 6 (ed. Delorme, "Huit questions," p. 281).

of Rome that being, or at least existence, had to be something absolute and not relative, he simply countered that for created things this was not the case.[63] A creature's being or existence was sustained only by dependence on God and was thereby truly "ad aliud," not absolute.

The repercussions of so baroque a theory of being and essence on Henry's understanding of the foundations for reality become apparent when one tries to pin down the philosophical status of his two sorts of being. For all the peculiarity of being of essence, Henry had no intention of establishing a second reality beside the here-and-now of God and creation. Instead his theory scrupulously distinguished between the question of being (*esse*) and that of actuality, so that although he spoke of ways something could be said to be (*esse*), either as essence considered absolutely or as existent, only the latter way expressly pointed to actual things. He was, he insisted, not positing a separate world of essences like the realm of ideas Aristotle accused Plato of arguing for.[64] Avicenna himself had been unambiguous in this regard, denying actuality to essence considered in and of itself, so that no one should dare attribute existential significance to the being of essence setting true essences apart from imaginary things.[65]

The corollary to this position was that so far as actuality was concerned, being of essence was absorbed into being of existence. Despite the fact that the former served as philosophical marker for an aspect of reality different from existence and capable of being considered apart from it, *in actuality* whatever had being of essence – that is,

---

[63] Henry, *Quodlibet* 10, q. 7 (Henrici Opera, 14:154). As the editor, Raymond Macken, has noted in the apparatus criticus to this text, Henry was responding to Giles of Rome's *De esse et essentia*, q. 9 (in *De esse et essentia, De mensura angelorum, et De cognitione angelorum* [Venice, 1503/repr. Frankfurt am Main, 1968], f. 19a).

[64] See Henry, *Quod.* 3, q. 9 (1:60vO): "Non autem dico quod quantum [certitudo naturae cuiuscumque vel essentia] est de se habet esse absolutum absque eo quod habet esse in intellectu vel singularibus, tamquam sit aliquid separatum. . . ." Also *Quodlibet* 7, qq. 1 & 2 (Henrici Opera, 11:18–19): "Quam tamen [essentiam absolute consideratam] esse nullus ponit secundum se extra singularia et extra intellectum, quali tamen modo Aristoteles ponit Platonem posuisse essentias rerum et quidditates secundum se existere separatas a rebus et extra intellectum et esse ideas rerum." Slightly further on, Henry contended that Plato was falsely accused by Aristotle on this score, a claim repeated in *Quodlibet* 9, q. 15 (Henrici Opera, 13:265, ll. 11–21). He thought Plato instead foreshadowed Augustine, recognizing that the ideas existed in God's mind.

[65] See Henry, *Quod.* 3, q. 9 (1:60vO and 61vO), which refers to Avicenna, *Liber de philosophia prima* V, 1 (ed. Van Riet, p. 234).

whatever actually was essence – also always possessed being of existence in some fashion.[66] Vital simply agreed.[67] Since the only two
expressions of being of existence were as object in mind or as extramental singular in the real, mostly created world, Henry sometimes
referred to two varieties of existence: conceptual being (*esse rationis*)
and natural being (*esse naturae*).[68] His language has encouraged the
notion that he saw a three-fold division of "being" into being of
essence, being in mind and natural being, as if these constituted
three alternative ways for something actually to be.[69] Yet he meant
only that actuality could take shape within mind or outside it, thus
giving rise to the two varieties of being of existence. Being of essence
taken by itself did not offer an alternate actuality but rather said
nothing about actuality at all.

All this meant that when one knew an essence, the mental object
had at least the actuality of something in mind – that is, it at least
possessed conceptual being (*esse rationis*) or, in a phrase already traditional in the schools, "diminuta rei entitas."[70] The connection between essence and conceptual being was in fact so strong for Henry

[66] See, for instance, the two passages quoted above, n. 64, as well as *Quod.* 3,
q. 9, ad 1. (1:62rS): "Nullo enim modo est ponere aliquam essentiam quin habeat
esse essentiae eo modo quo est eam ponere: ut si ponatur in intellectu habet esse
essentiae in intellectu; si in singularibus extra, habet et esse essentiae suae in singularibus extra. Quod si neutro modo ponatur essentia esse – scilicet nec in singularibus nec in intellectu – tunc nullo modo habet essentia esse essentiae alicuius,
neque similiter esse essentiae suae existit aliquo modo. . . ." See also above, n. 29,
on Henry's denial of real distinction between essence and existence.

[67] See Vital, *Quaestiones de cognitione,* q. 6 (ed. Delorme, "Huit questions," pp. 274
and 277).

[68] See *Quod.* 3, q. 9 (1:61rO); and *Quodlibet* 7, q. 13 (Henrici Opera, 11:93–94,
ll. 25–40), where he called them "esse in re extra" and "esse in intellectu." See
also *Summa,* a. 23, q. 1, ad 8.

[69] Among those who have proposed this interpretation are Godfrey of Fontaines
in Henry's day and John Wippel and Jean Paulus today – see Marrone, *Truth and
Scientific Knowledge,* pp. 105–6, n. 35. In addition to the first two passages cited in
the previous note, Henry's mention of a four-fold consideration of essence in *Quodlibet*
7, qq. 1 & 2 (Henrici Opera, 11:18, ll. 43–53), contributes to this view. My reasons for rejecting it are spelled out in *Truth and Scientific Knowledge,* pp. 105–7, a
position also taken by Antoni Siemianowski, "Teoria istnienia realnego i tzw. sposoby
istnienia u Henryka z Gandawy" ("La théorie de l'existence réelle et les 'modes
d'existence' chez Henri de Gand"), *Roczniki Filozoficzne* 13, no. 1 (1965): 33–41.

[70] On "diminuta rei entitas," see Armand Maurer, "*Ens Diminutum*: A Note on
its Origin and Meaning," MS 12 (1950): 216–22; and Marrone, *Truth and Scientific
Knowledge,* pp. 54–55, n. 47. For Henry's use of the phrase in the sense indicated
here, see, for example, *Summa,* a. 28, q. 4 (1:167vT); 34, q. 2 (Henrici Opera,
27:172, ll. 3–4); 34, q. 5, ad 1. (Henrici Opera, 27:235, l. 72); *Quod.* 4, q. 8 (1:96vI);
and *Quodlibet* 9, q. 2 (Henrici Opera, 13:31, ll. 53–56).

that he sometimes spoke as if mind were uniquely the location of absolute essence, though of course essence as essence was just as much resident in actual extra-mental things; indeed at times he nearly equated the "diminuta rei entitas" of mental objects with being of essence (*esse essentiae*) itself.[71] It was more valid to say, in Vital's words, that before having actual existence externally, all essence must exist in mind.[72] This was especially pertinent with regard to the mind of God. In knowing essence God necessarily provided it with the minimal actuality required of entity in general by constituting it in divine conceptual being, so that over eternity – outside creation and above time – that was precisely what the essences of creatures came down to: objects existing in divine mind and thus ultimately coincident with divine essence. In God's eternal present the exemplars or divine ideas and the essences they exemplified (*exemplata*) collapsed into the same thing.[73]

Yet if there was no separate realm of essentiality, so that outside instantiation in external singulars essence fell back on the actuality

---

[71] See Henry, *Quodlibet* 10, q. 8 (Henrici Opera, 14:202, ll. 9–12). In *Quod.* 3, q. 9 (1:62rR), he spoke of "esse rationis" as if it were equivalent to "esse essentiae," while in *Quod.* 8, q. 9, ad 1. (2:319v–20r[K]), he seemed to identify "esse essentiae" with "esse cognitivum." In *Quodlibet* 1, q. 9 (Henrici Opera, 5:53–54, ll. 69–74); *Quod.* 3, q. 9 (1:61rO); *Quod.* 5, q. 14 (1:177vR); and *Quodlibet* 10, q. 7 (Henrici Opera, 14:166, ll. 3–6), Henry revealed he appreciated the real basis for this potentially misleading connection: all essence must *at least* have existence in intellect.

[72] See Vital, *Quaestiones de cognitione*, q. 6 (ed. Delorme, "Huit questions," pp. 273): "Tale autem esse quod est esse essentiae, quod habet res antequam actualiter existat extra, solum habet in divino exemplari vel in mentis conceptu. . . ." See also the same question, p. 277. Henry realized this, as is evident from the last four citations given above, n. 71.

[73] My argument for this position, not universally ascribed to, is given in *Truth and Scientific Knowledge*, pp. 122–28. To the supporting passages cited there in nn. 93 and 94 (pp. 127–28) should be added *Quod.* 3, q. 9, ad 1. (1:62rS – following immediately after the text quoted above, n. 66); *Quod.* 8, q. 9, ad 1. (2:320rK); and *Quodlibet* 9, q. 2 (Henrici Opera, 13:27, ll. 45–48; 30–31, ll. 30–52; and 34, ll. 15–22). For reference to interpretations different from the one given here, see *Truth and Scientific Knowledge*, p. 123, n. 78. Those inclining towards a view like mine include Paulus, *Henri de Gand*, pp. 91–92, 95, 99, 371–72 (passages can also be found that seem to lean the other way); Ludwig Hödl, "Neue Begriffe und neue Wege der Seinserkenntnis," p. 609; Walter Hoeres, "Wesen und Dasein bei Heinrich von Gent und Duns Scotus," FS 47 (1965): 154; Anton C. Pegis, "A New Way to God: Henry of Ghent (II)," MS 31 (1969): 96, 98, and 116; and "Henry of Ghent and the New Way to God (III)," MS 33 (1971): 160; and Stephen D. Dumont, "The quaestio si est," p. 338, nn. 20 and 21. Heinrich Rüssmann, *Zur Ideenlehre der Hochscholastik unter besonderer Berücksichtigung des Heinrich von Gent, Gottfried von Fontaines und Jakob von Viterbo* (Würzburg, [1937]), pp. 49–50 and 71, described Henry's position as even verging on pantheism.

of the conceptual world constituted by active minds, Henry so focused
on absolute essence as the core of his metaphysics that he introduced a remarkable fluidity at just this point. Despite diverse acts
of existence in particular things or in the mind of God and human
beings, in some way any determinate essence was always really (re)
one and the same. The essence of an object as constituted in conceptual being in mind was really (re) identical to the essence as formally instantiated in an external thing.[74] Indeed essences as known
in human mind were really identical to the corresponding essences
as known in the mind of God. Henry was even prepared to say that
they were identical to the divine ideas themselves.[75] For all his efforts
at emphasizing the actuality of the particular world, there is a remarkable participationist, even Neoplatonic, cast to the vision of essence
upon which his structure of reality depended.[76]

These extraordinary undercurrents to Henry's metaphysics of essence
carried over into his theory of knowledge, where, ironically enough,
they were reinforced by Aristotelian elements otherwise unconnected
to his ontology. As already noted, essence, or quiddity, constituted
for Henry mind's proper object.[77] According to his taxonomy of

---

[74] Henry, *Quod.* 5, q. 15 (1:181vZ): "Unde . . . eadem re est forma quae est in
intellectu ut obiectum in cognoscente et quae est extra ut forma in formato et par-
ticipante." See also *Quod.* 4, q. 8 (1:96vI); and *Quodlibet* 9, q. 15 (Henrici Opera,
13:265, ll. 1–4). Vital tried to say the same in *Quaestiones de cognitione*, q. 6 (ed.
Delorme, "Huit questions," p. 294).

[75] Henry, *Quodlibet* 9, q. 15 (Henrici Opera, 13:262, ll. 29–31), quoted below,
Pt. 3, ch. 12, n. 90.

[76] A number of scholars (beginning with François Huet, *Recherches historiques et critiques sur la vie, les ouvrages et la doctrine de Henri de Gand* [Ghent, 1838], p. 96) have
noted what has even been characterized as an unusually pure Platonism in Henry's
thought. See Karl Werner, "Heinrich von Gent als Repräsentant des christlichen
Platonismus im dreizehnten Jahrhundert," *Denkschriften der kaiserlichen Akademie der
Wissenschaften*, Philosophisch-historische Classe, 28 (Vienna, 1878), p. 98; Braun, *Die
Erkenntnislehre*, pp. 108–9; Robert Bourgeois, "La théorie de la connaissance intel-
lectuelle chez Henri de Gand," *Revue de Philosophie*, n.s. 6 (1936): passim; Paulus,
Henri de Gand, pp. 386–89; Gómez Caffarena, *Ser participado*, p. 248; and Marrone,
Truth and Scientific Knowledge, p. 142. Maurice De Wulf, *Histoire de la philosophie sco-
lastique dans les Pays-Bas et la Principauté de Liège jusqu'à la Révolution Française*, Mémoires
Couronnés et Autres Mémoires publiés par l'Académie Royale des Sciences, des
Lettres et des Beaux-Arts de Belgique, 51 (Brussels, 1894–95), pp. 191–94 and
267–68; and Georg Hagemann, "De Henrici Gandavensis quem vocant ontolo-
gismo," *Index lectionum quae auspiciis augustissimi ac potentissimi Imperatoris Regis Guilelmi
II in Academia Theologica et Philosophica Monasteriensi . . . publice privatimque habebuntur*
(Münster, 1898), pp. 3–12 (Summer, 1898) and 3–13 (Winter, 1898/99), argued
against this view, saying Henry was no more Platonist than Aristotelian.

[77] See above, Pt. 3, ch. 10, n. 23.

"thing," this meant that the appropriate object of intellect was "thing" at the level of "res a ratitudine," which was essence considered absolutely in itself.[78] A similar convergence on absolute essence manifested itself in his theory of "being" as first concept of mind, for the "being" (*ens*) first known was metaphysically grounded at the level of "ens secundum essentiam" – indeed the objective content of the primitive concept of being was precisely essence or "res a ratitudine" generally conceived.[79] In knowing anything from its first concepts to the more complicated configurations built upon them, mind was therefore opened up to the very ontological horizon where for Henry the reality of external objects flowed into the conceptual environment of intelligible formalities only to touch eventually on the superessential shores of God's eternal wisdom. The cognitive world, anchored in essence, was from start to finish a world vibrant with God's presence.

Given this, it is obvious where Henry drew his confidence that a notion of being referring properly to God was present to mind at a cognitive stage just as primitive as that of the notion of being generally applicable to creatures. The natural origin of knowledge in the sensible world and the merely analogical connection between intellect's two fundamental concepts of being presented no barrier to its primary access to a concept with a uniquely divine referent, because from the broadest metaphysical perspective knowledge of sensible things yielded access to an intentional ground that ran unbroken right to God. The same idea could be corroborated by turning to Henry's account of the ontological import of essence's special being – that is, his suggestion that being of essence was an expression of, almost equivalent to, a relation between essence and God. Any intellect knowing essence or quiddity, and thereby perceiving an object on the level of being of essence, presumably had this relation cognitively available. From this it was only reasonable to infer

---

[78] See above, n. 22, and *Quod.* 3, q. 9 (1:61vO and 62rQ). Consult also *Quodlibet* 7, qq. 1 & 2 (Henrici Opera, 11:27–28); and *Quod.* 8, q. 12 (2:324rB).

[79] Henry, *Summa* (*Qg. ord.*), a. 34, q. 2 (Henrici Opera, 27:174–75, ll. 42–52): "... super illam rationem rei [dictae a reor reris] prima ratio quae fundatur, est ratio entis sive esse quiditativi ... a quo accipitur ratio rei dictae a ratitudine, quae eadem est cum ratione entis quiditativi. ... Ita quod ratio entis sit ratio primi conceptus obiective in intellectu, quia 'quod quid est est proprium obiectum intellectus'. ..." See also *Summa*, a. 21, q. 3 (1:126rE); and a. 24, q. 3 (1:138vP), showing how the primitive concept of being was tied to the being of essence attaching to ens and manifested its objectivity as essence. "Being" as first known pointed, therefore, not to existential reality but rather to the essential quality of things as possibles.

that it could see both extremes of the relation – not just absolute essence but also God himself.

If Henry never set out this argument himself, it nevertheless lay close to the surface of his thought. Time and again he noted how the proper object of intellect, "res a ratitudine" or essence, was formally such because of its relation to a divine exemplar.[80] And it was, after all, the formal aspect of a thing that determined the content the attendant mind picked up. Moreover, Henry's followers apparently recognized the argument as implicit in his works, some going so far as to draw it out explicitly for themselves.

One such was Richard of Conington. In a passage preserved because quoted by the English scholastic, William of Alnwick, Conington argued that "ens ratum," or what he also called "ens dictum a ratitudine" – Henry's "res a ratitudine" – was known only insofar as distinguished from "ens dictum a reor reris."[81] In other words "ens ratum," which amounted to essence, had to be perceived precisely

---

[80] For example, Henry *Quod.* 5, q. 2 (1:154rD); and q. 14 (1:177rR): "Ex hoc enim solo est aliquid scibile simpliciter quod est aliquid per essentiam habens rationem extra rem in Deo." Also *Quodlibet* 7, qq. 1 & 2 (Henrici Opera, 11:28, ll. 82–87): "Et hoc est per se quiditas et natura cuiuslibet creaturae.... Et est illud de quo iam diximus, quod habet per se ideam in Deo, unde et per se de ipso habet esse scientia." Porro, *Enrico di Gand*, pp. 135–36, esp. n. 14, reveals a reluctance to accept this explanation for Henry's confidence in his theory of a natural knowledge of God.

[81] The passage is transcribed by the editors in Duns Scotus, *Ordinatio* I, d. 8, p. 1, q. 3 (Opera Omnia [Vatican Edition] [Vatican City, 1956] 4:174–75, apparatus criticus [F]). In it, Conington was dealing with the same problem as that touched on in his *Quodlibet* 1, q. 2, arg. 7 (see above, n. 6), but his response in the latter work (ad 7.) (ed. Brown, p. 307) only hints at the argument laid out in Alnwick's quotation. Remember that Henry had also called "res a ratitudine" by a similar term: "ratum quid" – see above, n. 22.

Conington's reasoning rests on holding that knowledge of a relation in one extreme – perhaps he meant: knowledge of a relative orientation in one extreme – would cause knowledge of the other extreme, a principle Henry might have been reluctant to concede. For in at least one other context Henry maintained the opposite: that a relation could not be conceived in one extreme unless the other extreme was previously known independently – see Henry, *Quodlibet* 13, q. 1, ad 2. (Henrici Opera, 18:8, ll. 25–26). Conington might have found support for his position in John Pecham, who in *Quaestiones de anima*, q. 5, 16. (ad 5.) (ed. Spettmann, in *Quaestiones tractantes de anima*, p. 70), held that in simple cognition, but not complex, something could be known as compared to something else before it was known as absolute – see also Pecham, *Quaestiones de anima*, q. 8, ad 7. (ed. Spettmann, p. 88.) Since it is possible to imagine an argument similar to Conington's being made without recourse to the principle in question, none of this stands in the way of seeing Henry as fundamentally sympathetic to the stance Conington's reasoning was intended to defend.

for what it was, and this meant grasping its constituent conditions. Because what constituted "ens ratum" or essence was a relation to the first being, God himself, to which it was directed as to exemplary formal cause, in knowing essence mind conceived of its object not as formally absolute (*sub ratione absoluta*) but rather as relative (*sub ratione relativa*), relative, that is, to God. Since knowledge of a relation entailed knowledge of both correlative extremes, knowing the object as related to God required somehow having God as intellectual object, too. In short, despite the analogical character of "being," it was perfectly plausible that the concept of creaturely being seized by mind working naturally in the world should serve as vehicle for knowledge of a "proper concept of the first being," God. Cognitive access to divinity was an immanent, if hidden, feature of the process of knowing created essence.

A similar extrapolation from Henry's metaphysics is evident in Matthew of Aquasparta's handling, discussed above, of the kindred problems of knowing nonexistents and knowing immutable truth.[82] Like Henry, drawing on Avicenna, Matthew identified the simple object of mind as absolute quiddity, Avicenna's and Henry's absolute essence.[83] To answer the question of whether the actual, extra-mental existence of such an object was required for knowledge of it, he then made reference to a contrast between possibles and actuals plainly derivative of Henry's distinction between "res a ratitudine" and "res existens in actu."[84] Just as Henry, he claimed that only possible existence was necessary for knowledge, not actual.[85] For Matthew, however, this answer, at least on the surface implying no need in human cognition for an actual external object, was ultimately insufficient to meet the demands of immutable truth.[86] A deeper account of cognition incorporated, he thought, the notion of quiddity as dependent

---

[82] See the discussion above, Pt. 2, ch. 7, pp. 193–200.

[83] See Pt. 2, ch. 7, nn. 31–32.

[84] See Pt. 2, ch. 7, nn. 36–39.

[85] In fact Matthew would seem to have been drawing on a passage from Henry's *Summa* published shortly before his own work that gave exactly the same answer to the question of whether mind could know nonbeing and in similar language distinguished between two kinds of "non-entia," one knowable and the other not. Compare the response (especially f. 28rC) in Henry's *Summa*, a. 3, q. 1 (1:28r): "Utrum contingit hominem scire non entia," to the first passage cited above Pt. 2, ch. 7, n. 36 (from Matthew's *Quaestiones de cognitione*, q. 1). Like Matthew, Henry made reference to Avicenna's *Liber de philosophia prima* I, 5 as source for his ideas.

[86] See Pt. 2, ch. 7, nn. 40–44.

on a relation to divine exemplar, thus bringing in God himself as cognitive ground for whatever intellect knew.[87] It is evident how much this response depended on Henry's theory of essence, covering the same ground as Conington's subsequent defense of the primacy of a concept of being proper to God.

Vital apparently recognized Matthew's debt to Henry and adopted an identical line of reasoning in his own approach to the question about knowledge of nonexistents.[88] Avid supporter of Henry, he simply tailored Matthew's diction more closely to fit the contours of the master's thought. Reproducing Matthew's division of nonbeing into two kinds, he showed how Matthew's two could be defined in terms of the second and third of Henry's three types of "thing" – "ens secundum essentiam" and "ens secundum actum."[89] He then presented Matthew's initial answer – that possible being was sufficient to make something intelligible – carefully translating it into the language of being of essence and being of existence.[90] More cautious than Matthew, however, he satisfied himself with suggesting the final insistence on a divine ground for knowledge, merely reminding his reader that the cognitive object was such expressly because it had an exemplary cause in God.[91]

On the question of immutability, in fact, Henry himself seems at one point to have been ready to draw out the implications of his metaphysics and explicitly posit divinity as ground for human knowledge. He once noted that the truth of propositions concerning essential attributes was founded on essence as essence, thereby invoking

---

[87] See Pt. 2, ch. 7, nn. 52 and 53.

[88] Vital, *Quaestiones de cognitione*, q. 6 (ed. Delorme, "Huit questions," p. 272): "[U]trum intellectus coniunctus, ad hoc quod intelligat rem, indiget actuali existentia rei." Vital began his discussion of the question (p. 272) with what would seem to be an amalgam of the passage from Matthew's *De cognitione*, q. 1, and the heart of Henry's response in *Summa*, a. 3, q. 1, both cited above, n. 85.

[89] Vital, *Quaestiones de cognitione*, q. 6 (ed. Delorme, "Huit questions," p. 285). For Henry on these two kinds of "entia," see above, n. 30.

[90] Vital, *Quaestiones de cognitione*, q. 6 (ed. Delorme, "Huit questions," p. 293): "Si vero quaeras: Quid tunc est obiectum intellectus? cum non potest terminari ad nonens . . . respondeo . . . quod quamvis res tunc sint nihil privando actum existentiae, non tamen sunt nihil privando actum essentiae. . . ."

[91] Vital, *Quaestiones de cognitione*, q. 6 (ed. Delorme, "Huit questions," p. 291). Immediately following the passage quoted above, n. 90, Vital repeated the point about being of essence entailing existence of a divine exemplar, but drawing back from Matthew's concern about immutability he simply concluded (p. 294) that so far as knowledge of an object was concerned, being in mind constituted sufficient grounding.

an actuality not located in external things but rather in mind.[92] He
then added, in sharp contrast to his customary assurance that no
divine element was necessary to account for immutable truth, that
since essence as essence was eternal only in God's mind, the eternal truth-value of such propositions derived precisely from the divine
conceptual actuality of their exemplary component terms.[93] Unstated
but easy to surmise was the implication that human knowledge
acceded to immutability, and thus participated in eternity, just insofar as it obtained access to God by means of the special ontology
of essence. For all his concern to pull back from the dramatic theoretical condensation of divine illumination among the classic
Augustinians, Henry was to this degree party to the very homolo-
gizing of an Augustinian role for God in human knowledge seen in
Matthew of Aquasparta.[94]

[92] Henry, *Quod.* 3, q. 9 (1:62rQ): "Talis enim conceptus solius quiditatis et essentiae rei est ratione ea qua est quiditas et essentia, super quam secundum esse tale
quod habet in simplici mentis conceptu fundatur per se veritas enunciationum de
inhaerentia essentiali, ut quod homo est homo, vel animal, vel huiusmodi. Et per
accidens fundatur super hoc quod habet esse extra in particularibus."

[93] Just after the passage quoted above, n. 92, comes the following: "... res hoc
quod est in certitudinem [for: certitudine?] essentiae suae non habet ab alio
effective ... sed solum habet hoc quia est in alio formaliter, ut in intellectu divino ... in
quo est quid aeternum. Propter quod veritas enunciationum fundata super talem
certitudinem potest esse aeterna in intellectu aeterno. ..." Henry's usual approach
to cognitive immutability involved nothing more than the broadly Aristotelianizing
attitude seen since Grosseteste's *Commentary on the Posterior Analytics*, whereby it was
sufficient merely to locate the objects of science as mental entities, abstracted from
particular conditions of extramental existence and endowed with the universality of
conceptualization – see Henry, *Summa*, a. 2, q. 2, ad 1. (1:24rG); also *Quod.* 5, q. 14
(1:178vX); as well as similar ideas on the object of intellect in Vital, *Quaestiones de
cognitione*, q. 6 (ed. Delorme, "Huit questions," p. 292. For Grosseteste's views, see
above, Pt. 1, ch. 3, nn. 33–34.

[94] See above, Pt. 2, ch. 7, nn. 48–50.

CHAPTER TWELVE

ARISTOTLE AND AUGUSTINE REVISITED

Henry's philosophical accomplishments even as a new voice among Parisian theologians were stunning. He had separated the two fundamental elements of classic Augustinianism, a theory of normative illumination of mind by Eternal Truth and a notion of natural knowledge of God as first cognitive object, and then by means of an ingenious metaphysics rendered the latter, cut loose from classic moorings in an integrated doctrine of illumination, credible alongside a noetics where knowledge arose exclusively from sensation. But despite his apparent success, he was himself not satisfied with the ideological apparatus he had forged, and within a decade his approach to knowledge was shifting.

As already indicated, not every aspect of his early recasting of Augustinian epistemology and theory of mind was subjected to transformation. On natural knowledge of God his ideas remained basically the same to the end of his career. But when it came to knowledge of truth, he progressively distanced himself from the position established in his beginning years. The theory of normative illumination laid out in chapter 9 above is an artifact of his earliest work, summed up in the initial articles of the *Summa* and the first two Quodlibets. After 1277 he never again returned to the original schema with comparable clarity or conviction.

Some have argued that he simply abandoned the early view, leaving no room for it in his mature thought, but this surely goes too far. From time to time in his later work Henry referred back to his first account of truth-perception with approval, indicating an expectation that it be factored into his comments about knowledge and mind whether explicitly mentioned or not.[1] The break between his

---

[1] Paulus, *Henri de Gand*; and Stella, "La prima critical di Herveus Natalis," suggest that Henry turned away from his early views on illumination, while Macken, "La theorie;" Nys, *De werking*; and Prezioso, *La critica*, insist he never really abandoned the doctrine. On this question, and on instances where the later Henry mentioned the earlier theory, see Marrone, *Truth and Scientific Knowledge*, p. 8, nn. 14 and 15.

early and middle years was thus not a full repudiation, nor was it perfectly clean. Yet the fact remains that from 1279 or 1280, the notion of a divine light of truth took a back seat, its prominent place in the structure of his thought coming to be occupied instead by a view of truth and certitude in human knowledge, as well as a corresponding noetics, reflective of a more exclusively Aristotelianizing bent. And what was left of normative illumination in its new, recessive position was not exactly the same as before, entailing even less literally a divine intervention in the classic Augustinian sense than it had according to the already mitigated terms of his first work. Together, these developments mark an undeniable alteration in attitude towards the problems of truth and scientific cognition.

To a degree the evolution was inevitable. The tide of Aristotelianizing epistemology surging through the universities in the latter part of the thirteenth century ran deep and strong, and a scholar concerned for his professional status would have to find ways of trimming his sails to the demands of science conceived along Aristotelian lines. Henry was as sensitive as any of his colleagues to such pressure, perhaps even more determined than most to defend the apodictic character of his work.[2] Too zealous an attachment to the image of a truth-revealing Godly light must have weighed like so much heavy baggage in the intricate maneuverings of academic debate he engaged in year in, year out. But the classic Augustinians had been subject to pressure, too, and for all their concessions to Aristotle they did not reduce the theoretical importance of normative illumination, giving it instead a more salient, if more cautiously articulated, position in their thought. An additional factor must have intervened to make Henry, otherwise loyal member of the Augustinian camp, more susceptible to the impetus of the Aristotelianizing swell.

It has frequently been suggested above that a primary motive for the classic Augustinian condensation of a doctrine of divine illumination was the desire to highlight the cognitive intimacy of God to human intellect, particularly as manifested in the notion of a natural knowledge of divinity reaching far beyond the limits of a posteriori reasoning and loosely regarded as innate. Henry's metaphysics

---

[2] See, for example, Henry's extraordinary defense of efforts to explain theology as true science and his acerbic attack on those who considered it something less – *Quodlibet* 12, q. 2 (Henrici Opera, 16:20–21, ll. 43–51). This outburst was occasioned by criticism of his notion of a special intellectual light raising theological argument to the level of apodictic certainty, for which see above, Pt. 3, ch. 9, n. 19.

of essence had permitted him to give this intimacy a different theoretical basis, free of connection to illumination of truth. Once the idea of a primary knowledge of God in "being" was reinterpreted along these lines, the obligation to retain for the paradigmatic Augustinian light a central role in philosophy of knowledge practically disappeared. Henry must have recognized the opportunity for what it was – if only gradually and probably never in such explicit terms – and turned increasingly in an Aristotelianizing direction whenever he dealt with epistemic matters in his later work.

This is not to say that he consciously contrived to make his work more Aristotelian. He was all the same engaged in a less intentional process to comparable effect. At each turn in the ongoing philosophical debate of his later career when he came to questions of cognitive certitude, he looked to Aristotle for help in formulating a response, and with every step his voiced support for his early theories became more attenuated. The extraordinary ability of his system to validate Augustine's demand for intimacy between mind and God without recourse to the light of Truth relieved him even of the need to make clear his stand on the matter, so that, in contrast to the classic Augustinians, he could forego the ever more complicated affirmations of normative illumination in face of a growing reliance on an Aristotelianizing appraisal of truth and certitude. Gradually, almost imperceptibly, the theoretical balance of his epistemology shifted, and out of the change a new structure of thought emerged.

Such an account is hypothetical, and there can be no proof it is correct. But there is also no denying that the complexion of Henry's thinking modulated in just the way described. Beginning in 1279 or 1280 he began to attack formal questions of knowledge with something like the intensity of the earliest questions in the *Summa*, but now his answers emanated a new air, though his analysis still resonated with the structural harmonies of his early years. This new air – an Aristotelianizing motif – would carry through to the end of his career.[3]

---

[3] Maurice De Wulf, in *Histoire de la philosophie scolastique dans les Pays-Bas*, p. 268, characterized Henry as eclectic, while Paulus, *Henri de Gand*, pp. 5–6, said that in theory of knowledge – with the sometime exception of illumination – he was Aristotelian, although beneath everything lay an Augustinian view of cognition as judgment. Edward Dwyer, however, in *Die Wissenschaftslehre Heinrichs von Gent*, unequivocally claimed that Henry moved increasing towards Aristotle on all fronts over the course of his career. Nys, on the other hand, in *De werking*, pp. 117–18, 137 (see also *De*

In returning to the issues of science and certitude with which he had begun his *Summa*, Henry did so not as previously to establish a methodological basis for his work but rather to elucidate theological concerns like God's knowledge or the nature of the divine persons. Still, time and again he came up against the very foundational problem he had previously confronted: how to characterize the difference between true knowledge and knowledge of truth, which was of course also for him the boundary between non-scientific cognition and science. His early attempts at a solution had been complicated by his positing two levels of truth to know, first Aristotelian and "phantastic," second pure (*sincera*) and attainable only through divine illumination, and he had spent most of his efforts exploring the latter.[4] In contrast he now made no mention of a division and in discussing the way to accede to truth breathed not so much as a word about divine illumination. What had once been simply the lesser of two epistemic targets – Aristotelian and phantastic truth as opposed to lucid and pure – had become his sole interest.

It was not that Henry's fundamental vision of the truth-determining constituents of objective reality had changed. Article 34 of the *Summa*, composed in 1279 or 1280, went right back to his Augustinian, also Avicennian, roots, looking at truth as he had conceived of it in his earliest years. As he explained in question 2, truth could be defined as an accommodation (*adaequatio*) or rectitude tying together intellect and thing.[5] What was different this time was instead what he made of this vision for normal human cognition.

---

psychologia, p. 6), held that beginning as an Aristotelian in philosophy, Henry turned, under the influence of Averroes, more and more to Augustine, and Macken, in "La theorie," pp. 92–93, has traced a similar trajectory towards Avicenna and Augustine in the works leading up to Quodlibet 9. See also Marrone, *Truth and Scientific Knowledge*, pp. 143–44.

[4] On the distinction between true and truth, see above, Pt. 3, ch. 9, nn. 25 and 51; on the two truths and Henry's efforts to characterize them, nn. 52, 65, 69–70, 72–75 and 80–83.

[5] Henry, *Summa* (*Qg. ord.*), a. 34, q. 2 (Henrici Opera, 27:177, ll. 2–5): "... veritas, in communi significato . . . definitur sic, quod scilicet est adaequatio rei et intellectus et ita quasi quaedam mensura et rectitudo aequans ambo, quae sola mente percipitur. . . ." See also a. 34, q. 3 (Henrici Opera, 27:191, ll. 66–71). For the Avicennian "adaequatio" in Henry's early work, see above, Pt. 3, ch. 9, n. 44. The more Augustinian "rectitude perceived solely by mind" is described in explicitly these terms in Anselm's *De veritate* 11 (ed. Francis S. Schmitt, 1 191), which text is cited by Henry in *Summa* (*Qg. ord.*), a. 34, q. 2 (Henrici Opera, 27:177, ll. 5–6); and a. 34, q. 5 (Henrici Opera, 27:218–19, ll. 27–28; and 228, l. 61).

Question 1 of the same article had prepared the reader to believe that there were two ways to apply truth's definition, leading to two different species of truth: the truth of a thing (*veritas rei*) and the truth of a sign (*veritas signi*).[6] Applied to "thing," the definition of truth translated into doing what nature required, which came down to being what the thing, in essence, was.[7] This description not only provided Henry with the opportunity to reassert his long-held association between truth and quiddity; it also pointed the notion of accommodation back towards the relation between thing and divine mind, more specifically between created essence and uncreated exemplar, which latter was after all, for him as for all late-thirteenth-century thinkers, source of each object's essential core and thus in Augustinian terms the decisive condition of its truth.[8] But whereas in his early work Henry moved from this consideration directly to examining human perception of truth, from 1279 onwards he did not. Truth as reflective of a relation between object and divine exemplar now played no explicit role in his analysis of normal intellection. The terms of external reality expressed by such truth were not denied – on the contrary they were expressly reaffirmed – yet they were simply disregarded, as if irrelevant, when it came to the question of truth as known.

For the purpose of analyzing human knowledge, Henry turned to the truth of a sign. Following Anselm, he asserted that there were four types of sign pertinent to truth: sentences, concepts, desires and actions.[9] Since he was considering speculative knowledge, only two types were relevant to his concerns: concepts (*cogitationes*) and sentences or propositions (*orationes*). In line with his often evident Augustinian

---

[6] Henry, *Summa* (*Qg. ord.*), a. 34, q. 1 (Henrici Opera, 27:164, l. 18).

[7] Ibid. (p. 165, ll. 36–38): "... sic veritas rei oportet quod sit, quando res id existit quod natura sua requirit ut sit, videlicet quod in se contineat omne id quod ad naturam suam pertinet, et quiditatem."

[8] On truth and quiddity, see the pointed comments in *Summa* (*Qg. ord.*), a. 34, q. 2 (Henrici Opera, 27:171, ll. 65–69); and also a. 34, q. 4 (Henrici Opera, 27:196, ll. 26–27); q. 5 (Henrici Opera, 27:203, ll. 41–44; and 216, ll. 69–70); and n. 7, above. For Henry's early identification of the two, consult Pt. 3, ch. 9, nn. 29 and 50, above. On divine exemplar as source for quiddity or truth, see *Summa* (*Qg. ord.*), a. 34, q. 2 (Henrici Opera, 27:176, ll. 78–98); and q. 5, resp. and ad 2. (Henrici Opera, 27:216, ll. 72–75; and 235, ll. 94–96); on truth as arising out of a relative orientation (*respectus*) of thing to divine mind, a. 34, q. 3 (Henrici Opera, 27:192, ll. 96–97): "... veritas per se non est in aliqua re naturali creata nisi ex respectu ad intellectum increatum...."

[9] See again Henry, *Summa* (*Qg. ord.*), a. 34, q. 1 (Henrici Opera, 27:164, ll. 18–20), the source being Anselm, *De veritate* 2–5 (ed. Schmitt, 1, 177–83).

bias, he chose to focus not on propositions but rather on knowledge's simple constituents, taking the truth of concepts as his main concern.[10]

If one tailored the general definition of truth to the requirements of grammar, one could see that a sign was true when it signified properly, so the truth of a concept consisted in the concept's presenting its referent as it really was.[11] Knowledge of truth consequently constituted knowledge of a valid relation between concept and object. With this understanding as guide, Henry thus returned to the second line of analysis from his early examinations of truth, identifying it as a complex configuration grasped by an evaluative act of intellect.[12] Knowing truth meant judging knowledge of the true, "*simplex notitia*," according to the yardstick of the created referent outside mind.

It was in article 34, question 5, of the *Summa*, a piece principally devoted to analyzing truth and other reflexive relations in God, where he presented this version of his new approach to human knowledge of truth, specifically interpreting it in terms of intellect's reflexive capacity to turn back on and judge its own grasp of external quiddity.[13] By all appearances related to – maybe even dependent on – Aquinas's examination of complex truth along similar lines, the account is complicated, and there is no need here to go into details.[14] Suffice it to say that it not only raises a theory of truth dependent solely on factors found in the natural world to an eminence its counterpart did not possess in Henry's early work but also serves as corrective to several ambiguities in the description of truth of the Aristotelian, phantastic sort from his inaugural years.[15]

First of all, he had by now decided that the primitive level of knowledge mind was to judge by comparison to external reality – knowledge of the true – already pointed to quiddity, making the true

---

[10] See also above, Pt. 3, ch. 9, p. 281.

[11] Henry, *Summa* (*Qg. ord.*), a. 34, q. 1 (Henrici Opera, 27:164–65, ll. 33–36): ". . . veritas signi tunc est, quando signum facit hoc quod facere debet, sive quod natura sua requirit ut faciat, videlicet quod faciat omne id quod pertinet ad suam significationem, scilicet ut indicet ipsum significatum secundum quod est in re extra. . . ."

[12] See above, Pt. 3, ch. 9, pp. 276–79.

[13] See Henry, *Summa* (*Qg. ord.*), a. 34, q. 5 (Henrici Opera, 27:201–38).

[14] Instead, consult Marrone, *Truth and Scientific Knowledge*, pp. 50–69; and "Henry of Ghent in Mid-Career."

[15] Compare the discussion above, Pt. 3, ch. 9, pp. 282–84.

object (*verum*) grasped by intellect before it went on to know truth equivalent to essence itself.[16] Second, having come to the point of being prepared to give up the notion of impressed intelligible species, he now found it easier to say precisely what elements were implicated in the comparison. The mental words which he would substitute for impressed species could legitimately be regarded as themselves objects of knowledge and not – like species – just means for knowing.[17] He was consequently free to speculate that mind formed a mental word or "conceptus" at the level of knowledge of the true, reflected back on it to see how well it conformed to the external quiddity it was meant to express, and after consideration generated a second, evaluative word, conceptual marker of knowledge of truth.[18]

Finally, and most significantly, he now made no reference to any involvement of God or divine light. And lest his silence be taken as either a momentary lapse or a result of the limited purposes of the argument at hand – investigation of truth in God – it should be noted that he actually returned to the terminology of his earlier years but in a fashion revealing just how much his views had evolved. In article 34 Henry called knowledge mind obtained simply by reflecting back on itself and its created object knowledge of "pure truth" (*sincera veritas*), the very phrase his earlier lexicon had reserved exclusively for cognition arrived at with the aid of God.[19]

Yet despite its historical importance as an index of change, the description of knowledge in the *Summa*, article 34, does not represent Henry's usual position on epistemology in his later years. Indeed it constitutes the only significant occasion from 1279 onwards where he drew on the second of his early lines of truth-analysis, based on comparison or judgment. For a fully naturalistic – that is, worldly – reckoning of the standards for normal human cognition, the mature

---

[16] See Marrone, *Truth and Scientific Knowledge*, p. 58, n. 56; and also p. 41, n. 2. Contrast the description of "true" in Henry's early work: Pt. 3, ch. 9, nn. 27 and 29–31.

[17] On Henry's rejection of impressed species, see above, Pt. 3, ch. 9, n. 57; on the word, below, n. 24.

[18] See Henry, *Summa* (*Qq. ord.*), a. 34, q. 5 (Henrici Opera, 27:219–20, ll. 46–69); and the account in Marrone, *Truth and Scientific Knowledge*, pp. 61–62.

[19] In fact he called it "perfecta et sincera veritas" – *Summa* (*Qq. ord.*), a. 34, q. 5 (Henrici Opera, 27:215, l. 43). (Note that the reading "divino" in l. 42 of this passage is probably not preferable to the alternative, "omnino," presented in the apparatus, Henrici Opera, 27:214, l. 6 from bottom.) See also Marrone, *Truth and Scientific Knowledge*, p. 69, n. 92.

Henry more often reverted to the first of his early approaches, differentiating truth from the true simply according to an intrinsic quality of the object as perceived, in particular the clarity by which it manifested quiddity or essence.[20] Such a posture was even more authentically Aristotelianizing than that taken in article 34, since it hinged upon mind's efforts to seize Aristotle's *quod quid est*, basis for science in his epistemic scheme. Again the new account worked incidentally to clarify some of what Henry had said about knowledge of truth early on, but in this instance he was bringing to center stage a line of analysis only peripheral in his previous work.

Once more it is sufficient for present purposes to raise a few salient points.[21] Henry embarked upon his mature analysis of knowledge according to degree of perception of quiddity in Quodlibet 4, question 8, written in 1279 or 1280, shortly before article 34 of the *Summa*, and he continued along substantially the same path for the remainder of his career.[22] As outlined in Quodlibet 4, the process began when intellect, so far nothing more than a clean slate (*tabula complanata*), was confronted by a universal abstracted from some object's particular representation in a phantasm and moved by it to generate an act of cognition terminating in the object itself.[23] The formal marker of this act, summing up its cognitive content, was in Henry's words a mental "notion" (*notitia actualis*) or "word" (*verbum*), precisely the sort of conceptual entity he was, as just noted, increasingly substituting for intelligible species in his noetics. In Quodlibet 4 he commonly referred to it as a "forma expressiva," to contrast with the "forma impressa" or "impressiva" he identified with species, although "verbum" was the more authentic Augustinian term. Unlike impressed species, which rested in mind as accident in subject, the word for Henry amounted to the object itself having taken on intelligible existence, present to mind after its own special fashion "as known in the knower" (*ut cognitum in cognoscente*).[24]

---

[20] On this first line of analysis, see above, Pt. 3, ch. 9, pp. 426–27.

[21] For greater detail, see Marrone, *Truth and Scientific Knowledge*, pp. 69–92.

[22] Although Gómez Caffarena dated Quodlibet 4 to the Christmas recess of 1279, Paulus preferred a date of Easter 1280 – see Paulus, *Henri de Gand*, p. xv.

[23] *Quod.* 4, q. 8 (1:97rM and 98rP).

[24] *Quod.* 4, q. 8 (1:96vI and 97rL); and *Quod.* 5, q. 25 (1:204rI). On the word constituting object as present to mind, see also *Quod.* 5, q. 14 (1:175rD); for Henry's earlier references to a "word," see above, Pt. 3, ch. 9, n. 58. The first unambiguous sign of a complete and irrevocable rejection of impressed species came in this very *Quod.* 5, q. 14 (1:174rV and 177rR).

As in the epistemic scheme outlined in article 34 of the *Summa*, so in Quodlibet 4 this first word arose at the conceptual level of knowledge of the true, and Henry even called it the marker of a "simplicium comprehensio," a variant on his old "simplex intelligentia." Congruent with cognition at that stratum in his early works, it pointed to something close to what was perceived by the senses, though not formally under the aspect of singularity (*sub ratione particularis*).[25] To advance beyond it intellect had to ponder on what it knew and pose the fundamental Aristotelian question about the nature of simple objects: *quid est*?[26] Once it discovered the answer it produced a second formal marker of its understanding, a second word, which came now properly at the level of knowledge of truth, or science.[27] This second marker was legitimately a "word of truth," expressive, Henry hastened to make clear, of knowledge of Aristotle's *quod quid est*.[28]

Since the foregoing description made knowledge of truth dependent not on comparison of concept to object, as in the *Summa*, article 34, but rather on firmer grasp of object alone, Henry could now say that both knowledge of the true and knowledge of truth were directed to the same simple referent, continuously present to mind in the phantasm. What separated one stage from the other was simply deeper cognitive penetration.[29] Yet over and above this difference with the *Summa*'s nearly contemporary account, conspicuous once more were the modifications to the terms of Henry's early analysis – this time, naturally, to the first of his two basic approaches to truth. As in article 34, of course, so in Quodlibet 4 mind formed a word at both cognitive levels, not as previously only at the stage of

---

[25] Henry, *Quod.* 4, q. 8 (1:97r–v[M] and 98rP). On "simplex intelligentia" in the early Henry, see Pt. 3, ch. 9, nn. 27 and 41. In *Quod.* 4, q. 8 (1:97vM), he called this stage of knowledge "simplex notitia," and the word in which it was conceived, "verbum simplicis intelligentiae" (1:98rP). Mature references to "simplex intelligentia" in this sense can be found in *Quod.* 4, q. 8 (1:97vN) (quoted below, n. 26); *Quod.* 5, q. 14 (1:177rR); and *Summa*, a. 58, q. 2, ad 3. (2:130vH).

[26] Henry, *Quod.* 4, q. 8 (1:97vN): "Habita igitur in principio praedicta notitia simplicis intelligentiae . . . statim vis intellectiva comprehensa admiratur et format sibi quaestiones de incomplexo, ut quid est sol, quid est eclipsis et caetera huiusmodi."

[27] *Quod.* 4, q. 8 (1:97v–98r[O]), in which question (f. 98rP) Henry called it the "verbum scientiale."

[28] See Henry, *Quod.* 4, q. 8 (1:98rP); and *Quod.* 5, q. 14 (1:177rR).

[29] Henry, *Quod.* 4, q. 8 (1:98rP). On knowing truth as penetrating more deeply into the object, see *Summa*, a. 58, q. 2, ad 3. (2:130vI). Henry traced the language about penetrating deeper back to Avicenna, *Liber de philosophia prima* IX, 7 (ed. Van Riet, 2, 511–12).

knowledge of truth. Yet Henry did not hold to this position for very long, already by Quodlibet 6 having reinterpreted the initial understanding of an object – knowledge of the true – to be just the "simple manifestation of a thing" present to mind in the phantasm. According to this view, only at the level of science, knowledge of truth, did intellect formalize its cognition by generating a word.[30] Now, however, he declined to turn to impressed species to explain how intellect performed. Instead, the incompletely known object itself and the phantasm in the imagination sufficed to represent "the true" without further formal element in mind.

Of even greater moment was what this approach said about the technical distinction between knowing the true and knowing truth. The early Henry had maintained that knowledge of the true referred to something below quiddity, knowledge of truth alone to quiddity or essence. Article 34 of Henry's *Summa* demonstrates that by 1279 or 1280 he was ready to jettison that view, but without recourse to the line of analysis seeing truth as dependent on comparison between concept and object, how was he to establish the grounds for a difference?[31] Starting from Quodlibet 4, the mature Henry gradually elaborated a thoroughgoing response.

The division did not lie between particular and universal cognition, for Henry insisted that even at the level of "simplex intelligentia" mind's object was universal.[32] In Quodlibet 5, composed just after article 34 of the *Summa*, he drew upon the new views espoused there to confirm that knowledge of the true already amounted to knowledge of quiddity, adding now that cognition at the level of science or truth moved on, in contrast, to "quod quid est."[33] But exactly what did these words mean? Picking up on a motif detectable even in his earliest work, he finally settled on the opposition between knowing something as confused and knowing it as distinctly articulated into parts (*distincta per partes*).[34] As explained in a remarkable

[30] *Quodlibet* 6, q. 1 (Henrici Opera, 10:14, ll. 82–87; 14–15, ll. 93–07; 16, ll. 25–31; 17, ll. 53–55; and 19, ll. 82–91). See also *Summa*, a. 58, q. 2, ad 3. (2:130vI).

[31] See above, n. 16.

[32] See the first reference given above, n. 25.

[33] Henry, *Quod.* 5, q. 14 (1:176v–77r[O]). See also *Quod.* 4, q. 8 (1:97vN), where knowledge of the true is described as of "id cuius est quod quid est" – that is, of that from which knowledge of "quod quid est" could be drawn. The same phrase appears again in *Summa*, a. 58, q. 2, ad 3. (2:130vI).

[34] Henry, *Summa*, a. 54, q. 9 (2:104vC); and also *Summa*, a. 58, q. 2, ad 3. (2:130vI). In *Quod.* 14, q. 6 (2:566vE), Henry called the first level "intellectio con-

passage from Quodlibet 6, question 1, written in 1281 or 1282, knowledge of the true, "simplex intelligentia," was confused and indefinite in the sense that its object was definable but not yet defined. Making this knowledge distinct and raising it to the level of truth-perception entailed articulating the definition, thereby revealing the object's essential parts. Grasped by intellect, the definition constituted the object's "definitiva ratio," and as mind uttered this "ratio" to itself, it produced the mental word of truth, formal marker of scientific knowledge.[35]

Already in Quodlibet 4, question 8, Henry had charted the way for explaining how this process occurred. Intellect began with the broadest or most common conception of its object, and by sorting out variations and winnowing them down to the specific difference, it came up with the ingredients for a definition of the species to which the object belonged. In the case of "human being," that would be the phrase "rational animal."[36] All this was, of course, no more than the Aristotelian procedure of division, and Henry identified it as such – the "via divisiva" – directing his reader for instruction to the second book of Aristotle's *Posterior Analytics* and Boethius's *Liber de divisione*.[37] The discipline responsible for teaching the procedure was the traditional art of defining (*ars definitiva*).[38]

---

fusa simplicissima," his point apparently not just that it was literally incomplex knowledge, which was the case with knowledge of truth, too, but also that it constituted the simplest, most undifferentiated way of knowing a simple object. On Henry's early use of the idea of confused versus distinct cognition, see above, Pt. 3, ch. 9, nn. 32 and 33.

[35] Henry, *Quodlibet* 6, q. 1 (Henrici Opera, 10:14–15): "Est etiam ista notitia [simplex] de re quasi quaedam confusa et indefinita manifestatio eius, quia per ipsam cognoscitur res tamquam quiddam definibile confusum et indistinctum, ut circulus qui complete ab intellectu non cognoscitur donec formet in se eius definitionem, cognoscendo de eo quod est figura plana etc.

Ad formandum autem in se de re ipsum quod quid est, expressum per definitionem, se habet intellectus noster active discurrendo via artis investigandi quod quid est, dividendo et componendo generi alterum dividentium, quousque habeatur convertibile cum definito, iuxta regulas artis definitivae traditae in II° Posteriorum. . . .

Cum vero, ultima differentia adiuncta, concipit definitivam rationem, illa est verbum in intellectu de re iam perfectum et formatum per actum eius secundum . . . et in eo quiescit discursus intellectus, quia omnino perfectus est quoad notitiam simplicis intelligentiae de intelligibili incomplexo, cognoscendo ipsum tamquam quid distinctum et determinatum. . . ."

[36] Henry, *Quod.* 4, q. 8 (1:97vN). See also *Quodlibet* 6, q. 1 (quoted above, n. 35); and *Quod.* 14, q. 6 (2:566vE), where he said intellect began with the "genus supremum."

[37] Again Henry, *Quod.* 4, q. 8 (1:97vN).

[38] Henry, *Quod.* 14, q. 6 (2:566vE); and the passage from *Quodlibet* 6, q. 1 (quoted above, n. 35), where it is also called "ars investigandi quod quid est."

In the end, therefore, the distinction between knowledge of the true and knowledge of truth came down to a matter of logic. The object was the same in both cases but known to a different degree of conceptual articulation.[39] This vision of human cognition moreover mapped directly onto Henry's understanding of the relation between nominal knowledge and an Aristotelian grasp of "quid est." He held that Aristotle's nominal knowledge, preliminary to all other intellectual apprehension, was a kind of precognition of an object's quiddity (*cognitio eius quod quid ut est praecognitio*), followed not only by knowledge "si est" but also immediately thereafter by full quidditative comprehension as manifested in the definition.[40] He even characterized precognition of "quid est" in terms borrowed from the discussion of knowledge of the true, as confused knowledge of the named object (*intellectus confusus eius quod significatur per nomen*).[41] For clarification he introduced here the Aristotelian example of a circle, nominal knowledge of which entailed receiving the word "circle" but having only a vague idea what it meant, quidditative knowledge embracing the definition: a plane figure described by a single line.[42] The very same example would reappear in his detailed exposition of the difference between knowing the true and knowing truth found in Quodlibet 6, question 1.[43]

Such emphasis on defining naturally suggested that the way to knowledge of truth, even as conceived in these instances with regard

---

[39] See Henry, *Quod.* 14, q. 6 (2:566vE): "Licet enim quod quid est sit universale, quia est ratio definitiva universalis proprie dicti et convertibile cum ipso . . . differunt tamen proprie loquendo, quia ipsum commune esse definibile per genus et differentias, ut consideratur sub ratione confusi et indistincti secundum partes quae cadere debent in definitiva ratione, sic proprie dicitur universale, et dicitur esse eius quidditativum esse definitum continens ipsum distinctum secundum partes, ut homo animal rationale. . . ."

[40] On this progression, see Stephen D. Dumont, "The quaestio si est," pp. 342–47. Dumont (p. 343, n. 51) cites the revealing account in *Summa*, a. 24, q. 3 (1:138vO). See also above, Pt. 3, ch. 9, n. 34.

[41] Refer to the passage from Henry cited above, n. 40.

[42] Henry, *Summa*, a. 24, q. 3 (1:139rR), which calls upon Aristotle, *Physics* 1, 1 (184a26–b11). Dumont quotes this passage and gives the citation to Aristotle in "The quaestio si est," p. 346, n. 63

[43] See above, n. 35. All this, even the quotation from Aristotle, had been quickly sketched out in article 1, q. 12 from the *Summa* (see above, Pt. 3, ch. 9, n. 33), which thus serves as a reminder that Henry's mature views on truth constituted less a radical departure from his early ideas than a more forcefully articulated and prominent presentation of what had previously been present only in germ. Significantly, in *Summa*, a. 1, q. 12, he followed his early practice of reserving the term "quiddity" for what was known at the level of knowledge of truth.

to what was technically simple knowledge of "quod quid est," ultimately depended on complex activity of mind. Henry noted that
though the true, object of "simplex intelligentia," was grasped in a
purely simple intellective act, truth could be attained only after the
complicated procedure of compounding and dividing (*componendo et
dividendo*).[44] The realization led him to remark that in coming to know
the true, intellect could be said hardly to act at all, making it legitimate to characterize understanding as passive up through the first
stage of cognition, with authentic activity arising only at the second
stage required to know truth.[45] There emerges here a strongly Aristotelian sense of the purely receptive character of human intellection in at least its initial grades, agency coming into play only when
logical analysis was involved.

All told, Henry's mature analysis of truth along these lines offered
a coherent explanation of simple knowledge in the world, significantly
one that, like the more singular account in article 34 of the *Summa*,
at no point made mention of a divine role. Just as in article 34, the
second, illuminative stage of knowledge of truth, which occupied center stage in his earliest works, had simply dropped out of the picture, and again, its disappearance would scarcely seem attributable
to the mere fact that he was on most occasions investigating knowledge of truth not for itself but rather to apply the findings to other
issues of more immediate concern.[46] Not once among any of the

---

[44] Henry, *Quod.* 5, q. 25 (1:204vK); and *Quodlibet* 6, q. 1 (Henrici Opera, 10:14)
(quoted above, n. 35). For earlier mention of this distinction, see above, Pt. 3, ch. 9,
nn. 27 and 37.

[45] Henry, *Quod.* 4, q. 8 (1:97vN) on the first stage "sine studio," and (98rP) on
the second stage involving "negotiari et discurrere." For other discussions of intellect as purely passive in knowing the true, partly active in knowing truth, see *Quod.*
5, q. 25 (1:204r–v[I–K]), where the initial passivity is limited to possible intellect;
Quodlibet 6, q. 1 (Henrici Opera, 10:14, ll. 80–85 and 93–95); *Summa*, a. 54, q. 9
(2:104rC); and a. 58, q. 2, ad 3. (2:131rL), where again possible intellect is designated as passive. In *Summa*, a. 54, q. 9 (2:104vC); and a. 58, q. 2, ad 3. (2:130vI),
the secondary, active capacity of mind is explained in fully Augustinian terms, with
ample reference to Augustine's *De Trinitate*. Sometimes even reflexivity, associated
above with a Thomistic approach to truth, is invoked in this regard: see *Summa*, a.
54, q. 9 (2:104vC); and a. 58, q. 2, ad 3. (2:130v[I and K]). Henry's most subtle
discussion comes in the late *Quod.* 14, q. 6 (2:566vE), where he admits some "actio"
at all levels of knowledge, since even at the first stage the possible acts in an attenuated way, but confesses that only from the second stage does mind act to *form* its
knowledge.

[46] In fact, not all the passages examined just above analyze human cognitive
processes solely for the sake of producing models to use in resolving another problem. See, for instance, *Quod.* 14, q. 6.

aforementioned attempts from 1279 on to analyze the dichotomy between knowledge of the true and knowledge of truth was a model of cognition brought forth where God had a part to play. It was as if Henry had become so fully satisfied with an Aristotelianizing account of certitude that he no longer felt the need to call upon illuminationist theories of truth. If he had not fully abandoned such Augustinian ideas, they had surely receded far from the center of his attention. Following the precedent of article 34, he now even graced fully worldly cognition with an accolade once reserved for knowledge dependent upon God's light. His Aristotelianizing model for knowing truth brought intellect, he claimed, to "true and perfect knowledge" (*vera et perfecta de incomplexo notitia*), distant cry from the disparaging assessment of Aristotle's paradigm in his early years, more in line with the "perfect science" of his previous understanding of pure, illumined truth.[47]

Henry's followers evidently perceived the course of his thought in exactly this way. At least Vital sensed a change in direction and, even truer Augustinian than his more illustrious forebear, rejected the formulations of the master's later years. In the passage from *De cognitione*, question 8, already noted above, he summarized a view about knowing the true and knowing truth that in all essentials followed Henry's mature account, employing language lifted nearly verbatim from Quodlibet 4, question 8, and Quodlibet 6, question 1.[48] When he then, borrowing Roger Marston's words, rejected the whole position out of hand, he was expressly repudiating the Aristotelianizing vision of Henry's maturity.[49] For some Augustinians, even this champion of their cause could veer too far in Aristotle's direction.

For his own part, Henry went on enthusiastically to examine processes of mind, and their psychological concomitants, in which to ground his Aristotelianizing epistemology, revealing himself on

---

[47] Henry, *Summa*, a. 58, q. 2, ad 3. (2:130vI). For the early pejorative description of an Aristotelianizing model, see Pt. 3, ch. 9, nn. 70–71; for "perfect science," Pt. 3, ch. 9, n. 72. On re-estimation of Aristotelianzing knowledge in article 34, see above, n. 19.

[48] See above, Pt. 3, ch. 9, n. 35. Vital's complete presentation (*Quaestiones de cognitione*, q. 8 [ed. Delorme, "Huit questions," pp. 312–14]), which includes the passage referred to in that note, is drawn nearly verbatim from Henry's *Quod.* 4, q. 8 (1:97v[N–O]); and *Quodlibet* 6, q. 1 (Henrici Opera, 10:14–15, ll. 81–97), much of which material is either quoted or referred to in nn. 35–38 above, and nn. 65, 66 and 76 below.

[49] See above, Pt. 3, ch. 9, n. 36.

occasion to be an Averroist of considerable discernment.[50] As early as the first article of the *Summa* he had noted that some thinkers, most prominently Avicenna but also others among the Arabs, had held that a separate intellect provided human mind with knowledge through a formal process of participation. Such an intellect was necessarily a power higher than mind but close to it, by tradition the intelligence animating the tenth and lowest celestial sphere.[51] With respect to normal human knowledge, Henry rejected this position without reservation.[52] From his earliest to his very last work he committed himself instead to what he identified as Aristotle's point of view, that knowledge was not poured into mind from above but rather intellect, always potentially knowing, was moved to generate its own act of cognition in the presence of an active intellectual impulse (*activum aliquid*).[53]

In his mature writings Henry explained the relation of this active impulse to mind with reference to a third factor, the intelligible object. As already remarked, at the level of knowledge of both the true and truth mind's object was universal, Henry having insisted throughout his career that there could be no authentically intellectual perception – at least no direct perception – of anything else.[54]

---

[50] On Averroist elements in Henry's psychology, see Marrone, *Truth and Scientific Knowledge*, pp. 82–85, especially the comments on p. 83; more generally on his noetics and psychology, see Jerome V. Brown, "Abstraction and the Object of the Human Intellect according to Henry of Ghent," *Vivarium* 11 (1973): 80–104; "Henry of Ghent on Internal Sensation," *Journal of the History of Philosophy* 10 (1972): 15–28; and "Sensation in Henry of Ghent: A Late Medieval Aristotelian-Augustinian Synthesis," *Archiv für Geschichte der Philosophie* 53 (1971): 238–66; Paulus, "A propos de la théorie de la connaissance d'Henri de Gand," *Revue Philosophique de Louvain* 47 (1949): 493–96; and De Wulf, "L'exemplarisme et la théorie de l'illumination spéciale dans la philosophie de Henri de Gand," RNS 1 (1894): 53–75. Less reliable is Giuseppina Cannizzo, "La dottrina del 'verbum mentis' in Enrico di Gand," RFN 54 (1962): 243–66.

[51] Henry, *Summa*, a. 1, q. 4 (1:11vC). In *Quod.* 8, q. 12 (2:324rA), he referred to this position as the less common of two on the nature of agent intellect. For discussion of such a position as early as William of Auvergne and its attribution to Avicenna, see above Pt. 1, ch. 2, n. 31. On Henry's one explicit description of God as agent intellect, see below, nn. 96 and 98.

[52] Henry, *Summa*, a. 1, q. 4 (1:11vD).

[53] See Henry, *Summa*, a. 1, q. 4 (1:12r–v[E]). The phrase "aliquid activum" had also appeared in Pecham – see above, Pt. 2, ch. 6, n. 85.

[54] On the need for universality in the intellectual object, see Henry, *Quodlibet* 6, q. 6 (Henrici Opera, 10:68, ll. 53–54); *Quodlibet* 7, q. 14 (Henrici Opera, 11:98); *Quod.* 8, q. 12 (2:324rB); *Quod.* 14, q. 6 (2:566vE); *Quod.* 15, q. 9 (2:581rD); and *Summa*, a. 58, q. 2, ad 3. (2:130rG); on the impossibility of knowing singulars directly, see, for example, *Summa*, a. 58, q. 2, ad 3. (2:130r[G and H]). Vital, too, insisted

Since real essences were not universal in themselves, something was
needed to insure they be presented to intellect under the guise of
universality.[55] Here is where the active impulse came in, to prepare
a universal ground for mind to survey. Henry took it to be Aristotle's
opinion, which he accepted as correct, that this active impulse was
one of human intellect's two parts, thereby adopting the view seen
increasingly among Augustinians from Bonaventure on that there
were two varieties of intellect, each representing an inherent capacity possessed by every human soul.[56] He also followed Pecham in
saying that technically speaking these were not two different powers
(*potentiae*) of soul but rather two forces (*vires*), a less radical division.[57]
Vital agreed.[58] Both men were thinking, of course, of the agent and
possible intellects, by then the almost universally accepted scheme
for dividing functions of mind.

The complete description of how these forces worked evolved as
Henry moved from accepting impressed intelligible species to their
total elimination in favor of the mental word, but relevant to discussion here are only those mechanisms of mind not affected by the
change. It is important to remember that Vital never accepted Henry's
mature position on the erroneousness of positing intelligible species.[59]

From beginning to end of career Henry gave a virtually invari-
ant account of how the two forces operated in the first stage of the
procedure, leading to "simplex intelligentia" or knowledge of the true.
Agent intellect's primary role at this point was to render the cognitive material resident in phantasms suitable for understanding, and
it did so by denuding the phantasms of particular conditions so as

---

that what he called "cognitiones scientificae" had to be of the universal – see *Quaestiones
de cognitione*, q. 1 (ed. Delorme, "Huit questions," p. 180).

[55] See Henry, *Quod.* 4, q. 14 (1:178vX).

[56] Henry, *Summa*, a. 58, q. 2, ad 3. (2:129v–30r[D–F]). See above, Pt. 2, ch. 6,
nn. 81–82, for Bonaventure's views.

[57] Henry, *Summa*, a. 58, q. 2, ad 3. (2:129vD); and also *Quod.* 5, q. 14 (1:176vO);
and *Quodlibet* 13, q. 8, ad 1. (Henrici Opera, 18:56, ll. 75–80). See Pt. 2, ch. 6,
n. 87, for Pecham on this distinction. Matthew took the same route – see Pt. 2,
ch. 6, n. 95. Early on Henry was willing to call these two parts of the intellect
"potentiae" – see *Summa*, a. 1, q. 5 (1:14vB) – suggesting he had not yet read, or
understood, Pecham.

[58] Vital, *Quaestiones de cognitione*, q. 2 (ed. Delorme, "Huit questions," p. 197). As
indicated below, Vital disagreed with Henry on exactly how these two powers
worked.

[59] See Vital, *Quaestiones de cognitione*, q. 2 (ed. Delorme, "Huit questions," p. 207);
and also below, n. 71.

to reveal their universal core, the process called abstraction.[60] On this point Henry revealed himself as anxious as Matthew of Aquasparta to adopt an Aristotelianizing line on the necessity for all normal cognition to originate in the external world as apprehended through the senses.[61] Yet the agent had a secondary function directed not to the intelligible object but rather to possible intellect. Drawing on Aristotle's *De anima* Henry claimed that the initial processes of intellection were analogous to those of sight, so that agent intellect should be seen as a cognitive light, falling on phantasms in the way visible light illuminated colors and irradiating possible intellect just as visible light shone on the visible medium, the sensory organ and perhaps the power of sight itself. In this fashion, the agent prepared the possible for understanding by making it receptive of the abstracted universals.[62] By his later writings an even more complicated analysis appeared, with the agent performing two roles with regard to each target: working on phantasms by making them intelligible and giving them the capacity to act on the possible, on the possible by disposing it to receive universals and, as immanent in the universals themselves, determining it to a specific intellective act.[63] Here he explicitly evoked the idea seen in Grosseteste, that as the visual power necessarily possessed its own innate light of seeing, so intellect naturally contained an intelligible light within itself.[64]

The noetics of the second step, leading to knowledge of truth, Henry examined extensively only in his middle and later years. As noted above, he saw mind at this level as taking on a more active

---

[60] Henry, *Quod.* 8, q. 12 (2:324rB).

[61] On Matthew, see above, Pt. 2, ch. 6, nn. 35 and 37. In Aristotelian fashion Henry also insisted that mind in the world was capable of knowing only when a phantasm was present – see *Quod.* 5, q. 25 (1:204vK); *Quodlibet* 6, q. 6 (Henrici Opera, 10:68–69, ll. 55–77); and *Quod.* 8, q. 12 (2:324vC). Towards the end of his career he began to entertain exceptions to this rule, speaking of some kinds of knowledge from divine illumination or God's creative action that were independent of phantasms – see below, nn. 85–86 and 102.

[62] Henry, *Summa*, a. 58, q. 2, ad 3. (2:129v–30r[D–F]); and also *Summa*, a. 1, q. 5 (1:14vB); and *Quod.* 8, q. 12 (2:324rB). He traced the analogy back to Aristotle, *De anima* III, 5 (430a14–17). For description of the agent's act without recourse to this analogy, see *Quod.* 4, q. 8 (1:97rM). Quick sketches of the whole process from sensation to intellection also appear in *Quod.* 5, q. 14 (1:176v[M–O]); and *Summa*, a. 58, q. 2, ad 3. (2:130r–v[H]).

[63] Henry, *Quodlibet* 13, q. 8 (Henrici Opera, 18:50–52, ll. 28–73).

[64] Henry, *Quodlibet* 13, q. 8 (Henrici Opera, 18:50, ll. 35–41). On Grosseteste, see above, Pt. 1, ch. 1, nn. 31 and 35. Pecham and Matthew also held to this view – see above, Pt. 2, ch. 6, nn. 67–69.

mien in contrast to its predominant passivity while coming to know the true. For although agent intellect was operative in the business of "simplex intelligentia," possible intellect remained at that stage completely subject to the action of abstracted universals, but once it had been informed with knowledge of the true it arose from passivity to function along with the cooperating agent in actively searching out truth.[65] Indeed it was precisely possible intellect that performed the compounding and dividing revealing the object's definition.[66]

From Henry's description of possible intellect's workings in knowledge of truth it is evident that his understanding of this stage in the cognitive process drew heavily on Augustine's vision of the inherent activity of mind, from which he had, after all, taken the idea of a mental word exclusively associated with the second step in his earliest works.[67] To this degree even the mature Henry proved himself legitimate heir to the classic Augustinians, who likewise thought of mind as fundamentally active, Bonaventure claiming that the Aristotelian terms "agent" and "possible intellect" were by no means to be taken as implying total activity or passivity for either power of mind.[68] Apparently aware that he was in this respect distancing himself from Aristotle, Henry remarked how at the stage of "simplex intelligentia" both of mind's forces functioned "naturally," which was to say according to the precepts of a fully Aristotelianized natural world, but that subsequently intellect was "active," thus even willful, so far as either force was concerned.[69] Besides Augustine, however, he also drew inspiration on this matter from Averroes. Possible intellect, rendered active by its reception of knowledge of the true, was, he said, exactly what Averroes meant by the capacity of mind he called speculative intellect.[70]

---

[65] Henry, *Quod.* 5, q. 25 (1:204rI); and *Quod.* 14, q. 6 (2:566vE); see also *Quodlibet* 6, q. 1 (Henrici Opera, 10:14, ll. 80–85). For mention above of mind's initial passivity, see n. 45.

[66] Henry, *Summa*, a. 58, q. 2, ad 3. (2:130v[H–I]); and also *Quodlibet* 6, q. 1 (Henrici Opera, 10:14, ll. 93–95).

[67] See the passage from article 58 of the *Summa* cited above, n. 66. On this Augustinian side to Henry, see also above, n. 45.

[68] See above, Pt. 2, ch. 6, n. 81.

[69] Henry, *Summa*, a. 58, q. 2, ad 3. (2:130vH). On Henry's understanding of "natural," see above, Pt. 3, ch. 10, n. 48.

[70] Henry, *Summa*, a. 58, q. 2, ad 3. (2:131rL and 132vP). The term "intellectus speculativus" was drawn from Averroes, *Commentarium magnum in Aristotelis De anima libros* III, 5 (ed. Crawford, pp. 389–90 and 406). Consult other references in Marrone, *Truth and Scientific Knowledge*, pp. 83–84, n. 141. On Averroes's influence on Henry see also Nys, *De werking*, pp. 80–88 (*De psychologia*, pp. 34–37). In *Quodlibet* 13, q. 8

Predictably enough, as on other occasions where he seemed to stray from the path of Augustinian orthodoxy, so here, too, with this Averroizing facet of his later noetics Henry was rejected by his otherwise faithful followers. Vital summarized the master's views on the role of agent and possible intellects in a question in *De cognitione* the main purpose of which was to attack the rejection of impressed intelligible species. The body of the question made it clear that he was troubled not just by Henry's position on species but also by his whole description of mind's functioning, in particular the attribution of extreme passivity to possible intellect in the first stage of cognition and the power of compounding and dividing at the second stage, a power Vital reserved for the agent.[71] As for how mind took up impressed species, for which he retained a noetic function, Vital returned to Matthew of Aquasparta in distinction 39 of his *Commentary on the Sentences* and *De cognitione*, question 3, the latter providing his *texte de base*, mined according to form as source for verbatim borrowings.[72]

In keeping with Matthew, Vital chose to target a stance on mind's simple processes reminiscent of John Pecham's, for whom the senses played a merely occasional role by exciting intellect to immanent act. Vital altered Matthew's description of the targeted views, however, by eliminating intelligible species, a change almost certainly intended to bring the position in line with that of Peter Olivi.[73] It

(Henrici Opera, 18:54, ll. 25–31), Henry explained the two faces of possible intellect by saying that possible itself had two forces (*vires*) – by the first, "memoria," it was purely passive; by the second, "intelligentia," it was active and capable of seeking out truth.

[71] See Vital's conclusion, *Quaestiones de cognitione*, q. 2 (ed. Delorme, "Huit questions," p. 197), the question referred to above, n. 59. In the first article, Vital summarized Henry's views on noetics (pp. 185–92), especially those presented in Quodlibet 5, q. 14; Quodlibet 13, q. 8; and *Summa*, a. 58, q. 2, ad 3. – attributing them to "quidam magni" (p. 185) – and reproduced a list of reasons in their favor drawn sometimes verbatim from a work of Giles of Rome (pp. 192–96). He then relied heavily on the same work to reject these views in the second article (pp. 196–207). As Delorme notes in his edition of Vital, Giles's work was his *De cognitione angelorum*, q. 4 (in *De esse et essentia, De mensura angelorum, et De cognitione angelorum*, ff. 81d–86a).

[72] Vital, *Quaestiones de cognitione*, q. 3 (ed. Delorme, "Huit questions," pp. 211–32), dependent on Matthew even for the wording of the question (compare Vital, p. 211, with Matthew, *De cognitione*, q. 3 [BFS, 1:248]). For Matthew's analysis of the noetics of simple cognition, see above, Pt. 2, ch. 6, pp. 159–62.

[73] For Vital's description, see his *Quaestiones de cognitione*, q. 3 (ed. Delorme, "Huit questions," pp. 215–16), which draws sometimes word for word on Matthew, *De cognitione*, q. 3 (BFS, 1:259–60) – cited above, Pt. 2, ch. 6, nn. 26–30. On this as close to Pecham's views, see Pt. 2, ch. 6, nn. 48, 51 and 52. Among defenders of such ideas Vital quotes Olivi – see Vital, *Quaestiones de cognitione*, q. 3 (arg. 5–11) (ed.

is in fact possible he had only Olivi in mind, not realizing Matthew had originally been expressing doubts about ideas of the otherwise exemplary Pecham. Vital's own opinion, again greatly dependent on Matthew, was that mind really took something from external, sensible things in receiving intelligible species, even though this did not occur so as to subject it to material reality. Instead it acquired what it did simply by virtue of being an active power.[74] In short, he, like Matthew, championed a noetics that although Aristotelianizing enough not altogether to deny receptivity to mind, made ample room for an uncompromisingly Augustinian stand on its fundamental activity.

As for Henry, he realized that beyond the still technically simple knowledge discussed so far, there remained genuinely complex cognition, knowledge of propositions, where alone according to the strict Aristotelian lexicon "truth" came into play and the term "science" applied.[75] For these complex truths he also offered an epistemological analysis and underlying noetics, although much sparer than for what might be called "simple truth." Broadly speaking, he called all that had to do with knowledge of the assertions of science "syllogistic knowledge," observing that it was established upon the logical procedures outlined in the *Logica nova*, the latter part of Aristotle's organon.[76] More precisely, he conceded that this general rubric covered two different kinds of understanding, knowledge of propositions and knowledge of arguments, only the latter, of course, involving syllogism in the strict sense, or in the case of science, demonstration, and each dependent on a radically divergent intellective operation. For all that, in both cases possible worked actively along with agent intellect to carry the process forward.[77]

By his final years, quite plainly, Henry had developed a comprehensive vision of human knowledge in the world, remarkable in

---

Delorme, "Huit questions," pp. 217–18), all of which can be found in Olivi, *Quaestiones in secundum librum Sententiarum*, q. 58 (ed. Bernhard Jansen, BFS, 5:454–56 [Quaracchi, 1924]). In the same text, p. 477, Olivi makes clear his stand on intelligible species. Any jab at Olivi's rejection of intelligible species would naturally hit Henry as well.

[74] Vital, *Quaestiones de cognitione*, q. 3 (ed. Delorme, "Huit questions," pp. 218–19 – largely dependent on Matthew, *De cognitione* [BFS, 1:263–64] – and p. 224).

[75] On Henry's recognition of this fact about Aristotle, see above, Pt. 3, ch. 9, n. 47.

[76] Henry, *Quod.* 4, q. 8 (1:97vN). The *Logica nova* consisted of Aristotle's two *Analytics*, the *Topics* and *On Sophistical Refutations*.

[77] Henry, *Summa*, a. 58, q. 2, ad 3. (2:132vQ); and also (2:130vH). For more on his discussion of such fully complex processes of mind, see Marrone, *Truth and Scientific Knowledge*, pp. 83–85 and 88–90.

ARISTOTLE AND AUGUSTINE REVISITED

someone with his Augustinian proclivities for its dependence on an Aristotelianized epistemology explaining certitude and the attainment of science without reference to Godly intervention. As noted before, some historians have concluded that he consequently abandoned his early ideas on truth, rejecting in particular the second level, knowledge of "pure truth," revealed by divine illumination, but passages in his later work unequivocally reaffirming illumination of truth prove that this was not the case. Yet it has also been suggested that one should not think he held firm to the position on the issue mapped out early in his career. The normative illumination Henry had in mind in the scattered and for the most part unelaborated reaffirmations of his maturity was not precisely the same as the doctrine presented in the first articles of his *Summa*.

This chapter and the preceding two have shown how from mid-career on Henry not only worked out a greatly Aristotelianizing philosophy of knowledge and mind but also strengthened his appreciation of the way his theory of essence combined with his views on natural knowledge of God to promote an affirmation of divine intimacy to human intellect independent of Augustine's ideas about truth. It must now be added that he gradually perceived this same theory of essence as permitting his mature, Aristotelianizing epistemology to yield, with only modest effort at interpretation, something like those very Augustinian intuitions about God's place in cognition. Such tailoring of Aristotle to Augustine demanded a theoretical distancing from the literal image of a divine light of truth, which sat uneasily with the concrete processes of an Aristotelianized noetics, but it did not require abandoning the basics of Augustine's approach. Henry was now able simply to embrace Augustine without having to tack on, as had been the case in his early theories, a procedure involving God's action on mind as second stage in knowing truth above intellect's first, more Aristotelian operations. In light of his metaphysics, the two processes collapsed into one, with knowing truth in Aristotelian terms effectively equivalent to knowing it along Augustinian lines as well.

Another way to put this is that Henry's metaphysics of essence permitted the theory of knowledge he constructed in his later years to reproduce the fundamental epistemic conditions relegated in his early work to an explicit theory of divine illumination.[78] It was thus

---

[78] On the collapse of the two levels of science into one, see Marrone, *Truth and*

ultimately possible for him to account not only for divine intimacy to mind, already displaced onto his idea of natural knowledge of God, but also for divinity's function as guarantor of truth without referring to the paradigmatic Augustinian light. Increasingly Aristotelianizing, Henry could still plausibly claim he remained true to the end to the normative illuminationist theories prominently displayed in his early work just because his mature epistemology could be said to leave room for the truth-revealing dimensions of illumination whether or not he employed expressly illuminationist language or bothered to remind his readers that a divine role was involved.

For the same reason he could also draw back from the absolute separation introduced in his early years between natural knowledge of God and knowledge of truth, the former entailing divinity as object but the latter only as means of knowing. Henry's mature writings tapped into his metaphysics of essence to amplify God's role as somehow object even in truth-perception. Ironically he thus returned in his final years to a theoretical unity on the matter of God's place in cognition reminiscent of the classic Augustinians, this time, however, without recourse to the doctrinal glue of illumination by Eternal Truth.

A last look at what he had to say about knowledge of truth in his later years shows how all this was so. Scattered throughout his mature works are indications he realized how the truth mind was directed towards according to his fully developed theory of scientific knowledge, essence as signified by "quod quid est" and seized in the definition, was metaphysically identical to what he described in other contexts as absolute essence and had therefore to be located in his ontological scheme at the level of "res a ratitudine." He arrived at this understanding about the time Matthew, himself surely dependent on Henry, was coming to the same conclusion.[79] Already by Quodlibet 3, from 1278 or 1279, he had come to believe that the

---

Scientific Knowledge, pp. 139–40 and 146. Similar views on the role of metaphysics in Henry's later work were advanced by Gómez Caffarena, Ser participado, pp. 33–35; and Pegis, "A New Way to God: Henry of Ghent (II)," pp. 113–15, where the claim is made that the later Henry fused the Avicennian notion of absolute essence with Augustinian illumination. Prospero Stella, "La prima critica," also suggests that Henry progressively worked towards greater appreciation of Avicennian absolute essence, as well as a more active view of mind, while Dwyer, Die Wissenschaftslehre, pp. 38–43, remarks upon development of Henry's epistemology from early attachment to divine illumination to later emphasis on vision of the incorporeal reasons.

[79] On Henry, see the references given above, Pt. 3, ch. 11, n. 78; for Matthew's views, see Pt. 2, ch. 7, n. 56.

truth of propositions about essential attributes was founded on absolute essence, inferring from this that all science was ultimately grounded in the same.[80] Soon after, in article 34 of the *Summa*, he noted similarly that truth – this time, the objective truth of simple things to which knowledge was directed and according to which it had to conform to be true – was to be found in "res a ratitudine."[81] Vital meant the same thing when he claimed that the formality in virtue of which a thing should be labeled true was grounded in entity, a term both he and Henry used interchangeably with "res a ratitudine," as conceived absolutely (*per se*) by intellect.[82]

But the foundation for "res a ratitudine" was a relation between essence and divine ideal. Already of course in the *Summa*, article 34, Henry had drawn the inference that things possessed essential truth only by grace of a relative orientation (*respectus*) to God's mind, and within a year he was pointing out how human knowledge, by necessity directed toward essence, was possible only insofar as the object of intellection depended radically on a relation to divine exemplar.[83] It was a short step from this idea to appreciating that the underlying vision crucial to his discussion of mind's first object, the notion that normal human cognition opened onto a conceptual ground leading directly to God, applied as well to his account of knowledge of truth or science. Again, Henry's metaphysics of essence simply entailed the fact that already present in, if not explicitly expressed by, his

[80] See the quotation from *Quod.* 3, q. 9, given above, Pt. 3, ch. 11, n. 92. Shortly after this passage he noted: "Unde et ratio talis entis [i.e. essentiae absolutae conceptae], quia est aliquid secundum naturam et essentiam per se, est obiectum intellectus de quo habent esse scientiae. . . ." See also *Quod.* 8, q. 12 (2:324rB), where he explained that the intelligible objects perceived in phantasms under the universalizing illumination of agent intellect were known insofar as they were essences pure and simple (*sub ratione qua essentiae simpliciter sunt*) – that is, as absolute essences.
[81] Henry, *Summa (Qg. ord.)*, a. 34, q. 2 (Henrici Opera, 27:175–76, ll. 70–74): "Et ideo veritas cuiusque rei subsistentis in creaturis non dicitur fundari nisi in re secundo modo [i.e. secundum rationem rei dictae a ratitudine]. Quanto enim aliquid in re plus habet ratitudinis sive firmitatis, tanto plus habet entitatis, quare et veritatis. Ut ex hoc veritas dicatur esse in unoquoque, quia habet in se participatum id formae et essentiae, quod natum est habere secundum suam speciem. . . ."
[82] Vital, *Quaestiones de cognitione*, q. 6 (ed. Delorme, "Huit questions," p. 293): "Ratio autem veri non fundatur in actuali existentia rei . . . sed . . . in entitate ut concepta ab intellectu per se."
[83] Henry, *Summa (Qg. ord.)*, a. 34, q. 3 (Henrici Opera, 27:192, ll. 96–97), quoted above, n. 8, on truth and relative orientation; on objects intelligible because related to an exemplar, *Quod.* 5, q. 14 (1:177rR); and also *Quodlibet* 7, qq. 1 & 2 (Henrici Opera, 11:28), both quoted above, Pt. 3, ch. 11, n. 80.

Aristotelianizing description of truth-perception was the implication
that mind knowing truth had access to a divine object. It took a
mere signal to his readers, at most a short exposition, to give new
currency to the Augustinian account of knowledge of truth he seemed
otherwise to ignore in the epistemological and noetic explorations of
his mature works.

The first evidence Henry saw things this way comes in question
15 of Quodlibet 5, composed in late 1280 or early 1281. There he
brought together his notion of the intelligible object, interpreted
according to his metaphysics of essence, with specific recognition of
God's role as conceptual light. As he put it, God's function at the
level of essence was not just ontological, furnishing formal ground
for quiddity or objective truth, but also cognitive insofar as the very
fact of divine grounding insured intelligibility.[84] But he fully tipped
his hand, if only briefly, in Quodlibet 9, from 1286 and the height
of his career. Question 15 of that work asked whether there was in
mind a hidden knowledge (*intelligere abditum*) arising somehow beyond
the normal point of entry among phantasms in imagination, to which
he responded by insisting that Augustine had unambiguously answered
in the affirmative.[85] He then explained that Augustine had in mind
the ever-present and absolutely primary action of divine light on
human intellect requisite for access to pure truth, an action which
since not apparent to everyone, even those calling upon it, was properly designated "hidden."[86]

When he then went on to describe the process, his account matched
the analysis of the way to knowledge of pure truth given in his first
works, though at times with slightly modified terminology.[87] As before,

---

[84] Henry, *Quod.* 5, q. 15 (1:179vI): "Et . . . quia sicut lumen in corporibus est vis-
ibile primum et per se, per quod etiam alia videntur inquantum sunt luminis par-
ticipantia et inquantum sunt lumine exteriori illustrata, sic et in spiritualibus lux
prima quae Deus est, primum est et per se intelligibile, cuius participatione in esse
formali uniuscuiusque et illustratione omnia alia intelliguntur." Just before, Henry
had pointed out to his readers he was building on his understanding of the object
of intellect laid out in the preceding question of the Quodlibet, for which see above,
n. 83.

[85] Henry, *Quodlibet* 9, q. 15 (Henrici Opera, 13:258, ll. 2–5 and 11–18). Henry
referred to Augustine, *De Trinitate* X, 10; and XIV, 7 and 12 (eds. Mountain and
Glorie, 1, 329; and 2, 433–34 and 442–43).

[86] Henry, *Quodlibet* 9, q. 15 (Henrici Opera, 13:261, ll. 96–99) and also (13:265,
ll. 22–28). On how this action was not recognized by all, see q. 15, ad arg. (Henrici
Opera, 13:268, ll. 92–97).

[87] Ibid. (p. 262, ll. 23–28): "Est ergo intentio Augustini . . . quod postquam [anima]

there were here two separate stages in truth-perception, the first
revealing an "imaginaria veritas" reminiscent of the "phantastic knowledge of truth" of the initial articles of the *Summa*, only the second
yielding knowledge of pure truth, where God's intervention was critical.[88] Henry even referred his readers back to the beginning of the
Summa for details about how the illuminative procedure worked, as
if to imply that there had been no significant evolution in his thought.[89]
Yet in the middle of this unexceptional description appears an astonishing statement, unprepared for by anything he had said in his early
years. Immediately after indicating that for full knowledge of truth
mind must turn to the divine ideas or reasons, he remarked that the
abstracted objects known through or in the phantasms and the ideal
reasons in God – that is, the very two cognitive elements to be compared according to the early paradigm for knowing pure truth –
were in fact the same; indeed they were both identical with the
essences of things.[90]

One can understand this assertion only in light of the metaphysics
already laid out in Henry's other works, whereby, first of all, each
thing's essence in itself – that is, its absolute essence – remained really
the same throughout all instantiations in external reality or thinking
minds and, second, the exemplified essences known by God were,
over eternity, identical to the divine ideas.[91] Given these two presup-
positions, it was no more than inferring the obvious to state, as in

intelligibilia rerum sensibilium conspexerit in phantasmatibus per sensus receptis, a
sensibus se subtrahit et phantasmatibus, et per haec attingit praedictas incorporeas
rationes in ipsa veritate incorporea existentes." For full exposition of this account,
see Marrone, *Truth and Scientific Knowledge*, pp. 94–98.

[88] *Quodlibet* 9, q. 15 (Henrici Opera, 13:264, l. 97). On "phantastic knowledge,"
see above, Pt. 3, ch. 9, n. 70. Henry drew the term "imaginaria veritas" from
Augustine's mention of an "imaginarium conspectum" (or in Henry's words "imaginarium intellectum"), which he quoted several times (p. 264, ll. 75–76, 79 and 83).
See Augustine, *De Trinitate* IX, 6 (eds. Mountain and Glorie, 1, 303).

[89] *Quodlibet* 9, q. 15 (Henrici Opera, 13:264, ll. 85–87); also the same, p. 262, ll.
35–36.

[90] In *Quodlibet* 9, q. 15 (Henrici Opera, 13:262, ll. 29–31), Henry continued the
passage quoted above, n. 87, with the following words: "Sunt enim eadem cognita
et praedicta intellecta in phantasmatibus, et ipsae incorporeae rationes in ipsa veritate aeterna: non sunt enim aliud quam ipsae naturae et essentiae rerum."

[91] For fuller support of this interpretation, see Marrone, *Truth and Scientific Knowledge*,
pp. 134–40. On the first point, about the unicity of absolute essence, see also above,
Pt. 3, ch. 11, n. 74; on the second, about exemplified essences and divine ideas,
the same chapter, n. 73. That Henry used the term "ideal reasons" (*incorporeae
rationes*) as quoted above, n. 90, to refer specifically to the ideas (that is, God's

Quodlibet 9, that in progressing from the initial stages of knowledge, whether at the level of the true or in the first approach to truth, to the final act of knowing "pure truth," mind did not so much change referents or multiply formal objects, bringing in a second exemplar separate from the abstracted exemplar of "phantastic" cognition, as simply view the same item under different guise.[92] Beginning by perceiving essence as implicated externally in material things, it ended by considering the identical object as manifest in God's exemplary ideas, at which point it could fully judge the value of what it knew and thus attain knowledge of pure truth.[93]

By such a reading, the Augustinian notion of knowledge of truth could readily be seen as coincident with the Aristotelianizing epistemology and noetics of Henry's mature years. According to the latter, just as with the new reading of Augustine, coming to know truth meant not switching or multiplying objects but rather viewing the same object from a new perspective, specifically by penetrating beyond perception of the universal expressed concretely in the phantasm to rarer vision of the object as absolute essence alone. The process by which Henry had described Augustinian illumination in Quodlibet 9 might thus be thought of as another way of talking about knowledge of truth in more thoroughly Aristotelianizing terms. One could even combine both points of view to claim that mind, starting with apprehension of the object still limited by the phantasm, moved on to awareness of absolute essence, where it not only grasped the definition but, because absolute essence lay on the metaphysical plane where exemplar and exemplified were related, also in some way

"rationes cognoscendi") and not simply to the exemplified essences is clear from *Quodlibet* 9, q. 2 (Henrici Opera, 13:36–37, ll. 78–06); and *Summa*, a. 68, q. 5 (2:231rV).

[92] On the notion of two exemplars in his early view of truth, and the most extreme interpretation of it, whereby mind would compare the two as if they were two formal objects, see above, Pt. 3, ch. 9, nn. 52 and 104.

[93] Note especially Henry's language in *Quodlibet* 9, q. 15 (Henrici Opera, 13:264, ll. 80–91): "... tunc in illa luce et per hoc in illa aeterna veritate ex qua facta sunt omnia, mente conspicimus ... formas secundum quas habent esse illa de quibus imaginarium habemus intellectum, et secundum illas, ut secundum se conspicimus eas, iudicamus de *eisdem* ut habent esse in materia, et per hoc habemus de eis veracem notitiam. ... Et sic per formas quae sunt essentiae rerum, ut secundum se conspiciuntur illustratione lucis increatae, cognoscuntur vera notitia *ipsae eaedem* formae ut habent esse in materia, quae conspiciuntur in phantasmatibus illustratione lucis creatae quae est intellectus agentis. ..." (I have added emphases to call attention to the essential identity of object at all levels of cognition.) See also the same question, p. 265, ll. 1–4.

gained access to God. Since on this plane God's ideas stood as guar-
antors of a thing's truth, it was not farfetched to suggest that at this
conceptual level God's ideas were actually illuminating mind.[94]
Augustinian reliance on God as revealer of truth had simply become
immanent in an epistemic process that on the surface remained pre-
dominantly Aristotelian. It might require another step for this fact
to be brought to consciousness, but that was from Henry's perspective of little concern.[95]

These precious indications of a novel reading of Augustine stand
as eloquent testimony to the fact that, although much of Henry's
language in question 15, Quodlibet 9, reproduces what he said about
knowledge of pure truth early on, he was no longer thinking along
exactly the same lines, hoping now instead to steer clear of too literal a reliance on the illuminist image of much of Augustinian tradition. As if to make the point clear, for the first time he explicitly
called God an agent intellect for mind, working alongside the agent
properly part of the soul in the effort to know truth.[96] Although he
thereby incidentally reaffirmed terminology preferred by Pecham but
generally avoided by the rest of the classic Augustinians, on which
score he was faithfully seconded by Vital, his intention was plainly
that God be thought of as agent in a peculiar fashion, precisely
suited to his mature vision of knowledge of truth.[97] Drawing upon

---

[94] All this is implied in the suggestive language of *Quodlibet* 9, q. 15 (Henrici Opera, 13:265, ll. 4–7): "Propter quod dicit Augustinus . . . quod res per oculos nun- tiata imaginarium facit conceptum, sed mente aliud conspicio, licet non sit aliud re, licet differat intellectus agens qui Deus est, et qui est potentia animae rationalis. . . ."

[95] From a modern perspective, this might seem philosophically irresponsible. See the remarks in Marrone, *Truth and Scientific Knowledge*, p. 137, n. 122.

[96] Henry, *Quodlibet* 9, q. 15 (Henrici Opera, 13:264–65, ll. 92–00); and also the passage quoted above, n. 94. Macken, in "La théorie," pp. 92–93, discusses this as a salient aspect of Henry's later noetics, although I hesitate to make quite as much of it – see *Truth and Scientific Cognition*, pp. 98–99. Henry's characterization of God as agent intellect lies at the heart of what many historians identify as the "Avicennian Augustinianism" of his thought – see Prezioso, *La critica di Duns Scoto*, p. 62; Macken, "La théorie," pp. 92–93; and Pegis throughout his three perceptive articles, "Towards a New Way to God: Henry of Ghent," MS 30 (1968): 226–47; "A New Way to God: Henry of Ghent (II)," pp. 93–116; and "Henry of Ghent and the New Way to God (III)," pp. 158–79.

[97] On Pecham, see above, Pt. 2, ch. 6, nn. 100 and 104. Matthew of Aquasparta adopted the same language, but less enthusiastically – see Pt. 2, ch. 6, n. 106. For Vital's position, see *Quaestiones de cognitione*, q. 8 (ed. Delorme, "Huit questions," p. 329). From the middle of p. 328 to the middle of p. 329 of that question, Vital simply copied the collage of Augustinian texts presented in Henry's *Quodlibet* 9, q. 15 (Henrici Opera, 13:263–64), inserting additional comments about the two agents

an option already present in his earliest work, he insisted that the
divine agent acted not so much like light, which more befitted the
agent that was part of mind, as like art.[98] Regardless of how he had
conceived of "art" at the beginning of the *Summa*, here it surely
served to indicate a repository of ideas objectively available to mind
at the apex of its ascent to truth. According to this vision God
entered into the cognitive process less as authentic actor – for it was
mind itself that was active in the business of abstraction and definition –
than as a kind of ultimate, ideal epistemic ground.[99]

There is, however, still more to Henry's vision of mind's natural
capacity for divinely grounded understanding from the maturity of
his career. Once again taking Augustine as guide for the notion of
hidden knowledge, he explained in Quodlibet 9 that the workings
of God on mind entailed in the epistemic processes paradigmatically
associated with illumination left behind an impression that could provide the vehicle for cognition of divinity.[100] Such language is highly
reminiscent of Bonaventure's conviction that God as revealer of truth
supplied mind with an innate species or "effectus" through which
he, himself, was naturally known, and contrasts with Henry's more

---

summarizing Henry's views expressed in the same work (p. 264). Significantly, he
completely excised the indications of the ultimate identity of all essence in the passage from Henry quoted above, n. 93.

It is interesting to note that in *Quaestiones de cognitione*, q. 8 (ed. Delorme, "Huit
questions," p. 317), Vital presented Roger Marston's views on how God and a part
of the soul were both agent intellects – see Marston, *Quaestiones de anima*, q. 3 (in
BFS, 7:259) – only to reject (p. 321) this way of seeing the two agents, which made
the agent part of the soul an imperfect noetic actor. His rejection relied on an
argument Henry had advanced in *Quodlibet* 13, q. 8 (Henrici Opera, 18:53, ll. 9–11),
namely that mind was an image of God only insofar as its powers were considered
in act.

[98] Henry, *Quodlibet* 9, q. 15 (Henrici Opera, 13:265, ll. 7–10): "Agens enim qui
Deus est, agit sicut ars quae ponit formam in materia artificii; agens vero qui est
potentia animae, agit sicut lumen circa phantasmata. . . ." On Henry characterizing God as "art" in his earliest work, see above, Pt. 3, ch. 9, nn. 108, 111 and
113–14; for other indications of the inclination to separate the language of light
specifically from discussion of truth-perception, see Pt. 3, ch. 10, pp. 327–28. In
Quodlibet 13, q. 8 (Henrici Opera, 18:53, ll. 3–6), he would appear to contradict
the implication in Quodlibet 9 that God as agent did not act as intelligible light.

[99] Pecham's comments on God as agent can conceivably be read as approaching
the interpretation given here for Henry, especially the passage cited above, Pt. 2,
ch. 6, n. 105.

[100] Henry, *Quodlibet* 9, q. 15 (Henrici Opera, 13:265–66, ll. 23–34), which incor-
porates Augustine's own language from *De Trinitate* XIV, 15 (eds. Mountain and
Glorie, 2, 451).

typical, and early established, reservations about such views.[101] Similar indication that ideas not unrelated to Bonaventure's position on innate knowledge of God and other higher realities appealed to the later Henry emerges in brief remarks in question 12 of Quodlibet 8. There he used the term "hidden knowledge" to refer to innate cognitive habits (*habitus innati*) leading to knowledge of both divinity and universal objects present in all minds though not readily available once intellect had become enmeshed in phantasms after the Fall.[102] Clearly, the notion of God as mental object was coming to the fore in Henry's final thoughts about divinity's role in normal cognition of truth.

Indeed it appears he considered the traces God's activity left in mind to be not only markers providing a minimal natural knowledge of divinity but also the basis for a dynamic sweeping soul upwards, ultimately into a mystical vision. He noted that souls received these impressions or "descriptions" to greater or lesser degree according to their purity – that is, their freedom from material distractions – in the very fashion some pagan philosophers held minds to obtain greater or lesser illumination from higher intelligences according to intensity of intellectual disposition.[103] There was apparently a ladder of cognitive levels founded on God's hidden action on mind, viewed unambiguously now as leaving an impression, each higher level revealing divinity with greater clarity and all of them apportioned with an eye to the subject's intellectual cleanliness. At its top rung the ladder touched on the supernatural and even prophetic vision of divine things.[104]

In the full blush of his career, therefore, Henry was prepared to attach to a theory of knowledge most readily expressed in Aristotelianizing terms, a dynamic depiction of mind's orientation to God harking back to the rhetorical flights of Bonaventuran mysticism.

---

[101] For Bonaventure, see above, Pt. 2, ch. 8, nn. 41–47; on Henry's reservations, see the discussion above at Pt. 3, ch. 10, nn. 101–3, as well as n. 102 just below.

[102] Henry, *Quod.* 8, q. 12 (2:324vC). He advanced this idea despite early protestations against any notion of innate knowledge in human mind – see *Summa*, a. 1, q. 5 (1:15rB); and 1, q. 11 (1:21rC); as well as above, Pt. 3, ch. 10, nn. 17 and 116.

[103] Henry, *Quodlibet* 9, q. 15 (Henrici Opera, 13:266, ll. 33–44).

[104] Henry, *Quodlibet* 9, q. 15, ad arg. (Henrici Opera, 13:269, ll. 21–25): ". . . actus abdit[i] quos ponit Augustinus . . . in veritate ponendi sunt: in ipsis enim consistit perfectio cognitionis contemplantium modo naturae, et in ipsis fundatur perfectio contemplantium modo supernaturali secundum tertium genus visionis intellectualis eorum quae futura sunt modo prophetico. . . ."

Knowledge of truth, for all its worldly complexion, was also touch-
stone for the contemplative way, a matter more often alien to Henry's
scholarly concerns.[105] The same mature intuitions about the deep
structure of cognition also reached back to William of Auvergne and
the notion that knowledge of truth was initial testimony to the impetus of mind into the life beyond. Directed to truths in this world,
intellect started out on a path culminating in the vision of the absolute
and completely fulfilling truth, God himself.[106] It is ironic that at the
time of his greatest efforts at Aristotelianizing philosophy Henry felt
uncharacteristically free to tap into the most traditional elements of
the heritage associated with an Augustinian cast of mind.

---

[105] Bérubé has remarked on the almost Bonaventure-like dynamism of Henry's
mature vision – see especially his "Dynamisme psychologique," p. 12; and "De l'être
à Dieu chez Jean Duns Scot," in *Regnum hominis et Regnum Dei*, ed. Camille Bérubé,
I: 48, Acta Quarti Congressus Scotistici Internationalis (Rome, 1978). What is suggested here is in part what Bérubé had in mind, although not so fully, or authentically Bonaventuran, as he intended. On Henry's more typical reluctance to insinuate
the mystical path into his theory of knowledge, see above, Pt. 3, ch. 10, p. 330.

[106] On William, see above, Pt. 1, ch. 4, nn. 23–27. In *Quod*. 3, q. 1 (1:48r–v[V]),
Henry, like William, defended the notion of God as ultimate, beatifying object of
intellect by pointing to divinity as pure truth and thus naturally involved, by means
of illumination, in all true knowledge. In his *Quodlibet* 2, q. 1 (ed. Delorme, pp.
43–44), Vital inverted the argument: since mind was directed to God as to infinite
truth, so it was naturally capable of knowing all other, particular truths.

PART FOUR

THE NEW DISPENSATION 1290–1310
WILLIAM OF WARE AND JOHN DUNS SCOTUS

INTRODUCTION TO PART FOUR

If the classic Augustinianism of Bonaventure, Pecham and Matthew of Aquasparta had proven inherently unstable, the reforms introduced by Henry of Ghent were, for all their brilliance, subject to even more rapid decay. Henry's dramatic turn away from the search for a unified epistemology and noetics grounded in the image of divine illumination had singlehandedly reoriented thirteenth-century Augustinianism, opening a new chapter in the history of high medieval thought, and even contemporaries appreciated the significance of the achievement. Already in the last ten years of his life, and for several decades thereafter, his writings were the focus of extraordinary attention. Yet aside from a few supporters like Vital du Four and Richard of Conington, almost all who turned to Henry's work did so to criticize.

Attacks came from every direction, most readily to be sure from the ranks of those attracted to Thomistic Aristotelianism, but it was from fellow Augustinians that the most penetrating, and historically most fruitful, critique arose.[1] Already in Henry's day prominent Franciscan intellectuals had begun to question the wisdom of an epistemology relying on the notion of special illumination from God to explain the normative process of ascertaining truth, raising calls for rejection of this fundamental tenet of classic Augustinianism and Henry's early philosophy of knowledge as well. Peter Olivi throughout the 1280s, and towards the end of the decade or the beginning of the next his disciple, Peter of Trabes, launched a radical inquiry into cherished ideals of both Aristotelianizing and Neoplatonizing currents, one arm of which was insistence that the odor of ontologism attaching to the classic doctrine of divine illumination was an inevitable, intolerable concomitant of any such view.[2] From an entirely

---

[1] Among critics sympathetic to Thomas the most prominent were Godfrey of Fontaines and Giles of Rome. On their attitude towards Henry see, for a start, John Wippel, *The Metaphysical Thought of Godfrey of Fontaines*; and Robert Wielockx's "Commentaire" to Giles of Rome, *Apologia*.

[2] Camille Bérubé has had much to say about Olivi's critique of illuminationist theories – see Bérubé, "Jean Duns Scot: Critique de l'"avicennisme augustinisant,'" in *De doctrina Ioannis Duns Scoti*, I, 207–43, Acta Congressus Scotistici Internationalis, Oxford and Edinburgh, 11–17 September 1966 (Rome, 1968), esp. pp. 210 and

different perspective, uncharacteristically receptive to Thomistic positions on noetics and epistemology, Richard of Mediavilla revealed
similar reservations about traditional Augustinian ideas of a normative illumination from God.[3] The French master Raymond Rigaud
was yet another Franciscan calling for reconsideration of the classic
illuminationist position.[4]

But of course Henry's own enthusiasm for literal illumination of
mind by God in normal cognition had waned by the end of his
career. He thus shared in the increased scepticism about a natural
illumination leading to truth, his own mature ideas serving as a contributing if largely unrecognized factor in the eventual rejection of
classic illuminationism within Augustinian ranks and in particular the
Franciscan Order.[5] Far from countering the theoretical advances over
classic Augustinianism Henry put forth, the critics of illumination
should therefore more correctly be seen as accelerating the thrust of

240; "Henri de Gand et Mathieu d'Aquasparta," p. 170; and "Olivi, critique de
Bonaventure et d'Henri de Gand," pp. 57–58. Still the best general exposition of
Olivi's thought is Efrem Bettoni, *Le dottrine filosofiche di Pier di Giovanni Olivi* (Milan,
1959). For references about dating the primary work where Olivi confronts issues
of epistemology, his *Questions on the Sentences*, to the late 1280s, see David Burr, *The
Persecution of Peter Olivi*, Transactions of the American Philosophical Society, N.S. 66,
5 (Philadelphia, 1976), pp. 6a and 11a.

Long ago, Martin Grabmann, in *Der göttliche Grund menschlicher Wahrheitserkenntnis*,
pp. 41–43, noted Peter of Trabes's refusal to support the classic illuminationist doctrine. Friedrich Stegmüller, *Repertorium commentariorum in Sententias Petri Lombardi*
(Würzburg, 1947), 1, 339 (entry 696), dated Peter's *Commentary on the Sentences* to
more or less the same period as Olivi's. On Peter's rejection of the doctrine of
divine illumination (and Richard of Mediavilla's, as well, referred to in the next
note), see Patrick Doyle's excellent study, "The Distintegration of Divine Illumination
Theory in the Franciscan School, 1285–1300."

[3] Edgar Hocedez, *Richard de Middleton. Sa vie, ses oeuvres, sa doctrine* (Leuven, 1925),
pp. 152–54, observed that Richard cast doubt on the doctrine of illumination, a
fact widely appreciated in more recent literature. Hocedez dated Richard's *Sentences
Commentary* to around 1284, his quodlibetal disputations to 1284–87, which latter
dates Palémon Glorieux, "Maîtres franciscains régents à Paris. Mise au point,"
RTAM 18 (1951): 329, assigned to Richard's regency in theology at Paris.

[4] Ferdinand Delorme, "Quodlibets et questions disputées de Raymond Rigaut,
maître franciscain de Paris, d'après le Ms. 98 de la Bibl. Comm. de Todi," in *Aus
der Geisteswelt des Mittelalters. Studien und Texte Martin Grabmann . . . gewidmet*, ed. Albert
Lang et al., 2:826, Beiträge, Supplementband 3,2 (Münster, 1935); and Palémon
Glorieux, "Autour de Raymond Rigauld, O.F.M., et de ses Quodlibets," AFH 31
(1938): 532–33, concluded that the quodlibets generally attributed to Rigaud date
from 1287 to 1293. Glorieux, "Maîtres franciscains régents à Paris. Mise au point,"
p. 332, placed Rigaud's Parisian regency in theology in the years 1287–89. My
knowledge of Rigaud's positions derives from a reading of manuscript sources.

[5] See my comments in "Henry of Ghent and Duns Scotus on the Knowledge
of Being," p. 40; and the general analysis given above, Pt. 3, ch. 12.

change initiated by him. By the 1290s a new orthodoxy had been established. Franciscans almost without exception repudiated literal illumination of mind by divine light as given in the classical position of the 1260s and 1270s.[6]

All of which means that to progress beyond Henry's achievements to a further stage of development, Augustinians would have not just to criticize literal illumination but also respond to the more profound innovation he had introduced into the classic doctrine from his very earliest works, the separation between God's role as normative means in knowledge of truth and as natural and primitive object of mind in general cognition of being. And the scholastics who passed this milestone in the evolution of thirteenth-century Augustinianism, thereby completing the disengagement from the vision of Bonaventure and his followers, were not the critics of the late 1280s but rather those whose work began just as Henry was leaving the scene. As in the generation before the great secular master rose to prominence, the pertinent developments occurred here exclusively among Franciscans, making them once more sole bearers of the high-medieval Augustinian voice.

The two protagonists who figure most prominently in this fourth, and for the present study final, stage in the transformation of Augustinian epistemology and noetics are William of Ware and John Duns Scotus. They sit nicely together not only because their works display so many parallel lines of thought but also since there is reason to believe that William was, if not actually Duns's teacher, at least a formative influence on him during his years of theological study at Oxford.[7] In line with the new orthodoxy, but now more

---

[6] The most renowned exception was master Gonsalvus of Spain, often taken to be one of Duns Scotus's teachers (see André Callebaut, "Le B. Jean Duns Scot étudiant à Paris vers 1293–96," AFH 17 [1924]: 3–12) but most probably on the basis of a misreading of the evidence, as C.K. Brampton argues convincingly in "Duns Scotus at Oxford, 1288–1301," FrS 24 (1964): 6–8. Glorieux, "Maîtres franciscains régents à Paris. Mise au point," p. 332, assigned Gonsalvus's regency at Paris to 1301–3, making it likely he commented on the *Sentences* at the very end of the thirteenth century. On his theory of knowledge, see Benoît Martel, *La psychologie de Gonsalve d'Espagne* (Montreal, 1968).

[7] The number of fourteenth-century testimonies found for the assertion that Ware was Duns's teacher has been continually augmented by research in this century, but none of them furnishes conclusive proof. See Hubert Klug, "Zur Biographie der Minderbrüder Johannes Duns Skotus und Wilhelm von Ware," FS 2 (1915): 377–85; Augustinus Daniels, "Zu den Beziehungen zwischen Wilhelm von Ware und Johannes Duns Skotus," FS 4 (1917): 222; Franz Pelster, "Handschriftliches zu

explicitly than ever, William and Duns repudiated any literal notion of divine illumination in normal processes of the wayfarer's thought, including even a minimally Augustinian normative intervention for knowledge of truth. In its place emerged an aggressively Aristotelianizing worldliness and a willingness to speculate on epistemic standards linking mind ever more indissolubly to the created world of here and now. To compensate for the loss, both elaborated on the insights of Henry as well as classic Augustinians concerning the connection between knowing "being" and knowing God, thus maintaining a positive and fully natural way for intellect to grasp divinity in this life. But here, too, a characteristic readiness to run the risk of philosophical innovation led to doctrinal maneuvers unlike those of either Augustinians or Aristotelianizers in earlier years, making at least Duns's ideas on "being" not only controversial and influential in his time but also a landmark for historians of medieval thought.

With their determination to go Henry of Ghent one better in shattering the unity Augustinian epistemology and noetics had achieved under Bonaventure and his followers, William and Duns thus complete the circle of our story, in some way returning the language of divine illumination to the ambiguous status it possessed in the 1220s

---

Skotus mit neuen Angaben über sein Leben," FS 10 (1923): 2–4; Andrew G. Little, "The Franciscan School at Oxford in the Thirteenth Century," AFH 19 (1926): 867; Heinrich Spettmann, "Die philosophiegeschichtliche Stellung des Wilhelm von Ware," *Philosophisches Jahrbuch der Görres-Gesellschaft* 40 (1927): 404–5; Ephrem Longpré, "Le Commentaire sur les Sentences de Guillaume de Nottingham," AFH 22 (1929): 232–33; and Francisco de Guimaraens, "La doctrine des théologiens sur l'Immaculée Conception de 1250 à 1350," EF n.s. 10 (1953): 27. Josef Lechner, "Wilhelm v. Ware," in *Lexikon für Theologie und Kirche*, ed. Michael Buchberger, 2nd ed., 10:910 (Freiburg im Br., 1938); and "Die mehrfachen Fassungen des Sentenzenkommentars des Wilhelm von Ware O.F.M.," FS 31 (1949): 16–17; and Pelster, "Handschriftliches zu Skotus," pp. 2–4, preferred to leave the question open, but most scholars have leaned towards taking the assertion as true – for instance, Ephrem Longpré, "Guillaume de Ware O.F.M.," *La France Franciscaine* 5 (1922): 75–76; and "Le Commentaire," p. 232; Pierre Muscat, "Guillelmi de Ware quaestio inedita de unitate Dei," *Antonianum* 2 (1927): 336; Charles Balić, "Quelques précisions fournies par la tradition manuscrite sur la vie, les oeuvres et l'attitude doctrinale de Jean Duns Scot," *Revue d'Histoire Ecclésiastique* 22 (1926): 551–66; and Athanasius Ledoux, "De gratia creata et increata iuxta quaestionem ineditam Guillelmi de Ware," *Antonianum* 5 (1930): 137–56. Given the unanimous if not unassailable testimonial evidence from the fourteenth century and the striking parallels between William's and Duns's thought, the latter seems to be the wisest course. As both Guimaraens, "La doctrine des théologiens," p. 28; and Charles Balić, "The Life and Works of John Duns Scotus," in *John Duns Scotus, 1265–1965*, ed. John K. Ryan and Bernardine M. Bonansea (Washington, D.C., 1965), pp. 10–11, suggest, the most likely scenario is that Duns audited William's bachelor lectures on the *Sentences* at Oxford in the early 1290s.

and 1230s. Theirs was, however, no historical retreat but rather an ambitious step forward, for they revisited the issues raised by William of Auvergne and Robert Grosseteste with the seasoned eye of experienced campaigners who had witnessed the heroic attempts at an Augustinian synthesis and were now equipped to offer a more subtle resolution. The radicalism of their ideas permitted them – Duns in particular – to surpass any of their predecessors in seizing the cognitive dynamism at the heart of the traditions of divine illumination and giving it a place, even domesticating it, in the matter-of-fact, almost pedestrian world of Aristotelianizing epistemology. They bring to culmination thirteenth-century efforts to preserve the uniqueness of the Augustinian heritage, in particular its vibrant sense of intellect's intimacy with God, in an academic arena where specificity and concreteness as well as systematic coherence weighed heavily. Among Augustinians, they represented the philosophical future.

William was probably the elder of the two. Born in Hertfordshire, England, sometime early in the second half of the thirteenth century, he entered the Franciscan Order while a youth, but little more is known of his life. It is certain that he studied at Oxford, nearly so that he lectured there on the *Sentences* as a bachelor in the early 1290s, and some have said he also taught as master of theology at Paris, although that is largely a matter of conjecture.[8] His only work to survive is a collection of *Quaestiones super quatuor libros Sententiarum*,

---

[8] On William's biography, see Klug, "Zur biographie der Minderbrüder"; Longpré, "Guillaume de Ware O.F.M.," pp. 74–77; Little, "Franciscan School at Oxford," pp. 866–67; Spettmann, "Die philosophiegeschichtliche Stellung"; Gedeon Gál, "Gulielmi de Ware, O.F.M. Doctrina philosophica per summa capita proposita," FrS 14 (1954): 155–56; and Aquilinus Emmen, "Wilhelm v. Ware," in *Lexikon für Theologie und Kirche*, ed. Josef Höfer and Karl Rahner, 2nd ed. fully revised, 10:1154–56 (Freiburg im Br., 1965). Ledoux, "De gratia creata et increata," made the now unlikely suggestion that William lectured at Oxford and Duns attended his lectures as late as 1300–1302. Palémon Glorieux, "D'Alexandre de Halès à Pierre Auriol. La suite des maîtres franciscains de Paris au XIIIe siècle," AFH 26 (1933): 277; and "Maîtres franciscains régents à Paris. Mise au point," pp. 325 and 332, assumed that William was master of theology at Paris, and in the latter work proposed 1296–99 as tentative dates for his regency, but as Guimaraens ("La doctrine des théologiens," pp. 25–26) reminds us, there is no proof he taught there. Franz Pelster, "Die Kommentare zum vierten Buch der Sentenzen von Wilhelm von Ware, zum ersten Buch von einem Unbekannten und von Martin von Alnwick im Cod. 501 Troyes," *Scholastik* 27 (1952): 347, n. 8, is on firmer ground in concluding that it is unlikely William was ever master at Paris or regent, indeed, at any university. Elia Magrini, "La produzione letteraria di Guglielmo di Ware," *Miscellanea Francescana* 36 (1936): 312–32; 38 (1938): 411–29, is unreliable.

based at least originally on lectures delivered at Oxford and for
which there are probably three redactions, only scattered excerpts
of which have been published, none in a critical edition.[9] Given the
indeterminateness of both text and biography, it is safest to assume
that what remains of William's teaching dates from the early or mid-
1290s, with the likelihood that some manuscript versions present revisions or reconsiderations from slightly later on.[10]

More evidence exists about the life and works of Duns Scotus, so
that although here, too, there is uncertainty, it is at least possible to
construct a plausible chronology of events.[11] He was born in Scotland,

---

[9] In addition to the references given above, n. 8, see also Josef Lechner, "Beiträge
zum mittelalterlichen Franziskanerschrifttum, vornehmlich der Oxforder Schule des
13./14. Jahrhunderts, auf Grund einer Florentiner Wilhelm von Ware-Hs." FS 19
(1932): 99–127. In "Wilhelm von Ware" (1938), col. 910, Lechner suggested that
there were at least two redactions of the work, along with various *reportationes*, while
by "Die mehrfachen Fassungen" (1949), pp. 28–30, he had decided that the authentic work existed in at least three versions.

[10] Numerous manuscripts purport to contain the whole of William's collected
Quaestiones, but in addition to textual variations among the three versions the manuscripts also show differences in the order and even number of questions included.
Augustinus Daniels, "Zu den Beziehungen," pp. 230–38, offered what he thought
was a complete listing, numbering 230 questions in all, and though his list should
not be taken as exhaustive or authoritative, expediency requires using his numera-
tion in referring to William's questions no matter how they are ordered or identified
in the specific manuscript or edited version cited. Thus, questions 14 and 21 in the
Daniels list have been edited by Daniels himself in *Quellenbeiträge und Untersuchungen
zur Geschichte der Gottesbeweise im dreizehnten Jahrhundert*, 89–104, Beiträge, 8, 1–2 (Münster,
1909); question 15 by Muscat in "Guillelmi de Ware quaestio inedita," pp. 344–50;
question 19 by Daniels in "Wilhelm von Ware über das menschliche Erkennen,"
in *Festgabe zum 60. Geburtstag Clemens Baeumker*, 311–18, Beiträge, Supplementband 1
(Münster, 1913); and question 85 among others by Michael Schmaus in *Der Liber
propugnatorius des Thomas Anglicus und die Lehrunterschiede zwischen Thomas von Aquin und
Duns Scotus. II: Die Trinitarischen Lehrdifferenzen*, 234*–85*, Beiträge, 29 (Münster, 1930).
Excerpts of other questions (of special interest here, questions 20 and 45) appear
in Gal, "Guilielmi de Ware, O.F.M. doctrina philosophica"; while further excerpts
(notably of questions 45, 46, 101 and 129) are given in Doyle, "The Disintegration
of Divine Illumination Theory." At times these excerpts will be cited below. All
other citations of William's work will be made to transcriptions I have taken from
MS Bibl. Vat., Chigi. B. VIII. 135, with occasional reference to the slightly different
version offered in MS Vat., Chigi. B. VII. 114. A German translation of question
129 in Daniels's list is given in Hieronymus Spettmann, ed. and trans., *Die Erkenntnislehre
der mittelalterlichen Franziskanerschulen von Bonaventura bis Skotus*, 80–85 (Paderborn, 1925),
but the text is so condensed that it offers nothing over the transcriptions I have
made of the same question and the excerpts given in Doyle.

[11] The following account of Duns's life is based on conclusions presented in three
recent works: C.K. Brampton, "Duns Scotus at Oxford" (1964); Charles Balić, "The
Life and Works of John Duns Scotus" (1965); and Allan B. Wolter, "Duns Scotus
on Intuition, Memory and Our Knowledge of Individuals," in *History of Philosophy*

probably in the mid-1260s, received into the Franciscan Order at an early age, and sent to study theology at Oxford perhaps in the fall of 1288. Here he likely came under the influence of William of Ware, possibly attending Ware's bachelor lectures on the *Sentences*.[12] It is probable that he offered his own lectures on the *Sentences* as *baccalaureus theologiae* during the academic year, 1298–99, spending the next year reworking them for potential publication. This revision of his notes for the Oxford *Sentences* lectures has come down to us as the *Lectura oxoniensis*, probably the first theological opus from Duns's pen.[13]

In the year 1300–1301, Duns may have delivered bachelor lectures on the Bible, or, having finished his requisite bachelor lecturing, he may have disputed under various masters at Oxford as *baccalaureus formatus*. His whereabouts in 1301–2 are unknown, but it is not inconceivable that he taught at a Franciscan convent elsewhere in England. On the other hand, he may have gone to Paris.[14] Already he had begun what was to be his largest and most authoritative

---

in the Making. A Symposium of Essays to Honor Professor James D. Collins on his 65th Birthday, ed. Linus J. Thro, 83 (Washington, D.C., 1982). For further biographical references, consult these works and Felix Alluntis and Allan B. Wolter, "Introduction," in John Duns Scotus, *God and Creatures. The Quodlibetal Questions*, xvii–xxxiv (Princeton, 1975). The compendiary efforts of Efrem Bettoni, *Vent'anni di studi scotisti (1920–1940)* (Milan, 1943); and Maurice Grajewski, "Duns Scotus in the Light of Modern Research," *Proceedings of the American Catholic Philosophical Association* 18 (1942): 168–85, are now out of date.

[12] See above, n. 7.

[13] The *Lectura* covers only the first three of the four books of *Sentences*. Books I and II have been edited in the projected complete edition of Duns's works being published at the Vatican City (Opera Omnia, 16–19 [Vatican City, 1960–93]). Henceforth all citations to this work will be to Vatican, followed by volume, page and paragraph number. In "De Ordinatione I. Duns Scoti disquisitio historico-critica," in Duns Scotus, Opera Omnia, 1:160* (Vatican City, 1950), the editors note that Duns probably kept his own notes in quires from which he lectured, on the basis of which he compiled the more polished text called the *Lectura*. Luka Modrić, "Rapporto tra la 'Lectura' II e la 'Metaphysica' di G. Duns Scoto," *Antonianum* 62 (1987): 508; and the editors in "Prolegomena" to Duns Scotus, *Lectura* (Vatican, 17:13*), locate the *Lectura*'s composition between 1296 and 1302, but it would appear that a narrower range of dates (1298–1300) is even more likely.

[14] In an important pair of papers delivered originally in Rome in 1993, William Courtenay, "Scotus at Paris," in *Via Scoti. Methodologica ad mentem Joannis Duns Scoti*, ed. Leonardo Sileo, 1, 149–63, Atti del Congresso Scotistico Internazionale, Rome, 9–11 March 1993 (Rome, 1995); and Allan Wolter, "Duns Scotus at Oxford," in *Via Scoti*, ed. Sileo, 1, 183–92, debate the precise lines of Scotus's career from 1297 to 1302. In the end, Wolter keeps alive the supposition that Scotus lectured on the Bible, which Courtenay had cast into doubt, and Courtenay, while reinforcing the current consensus that Duns did not study in Paris before 1300, opens the possibility that he was resident there before 1302.

composition, the ordered collection of questions on the *Sentences* known by the name of *Ordinatio*, material for which was lifted primarily from the *Lectura* though Duns greatly reworked his original ideas and eventually drew also upon another set or sets of lectures he gave on the *Sentences* in Paris.[15] It has been established that he was laboring on the *Ordinatio*'s Prologue in the middle of 1300, that he had probably finished Book II before the fall of 1302, and that he was still engaged with Book IV in 1304 or later.[16] The work never received his finishing touches, so that even in its fullest redaction it is incomplete and occasionally ambiguous.[17]

In June 1302, the Franciscan General Chapter, recognizing the young theologian's extraordinary talent, assigned him to lecture on the *Sentences* in the order's studium at the University of Paris, a commission he fulfilled, still as bachelor, during the academic year, 1302–3.[18] He may not have been quite done when he was banished

---

[15] On the genesis of this work, see "Adnotationes," in Duns Scotus, *Ordinatio* (Vatican, 7:1* and 4*–6*). A critical edition of it has also been begun in the Opera Omnia published at the Vatican City, beginning with volume 1 in 1950. Henceforth references to this edition will be made, as with the *Lectura*, to Vatican, followed by volume, page and paragraph number. Those parts of the *Ordinatio* not yet available from the Vatican press will be cited from the edition by Luke Wadding, reissued in the collection of Duns's Opera Omnia published by Vivès at the end of the nineteenth century (volumes 8–21 [Paris, 1893–94]). References to this edition will be made to Vivès, followed by volume and page number. In "Duns Scotus on Intuition," pp. 98, n. 7, and 104, n. 64), Wolter reminds us that the version given by Vivès (most correctly referred to as *Opus oxoniense*) was probably written later than the authentic *Ordinatio* and does not always read the same, although the differences would seem to be greater for the first two books than for the third and fourth. Vladimir Richter, *Studien zum literarischen Werk von Johannes Duns Scotus* (Munich, 1988), attacked the authenticity of what is known as the *Ordinatio*, but the reply by Luka Modrić, "Osservazioni su una recente critica all'edizione Vaticana dell' *Opera omnia* di Giovanni Duns Scoto," *Antonianum* 58 (1983): 336–57, made on occasion of the original appearance of Richter's critique, speaks for the majority of scholars, who recognize the work as belonging to Duns.

[16] See Brampton, "Duns Scotus at Oxford," pp. 8–10; and Wolter, "Duns Scotus on Intuition," p. 104, n. 64.

[17] See "Disquisitio historico-critica," Duns Scotus, *Ordinatio* (Vatican, 1:172*–73*).

[18] Brampton, "Duns Scotus at Oxford," p. 8, argued persuasively that contrary to frequent assumption there is no reason to think Duns either studied or taught theology at Paris prior to 1302, but as Courtenay ("Scotus at Paris," p. 162) and Wolter ("Duns Scotus at Oxford," pp. 183 and 192), agree, all that can be said for certain now is that nothing indicates Scotus was at Paris before 1300. Although there exist manuscript references to his presence sometime at the University of Cambridge, Brampton believes (p. 18) that there is no compelling indication he lectured on the *Sentences* there. Still, Alluntis and Wolter, in "Introduction" to *God and Creatures*, p. xxii, suggest that he may have given *Sentences* lectures at Cambridge in

from France along with other Franciscans in June of 1303 for refusing to side with King Philip IV in his dispute with Boniface VIII. Tensions subsided in less than a year, and by May 1304 Duns was back in Paris, perhaps completing the series of lectures interrupted the previous spring. It is even possible that in 1304–5 he undertook a course of lectures on the *Sentences* at Paris for a second time.[19] The record of all such lecturing is extant only in the form of student notes collectively referred to as the *Reportatio parisiensis*, for which there are numerous versions, one, known as the *Reportatio examinata* or *magna*, almost surely examined and corrected by the lecturer himself and thus carrying greater authority than the rest.[20]

Gonsalvus of Spain, acting in his capacity as General Minister of the order, wrote the Parisian Franciscans in the fall of 1304 urging them to persuade the chancellor to grant Duns the license to teach. The latter incepted as master of theology sometime in 1305, officiating as regent in the Franciscan studium at Paris during the academic year 1306–7. In that same year he held his only quodlibetal disputation, the written revision of which was never quite finished and stands along with the final distinctions of the *Ordinatio* as his last theological production.[21] By fall of 1307 Duns had been transferred to the Franciscan studium at Cologne, where he served as principal lecturer until his death, traditionally assigned to November 8, 1308.

1303–4 when he was back in England from Paris. At present no firm conclusion can be drawn about Duns's connections to Cambridge.

[19] For the most recent conjectures on this second series of Parisian lectures, see Courtenay, "Scotus at Paris," pp. 160–62; and Wolter, "Duns Scotus at Oxford," pp. 190–91.

[20] The *Reportatio examinata* (generally referred to as Reportatio IA, IIA, IIIA and IVA) is almost entirely unedited. Reportatio IA, dist. 2, qq. 1–4, will be cited below according to the edition in Allan B. Wolter and Marilyn McCord Adams, "Duns Scotus' Parisian Proof for the Existence of God," FrS 42 (1982): 252–321. All other references to the *Reportatio parisiensis* will be to the version offered in the Vivès edition (vol. 22–24 [Paris, 1894]), cited below to Vivès, followed by volume and page. Book I in this edition actually gives the *Additiones magnae in I. Sententiarum*, and Book II the *Additiones in II. Sententiarum*, both reworkings of Scotus's Oxford and Parisian lectures compiled by William of Alnwick and not Duns himself – see "Disquisitio historico-critica," Duns, *Ordinatio* [Vatican, 1:39*–40* and 144*–49*]; and "Adnotationes," *Ordinatio* [Vatican, 7:4*]. Stephen D. Dumont, "Theology as a Science," p. 585, n. 25, notes however that for the prologue, the text given by Vivès is quite close to that of the examined version.

[21] The text of *Quaestiones quodlibetales* used here is the edition available in Vivès (vol. 25–26 [Paris, 1895]). References to this text will be to Vivès, followed by volume and page.

Besides the commentaries on the *Sentences* and the quodlibetal questions, Duns also delivered occasional independent lectures or *collationes* in question form throughout his theological career, the record of forty-six of which has been preserved, nineteen definitely issuing from his stay at Paris and at least some of the rest from Oxford.[22] Significant for this study are also commentaries on the logical works of Aristotle and Porphyry, all of which can reasonably be presumed to date from before Duns's years as student of theology.[23] There is finally the sprawling commentary on Aristotle's *Metaphysics*, the *Quaestiones super libros Metaphysicorum*.[24] Scholars diverge widely on the date of this work, but it is increasingly apparent that the surviving text is the product of several rewritings, its base either predating Duns's studies in theology or hailing from the early 1290s but some additions being inserted at least after the composition of the *Lectura*.[25] Even the most careful editing cannot render it fully consistent, and it was probably abandoned by Duns without a definitive polishing. Whatever the case, it is a fascinating work that must be considered in any examination of his thought.

[22] See Charles Balić, "De Collationibus Ioannis Duns Scoti doctoris subtilis ac mariani," *Bogoslovni Vestnik* 19 (1929): 185–219. The text of the *collationes* used here will be that given in Vivès (vol. 5 [Paris, 1892]), cited as Vivès, followed by volume and page. Those *collationes* not included in the Vivès edition will be cited either according to the text given in Charles R.S. Harris, *Duns Scotus*, 2:361–78 (Oxford, 1927); or that in Charles Balić, "De collationibus Ioannis Duns Scoti," pp. 201–12; occasionally by way of a combination of the two.

[23] When any of these works is used below, the reference will be to the editions given in Vivès (vol. 1–2 [Paris, 1891]), cited as Vivès, followed by volume number and page.

[24] This work will be cited according to the new edition, *Quaestiones super libros Metaphysicorum Aristotelis*, eds. R. Andrews et al., B. Ioannis Duns Scoti Opera Philosophica, 3–4 (St. Bonaventure, N.Y., 1997), reference made to Opera Phil. followed by volume, page and paragraph number. Only Books I–IX of Duns's authentic *Questions* are extant.

[25] On dating the *Questions on the Metaphysics*, see Timotheus Barth, "Zum Problem der Eindeutigkeit," *Philosophisches Jahrbuch* 55 (1942): 314–15; Odon Lottin, "L''Ordinatio' de Jean Duns Scot sur le livre III des Sentences," RTAM 20 (1953): 117; Balić, "The Life and Works of John Duns Scotus," pp. 21–22; Wolter, "Duns Scotus on Intuition," p. 83; Modrić, "Rapporto," pp. 507–8; Dumont, "Theology as a Science," p. 581, n. 7; Marrone, "The Notion of Univocity in Duns Scotus's Early Works," p. 391; and Giorgio Pini, "Duns Scotus's Metaphysics: The Critical Edition of his *Quaestiones super libros Metaphysicorum Aristotelis*," RTAM 65 (1998): 357–58 and 365–66.

CHAPTER THIRTEEN

REJECTION OF ILLUMINATION AND A WORLDLY THEORY OF KNOWLEDGE

Preoccupied with the fact that Duns Scotus turned away from Henry of Ghent's theory of illumination in normal knowledge of truth, modern scholarship has long taken this rejection as marking the fundamental shift in late thirteenth-century Augustinian epistemology and noetics.[1] Yet as shown above, not only was Duns – as well as William of Ware, with whom he is here paired – unoriginal on this score, serious questions about divine illumination having been floated among Franciscans already in Henry's lifetime, but Henry himself had actually taken significant steps in that direction. Indeed, the more is known about all three scholastics, the clearer it is how much the thought of William and Duns is derivative of Henry's just where it would appear to be most resolutely opposed, with Henry bequeathing his two successors the very problematic for many of the issues they addressed.[2] Even in the matter of knowing truth, where the contrast

---

[1] An exemplary account of Duns's rejection of divine illumination, emphasizing its break with earlier Augustinian thought, can be found in Bettoni, *Duns Scotus. The Basic Principles of his Philosophy*, trans. Bernardino M. Bonansea (Washington, D.C., 1961), esp. pp. 16–17, 43 and 46 (the preceding an English translation of *Duns Scoto* [Brescia, 1946]), but the classic statement appeared in Gilson's "Pourquoi saint Thomas a critiqué saint Augustin," p. 5.

[2] Hadrianus Borak, "Aspectus fundamentales platonismi in doctrina Duns Scoti," in *De doctrina Ioannis Duns Scoti*, I, 114, Acta Congressus Scotistici Internationalis, Oxford and Edinburgh, 11–17 September 1966 (Rome, 1968); and Anton Pegis, "Toward a New Way to God" (1968), p. 246, have made the latter point about Duns, while both Efrem Bettoni, *Duns Scotus*, p. 20; and Olivier Boulnois, intr., trans. and comm. for Jean Duns Scot, *Sur la connaissance de Dieu et l'univocité de l'étant* (Paris, 1988), pp. 30 (n. 51), 35 and 43, call attention to Duns's dependence on Henry, despite the changes he introduced. Although Paulus, in "Henri de Gand" (1935–36), pp. 103 and 135, said Duns Aristotelianized Henry's Platonism, by *Henri de Gand*, pp. 133–35, he admitted how much of at least the structure of Henry's Platonism remained in Scotus. Numerous scholars have noticed Henry's influence on William: see Hieronymus Spettmann, "Die philosophiegeschichtliche Stellung des Wilhelm von Ware," pp. 42–49; Pelster, "Die Kommentare zum vierten Buch"; Gál, "Doctrina philosophica," p. 291; and Doyle, "The Disintegration," pp. 363–65. In this light it is also worth noting Gál's assertion ("Doctrina philosophica," p. 291) that among all Franciscans of the late thirteenth century, William was closest to Scotus in content and structure of thought.

would seem to be unambiguous and profound, one must therefore
be careful not to draw too sharp a dividing line between Henry's
ideas and those of his successors.

Not surprisingly, William and Duns approached the problem of
truth with a recognition of the primacy of the division between simple and complex cognition, the Aristotelian commonplace accepted
even among thirteenth-century Augustinians as central in discussions
of epistemology. They openly acknowledged Aristotle as source for
the idea that truth had to do exclusively with complex knowledge,
Duns going on to make clear he agreed, holding in Aristotelian fashion that judgment alone, an option available to mind only in its
complex acts, lay at the heart of what it was to know truth.[3] Yet
both scholastics adopted this Aristotelian posture with a nod to the
decidedly un-Aristotelian application it had received immediately preceding them in Henry's distinction between the simple procedure of
knowing a "true" object and the semi-complex one of knowing an
object "as true," defining attribute of knowledge of "truth."[4]

In fact, William reminded his readers that Henry had corroborated his position by insisting that among the most basic concepts,
"being" came to mind before "true," making it only logical that
there be a stage of knowledge prior to consideration of truth or falsehood, which reminder Duns repeated at greater length.[5] Just as
important, both thinkers were aware that Henry had called the more

---

[3] William cited the *Metaphysics* as authority for the connection between truth and
complex cognition in his *Quaestiones*, q. 19 (ed. Daniels, in "Wilhelm von Ware,"
pp. 313–14). In *Quaestiones quodlibetales*, q. 14 (Vivès, 26:5a–b), Duns referred to book
3 of *De anima* for the distinction between simple and complex cognition, a reference previously made in *Quaestiones super libros Metaphysicorum* I, q. 4 (Opera Phil.,
3:99, n. 12), where he went on to tie complex cognition specifically to knowledge
of truth(Opera Phil., 3:99–100, n. 14). He pointed out the importance of judge-
ment in knowing truth in *Quaestiones super libros Metaphysicorum* I, q. 4 (Opera Phil.,
3:110, n. 47). For the authoritative Aristotelian texts, see above, Pt. 1, ch. 1, n. 2.

[4] On Henry's distinction, see above, Pt. 3, ch. 9, nn. 25, 27, 42–45, and 51.
William drew attention to this position in *Quaestiones*, q. 19 (ed. Daniels, in "Wilhelm
von Ware," p. 313); Duns laid out his understanding in *Lectura* I, d. 3, p. 1, q. 3
(Vatican, 16:299, n. 187); and *Ordinatio* I, d. 3, p. 1, q. 4 (Vatican, 3:157, n. 258).
It is interesting to note that William, and Duns in the *Lectura*, mentioned only one
level of knowledge of truth. By the *Ordinatio*, Duns, having apparently refined his
understanding of Henry, faithfully represented him as positing two levels at which
truth could be known. It may be that the early Duns saw Henry through William's
eyes, only later coming to appreciate him more in his own right.

[5] William, *Quaestiones*, q. 19 (ed. Daniels, in "Wilhelm von Ware," p. 314); and
Duns, *Lectura* I, d. 3, p. 1, q. 3 (Vatican, 16:283–84, n. 153); as well as *Ordinatio* I,
d. 3, p. 1, q. 4 (Vatican, 3:126–27, n. 208).

primitive of his two kinds of cognition "simple understanding" (*simplex intelligentia*), a term they were prepared at times to use the same way themselves.[6] Since for Henry the contrast between simple understanding and the composite mental act associated with knowing truth did not coincide with Aristotle's separation of simple from complex apprehension – knowledge of a term from knowledge of a proposition – it is suggestive, to say the least, to find the theme repeated in William and Duns.[7]

Of the two scholastics, only Duns characterized each of the contrasting operations precisely enough to reveal exactly what the distinction entailed for him. Scotus was familiar with all the definitions of truth current in thirteenth-century Augustinianism: Avicennian "adequation of object to intellect," "conformity of exemplar to exemplified" as seen in Grosseteste's work, and "mental rectitude" drawn from Anselm.[8] In one of his early logical commentaries, he carefully explained that, because something was true only insofar as it was accommodated to its proper measure, and since the measure here was intellect, truth arose by comparison to intellect or understanding.[9] But there were two types of intellect to consider: one exclusively measure of other things and the other just as often measured by something else. With regard to intellect that was always measure – God, himself – all things were true to the degree they imitated a divine idea, which was to say that they were true insofar as they

---

[6] See the passage from William's *Quaestiones*, q. 19, cited above, n. 3, for Duns, *Ordinatio* I, d. 3, p. 1, q. 4 (Vatican, 3:127, n. 208), possibly derivative of the aforementioned passage from William, and also *Ordinatio* I, d. 35, q. un. (Vatican, 6:247, n. 9). On the term in Henry, see above, Pt. 3, ch. 9, n. 41.

[7] Since Duns appreciated the nature of the authentic Aristotelian distinction, he sometimes employed the contrasting terms "simplex apprehensio" and "compositio terminorum" with it in mind – for instance, *Ordinatio* III, d. 23, q. un., n. 9 (Vivès, 15:15b); and *Quaestiones quodlibetales*, q. 6, n. 7 (Vivès, 25:243b). A fully Aristotelianizing exposition of the difference appears in Duns's *Quaestiones super libros Metaphysicorum* II, q. 1 (Opera Phil., 3:194, n. 4).

[8] Duns, *Collationes* 19, n. 1 (Vivès, 5:221a–b) for the former two; *Ordinatio* I, d. 3, p. 1, q. 3 (Vatican, 3:105, n. 170) for Anselm's rectitude. On the three definitions, consult above, Pt. 1, ch. 1, nn. 7 and 8.

[9] Duns, *In duos libros perihermenias quaestiones*, q. 3, n. 2 (Vivès, 1:588a). The same conclusion reappears in *Ordinatio* I, d. 3, p. 1, q. 3 (Vatican, 3:111, n. 183), where Duns added that "true" entailed a formal relation (*respectus*) to intellect. More precisely, he admitted that the measure of truth was an idea or formal nature residing in intellect, so that it was only in a secondary or mediated sense that "true" related object to intellect itself (see *In duos libros perihermenias*, q. 3, n. 3 (Vivès, 1:588a).

approximated the contours of their specific nature. With regard to
all other intellects – among them human mind – which might be the
measure of artifacts but, when it came to natural objects, were themselves to be measured, the accommodation pointed in the other direction. These intellects were said to be true by conformity to object
known.[10]

By the *Questions on the Metaphysics*, Duns had developed the idea
so far as to say there were two varieties of truth, one in things and
another in intellects.[11] His words call to mind Henry's mid-career
distinction between truth of a thing and truth of a sign, the latter
finding its most significant epistemological manifestation either in or
from intellect, and Duns admitted he was drawing upon other,
unnamed thinkers.[12] Turning initially to the first of the two varieties,
he explained that *things* were true either by comparison to a pro-
ducer or by comparison to a knowing subject.[13] So far as the former configuration was concerned, reproducing his earlier notion of
conformity between object and an intellect that was measure but not
measured, further division could be made into two sub-varieties. If
the conformity to the unmeasured measure, which was God, were
drawn in fullness (*adaequatio*), then there was only one true object,
Christ, the Son, but if standards were relaxed to imply just imitation (*imitatio*), then every created object was thereby true.[14] Plainly,
Duns accepted the universal scholastic attribution of objective truth
to all creation on grounds of the exemplarity of God. But like the
mature Henry before him, as epistemologist Duns quickly passed
over the truth binding things to God and looked instead to the comparison between thing and knowing subject, most especially human
mind. Here the truth in things led to a description of "true," already
familiar from the works of Henry, as capable of manifesting itself to
intellect or assimilating intellect to itself.[15]

---

[10] See again, *In duos libros perihermenias*, q. 3, n. 3 (Vivès, 1:588a).
[11] Duns, *Quaestiones super libros Metaphysicorum* VI, q. 3 (Opera Phil., 4:65, n. 22):
"Est enim veritas in rebus et veritas in intellectu."
[12] On Henry, see above, Pt. 3, ch. 12, nn. 6, 7 and 9; for Duns's admission of
dependence, *Quaestiones super libros Metaphysicorum* VI, q. 3 (Opera Phil., 4:60–61, nn.
13–14). Duns even used the terms "verum in re" and "verum in signo" to make
essentially Henry's point – see *Quaestiones super libros Metaphysicorum* VI, q. 3 (Opera
Phil., 4:72, nn. 44–45).
[13] *Quaestiones super libros Metaphysicorum* VI, q. 3 (Opera Phil., 4:65, n. 23).
[14] *Quaestiones super libros Metaphysicorum* VI, q. 3 (Opera Phil., 4:65–66, n. 25).
[15] Duns, *Quaestiones super libros Metaphysicorum* VI, q. 3 (Opera Phil., 4:66, n. 26);

Of course, the notion of manifestation pointed conspicuously to something arising in the knowing intellect, either as a quality resident in it or, more properly, as the objective presence of what was known in the knower.[16] Inexorably, therefore, consideration of the thing's truth gave way to consideration of truth in an intellect, where it was mind and not object that was measured, measured indeed by comparison to the object understood. And here Duns laid bare the precise dimensions of his dependence on Henry's division between knowing the true and knowing truth.

As he said, there were two ways there might be something "true" in intellect: either as intellect perceived a simple object, generating a single concept expressing its understanding, or as it united different concepts in an act of complex cognition.[17] In the first case, which pertained to all acts of simple cognition, most emphatically those yielding concepts that were absolutely simple (*simpliciter simplex*), truth followed understanding immediately and necessarily, for no matter what concept mind formed, that concept represented a referential content to which it could be said to correspond. The idea of white conformed to whiteness and was in that sense true, regardless of conditions in the external world.[18] On this matter Duns simply confirmed Henry's confidence in the building blocks of knowledge, adding that what competed with truth at the level of simple understanding was not falsehood but ignorance, the total absence of knowledge.[19] Yet such cognition – perception of what was true – was not tantamount to knowledge of truth, for like Henry, Duns conceded that at this primitive level of understanding intellect was not cognizant of the truth it contained.[20]

---

a description repeated in *Lectura* I, d. 3, p. 1, qq. 1–2 (Vatican, 16:274–75, n. 128); *Ordinatio* I, d. 3, p. 1, q. 3 (Vatican, 3:105, n. 169); and *Reportatio parisiensis* Prol., q. 1, n. 37 (Vivès, 22:26b). For Henry on truth as manifestive or declarative of itself, see his *Summa*, a. 34, q. 2 (1:211v[N & O]; and q. 4 (1:215vB); and Marrone, *Truth and Scientific Knowledge*, p. 51; as well as related formulations in the passage cited above, Pt. 3, ch. 9, n. 15.

[16] Duns *Quaestiones super libros Metaphysicorum* VI, q. 3 (Opera Phil., 4:66, n. 26), where, concerning the latter, he explained: ". . . facta manifestatione vel assimilatione, res est in intellectu, sicut cognitum in cognoscente."

[17] *Quaestiones super libros Metaphysicorum* VI, q. 3 (Opera Phil., 4:67–69, nn. 31–35).

[18] See n. 17, above, and also *Quaestiones super libros Metaphysicorum* I, q. 4 (Opera Phil., 3:112–13, n. 56).

[19] *Quaestiones super libros Metaphysicorum* VI, q. 3 (Opera Phil., 4:68, n. 32). On Henry, see above, Pt. 3, ch. 9, p. 273, especially n. 14, and pp. 275–76.

[20] Duns, *In duos libros perihermenias*, q. 3, n. 3 (Vivès, 1:588b): "Licet autem sensus dicatur verus, et intellectus similiter . . . tamen sensus secundum se non cognoscit conformitatem sui ad id, quod cognoscit. . . . Similiter est de intellectu simplici. . . ."

Knowledge of truth entered the picture only at the complex level, where the activity of compounding and dividing permitted mind to consider correspondence or conformity and judge whether its knowledge was true or not.[21] For complex cognition, therefore, the alternatives to truth were not just ignorance but also falsehood.[22] Influenced by Henry and his other predecessors in the Augustinian tradition, Duns did not invariably insist that the judgment in question entail an authentically Aristotelian assessment of a complex condition in the world, granting sometimes that it might consist in merely ascertaining whether a simple intellective content corresponded faithfully to a specific object outside.[23] Like Henry, he also held that the ability to deliver such judgment depended on mind's capacity to reflect back upon itself.[24] He even went so far as to make gestures towards Henry's idea of a mental word, claiming that only after intellect had reflected on its own knowledge could it be said that truth emerged not as merely a formally inhering quality (*formaliter*), as with simple understanding, but as something directing intellect to a separate objective content (*obiective*).[25]

Yet despite these signs of leanings in Henry's direction, more often Duns adhered strictly to Aristotle, declaring even in the *Questions on the Metaphysics* that the complex cognition through which mind attained knowledge of truth was precisely propositional.[26] On these occasions he countered the Augustinian contention that intellect ought to be

[21] The passage quoted above, n. 20, continues: ". . . sed intellectus componens cognoscit illam conformitatem sui ad rem" – a view which lay at the heart of Duns's Aristotelianizing statement: "Dicendum, quod verum et falsum sunt circa compositionem et divisionem intellectus tantum, sicut in cognoscente" (*In duos libros perihermenias*, q. 3, n. 2 (Vivès, 1:588a). See also *Quaestiones super libros Metaphysicorum* I, q. 4 (Opera Phil., 3:112–13, n. 56).

[22] *Quaestiones super libros Metaphysicorum* VI, q. 3 (Opera Phil., 4:69, n. 35).

[23] *In duos libros perihermenias*, q. 3, n. 3 (Vivès, 1:588b): "Non enim intellectus componit per hoc, quod dicit unam speciem intelligibilem esse aliam; sed per hoc, quod judicat ita esse in re, sicut intellectus conformatur rei."

[24] See the last passage from Scotus cited above, n. 3. On Henry and reflection, consult Pt. 3, ch. 12, nn. 13 and 14.

[25] *Quaestiones super libros Metaphysicorum* VI, q. 3 (Opera Phil., 4:69, n. 36), and the same question, p. 60, n. 13. The idea is related to Duns's description, plainly evocative of Henry, of object residing in mind as "the known in the knower," for example in the second passage just cited; the passage quoted in n. 16; *Quaestiones super libros Metaphysicorum* VII, q. 14 (Opera Phil., 4:289, n. 27); and *In duos libros perihermenias*, q. 3, n. 3 (Vivès, 1:588b). On Henry's notion of "word," see above, Pt. 3, ch. 9, nn. 58 and 59; and more importantly, Marrone, *Truth and Scientific Knowledge*, pp. 22–23 and 41–42.

[26] *Quaestiones super libros Metaphysicorum* VI, q. 3 (Opera Phil., 4:69, nn. 36–37).

just as able to judge conformity to objective conditions in the case of simple knowledge as propositional by insisting that such an argument overlooked an important difference between the two kinds of knowing. The authentic referent (*signatum*) of a simple concept was not, he contended, an external object but rather the cognitive content of the concept itself. There was therefore no separate measure against which to test a simple concept for truth or falsity. With propositional knowledge, on the other hand, the conjunction of terms exhibited in an assertion could be set against the evidence of the terms as they existed separately, which separation was naturally prior to their combination.[27] Judgment was therefore possible in complex cognition insofar as one took the measure of terms or logical entities as they existed at one stage of knowing and at another, and since judgment lay at the heart of knowing truth, at the complex level knowledge was at last capable of being either true nor false. Mind inquiring after truth did so, in short, by comparing a proposition to its separate terms, or rather to the mutual relationship habitually existent in each of them.[28]

This final claim not only cemented the bond to Aristotle but also effectively severed any necessary tie between knowledge of truth and conditions outside mind. Knowing truth, even if regarded solely as a matter of evaluating the validity of a proposition, depended less on checking a mental configuration against real composition or disjunction of external objects than on judging how well it represented the inherent properties of terms. Duns had dared, in short, to go further than any Augustinian since William of Auvergne towards eliminating the question of existential import and emphasizing the logical nature of truth.[29] His "terminism," moreover, should prepare

---

[27] Duns laid out the Augustinian argument in *Quaestiones super libros Metaphysicorum* VI, q. 3 (Opera Phil., 4:72–73, nn. 45 and 47), giving his answer in the same question, p. 73, n. 48. Note that this reading involves interpreting Duns in n. 47, contrary to what the editors of the new edition suggest, to be referring with "ad primum" to n. 45, with "quod praedictum est" to n. 36 (p. 69).

[28] *Quaestiones super libros Metaphysicorum* VI, q. 3 (Opera Phil., 4:74, n. 51): "Nota . . . quare complexum est verum. Quia complexionem, quae est a ratione, praecedit naturaliter identitas extremorum, vel alia habitudo virtualiter inclusa in ipsis, cui actum rationis conformari ut mensurae est ipsum verum esse." In the same question, pp. 81–82, n. 69, doubt is raised about this theory of truth dependent on a virtual habit, but rather than resolve the matter Duns simply invites his reader to investigate the question.

[29] On William of Auvergne, see above, Pt. 1, ch. 3, especially nn. 24 and 26; for Duns's attitude on existential import, his *In primum librum Perihermenias quaestiones*,

the reader for the subsequent repudiation, despite the undeniable echoes of Henry's ideas about true and truth, of his forebear's early reliance on divine illumination to account for the wayfarer's natural knowledge, the side of Duns's relation to Henry upon which modern scholarship has focused.

Although Duns's Franciscan predecessors had blazed the way for this rejection, even more profoundly influential was William of Ware. There can be no doubt that both William and Duns took Henry's ideas on illumination as a foil to their own views. In question 19, where he specifically addressed God's illuminative role in human cognition, William devoted his primary efforts to delineating the position of those (*alii*) who, having distinguished knowing the true from knowing truth, held that "pure truth" (*sincera veritas*) could be seen only in the divine light.[30] He presented three arguments deployed by the proponents of this theory to support it, the very three reasons Henry himself had highlighted in his classic exposition of special illumination in article 1 of the *Summa*, which text William most likely had before him as he wrote.[31] When Duns turned to theories of illumination in both the *Lectura* and the *Ordinatio*, he followed William's lead, taking stock of exactly the same passage from Henry's work.[32]

It is illustrative of the way Duns made use of William that his account of Henry's theory is on the whole sharper and more faithful to the original than is that of his teacher. Whether out of ignorance or by design, William simply overlooked the level of truth Henry

---

q. 8, n. 13 (Vivès, 1:555b). Matthew of Aquasparta had made a similar claim, only to insist that it was theologically deficient – see above, Pt. 2, ch. 7, nn. 38, 40–43.

[30] William, *Quaestiones*, q. 19 (ed. Daniels, in "Wilhelm von Ware," pp. 313–14).

[31] William, *Quaestiones*, q. 19 (ed. Daniels, in "Wilhelm von Ware," p. 314). The passage from Henry is in *Summa*, a. 1, q. 2 (1:5vE).

[32] Duns, *Lectura* I, d. 3, p. 1, q. 3 (Vatican, 16:283–89, nn. 152–61 [nn. 157–59 reproducing Henry's three arguments in the *Summa*]); and *Ordinatio* I, d. 3, p. 1, q. 4 (Vatican, 3:126–32, nn. 208–17 [nn. 211–13 on the three arguments]). Jerome V. Brown has extensively analyzed Duns's arguments in Book I, dist. 3 of both works in "John Duns Scotus on Henry of Ghent's Arguments for Divine Illumination: The Statement of the Case," *Vivarium* 14 (1976): 94–113; "John Duns Scotus on Henry of Ghent's Theory of Knowledge," *The Modern Schoolman* 56 (1978–79): 1–29; and "Duns Scotus on the Possibility of Knowing Genuine Truth: The Reply to Henry of Ghent in the 'Lectura Prima' and in the 'Ordinatio'," RTAM 51 (1984): 136–82; but his interpretation differs from the one given here. Even more at variance are the conclusions of Ruggero Rosini, "Gli 'intelligibili' nella dottrina di Giovanni Duns Scoto," in *Deus et homo ad mentem I. Duns Scoti*, Acta Tertii Congressus Scotistici Internationalis, Vienna, 28 September–2 October 1970, 673–91 (Rome, 1972).

placed between the plain "true" of the object and "pure truth" of special illumination. By his account, Henry's theory allowed just two alternatives: to know the true without divine light or truth with it.[33] Duns, on the other hand, took pains to lay out the complexity of his source, with his rendition correctly positing two levels of knowing truth, only the second of which required intervention of divine light.[34] He was also more informed, or more revealing, about Henry's terminology. In both *Lectura* and *Ordinatio* Henry's higher level is referred to not only as "pure" truth, the word found in William, but also as "certain" and "infallible" truth, both descriptions of considerable importance for Henry.[35]

William and Duns were mindful of Henry's attempt to elude ontologism by differentiating between reliance on divine exemplar as merely means of knowing and as both means and object, too.[36] They also called attention to the three-fold presentation of God's action from Henry's *Summa*, article 1, question 3, which compared the divine

---

[33] William, *Quaestiones*, q. 19 (ed. Daniels, in "Wilhelm von Ware," p. 313).

[34] Duns, *Lectura* 1, d. 3, p. 1, q. 3 (Vatican, 16:286, nn. 156–57); and *Ordinatio* 1, d. 3, p. 1, q. 4 (Vatican, 3:127–28, nn. 210–11). A more primitive version of an illuminationist theory of truth appears in Duns's *Quaestiones super libros Metaphysicorum* II, qq. 2–3 (Opera Phil., 3:212, n. 36), where, as in William, truth is unitary and involves comparison with the divine exemplar. It is not clear in that question what Duns thought of the theory or in any case how he would have related it to Henry's views.

[35] For Henry's use of these three terms, see Pt. 3, ch. 9, nn. 80, 81 and 83; for Duns's, *Lectura* 1, d. 3, p. 1, q. 3 (Vatican, 16:281, 286 and 289, nn. 144, 157 and 161); and *Ordinatio* 1, d. 3, p. 1, q. 4 (Vatican, 3:123, n. 202). In *Ordinatio* 1, d. 3, p. 1, q. 4 (Vatican, 3:128, n. 211), Duns even quotes Henry's phrase: "omnino certa et infallibilis notitia veritatis" (see above, Pt. 3, ch. 9, n. 82). *Ordinatio* 1, d. 3, p. 1, q. 4 (Vatican, 3:130, n. 214), refers to "certa scientia et infallibilis veritas," echoing the "infallibilis scientia" of Henry's illuminative knowledge of truth (see again Pt. 3, ch. 9, n. 83).

[36] In *Quaestiones*, q. 19 (ed. Daniels, in "Wilhelm von Ware," pp. 314–15), William characterized the distinction as between a light seen "obiective" or "directo aspectu" and one seen "indirecto aspectu" or "oblique." Duns picked up on this language but also employed the more authentic terminology referring to a "ratio cognoscendi" – see *Lectura* 1, d. 3, p. 1, q. 3 (Vatican, 16:288–89, n. 160); and *Ordinatio* 1, d. 3, p. 1, q. 4 (Vatican, 3:130–31, n. 215). On Henry, see above, Pt. 3, ch. 9, nn, 86 and 92. Duns also used the distinction elsewhere in his thought, for Henry's "ratio tantum" sometimes substituting the term "praecise ratio cognoscendi" – see *Quaestiones quodlibetales*, q. 14, n. 2 (Vivès, 26:3a–b); and n. 26 (Vivès, 26:108a). In *Ordinatio* 1, d. 3, p. 1, q. 4 (Vatican, 3:130, n. 214), he perceptively remarked how for Henry God served as means of knowing in understanding pure truth insofar as he was "nudum exemplar," in contrast to being grasped as object known in this world merely in a general attribute. For Henry's views on this, see Pt. 3, ch. 10, nn. 7 and 8.

contribution in knowledge of truth first to light, then to a species and finally to a character or figure. William even commented how beautifully this encapsulated Henry's thought.[37] For his part, Duns interpreted the whole description as a theory of two exemplars at work in knowledge of pure truth, thus amplifying the feature of Henry's illuminationism tying him most closely to the classic Augustinians, especially Pecham. He recognized nonetheless how careful Henry was to stipulate that the divine exemplar did not take part in the process as something actually inhering in mind.[38]

Above all, William and Duns were sensitive to the ostensibly Augustinian pedigree of illuminationist views, and they realized that Henry had called explicitly upon Augustine as authority in his behalf, both pointedly remarking upon the Augustinian origin of Henry's term, "pure truth."[39] But for all the careful argumentation and despite the impressive genealogy claimed for the ideas, neither lent Henry his support. Instead, they stoutly denied any validity to the presumed connection between illumination and normal knowledge of truth. Their position was that there was no need for a special light of truth, since indubitable certitude could be obtained by mind working solely in its own natural light.[40] Duns suggested it was only the appeal to Augustine, which he considered fundamentally misdirected, that gave

---

[37] William, *Quaestiones*, q. 19 (ed. Daniels, in "Wilhelm von Ware," p. 315); and Duns, *Lectura* 1, d. 3, p. 1, q. 3 (Vatican, 16:288, n. 160), merely noting that the theory described God's action "tripliciter"; and *Ordinatio* 1, d. 3, p. 1, q. 4 (Vatican, 3:131, n. 216), listing the three ways. On Henry, see Pt. 3, ch. 9, n. 95.

[38] Duns, *Lectura* 1, d. 3, p. 1, q. 3 (Vatican, 16:289, n. 161); and *Ordinatio* 1, d. 3, p. 1, q. 4 (Vatican, 3:131–32, n. 217). For this theme in Henry and the classic Augustinians, see Pt. 3, ch. 9, nn. 104–7.

[39] William, *Quaestiones*, q. 19 (ed. Daniels, in "Wilhelm von Ware," p. 312); and on Augustine's reliance on a theory of divine illumination in knowledge of truth for proving the existence of God, *Quaestiones*, q. 14 (ed. Daniels, in *Quellenbeiträge und Untersuchungen*, p. 92). In *Lectura* 1, d. 3, p. 1, q. 3 (Vatican, 16:287, n. 157), Duns traced Henry's term "sincera veritas" back to Augustine's *83 Quaestiones*, a connection mentioned without regard to Henry in *Quaestiones super libros Metaphysicorum* I, q. 4 (Opera Phil., 3:96, n. 6). *Ordinatio* 1, d. 3, p. 1, q. 4 (Vatican, 3:129, n. 211) – parallel to the passage cited above from *Lectura* – omitted the word "sincera" from the Augustine quotation. William identified Augustine as the specific source for "sincera veritas" in *Quaestiones*, q. 19 (ed. Daniels, in "Wilhelm von Ware," p. 314). On Henry's, and Matthew of Aquasparta's, debt to Augustine, consult above, Pt. 3, ch. 9, n. 80.

[40] Duns, *Lectura* 1, d. 3, p. 1, q. 3 (Vatican, 16:290–91, nn. 165–66); and William, *Quaestiones*, q. 19 (ed. Daniels, in "Wilhelm von Ware," pp. 315–16). In *Ordinatio* 1, d. 3, p. 1, q. 4 (Vatican, 3:156–57, n. 258), Duns explained that infallible truth could be known "ex puris naturalibus."

such otherwise implausible theories whatever credibility they possessed.[41] In the end, this was all he and William would make of the celebrated tradition of divine illumination in the Augustinian school.

As for the specific arguments Henry had put forth, William and Duns concurred that they effectively invalidated themselves. In Duns's words, the three reasons of the *Summa*, article 1, did not simply fail to establish a role for divine light in normal human cognition but actually worked to deny the possibility of cognitive certitude under any conditions, thus completely missing the mark.[42] Among Duns's counterarguments, perhaps the most interesting had to do with Henry's third reason, concerning the need for a reliable exemplar against which to measure knowledge fashioned by means of cognitive species drawn from below. Returning to the two-exemplar interpretation of Henry's views, he reminded his readers that no chain was stronger than its weakest link, so that as long as mind relied, if even partially, on an intellective exemplar extrapolated from created objects, its knowledge could not overcome that exemplar's inherent limitations.[43] William, too, had found this rebuttal particularly convincing, it being the only argument to appear in his work in precisely the form it would later take with Duns.[44]

It is worth observing how William held that direct involvement of the divine in human cognition, even if it could compensate for the limitations of creaturely agency, would so overshadow mind's native contribution as to make Henry's illumined knowledge not the natural cognition he was aiming for but rather something of an entirely supernatural kind.[45] Here was one of the rare arguments

---

[41] In *Lectura* 1, d. 3, p. 1, q. 3 (Vatican, 16:282, n. 144), Duns introduced the opening arguments in favor of special illumination by saying: "Et quod requiritur specialis influentia, probatur per auctoritates Augustini, quae faciunt difficultatem in hac quaestione."

[42] Duns, *Lectura* I, d. 3, p. 1, q. 3 (Vatican, 16:291–92, nn. 168–70); and *Ordinatio* I, d. 3, p. 1, q. 4 (Vatican, 3:133–35, nn. 219–22). *Ordinatio* I, d. 3, p. 1, q. 4 (Vatican, 3:132 and 135, nn. 218 and 222) claims that Henry's three reasons lead to the error of the Academics, scepticism. On the arguments in Henry, see above, n. 31.

[43] Duns, *Lectura* I, d. 3, p. 1, q. 3 (Vatican, 16:292, n. 170); and *Ordinatio* I, d. 3, p. 1, q. 4 (Vatican, 3:134, n. 221).

[44] William, *Quaestiones*, q. 19 (ed. Daniels, in "Wilhelm von Ware," p. 317). Duns's language in the *Ordinatio* passage cited above, n. 43, is especially close to William's.

[45] William, *Quaestiones*, q. 19 (ed. Daniels, in "Wilhelm von Ware," p. 316): "Item si lumen supernaturale requiritur in omni cognitione intellectuali, cum omnis actus accipiat denominationem et qualificationem ex modo et ratione operandi, sequitur quod omnis talis operatio esset supernaturalis." This appears to be the criticism of

William leveled against Henry that Duns declined to adopt even in qualified form. Instead, in a question not specifically about illumination and truth, he drew attention to an anomalous instance where Henry himself had presumed a conflict between natural and supernatural action not unlike the one William called upon to advance his argument against Henry. Noting how Henry had maintained that the impossibility of raising natural knowledge to an unambiguous understanding of the divine argued for the necessity of supernatural revelation for the fullness of faith, he commented that this argument was elsewhere contradicted by Henry's own illuminationist claim that God could work directly in knowledge of pure truth without obliterating the naturalness of the act.[46] Clearly, Duns was saying, Henry's reasoning about revelation was inconsistent with his own avowed principles concerning the relation between natural aptitude and the efficacy of divine assistance.

The point was well taken, and damaging to Henry's case, yet Duns was on to even more than would at first appear. Both Henry before him and Matthew, too, had sensed the difficulty of sustaining a role for divine illumination in normal cognition without effacing the natural character of the intellective act, anticipating William's challenge. Their solution was to concede that the illuminative action yielding knowledge of pure truth did not arise from nature while insisting nevertheless that neither act nor resultant knowledge was incompatible with the natural character of intellect and thus not entirely unnatural.[47] Duns accepted their reasoning, as usual adding his own precision in articulation.

He said there were two ways one could look at the division between natural and supernatural acts.[48] The first way, dependent on calibrating a receptive power against the act formally received or generated in it, every act was natural, violent or neutral according to whether or not the power was positively inclined to receive the particular act. From this perspective there was no such thing as super-

Henry's illuminationism that Doyle, "The Disintegration" pp. 338–39, takes as most important for William.

[46] Duns, *Lectura* Prol., p. 1, q. un. (Vatican, 16:12–13, n. 30): and *Ordinatio* Prol., p. 1, q. un. (Vatican, 1:31, n. 52). Henry's argument about revelation appears in his *Summa*, a. 3, q. 4 (1:29vP). Duns once made a similar charge about Henry's inconsistency in a question dealing explicitly with illumination – see *Ordinatio* I, d. 3, p. 1, q. 4 (Vatican, 3:158–59, n. 260).

[47] See above, Pt. 3, ch. 9, nn. 128–31; and Pt. 2, ch. 5, n. 108.

[48] Duns, *Lectura* Prol., p. 1, q. un. (Vatican, 16:13–14, nn. 31–32); and *Ordinatio* Prol., p. 1, q. un. (Vatican, 1:35, n. 57).

natural action, for if the term "supernatural" were to add anything
to the three alternatives already presented it would have to entail
not merely countermanding a power's natural inclination but violating its very receptive nature, effectively evacuating the possibility
of any action whatsoever. No power could receive that which it was
by nature absolutely unsuited to receive, and no degree of mediation, no matter how supernaturally potent, could make things otherwise.[49] On this score, Duns would have been prepared to go even
farther than William's argument against Henry and insist that if the
theory of divine illumination was intended to overcome natural limitations on the receptiveness of mind, it simply would not work.

Yet there was a second way of categorizing acts, relying on calibrating a power against the agent from which it received the form
determining its act.[50] Here lay room for distinguishing between natural and supernatural acts, since the natural order of things linked
each power with some agents and not with others. When a receptive power received a form from an agent naturally ordered to act
upon it, the act was natural; when from an agent operating outside
the order of nature, the act was supernatural. Both cases were possible, for in both the formal action was not unsuited to the power
that received it and in neither was the nature of the receptive power
expunged. It was surely supernatural action of this sort that Henry
and Matthew were getting at with their defense of special illumination as not entirely natural but not completely unnatural either, and,
when it suited his purpose, Duns was prepared to state the principle

---

[49] Duns made this point often with regard to first object of intellect and knowledge of separate substances, as in *Quaestiones super libros Metaphysicorum* II, qq. 2–3
(Opera Phil., 3:210, n. 32); *Ordinatio* I, d. 3, p. 1, q. 3 (Vatican, 3:71 and 114–15,
nn. 114 and 188); and *Quaestiones quodlibetales*, q. 14, n. 12 (Vivès, 26:46b). It is
ironic that despite the sentiment indicated above, n. 45, when it came to the questions of adequate object of intellect and knowledge of God, William of Ware was
willing to admit that a special, presumably beatific, illumination could sufficiently
"strengthen" the power of mind to enable it to see objects it was otherwise naturally incapable of attaining – see William, *Quaestiones*, q. 12 (MS Vat., Chigi. B.
VIII. 135, f. 2rb–va), a fragment of which is quoted (from another manuscript) in
Gál, ed., "Gulielmi de Ware," p. 169.

[50] See above, n. 48. In the *Lectura* passage, Duns said literally that the comparison lay between the power and "the form as received from the agent," while by
the *Ordinatio* he had abandoned so ambiguous a description of the latter *comparan-
dum*, replacing it with "agent" alone. For more on this second way and the possibility of supernatural acts, see *Lectura* Prol., p. 1, q. un. (Vatican, 16:15–16, n. 36);
and *Ordinatio* Prol., p. 1, q. un. (Vatican, 1:37, n. 60); on how even supernatural
acts would not excede the natural perfectibility of a power, *Quaestiones quodlibetales*,
q. 14, n. 2 (Vivès, 26:2b).

in language quite close to Henry's. Talking about knowledge of God, he insisted that one must distinguish between mind's power to receive a particular understanding and its power to attain such understanding on its own or by order of natural causation.[51] What lay within its power in the first sense might well lie outside it in the second. Surely this fundamental agreement with Henry on what constituted the supernatural explains why he passed over William's argument against special illumination on grounds it violated mind's natural powers. For Duns as well as Henry, God might well intervene with no such violation.

To Duns's eyes, the aspect of Henry's special illumination that called the theory into question had to do not with the nature of the agent or the character of the act but rather the identity of the object known. He was bothered by the ontologism long haunting the Augustinian point of view. In his opinion, Henry's explanation for knowledge of pure truth obliged mind to know both created object and ideal exemplar in the divine mind, for otherwise it could not draw the requisite comparison. Yet Henry would surely have admitted, like every orthodox theologian of his time, that the viator normally had no such cognitive access to God or what lay within his mind. In short, all Henry's talk about God's light acting as means of knowing but not object known was inadequate to the demands of his theory of truth.[52]

Most likely because of this sensitivity to the threat of ontologism, in the earliest of his commentaries on the *Sentences* Duns presented Henry's theory of knowing pure truth as stipulating recourse to a "special influence" from God. Access to merely an influence would of course relieve mind of the necessity for gazing upon divinity itself, which was precisely why the notion had surfaced occasionally among

---

[51] See Duns, *Quaestiones quodlibetales*, q. 14, n. 2 (Vivès, 26:2b–3a); and also below in discussion of the adequate object of intellect, Pt. 4, ch. 16, n. 34.

[52] Duns, *Lectura* I, d. 3, p. 1, q. 3 (Vatican, 16:300, n. 187); and *Ordinatio* I, d. 3, p. 1, q. 4 (Vatican, 3:157, n. 258): "... alio modo, intelligit per veritatem, conformitatem ad exemplar . . .; si autem ad exemplar increatum, conformitas ad illud non potest intelligi nisi in illo exemplari cognito, quia relatio non est cognoscibilis nisi cognito extremo. Ergo falsum est quod ponitur exemplar aeternum esse rationem cognoscendi et non cognitum." William made nearly the same point, though not quite, in *Quaestiones*, q. 19, arg. 1 contra (ed. Daniels, in "Wilhelm von Ware," p. 312).

the classical Augustinians and why Henry's language at times seemed
to lend it support.[53] But for Duns there was just one way to interpret reference to a special influence in knowledge of truth, and this
was to see it in light of the tradition going back to John of La
Rochelle as signifying the created agent intellect, concrete manifestation of God's cognitive solicitude for soul. Duns was dubious Henry
meant his own theory to be read this way.[54] Incidentally, William,
too, had proffered such a reading of language traditionally associated with divine illumination, saying that the Psalmist's *signum* or
signaculum of God in mind was meant to indicate something lower
than divinity itself.[55] It stood for the intellective power, or what could
be called the natural light (*naturale lumen*) of intellect, in which all
truth was seen.[56]

Yet if Henry's arguments could be so easily dismissed, there
remained the problem Duns had initially alluded to that Augustine's

---

[53] For this formulation, see Duns's *Lectura* I, d. 3, p. 1, q. 3 (Vatican, 16:281,
n. 144): "Utrum intellectus alicuius viatoris possit naturaliter intelligere aliquam certam veritatem et sinceram absque speciali influentia a Deo"; and also the same
question (Vatican, 16:286, n. 157). By *Ordinatio* I, d. 3, p. 1, q. 4 (Vatican, 3:123,
n. 202), the wording had been changed to: ". . . an aliqua veritas certa et sincera
possit naturaliter cognosci ab intellectu viatoris, absque lucis increatae speciali illustratione." The use of the term "special illustration" reflects in my opinion a more
accurate reading of Henry's intentions, but for modern interpretations of his theory as requiring only a special influence, see above, Pt. 3, ch. 9, n. 120. Only once
in the *Ordinatio* (I, d. 3, p. 1, q. 4 [Vatican, 3:131, n. 216]) did Duns speak of a
special influence, and this would appear to be because he could find no other way
to understand the third of Henry's three descriptions of God's illuminative action:
as a character impressed on mind (see above, n. 37).

[54] On this reading of Henry, see Duns, *Ordinatio* I, d. 3, p. 1, q. 4 (Vatican,
3:158, n. 260). The version given in *Lectura* I, d. 3, p. 1, q. 3 (Vatican, 16:300,
n. 188) is somewhat different. See above, Pt. 2, Intro., n. 4, for Rochelle's views,
and the discussion of God's "influence" in Pt. 2, ch. 5, pp. 135–36.

[55] William *Quaestiones*, q. 19 (ed. Daniels, in "Wilhelm von Ware," p. 318), also
quoted by Doyle in *The Disintegration of Divine Illumination*, p. 335, n. 153. On how
other Augustinians interpreted this Psalm, see above, Pt. 2, ch. 6, n. 82; and ch. 8,
nn. 18, 20, 22 and 25.

[56] On this natural light, see William, *Quaestiones*, q. 19 (ed. Daniels, in "Wilhelm
von Ware," pp. 315–16): "Sicut lumen glorie sufficit ad cognoscendum omnia que
spectant ad cognitionem gloriosam . . . ita lumen naturale ad cognoscendum que
subsunt cognitioni naturali, subposita, dico, influentia universali divina." See also
Quaestiones, q. 2 (MS Vat., Chigi. B. VIII. 135, f. 2rb): "Sed omnis operatio naturalis intellectus nostri est mediante lumine naturali tamquam instrumento." Duns
referred similarly to the natural light of mind in *Quaestiones super libros Metaphysicorum*
I, q. 4 (Opera Phil., 3:120, n. 83); and *Ordinatio* III, d. 24, q. un., nn. 1 and 21
(Vivès, 15:35a and 52b).

writings were interpreted by so many to support a similar conclusion. Neither William nor Duns considered this any greater obstacle than Henry's reasons themselves, for both were convinced that an honest appraisal of Augustine would disclose his views to be quite different from what Henry, or the classic Augustinians for that matter, had held them to be.[57] In particularly revealing comments capitalizing, ironically enough, on a suggestion appearing in Henry's work, both took Augustine's famous mention of mind working in a "lux sui generis" to refer not to special divine light but again simply to intellect's own natural power to know.[58]

Of course, both scholastics assumed that in all human understanding God worked in the background as a general influence in contrast to the special influence or light posited in the "Augustinian" noetics against which they were arguing. No one of any ideological stripe denied this general role to divinity.[59] In Duns's words, God acted thus as ultimate cause (*generalis causa*) of all natural effects.[60] William quoted Augustine on God's power as revealed in the world

[57] See Duns, *Lectura* I, d. 3, p. 1, q. 3 (Vatican, 16:289–91, nn. 162–64, 167); *Ordinatio* I, d. 3, p. 1, q. 4 (Vatican, 3:135–36, nn. 223–24); and a reference back to the question in the *Lectura* (Vatican, 16:306, n. 201), in *Lectura* I, d. 35, q. un. (Vatican, 17:456, n. 32). William made the same general point in *Quaestiones*, q. 19 (ed. Daniels, in "Wilhelm von Ware," p. 317), shortly before offering the alternate explanation (ed. Daniels, in "Wilhelm von Ware," p. 318) that Augustine had once held a view similar to Henry's but repudiated it upon retracting his early acceptance of Plato's theory of reminiscence.

[58] For earlier interpretations of Augustine's phrase, see above, Pt. 3, ch. 9, nn. 67–68. On William, see *Quaestiones*, q. 19 (ed. Daniels, in "Wilhelm von Ware," p. 316): "Item Augustinus XII *De Trinitate* capitulo ultimo: credendum est ita conditam esse naturam mentis intellectualis, ut rebus naturalibus naturali ordine disponente subiecta sic illa videat in quadam luce sui incorporea...." In *Quaestiones*, q. 129 (MS Vat., Chigi. B. VIII. 135, f. 88rb), he identified this light as the soul's inherent agent: "Intellectus autem possibilis presupponit ante se potentiam generis sui, videlicet intellectum agentem disponentem ipsum fantasma...." In *Lectura* I, d. 3, p. 1, q. 3 (Vatican, 16:290, nn. 164–65), Duns echoed William's q. 19 by freely quoting Augustine and associating the "lux sui generis" with the natural light of mind. It is interesting to note that in *Quaestiones super libros Metaphysicorum* I, q. 4 (Opera Phil., 3:125–27, nn. 99 and 102–5), Duns said one could interpret Augustine's statements on pure truth as either, in Aristotelian fashion, contrasting knowledge of pure truth, available only to mind, with sensation, insufficient for manifesting truth, or positing a special revelation far beyond mind's normal natural processes.

[59] For earlier references to God's general influence, see above, Pt. 2, ch. 5, n. 82; and Pt. 3, ch. 9, nn. 21–23. William mentioned the idea in the passage quoted above, n. 56; on Duns's views, see *Lectura* I, d. 3, p. 1, qq. 1–2 (Vatican, 16:259, n. 91); and, more specifically on interpreting Augustine in this light, *Ordinatio* I, d. 3, p. 1, q. 4 (Vatican, 3:165 and 166, nn. 269 and 272).

[60] Duns, *Ordinatio* III, d. 24, q. un., n. 12 (Vivès, 17:43b).

through a dual operation, one falling under general and the other under special providence, concluding that so far as intellection was concerned, general providence came down to God's providing all minds with their own natural light.[61] Duns was in fact so bold as to designate as the "common opinion" of Christian speculation the view that Augustine assigned to divine light the role of remote or general cause in truth-perception, thereby shutting Henry out of the mainstream. He even turned Henry's preferred term, "pure truth" (*sincera veritas*), to his own purposes, taking a rare opportunity to evoke it here for this non-illuminationist version of Augustine on truth.[62]

In his *Lectura* – but no longer in the *Ordinatio* – Duns reached all the way back to Matthew of Aquasparta, who had drawn on Pecham's notion of a double agent intellect to explain how both God and mind's inherent light acted as efficient causes (*effective*) in human knowledge of truth.[63] Like Matthew before him, Duns insisted that it was proper to the intellective agent to act efficiently (*effective*) but not formally (*formaliter*) in causing understanding. Thus just as mind had its own natural light to act as efficient cause of knowing, so divinity served as remote agent for human cognition by cooperating in the efficient causality of the natural light.[64] Such ideas ranged Duns along with Matthew against those like Pecham who resisted the claim that God acted in human intellection primarily as efficient cause.[65] And in the very fashion that Matthew held God to be primary and principal efficient cause in the process, so Duns reasoned, though not in exactly the same spirit, that one should indeed more

---

[61] William, *Quaestiones*, q. 2 (MS Vat., Chigi. B. VIII. 135, f. 2rb): "Ideo aliter dicitur quod, cum secundum beatum Augustinum 8 *Super Genesim*, c. 9: 'Gemina operatio dei reluct in mundo, una ex prouidentia generali qua mouet res secundum naturas eorum, alia ex prouidentia speciali qua mouet eas per potentiam obedialem in eis existentem,' congruum est quod regat creaturam rationalem prouidentia uniuersali et speciali: uniuersali secundum quod indidit sibi lumen naturale ad omnia cognoscibilia naturaliter cognoscenda que subsunt sue potentie, particulari seu speciali qua cognoscat et diligat aliquid supra se."

[62] *Ordinatio* I, d. 3, p. 1, q. 4 (Vatican, 3:159, n. 260): "Si dicas quod lux increata cum intellectu et obiecto causet istam veritatem sinceram, haec est opinio communis, quae ponit lucem aeternam sicut 'causam remotam' causare omnem certam veritatem." The point is made less dramatically in *Lectura* I, d. 3, p. 1, q. 3 (Vatican, 16:301, n. 188). See also below, n. 153.

[63] See above, Pt. 2, ch. 6, n. 104 for Pecham; nn. 116 and 118 for Matthew.

[64] Duns, *Lectura* I, d. 3, p. 1, q. 3 (Vatican, 16:301–2, n. 189). On Matthew, see above, Pt. 2, ch. 6, n. 113.

[65] For Pecham, see above, Pt. 2, ch. 5, nn. 66 and 68; for Matthew's critique, nn. 77–78 and 99–100.

properly be said to see intelligible objects in divine light than in the light of one's own agent intellect, since first, not proximate, causes always exercised greater influence over any act.[66]

In place of Henry's illuminationist explanation for knowledge of truth from the early articles of the *Summa*, Duns settled instead on a fully natural account of more literally Aristotelianizing inspiration. Significantly, this account is reminiscent of Henry's ideas from middle and later career, a reminder that despite Duns's attacks on his predecessor's work, he continually depended on him to blaze the path to a new noetics and epistemology. Yet where Henry had only begun to open up a more purely Aristotelian clearing in the thickets of traditional Augustinianism, Duns carried the project several stages beyond. More than any of his intellectual soulmates, he suggested the possibility of constructing a naturalism escaping even the principles of Aristotelian thought, plainly leaving William of Ware behind, whose works give but a premonition of his disciple's audacious conceptualizing.

To establish the notion of a knowledge of truth unencumbered by divine illumination, Duns had to lay out the criteria for calling knowledge true. This brought him back to the concept of certitude, the subjective quality most prominently associated with knowledge of truth throughout the thirteenth century. Curiously enough, it was only in his mature works, from the *Ordinatio* on, that he defined "certitude," and he did so in terms taken from Henry of Ghent. Picking out precisely the two features Henry had associated with his first and lower level of science, he explained that cognitive certitude consisted in freedom from doubt and deception.[67] For Henry, of course, there had been a second degree of science, knowledge of pure truth, which advanced beyond the first by adding infallibility, but for Duns infallibility was already implicit in knowledge where mind had no doubt it was not deceived.[68]

---

[66] Consult Duns as cited above, n. 64, again explicitly echoing Augustine, and undermining Henry, by employing the term "pure truth." On Matthew, see above, Pt. 2, ch. 6, n. 117.

[67] Duns, *Ordinatio* I, d. 3, p. 1, q. 4 (Vatican, 3:136, n. 225): "... nam certitudo habetur quando excluditur dubitatio et deceptio." Nearly identical wording is found in *Ordinatio* Prol., p. 4, qq. 1–2 (Vatican, 1:141, n. 208); *Ordinatio* III, d. 24, q. un., n. 13 (Vivès, 15:44b); *Reportatio parisiensis* Prol., q. 1, n. 4 (Vivès, 22:8a); and *Quaestiones quodlibetales*, q. 17, n. 11 (Vivès, 26:220b – cited below, n. 80). For Henry on these two features, see above, Pt. 3, ch. 9, nn. 18 and 61.

[68] On Henry and the infallibility required for knowing pure truth, see above,

Having set these parameters, Scotus then insisted that mind could meet the two conditions for certitude – freedom from deception and indubiety – solely on its own without special divine aid (*ex puris naturalibus*).[69] Psychologically speaking, this was because soul possessed within itself, as Duns always held, adequate cognitive light, the natural power of mind mentioned in connection with Augustine above.[70] Yet like Henry, and most of the classic Augustinians, he conceded that intellect drew its knowledge naturally from sensation, making sense data a contributing cause of natural cognition and thus partial basis for whatever certitude was achieved. Here arose the age-old dilemma: Might not recourse to sensation leave an opening for error?

It has already been shown how Duns, in an Aristotelianizing mood, stressed that simple knowledge, which was what the senses yielded most immediately, was always true.[71] In other words, as William of Ware had also maintained, intelligible species taken from sensation provided mind with absolutely reliable understanding.[72] The difficulty arose with judgment. If the senses were indisposed, then intellect might refer a mental image or idea to the wrong real object or implicate it in a presumed condition which did not really obtain.[73]

---

n. 35, and also Pt. 3, ch. 9, n. 83. That Duns thought infallibility was included in the first two conditions is clear from *Ordinatio* I, d. 3, p. 1, q. 4 (Vatican, 3:156, n. 258), quoted below, n. 69. In *Ordinatio* III, d. 23, q. un., n. 16 (Vivès, 15:23a), he associated infallibility simply with freedom from deception, and indeed *Ordinatio* I, d. 3, p. 1, q. 4 (Vatican, 3:136, n. 225), partially quoted above, n. 67, had plainly used the phrase "non fallimur" to express such freedom.

[69] Duns, *Ordinatio* I, d. 3, p. 1, q. 4 (Vatican, 3:156–57, n. 258): ". . . quaero quid intelligit per veritatem certam et sinceram? Aut veritatem infallibilem, absque dubitatione scilicet et deceptione, – et probatum est prius et declaratum . . . quod illa potest haberi ex puris naturalibus." See also *Ordinatio* I, d. 3, p. 1, q. 4 (Vatican, 3:135–36, n. 224).

[70] See above, n. 58. Further mention of the sufficiency of natural light for the philosophical sciences comes in *Reportatio parisiensis* Prol., q. 3, n. 13 (Vivès, 22:52a); see also *Quaestiones super libros Metaphysicorum* I, q. 4 (Opera Phil., 3:98, n. 11). In *Quaestiones super libros Metaphysicorum* Prol. (Opera Phil., 3:4, n. 3), Duns explained how mind's cognitive certitude could be traced to its immateriality.

[71] See above, nn. 18 and 19.

[72] Duns's marginal note in *Ordinatio* I, d. 3, p. 1, q. 4 (Vatican, 3:149, ll. 17–19): ". . . sic species intelligibilis – non phantasma – est delebilis, sed immutabilis a vera repraesentatione in falsam." See also the same question (Vatican, 3:153, n. 251). Duns explained that this meant any intelligible object was, alone and in itself, always an adequate source of true knowledge – see *Ordinatio* I, d. 3, p. 1, q. 4 (Vatican, 3:149, ll. 19–22); and *Lectura* I, d. 3, p. 1, qq. 1–2 (Vatican, 16:275, n. 129). For William's views, see *Quaestiones*, q. 19 (ed. Daniels, in "Wilhelm von Ware," p. 317).

[73] See Duns, *Ordinatio* III, d. 23, q. un., n. 16 (Vivès, 15:23a–b); and William, *Quaestiones*, q. 19 (ed. Daniels, in "Wilhelm von Ware," p. 317).

But sensation in no way bound mind to any judgment or even authentically caused it. As Duns said, the senses were, so far as concerned judgment of truth, merely the *occasion* for knowledge, for although reason received the simple content of its understanding from sensation, it decided how to apply this content on its own.[74] In short, mind had the power to override whatever misreckoning might arise from indisposed senses and bring its own instinct for certainty to bear on the search for truth.[75] In one of the most remarkable uses of the dichotomy "occasion" and "cause" since William of Auvergne – but one paralleling a similar application by John Pecham – Duns simply severed intellectual certitude from the conditions of sensory perception.[76]

Certain judgment was thus fully within the power of mind and, as he saw it, most perfectly attained in a few basic types of cognition. Absolutely indubitable, these types provided the principles, in the broadest sense of the word, upon which the entire structure of certain knowledge would be built. All in all there were three: first principles, or immediately self-evident truths, within whose shadow fell the conclusions drawn from them as well, statements known to be true by experience, and assertions about one's own acts, especially internal or mental acts.[77] In a later note he added a fourth type, statements known "ut nunc" by sensation, by which he clearly meant to bring into play his controversial concept of intuitive knowledge, but this is a topic with which the present study is not concerned.[78] Both the *Lectura* and the *Ordinatio* produce arguments for

---

[74] Duns, *Ordinatio* I, d. 3, p. 1, q. 4 (Vatican, 3:140–41, n. 234 – strictly speaking on judgments of immediately evident truth – and 138, ll. 13–14); *Lectura* I, d. 3, p. 1, q. 3 (16:308–9, nn. 205 and 207); and *Quaestiones super libros Metaphysicorum* I, q. 4 (Opera Phil., 3:101–2, nn. 17 and 19).

[75] Duns, *Quaestiones super libros Metaphysicorum* I, q. 4 (Opera Phil., 3:109, n. 45; also 101, n. 18). In the same question, pp. 113–14, nn. 57–61, he even defended Henry by name from criticism on this score. For theoretical defense of the evident disposition of intellect for certain judgment, see *Ordinatio* I, d. 3, p. 1, q. 4 (Vatican, 3:154 and 156, nn. 253 and 257).

[76] On William, see Marrone, *New Ideas*, pp. 61–69; for Pecham, above, Pt. 2, ch. 6, n. 52.

[77] Duns, *Ordinatio* I, d. 3, p. 1, q. 4 (Vatican, 3:138, n. 229): "Quantum ad secundum articulum – ut in nullis cognoscibilibus locum habeat error academicorum – videndum est qualiter de tribus cognoscibilibus praedictis dicendum est, videlicet de principiis per se notis et de conclusionibus, et secundo de cognitis per experientiam, et tertio de actibus nostris, – utrum possit naturaliter haberi certitudo infallibilis." A parallel passage can be found in *Lectura* I, d. 3, p. 1, q. 3 (Vatican, 16:292, n. 172).

[78] *Ordinatio* I, d. 3, p. 1, q. 4 (Vatican, 3:137, ll. 9–12). There is a considerable

why the certitude of each of these cognitive foundations was obvious and irrefragable.

With regard to knowledge of internal acts, Duns took the almost
Cartesian stance that it was simply indisputable that mind was directly
open to such acts and possessed reliable understanding of them. Not
unlike Descartes, he considered the inerrant access of intellect to its
own activity as the indispensable condition for all other knowledge
of truth.[79]

To account for the certitude of the other two foundational types
required going beyond mind to locate a separate factor permitting
it to deliver judgment with confidence. Thus Duns here came up
against the problem of evidence, even in cases of *per se* or self-evident truth, for he readily admitted that what distinguished certain
from uncertain knowledge – except, of course, in the case of intellect's awareness of its own acts – was the ability to point to something other than mind by which judgment could be justified, whether
that be an aspect of a proposition or simple object in itself or some
other sufficient cause for knowing.[80] As is clear at several points, a
comparable problem applied to knowledge by faith, where certitude
rested upon the reliability of confirming testimony.[81] But since only

literature on the notion of intuition in Duns's thought and much disagreement about
what it meant for him. Early on Déodat-Marie de Basly, "L'intuition de l'extramental matériel," EF 48 (1936): 267–79, argued Duns held for some form of intellectual intuition in the life of the viator, while Léon Veuthey, "L'intuition scotiste
et le sens du concret," EF 49 (1937): 76–91; "Cohérence: Eclectisme ou synthèse,"
EF 49 (1937): 324–32; and "L'esprit du concret," RFN 29 (1937): 44–58, insisted
he did not. The classic account of intuition in Scotus is Sebastian J. Day, *Intuitive
Cognition. A Key to the Significance of the Later Scholastics* (St. Bonaventure, N.Y., 1947),
though Day's conviction that the idea of intuition was relatively unproblematic for
Duns has come under criticism of late. See, for a beginning, Allan B. Wolter, "Duns
Scotus on Intuition, Memory and Our Knowledge of Individuals"; and Richard E.
Dumont, "Scotus' Intuition Viewed in the Light of the Intellect's Present State," in
De doctrina Ioannis Duns Scoti, Acta Congressus Scotistici Internationalis, Oxford and
Edinburgh, 11–17 September 1966, 2, 47–64 (Rome, 1968).

[79] For Duns's discussion of certain knowledge regarding mental acts, see *Lectura*
I, d. 3, p. 1, q. 3 (Vatican, 16:296–97, n. 181); *Ordinatio* I, d. 3, p. 1, q. 4 (Vatican,
3:144–46, nn. 238–39); and *Ordinatio* III, d. 23, q. un., n. 17 (Vivès, 15:26b). Consult
also Peter C. Vier, *Evidence and its Function according to John Duns Scotus* (St. Bonaventure,
N.Y., 1951), pp. 121–35. On this as the basis for all other evidence, see Duns,
Lectura I, d. 3, p. 1, q. 4 (Vatican, 3:137, l. 12–138, l. 11): ". . . tertium [i.e., cognitio de actibus nostris] concluditur esse per se notum, alias non iudicaretur quid
esset per se notum. . . ."

[80] Duns, *Quaestiones quodlibetales*, q. 17, n. 11 (Vivès, 26:220a–b).

[81] On firm adherence by faith, see Duns, *Ordinatio* III, d. 23, q. un., n. 5 (Vivès,
15:8b); and *Reportatio parisiensis* III, d. 23, q. un., n. 6 (Vivès, 23:435b–36a). Elsewhere
he commented that faith did not exclude absolutely all doubt – see *Ordinatio* III,

natural knowledge is presently of concern, it is with regard to naturally known truths alone that one needs to examine his account of
the evidence sufficient to induce certitude.[82] This constituted evidence
in the most proper sense of the word, an identifiable something
drawn from or materially related to a cognitive object and by which
science was distinguishable from faith.[83]

Duns constructed his theory of evidence with an eye to Aristotle's
scheme for certain knowledge – that is, within the framework of what
was by then the standard notion of the formal constitution of science. He was more precise about this than any of the Augustinians
who came before him, though like all since Grosseteste he took his
understanding of science from the portrayal given in the *Posterior
Analytics*.[84] By these terms science proper had to do with knowledge
of universals, but equally importantly it was confined to knowledge
of conclusions drawn from appropriately arranged principles or
premises.[85] Since Duns accepted Grosseteste's exposition of the dis-

---

d. 24, q. un., n. 17 (Vivès, 15:48a); and *Reportatio parisiensis* III, d. 24, q. un., n. 21
(Vivès, 23:457a). On faith, because in its own way certain, as a subcategory of "scientia" broadly construed, see *Ordinatio* III, d. 24, q. un., n. 13 (Vivès, 15:44a–b);
and *Reportatio parisiensis* III, d. 24, q. un., n. 15 (Vivès, 23:453b–54a). Strictly speaking, however, "science" did not include faith, for there could be no demonstration
from propositions held on faith – see *Lectura* I, d. 2, p. 1, qq. 1–2 (Vatican, 16:138,
n. 76).

[82] Such truths made up what Duns called speculative knowledge derived naturally, or, in other words, by way of sensation – see *Quaestiones super libros Metaphysicorum*
VI, q. 1 (Opera Phil., 4:18, n. 45).

[83] Duns, *Ordinatio* III, d. 23, q. un., nn. 5, 6 and 17 (Vivès, 15:8b, 10a–b and
26a); *Reportatio parisiensis* III, d. 23, n. 6 (Vivès, 23:436a); and d. 24, q. un., nn. 2
and 10 (Vivès, 23:447b and 451b).

[84] See *Ordinatio* Prol., p. 1, q. un. (Vatican, 1:7, n. 9), although *Quaestiones super
libros Metaphysicorum* VI, q. 2 (Opera Phil., 4:43, n. 20) conceded that broadly speaking any argued knowledge could be called scientific. Duns was familiar with
Grosseteste's analysis of Aristotle on science and even referred to him as an authority on the subject – see *Collationes* 13, n. 1 (Vivès, 5:200a).

[85] On science as only of universals, see Duns, *Super Universalia Porphyrii quaestiones*,
qq. 7–8, nn. 1 (arg. 2) and 8 (ad 2.) (Vivès, 1:118b and 121b); and *Ordinatio* III,
d. 24, q. un., n. 4 (Vivès, 15:38b); as of conclusions, see *Quaestiones super libros
Metaphysicorum* VI, q. 1 (Opera Phil., 4:5, n. 8); *Lectura* Prol., p. 3, q. 1 (Vatican,
16:39, n. 107); *Ordinatio* Prol., p. 4, qq. 1–2 (Vatican, 1:141, n. 208); and *Reportatio
parisiensis* Prol., q. 1, n. 4 (Vivès, 22:8a–b). William of Ware suggested that science
could be of both universals and particulars – see his *Quaestiones*, q. 2 (MS Vat.,
Chigi. B. VIII. 135, f. 2rb): "Item, omnis scientia acquisita vel est universalis, vel
particularis." For Duns on science and particulars, see below, pp. 434–38, and
Marrone, "Concepts of Science among Parisian Theologians in the Thirteenth
Century," in *Knowledge and the Sciences in Medieval Philosophy*, ed. Reijo Työrinoja

tinction between principles and conclusions, the former known immediately by means of understanding (*intellectus*), the latter discursively
by reason (*ratio*), unique instrument of scientific thought (*scientia*), his
first job was simply to lay out the full scheme in detail.[86]

As with Grosseteste in his *Commentary on the Posterior Analytics*, he
viewed Aristotle's plan as specifying levels of relative authenticity of
knowing, so that in his own *Questions on the Metaphysics* he explained
that above mere belief in the truth of a proposition there were three
types of complex true cognition. First came experiential knowledge
of a fact or condition (knowledge *quia est*), then the nondiscursive
knowledge of principles, and finally demonstrated knowledge of the
reasoned fact (knowledge *propter quid*).[87] Of these, knowledge of the
reasoned fact fell under the category of knowledge of conclusions, or
science proper, where evidence was discursive and thus not relevant
to the matter of primary certitude at issue here. This left nondiscursive
knowledge of principles and knowledge of fact – in other words, cognitive acts directed towards first principles and statements known by
experience, the very two of Duns's three foundational types whose
certitude remained to be explained. To fill out the picture specifying the conditions of evidence for all primary cognition, one might

---

et al., III: 130–31, Proceedings of the Eighth International Congress of Medieval
Philosophy (Helsinki, 1990).

[86] See Duns's use of the pair *intellectus/scientia* in *Quaestiones super libros Metaphysicorum*
II, q. 1 (Opera Phil., 3:195, n. 6); VI, q. 1 (Opera Phil., 4:6, n. 10), and briefly
in *Ordinatio* Prol., p. 3, q. 1–3 (Vatican, 1:98, n. 145); for the contrast between *intellectus* and *ratio*, see *Quaestiones super libros Metaphysicorum* I, q. 4 (Opera Phil., 3:112,
n. 55). On whether the significant distinction lay between two types of knowledge
or two processes of knowing, see Marrone, "Certitude of Induction," p. 482. Duns
also recognized another use of the word "scientia," as the aggregate of all principles and conclusions about a single subject – see *Quaestiones super libros Metaphysicorum*
I, q. 1 (Opera Phil., 3:50–51, n. 103; and 60, n. 131); and VI, q. 1 (Opera Phil.,
4:7, n. 13); and for both uses, VI, q. 1 (Opera Phil., 4:15–16, nn. 39–40). It was
this second meaning he had in mind in *Ordinatio* Prol, p. 3, qq. 1–3 (Vatican, 1:98,
n. 145), and which presumably allowed him to speak loosely of knowledge of principles as "science" in *Ordinatio* III, d. 23, q. un., n. 7 (Vivès, 15:11a). This usage,
too, went back to Grosseteste – see Marrone, *New Ideas of Truth*, p. 226.

[87] Duns, *Quaestiones super libros Metaphysicorum* I, q. 4 (Opera Phil., 3:118, n. 79):
"Expertus vero, demonstratione carens, sciet quia est certitudinaliter et sine dubitatione cognoscet, quia videt et certus est naturam, ut in pluribus, uniformiter et
ordinate agere. Principium vero intelligens, absque applicatione ad conclusionem,
sciet 'in virtute'; demonstrationem vero habens sciet 'propter quid.'" These three
types of knowing are practically the same as the last three levels of "science" listed
by Grosseteste in his *Commentary* I, ch. 2 – see Marrone, *New Ideas of Truth*, pp.
224–26).

also add a further sort of principle about which Duns had little to say: immediate propositions derived from the subject of a science.[88]

Among these three types of principle, most basic were those that were such in the strictest sense of the word, what Grosseteste had called axioms (*dignitates*) or first common principles and William of Auvergne simply first principles.[89] Another traditional name for them was common conceptions of mind.[90] Duns referred to them from the beginning as first principles or common conceptions and, following the oft-quoted passage from Aristotle's *Posterior Analytics*, said that they were known to be true, once composed in propositional form, immediately from knowledge of their constituent terms.[91] Like Grosseteste and William of Auvergne, he observed that some among them were absolutely first, others less strictly so.[92] Examples included the proposition: "It is impossible for the same thing both to be and not to be" – a radically metaphysical application of the principle of non-contradiction – and the commonly cited: "The whole is greater than any of its parts."[93]

As with all principles, the certitude attaching to knowledge of such propositions was greater than that of conclusions derived from them, since less dependent on mediating processes of inference.[94] On the

---

[88] On these three sorts of principal knowledge in Grosseteste, see *New Ideas of Truth*, pp. 256, 260–62.

[89] Consult the reference to Grosseteste in n. 88, above, and for William, *New Ideas of Truth*, p. 109; see also above, Pt. 1, ch. 1, nn. 52 and 53.

[90] See Marrone, *New Ideas*, p. 109, n. 68.

[91] Duns, *In librum Praedicamentorum quaestiones*, q. 4, n. 12 (Vivès, 1:449a): "Ad aliud dico, quod 'principia cognoscimus inquantum terminos cognoscimus,' ut dicitur 1. *Posteriorum*. . . ."; as well as *Quaestiones super libros Metaphysicorum* I, q. 4 (Opera Phil., 3:100, n. 14); *Ordinatio* Prol., p. 1, q. un. (Vatican, 1:8, n. 10); and *Reportatio parisiensis* Prol., q. 1, n. 4 (Vivès, 22:8b). For the citation to Aristotle, already present as early as Bonaventure, see Pt. 2, ch. 6, n. 5. Duns referred to "prima principia" again in *Ordinatio* III, d. 24, q. un., n. 1 (arg. 7) (Vivès, 15:35a–b); to "communes conceptiones" in *Quaestiones super libros Metaphysicorum* I, q. 4 (Opera Phil., 3:108, n. 44); and occasionally to "principia immediata," as in *Ordinatio* III, d. 24, q. un., n. 11 (Vivès, 15:42a).

[92] Duns, *Quaestiones super libros Metaphysicorum* II, q. 1 (Opera Phil., 3:195–96, n. 8); also I, q. 4 (Opera Phil., 3:108–9, n. 44); and *Reportatio parisiensis* Prol., q. 2, n. 5, and q. 3, n. 16 (Vivès, 22:35b and 53a). For William and Grosseteste, see *New Ideas of Truth*, pp. 111, 270–71.

[93] Duns, *Lectura* I, d. 2, p. 1, qq. 1–2 (Vatican, 16:117, n. 20); and the first passage cited above, n. 92. See also William of Ware, *Quaestiones*, q. 2 (MS Vat., Chigi. B. VIII. 135, f. 2ra): "Primum uero principium complexum est: De quolibet est affirmatio vel negatio."

[94] Duns, *Quaestiones super libros Metaphysicorum* Prol. (Opera Phil., 3:10, n. 21): ". . . certissima cognoscibilia sunt principia et causae, et tanto secundum se certiora

part of intellect, it was the naked light of mind and no more complicated mental maneuver that accounted for this certainty, which is
to say that mind knew first principles as true without having to make
a judgment about their relation to something else.[95] Of course it had
to compose the propositions, so that two acts were required of intellect in knowing the truth of a first principle besides just receiving
simple terms: forming the proposition and then recognizing its truth.[96]
It is likely Duns assigned these acts to different powers of mind, like
some of his predecessors attributing the proposition-forming function
to possible intellect in contrast to the agent, which had already
abstracted the simple terms.[97] Yet neither act constituted authentically discursive thought.

The evidence compelling mind to recognize truth in these instances
consisted in the terms themselves, which offered patent testimony of
the conformity of principal propositions to their inherent interrelation-
ship.[98] The fact that this evidence was not separate from the components of the propositions themselves meant that first principles
could be said to be known as true "per se" – that is, that they were
self-evident or immediate truths.[99] Since the terms were universal,

---

quanto priora. Ex illis enim dependet tota certitudo posteriorum." See also *Ordinatio*
III, d. 23, q. un., nn. 7 and 8 (Vivès, 15:11a and 12a). The idea can be seen as
early as William of Auvergne, for whom it sometimes carried pejorative overtones –
see Marrone, *New Ideas*, pp. 35–36.

[95] See Duns, *Quaestiones super libros Metaphysicorum* I, q. 4; and II, q. 1 (Opera
Phil., 3:100, n. 14; and 194, n. 4); and also *Reportatio parisiensis* Prol., q. 2, n. 20
(Vivès, 22:44b): ". . . lumen naturale . . . sufficit ad cognoscendum per se notam ex
terminis. . . ."

[96] On composing the proposition, see Duns, *Quaestiones super libros Metaphysicorum*
I, q. 4 (Opera Phil., 3:108, n. 44);and *Ordinatio* I, d. 3, p. 1, q. 4 (Vatican, 3:140,
n. 234); on then recognizing truth, *Quaestiones super libros Metaphysicorum* VI, q. 3
(Opera Phil., 4:69–70, n. 38): "Contra . . . videtur quod principia, statim cum appre-
henduntur, cognoscuntur esse vera. – Responsio: propter evidentem habitudinem
terminorum, intellectus componens statim percipit actum componendi esse con-
formem entitati compositorum. Posset ergo dici quod ibi est alius actus, et reflexus
sed imperceptus, quia simul tempore." *Quaestiones* II, q. 1, n. 2 (Vivès, 7:96b) lays
out all three stages: simple perception of terms, composition of principles and assent
to their truth.

[97] Duns, *Quaestiones super libros Metaphysicorum* I, q. 4 (Opera Phil., 3:120–21, n. 85).
On a similar view in Henry, see above, Pt. 3, ch. 12, n. 77.

[98] In *Quaestiones super libros Metaphysicorum* VI, q. 3 (Opera Phil., 4:74, n. 52), Duns
spoke of the terms as containing a virtual habit, presumably of their mutual relation, to which their composition in the principal proposition was seen to conform.
By *Lectura* I, d. 3, p. 1, q. 3 (Vatican, 16:292–93, n. 173); and *Ordinatio* I, d. 3,
p. 1, q. 4 (Vatican, 3:138–39 and 141, nn. 230 and 234), he had abandoned such
language to speak more simply of the evident conformity of composition to terms.

[99] Duns, *Lectura* I, d. 2, p. 1, qq. 1–2 (Vatican, 16:114–17, nn. 14, 19 and 20);

there was furthermore no necessary connection between such principles and actual conditions of existence in the extra-mental world.[100]
Of course, the terms had originally to be drawn from existing objects
via sensation and abstraction, but both objects and act of sensation
again served only as occasions for mind's knowledge and not in any
real sense compelling causes.[101] In this restricted sense alone could
first principles be said to be induced, not because there was a logical process of inductive argument leading to their acceptance.[102]
Much like Grosseteste long before, Duns insisted that even if mind
were to observe in the extramental world the conjunction of relevant real objects, such as a whole and its parts, that would not add
to the certainty with which it affirmed the principle's truth. Perception
of a complex particular instance would not serve in such a case as
in any way proof but merely a kind of assistance (*manuductio*) to mind
which could easily be done without.[103]

Knowledge of first principles was, moreover, so directly consequent upon sensation of the appropriate simple objects from which
the constituent terms could be extracted that Duns held it to be,
like simple cognition, always true, which was to say mind never perceived first principles without granting their truth.[104] One might even
say such knowledge was innate, not in the Platonic sense, by which
it would actually be in us from birth, but rather along lines already
laid out in Bonaventure and the classic Augustinians, because the
inborn light of intellect sufficed to explain true knowledge of prin-

Ordinatio I, d. 2, p. 1, qq. 1–2 (Vatican, 2:131, n. 15); and *Quaestiones quodlibetales*,
q. 7, n. 5 (Vivès, 25:287a); also *Quaestiones quodlibetales*, q. 17, n. 11 (Vivès, 26:220a).
William of Ware made the same point in *Quaestiones*, q. 21 (ed. Daniels, in *Quellenbeiträge
und Untersuchungen*, p. 101).

[100] On the demand for universality, see Duns, *Quaestiones super libros Metaphysicorum* I,
q. 4 (Opera Phil., 3:115, n. 66); on the relation to actual existence, *Lectura* I, d. 2,
p. 1, qq. 1–2 (Vatican, 16:124, n. 37); *Ordinatio* I, d. 2, p. 1, qq. 1–2 (Vatican,
2:147–48, n. 38); and III, d. 24, q. un., n. 19 (Vivès, 15:49a).

[101] Duns, *Ordinatio* I, d. 3, p. 1, q. 4 (Vatican, 3:140–41, n. 234), cited above,
n. 74.

[102] Duns, *Quaestiones super libros Metaphysicorum* I, q. 4 (Opera Phil., 3:115, n. 67);
Ordinatio III, d. 24, q. un., n. 19 (Vivès, 15:49a–b); and *Reportatio parisiensis* III,
d. 24, q. un., n. 23 (Vivès, 23:457b–58a).

[103] Duns, *Quaestiones super libros Metaphysicorum* I, q. 4 (Opera Phil., 3:100–101, nn.
14–15 and 17); and also the passage from the same work cited in the preceding
note. For Grosseteste, see Marrone, *New Ideas*, pp. 277–78.

[104] Duns, *Quaestiones super libros Metaphysicorum* I, q. 4 (Opera Phil., 3:128, n. 107);
and *Ordinatio* II, d. 6, q. 2, n. 11 (Vivès, 12:356a).

ciples immediately upon simple cognition of the appropriate terms.[105] Duns was willing here to concede as well the familiar language of John of Damascus, according to whom knowledge of this kind was "inserted" into mind, though he was surely more comfortable with his own terminology, by which first principles were said to be naturally known (*naturaliter nota*).[106] And with this "naturalism" of the intellective act he associated a metaphysical naturalism remarkable for a scholar of Augustinian bent, for according to Duns there was a "naturalitas" – what might even be called a natural necessity (*necessitas naturalis*) – about the truth of first principles precedent even to God's will.[107]

As for the type of principle taken from the subject of a science, added incidentally to the list above but about which Duns had nothing explicit to say, implied in his writings is the standard Aristotelianizing view already presented by Grosseteste. Such truths were known immediately once the definition of the subject had been revealed.[108] This is presumably what Duns was talking about in a passage from the *Ordinatio* contrasting strictly *per se* cognition of first principles with the immediately evident knowledge of propositions formed from a term conjoined to definition.[109] By the *Quodlibetal Questions* he was prepared to embrace a profoundly Aristotelian notion

[105] In *Quaestiones super libros Metaphysicorum* I, q. 4 (Opera Phil., 3:105–8, nn. 32–42), Duns presented the Platonic interpretation and gave reasons for rejecting it. He agreed with Henry (see above, Pt. 3, ch. 10, nn. 17 and 19; and also ch. 9, n. 112) that all natural human cognition arose out of sensation (see *Quaestiones super libros Metaphysicorum* II, q. 1 [Opera Phil., 3:194, n. 4]). For his analysis of the language of "innate" along classic lines, see the same question, in *Quaestiones* (Opera Phil., 3:194–95, nn. 5–6). Vier, *Evidence and its Function*, p. 104, comments on this aspect of Duns's thought and gives a further citation. On Bonaventure and Matthew, see above, Pt. 2, ch. 6, nn. 2, 4, 5, 18 and 20.

[106] For Duns quoting Damascene, see *Lectura* I, d. 2, p. 1, qq. 1–2 (Vatican, 16:113, n. 8); and *Ordinatio* I, d. 2, p. 1, qq. 1–2 (Vatican, 2:128–29, n. 10). On the passage from John of Damascus itself, see above, Pt. 2, ch. 8, n. 32.

[107] See the extraordinary passage in *Ordinatio* I, d. 3, p. 1, q. 4 (Vatican, 3:164–65, nn. 268–69), including the sentence: "Et in talibus [veris necessariis ex vi terminorum] est maxima naturalitas – tam causae remotae quam proximae – respectu effectus, puta tam intellectus divini ad obiecta moventia, quam illorum obiectorum ad veritatem complexionis de eis." Corollary matters were mind's lack of freedom to deny the truth of such propositions (*Ordinatio* II, d. 6, q. 2, n. 11 [Vivès, 12:355b]) and Duns's comment that this was why Augustine, contrary to Aristotle, said mind made no judgment in affirming such truths (*Ordinatio* I, d. 3, p. 1, q. 4 [Vatican, 3:149, l. 23–150, l. 16]).

[108] See Marrone, *New Ideas*, pp. 256–59.

[109] Duns, *Ordinatio* I, d. 2, p. 1, qq. 1–2 (Vatican, 2:132–34, nn. 16, 18–19).

of the central importance of the latter for science, contending that knowledge of definitions lay at the heart of all scientific thought.[110]

More explicit, and far more interesting, were his comments on the remaining type of speculative principle, statements drawn from experience, constituting most of the principal truths peculiar to the natural sciences. Here, in contrast to first principles proper, which were known as true immediately from their terms, there was a place for frequent observation and something like inductive argumentation. Here, too, one sees dramatic development in Duns's thought from his early to later years.

His first remarks on the matter were prompted by examination of the difference between demonstration of a fact (*quia*) – that is, a posteriori argument to cause from effect – and demonstration of the reasoned fact (*propter quid*) – a priori explanation of a complex configuration by revealing its proper cause.[111] At this early stage he apparently saw the distinction between the two as pertinent just to the conclusions of science, and reasonably enough, since only conclusions were demonstrated in the narrow sense of the word. As his *Questions on the Metaphysics* explained, sensory cognition could contribute to knowledge of conclusions not merely, as in the case of first principles, by providing simple terms for propositions, but also by enabling mind to grasp by experience – by frequent acquaintance with the facts – the truth of a general statement of affairs. There was, then, an authentic evidential role in science for induction, one suggested by Aristotle's remarks at the beginning of his own *Metaphysics*, and Duns went on to note that such inductive or experiential knowledge of fact (*quia*) could lead to scientific knowledge in a more proper sense (*propter quid*) by propelling intellect to inquire about the reason or cause for the conditions it knew to be true.[112]

The problem with experiential knowledge of fact was the difficulty of defending its reliability. Duns recognized first of all that by the standards of Aristotelian inferential logic, knowledge of fact was less

---

[110] Such knowledge was, he said, "cognitio praevia scientiae" – see *Quaestiones quodlibetales*, q. 7, n. 7 (Vivès, 25:289b), quoted below, n. 156.

[111] On this distinction, see Duns, *Quaestiones quodlibetales*, q. 7, n. 3 (Vivès, 7:283b), which refers to the classic Aristotelian discussion in *Posterior Analytics* I, 13.

[112] On this idea and citation of Aristotle's *Metaphysics*, see Duns, *Quaestiones super libros Metaphysicorum* I, q. 4 (Opera Phil., 3:95, ll. 3–4; 101–2, nn. 19–20; and 116, n. 69); and also the late *Quaestiones quodlibetales*, q. 7, n. 3 (Vivès, 284a), which adds reference to the *Posterior Analytics*. The locus classicus was Aristotle's *Metaphysics* I, 1 (980b28–981a3).

certain than knowledge of reasoned fact, since as a posteriori it was less immediately apodictic.[113] Second, and even more worrisome, was the inherent insecurity of any premise, regardless of order of argumentation, dependent on particular observations, because no matter how many supporting cases one could point to, there might remain an instance as yet unnoticed to disprove the rule. In any case, a proper explanation had to reveal essential connections and not just accidental coincidence of effects, but to assume that an induction from experience involved essential relations begged the question, since that was something the induction itself would have to prove. It would seem that the best to expect from experience was, as Grosseteste had once suggested, plausible or dialectical argument, and nothing like the demonstration required of science.[114]

Duns had an answer for both concerns. Regarding the second he said that when one brought to sensory data, particular though they were, the premise that nature acts with regularity, then one could extrapolate from them fully universal knowledge.[115] Such an Aristotelianizing invocation of the principle of uniformity of nature had, of course, already been made by others in the Augustinian tradition, and Duns explicitly referred to Henry of Ghent as source for the idea.[116] He was satisfied that it sufficed to make experiential knowledge of the fact fully certain, adequate to the demands of science even if technically nondemonstrative.[117] As for the first concern, concerning the logical ordering of complex knowledge drawn from experience, he had already maintained that mind could transform knowledge of fact (*quia*) into fully scientific knowledge of reasoned fact (*propter*

---

[113] Duns, *Quaestiones super libros Metaphysicorum* I, q. 1 (Opera Phil., 3:27, n. 30).

[114] See Duns's comments in *Quaestiones super libros Metaphysicorum* I, q. 4 (Opera Phil., 3:102–4, nn. 21–28; and 116–17, nn. 70–75). On Grosseteste's admission that knowledge induced from experience might not be strictly scientific, see Marrone, *New Ideas*, pp. 225–26.

[115] Duns, *Quaestiones super libros Metaphysicorum* I, q. 4 (Opera Phil., 3:115–16, n. 68): "Ad primum argumentum principale dicendum quod ex multis singularibus cum hac propositione 'natura agit ut in pluribus, nisi impediatur,' sequitur universalis. Et si non sit causa impedibilis, sequitur simpliciter quod in omnibus." Consult Vier, *Evidence and its Function*, pp. 136–52, which brings Duns's ideas on the matter together into a unified theory, in contrast to treatment here, highlighting development over the course of his career.

[116] See *Quaestiones super libros Metaphysicorum* I, q. 4 (Opera Phil., 3:113, nn. 57–58); and for Grosseteste on the relation between science and natural regularity, Marrone, *New Ideas*, pp. 262–63, nn. 126–27.

[117] See the passage quoted above, n. 87.

quid).[118] What remained was to show how the transformation was possible.

The way led through the logical process of division.[119] Duns had complete confidence in the reliability of this process, insisting that while one could not literally prove in any case that division had worked to select the immediate and proper cause of an effect, the validity of the result would nevertheless be apparent from the nature of the terms produced.[120] It was as if truth obtained by applying division to a posteriori knowledge of conditions in the world was virtually as self-evident as that of knowledge of first principles. Duns even hinted at a parallel between the sort of experiential cognition he was thinking of and the authentically immediate knowledge of principles, for he used the word "intellectus," paradigmatic Aristotelian term for principal cognition, to refer to the type of evident but undemonstrated knowledge he had in mind.[121]

Such comments on the scientific role for experience in the *Questions on the Metaphysics* established the parameters of Duns's approach for the rest of his career, but they only suggested the ultimate reach of his ideas. By the time of the *Lectura* he had gone a step further. Most important was that the parallel between experience and principal cognition hinted at in the *Questions* now emerged explicitly with admission that it might be not just conclusions but also some principles of science that experience could reveal.[122] Beyond this, he worked to clarify, perhaps having familiarized himself more fully with the Aristotelianizing literature, the defense of the certitude that experience could bring. His treatment of the principle of uniformity in nature was now more precise, the explanation of where it might apply fleshed out with reference to two instances most likely drawn

---

[118] See above, n. 112.

[119] Duns, *Quaestiones super libros Metaphysicorum* I, q. 4 (Opera Phil., 3:119, n. 81).

[120] Duns, *Quaestiones super libros Metaphysicorum* I, q. 4 (Opera Phil., 3:119–20, n. 82): "Dividendo enim multa praedicata dicta de subjecto propositionis mediatae probandae, invenietur unum quod mediat inter ipsum et praedicatum de ipso probandum. Quod unum, an mediate an immediate insit subjecto, patebit ex ratione terminorum; et similiter si praedicatum probandum sibi immediate insit, vel non."

[121] Duns, *Quaestiones super libros Metaphysicorum* I, q. 4 (Opera Phil., 3:117–18, n. 77).

[122] Duns, *Lectura* I, d. 3, p. 1, q. 3 (Vatican, 16:294, n. 177): "De certitudine veritatis secundae cognitionis, acquisitae per experientiam, est sciendum quod per experientiam acquiritur certa cognitio veritatis tam de conclusione quam de principio." For a later comment on knowing principles from experience, see *Reportatio parisiensis* Prol., q. 2, n. 5 (Vivès, 22:35b).

from Grosseteste's *Commentary on the Posterior Analytics*. One was the case, traceable originally to Avicenna, of frequent healing observed in connection with a particular herb, the other Aristotle's example of a lunar eclipse, which Duns used to show at greater length how he thought division might work.[123] Yet he still had little to say about exactly how all this applied to the business of acquiring scientific principles. Just when he appeared to be raising the issue, he turned instead to a circumscribed discussion of mind's ability to judge an erring sense.[124]

The dramatic theoretical advance came with the *Ordinatio*, in a reworking of the passage on certitude and experience from the *Lectura*. Here Duns enhanced the precision about the rule of uniformity of nature already seen in the earlier work and added a dialectical defense of its truth. Apparently he now reckoned this rule among the first principles of science, known by mind as true immediately from the terms of which it was composed.[125] Then he turned to the two examples previously introduced in the *Lectura*. It was in explaining them that he moved significantly beyond anything he had yet said, at last capitalizing fully on the kind of Aristotelianizing analysis made by Grosseteste three-quarters of a century before.

The case of a lunar eclipse offered occasion to show how mind could turn experiential knowledge of fact (*quia*) into true *propter quid* knowledge of a scientific conclusion.[126] Repeating the claim from the *Questions on the Metaphysics* that mind acquainted with a condition known to hold true by experience would seek out its cause, he almost casually observed that technically speaking intellect had to hypothesize the conclusion and then search, by way of division, for a *per se* principle or principles to explain how it had come to be.[127] For all its brevity, the reference to hypothesis, or *suppositio*, is striking in

---

[123] Duns, *Lectura* I, d. 3, p. 1, q. 3 (Vatican, 16:294–95, nn. 177–78). For Grosseteste's use of the two examples, see Marrone, *New Ideas*, pp. 273–74, nn. 154 and 155; and 278, nn. 159 and 160.

[124] See Duns, *Lectura* I, d. 3, p. 1, q. 3 (Vatican, 16:295–96, n. 180); and on the same issue, also *Quaestiones super libros Metaphysicorum* I, q. 4 (Opera Phil., 3:112–13, n. 56; and 128, n. 107).

[125] Duns, *Ordinatio* I, d. 3, p. 1, q. 4 (Vatican, 3:141–43, n. 235; and 138, ll. 15–17).

[126] Duns, *Ordinatio* I, d. 3, p. 1, q. 4 (Vatican, 3:143, n. 236).

[127] Duns, *Ordinatio* I, d. 3, p. 1, q. 4 (Vatican, 3:143, n. 236): "Sed ulterius notandum quod quandoque accipitur experientia de conclusione . . . et tunc, supposita conclusione quia ita est, inquiritur causa talis conclusionis per viam divisionis: et quandoque devenitur ex conclusione experta ad principia nota ex terminis. . . ."

its novelty for Duns, and reveals a profound awareness of Aristotel-ianizing theories of science, especially the tradition of Aristotle com-mentary running from Grosseteste through Albert the Great and Thomas.[128] Such awareness moreover enabled him finally to put aside all doubts about the relative reliability of knowledge obtained the experiential way. Intellect beginning with experience and moving through hypothesis and division to discovery of cause could be said to know with the certitude of strictly scientific demonstration.[129]

Even more fascinating is the approach to the example of herbal healing. Here Duns faced head-on the theoretical challenge of ground-ing principles of natural science in a logic of particular experience, candidly assessing for the first time the extent to which induction might find a foundational and not simply propaedeutic place in the construction of scientific argument. In doing so, he not only returned the Augustinian tradition to Grosseteste's promising speculations on induction but actually moved the discussion a stage beyond.[130]

As Duns saw it, an intellect grasping the truth of a factual con-dition (*quia*) sometimes might not be able to work by division to a *per se* or self-evident principle by which to explain the circumstances in fully demonstrative form. In such cases, it would have to rest con-tent with experiential knowledge of the fact as the only principle upon which to ground further scientific argumentation.[131] For exam-

---

[128] For Grosseteste, Albert and Thomas on hypothesis, see Marrone, *New Ideas*, pp. 229–30 and 242–44; and above, Pt. 1, ch. 3, nn. 40 and 41. See also Vier's comments, *Evidence and its Function*, pp. 150–52. As noted above, Pt. 2, ch. 7, at nn. 23 and 24, Bonaventure revealed a similar appreciation of hypothesis but hardly worked it deeply into his thought.

[129] Again, Duns, *Ordinatio* I, d. 3, p. 1, q. 4 (Vatican, 3:143, n. 236): "Et si [prin-cipium per se notum] inventum fuerit per divisionem . . . scietur certissime demon-stratione propter quid (quia per causam), et non tantum per experientiam, sicut sciebatur ista conclusio ante inventionem principii." Related is the explanation in *Ordinatio* I, d. 3, p. 1, q. 4 (Vatican, 3:151, n. 247), that natural truths could be considered immutable in any case where the posited condition invariably held true whenever the terms were instantiated in reality. Also see *Reportatio pariesiensis (exam-inata)* I, d. 2, p. 1, qq. 1–3 (ed. Wolter and Adams, in "Parisian Proof," pp. 258 and 266), on how an argument from contingents might be rendered demonstrative by couching the premises in the language of possibility.

[130] On Grosseteste and induction of principles, see again Marrone, *New Ideas*, pp. 225–26; as well as the discussion of experiment and quick wit, pp. 272–81.

[131] The passage is important enough to be quoted in its entirety – Duns, *Ordinatio* I, d. 3, p. 1, q. 4 (Vatican, 3:143–44, n. 237): "Quandoque autem est experientia de principio, ita quod non contingit per viam divisionis invenire ulterius princip-ium notum ex terminis, sed statur in aliquo 'vero' 'ut in pluribus,' cuius extrema per experimentum scitum est frequenter uniri, puta quod haec herba talis speciei

ple, one might be able to discover by experience that a species of herb was hot and take this as the reason why such herb was therapeutic for specific ills, without being able to discover a more immediate middle term to account for the herb's hotness, and thus its curative power. In this instance, one could therefore never offer a truly *propter quid* explanation for the healing process, based exclusively on proper first principles.

Knowledge obtained in this fashion was, Duns insisted, fully certain and free of fallibility. But the certitude, as initially in all cases of knowledge of conditions drawn from experience in the real world, depended upon the principle of uniformity of nature, which in light of the failure of division to produce an obvious immediate middle term, remained the sole justification for granting the induction of universal truth.[132] Although such knowledge was scientific, it was just barely so, falling, as Duns said, into the last and least grade of science. The problem went beyond logic, beyond the fact that one of the ultimate premises, multiple experience, was not truly a priori. The real difficulty was metaphysical. For as Duns reminded his reader, a predicate signifying a property that might not be truly part of its subject and logically implicated in it – like "hotness" with respect to an herb – might point to something that could be separated from the subject, even if only by the absolute power of God. Argument employing such a predicate was, in short, more about the "aptitude" of things than, as in the case of strictest science, about an absolute necessity in every possible case.

With these comments on induction from experience, Duns completed his survey of the evidential basis for all principles of scientific truth. Were one to pose the further question of how such evidence translated into support for scientific conclusions at the other end of demonstrative argumentation, the answer could have been easily provided by anyone schooled in the medieval curriculum in arts. Duns's

---

est calida, – nec invenitur medium aliud prius, per quod demonstretur passio de subiecto propter quid, sed statur in isto sicut primo noto, propter experientias: licet tunc incertitudo et fallibilitas removeantur per istam propositionem 'effectus ut in pluribus alicuius causae non liberae, est naturalis effectus eius,' tamen iste est ultimus gradus cognitionis scientificae. Et forte ibi non habetur cognitio actualis unionis extremorum, sed aptitudinalis. Si enim passio est alia res, absoluta, a subiecto, posset sine contradictione separari a subiecto, et expertus non haberet cognitionem quia ita est, sed quia ita aptum natum est esse."

[132] On Duns's expectation that, in the best of cases, division would produce such a term, see above, n. 120.

treatment of the matter was not surprisingly terse, almost offhand. He had unshakable confidence in the principles of inferential logic. Having accounted for true knowledge of principles, he could simply point to the obvious indubitability of syllogism to justify assent to conclusions demonstrated from them as premises.[133] In a way reminiscent of the case of first principles, the power of mind alone was capable of recognizing the validity of a true inference with no more evidence than the formal structure of the argument itself.[134] Indeed, so transparent was inference that the certitude of conclusions could be said to depend entirely and directly upon the evident certitude of principles.[135]

In all this, Duns's understanding of scientific cognition and the evidence it required represented an intensification of already powerful Aristotelianizing drives within the Augustinian tradition. Yet his appreciation of the possibilities of natural knowledge articulated in line with Aristotle's science, even where surpassing Grosseteste's insights, was not radically innovative by the general standards of late thirteenth-century Scholasticism. One might say Duns had merely reclaimed for Augustinians an interest partially surrendered to other schools of thought after Grosseteste's death. Where Duns's epistemology made unique strides forward was instead in his willingness to contemplate an extension of these same impulses beyond anything Aristotle had dreamed of.

Most significant in this regard was his occasional determination to shift the criteria for scientific knowledge – or, if not strictly "science," a new epistemic category of comparable prestige – away from the formal requirements of demonstration, especially to allow for

---

[133] Duns, *Ordinatio* I, d. 3, p. 1, q. 4 (Vatican, 3:140, n. 233): "Habita certitudine de principiis primis, patet quomodo habebitur de conclusionibus illatis ex eis, propter evidentiam formae syllogismi perfecti, – cum certitudo conclusionis tantummodo dependeat ex certitudine principiorum et ex evidentia illationis." See also *Lectura* I, d. 3, p. 1, q. 3 (Vatican, 16:290–91, n. 166).

[134] Duns, *Quaestiones super libros Metaphysicorum* I, q. 4 (Opera Phil., 3:109, n. 45): "... statim virtute luminis sui assentit [intellectus] conexioni [terminorum in syllogismo], quia 'syllogismus perfectus est' etc. ..." On Duns's confidence in mind's ability to recognize a valid syllogism, see *Ordinatio* II, d. 6, q. 2, n. 11 (Vivès, 12:355b); and *Reportatio parisiensis* Prol., q. 2, n. 6 (Vivès, 22:36b).

[135] Duns, *Ordinatio* III, d. 24, q. un., n. 11 (Vivès, 15:42a): "... tota evidentia conclusionis dependet essentialiter a principiis." See also *Reportatio parisiensis* Prol., q. 1, n. 5 (Vivès, 22:9a); and *Quaestiones quodlibetales*, q. 17, n. 11 (Vivès, 26:220a): "Conclusio autem est certa per principium, tanquam per causam suae certitudinis. ..."

inclusion of God's knowledge of singular, contingent events, absolutely certain but by Aristotelian standards patently unscientific. It makes no sense to go deeply into the matter here, but some account is due if only to reveal the range of Duns's thought.[136] The issue arose in the context of discussing the scientific value of theological knowledge, a topic raised by the familiar questions whether theology was a science and whether a scientific grasp of the truths of theology would be compatible with faith in those same truths. Duns's response made use of suggestions put forth by Henry of Ghent at a similar juncture in his own thought, but in a fashion more poignantly indicative of their radical potential for breaching the limits of an Aristotelianizing perspective.[137]

Five times when he examined the scientific status of theology Duns listed the criteria for strictly scientific cognition, construed according to Aristotle's definition. All five listings are similar, but the first three are so much alike in wording and application that they can be taken as virtually identical renditions.[138] The first criterion was that the knowledge be certain, which for Duns of course meant that it had to exclude both error and doubt.[139] The second was that it be necessary, a quality alternately ascribed to the object of knowledge or to the knowledge itself.[140] The third criterion stipulated that such knowledge be produced by a cause evident to intellect, and the fourth, that it result from discursive, specifically syllogistic, reasoning.

Twice, in the prologues to the *Lectura* and the *Ordinatio*, Duns asserted that the last criterion, requiring syllogistic reasoning – as well as, by implication, so much of the third as implicated discursive

---

[136] For more on the problem, see Marrone, "Concepts of Science among Parisian Theologians."

[137] On Henry, see Marrone, "Concepts of Science among Parisian Theologians," nn. 21 and 22. The crucial texts are Henry's *Summa*, a. 6, q. 1; and a. 7, q. 2.

[138] Duns, *Lectura* Prol., p. 3, q. 1 (Vatican, 16:39, n. 107); *Ordinatio* Prol., p. 4, qq. 1–2 (Vatican, 1:141, n. 208); and *Ordinatio* III, d. 24, q. un., n. 13 (Vivès, 15:44b). The listing in *Reportatio parisiensis* III, d. 24, q. un., n. 16 (Vivès, 23:454a–b) is much the same, except that Duns does not follow up with an attempt to modify Aristotle. For the fifth, more pertinent passage, see below, n. 149. As explicitly indicated in *Ordinatio* Prologue and III, d. 24; and *Reportatio parisiensis* III, d. 24, the lists were intended to synopsize Aristotle's ideas from *Posterior Analytics*, I, 2 (71b9–22).

[139] On Duns's view of certitude, see above, n. 67.

[140] Duns's words implied the former ascription in the Prologue to both *Lectura* ("de necessariis") and *Ordinatio* ("de cognito necessario"), the latter in *Ordinatio* III, d. 24 ("cognitio necessaria"). The two remaining passages both ascribe the quality to the object of knowledge.

appeal to a cause – was actually a token of cognitive imperfection. Immediate knowledge was manifestly superior to that dependent on a process of inference. Accordingly, the finest forms of understanding, such as theology in the divine mind or even theology considered absolutely and in itself, should not be held to this standard.[141] One could discard Aristotle's requirement for discourse or syllogism without in any way diminishing epistemic prestige and authenticity.

He also believed it possible to go beyond Aristotle on the question of necessity. Because theology frequently concerned contingent propositions, such as the fact that Christ was made flesh to save humankind, then if it were to be considered scientific, the criterion of necessity would have to be modified to accommodate an objective contingency Aristotle would never have tolerated. Once more in the two prologues he explained how this might be done.[142] One could say that, in excluding contingent propositions from science, Aristotle had considered necessity only as applicable to the cognitive object, not thinking of it as a potential attribute of knowledge itself. This was plausible with regard to human cognition, where any instance of knowledge was in itself not necessary but contingent, liable to be forgotten as quickly as learned. Yet one could imagine knowledge of a more perfect kind. Looking to God, one saw a mind for which contingency in knowing was out of the question. Divine knowledge was itself always necessary, at least in the sense that it was absolutely perpetual and unchanging even when about contingent propositions or events.[143] The same was effectively true of theology in itself, since the evidence for theological truths lay in their

---

[141] *Lectura* Prol., p. 3, q. 1 (Vatican, 16:39, n. 107); and *Ordinatio* Prol., p. 4, qq. 1–2 (Vatican, 1:141–42, n. 208): "Ultimum, videlicet causatio scientiae per discursum a causa ad scitum, includit imperfectionem, et etiam potentialitatem intellectus recipientis. Ergo theologia in se non est scientia quantum ad ultimam condicionem scientiae. . . ." The *Lectura* passage added, by parallel reasoning, the exclusion of the requirement that such knowledge be effected by a cause – after all, neither God nor his understanding was subject to a cause. For the time being, Duns made nothing more of this point, but see below, n. 149, for a place where he took it as occasion for more dramatic speculation.

[142] Duns, *Lectura* Prol., p. 3, q. 1 (Vatican, 16:41, n. 112); and *Ordinatio* Prol., p. 4, qq. 1–2 (Vatican, 1:144–45, n. 211).

[143] See the passage from the *Ordinatio* cited above, n. 142, in particular: "Si igitur aliqua alia cognitio est certa et evidens, et, quantum est de se, perpetua, ipsa videtur in se formaliter perfectior quam scientia quae requirit necessitatem obiecti. Sed contingentia ut pertinent ad theologiam nata sunt habere cognitionem certam et evidentem et, quantum est ex parte evidentiae, perpetuam."

perpetual manifestation in the divine mind, lending them a necessity not of object but rather of habit of knowledge, derived from
God's own mental acts. In short, there was a sort of necessity theological truths could aspire to different from the necessity demanded
by Aristotelian science but much more perfect.[144] Again one could
depart from Aristotle without devaluing what it meant to know.
Indeed, such a departure, by improving upon Aristotle's criterion of
necessity, would render knowledge more truly "scientific."[145]

Combining his two reservations, Duns was even so bold as to
propose that all that was required to reach the height of cognitive
perfection were the two scientific criteria of certitude and evidence –
just the first and third on his list.[146] The idea had already been
advanced by Henry, who used it to defend his special *lumen medium*
of the theologian's knowledge, but Duns invested it with even greater
prominence.[147] If Aristotle had constructed his "science" so as to
coincide with cognitive perfection, then he had inconveniently introduced a pair of needless constraints. Science, or more impartially,
cognition, that truly aspired to being the best knowledge of all had
to worry only about attaining certitude and producing evidence upon
which it could rest.

Duns was conscious that in saying this he was abandoning the
Aristotle of historical record. Thus he once suggested that although
the perfect "science" of God's knowledge and of theology in itself
might violate the criteria of the *Posterior Analytics*, perhaps it was compatible with a more capacious definition offered in the *Nicomachean*

---

[144] Again the same passage as cited in n. 143: "Igitur contingentia ut pertinent
ad theologiam nata sunt habere perfectiorem cognitionem quam scientia de necessariis acquisita."

[145] See the passage from *Lectura* cited above, n. 142: "Et ideo theologia in se est
vera scientia, licet sit de contingentibus; quod non contingit de alia scientia naturaliter acquisita."

[146] Duns, *Ordinatio* Prol., p. 4, qq. 1–2 (Vatican, 1:144, n. 211): "Hic dico quod
in scientia illud perfectionis est, quod sit cognitio certa et evidens. . . ." The same
point is assumed in *Ordinatio* III, d. 24, q. un, n. 1 (Vivès, 15:34a); and also n. 17
(Vivès, 15:47b): "Nunc autem si res ipsae de quibus Scriptura tractat, essent clare
apprehensae et intuitive, generarent notitiam certam absque omni dubitatione, et
haec notitia, quia evidens est, diceretur scientia." Vier, *Evidence and its Function*, pp.
117–20 and 165–66, has given considerable attention to Duns's emphasis on these
two criteria.

[147] See Marrone, "Concepts of Science among Parisian Theologians," p. 129;
and Dumont, "Theology as a Science," pp. 586–87. For Duns's take on this special science available to theologians, see below, Pt. 4, ch. 15, nn. 126–32.

Ethics.[148] More often, he simply accepted the fact that for his purposes Aristotle had to be left behind. Perhaps he was talking about what should be called "wisdom" rather than "science," reserving the latter description for more strictly Aristotelian intents.[149] Whatever his words, however, and whatever latitude he read into Aristotle's work, he plainly intended to continue playing Aristotle's game. Like the latter, he was looking for a formal description of cognitive perfection, although he thought he could follow this ideal even beyond Aristotle's own rules. If this meant foregoing the term "science," so be it. But in laying out his new criteria Duns was, to his mind, only furthering the quest fascination with Aristotelian science had inspired. He was merely refining the standard by which knowledge should be judged.

Duns's examination of theology as a science generated the most radical epistemological ideas he was to produce, carrying his theory

---

[148] Duns, *Ordinatio* Prol., p. 4, qq. 1–2 (Vatican, 1:145–46, n. 212), the passage he had in mind being *Nicomachean Ethics* VI, 3 (1139b15–35).

[149] Duns, *Lectura* Prol., p. 3, q. 1 (Vatican, 16:41, n. 113): "Et ideo proprie theologia dicitur sapientia et non scientia, quia est evidens notitia, non mendicata per discursum nec per causam, sed ex evidentia extremorum." See also *Ordinatio* Prol., p. 4, qq. 1–2 (Vatican, 1:146, n. 213): "Magis tamen proprie potest dici quod theologia est sapientia secundum se.... Quantum ... ad contingentia, habet evidentiam manifestam de contingentibus in se visis ... et non habet evidentiam mendicatam ab aliis prioribus; unde notitia contingentium ut habetur in ea magis assimilatur intellectui principiorum quam scientiae conclusionum." Both passages identify the absence of discursive thought as reason not to call theology in itself a science. (In contrast, in *Ordinatio* III, d. 24, q. un., n. 17 (Vivès, 12:48a), when speaking of the special theological science God sometimes revealed to mankind (see above, n. 147), Duns said it might not be properly designated science because it did not involve full and proper understanding of its simple terms.) In this regard it should be noted that in the fifth of the passages (see above, n. 138) listing the criteria for science – *Reportatio parisiensis* Prol., q. 1, n. 4 (Vivès, 22:7b–8b) – Duns modified his third criterion so as to stipulate that the knowledge had to be not only evident but also from some prior element (*ex prius evidente*). This change was important, for now when he affirmed the third criterion of God's knowledge he could insist that for God there was some ordering of propositions even if not the strictly discursive arrangement Aristotle had in mind. In short he was back to the problem of God's absolute impassivity once briefly alluded to in the *Lectura* (see above, n. 141), now ready to offer a new solution. As he showed in the same question in *Reportatio parisiensis*, articles 3 and 4 (Vivès, 22:16a–33b), not all God's knowledge was precisely like mankind's knowledge of self-evident principles, for there was in God an ordering of concepts and propositions, even if only by nature and not actually in time as would be necessary for true discourse. By making this claim Duns was apparently preparing to shed his hesitation noted in the second *Ordinatio* passage quoted above about calling theology a true science because it imitated principal more than discursive knowledge. Note, too, that in *Reportatio parisiensis* Prol, q. 3, quaestiuncula 2 and 3, nn. 12 and 15 (Vivès, 22:51b and 52b), he admitted that his expanded idea of science meant that singulars could be the object of scientific cognition.

of knowledge farther than even the most suggestive of Henry of Ghent's departures from Aristotelian orthodoxy. Yet there remain aspects of his analysis of the terms of cognitive certitude bringing us back to a more familiar face of late thirteenth-century Augustinianism and Henry's attempts in his later years to insinuate a more faithful Aristotelianism. Here he took up threads in Henry's thought neglected by otherwise doctrinaire disciples like Vital du Four. The subject on these occasions was not so much science itself as its foundation in a type of simple cognition sufficiently perfect or replete to sustain the propositions of scientific reason. He was in effect probing the divide between what Henry had called simple understanding (*simplex intelligentia*) and his initial level of knowledge of the truth.[150]

First of all, Duns laid hold of Henry's early view, which the latter himself shunned in his mature years, that to pass from knowledge below science to the level of truth meant moving to an authentic concept of quiddity from something less.[151] Citing a passage from *De Trinitate*, he explained in both *Lectura* and *Ordinatio* that he took Augustine's comments about seeing an object in the eternal reasons to refer to knowing it in itself (*secundum se*) in contrast to grasping it as terminus of an accidental intellective act (*ens per accidens*).[152] By this distinction he meant to separate mind's inchoate focus on a farrago of accidental qualities as perceived in the phantasm, which in the *Ordinatio* he described as yielding an accidental concept (*conceptus per accidens*) of the thing, from the more perfect grasp of authentic essence in a simple concept of quiddity (*conceptus simplex quidditatis*). As he said, only when intellect understood its object in the latter way did it seize the precise or proper nature of a term (*propria, praecisa ratio termini*).[153] This was the understanding opening the way to genuine scientific knowledge of truth.

---

[150] On Henry's distinction, see above, Pt. 3, ch. 9, nn. 25 and 27; and ch. 12, pp. 367–69.

[151] For Henry's early views, see Pt. 3, ch. 9, nn. 27, 29, 30 and 31; for his later, Pt. 3, ch. 12, nn. 32–33.

[152] Duns, *Lectura* I, d. 3, p. 1, q. 3 (Vatican, 16:307, n. 202); and *Ordinatio* I, d. 3, p. 1, q. 4 (Vatican, 3:167–69, nn. 275–76). On *ens per accidens* in this sense, as an intelligible object incorporating elements of various logical kinds or genuses, see Duns, *Quaestiones super libros Metaphysicorum* VI, q. 2 (Opera Phil., 4:40–41, nn. 15–16). The reference to Augustine was to *De Trinitate* XII, 14 (eds. Mountain and Glorie, 1, 376–77).

[153] Duns, *Ordinatio* I, d. 3, p. 1, q. 4 (Vatican, 3:167–68, n. 275): "Veritates autem primae sunt praecise tales ex propria ratione terminorum, in quantum illi termini

Second, he developed the idea, which Henry had adhered to throughout his career, that moving towards science entailed coming to know an object's definition.[154] His clearest statement on the matter appears in the *Ordinatio*, where he asserted that the most perfect knowledge attainable at the level of simple cognition was apprehension of the definition, obtained through the logical process of division. Upon this was built knowledge of principles and then the conclusions inferred from them.[155] Though he conceded that one might loosely characterize definitive knowledge as scientific, technically speaking it was immediately prior to science, marking the last grade of intellection before advancing to complex certitude.[156] The difference between it and the more primitive understanding, literally that between knowing the definition and knowing just the *definitum*, like Henry he traced back to Aristotle's notion of a "nominal knowledge" signifying the object only by name and thus unsuitable to be employed in scientific reasoning.[157] Following Henry as well, he reserved for definitive cognition the strict Aristotelian designation, knowledge of "quod quid est," or even more precisely than Henry, "quod quid erat esse."[158]

Here he also employed Henry's distinction between confused and distinct knowledge, another maneuver rejected by Vital du Four.[159] Developed by Duns to a far greater degree than by Henry, the division became a virtual leitmotif for his thought. His views are laid

---

abstrahuntur ab omnibus per accidens coniunctis cum eis. . . . Et ideo intellectus qui numquam intelligit totalitatem nisi in 'conceptu per accidens' . . . numquam intelligit sinceram veritatem . . . quia numquam intelligit praecisam rationem termini per quam est veritas."

[154] See Pt. 3, ch. 9, n. 33; and ch. 12, n. 35.

[155] Duns, *Ordinatio* I, d. 3, p. 1, q. 4 (Vatican, 3:157, n. 259).

[156] *Quaestiones quodlibetales*, q. 7, n. 7 (Vivès, 25:289b): ". . . ultimus tamen gradus cognoscendi aliquod incomplexum cognitione scientifica, sive praevia scientiae, est cognitio definitiva. . . ." This passage is cited above, n. 110.

[157] On the literal distinction, Duns, *Ordinatio* I, d. 8, p. 1, q. 3 (Vatican, 4:178, n. 58); on "nominal knowledge," *Collationes* 13, n. 1 (Vivès, 5:200a): "Dico secundum eum [i. e. Philosophum], quod notitia prima et confusissima, quae habeatur de re, est notitia qua scitur quid significatur per nomen, et ista est magis suppositio quam scientia, vel notitia. . . ." See also *Ordinatio* I, d. 2, p. 1, qq. 1–2 (Vatican, 2:133, n. 18); I, d. 3, p. 1, q. 3 (Vatican, 3:101, n. 164); IV, d. 1, q. 2, n. 2 (Vivès, 16:100a); and *Quaestiones quodlibetales*, q. 7, n. 7 (Vivès, 25:289b). For Henry on this, see above, Pt. 3, ch. 12, nn. 40–42.

[158] For "quod quid est" see *Ordinatio* I, d. 2, p. 1, qq. 1–2 (Vatican, 2:132, n. 17); for "quod quid erat esse," *Ordinatio* IV, d. 1, q. 2, n. 3 (Vivès, 16:101a).

[159] For Henry, see above, Pt. 3, ch. 12, n. 34; on Vital's rejection, Pt. 3, ch. 9, nn. 35 and 36.

out most fully in parallel passages in the *Lectura* and the *Ordinatio*, and though the latter exposition is somewhat more refined, both present the same basic scheme. Each carefully differentiates one disjunctive pair: knowing a confused object (*confusum intelligere*) and knowing a distinct object (*distinctum intelligere*), from another: knowing confusedly (*confuse intelligere*) and knowing distinctly (*distincte intelligere*).[160] A confused object was one with sufficient integrity to be seized by mind in a simple act corresponding to a simple concept but still in itself divisible into what might be called simpler logical constituents, either the "essential parts" of a complete essence – such as the matter and form of a composite – or the "subjective parts" of a universal – like the various species of a genus. A distinct object was one that could not be so divided, such as an ultimate species or an individual. The distinction in this case was thus effectively between more and less general, or universal, levels of representation.[161] Knowing confusedly, on the other hand, entailed knowing an object, as by name alone, without resolving it into definitive elements or formal parts. Knowing distinctly demanded making that resolution – that is, finding the definition. One might know either confusedly or distinctly at the same level of generality.

Duns insisted that when it came to knowing things confusedly, that which was more specific and less common or general – that is, the more "distinct" object – was known by human intellect before that which was more common or "confused." Thus, mind attained a nominal grasp, as opposed to definitive understanding, of "man" before "animal," of "white" and "black" before "color."[162] In contrast, in the business of knowing things distinctly – that is, by definition – the more common or "confused" object or concept was arrived at first. One had to know the definition of "animal" before being able

---

[160] Duns, *Lectura* I, d. 3, p. 1, qq. 1–2 (Vatican, 16:250, n. 69); and *Ordinatio* I, d. 3, p. 1, qq. 1–2 (Vatican, 3:49–50, n. 72). In *Lectura* I, d. 3, p. 1, qq. 1–2 (Vatican, 16:251, n. 70); II, d. 3, p. 2, q. 2 (Vatican, 18:324, n. 292); and *Ordinatio* II, d. 3, p. 2, q. 2 (Vatican, 7:555, n. 324), he used the term "cognitio confusa" for knowing confusedly, echoing more closely Henry's words (see again, Pt. 3, ch. 12, n. 34).

[161] In *Quaestiones super libros Metaphysicorum* VI, q. 1 (Opera Phil., 4:35–36, n. 94), in either a much earlier or an even later statement of his ideas, Duns spoke of what he usually called "confusum" as "communissimum" and what he usually called "distinctum" as "particularium," much as we might be inclined to do today.

[162] Duns, *Lectura* I, d. 3, p. 1, qq. 1–2 (Vatican, 16:251, n. 70); and *Ordinatio* I, d. 3, p. 1, qq. 1–2 (Vatican, 2:50, n. 73). For the example of "white," "black" and "color," see *Lectura* I, d. 3, p. 1, qq. 1–2 (Vatican, 16:254, n. 78).

to compose that of "man."[163] Moreover, if the very process of knowing things confusedly were compared to the process of knowing things
distinctly, then absolute priority would go to knowing confusedly.[164]
Thus, intellect grasped any object confusedly, as a simple *definiendum*,
before knowing its definition.

For Duns there was no doubt that knowing distinctly was more
perfect and more to be valued than knowing confusedly.[165] The
difference between the two therefore served ideally to convey his
views on the move from an initial imperfect grasp of an object to
the deeper simple understanding precedent to scientific reasoning.
Coming to know quiddity, which amounted in logical terms to finding
the definition, could be legitimately described as passing from knowing confusedly to knowing distinctly, or more simply from confused
to distinct cognition.[166] The same description suited the equivalent
process of going from accidental concept of an object to concept of
the object in itself.[167] In short, Duns could adopt almost without
reservation the ideas and even much of the terminology of the later
Henry concerning the simple cognitive foundation for Aristotelianizing
science.

Although Duns realized that for Henry the formal marker of most
perfect simple cognition, Henry's knowledge of truth as basis for sci-

---

[163] Duns, *Lectura* I, d. 3, p. 1, qq. 1–2 (Vatican, 16:252, n. 75); and *Ordinatio* I,
d. 3, p. 1, qq. 1–2 (Vatican, 3:54, n. 80). He made the same two points, but again
in an atypical formulation – compare n. 161, above – in *Quaestiones super libros Metaphysicorum* I, q. 10 (Opera Phil., 3:184–85, n. 18).

[164] Duns, *Lectura* I, d. 3, p. 1, qq. 1–2 (Vatican, 16:253–54, nn. 78–79); and
Ordinatio I, d. 3, p. 1, qq. 1–2 (Vatican, 3:56, n. 82): "Sed comparando ordinem
confuse concipiendi ad ordinem distincte concipiendi, dico quod totus ordo confuse
concipiendi prior est. . . ."

[165] See Duns, *Quaestiones quodlibetales*, q. 14, n. 2 (Vivès, 26:3a): ". . . cognitio intellectiva . . . potest intelligi perfecta, aut imperfecta; et intelligo . . . quod scilicet illa
intelligatur perfecta, qua attingitur objectum sub perfecta ratione suae cognoscibil-
itatis, hoc est, per se propria et distincta; et per oppositum, imperfecta dicatur illa,
qua attingitur tantum per accidens, vel tantum in aliquo conceptu communi, vel
confuso."

[166] For example, Duns, *Lectura* I, d. 2, p. 1, qq. 1–2 (Vatican, 16:115, n. 16);
Ordinatio I, d. 2, p. 1, qq. 1–2 (Vatican, 2:133, n. 18); *Quaestiones quodlibetales*, q. 7,
n. 7 (Vivès, 25:289b) – the latter two referred to above, n. 157. See also the lucid
passage cited above, n. 155. In *Ordinatio* III, d. 24, q. un., n. 19 (Vivès, 15:49a–b);
and *Reportatio parisiensis* III, d. 24, q. un., n. 23 (Vivès, 23:458a), Duns expatiated
on the unsuitability of knowing confusedly for the construction of science, except
in the case of subalternated science.

[167] The language of confused and distinct cognition appears in the discussions in
the *Lectura* and *Ordinatio* cited in this regard above, nn. 152 and 153.

ence, was a mental word (*verbum*), he did not adopt such language himself.[168] The omission was surely no accident, for unlike his forebear he never rejected intelligible species and thus had no reason to turn to so controversial a description of processes of mind. William of Ware was more hospitable. Despite an attempt to dissociate himself from Henry's precise position on mental words, he was broadly tolerant of it, especially inclined to the early stance that Henry abandoned only to embrace again in Quodlibet 6 and later, according to which the mental word emerged just at the level of knowledge of truth, simple cognition adequate to science.[169] Duns's and William's differing reactions on this same point serve as a reminder that many particulars of Henry's understanding of truth and science, and the noetics that went with it, found a resonance at Oxford and Paris early that would not survive Scotus's critical winnowing.

---

[168] Duns traced the term "verbum veritatis" to Henry – see *Ordinatio* I, d. 3, p. 1, q. 4 (Vatican, 3:132, n. 217). On Henry and "word," see above, Pt. 3, ch. 9, nn. 58–59; and ch. 12, nn. 18, 24, 27, 28 and 30 (especially n. 24 for the "word" as "cognitum in cognoscente"). Duns at times deigned to use the latter phrase to describe the objective content of knowledge – see above, nn. 16 and 25.

[169] In *Quaestiones*, q. 84 (MS Vat., Chigi. B. VIII. 135, f. 49vb), William commented favorably on those seeing the word as a "quidditas formata . . . per intellectum," evoking Henry's language of "formata notitia" in *Quod.* 4, q. 8 (1:974b), though later he took steps to distance himself from any such position. In *Quaestiones*, q. 85, he characterized one of three opinions on "the word" as describing it as *terminus* of intellection and *declarativum*, which description he later explicitly tied to Henry – see ed. Schmaus, in *Der Liber propugnatorius*, pp. 259* and 270*. While never specifically adopting this position himself, preferring instead to characterize the word as identical to the act of intellection (ed. Schmaus, in *Der Liber propugnatorius*, p. 264*), he admitted it could be accommodated to his own view (ed. Schmaus, in *Der Liber propugnatorius*, p. 270*). As for William's preference for the early version, see his general description (in *Quaestiones*, q. 85 [ed. Schmaus, in *Der Liber propugnatorius*, p. 259*]) of Henry's position, which he said could be accommodated to his own, and his account of Henry's views (ed. Schmaus, in *Der Liber propugnatorius*, p. 264*) in an argument he felt could possibly be made against them. For Henry's change of mind, see above, Pt. 3, ch. 12, n. 30.

CHAPTER FOURTEEN

NOETICS AND THE CRITIQUE OF HENRY'S ONTOLOGY OF ESSENCE

Although William of Ware, and Duns Scotus even more, had been eager to transcend Henry of Ghent's approach to the nature of truth and the precise configuration of scientific knowledge, in the final analysis neither put forth an epistemology radically different from their predecessor's in the more Aristotelianizing moments of his middle and later years. The rejection of classic Augustinian views on the normative epistemic function of divine illumination in this last, Scotistic phase of thirteenth-century Augustinianism thus constituted not so much a revolution as amplification of what Henry had already dared to suggest.

The same is not true with regard to those aspects of classic illumination falling on the other side of Henry's functional divide – matters of ideogenesis, object of intellect and ontological grounding of reference – where he had introduced a different set of novelties with his complicated metaphysics of essence. By astutely manipulating this metaphysics Henry had been able to validate the Aristotelianizing worldliness emergent in theory of mind even among classic Augustinians – indeed, greatly intensify it by stripping away the language of a Godly light or divine intervention from his description of how mind generated ideas – while at the same time insuring intellect direct and intimate access to divinity in a manner designed to elude the charge of ontologism. Here again Duns capitalized upon these precedent innovations on his way to revisionary reconstruction of the Augustinian heritage. Yet this time he cannot be said merely to have ridden Henry's coattails.

When it came to questions of mind's object and the metaphysics against which it was to be seen, Duns, though admittedly not William, veered off in a direction neither Henry nor any of the classic Augustinians had contemplated. It is not just that he subjected Henry's metaphysics of essence to a withering critique, for which, in contrast to the criticism of divine illumination, no precedent can be found in a late, mature phase of Henry's work. For despite a considerable debt to his forebear's ontology evident in both the structure and language of his own metaphysics, in this instance Duns saw in such novel efforts possibilities not merely that Henry had not realized but that he would have rejected had they been presented to him. On these matters where noetics and metaphysics intersected, Duns broke with the past so cleanly that the crucial discontinuity in the Augustinian tradition must be located with him and not with Henry of Ghent.

Understanding this side of Duns's and, so far as necessary, William's thought means beginning with noetics and the questions of where human knowledge originates and how, in this life, it is obtained. Among these issues continuities with Henry still predominated.

From the outset Duns made clear he would concede no direct role in the normal genesis of human cognition to divine ideas or ideal reasons, whether they be thought of as separate entities or as intelligibles residing solely in God's mind. So far as he was concerned, the understanding of ideas as essences existing on their own was inherently unacceptable. Explaining in the *Ordinatio* that according to Aristotle's report such a position had been defended by Plato, he turned approvingly to Augustine's counterproposal that ideas were the quiddities of things made manifest in divine intellect, a view he took as actually closer to what the authentic Plato had intended to suggest.[1] Of course Henry, with his eternal *exemplata*, had been accused of positing the very separate essences Duns was here at pains to criticize, but it has been argued above that this accusation passed wide of the mark.[2] Instead, Henry probably pointed the way for Duns. He had gone on record holding that Aristotle wrongly interpreted Plato as locating the ideas separate from God, and like Duns he felt the notion was in any case philosophically untenable.[3]

Yet even if one should accept ideas as separate essences, Duns insisted that no role need be ascribed to them in human knowledge of the world. In the *Questions on the Metaphysics*, he confessed that although it was not absolutely contrary to the principles of ontology that separate ideal essences should exist, there was no necessity to invoke them in accounting for natural human cognition, and consequently no philosophically compelling reason to concede them a

---

[1] Duns, *Ordinatio* I, d. 35, q. un. (Vatican, 6:262, n. 41).
[2] See above, Pt. 3, ch. 11, n. 73; and *Truth and Scientific Knowledge*, pp. 122–23.
[3] See above, Pt. 3, ch. 11, n. 64.

place.[4] Concerning them he took the position Grosseteste and William of Auvergne had assumed long before with respect to any reason or idea above the particulars of the world. A case could simply not be made that such unworldly elements were implicated in normal conditions of predication.[5]

As for ideas viewed as the quiddities of things resident in God's mind, the argument against a semantics appealing to independent intelligible essences outside the world suggests that Duns was not likely to make room among the referents of natural human knowledge for ideal objects under this guise either. The ontology of essence and theory of reference outlined below confirm this to be the case.[6] But questions about reference aside and looking simply to noetic processes or the mechanics of the mental act, Duns still could not envision a normal role for divine ideas. Ideal intelligible forms, even when Christianized according to the traditional Augustinian interpretation, were not to be seen as part of the day-to-day workings of intellect.

The easiest way to make this clear is to look at Duns's, and where relevant William's, account of the generation of knowledge here below. Duns insisted that three primary factors entered into human cognition: object, intellect and means of knowing (*ratio intelligendi* or *cognoscendi*).[7] By limiting himself to just these three he managed to affirm a simple naturalism of intellection in the world, linking up with an even more purely Aristotelianizing noetics than was to be found in Henry of Ghent.

Concerning the first factor, the objective origin of knowledge, there can be no question about his views. As all his Augustinian forebears since Bonaventure had conceded, human cognition arose from below – from the world – and not above. In the *Questions on the Metaphysics* Duns explicitly dissociated himself from either of the most famous Platonizing depictions of a source for human intellection in a world above mind.[8] Avicenna's theory of the infusion of intellectual species

---

[4] Duns, *Quaestiones super libros Metaphysicorum* VII, q. 18 (Opera Phil., 4:340–41, n. 14).
[5] Duns, *Quaestiones super libros Metaphysicorum* VII, q. 18 (Opera Phil., 4:341, n. 15); on William and Grosseteste, see above, Pt. 1, ch. 2, pp. 62–64.
[6] See below, pp. 458–75 and 479–81.
[7] Duns, *Lectura* I, d. 35, q. un. (Vatican, 17:446, n. 7); and *Ordinatio* I, d. 35, q. un. (Vatican, 6:247, n. 7).
[8] Duns, *Quaestiones super libros Metaphysicorum* I, q. 4 (Opera Phil., 3:105, nn. 31–32),

from a superior intelligence was barely worth mentioning, generally discredited among Augustinians since the days of William of Auvergne, or at least the death of Grosseteste. Yet Plato's theory of reminiscence was no more satisfactory, as Duns believed he could demonstrate with a variety of arguments drawn from Aristotle, Augustine and plain good sense. In the classic phrase invoked by William of Ware, human mind was created as a blank slate.[9] Calling upon Aristotle as authority, both Duns and William affirmed that all that was written upon this slate emerged from the senses.[10] Each echoed the phrase already seen in Henry of Ghent, that human understanding took its origin (*ortus*) from sensation.[11]

More correctly, it was knowledge of simple terms, necessary for the subsequent grasp of complex cognitive objects, that derived precisely from sensory cognition.[12] As already mentioned above, Duns thought knowledge of complex truths, particularly those of science, was not dependent directly upon the evidence of sensory acts.[13] He

---

for the presentation of Avicenna's and Plato's views. The arguments against Plato follow on pp. 106–8, nn. 35–42.

[9] William, *Quaestiones*, q. 129 (MS Vat., Chigi. B. VIII. 135, f. 88rb): "Et quantum ad huius determinationem creata est anima sicut tabula rasa." See the full passage from which this comes, n. 26, below.

[10] William, *Quaestiones*, q. 2 (MS Vat., Chigi. B. VIII. 135, f. 2ra): "Item in potentiis ordinatis ad inuicem, numquam aliquid potest esse obiectum potentie superioris nisi fuerit obiectum potentie inferioris, ut patet de sensu communi et particulari. Cum ergo sensus et intellectus sunt potentie ordinate ad inuicem, non poterit aliquid esse obiectum intellectus quod non fuerit obiectum sensus naturaliter loquendo." Duns, *Quaestiones super libros Metaphysicorum* I, q. 4 (Opera Phil., 3:99–100, n. 14): "Igitur nullo actu intellectus cognoscitur aliquid a nobis nisi praecesserit cognitio sensibilium in sensu."

[11] William, *Quaestiones*, q. 2 (MS Vat., Chigi. B. VIII. 135, f. 2rb): "Item omnis cognitio nostra naturalis ortum habet a sensu, ex 2° *De anima* et ex primo *Posteriorum*. Quod patet ex hoc quia in omnibus potentiis ordinatis non potest esse aliquod obiectum superioris potentie, nisi aliquo modo prius fuerit in inferiori . . ." Duns, *Quaestiones super libros Metaphysicorum* II, q. 1 (Opera Phil., 3:194, n. 4): "Dicendum quod non habet aliquam cognitionem naturalem secundum naturam suam, neque simplicium neque complexorum, quia 'omnis nostra cognitio ortum habet a sensu.'" See also the phrase: "cognitio oritur a sensu," in Duns, *Quaestiones super libros Metaphysicorum* VI, q. 1 (Opera Phil., 4:18, n. 45); and *Ordinatio* III, d. 24, q. un, n. 19 (Vivès, 15:49a). Henry employed the phrase about the origin of knowledge in a somewhat different context, natural knowledge of God, but with the same general point in mind – see above, Pt. 3, ch. 10, n. 19. On Duns's insistence that knowledge began with sensation, see also above, Pt. 4, ch. 13, pp. 419–20.

[12] Duns, *Quaestiones super libros Metaphysicorum* I, q. 4 (Opera Phil., 3:100, n. 15); II, q. 1 (Opera Phil., 3:194–95, nn. 5–6); and *Ordinatio* I, d. 3, p. 1, q. 4 (Vatican, 3:140, n. 234).

[13] See above, Pt. 4, ch. 13, nn. 74–75.

furthermore wanted to distance himself from an Aristotelianizing
position he surely associated with Thomas and his followers, which
saw the sensible origin of simple cognition as restricting mind to
knowing only material substances in this life. Denial of this limitation would be particularly important in Duns's arguments about the
wayfarer's knowledge of God.[14] Instead he insisted that intellect could
extrapolate from sensation, through a process of cognitive composition, an understanding of objects in no way subject to the senses.[15]

To explain how the sensible object, located in the extramental
material world, brought about the cognitive act, Duns resorted to
language seen before in several others of the Augustinian tradition
and detected above in his own theory of science. He maintained
that the sensible, and likewise sensation of it, acted to a degree as
efficient cause of knowledge, but only instrumentally, or more exactly,
as "occasion" for mind's intellective act.[16] This less-than-perfect causal
efficacy was manifested among other ways by the fact that simple
knowledge did not arise from sensible object directly but only from
the phantasm in the imagination under the influence of the agent
intellect.[17] William of Ware made a related point when he commented

---

[14] See *Quaestiones super libros Metaphysicorum* II, qq. 2–3 (Opera Phil., 3:206, n. 22)
for the inference; and pp. 215–23, nn. 51–75, for Duns's arguments against it. On
these arguments' later importance for Duns, see below, Pt. 4, ch. 15, pp. 521–23
and 528–30; but also ch. 16, pp. 539–47.

[15] Duns, *Quaestiones super libros Metaphysicorum* II, q. 3 (Opera Phil., 3:227, n. 90);
and for a more mature version of the same, *Ordinatio* I, d. 3, p. 1, qq. 1–2 (Vatican,
3:44, n. 63).

[16] See Duns, *Quaestiones super libros Metaphysicorum* I, q. 4 (Opera Phil., 3:120, n. 83),
which refers back to the principal argument on p. 95, n. 1; and also the first two
references given above, Pt. 4, ch. 13, n. 74. This "occasionalism," which was really
a kind of partial or imperfect efficient causality, must be distinguished from the
more authentic occasionalism attacked by Matthew in his account of simple cognition – see above, Pt. 2, ch. 6, nn. 26–32.

[17] Duns, *Quaestiones super libros Metaphysicorum* VII, q. 18 (Opera Phil., 4:352–53,
n. 51); *Lectura* Prol., p. 1, q. un. (Vatican, 16:14, n. 32); *Ordinatio* Prol., p. 1, q. un.
(Vatican, 1:37, n. 61) – these latter two cited below, n. 22 – and *Lectura* I, d. 8,
p. 1, q. 3 (Vatican, 17:20, n. 62): "Nihil naturaliter causatur in intellectu nostro
nisi a phantasmate cum intellectu agente. . . ." When the last of these passages was
taken up again in Duns's *Ordinatio* I, d. 8, p. 1, q. 3 (Vatican, 4:173–74, n. 51),
the list of contributing causes was increased to three, more in line with the three
elements mentioned above, n. 7: ". . . quidquid enim est naturaliter movens intellectum nostrum pro statu isto, sive intellectus agens sive phantasma sive species rei
intelligibilis, habet pro effectu adaequato causare in nobis conceptum. . . ." See also
the lapidary statement in *Ordinatio* I, d. 3, p. 1, qq. 1–2 (Vatican, 3:21, n. 35): ". . .
nullus conceptus realis causatur in intellectu viatoris naturaliter nisi ab his quae sunt

that both intellect and object – or to put it another way, both knower and known – cooperated in the act of cognition.[18] Indeed William probably had the very same process in mind, for he, like Duns later on, noted that intellect did not accept knowledge from its object directly but relied instead on the mediation of the phantasm.[19] So great was this dependence that, although the phantasm was not an intelligible entity, mind could manage the act of simple intellection only when a phantasm was present.[20]

For all its extraordinarily Aristotelianizing tenor, this position must not be confused with that of purer Aristotelians like Thomas Aquinas. Arguing from a perspective crucial to his theory of intuition, Duns held at least by end of career that, absolutely speaking, the external object could present itself directly to intellect without mediation of any phantasm, while soul was likewise not constrained by nature to turn to phantasms for intellection.[21] Only "in via" was a phantasm required, and thus only after the Fall was it "natural" for mind to know things in a mediated way.[22] This is what Duns meant with

---

naturaliter motiva intellectus nostri; sed illa sunt phantasma, vel obiectum relucens in phantasmate, et intellectus agens. . . ."

[18] William, *Quaestiones*, q. 127 (MS Vat., Chigi. B. VIII. 135, f. 85vb): "Uel aliter potest dici quod hoc diceretur pro tanto quod ipse actus intelligendi uel uidendi, quia fit siue pariter ab utroque, uidelicet cognoscente et cognosendo – hoc est, pariter ab obiecto et a potentia . . . ideo dicitur quod idem est actus sensibilis et sensus; non quod intellectus siue sensus nullum actum habet, sed quia ab utroque causatur, scilicet a cognoscente et cognito."

[19] William, *Quaestiones*, q. 130 (MS Vat., Chigi. B. VIII. 135, f. 88vb): ". . . intellectus noster non accipit cognitionem suam immediate a re, sed a fantasmate."

[20] Duns, *Lectura* I, d. 3, p. 1, qq. 1–2 (Vatican, 16:237, n. 32): ". . . intellectus non intelligit nisi dum phantasia phantasiatur singulare, quod intellectus intelligit universaliter. . . ." Also *Ordinatio* I, d. 3, p. 1, q. 3 (Vatican, 3:113, n. 187). This meant that intellect could remember something only when sensitive memory had retained a sensible species to be used in generating a phantasm in the imagination: see *Ordinatio* IV, d. 45, q. 3, n. 16 (Vivès, 20:341a). Even mind's self-knowledge depended on phantasms of material objects – see *Lectura* II, d. 3, p. 2, q. 1 (Vatican, 18:310, n. 256); and *Ordinatio* II, d. 3, p. 2, q. 1 (Vatican, 7:537, nn. 291–92).

[21] On object's power, see Duns, *Ordinatio* IV, d. 45, q. 3, nn. 8 and 12 (Vivès, 20:302a–b and 305a); on soul's, *Ordinatio* I, d. 3, p. 1, q. 3 (Vatican, 3:113–14, n. 187).

[22] Duns, *Lectura* Prol., p. 1, q. un. (Vatican, 16:13–14, n. 32): "Unde comparando intellectum ad movens naturaliter natum movere ipsum, in via solum est cognitio naturalis quae causatur a phantasmate et ab intellectu agente, quia illa sola nata sunt movere ipsum; et ideo talis tantum est cognitio naturalis hic." See also *Ordinatio* Prol., p. 1, q. un. (Vatican, 1:37, n. 61); and *Quaestiones quodlibetales*, q. 7, n. 11 (Vivès, 25:293b). Duns made the same point by referring to the "status vitae praesentis" – see *Lectura* II, d. 3, p. 2, q. 1 (Vatican, 18:309, n. 254); and *Ordinatio* II, d. 3, p. 2, q. 1 (Vatican, 7:535, n. 289).

his stipulation that by the normal laws of nature (*de communi lege*) intellect needed a phantasm in order to act.[23] And the reason was not, as most of Neoplatonic tradition would suggest, because in the world soul had been consigned to a body necessarily constraining its activity but simply because, as may have been suggested to Duns by William of Ware, in the present life things had been ordered by God so that mind should have recourse to phantasms.[24] Whether the divinity had laid down this order as punishment for original sin or on no other grounds than its own free and inscrutable will, Duns admitted he did not know.[25]

Of course mind could make use of the phantasm just because it had its own power of understanding, the active ingredient permitting material object to elicit intellective act and the second of Duns's three primary factors of cognition. Of the three, this was the one – intellect – most qualified to be counted as efficient cause in the strict sense of the word. William of Ware assessed its contribution to cognition by referring to two ways something could be said to be in potency: either accidentally or essentially.[26] With regard to the general

---

[23] Duns, *Lectura* I, d. 3, p. 1, qq. 1–3 (Vatican, 16:243, n. 46); and *Quaestiones quodlibetales*, q. 7, n. 11 (Vivès, 25:293b).

[24] Duns, *Ordinatio* I, d. 3, p. 1, q. 3 (Vatican, 3:113–14, n. 187); and *Ordinatio* IV, d. 45, q. 3, n. 20 (Vivès, 20:366a): "... nec modo possumus uti specie intelligibili sine phantasmate, tunc autem poterimus, non propter novam perfectionem, sed quia non est ibi ille ordo illarum potentiarum in operando, qui nunc est." Compare William, *Quaestiones*, q. 130 (MS Vat., Chigi. B. VIII. 135, f. 89ra): "Sed nunc est sic quod intellectus noster, qui est ultimus in genere intelligentium, non accipit cognitionem immediate ab ipsis rebus. . . . [P]ropter ordinem uniuersi de ratione intellectus nostri est accipere cognitionem a rebus mediante sensu. . . ."

[25] Duns, *Ordinatio* I, d. 3, p. 1, q. 3 (Vatican, 3:113–14, n. 187). *Lectura* II, d. 3, p. 2, q. 1 (Vatican, 18:309–10, n. 255), suggested that human intellect might have been ordained to know via phantasms even in the state of innocence, but by *Ordinatio* II, d. 3, p. 2, q. 1 (Vatican, 7:536–37, n. 290), Duns had revised his thinking to make it clear that only in the state of sin was it natural for mind to turn to phantasms. There he seemed to determined to show that it could not have been sin alone that accounted for this state of affairs but also God's decision to establish a natural order of powers.

[26] William, *Quaestiones*, q. 129 (MS Vat., Chigi. B. VIII. 135, f. 88rb): "Ad aliud dicitur quod aliquid esse in potentia est duobus modis, uidelicet in potentia accidentali et in potentia essentiali. Modo igitur dico quod intellectus non est nisi in potentia accidentali actiue loquendo ut actum eliciat, et non requiritur quod aliquid sibi imprimatur a motore essentialiter ut actiue actum elıcıat, sed solum remoto siue soluto prohibitante potest de se exire in actum. Sed intellectus est in potentia essentiali ad determinationem actus sui antequam habeat speciem terminantem suum actum, et ideo requiritur quod a motore extrinseco aliquid sibi imprimatur, uidelicet ipsa species, nec potest habere actum intellectionis antequam ipsa species imprimatur. Non quod sit in potentia essentiali actiue, sed solus sic est in potentia determinatiue,

capacity to produce a cognitive act, intellect was only accidentally in potency. It could in other words cross over into act entirely of itself so long as there was no impediment, for such purposes standing in need of no extrinsic force or active formal principle beside its own power to know. In a noetic context, accidental potency thus stood for mind's implicit intellective actuality. Yet with respect to any particular act of intellection, mind was in essential potency, requiring a formal contribution from outside directing the internally generated act to this or that determinate thing. This formal addition arose from the phantasm and was impressed in a receptive intellective capacity reflective of the fundamental potentiality for knowing things. The whole account was, quite obviously, a general restatement of the standard Aristotelian doctrine of intellect as divided into active and passive powers – agent and possible intellects – a doctrine accepted even among Augustinians since the days of Bonaventure and Matthew and almost universally conceded by William's and Duns's time.[27]

Concerning agent intellect, Duns, following the position traced above to John of La Rochelle, commented that it was an effect of divine light and as such sufficient to act without further intervention by divinity or reinforcement through any other of divine light's effects – effects, presumably, of the sort posited by Gilbert and later Matthew under the rubric of "influence."[28] As noted previously, along

---

sicut dictum est. Et quantum ad huius determinationem creata est anima sicut tabula rasa. Et ideo propter huius determinationem oportet quod recipiat speciem qua determinatur non ad actum simpliciter sed ad talem actum." See the same passage from another manuscript version in Doyle, "The Disintegration," p. 325, n. 97; and a related passage from the same question in the succeeding n. 98. William's language is echoed in Duns, *Ordinatio* II, d. 3, p. 2, q. 1 (Vatican, 7:534, n. 287); and even more resoundingly in the earlier version of the same, *Lectura* II, d. 3, p. 2, q. 1 (Vatican, 18:309, n. 253).

[27] See early endorsement of the doctrine in Duns's *Super Universalia Porphyrii*, q. 5, n. 3 (ad 2.) (Vivès, 1:106a): ". . . intellectus possibilis est virtus passiva, et illa praesupponit suum objectum: sed intellectus agens non praesupponit, quia non est virtus passiva." Another early mention can be found in *Lectura* I, d. 3, p. 1, qq. 1–2 (Vatican, 16:246–47, n. 57). On agent and possible intellect in the classic Augustinians, see above, Pt. 2, ch. 6, pp. 171–78; in Henry and Vital, Pt. 3, ch. 12, nn. 56–58. Note how in the first passage cited above Duns uses neither the term "potentia" nor "vis" but rather "virtus." On this, compare Pt. 2, ch. 6, nn. 81, 87 and 95; Pt. 3, ch. 12, n. 57.

[28] See the extraordinarily clear statement to this effect in Duns, *Lectura* I, d. 3, p. 1, q. 3 (Vatican, 16:300, n. 188). On John of La Rochelle, see above, Pt. 2, Intro., n. 4; on Gilbert and Matthew, Pt. 2, ch. 5, nn. 59, 61–62 and 74–81.

these lines alone – that is, just because divine light was efficient cause of mind's intrinsic agent – had Duns found it possible to accept the occasional characterization of God's light itself as agent intellect for human mind, his minimalist concession to the Baconian language commonly referred to as Avicennian Augustinianism.[29] More to the point, since the intrinsic agent was an effect of a higher light, it was legitimate to refer to it in standard Aristotelian terms as a light itself, a description proffered by both William and Duns.[30] This light acted, Duns made clear, efficiently but not formally, which was to say, more truly than any other contributor as efficient cause of intellection yet not as determinant of its formal content.[31] The idea was cognate, of course, to William of Ware's contrast between two kinds of intellective potency, accidental and essential, and in either form, whether Duns's or William's, surely drew upon Matthew of Aquasparta's distinction between formal and efficient factors in the cognitive act.[32]

As for exactly what agent intellect caused, and on or in what it acted, Duns explained that one of its operations was to impose directly on the phantasm a form or active principle by virtue of which the latter could move possible intellect to understanding and which could itself be described, like the agent generating it, as a light or "lumen."[33] William of Ware meant much the same thing when he said that a task of the agent was to "actuate" the phantasm by irradiation.[34] Yet the agent also abstracted simple concepts or, in what was in Duns's lexicon a virtually synonymous process, produced cognitive universality, and this was an effect not directly

---

[29] Refer to Pt. 4, ch. 13, n. 64, above. See also a more oblique version of the same schema in Duns, *Ordinatio* I, d. 3, p. 1, q. 4 (Vatican, 3:159, n. 260). Duns's language in these passages, with its reference to efficient causality, recalls Matthew's formulation that God acts in human intellection as "primary efficient cause" – see above, Pt. 2, ch. 6, nn. 117–18; also Pt. 4, ch. 13, n. 65.

[30] See Duns, *Lectura* I, d. 3, p. 1, q. 3 (Vatican, 16:301, n. 189) for an analogical application of this language to God. Consult also William, *Quaestiones*, q. 19 (ed. Daniels, in "Wilhelm von Ware," p. 317); q. 28 (MS Vat., Chigi. B. VIII. 135, f. 19vb), quoted below, n. 40; and more obliquely, q. 128 (MS Vat., Chigi. B. VIII. 135, f. 86vb): "Sic dicam quod tale fantasma existens sub tali lumine poterit facere unam speciem in intellectu possibili, singularem subiectiue loquendo, tamen uniuersalem representatiue."

[31] Again, see the passage cited above, Pt. 4, ch. 13, n. 64.

[32] For Matthew, see again above, Pt. 2, ch. 6, n. 117; also Pt. 2, ch. 5, n. 99 (cited above, Pt. 4, ch. 13, n. 65).

[33] See Duns, *Quaestiones super libros Metaphysicorum* I, q. 4 (Opera Phil., 3:100, n. 14); and for "lumen," the same question, pp. 121–22, n. 89 – quoted below, n. 35.

[34] William, *Quaestiones*, qq. 28 and 129, both as quoted below, n. 40.

induced in the phantasm but rather secondarily resultant from agent's initial act.[35] Duns realized that some had described abstraction as a discursive process following and not formally included in agent's action – elements of such a view were evident in Henry of Ghent – but early on he rejected any such description.[36] Instead, he took abstraction to mean the act whereby agent intellect, working in conjunction with the object's nature as manifest in the phantasm, caused the object to take on intelligible being – first and foremost as a mental habit and secondarily and only intermittently in actuality – as a determinate formal content in the possible intellect.[37]

William went so far as to characterize abstraction as the process by which agent removed from object as resident in phantasm the particular conditions impeding its intelligibility, a variety of Aristotelianizing fare already served up by previous Augustinians.[38] Duns, with his conviction that the natures of things were ultimately intelligible in themselves, found it hard to adopt such language.[39] To understand fully how he viewed the object's intelligibility would entail going into his idea of common nature and his account of the principles of individuation, a far remove from the theme of this study, but it should be pointed out nonetheless that his novel vision on this score left his advocacy of an agent intellect resting on a weak reed. He could never say precisely what the agent did besides lending a power of agency to the phantasm – that is, he could never exactly

---

[35] Duns, *Quaestiones super libros Metaphysicorum* I, q. 4 (Opera Phil., 3:120, n. 85) for abstraction; and pp. 121–22, n. 89 for universality: ". . . ultimus terminus actionis intellectus agentis est universalitas. Non autem terminus proximus, quem producit in phantasmate, ut mediante illo inducat ultimum terminum; immo productum in phantasmate est aliquod lumen." See also *Super Universalia Porphyrii*, q. 5, n. 3 (ad 2.) (Vivès, 1:106a): "Universale etiam non est objectum [intellectus agentis], sed quod quia [sic for: quid] est, in phantasmatibus, et universale est finis ejus."

[36] For Henry's view, consult above, Pt. 3, ch. 9, nn. 37–39; and ch. 12, nn. 35, 44 and 45; on which, see Duns, *Quaestiones super libros Metaphysicorum* I, q. 4 (Opera Phil., 3:122, n. 89) – the passage following that quoted above, n. 35. That Duns rejected this description is clear from *Quaestiones super libros Metaphysicorum* VII, q. 18 (Opera Phil., 4:352–53, n. 51), where he claimed that the agent was partial cause of a real universal species.

[37] Duns, *Quaestiones super libros Metaphysicorum* VII, q. 18 (Opera Phil., 4:350–51, nn. 46–48). On references in this passage to first and second being, see the same question, p. 348, n. 44.

[38] William, *Quaestiones*, q. 26 (in Doyle, "The Disintegration," p. 327, n. 105; for a similar position in Henry, above, Pt. 3, ch. 12, n. 60.

[39] On the object as directly intelligible without the phantasm, see the passage from *Ordinatio* IV, d. 45, q. 3, cited above, n. 21.

delineate its other, abstractive function – yet by his view of the object, phantasms could be completely done without.

William had a theory that might have served Duns well. Agent intellect operated not merely to dispose the phantasm to act – which was, he said, all that the ancients had known about its function – but also to prepare the possible for receiving understanding.[40] As if to underline the broader significance of his point, he commented on how it made an agent indispensable regardless of whether or not objects were intelligible without recourse to phantasms.[41] He even assigned the agent two roles vis-à-vis phantasm and two others vis-à-vis possible intellect, precisely the position Henry of Ghent had taken in late career, a passage from Henry's Quodlibet 13, q. 8 providing the likely source for his words.[42] With his own quite different

---

[40] William, *Quaestiones*, q. 129 (MS Vat., Chigi. B. VIII. 135, f. 88rb): "Dicit quod duplex est operatio intellectus agentis. Quarum una est disponere fantasma ut potest mouere ipsum intellectum possibilem, et philosophi solum propter illam opinionem posuerunt intellectum agentem, sicut potest haberi a Commentatore 3º *De anima*, ubi dicit quod si essent res separate, sicut posuit Plato, non esset necesse ponere intellectum agentem. Alia autem operatio intellectus agentis est disponere intellectum possibilem ut possit recipere speciem et intelligere." This passage synopsizes Henry's views as given in the passages cited in Pt. 3, ch. 12, n. 62. For the reference to Averroes, see *Commentarium magnum in De anima* III, 18 (ed. Crawford, p. 440). In another question, William drew even more clearly on Henry's assertion in *Summa*, a. 1, q. 5; and a. 58, q. 2, that agent was to phantasm as light to color, agent to possible as light to the medium – or, Henry added, to the *visus*: see William's *Quaestiones*, q. 28 (MS Vat., Chigi. B. VIII. 135, f. 19vb): "De primo sciendum est quod secundum Philosophum 3º *De anima*, intellectus agens est habitus ut lux. Sicut enim lux non habet solum actuare colorem ut faciat de potentia uisibili actu uisibile, sed etiam disponere medium ad susceptionem speciei, ita intellectus agens habet irradiatione sua fantasmata actuare, ut de potentia intelligibilibus faciat actu intelligibilia; habet etiam disponere intellectum possibilem, seu memoriam, ad receptionem specierum intelligibilium." Compare the somewhat less satisfactory version in Doyle, "The Disintegration," p. 328, n. 108. For Aristotle, consult *De anima* III, 5, also cited above, Pt. 3, ch. 12, n. 62.

[41] William, *Quaestiones*, q. 28 (MS Vat., Chigi. B. VIII. 135, f. 20ra): "Ad aliud dico quod intellectus agens comparatur ad intellectum possibilem et ad alias potentias, et ad fantasmata. Licet ergo non requiratur intellectus agens propter fantasmata – et hoc si res essent abstracte, ut posuit Plato – requiritur tamen per comparationem ad intellectum possibilem."

[42] William, *Quaestiones*, q. 28 (MS Vat., Chigi. B. VIII. 135, f. 19vb): "Sic lumen intellectus agentis duo facit circa fantasmata: unum quod facit intelligibile quod est ibi in potentia esse actu intelligibile, et aliud quod dat sibi actualitatem per quam possit mouere intellectum possibilem. Similiter circa intellectum possibilem duo facit: unum quod disponit ipsum ad receptionem speciei, aliud quod dat sibi actualitatem per quam possit elicere actum secundum." On Henry, see above, Pt. 3, ch. 12, n. 63. Gál pointed out the connection to Henry in "Guilielmi de Ware doctrina," pp. 162–63.

vision of quiddity, Duns simply ignored all this from his two predecessors, ultimately leaving ambiguous the place of the agent in his
noetics.

Concerning possible intellect, William and Duns agreed that its
role was to receive from the phantasm the intelligible abstraction of
the object.[43] In line again with Henry, they also insisted that once
this reception had occurred, the possible generated its own activity
by which mind came at last to actual simple intellection – what had
amounted in Henry's system to the formation of an expressed species
or word.[44] Duns was in fact prepared to assert, once more like Henry
but taking his ideas a step further, that possible intellect was then
responsible on its own for subsequent complex acts not only of compounding and dividing received simple concepts but also recognizing whether the resultant propositions were true or false.[45]

What passed from phantasm to the receiving possible intellect
under the agent's influence was an intelligible species, a formal principle that could inhere in the possible and thereby serve as concrete
vehicle conveying information about the object to mind. This was,
of course, the third of Duns's primary factors of simple cognition –
the means of knowing – and both he and William defended its place
in noetics in the face of the Henry's rejection of it as a threat to
cognitive objectivity.[46] As William had illustrated by means of his

---

[43] William, *Quaestiones*, q. 28 (MS Vat., Chigi. B. VIII. 135, f. 19vb), quoted
above in nn. 40 and 42. In Duns the point is continually implied, rarely explicitly
stated, although Duns does talk about reception by possible intellect in *Quaestiones
super libros Metaphysicorum* VII, q. 18 (Opera Phil., 4:351, n. 47).

[44] William, *Quaestiones*, q. 28 (MS Vat., Chigi. B. VIII. 135, f. 19vb), quoted
above, n. 42; Henry's views are outlined above, Pt. 3, ch. 12, nn. 65 and 67. As
might be expected, given Duns's radical ideas about the intelligibility of the object,
he was more tentative about a second act, but he, too, seems to have accepted it
to the extent of recognizing the difference between the inhering of the intelligible
species in the possible and a concomitant actual cognition – see the passages from
Quaestiones super libros Metaphysicorum VII, q. 18, cited above, nn. 36 and 37.

[45] Duns, *Quaestiones super libros Metaphysicorum* I, q. 4 (Opera Phil., 3:100, n. 14):
"Ille [intellectus possibilis] igitur sic, conceptis simplicibus, potest virtute propria ipsa
componere vel dividere." Also the same question, pp. 120–21, nn. 84–85: "Responsio:
quod in demonstratione intellectus possibilis est principalis causa, quia in ipso est
habitus principiorum et conclusionum. Sed quid hic? – Responsio: si experimentum
sit in parte sensitiva, tunc intellectus agens abstrahit incomplexa, et intellectus possibilis componit illa, et adhaeret illi complexioni per se si est principium, vel ex cognitione sensitiva, quae vidit extrema coniungi in singulari saepe." Compare Henry's
views – Pt. 3, ch. 12, n. 66, 76 and 77 – which were, in contrast, partly about
simple cognition and in any case attributed a complementary role to agent intellect.

[46] See mention of intelligible species in Duns's *Quaestiones super libros Metaphysicorum*

distinction between accidental and essential potency, the species provided the determinative complement to intellect regarded as in potency
to every specific instance of understanding, marking a cognitive operation as *such* an act – that is, one referring to this or that object.[47]

For all this, William as well as Duns affirmed that there was no
absolute necessity for intelligible species in human intellection, which
could and, under the right circumstances, did occur without species
at all. William defended his position with reference to the principle
of parsimony and an argument about the true nature of formal causation.[48] It was a matter of considerable significance for the history

VII, q. 18, cited above, n. 36. The same question, p. 349, n. 45, identified as the
"common opinion" (*via communis*) the view that there were intelligible species and
that they were retained by mind after the initial act of intellection. Duns realized
that Henry, whom he did not mention by name, denied intelligible species – see
again the same question, pp. 349, n. 44; and 351, n. 50; and *Reportatio parisiensis*
Prol., q. 1, n. 14 (Vivès, 22:14b) – and in *Lectura* I, d. 3, p. 1, q. 3 (Vatican, 16:299,
n. 185), he expressly contrasted his own position to Henry's. For William of Ware,
see *Quaestiones*, q. 129 (MS Vat., Chigi. B. VIII. 135, f. 88rb), quoted above, n. 40.
    [47] William, *Quaestiones*, q. 129, as quoted above, n. 26; and also the same ques-
tion, (MS Vat., Chigi. B. VIII. 135, f. 88rb): "Nunc autem est ita quod intellectus
agens non presupponit ante se aliam potentiam disponentem suum obiectum, nec
in se recipit aliquid quod determinatiue terminet suum actum. Intellectus autem
possibilis presupponit ante se potentiam generis sui – uidelicet intellectum agentem – disponentem ipsum fantasma ut possit mouere ipsum intellectum, et recipit
aliquid in se quod determinatiue terminet suum actum – uidelicet ipsam speciem
obiecti – que cadit etiam media inter obiectum et actum, sicut dictum est." See
also from the same question, f. 87vb, quoted below, n. 49.
    [48] William, *Quaestiones*, q. 129 (MS Vat., Chigi. B. VIII. 135, f. 87va): "Sed quia
nullam speciem oporteat ponere in intellectu possibili propter defectum a parte
potentie, uidetur, secundum Philosophum primo *Physicorum*, qandocumque aliquid
eque bene fieri potest per pauciora sicut per plura, ponendum est id fieri per pauciora – quare enim secundum Philosophum idem potest saluari per tria principia,
quod posset per infinita si ponerentur, ideo, dicit, tria principia esse ponenda –
cum, igitur, illud idem quod saluatur ipsi siue illi ponendo speciem requiri a parte
potentie – ut scilicet a tali potentia cum tali specie actus eliciatur – possumus salu-
are nos per potentiam nudam nullam speciem in ea ad hoc ponendo, melius est
ponere ipsam non requiri quam requiri. . . . Ergo potentia intellectiua, cum sit multo
actualior caliditate, quia est forma immaterialis plus habens de entitate quam calid-
itas, que est forma materialis, poterit per se sine aliqua forma sibi superaddita in
suum actum, qui est intelligere. . . . Sed si species requireretur a parte potentie ut
causa formalis respectu intellectionis, igitur ipsa magis esset potentia intellectiua
actiua intellectionis quam ipsa potentia intellectiua. Et confirmatur hoc ex 9° *Meta-
physice*, ubi dicit quod illud est potentia actiua quo aliquid agit, et illud potentia
passiua quo aliquid patitur. Cum igitur talis species esset illud quo potentia intellectiua intelligeret, ipsa esset intellectiua actiue loquendo, quod est inconueniens."
For the references to Aristotle, see *Physics* I, 6 (189a14–17); and *Metaphysics* IX, 1
(especially 1046a11–15). William's argument against species as active formal principle
may have implicitly contradicted Matthew of Aquasparta on the formal principles

of thought that this conditional exclusion of intelligible species rested on grounds quite different from those of Henry's unconditional rejection, his insistence that there be no impressed or inhering intellective form in any act of intellection – that is, it rested on the conviction instead that if an object could be present in itself, there was no need for species, too.[49] Duns in particular took such reasoning as invitation to expand beyond what anyone had previously thought prudent the number of cases in which object presented itself directly to intellect, opening the way for his famous notion of intuitive cognition – knowledge without species being the hallmark of Scotistic intuition, with species playing a role only in what he called abstractive intellection.[50] Though William never used the term "intuitive" for knowledge

---

of understanding – see above, Pt. 2, ch. 5, n. 102; and ch. 6, pp. 182–85, especially n. 115.

[49] On Duns's explicit rejection of Henry's view on species, see above, n. 46. William also mentioned Henry's opinion and made clear it differed from his own – see *Quaestiones*, q. 129, (MS Vat., Chigi. B. VIII. 135, f. 87vb): "Secundus modus dicendi est quod intellectio in homine fit tantum modo per speciem expressam in fantasmate uirtute luminis agentis uniuersale representantem ut intellectus possit uniuersale intelligere. Secundum quam opinionem patet etiam speciem tantum poni propter representationem obiecti absentis ut potentia intellectiua informetur, cum nec aliquam formam isti ponant recipi in ipso intellectu." William's description of Henry as allowing an inhering species only insofar as object was represented in phantasm is echoed in Duns's later criticism of Henry on species: see *Lectura* I, d. 3, p. 1, q. 3 (Vatican, 16:299, n. 185); and *Ordinatio* I, d. 3, p. 1, q. 4 (Vatican, 3:153, n. 251). On why species were needed in those instances where they came into play, see William, *Quaestiones*, q. 129 (MS Vat., Chigi. B. VIII. 135, f. 87vb): "Alia uero est potentia que nullam presupponit formam ex parte sui propter actum suum, sed tamen presupponit et requirit rem ipsam uel speciem in se ipsa, que suum actum terminet – rem si sit in ipsa res presens intellectui, uel speciem rei si res sit absens. Nam ad hoc solum ponitur species in intellectu possibili ut res representetur que absens est. . . . Species uero ponitur magis propter absentiam obiecti – videlicet, quia non est obiectum presens, ideo ponitur species ipsum representans. . . . Ex iam dictis potest patere qui sunt modi ponendi circa modum intelligendi in nobis et in angelo. . . . Quartus modus est, quem magis intelligo, quo dicitur quod ipsa potentia intellectiua secundum se sine alio superaddito potest actum intellectionis elicere non requirens speciem nisi ut obiectum, quando est absens, representet. Et si obiectum esset presens, nulla species requireretur." See also the same question, excerpted in Doyle, "The Disintegration," p. 238, n. 109. Duns made the same point, but more obliquely, in his *Reportatio parisiensis* Prol., q. 1, n. 11 (Vivès, 22:13a): ". . . quia nihil potest esse in intellectu objective, nisi vel objiciatur intellectui principaliter in se ipso, vel in aliquo repraesentativo ejus realiter existente."

[50] See, for instance, Duns, *Lectura* II, d. 3, p. 2, q. 2 (Vatican, 18:322, n. 388): ". . . non autem dicitur esse cognitio 'intuitiva' quia non est 'discursiva,' sed prout distinguitur contra abstractivam qua per speciem cognoscitur res in se." Dumont's argument ("Theology as a Science," nn. 28 and 30) pointing to Henry's 3 – fold typology of knowledge as source for Duns's idea of a kind of knowledge by the

of an object present in itself, he clearly accepted the phenomenon in much the same terms as Duns, holding that it applied to human cognition at least in the case of the beatific vision.[51]

Despite the obvious departures, William's and Duns's theory of mind was in the end, on the themes of major concern for the present study, fundamentally like what had already appeared in Henry of Ghent, often directly derivative of him. All three theologians offered a strongly naturalizing noetics with regard to normal circumstances in the world of sin, and most important, for none of them, neither William nor Duns at any point nor Henry after mid-career, was there even the trace of a direct role for God. But as remarked at the beginning of this chapter, Henry's noetics and his theory of the object of mind had been considerably enriched – one might say transformed beyond appearances – by his ontology and his metaphysics of essence. Through these aspects of his philosophy God was drawn back in, notwithstanding his absence from the technical account of noetic procedures. Here is where Henry had brought his greatest inventiveness to bear on issues of mind and cognitive object, and where he retained an intimate role for divinity regardless of what was to be believed about normative questions of truth and illumination.

At this point Duns, although probably not William, resolutely broke with Henry. He adamantly, and quite conspicuously, rejected the latter's theory of essence and all its implications for mind's road to God. In so doing, he made his most dramatic contribution to the Augustinian tradition of which he was part. Still, even in rejection, it is striking how much of the structural underpinnings of Henry's metaphysics remained. Duns worked out his own quite contrary ontology in a philosophical context where the terms as well as many of the formal relations among them came from Henry, were indeed incomprehensible without an understanding of his thought.

Like Henry, and in line with the Aristotelianizing currents of the day, William and Duns held the object of mind to be quiddity.[52]

---

presence of the object (Henry's "visio") is strengthened by the appearance in William of Ware of reference to the very same 3–fold scheme – see William, *Quaestiones*, q. 20, as quoted in Doyle, "The Disintegration," p. 326, n. 101.

[51] William, *Quaestiones*, q. 129 (MS Vat., Chigi. B. VIII. 135, f. 88va): "Similiter ex hoc soluitur utrum essentia diuina in patria uideatur per speciem, quia patet per eandem rationem [i.e. quod non ponitur species nisi propter absentiam a parte obiecti,] quod non."

[52] On Henry, see above, Pt. 3, ch. 10, n. 23.

More precisely, it was, as William said, the quiddity of material things, to which Duns agreed, adding by way of more generous terms he set in mid-career that this included whatever was logically contained in or inferred by material objects.[53] As will be clear below, Duns had a yet vaster notion of the domain of intellectual objects when it came to what mind was by nature directed towards, but of concern now is only what could be known in the world of sin.[54]

William and the early Duns appear to have concurred, like purer Aristotelianizers, that mind's quidditative object was necessarily known as a universal, though Duns eventually abandoned this view.[55] Even in his early works he had conceded that the universal was not precisely the same as quiddity or *quod quid est*, a sign that he, like Henry, was prepared to consider the mental object in a strongly Avicennian light. As he well knew, for Avicenna absolute essence, equivalent to quiddity in his system, was prior to universality or singularity.[56] By

---

[53] William, *Quaestiones*, q. 26 (in Doyle, "The Disintegration," p. 327, n. 105); and q. 130 (MS Vat., Chigi. B. VIII. 135, f. 88vb): "... obiectum intellectus nostri est ipsa quidditas rei, et non esse ipsius rei, siue quidditas in sensibus." For Duns's earliest statement, see *Super Universalia Porphyrii*, q. 5, n. 3 (Vivès, 1:106a): "... quia intelligitur de primo subjecto [here, in the sense of "object"], quod est quod quid est rei materialis." For the later, more generous version, see *Lectura* I, d. 8, p. 1, q. 3 (Vatican, 17:20–21, n. 62); *Ordinatio* Prol., p. 1, q. un. (Vatican, 1:20, n. 33); and I, d. 3, p. 1, q. 3 (Vatican, 3:76, n. 123): "Concordant hic Aristoteles et 'articulus,' quod quiditas rei sensibilis est nunc obiectum adaequatum, intelligendo 'sensibilis' proprie, vel inclusi essentialiter vel virtualiter in sensibili."

[54] The point about a more inclusive object by nature if not in actual fact is made most explicitly in Duns, *Quaestiones quodlibetales*, q. 14, n. 12 (Vivès, 26:46b–47a). For discussion of object of mind absolutely speaking, see below, Pt. 4, ch. 16, pp. 539–45, also cited above, n. 14.

[55] William, *Quaestiones*, q. 130 (MS Vat., Chigi. B. VIII. 135, f. 88vb): "Ex hoc sequitur differentia secunda, scilicet quod obiectum intellectus nostri est uniuersale tantum. Quia ex quo quidditas tantum est obiectum que induit rationem uniuersalis tantum, uniuersale ipsum erit obiectum intellectus nostri." On Duns, see *Super Universalia Porphyrii*, q. 4, n. 2 (Vivès, 1:96b); and q. 5, n. 2 (Vivès, 1:106a): "... primum objectum intellectus, scilicet quod quid est, intelligitur sub ratione universalis."

[56] The passage from *Super Universalia Porphyrii*, q. 5, n. 2 (Vivès, 1:106a), quoted in the preceding note, continues as follows: "Illa vero ratio non est idem essentialiter cum illo quod quid est, sed modus ejus accidentalis." For a related idea, expressed in even more Avicennian terms, see Duns, *In primum librum Perihermenias*, qq. 5–8, nn. 4 and 14 (Vivès, 1:552a and 556a). In *Quaestiones super libros Metaphysicorum* VII, q. 18 (Opera Phil., 4:351, n. 49), Duns cited the classic passage from Avicenna on absolute essence that Henry had set at the foundation of his own metaphysics (see above, Pt. 3, ch. 11, n. 15). William of Ware was also aware of Avicenna's position and referred to the same text, though he did not draw from it any conclusions about the intellectual object – see William, *Quaestiones*, q. 45 (in Doyle, "The Disintegration," p. 311, n. 20).

the time Duns wrote the *Questions on the Metaphysics*, he had drawn
the obvious conclusion with regard to his own philosophy. Henceforth
mind's object in the first instance, outside intellect, was for Duns
universal only in the sense that as absolute essence it was open to
being considered under the guise of universality.[57] William seems
never to have fallen so fully under the spell of Henry's Avicennianism.

Regardless of this disagreement, however, both scholastics came
together again in borrowing extensively from the peculiar structure
of reality with which Henry had undergirded his notion of the cognitive object, a structure of deeply Avicennian hue. In particular,
each made liberal use of the distinctive terminology of Henry's metaphysics of essence, especially the odd designation of a being of essence
separate from being of existence, the former more typically described
by Duns as quidditative being (*esse quidditativum*).[58] This phenomenon
was not unique in the late thirteenth century, for Henry's terms
appeared in the work of other scholastics, too.[59] But William and
Duns knew Henry exceptionally well and took unusual care to reproduce the exact array of metaphysical categories found in his thought.

More laconic on the matter than his sometime disciple, William
focused on the distinction between essence and the two kinds of
being that came to it.[60] In contrast, Duns was lavish in his description, by his later works laying out essentially the entirety of his predecessor's ontology. Indeed, he revealed himself an extraordinarily
perceptive reader of Henry, adept at using and reformulating his
distinctive ideas. For instance, he carefully sketched out the schema
of three levels of thing (*res*) and their relation to God, and while
reproducing the fundamental categories in Henry's own words – "res

---

[57] Duns, *Quaestiones super libros Metaphysicorum* VII, q. 18 (Opera Phil., 4:347, n. 41).
See also the same question, p. 354, n. 59; and at the end of his career, *Quaestiones
quodlibetales*, q. 13, n. 9 (Vivès, 25:522a). Of course, such a shift in position would
not force Duns to change his description of science as of *quod quid est* (see Pt. 4,
ch. 13, n. 158) although it might dramatically recast the ontological implications of
his language.

[58] William, *Quaestiones*, q. 45 (in Doyle, "The Disintegration," pp. 306, n. 1; and
311, n. 20). Duns was already using "esse existere" in *In primum librum Perihermenias*,
qq. 5–8, nn. 9 and 10 (Vivès, 1:554a–b); and "esse existentiae" and "esse quiditativum" in *Quaestiones super libros Metaphysicorum* VI, q. 3; and IX, qq. 1–2 (Opera
Phil., 4:59, n. 10; and 521, n. 34). Henry had also occasionally used the term "esse
quidditativum" – see above, Pt. 3. ch. 11, n. 35.

[59] See Marrone, "Knowledge of Being," p. 41, n. 68.

[60] For instance, William, *Quaestiones*, q. 45 (in Doyle, "The Disintegration," p. 311,
nn. 19 and 20).

a reor-reris," "res a ratitudine" and "res actualis exsistentiae" – he also felt free to offer language he found philosophically more revealing, for the first category substituting "realitas opinabilis," for the second, "realitas quiditativa."[61] He likewise realized how Henry's notion of progressively denser levels of being implied that there were more and less empty varieties of "nothing" as well, capturing at least the second and third of the three ways Henry had used the term.[62]

Yet beyond being at home with Henry's terminology and willing to draw extensively upon it, both scholastics were prepared to accept much of the accompanying metaphysical analysis or understanding of reality. This receptivity is plainest and strongest in William, who seems to have adopted Henry's vision virtually without critique. He endorsed the position that the dissimilar ontological status given to essence by being of essence and to an actual thing by being of existence precisely reflected essence's divergent relation (*respectus* or *comparatio*) to God as to formal and to efficient cause.[63] He also apparently conceded, or at least never denied, that the division between being

---

[61] Duns, *Ordinatio* I, d. 3, p. 2, q. un. (Vatican, 3:188–89, n. 310); compare Henry's three levels, above, Pt. 3, ch. 11, pp. 340–43. Already in *Lectura* I, d. 36, q. un. (Vatican, 17:462, n. 4), Duns had commented on these three levels, a description reduced in *Ordinatio* I, d. 36, q. un. (Vatican, 6:273, n. 4) to simple reference to Henry's *Summa*, a. 21, q. 4. Later, in *Reportatio parisiensis* II, d. 1, q. 2, n. 3 (Vivès, 22:523a-b), he offered a fuller summary, including explanation of the relation to God entailed at each stage. This late question is remarkable, constituting a compendium of ideas found in Book I of both *Lectura* and *Ordinatio*, dd. 3, p. 2, q. un.; 36, q. un.; and 43, q. un. It should be noted that the scheme of three levels of *res* or *ens* given in *Quaestiones quodlibetales*, q. 3, nn. 2–3 (Vivès, 25:114a–15b), is idiosyncratic and not intended reproduce Henry's ideas. On Duns's use of modified terminology, see again *Ordinatio* I, d. 3, p. 2, q. un. (Vatican, 3:188, n. 310). He also continued to prefer the term "esse quiditativum" (see above, n. 58) to Henry's "esse essentiae," as in *Quaestiones super libros Metaphysicorum* VI, q. 3 (Opera Phil., 4:59, n. 10); *Lectura* I, d. 36, q. un. (Vatican, 17:464, n. 13); and *Ordinatio* I, d. 2, p. 1, qq. 1–2 (Vatican, 2:209, n. 138). In *Ordinatio* I, d. 30, qq. 1–2 (Vatican, 6:193, n. 53), he showed he thought "esse quiditativum" could also be called, in language true to Henry's ideas, "esse exemplatum." In general, I feel Jerome Brown, in "John Duns Scotus on Henry of Ghent's Arguments; and "John Duns Scotus on Henry of Ghent's Theory of Knowledge," has underestimated Duns's insight into Henry's ideas.

[62] Duns, *Lectura* II, d. 1, q. 2 (Vatican, 18:24, n. 75); and *Ordinatio* II, d. 1, q. 2 (Vatican, 7:41–42, nn. 76–77). On Henry's three kinds of nothing, see above, Pt. 3, ch. 11, nn. 18, 34, and 37; and also below, n. 129.

[63] William, *Quaestiones*, q. 45 (in Doyle, "The Disintegration," pp. 310, n. 18(b); 311, n. 20). For Henry's views, see above, Pt. 3, ch. 11, nn. 48–50, 52 and 57–58. Doyle agrees that William was generally "comfortable" with Henry's views on being of essence and being of existence – see his "The Disintegration," p. 262.

of essence and being of existence was so sharp that the latter could be withdrawn from essence by God while the former in some way – for Henry, of course, in divine mind – survived.[64]

He did make a minor criticism of Henry's view on how the three fundamental elements – essence, being of essence and being of existence – differed, characterizing his predecessor as holding that essence and being of existence were distinguishable by intention, essence and being of essence only conceptually.[65] This was, as noted, Henry's authentic position at times, although there is evidence he changed his mind temporarily in mid-career.[66] While William agreed that the three were not really (*re*) diverse, he faulted Henry for introducing a two-fold distinction below real difference.[67] To his eyes, such fine-tuning went too far. There was no such thing as Henry's "intentional difference," and he suggested instead that all three elements differed the same way – that is, conceptually – a stance found at no point in Henry's work.[68]

Despite the fact that Duns never embraced Henry's metaphysics so warmly as William, he, too, adopted much of the basic approach, at least early on. Naturally, he began with the vital Avicennian notion that essence, also called nature or quiddity and corresponding to

---

[64] William, *Quaestiones*, q. 46 (in Doyle, "The Disintegration," p. 314, n. 32 – surely a slightly defective transcription). Doyle's comment that William seems here to accept Henry ("The Disintegration," p. 261) is my reason for saying he "apparently" did, for the matter is not absolutely clear to me and could only be resolved by further reading in William's work. Gál quotes from the same question 46 (see Gal, "Guilielmi de Ware doctrina," p. 267) a passage that might reflect Henry's views – that outside the world all essence fell back on existence in divine mind (see above, Pt. 3, ch. 11, nn. 70, 71 and 73) – but could just as well anticipate Duns's opinion that being of essence was not preserved by object's presence in mind.

[65] William, *Quaestiones*, q. 45 (in Doyle, "The Disintegration," pp. 311–12, nn. 21 and 22), reproducing the very examples of the three kinds of distinction Henry had given in Quodlibet 11, q. 3 – see Pt. 3, ch. 11, n. 43.

[66] See above, Pt. 3, ch. 11, n. 44.

[67] William defended the real identity of the three by noting that the two kinds of being added only a "modus positivus" to essence – see *Quaestiones*, q. 45 (in Doyle, "The Disintegration," p. 312, n. 23). His arguments against Henry's particular view are found in the same question (Doyle, "The Disintegration," pp. 312–13, nn. 24–27). The transcription Doyle gives in n. 24 is defective and should be corrected by Gál's version of the same in "Guilielmi de Ware doctrina," p. 266.

[68] William, *Quaestiones*, q. 45 (in Doyle, "The Disintegration," p. 313, n. 29) – also quoted by Gál in "Guilielmi de Ware doctrina," p. 266. Relying on Gál's arguments, Doyle sees William's version of the conceptual distinction in this case as foreshadowing Duns's formal distinction – see Doyle, "The Disintegration," pp. 260–62, esp. at n. 30; and Gal, "Guilielmi de Ware doctrina," pp. 176–79 and 265–66.

Henry's "res a ratitudine," did not connote existence, which is what justified considering it exclusively under the aspect of its own special being, Duns's "esse quiditativum."[69] From this, he inferred that the question of whether something had essence, or was *ens*, was separate from the question of existence, and like Henry he believed it corresponded to what Aristotle meant by asking *si est*.[70] Moreover, just as for Aristotle the question *si est* was immediately followed by inquiry after *quid est*, seeking the essential definition, so asking about essence in Duns's terms ineluctably prompted a search for the quiddity of a thing, thus providing the basis for science. Indeed, precisely at the level of being of essence – again, for Duns, "esse quiditativum" – was the object of knowledge to be located, so that essence properly speaking was the same as "ens ratum," which comprised all things available for mind to know.[71] Essence was as such fundamentally opposed to fiction (*figmentum*), which could never legitimately be object of knowledge.[72] Equally important, possessing essence meant being "apt to exist," which was to say, "being possible," a phrase Duns sometimes used substantively as synonymous with "quidditative being."[73] In short, he and Henry appeared to agree that the domain of essence, stripped of all but its own special

[69] Duns, *In primum librum Perihermenias*, qq. 5–8, n. 7 (Vivès, 1:553a–b).

[70] Duns, *In primum librum Perihermenias*, qq. 5–8, n. 9 (Vivès, 1:554a). On the ways something could be called "ens," see the same question, n. 10 (Vivès, 1:554b–55a), while for Henry on *ens* as at the level of *res a ratitudine*, see above, Pt. 3, ch. 11, nn. 29, 30 and 79. For the larger issue, consult Dumont, "The quaestio si est," pp. 344–45 and 350.

[71] On *esse quiditativum* and the object of knowledge, see Duns, *Quaestiones super libros Metaphysicorum* VI, q. 2 (Opera Phil., 4:45–46, n. 25); and q. 3 (Opera Phil., 59, n. 10); for *ens ratum*, the following note. Henry's use of the cognate term, "ratum quid," is cited above, Pt. 3, ch. 11, n. 22. As shown below, n. 107, Duns later made the significant move of divorcing "ens ratum," at least according to its primary sense as "possible," from "esse quiditativum."

[72] Duns, *Ordinatio* I, d. 3, p. 2, q. un. (Vatican, 3:192–93, n. 317); and I, d. 36, q. un. (Vatican, 6:290, n. 48).

[73] Duns, *In primum librum Perihermenias*, qq. 5–8, n. 9 (Vivès, 1:554a): "Nihil enim habet essentiam, nisi quod aptum natum est existere," echoing Henry's language from *Summa*, a. 21, q. 4 (1:127rO) that something that was essence "nata est produci in actuali esse." In *Quaestiones super libros Metaphysicorum* IX, qq. 1–2 (Opera Phil., 4:518, n. 27), Duns said that essence was "possibilis esse," a phrase which by *Lectura* I, d. 2, p. 1, qq. 1–2 (Vatican, 16:131, n. 57) had developed into the substantive "esse potentiale" and the near-substantive "esse possibile." Finally in *Ordinatio* I, d. 2, p. 1, qq. 1–2 (Vatican, 2:162, n. 56), "esse possibile" appears in fully substantive form as synonymous with "esse quiditative."

being, was both situs of science and coincident with the realm of possibles.[74]

Unlike William, however, Duns quickly developed serious reservations about the ontological implications of all this, especially so far as concerned "res a ratitudine," the tenuous something at the level of quidditative being which was presumed to constitute the locus of possibility. In the first two questions, Book IX, of the *Questions on the Metaphysics*, dealing with potentiality and act, he outlined two primary ways of taking the word "potency," either as referring to a concrete principle of motion and change or as denoting a state or mode of being, and two secondary usages derived by extension from the latter, mathematical powers and logical possibility.[75] It was potency as a mode of being, which he labeled the metaphysical sense of the word, that interested him, and under it lay three subtypes: first, potentiality as equivalent to possibility in general and opposed to impossibility; second, potentiality as possibility in contrast to necessity, or what we would call contingency; and third, potentiality as possibility shorn of actuality, or rather the capacity for something to come to be which did not yet exist. Each type applied, of course, not to the complex possibility and impossibility of propositions, which had already been set aside as "logical," but only to that of simple objects or things. Of the three, both the first and the third readily evoked Henry's notion of essence or "res a ratitudine," but the third most clearly presented that elusive object as resident somehow solely in being of essence or quidditative being and separate from existence. For the purposes of discussion, Duns said he would focus attention on just this third.

---

[74] On possibles, see Duns, *Lectura* II, d. 1, q. 2 (Vatican, 18:24, n. 76); and *Ordinatio* II, d. 1, q. 2 (Vatican, 7:42, n. 78). As will be clear below, n. 107, by the time Duns wrote the latter passage he had decided that primitive possibility was not located at the level of quidditative being or being of essence, so that in Vatican, 7:41–42, nn. 77–79, he was merely giving Henry's views, immediately followed by his own refutation on p. 43, nn. 80–81.

[75] For the full schema laid out in this paragraph, see Duns, *Quaestiones super libros Metaphysicorum* IX, qq. 1–2 (Opera Phil., 4:512–16), nn. 14–22). Lengthier analysis of these two questions and the issues they raise appears in Marrone, "Dun Scotus on Metaphysical Potency and Possibility," in *Essays in Honor of Girard Etzkorn*, ed. Gordon A. Wilson and Timothy B. Noone, 265–89 (FrS 56 [1998]) (St. Bonaventure, N.Y., 1998). There is beginning to be a considerable literature on Duns's understanding of possibility – in particular, his approach to what is called "modality" in current philosophy – for which see the references, especially to Simo Knuuttila, in Marrone, "Revisiting Duns Scotus and Henry of Ghent on Modality," in *John Duns Scotus: Metaphysics and Ethics*, ed. Ludger Honnefelder et al., 175–89 (Leiden, 1996).

Of particular importance was the question of ontological density that arose when trying to explain exactly what the third type of metaphysical potentiality amounted to. Whatever this third type consisted in, it did not entail actual existence, for it designated what was potential to actuality.[76] But then what was it? And was not some sort of entity required of it, marking it off from absolutely nothing and raising it into the realm of potential being? Duns's initial answer was that a kind of entity was indeed involved, something ontologically more tangible than logical possibility but less than existence. This something was the entity separating possible essences from fictions, like the Chimera, which had no entity at all.[77]

If Duns meant this to represent his position on the ontological status of metaphysical potentiality, it us astonishing how great the resemblance to Henry's vision of possibility as founded in essence at the level of quidditative being. And there is every reason to believe that he composed his words with Henry in mind. Shortly before in the same question he had commented on his third type of metaphysical potentiality in terms that could easily have come from Henry's pen, exhibiting the same focus on essence with its own special purchase on being, while much later, in Book II of the *Ordinatio*, when explicitly describing Henry's opinion on the potentiality of essence, this time overtly linked to quidditative being, he employed the very same philosophical terms.[78] Of course, such a view of essence had gotten Henry into trouble, eliciting charges that he was positing a separate realm of possibility apart from the actual world.[79] Already in the *Questions on the Metaphysics* Duns seems to have sensed a similar danger himself. Rather than explore the "entitas" of metaphysical possibility any further, he simply confessed that the difficulties

---

[76] Duns, *Quaestiones super libros Metaphysicorum* IX, qq. 1–2 (Opera Phil., 4:520, n. 30).

[77] Duns, *Quaestiones super libros Metaphysicorum* IX, qq. 1–2 (Opera Phil., 4:520–21, n. 33): ". . . potentiae activae cuicumque necesse videtur ponere aliquid possibile correspondens; quia respectu eius quod non est in se possibile, nulla est potentia activa. Deus autem est creativus antequam creet, ergo creabile est possibile creari, non tantum potentia logica. . . . Propter hoc ergo ponitur potentia illa metaphysica in essentia possibili – aliqua entitas qualis non est in chimaera."

[78] Duns, *Quaestiones super libros Metaphysicorum* IX, qq. 1–2 (Opera Phil., 4:518, n. 27): ". . . potentia metaphysica praecise sumpta . . . fundatur praecise in essentia, quae dicitur possibilis esse, et est ordo illius essentiae ad esse tamquam ad terminum. . . ." Compare this quotation, along with that given above, n. 77, to *Ordinatio* II, d. 1, q. 2 (Vatican, 7:42, n. 78).

[79] See above, Pt. 3, ch. 11, especially nn. 64, 69 and 76.

of accounting for it were great and better deferred to a time when
they could be given more attention.[80]

But Duns had a surprise in store, for having as much as endorsed
Henry's view, he then introduced another way of accounting for
metaphysical potentiality that took quite a different ontological route.
Some, he said, simply conceded that the potentiality for being something possessed no entity at all but was in itself nonentity or nonbeing.[81] If such potentiality appeared closer to entity than did absolute
nothing, the reason was that it constituted the sort of nonbeing to
which being might succeed, or to put it another way, that it consisted in the privation of being but not its negation. Here at last was
a metaphysical interpretation of possibility which abandoned Henry
and the complicated ontology of essence he had devised. What is
more – the real surprise – Duns added that this second interpretation struck him as more probable than the first. It was, he noted,
especially compelling if one took essence and being, by which latter
he evidently meant being of existence, to differ only conceptually,
exactly as William of Ware had thought Henry's metaphysics ought
to be construed.[82]

The doubts about Henry's ontology that surfaced in the *Questions
on the Metaphysics* swelled to a flood tide of criticism in the commentaries

---

[80] The passage quoted above, n. 77, continues (p. 521, n. 33): "Sed de fundamento eius, qualem entitatem habet antequam exsistat, difficultas est magna, nec
hic pertractanda; forte videretur diffusius et prolixius principali."

[81] Duns, *Quaestiones super libros Metaphysicorum* IX, qq. 1–2 (Opera Phil., 4:522–23,
n. 35): "Aliter dicitur quod ens in potentia simpliciter est non-ens.... [S]ic in
proposito 'ens in potentia' nihil formaliter dicit nisi non-ens quoddam, cui scilicet
potest succedere ens.... Et pro tanto videtur ens in potentia magis ens quam negatio entis, sicut privatio videtur magis ens quam negatio ... secundum illos qui ponunt
essentiam nullam habere entitatem omnino nisi quando exsistit actu." See a
confirmation of this view in the same question, p. 533, n. 64. Later Duns apparently decided that potentiality was indeed the negation of nonbeing, but perhaps
not so much a negation as total nonentity – consult below, n. 129.

[82] The passage quoted above, n. 81, continues as follows (Opera Phil., 4:523,
n. 36): "Videtur haec via secunda probabilis, et maxime si ponant essentiam et esse
non differre nisi ratione." Indeed, in *Ordinatio* II, d. 1, q. 2 (Vatican, 7:49, n. 93)
– quoted in part below, n. 117 – Duns presented as his own an interpretation of
possibility or potentiality exactly like the one introduced here in opposition to
Henry's. Bérube has already called attention to this preview in the *Questions on the
Metaphysics* of a shift in Duns's opinion: see Bérubé, "Pour une histoire des preuves
de l'existence de Dieu chez Duns Scot," in *Deus et homo ad mentem I. Duns Scoti*, Acta
Tertii Congressus Scotistici Internationalis, Vienna, 28 September–2 October 1970
(Rome, 1972), p. 21. For Duns's full-blown mature position on the matter, see
below, n. 116. On William's views, see above, nn. 67 and 68.

on the *Sentences*. First of all, Henry's views were attacked for their implications about the theology of creation. Duns felt that the peculiar way both being of essence and being of existence were defined as merely relative orientations (*respectus*) towards God would lead logically to the denial of creation in time.[83] Alternatively, since according to Henry the object as known eternally by God possessed being of essence – in Duns's words, quidditative being – then it was hard to see what remained of creation *ex nihilo*.[84] But perhaps more significantly, Duns questioned the philosophical coherence of Henry's ideas. Again he focused on the feature of the latter's metaphysics positing the two kinds of being as arising out of relative orientations, or even consisting in nothing more than relations, to God.[85] Most troublesome was the relation accounting for essence or "res a ratitudine."

The immediate target of criticism was an extreme formulation of the theory, a version of which had appeared, as shown above, in the works of Richard of Conington. By this, "res a ratitudine" or "ens ratum" – Richard's term, which Duns pointedly reproduced – was so radically constituted by relation to God that one could not know it without in some way knowing the relation, too.[86] Of course this general idea had been crucial for the noetic implications of Henry's ontology, most especially for the inferences he and his

[83] Duns, *Ordinatio* I, d. 30, qq. 1–2 (Vatican, 6:174–75, nn. 15–16), much of which reappears with slight variants in *Reportatio parisiensis* II, d. 1, q. 2, nn. 5–6 (Vivès, 22:524a–25b); *Lectura* I, d. 36, q. un. (Vatican, 17:464–65, nn. 14–15, 17); and *Ordinatio* I, d. 36, q. un. (Vatican, 6:276–77, nn. 15–17). The latter two texts are referred back to respectively in *Lectura* II, d. 1, q. 2 (Vatican, 18:25–26, n. 79); and *Ordinatio* II, d. 1, q. 2 (Vatican, 7:43, n. 81). See also the arguments listed in *Collationes*, 33, nn. 1–2 (Vivès, 5:278a–b). Paulus has interesting comments on all this: *Henri de Gand*, pp. 131–33.

[84] Duns, *Lectura* I, d. 36, q. un. (Vatican, 17:464, n. 13); and *Ordinatio* I, d. 36, q. un. (Vatican, 6:276, n. 13). For Henry on *esse essentiae* through eternity, see above, Pt. 3, ch. 11, n. 73. Consult Marrone, "Knowledge of Being," p. 43, n. 77, for other criticisms of Henry on these points.

[85] See Henry's position above, Pt. 3, ch. 11, n. 62.

[86] Duns laid out this view many times: *Lectura* I, d. 3, p. 2, q. un. (Vatican, 16:317 and 318, nn. 226 and 228); *Ordinatio* I, d. 3, p. 2, q. un. (Vatican, 3:185–86 and 193, nn. 303–5 and 318) – for the meaning of "respectus vestigialis," see the same, p. 176, n. 287 – *Lectura* I, d. 8, p. 1, q. 3 (Vatican, 17:21, n. 63); *Ordinatio* I, d. 8, p. 1, q. 3 (Vatican, 4:174–75, n. 52); *Lectura* I, d. 36, q. un. (Vatican, 17:461, n. 1); *Ordinatio* I, d. 36, q. un. (Vatican, 6:271, n. 1); and a revision of the preceding two in *Reportatio parisiensis* II, d. 1, q. 2, n. 1 (Vivès, 22:522b–23a). On Conington, see above, Pt. 3, ch. 11, n. 81. In Duns's Opera Omnia 3:175, note 3, the editors commented that Duns was referring to someone other than Henry himself but admitted they did not know to whom, while by Opera Omnia 4:174, note 5, they had identified Richard of Conington as the likely referent.

followers drew about the wayfarer's knowledge of God. Even Matthew
of Aquasparta had succumbed to the charm of Henry's theories on
this score.[87] Perspicacious reader of his "adversaries," Duns recognized that although explicit statement of the position could not be
found in Henry's own works, the idea was nourished by them. He
seems in fact to have located a peculiar theoretical convolution of
Henry's that could be applied so as to render it formally precise:
mention of an "aliquid", or what Duns called "aliquitas," even more
fundamental than essence, a baroque twist most modern observers
have overlooked.[88]

Duns excoriated any such vision of the constitution of essence or
the "ratitudo" of a thing and said it could not be made consistent
with the rest of the metaphysics of the thinker upon whose ideas it
was founded – Henry, that is.[89] Setting inconsistency aside, however,
there remained the more intrinsic problem that if a thing were not
in itself essentially firm and determinate – "ratum" in Richard's and
Duns's language – there was nothing one could add to it, especially
not a mere relation or relative orientation, by which to make it so.
Whatever a thing was in essence it had to be so absolutely (*ad se*)
and not with reference to something else.[90] Thus, against both Henry

---

[87] For the implications in Henry, see above, Pt. 3, ch. 11, pp. 354–55; on
Matthew, the same chapter, nn. 82–87.

[88] Duns, *Lectura* I, d. 3, p. 2, q. un. (Vatican, 16:317, n. 225); and *Ordinatio* I,
d. 3, p. 2, q. un. (Vatican, 3:184–85, n. 302). For the theory in Henry, see Marrone,
Truth and Scientific Knowledge, pp. 113–14, n. 60. To the citation given there to Henry's
Quodlibet 10, q. 7, must be added *Quod.* 5, q. 2 (1:154r–v[D]); *Summa*, a. 28,
q. 4 (1:168rV); and *Quod.* 10, q. 8 (Henrici Opera, 14:202, ll. 95–98). The reference to Henry provided by the editors to Duns's Opera Omnia (3:184, note 3) is
less appropriate.

[89] Duns, *Lectura* I, d. 3, p. 2, q. un. (Vatican, 16:319–20 and 323, nn. 234–35
and 241); *Ordinatio* I, d. 3, p. 2, q. un. (Vatican, 3:188–93, nn. 310, 311–14 and
317); and references back to these treatments in *Lectura* I, d. 8, p. 1, q. 3 (Vatican,
17:22, n. 66); *Ordinatio* I, d. 8, p. 1, q. 3 (Vatican, 4:176, n. 54); and *Ordinatio* I,
d. 36, q. un. (Vatican, 6:291, n. 51). See also *Collationes* 32, n. 2 (Vivès, 5:273b–74a),
and *Collatio* 24 (ed. Balić, p. 217; also given in Harris, *Duns Scotus*, 2, 375), criticizing
the presumption that such a notion of "res a ratitudine" could explain how mind
got a proper concept of God. Also compare *Lectura* I, d. 3, p. 2, q. un. (Vatican,
16:323, n. 243). As noted above, Pt. 3, ch. 11, n. 81, there is reason to believe
Henry himself would have been forced to reject a formulation precisely like Richard's
had he been confronted with it, and for the very reasons Duns pointed to.

[90] Duns, *Ordinatio* I, d. 3, p. 2, q. un. (Vatican, 3:194–95, n. 323); also *Lectura*
I, d. 8, p. 1, q. 3 (Vatican, 17:22, n. 66). On this, see Ludger Honnefelder, "Die
Lehre von der doppelten ratitudo entis und ihre Bedeutung für die Metaphysik des
Johannes Duns Scotus," in *Deus et homo ad mentem I. Duns Scoti* (Rome, 1972), pp.
664–65.

and Richard, Duns maintained that a thing was "ens ratum," a possible essence, completely and formally on its own (*de se formaliter*) and so in need of no extrinsic cause for its essential identity.[91] The same was true for whatever was not "ens," whatever was impossible.[92] In Duns's lapidary pronouncement: "There is no reason (*causa formalis*) why 'man' is the sort of thing to which being is not repugnant and 'Chimera' [the sort] to which it is, except [the fact] that Chimera is Chimera and man is man."[93]

Yet it was not enough simply to deny Henry's ontology of essence. Contemporary debate demanded a positive accounting of the metaphysical foundations for essence or simple possibility: Duns himself had raised the issue, if a bit tentatively, in his *Questions on the Metaphysics*.[94] Moreover, it could hardly be said that Henry had made no attempt to put forth a nuanced, philosophically engaged explanation. Although accused by many of making absolute essence too actual or real, he intended his claim that being of essence was a relation, or based on one, to demonstrate how essence by itself did not constitute actuality. The same motive lay behind his insistence that being of essence and being of existence were never found alone in any actual case.[95] Insofar as some actuality on the part of the object was required to explain the possibility of nonexistents, he located it in mental entity (*ens rationis*): outside objects' realization

---

[91] Duns, *Lectura* I, d. 36, q. un. (Vatican, 17:472, n. 32): ". . . quando arguitur quod humanitas de se non est ens ratum, dicendum quod si intelligatur per 'ens ratum' ens prout distinguitur ab impossibili, cui non repugnat esse, sic homo de se est ens ratum formaliter, – et a quo habet quod sit ens, ab eodem habet quod sit ens ratum de se formaliter: nec huius est aliqua causa. . . ." See also *Ordinatio* I, d. 36, q. un. (Vatican, 6:296–97, nn. 60 and 62); and I, d. 43, q. un. (Vatican, 6:354, n. 6): "Sed lapis est possibilis esse ex se formaliter." As Duns admitted in *Reportatio parisiensis* II, d. 1, q. 2, n. 16 (Vivès, 22:529a), this did not mean that created things were uncaused, just that there was no extrinsic explanation for the contours of their quiddity: "Dico igitur, quod formaliter ratum seipso est ratum formaliter, si per 'ratum' intelligatur, cui non repugnat esse, et causaliter est a Deo."
[92] Duns, *Lectura* I, d. 43, q. un. (Vatican, 17:532, n. 12); and *Ordinatio* I, d. 43, q. un. (Vatican, 6:353, n. 5): "Illud ergo est simpliciter impossibile cui per se repugnat esse, et quod ex se primo est tale quod sibi repugnat esse, – et non propter aliquem respectum ad Deum, affirmativum vel negativum. . . ." See also *Lectura* II, d. 1, q. 2 (Vatican, 18:29, n. 89).
[93] Duns, *Reportatio parisiensis* II, d. 1, q. 2, n. 15 (Vivès, 22:528b): "Nec est alia causa formalis, quare homo est talis naturae, cui non repugnat esse, et chimaera cui repugnat esse, nisi quia chimaera est chimaera, et homo est homo."
[94] See above, nn. 77 and 80.
[95] See above, Pt. 3, ch. 11, n. 66. For discussion of other critics of Henry's theory of essence before Duns, see Paulus, *Henri de Gand*, pp. 123–29.

externally in things of nature, their essence and being of essence
could be found in them as conceived by mind, human or divine,
where they were sustained by intellect's own being of existence.[96]

Duns chose to make his break with Henry complete by challeng-
ing even this effort to ward off the charge of Platonism. Like his
predecessor, he emphasized that being of essence and being of existence were in actuality inseparable, yet in sharp contrast he refused
to attribute any sort of borrowed being of existence, and *pari passu*
any being of essence, to an object as conceived in mind – to anything other than the fully real thing in the extramental world.[97] For
Duns, the actuality of an act of cognition did not pass over to object

---

[96] See above, Pt. 3, ch. 11, nn. 70, 71 and 73; and Marrone, *Truth and Scientific
Knowledge*, p. 125, n. 88.

[97] In *Ordinatio* I, d. 36, q. un. (Vatican, 6:290, n. 48), Duns, speaking of "esse
essentiae" and "esse exsistentiae" said: ". . . unum non est sine altero, qualitercumque distinguantur;" and referring back to this passage later in *Lectura* II, d. 1,
q. 2 (Vatican, 7:43, n. 82), he reaffirmed: ". . . numquam esse essentiae realiter sep-
aratur ab esse exsistentiae." He developed his argument that the object as understood – by God or man – did not have either *esse existentiae* or *esse essentiae* in *Lectura*
I, d. 36, q. un. (Vatican, 17:468–69, nn. 23, 24 and 26); and *Ordinatio* I, d. 36,
q. un. (Vatican, 6:281–82 and 292, nn. 27, 28 and 53–-in the latter question especially (pp. 281–82, n. 28): "Quia si aliquid non sit, potest a nobis intelligi (et hoc
sive essentia eius sive exsistentia eius), et tamen non propter intellectionem nostram
ponitur quod illud habeat verum esse essentiae vel exsistentiae." This is a philosophically stronger claim than maintaining merely that knowledge does not require
the object's existence, which all scholastics would have agreed to, for by such weaker
terms one would need only admit that object as understood does not have authentic *esse existentiae*. See this weaker claim in William of Ware, *Quaestiones*, q. 130 (MS
Vat., Chigi. B. VIII. 135, f. 88vb): "Fantasma autem potest esse in anima sensitiua
non existente re extra. Hec enim est differentia inter sensus exteriores et interiores,
quia exteriores non possunt esse in actu nisi presentibus sensibus [sic for: sensibilibus?]; interiores uero possunt, sicut patet de fantasia. Et ideo obiectum exterio-
rum est ens in actu; non oportet autem quod obiectum interiorum sit ens in actu."
Duns himself, holding to the stronger claim, was naturally free to make the weaker
one as well: see *Reportatio parisiensis* II, d. 1, q. 2, n. 11 (Vivès, 22:527a); and *Quaestiones quodlibetales*, q. 6, n. 7 (Vivès, 25:243b). Of course, neither he nor anyone else
intended to deny that mental phenomena, considered as mental phenomena and
not for their cognitive content, had their own actuality or being of existence – see
below, nn. 136 and 146.

Bérubé has called attention to Duns's decision to break with Henry on being of
essence and object of mind, referring to the same passage from the *Lectura* cited
just above – see Bérubé, "Pour une histoire des preuves," p. 25. Although not generally reliable in his description of Henry, Otto Wanke, *Die Kritik Wilhelms von Alnwick
an der Ideenlehre des Johannes Duns Scotus* (Bonn, 1965), pp. 63–64, also recognized
Duns's turn against him on this point, while other scholars have failed to notice so
important a shift in perspective: for instance, Bettoni, "Il problema degli universali
in Duns Scoto," *Studi Francescani* 38 (1941): 54; and Tamar M. Rudavsky, "The
Doctrine of Individuation in Duns Scotus," FS 62 (1980): 68.

and thus in no way provided grounding for the object's own being – no grounding for its being of existence and none for its quidditative being as well.

This difference signals a profound structural discord between Duns's and Henry's metaphysics. Henry set "res a ratitudine" or absolute essence in the first instance against "res in actu" or actual thing, and then for the latter recognized two kinds: thing as object in mind and thing outside in the extramental world. Duns, on the other hand, set "ens in anima" or conceptual thing against "ens extra animam" or real object, with the latter distinguished by two aspects: quidditative being and being of existence – or, more simply, essence and existence.[98] Where in Henry's system essence was primary, to be taken as in some way prior even to actuality, for Duns it was just an aspect of what it was actually to be.

By Duns's scheme, only the objective domain located outside mind was truly being (*verum esse*) or being in an absolute sense (*simpliciter esse*), a category that inextricably combined both being of essence and being of existence.[99] Early on, in the *Lectura*, he had called the same category "real being" (*esse reale*) or "truly real being" (*verum esse reale*) as opposed to "intelligible being" (*esse intelligibile*) or "being only

---

[98] For Henry, see above, Pt. 3, ch. 11, pp. 351–53; and Marrone, *Truth and Scientific Knowledge*, p. 125; for Duns, *Ordinatio* I, d. 36, q. un. (Vatican, 6:285, n. 36): ". . . prima distinctio entis videtur esse in ens extra animam et in ens in anima, – et illud 'extra animam' potest distingui in actum et potentiam (essentiae et exsistentiae). . . ." Also the same question (Vatican, 6:298, n. 66): ". . . 'esse intellectum' est esse distinctum contra totum esse reale, tam quiditativum quam exsistentiae." Consult the discussion in Marrone, "Knowledge of Being," pp. 44–45.

[99] As early as *In primum librum Perihermenias*, qq. 5–8, nn. 1 and 5 (Vivès, 1:549b and 552b), Duns was using "verum ens" as equivalent to "simpliciter ens," both in the sense of "existing." Likewise in *Ordinatio* I, d. 36, q. un. (Vatican, 6:282, nn. 28–29); and d. 43, q. un. (Vatican, 6:355, n. 9), he used "esse simpliciter" to mean actual existence, comprising both being of essence and being of existence and found only outside mind (see *Ordinatio* I, d. 36, q. un. [Vatican, 6:285, n. 36]). For "verum esse" used this way in the later works, see *Lectura* I, d. 36, q. un. (Vatican, 17:468, n. 23); *Ordinatio* I, d. 36, q. un. (Vatican, 6:290, n. 48); *Ordinatio* II, d. 1, q. 2 (Vatican, 7:43, n. 81); and *Reportatio parisiensis* II, d. 1, q. 2, n. 15 (Vivès, 22:528a). *Ordinatio* I, d. 36, q. un. (Vatican, 6:292, n. 54), offers the variant, "entitas simpliciter." The only exception to strict identification of both being of essence (quidditative being) and being of existence with true being outside of mind is more apparent than real: *Reportatio parisiensis* II, d. 1, q. 2, n. 12 (Vivès, 22:527a), where Duns coined the amphibious term "esse quidditativum intelligibile," contrasting it to "esse in re." For Henry's contrasting use of the substantives "ens simpliciter dictum," "esse simpliciter dictum" or "esse simpliciter" to mean "esse essentiae," see his *Summa*, a. 21, q. 4; and a. 26, q. 1 (1:127rM and 157r–v[C]).

in mind" (*esse secundum rationem*).[100] He sometimes referred to the latter as "intentional being" (*esse intentionale*), "cognitive being" (*esse cognitum* or *esse cognoscibile*), or even, with respect to God's mind, "exemplified being" (*esse exemplatum*).[101] Just as frequently he took up the traditional scholastic designation, describing it as a diminished version (*ens deminutum, esse deminutum*) of the real thing.[102] In contrast to the true being of an object in the extramental world, such ephemeral manifestation merely as conceived or understood could be called the object's being only improperly or in a manner of speaking (*secundum quid*).[103]

---

[100] Duns, *Lectura* I, d. 36, q. un. (Vatican, 17:464 and 467, nn. 13 and 21); d. 43, q. un. (Vatican, 17:533, n. 14), which language reappears in *Quaestiones quodlibetales*, q. 3, n. 2; and q. 13, n. 12 (Vivès, 25:114a and 525b).

[101] For *esse intentionale*, see *Lectura* I, d. 3, p. 1, q. 3 (Vatican, 16:300, n. 188); and *Ordinatio* I, d. 3, p. 1, q. 4 (Vatican, 3:258, n. 260); for *esse cognitum* or *esse cognoscibile*, the remarkably Avicennian passage in *Super Universalia Porphyrii*, q. 3, n. 2 (Vivès, 1:136a); and also *Lectura* I, d. 30, qq. 1–2 (Vatican, 17:412–13, n. 48); d. 36, q. un. (Vatican, 17:469, nn. 27 and 28); d. 43, q. un. (Vatican, 17:534, n. 19); *Ordinatio* I, d. 36, q. un. (Vatican, 6:284, n. 34); II, d. 1, q. 2 (Vatican, 7:49, n. 93); and *Quaestiones quodlibetales*, q. 13, nn. 10, 12, and 14 (Vivès, 25:522b, 525b and 541a); for *esse exemplatum*, *Ordinatio* I, d. 30, qq. 1–2 (Vatican, 6:194, n. 56); and d. 36, q. un. (Vatican, 6:284, n. 34). The phrase "cognitive being" as applied here to manifestation in mind of object as understood must be kept separate from Duns's more particular use of "ens rationis" to designate a logical second intention (see *Ordinatio* IV, d. 1, q. 2, n. 3 [Vivès, 16:100b–101a]), what in *Quaestiones quodlibetales*, q. 3, n. 2 (Vivès, 25:114a–b) he called "res rationis."

[102] The term is used early on in *Quaestiones super libros Metaphysicorum* VI, q. 3 (Opera Phil., 4:59, n. 9). For later examples, see *Lectura* I, d. 36, q. un. (Vatican, 17:469, nn. 26–27); *Ordinatio* I, d. 35, q. un. (Vatican, 6:254, n. 24); d. 36, q. un. (Vatican, 6:285, 286, 288 and 289, nn. 36, 39, 44 and 46); and *Reportatio parisiensis* II, d. 1, q. 2, nn. 13 and 15 (Vivès, 22:528a–b). Duns sometimes called this "ens deminutum" the "obiectum formale" of mind – see *Ordinatio* I, d. 8, p. 1, q. 3 (Vatican, 4:226, n. 146). On use of the term "diminished being" before Duns, see above, Pt. 3, ch. 11, nn. 70–71.

[103] Duns, *Lectura* I, d. 2, p. 1, qq. 1–2 (Vatican, 16:114, n. 11); d. 30, qq. 1–2 (Vatican, 17:416, n. 62); d. 36, q. un. (Vatican, 17:471, n. 31); and *Ordinatio* I, d. 36, q. un. (Vatican, 6:284, 285 and 288–89, nn. 34, 36 and 44–45). See also *Lectura* II, d. 1, q. 2 (Vatican, 18:26, n. 82); *Ordinatio* II, d. 1, q. 2 (Vatican, 7:43–44, nn. 83 and 84); and *Reportatio parisiensis* II, d. 1, q. 2, nn. 13 and 19 (Vivès, 22:527b and 530a), which states quite succinctly: ". . . esse lapidis in cognitione est esse diminutum lapidis, et secundum quid." Duns occasionally employed the term "esse verum" more broadly to include cognitive being, but such cases can be clearly identified by context and must be kept separate from the more typical usage cited above, n. 99. See, for instance, *Lectura* I, d. 36, q. un. (Vatican, 17:468–69, nn. 26–27), where it is said that being in a mind is a kind of "verum esse" but not "esse verum essentiae vel existentiae" (the latter phrase also in *Ordinatio* I, d. 36, q. un. [Vatican, 6:282, n. 28]). In *Ordinatio* I, d. 36, q. un. (Vatican, 6:288, n. 44), Duns repeated this peculiar usage of "verum esse" but noted (Vatican, 6:289, n. 46 – quoted below, n. 146) more meticulously that such being of the object was really "verum esse secundum quid." Towards the end of his life, in *Ordinatio* IV,

From such a perspective it was hard not to view Henry, despite his protestations, as lending essence a kind of actuality all its own. How else was one to explain divorcing an object's being of essence from its own proper existence as a real thing and giving it expression in the cognitive activity, or noetic ambience, of a knowing mind? Moreover, having come to this unfavorable judgment of Henry's metaphysics, it was nearly impossible not to criticize him as well for positing two moments in each object's ontological history. For Duns there was not only no need for quidditative being to precede actual existence; it was in fact inconceivable that it did.[104] Likewise, he felt compelled to deny Henry's contention that an object was constituted by two differing relations to God, one to divinity as exemplary form and another to it as efficient cause. Instead he insisted that God as efficient cause created a thing simultaneously in essence and existence, establishing a single relationship between exemplified, created thing and himself.[105] It is worth remembering that William of Ware had also laid out the double-relation aspect of Henry's theory of essence but unlike Duns had given it his blessing.[106] Here, as so often on

---

d. 1, q. 2, n. 2 (Vivès, 16:100a); and d. 8, q. 1, n. 2 (Vivès, 17:7a), he did use "verum esse" and "aliquid reale" to designate "having quiddity" in such a way as clearly to include possessing it solely in a mind, exceptional behavior more like what one would expect from Henry.

[104] Duns, *Reportatio parisiensis* II, d. 1, q. 2, n. 11 (Vivès, 22:526b): ". . . nulla necessitas est ponere tale esse quidditativum praecedens esse in effectu. . . ." For Henry's notion of movement through being of essence to existence, see above, Pt. 3, ch. 11, nn. 46–47.

[105] Duns, *Lectura* I, d. 36, q. un. (Vatican, 17:466, n. 19); and *Ordinatio* I, d. 36, q. un. (Vatican, 6:279–80, n. 23). Especially revealing is the passage from the question in the *Lectura* (Vatican, 17:472, n. 32): "Et quando dicitur quod habet tunc [i.e. in esse essentiae] respectum ad Deum et non ad Deum ut efficiens est, quia 'efficiens' non terminat quaestionem 'quid est' sed definitio, dico quod illud esse ratum, quod est esse essentiae, non est nisi causa esse actualis exsistentiae; et ideo Deus sic terminat rationem utriusque, in quantum dat utrumque esse effective." The discussion in d. 36 clarified a more ambiguous handling of the issue earlier in *Lectura* I, d. 2, p. 1, qq. 1–2 (Vatican, 16:124–25, n. 39), whose corresponding text in *Ordinatio* I, d. 2, p. 1, qq. 1–2 is terser, probably because by then Duns had already written the more complete analysis of *Lectura* I, d. 36. The criticism is repeated in *Reportatio parisiensis* IA (examinata), 2, qq. 1–3 (ed. Wolter and Adams, in "Parisian Proof," p. 256); and II, d. 1, q. 2, nn. 6–8 (Vivès, 22:525a–b). On Henry's views, see above, Pt. 3, ch. 11, nn. 52, 53, 58 and 61.

[106] In *Quaestiones*, q. 45, William laid out Henry's views (see Doyle, "The Disintegration," pp. 311 and 312, nn. 20 and 25) and then showed he accepted them as valid (Doyle, "The Disintegration," p. 313, n. 29; and the same in Gál, "Guilielmi de Ware doctrina," p. 266). All these passages are referred to above, nn. 63, 67 and 68.

matters of metaphysics, the latter revealed how for all his debt to William he was quite prepared to leave both him and Henry behind.

Naturally, since Duns agreed that before creation all creatable things were possible, his criticism of Henry on the metaphysical location of essence forced him to cut the tie so important in Henry and even in his own early work between "the possible" and "essence," or between "possible being" and "being of essence" or "quidditative being."[107] In short, "possible" became for Duns a more inclusive category than either "being in act" or "being in essence" – that is, either being of existence or quidditative being.[108] Possibility included things that were purely and simply nonbeing.[109] Dividing reality this way altogether circumvented Henry's difficulties in explaining how his theory of essence did not entail eternal actualities other than God, since possibility was no longer to be associated with anything Duns would call "truly being."[110] By the same token, God's ideal

---

[107] In *Lectura* I, d. 36, q. un., Duns laid out Henry's position (Vatican, 17:462–63, nn. 6–7) on possibles having a type of quidditative being before existence and then (Vatican, 17:464, n. 13) showed how his conviction that quidditative being or being of essence was "truly being" required rejecting such a view. By *Ordinatio* II, d. 1, q. 2 (Vatican, 7:43, n. 81), he was arguing that "esse possibile" was therefore not the same as "esse essentiae," thus contradicting his own earlier usage (see above, n. 73 – already in *Ordinatio* I, d. 43, q. un [Vatican, 6:359, n. 16] he had used "esse possibile" in the newer sense). *Lectura* I, d. 36, q. un. (Vatican, 17:472, n. 32) reveals Duns willing to apply the term "ens ratum" equivocally to either possible being or quidditative being, so long as it was clear that the two were not the same, a point made again in *Reportatio parisiensis* II, d. 1, q. 2, n. 15 (Vivès, 22:528a–b); and less clearly in *Ordinatio* I, d. 36, q. un. (Vatican, 6:290–91, nn. 48–50). In *Reportatio parisiensis* II, d. 1, q. 2, n. 14 (Vivès, 22:528a), he explained that possible being was, in contrast to quidditative being, being only in a manner of speaking (*secundum quid*). However, *Reportatio parisiensis* IA (*examinata*), d. 2, qq. 1–3 (ed. Wolter and Adams, in "Parisian Proof," p. 266), shows Duns quite late still capable of reverting to his earlier usage of "quidditative being" and "possible being" as synonyms.

[108] Duns, *Lectura* I, d. 36, q. un. (Vatican, 17:473, n. 36): "'Possibile' est communius quam ens in actu vel ens secundum esse essentiae. . . ." As shown below, n. 113, there was a way Duns used "ens" as synonymous with possibility.

[109] That is, possibility included things that were not, in his terms, "being pure and simple" (*simpliciter esse*) – see above, n. 99. A sign of Duns's ineradicable debt to Henry is that, despite this attempt at clear and categorical language, he was also willing to talk, like Henry, of levels of nothing or nonbeing – see above, n. 62, and below, n. 129.

[110] See the discussion in *Collationes* 33, nn. 1–2 (Vivès, 5:278a–b); and Duns's statements in *Lectura* I, d. 30, qq. 1–2 (Vatican, 17:416, n. 62): ". . . potest dici quod si ponatur quod res non habuerunt ab aeterno esse reale, ex hoc quod fuerunt possibilia-esse, sed tantum esse secundum quid, tunc . . ."; and d. 36, q. un. (Vatican, 17:468, n. 26): "Ideo dico quod res ab aeterno non habuit esse verum essentiae vel exsistentiae. . . ."

understanding of things, the basis for his eternal exemplarity, could now be detached from anything objectively so "real" as the *cognitum*'s being of essence.[111]

Yet Duns went even further to dismantle Henry's ontology. Having uncoupled simple possibility from quidditative being and eliminated the requirement that it rest on any true being at all, he then proceeded to establish it on purely formal grounds. Duns's classic definition of the possible was simply that to which being was not repugnant, while conversely the impossible was that to which being was repugnant.[112] This definition of "possible" could at times be loosely extended to "being" (*ens*) itself, although strictly speaking "being" in the active sense of "esse" – either of essence or of existence – was for the mature Duns a much more restrictive ontological category.[113] In rare instances he actually referred to "the possible" defined this way as "quiddity," though it was more proper to say quiddity was ultimately founded in it, quidditative and possible being constituting two very distinct things.[114] Regardless of such lapses from semantic strictness, however, he remained insistent that "the possible" was such formally of itself (*de se formaliter*), requiring no external reason or cause, such as Henry's exemplary relation to God, to account for its status.[115]

---

[111] Duns, *Lectura* I, d. 36, q. un. (Vatican, 17:467, nn. 21–22), produces two arguments for why Henry was wrong to demand that the thing in "esse essentiae" be simultaneously correlative to God's knowledge of it, which arguments are reproduced in reverse order in *Ordinatio* I, d. 36, q. un. (Vatican, 6:278–79, nn. 20–21). For Duns's own view, see *Lectura* I, d. 36, q. un. (Vatican, 17:468, n. 23): "Ideo dico ... quod creatura (ut lapis), ut est fundamentum relationis idealis, non est verum ens secundum esse essentiae, nec secundum esse exsistentiae."

[112] Duns, *Lectura* I, d. 36, q. un. (Vatican, 17:472, n. 32), on "the possible" as "cui non repugnat esse;" and the same question (Vatican, 17:475, n. 39), on "the impossible": "... chimaera dicitur nihil – et quodlibet impossibile – propter formalem repugnantiam ad positivum ens." See also *Lectura* I, d. 43, q. un. (Vatican, 532, n. 12 – quoted below, n. 122); and *Ordinatio* I, d. 36, q. un. (Vatican, 6:291, n. 50); and d. 43, q. un. (Vatican, 6:353, n. 5). Once he called "the possible" that which was not *contradictory* to being – see *Lectura* I, d. 2, p. 1, qq. 1–2 (Vatican, 16:131, n. 57): "... ['possibile esse'] ... non includit contradictionem ad esse...."

[113] Duns, *Lectura* I, d. 36, q. un. (Vatican, 17:472, n. 32); and *Ordinatio* IV, d. 1, q. 2, n. 8 (2! in text) (Vivès, 16:108b–9a); and d. 8, q. 1, n. 2 (Vivès, 17:7b).

[114] *Quaestiones super libros Metaphysicorum* I, q. 1 (Opera Phil., 3:69, n. 155); *Lectura* I, d. 2, p. 1, qq. 1–2 (Vatican, 16:131, n. 57); *Ordinatio* IV, d. 1, q. 2, n. 8 (2! in text) (Vivès, 16:109a), and the reference to the same question given above, n. 103; and the citations to the *Reportatio parisiensis examinata* given above, n. 107. This use of "quiddity" resounded greatly of the metaphysics of Henry of Ghent.

[115] See above, nn. 90, 91 and 93; as well as *Lectura* I, d. 43, q. un. (Vatican, 17:532, n. 12); *Ordinatio* I, d. 36, q. un. (Vatican, 6:291, nn. 50–51); and d. 43, q. un. (Vatican, 6:353–54 and 360, nn. 5 and 17). Hadrianus Borak, "De radice

Bereft of being, possibility came down to logic. In fact, by his
mature works Duns was willing to say that what could be called
"objective potentiality," corresponding precisely to the third type of
"metaphysical potentiality" in his *Questions on the Metaphysics*, was
immediately emergent out of a logical potential independent of any
ontological considerations:

> Nor should we imagine that [being] is not repugnant to "man" because
> ["man"] is being in potentiality, and that [being] is repugnant to
> "Chimera" because ["Chimera"] is not being in potentiality. Instead,
> the contrary is true: because [being] is not repugnant to "man," there-
> fore ["man"] is "a possible" in logical potentiality, and because [being]
> is repugnant to "Chimera," therefore ["Chimera"] is "an impossible"
> in the corresponding impotentiality. And upon the logical potentiality
> [of such as "man"] there follows an objective potentiality [for real
> being].[116]

In short, he had at last decided conclusively between the alternative
explanations offered for metaphysical potentiality in the *Questions on
the Metaphysics*, opting for the way implicating no real conditions of
being, no objective "entity" at all, and was besides prepared now
explicitly to connect metaphysical potentiality to logical, grounding
the former in the latter.[117] As he repeated over and over, even if *per*

---

ontologica contingentiae," *Laurentianum* 2 (1969):138; and Ludger Honnefelder, "Die
Lehre von der doppelten ratitudo entis," pp. 228–69, have pointed to this significant
aspect of Duns's mature notion of possibility.

[116] Duns, *Ordinatio* I, d. 36, q. un. (Vatican, 6:296, n. 61): "Nec est hic fingendum
quod homini non repugnat quia est ens in potentia, et chimaerae repugnat quia
non est ens in potentia, – immo magis e converso, quia homini non repugnat, ideo
est possibile potentia logica, et chimaerae quia repugnat, ideo est impossibile impos-
sibilitate opposita; et illam possibilitatem consequitur possibilitas obiectiva...." In
Quaestiones super libros Metaphysicorum IX, qq. 1–2 (Opera Phil., 4:524–25, n. 41),
Duns had already labeled his third type of metaphysical potentiality "potentia objec-
tiva." On this, again consult Marrone, "Duns Scotus on Metaphysical Potency,"
pp. 272 and 287–89.

[117] For the earlier alternate explanations, see above, nn. 77 and 81. The passage
in *Ordinatio* II, d. 1, q. 2 (Vatican, 7:49, n. 93), cited above, n. 82, makes clear
Duns's choice between them: "Concedo enim quod omne creabile prius erat possibile
ex parte sui, sed ista possibilitas vel potentialitas non fundatur in aliquo esse simpliciter...." On metaphysical and logical potentiality, see above, n. 75. Since for Duns
metaphysical potentiality succeeds logical, the passage quoted above, n. 116, is for
the most part technically consistent with that quoted from the *Questions on the Metaphysics* in n. 77, indicating that on this matter he may simply be clarifying views
he held early on. What is, again, significantly different about the position in the
Ordinatio is the rejection of the previous identification of metaphysical or objective
potentiality with entity or essence – contrast the end of the quotation in n. 77 (and
the passage in n. 78) with the text from *Ordinatio* II, quoted just above.

impossibile God did not exist, possibility – or more precisely, its logical dimension – would remain, and if, again *per impossibile*, some
non-divine mind were to appear, that mind would be able to comprehend it.[118] Henry's whole ontology of essence, and with it the set
of implications to be drawn from it for theory of mind, most especially with regard to natural knowledge of God, fell at a single blow,
as Duns effectively conceded by the very end of his career.[119]

It could be asked, of course, how logic bore on the kind of primitive potentiality Duns had in mind. Since in the *Questions on the Metaphysics* he had said that logical potentiality applied to complex mental
objects like propositions, what sense did it make to maintain now
that simple objects, or simple ideas, were either logical or illogical?[120]
Duns held already early on that absolutely simple (*simpliciter simplex*)
objects, or their respective concepts, were always logically valid or
compelling.[121] It was thus only in the case of simple objects capable
of yet further division or analysis that doubts about logicality might
arise. The reason was, he eventually explained, that the formal constituents of not-absolutely-simple objects might themselves prove mutu-
ally incompatible, in which case the objects could not be taken as

---

[118] Duns, *Lectura* I, d. 36, q. un. (Vatican, 17:472, n. 33): ". . . si Deus non esset,
nec aliquid determinatum in metaphysica, adhuc aliquis vere posset scire meta-
physicam, si posset esse." Also *Ordinatio* I, d. 43, q. un. (Vatican, 6:353–54, n. 5):
"Illud ergo est simpliciter impossibile cui per se repugnat esse, et quod ex se primo
est tale quod sibi repugnat esse, – et non propter aliquem respectum ad Deum,
affirmativum vel negativum; immo repugnaret sibi esse, si per impossibile Deus non
esset." (Given the parallelism between possibility and impossibility, the latter argument naturally applied to "possible" as well as "impossible.") See also the continuation of the passage quoted above, n. 116; and *Reportatio parisiensis* Prol., q. 3,
q'uncula 4, n. 17 (Vivès, 22:53b). Duns had in fact already taken this stand on logical potentiality in *Quaestiones super libros Metaphysicorum* IX, qq. 1–2 (Opera Phil.,
4:518, n. 18), which discussion is effectively reproduced in *Lectura* I, d. 39, qq. 1–5
(Vatican, 17:494, n. 49). Once more, the difference lies in the way with his later
position he insinuates this logical possibility into objective possibility, removing from
the latter all entity or essence.

[119] Duns, *Reportatio parisiensis* II, d. 1, q. 2, n. 11 (Vivès, 22:527a): "Non enim
novit [intellectus creatus] rosam solum ut in intellectu divino, sed rosam, quam
novit in existentia in effectu, ita quod si, per impossibile, intellectus divinus non
esset, nec per consequens rosa in mente divina, adhuc si intellectus creatus maneret,
cognosceret rosam non existentem."

[120] On logical potentiality, and its difference from metaphysical potentiality, see
again n. 75, above.

[121] One can draw this conclusion already from what is said in *Quaestiones super
libros Metaphysicorum* VI, q. 3 (Opera Phil., 4:68, n. 32), about truth or falsity of
concepts, but the point is made much more clearly in the presumably later *Ordinatio*
I, d. 3, p. 1, q. 3 (Vatican, 3:91, n. 147).

candidates for real being and would have to be declared impossible.[122] On grounds of the consistency or inconsistency of composition, therefore, the language of contradiction, normally restricted to
the logic of propositions, found a legitimate place even in discussion
of simple ideas.[123]

Though Duns neglected to say so, he was here drawing on a
theme originally developed by Henry: the notion that anything which
could be conceived by mind, even if it were not a proper intellectual object but only a figment in the class of *res a reor reris*, had to
be constructed from concepts that were themselves possible and
signified *res a ratitudine*.[124] He merely added explicit reason for what
Henry had not seen fit to explain, noting that it was precisely a logical property which decided whether such constructions would themselves be *res a ratitudine* or not – that is, "possibles" or "impossibles."
Simply put, the conceptual parts of anything intellect could in any
way conceive were each fully legitimate, as Henry's account made
clear, but the chance of an inherent mutual repugnance, a property
analogous to the logical incompatibility of contradictory extremes,
meant that even though mind had brought such constituents together
in an "imagined" object, that did not ensure they could be conjoined in the extramental world.[125] Taking up an idea of Aristotle's,

---

[122] Duns, *Lectura* I, d. 43, q. un. (Vatican, 17:532, n. 12): "... nihil est simpliciter
impossibile nisi cui repugnat esse; nulli autem primo repugnat esse quia non est
respectus alterius ad ipsum, sed ratio prima quare alicui repugant esse erit intrin-
seca ex repugnantia formali ex quibus constituitur: quia enim unum illorum formaliter repugnat alteri, ideo non possunt constituere unum, sed illi propter eorum
incompossibilitatem repugnat esse...": also (Vatican, 17:534, n. 16). *Ordinatio* I,
d. 43, q. un., makes the same point – see Vatican, 6:353, n. 5; 359, n. 16; and
especially 356, n. 10: "... quia illa impossibilitas in creatura est propter formalem
repugnantiam partium." Compare the similar treatment, in terms now of a "ratio
in se vera" (or "falsa"), in *Lectura* I, d. 2, p. 1, qq. 1–2 (Vatican, 16:120, n. 26);
and *Ordinatio* IV, d. 1, q. 2, n. 5 (Vivès, 16:106a) – both cited below, n. 126.
Language nearly identical to that from *Ordinatio* I, d. 43, occurs in *Reportatio parisiensis* II, d. 1, q. 2, n. 16 (Vivès, 22:529a): "... neque potest esse aliquid, quin sit
res rata isto modo, nisi sit res talis, quae est incompossibilis esse ratione formalis
repugnantiae partium." Matthew of Aquasparta had used the term "incompossibile"
in just this way: *Quaestiones de cognitione*, q. 1 (BFS, 1:213, l. 14).
[123] The use of such language appears, without explanation, already in *Quaestiones
super libros Metaphysicorum* IX, qq. 1–2 (Opera Phil., 4:515, n. 21), but is presented
fully in *Ordinatio* I, d. 2, p. 1, qq. 1–2 (Vatican, 2:209, n. 137) – both cited below,
n. 126. See also the final *Lectura* passage quoted above, n. 112.
[124] See Marrone, *Truth and Scientific Knowledge*, pp. 110–11 and 120–21; also above,
Pt. 3, ch. 11, n. 28.
[125] Duns, *Lectura* I, d. 43, q. un. (Vatican, 17:533, n. 15): "... illud enim quod

Duns called those mental objects that, due to the formal coherence of their parts, were indeed possible "concepts in themselves true" (*rationes in se verae*), distinguishing them, with their inherent "truthfulness," from objects "true of something else" (*rationes de aliquo verae*) – for instance, propositions. Concepts lacking such inherent integrity were "in themselves false."[126]

The same phenomenon explained why only possible objects were truly understandable and thus proper objects of intellection.[127] Although mind had the power to form a mental image of an "impossible" – Henry's fiction or object precisely and exclusively *res a reor reris* – such an image was, because of its inherent incongruity or "false-hood," nothing more than a nominal object (*quid nominis*), incapable of representing a quiddity or forming the basis for authentic knowl-edge.[128] On this score, Duns was actually willing to approach Henry's

---

non potest esse in rerum natura, imaginatur ut aliquod compositum ex pluribus repugnantibus, quae non faciunt unum nec possunt facere unum (sicut est chimaera et huiusmodi); illas autem partes potest Deus producere, ut caput hominis et cau-dam leonis et huiusmodi. . . ." Note again, as above at n. 116, how Duns employs as example the Chimera, paradigm of *res a reor reris* for Henry.

[126] Duns, *Quaestiones super libros Metaphysicorum* VI, q. 3 (Opera Phil., 4:68, n. 33): "Nam intellectus simplex circa conceptum non simpliciter simplicem, licet non pos-sit esse formaliter falsus, potest tamen esse virtualiter falsus, apprehendendo aliquid sub determinatione sibi non convenienti. Et hoc modo dicitur in V, cap. 'De falso,' quod est ratio aliqua in se falsa, non solum de aliquo falsa. . . ." The reference to the *capitulum* "De falso" was to Aristotle, *Metaphysics* V, 29 (1024b17–19). See also *Quaestiones super libros Metaphysicorum* IX, qq. 1–2 (Opera Phil., 4:515, n. 21 – cited above, n. 123); *Lectura* I, d. 2, p. 1, qq. 1–2 (Vatican, 16:120, n. 26): *Ordinatio* I, d. 2, p. 1, qq. 1–2 (Vatican, 2:141–42, n. 30); d. 3, p. 1, q. 3 (Vatican, 3:91, n. 147); and IV, d. 1, q. 2, n. 5 (Vivès, 16:106a); d. 8, q. 1, n. 2 (Vivès, 17:7a); and *Quaestiones quodlibetales*, q. 13, n. 24 (Vivès, 25:569b); and q. 14, n. 4 (Vivès, 26:6a).

[127] Duns, *Ordinatio* I, d. 2, p. 1, qq. 1–2 (Vatican, 2:209, n. 137): ". . . in cuius cognitione vel cogitatione includitur contradictio, illud dicitur non cogitabile, quia sunt tunc duo cogitabilia opposita nullo modo faciendo unum cogitabile, quia neut-rum determinat alterum." See also *Quaestiones quodlibetales*, q. 3, n. 2 (Vivès, 25:114a): "Verissime enim illud est nihil quod includit contradictionem, et solum illud, quia illud excludit omne esse extra intellectum et in intellectu. . . ."; and q. 14, n. 4 (Vivès, 26:6a). In *Quaestiones quodlibetales*, q. 3, Duns made room for a kind of concept that could be properly understood yet never find a real, extra-mental referent, so as to allow for second intentions – see Vivès, 25:114a–b. On Henry's view that what explained intelligibility was being of essence or quidditative being, see above, n. 71.

[128] The passage quoted above, n. 126, from *Quaestiones super libros Metaphysicorum* VI, q. 3 (Opera Phil., 4:68, n. 33), continues: ". . . et tamen ratio illa in se falsa simplici apprehensione intelligibilis est, sed ipsa non exprimit aliquod 'quid' nisi forte aliquando quid nominis." As Duns explained, *Quaestiones super libros Metaphysicorum* VI, q. 4 (Opera Phil., 4:87, n. 10), when the Aristotelian question "si est" was asked of such an object, the answer was negative – it had no quidditative being. For Duns and Henry on "si est," see above, n. 70.

notion that "impossibles" – again, objects exclusively *res a reor reris* –
were "more nothing" than "possibles" before actualization, though
unlike Henry he accounted for the difference in purely logical terms.
The Chimera could be said to be "more" nothing than man even
before creation, not because it involved greater negation of being –
for negation did not come in degrees – but rather because there
were more ways it was opposed to being than was "man".[129]

Clearly Duns drastically attenuated the ontological grounding of
possibles as presented by Henry of Ghent, pushing the metaphysics
of potentiality far in the direction of logic. It is just as important to
recognize, however, that he simultaneously expanded the domain of
objects accessible to direct reference and available for supposition;
perhaps one should say he enriched the metaphysical spectrum of
intelligible objects. Like Henry, he took pains to show that the ontological status of object as known had to be divorced from extramental
conditions and, as will be clear below, resorted to locating whatever
actuality was necessary for the act of knowing solely in the intellective subject.[130] But Henry had allowed something of the existence of
the subject to spill over into the object as object, enough to provide
ground for the being of essence of what was known, while Duns,
with a more austere metaphysics, had made object's being of essence
or quidditative being absolutely inseparable from full objective actuality, thus placing an impermeable barrier between being known and
"being" in any true sense of the word, whether quidditative or existential.[131] It was just this greater austerity that in turn freed him to hold
a wider range of objective conditions subject to cognition.

In the same breath with which he reminded his readers that a
mental object as known – an intellectively constituted "objective possible" in his metaphysical scheme – possessed an ontological status
prescinding not only from the object's actual being of existence but

---

[129] Duns, *Lectura* I, d. 36, q. un. (Vatican, 17:474–75, nn. 38–39). By *Ordinatio* I,
d. 36, q. un. (Vatican, 6:294–296, nn. 58–60), Duns had softened his language so
than the Chimera was not "more" nothing than man but just nothing in a different
way. Even later, *Reportatio parisiensis* II, d. 1, q. 2, n. 18 (Vivès, 22:530a), he decided
to offer both formulations without choosing between them. On Henry's levels of
nothing, see above, n. 62. In a similar vein, William of Ware had talked about
levels of impossibility, which were, like Duns's levels of nothing in the *Lectura*, to
be explained in purely logical terms – see William, *Quaestiones*, q. 21 (ed. Daniels,
in *Quellenbeiträge und Untersuchungen*, p. 101).
[130] See below, nn. 135 and 136.
[131] See above, nn. 96 and 97.

also from its being of essence, he went on to say that over all eternity any mind, whether God's or, *per impossibile*, a human being's, could know both essence and existence of any possible object. Thus any object could be known as it would be in actual being of essence or being of existence at the very moment it possessed neither.[132] Such a position encouraged what would have been to Henry's ear the peculiar language that intellect could know quiddity even when there was no quiddity, or existence even when no object existed.[133] For Duns, the peculiarity was more apparent than real. To his way of seeing things, knowing placed no ontological burden on object as object, a radical divorce between circumstances of cognition and objective content that nonetheless in no way diminished the reality of what was known. At any time an object could be known in the fullness of being or existence regardless of actual conditions.

On three occasions in his commentaries on the *Sentences* he explained in technical detail how this was so.[134] The being of an object as

---

[132] Duns, *Lectura* I, d. 36, q. un. (Vatican, 17:469, n. 26): "... sicut si ponatur quod ego fuissem ab aeterno et quod ab aeterno intellexissem rosam, ab aeterno tunc intellexi rosam secundum esse suum essentiae et secundum esse exsistentiae; et tamen non habuit esse nisi cognitum...." Also *Ordinatio* I, d. 36, q. un. (Vatican, 6:281–82, nn. 27–28): "... praecognovit ergo [Deus] esse exsistentiae sicut esse essentiae, – et tamen propter istam relationem fundatam non concedit aliquis 'esse exsistentiae' fuisse verum esse tale, scilicet verum esse exsistentiae ab aeterno; ergo pari ratione nec concedendum est de esse essentiae.... Quia si aliquid non sit, potest a nobis intelligi (et hoc sive essentia eius sive exsistentia eius), et tamen non propter intellectionem nostram ponitur quod illud habeat verum esse essentiae vel exsistentiae...." The same point is made in *Ordinatio* I, d. 30, qq. 1–2 (Vatican, 6:176, n. 17), while the argument in *Ordinatio* I, d. 36, cited just above, is paralleled by that in *Reportatio parisiensis* II, d. 1, q. 2, n. 11 (Vivès, 22:526b), where the principle of parsimony is used to show that God's eternal knowledge of both essence and existence requires neither the actual essence nor existence of the object. See also the continuation of this last passage, as quoted above, n. 119.

[133] Duns, *Lectura* I, d. 36, q. un. (Vatican, 17:471, n. 30): "Sic in proposito intelligo quiditatem rosae, quando non est nec sua quiditas ponitur: quiditas rosae absolute est obiectum respectu cognitionis meae...." See also the discussion in *Ordinatio* I, d. 36, q. un. (Vatican, 6:290, n. 49), with respect to *ens ratum* in the sense of fully existent: "Distincta autem cognitio potest esse alicuius, licet ipsum non sit ens ratum; non enim oportet nisi quod ens ratum terminet cognitionem definitivam...." (On the two ways Duns used "ens ratum," see above, n. 107.) Duns drew on the ironies of language even more in *Reportatio parisiensis* II, d. 1, q. 2, n. 15 (Vivès, 22:528b): "Proinde sicut non est ens ratum, nisi quando est, sic non habet esse, quod exprimitur per definitionem, nisi quando est, et non sequitur quod definitio potest terminare quaestionem an est, quia potest habere esse definitivum, loquendo de esse definitivo, hoc est, distincte cognito, quando non est; non tamen tunc habet esse definitivum, quod exprimitur per definitionem."

[134] Duns, *Lectura* I, d. 36, q. un. (Vatican, 17:471, n. 30); and the much longer,

known – its actuality *in* the act of cognition – was, as he had said,
a diminished or attenuated being (*esse deminutum*); it was the cognitive being supplied vicariously by the acting mind.[135] But the diminution of, or divorce from, an object's fully actualized being at the
time of cognition did not mean that what mind knew was the object
as diminished and divorced. In other words, the ontological diminution entailed in the act of cognition did not extend to object as
object, and it was object as object to which mind was directed, not
object as known.

The philosophical commitment entailed by such a position becomes
especially poignant in Duns's description of the creative process arising out of God. Having conceded, like Henry, that there must be
some actuality in all knowledge, at minimum the actuality of the
knowing mind and its ideas, he offered an account of creation yielding a significant place for the object as known (*obiectum cognitum*) and
at least superficially reproducing Henry's theory of the process, by
implication accepting even its more controversial aspects.[136] Most
important of these was the idea that created things arose by a two-
stage procedure out of nothingness and into existence, the same
vision of creation which, when interpreted strictly according to Henry's
metaphysics, Duns repudiated in his Parisian lectures.[137] As he explained
it now, in the very first moment after God knew himself he produced all other possible objects in their cognitive being (*esse intelligibile*) by the simple act of thinking of them. Only then, after all
available objects were known, were some of them created by being
raised to the actuality of being of existence, which for Duns of course

parallel accounts in *Ordinatio* I, d. 36, q. un. (Vatican, 6:283–85, nn. 32–36); and
Reportatio parisiensis II, d. 1, q. 2, nn. 12–13 (Vivès, 22:527a–28a). See also *Ordinatio*
I, d. 36, q. un. (Vatican, 6:288–89, n. 45). The heart of the matter is perhaps best
expressed in an excerpt from the version in *Ordinatio* I, d. 36, q. un. (Vatican, 6:284,
n. 34): ". . . esse enim hominis simpliciter – et non deminutum – est obiectum opin-
ionis, sed istud 'esse simpliciter' ut in opinione, est esse 'secundum quid'; et ideo
non sequitur 'Homerus est in opinione, ergo Homerus est,' nec etiam 'Homerus est
exsistens in opinione, ergo Homerus est exsistens,' – sed est fallacia secundum quid
et simpliciter." All these accounts represent a shift from an earlier view, in which
Duns appears to have held that the referent of knowledge was in the first instance
the object as known, an "ens per intellectum" – see *In primum librum Perihermenias*,
qq. 5–8, nn. 4 and 13 (Vivès, 1:551b–52a and 555b); and *In duos libros Perihermenias*,
q. 2, nn. 3 and 5 (Vivès, 1:586a–b).
[135] See above, nn. 100–2.
[136] On Duns and the minimum of actuality required in being known, see above,
nn. 132 and 135; for Henry, n. 96.
[137] See above, n. 104.

implicated being of essence as well.[138] In apparent contradiction to his efforts to sever possibility from even the minimal "true being" implied in Henry's being of essence, here was Duns admitting that before creation things were "produced" in possibility.[139] What is more, this production of possibles, though not to be confused with creation, was still movement out of nothing (*de simpliciter nihilo*) into a condition of other than absolute nonbeing.[140]

Yet beneath the similarities of structure and language lay profound metaphysical disparities between Duns's and Henry's view. The notion that any possible object had first to take shape in intelligibile being before it could be brought to existence had implied for Henry that God was precise, or exclusive, cause of "the possible" as possible. Duns, on the other hand, made it plain that his understanding of possibility as due to the absence of a formal repugnance of constituent conceptual parts, a logical quality in no way dependent on God or derived from his power to produce, meant that God was not sole, perhaps not even most significant, cause of possibility in possible objects.[141] In his words, a thing was possible formally on its own (*ex se formaliter*), although so far as principiant causes were concerned (*principiative*) – we might say, causes that had the capacity to bring about real effects – possibility arose from the divine

---

[138] Duns laid out this two-stage process in a pair of passages devoted more specifically to explaining divine ideas: *Lectura* I, d. 35, q. un. (Vatican, 17:452, n. 22); and *Ordinatio* I, d. 35, q. un. (Vatican, 6:258, n. 32). See also references to the same view in *Lectura* I, d. 43, q. un. (Vatican, 17:533–34, nn. 14, 17 and 19); *Ordinatio* I, d. 43, q. un. (Vatican, 6:358, n. 14); *Lectura* II, d. 1, q. 2 (Vatican, 18:26, n. 80); and *Ordinatio* II, d. 1, q. 2 (Vatican, 7:43, n. 80).

[139] Duns, *Ordinatio* I, d. 43, q. un. (Vatican, 6:358–59, n. 14): "Si tamen res intelligatur esse possibilis antequam Deus per omnipotentiam producat, illud sic est verum, sed in illa possibilitate non est simpliciter prius, sed producitur ab intellectu divino." See also *Ordinatio* II, d. 1, q. 2 (Vatican, 7:43, n. 80). On Duns cutting "possibility" from quidditative being, see above, nn. 107 and 108.

[140] Duns, *Ordinatio* II, d. 1, q. 2 (Vatican, 7:44, n. 84): "Potest aliquid produci (licet non creari) de simpliciter nihilo, . . . istud tamen 'produci' non est creari, quia non creatur aliquid in esse simpliciter, sed producitur ad esse secundum quid." Similar language, but mixed with uncharacteristic use of "quidditative being," can be found in *Collationes* 33, n. 4 (Vivès, 5:279b). Duns's position in *Ordinatio* II, d. 1, q. 2 (Vatican, 7:43–44, n. 83), that creation proper could not be "simpliciter de nihilo", revised his earlier view finding such language perfectly acceptable – see *Lectura* II, d. 1, q. 2 (Vatican, 18:26–27, nn. 81–82).

[141] Duns, *Lectura* I, d. 43, q. un. (Vatican, 17:534, n. 17): "Ex hoc autem apparet quod potentia Dei non est praecisa causa quare aliquid est factibile et producibile, sed cum illa requiritur quod non sit formalis repugnantia partium."

mind, the ultimate extrinsic principle (*primum extrinsecum principium*) by which a "possible" was produced in cognitive being.[142]

More to the point, he insisted that any description of creation as proceeding by stages be held to the terms of his absolute divide between cognitive and real being, the latter inseparably embracing being of existence and of essence.[143] Consequently, the object as known by God and residing before creation as "objective possible" in divine mind was not to be formally identified with the object as object that God knew, either its existence or its essence. Cut off completely from the reality attaching to the created world, such a "possible" in mind had only "diminished being": it was merely a diminished and not authentic version of the thing.[144] Thus despite the common practice of calling it the object known, the appellation was valid only in a manner of speaking (*secundum quid*), as if by a philosophical figure of speech.[145] Of course, since this same "possible," taken as a mental phenomenon produced by God's intellect, subjectively possessed the true being of a cognitive act, Duns admitted that if forced to identify an objective actuality associated with it one could reply that the being in a manner of speaking (*esse secundum quid*) of the object God knew was in a sense reducible to the

---

[142] Duns, *Ordinatio* I, d. 43, q. un. (Vatican, 6:354, nn. 6–7): ". . . sed lapis est possibilis esse ex se formaliter; ergo et reducendo quasi ad primum extrinsecum principium, intellectus divinus erit illud a quo est prima ratio possibilitatis in lapide. . . . [E]rgo [lapis] est ex se formaliter possibilis et quasi principiative per intellectum divinum." The same was true of impossibility – see the same question (Vatican, 6:360, n. 17). In *Reportatio parisiensis* II, d. 1, q. 2, n. 16 (Vivès, 22:529a), Duns said a thing was possible "formaliter" on its own, "causaliter" from God. In *Lectura* II, d. 1, q. 2 (Vatican, 18:26, n. 82); and even more in *Ordinatio* I, d. 43, q. un. (Vatican, 6:358–59, n. 14), he located a thing's production in cognitive being by God and its becoming a possible in itself in successive instants of nature, while in *Ordinatio* II, d. 1, q. 2 (Vatican, 7:49–50, nn. 93–94), he made sure it was clear that there was no temporal progression here by noting that possibility, which was formally from the object *ex se*, was always accompanied by cognitive being, even though cognitive being and possibility were not formally exactly the same. See also the more detailed analysis of "principiative" causation with regard to possibility in Marrone, "Duns Scotus on Metaphysical Potency," pp. 284–87.

[143] On the divide, see above, nn. 99–101.

[144] See above, nn. 102 and 135.

[145] On "the possible" as the object itself only *secundum quid*, see above, n. 103; and also the passage from *Reportatio parisiensis* II, d. 1, q. 2, n. 14, cited above, n. 107. On "the possible" as having less than "true being" before creation, see the passages from *Lectura* II, d. 1, q. 2; and *Ordinatio* II, d. 1, q. 2, cited above, nn. 103 and 140; as well as the quotations from the *Lectura* given in n. 110. Also consult the discussion of this point in Marrone, "Knowledge of Being", pp. 45–46.

being pure and simple (*esse simpliciter*) of a *cognitum* in the divine mind.
But in contrast to Henry when faced with same noetic configuration,
he returned to his claim that the actuality in question was not part
of the true being of the object; formally it remained forever the
being pure and simple of God's thoughts.[146] As always for Duns,
actuality of knowledge implied actuality of mind but said nothing
about actuality of object. Objects were known as determined by conditions at some point or points in their extramental history, not necessarily conditions at the time of cognition and most assuredly not
those attaching to the knowing intellect.

From this it should be obvious how Duns would resolve the problem of immutability in special complex truths like the truths of science. He naturally recognized that certain knowledge, at least with
reference to universal truth, did not require actual existence of its
immediate objects in the created world, a position nearly unani-
mously accepted in the schools since the days of William of Auvergne.[147]
Yet scholastics such as Matthew of Aquasparta had conceded this
fundamental principle and still contended that the immutability of
such knowledge ultimately rested on some tie with God and his ideas,
the only truly immutable and eternal reality in all existence. Even
Henry had once implied as much.[148] William of Ware seems to have
yielded to such Augustinianizing attitudes, too, although the evidence
he did so is only indirect.[149]

Duns resolutely rejected all such appeals to an ontological underpinning of cognitive immutability in God or God's eternal understanding. Just as Henry on occasion, and Grosseteste more consistently

---

[146] Duns, *Ordinatio* I, d. 36, q. un. (Vatican, 6:289, n. 46 – also cited above,
n. 103): "Et si velis quaerere aliquod esse verum huius obiecti ut sic, nullum est
quaerere nisi 'secundum quid,' nisi quod istud 'esse secundum quid' reducitur ad
aliquod esse simpliciter, quod est esse ipsius intellectionis; sed istud 'esse simpliciter'
non est formaliter esse eius quod dicitur 'esse secundum quid,' sed est eius termi-
native vel principiative, ita quod ad istud 'verum esse secundum quid' reducitur sic
quod sine isto vero esse istius non esset illud 'esse secundum quid' illius." See also
Ordinatio I, d. 36, q. un. (Vatican, 6:267, n. 51); and II, d. 1, q. 2 (Vatican, 7:49,
n. 93) – the latter cited above, nn. 82, 117 and 142.
[147] Duns, *Ordinatio* II, d. 3, p. 2, q. 2 (Vatican, 7:552, n. 319); *Reportatio parisiensis* Prol., q. 2, n. 5 (Vivès, 22:41b–42a); and *Quaestiones quodlibetales*, q. 7, nn. 8–9
(Vivès, 25:290a–b).
[148] On Matthew, see above, Pt. 2, ch. 7, nn. 44–45; for hints of the same in
Henry, and also Vital du Four, Pt. 3, ch. 11, nn. 91–93.
[149] William, *Quaestiones*, q. 14 (arg. "sexto") (ed. Daniels, in *Quellenbeiträge und
Untersuchungen*, p. 92).

before him, so he refused to accept the Augustinian argument –
seen, for instance, in Bonaventure – that mutability in the natural
world made divine intervention necessary to sustain immutability at
the level of science. As he said in the *Lectura*, such reasoning simply
failed to take account of the fact that whatever permanence attached
to human knowledge depended not on external objects but rather
intelligible species representing objects to mind, species free of the
ontological restraints of the extra-mental world.[150]

By the time these ideas were revised for the *Ordinatio*, Duns had
only sharpened his opposition to the Augustinian point of view, with
the invocation of species serving merely to introduce a more subtle
way of considering the cognitive object. He now explained that it
was the "nature" of things – that is, their absolute essence in his
sense of the term – and not precisely the particular objects themselves that generated species in the mind, so that these natures (*naturae per se*) constituted the authentic object of scientific knowledge. It
was thus in conformity with fixed relations among natures, not connections among particular things, that intellect formulated propositions representing immutable truth.[151] Given Duns's insistence on
ontologically separating object from conditions of cognition and his
determination to anchor the validity of concepts to their inherent
logical coherence, the new emphasis on "nature" could only point
even further away from actual existence, whether in the world or,
as Augustinians would suggest, in the divine mind, and towards the
ephemeral realm of logic itself. Less and less was appeal to extramental
support necessary to sustain immutability. Indeed, by his Parisian
lectures Duns would go so far as to say that there could be science,
certain and immutable, even if, *per impossibile*, there were no God.[152]

Yet still he felt compelled to explain how it was admissible to
apply a term like "immutable," with its metaphysical concreteness
and the echo of eternal existence, to human cognition. The answer,
inserted as a further revision to the text, was that in the cases of

---

[150] Duns, *Lectura* I, d. 3, p. 1, q. 3 (Vatican, 16:298, n. 183); the Augustinian
reasoning is presented in the same question, p. 287, n. 157. For the latter's appearance
in Bonaventure, see above, Pt. 2, ch. 7, n. 10. On Henry, consult Pt. 3, ch. 11,
n. 93; on Grosseteste, Pt. 1, ch. 3, nn. 33–34.
[151] Duns, *Ordinatio* I, d. 3, p. 1, q. 4 (Vatican, 3:150–51, n. 246). On this, see
also above, Pt. 4, ch. 13, n. 29.
[152] Duns, *Reportatio parisiensis* Prol., q. 3, q'uncula 4, n. 17 (Vivès, 22:53b), also
cited above, n. 118.

intelligibile species in their role as signifiers, of the intellectual object no matter how defined, or most especially of immutable complex truths – for instance, scientific principles or self-evident propositions – "immutability" need not imply unchanging reality perduring through all time. Instead all such things were "immutable" if, whenever they existed, they were incapable of shifting from true to false or vice versa, remaining unalterably, necessarily – one might even say "always" – univalent.[153] With regard to such objects, therefore, once mind had perceived them correctly it could not fall into error, since their truth-value, although not their being, never varied.[154]

Here Duns turned to a distinction already seen in Bonaventure's work, whether or not that was actually his source. The latter had separated absolute (*simpliciter*) immutability – the existentially eternal variety seen in God – from immutability by supposition (*ex supposi-tione*) – undeviating in value whenever its subject was found to exist – and upon these two established two sorts of cognitive certitude, absolute (*simpliciter*) and qualified (*secundum quid*).[155] Along the same lines, Duns distinguished absolute (*simpliciter*) necessity or incorrupt-ibility, semantically equivalent to immutability in this context, from necessity or corruptibility in a qualified way (*secundum quid*). The first attached to whatever existed and remained the same for eternity, the second to whatever remained the same whenever it happened to be. It was according to the latter sort of necessity that human mind attained to necessary truth, making immutability of this sort what science could aspire to.[156]

Duns thought this sufficed: for human knowledge to be called

---

[153] For complex truths, see Duns, *Ordinatio* I, d. 3, p. 1, q. 4 (Vatican, 3:151, n. 247); for truths, species and objects, the same question, (Vatican, 3:149, ll. 16–22).

[154] Duns, *Ordinatio* I, d. 3, p. 1, q. 4 (Vatican, 3:152–53, n. 250).

[155] See above, Pt. 2, ch. 7, nn. 21 and 23; for the same in Matthew, n. 25.

[156] Duns, *Ordinatio* I, d. 3, p. 1, q. 4 (Vatican, 3:151–52, n. 248): "Contra: quo-modo propositio 'necessaria' affirmatur, si identitas extremorum potest destrui? Respondeo: quando res non est, non est identitas eius realis, – sed tunc si est in intellectu, est identitas ut est obiectum intellectum, et necessaria secundum quid, quia in tali 'esse' extrema non possunt esse sine tali identitate; tamen illa potest non esse, sicut extremum potest esse non intellectum. Ergo 'propositio necessaria' in intellectu nostro secundum quid, quia immutabilis in falsam; sed 'simpliciter nec-essaria' non nisi in intellectu divino, sicut nec extrema habent identitatem simplici-ter necessario in aliquo 'esse' nisi in illo 'esse' intellecto." Duns used the term "simpliciter incorruptibilis" for the same idea earlier in the question, (Vatican, 3:149, l. 17). In *Quaestiones quodlibetales*, q. 7, n. 43 (Vivès, 25:317a–b) he employed what he considered more Aristotelianizing language: "necessitas a se" and "necessitas formalis."

immutable, it need attain no more than immutability *secundum quid*. Unlike Bonaventure, he felt no urgency to resort to divine support to shore up the weakness of mankind's cognitive grasp and was simply willing to sever the tie between immutable knowledge in the world of sin and the authentic eternity of God.[157] Regardless of his debt to Henry and his borrowing from the classic Augustinian tradition, he thus differed radically from previous Augustinians. He wanted to bring Augustinian metaphysics down to earth, and more than anyone else before, even William of Auvergne and Grosseteste at their most Aristotelianizing, he succeeded.

---

[157] See discussion of the eternity *secundum quid* of immutable truths in *Ordinatio* I, d. 3, p. 1, q. 4 (Vatican, 3:160, n. 262), a passage drawing on *Lectura* I, d. 3, p. 1, q. 3 (Vatican, 16:303, n. 192), where Duns made clear how human mind does not grasp immutable truths as they are related to God, thus explicitly abandoning Matthew of Aquasparta's and Richard of Conington's invocation of Henry's metaphysics to reaffirm Augustinian noetics. A related passage, severing cognitive necessity from the ontology of actuality, can be found in *Ordinatio* I, d. 2, p. 1, qq. 1–2 (Vatican, 2:147–48, n. 38).

CHAPTER FIFTEEN

FULLY NATURAL KNOWLEDGE OF GOD

Both William of Ware and Duns Scotus had borrowed the technical lexicon and much of the structure for their metaphysics of being and essence from Henry of Ghent. But unlike William, Duns had jettisoned the ontological freight Henry designed this analytical framework to carry, particularly a number of controversial assumptions about reality that had seemed to assign absolute essence special ontological status tied to its exemplary relation to God. For Duns, there was little about the constitution of essence that resonated of anything more than a simple logic of noncontradiction.

Yet Henry's theory of essence, precisely because of its ontological implications, had permitted his otherwise worldly and Aristotelianizing noetics to accommodate profoundly Neoplatonizing inferences about the object of cognition. And the latter had proven crucial to his explanation of the wayfarer's knowledge of God, even strengthening Augustinian claims for intimate access to divinity within the limits of normal intellective activity. Duns's attack on Henry at just this point in his metaphysics would presumably weaken such claims, in light of his anti-illuminationism perhaps extinguish them altogether. So far as natural knowledge of God was concerned, one might expect Duns to have been forced to quit the Augustinian camp.

In fact, the historical upshot was quite different. No doubt the rejection of divine illumination in normal cognition of truth and Duns's distaste for Henry's ontology of essence stretched to the limit his ties to the intellectual currents examined in the chapters above. But rather than signal the end of a tradition, his ideas on natural knowledge of God breathed new life into many of the most fundamental Augustinian demands. Here, as with metaphysics pure and simple, Duns's thought marked a dramatic turning point, a discontinuity within the Augustinian tradition, but no abandonment of it. Relying once more on prodigious insight and originality, he moved beyond the mere presentiment of critical Augustinians like William of Ware that Henry's elaborate vision could not stand to an altogether reconstructed formulation of traditional concerns.

The engine driving Duns's reworking of the theory of a natural knowledge of God was denial of immediate access to divinity, the resolute elimination of any process or mechanism smacking of supernaturalism or divine intervention tucked inside the order of nature. His determination to avoid so much as the hint of ontologism had indeed provided a powerful corroborative motive for eschewing Henry's subtle efforts to bind reality to God through metaphysical convolutions in essence in the first place. On this score he was not content simply to follow Henry's, and Matthew of Aquasparta's, lead in naturalizing Augustinianism, purging it of the quasi-mystical dynamic that had emerged so often up through Bonaventure, but insisted on carrying his predecessors' initial, and sometimes halting, steps all the way to their logical conclusion.

Still, with all his naturalizing he was not striving for the kind of Aristotelianism championed by such as Thomas and his followers. He valued the Augustinian cast of mind, most especially its assurance that intellect had access to a special opening onto God by way of the very cognitive evidence it garnered from the senses. Duns was confident he could preserve this perspective alongside an uncompromising worldliness. Translated by him into a philosophical language fully accommodated to Aristotelianizing attitudes about nature and natural processes, Augustine's seductive vision of a harmony between mind and its divine object was at last equipped with adequate means to withstand the ideological pressures threatening to overwhelm it in the years when Henry's metaphysically more luxuriant defense of Augustinianism came under attack. Duns's ideas about natural knowledge of God thus represent the culmination of a seventy-five year process of adaptation and clarification engaging the Augustinian current since William of Auvergne. His was the final step in an effort to accommodate a powerful version of Neoplatonism to the new scholastic standards of the university world.

As often, what strikes one initially is how much Duns retained of Henry's general approach. There can be no doubt he began his thinking about natural knowledge of God with Henry as his guide, and the same could be said for William of Ware, at least from what little is known of his ideas on the matter. Just like Henry, Duns stipulated that the mind of the wayfarer could by natural means know something of God's essence, even "quiddity."[1] He was if anything

---

[1] Duns, *Ordinatio* I, d. 3, p. 1, qq. 1–2 (Vatican, 3:16–17, n. 25): "Dico ergo

more sanguine on this score than his predecessor, criticizing Henry for qualifying intellect's knowledge of God's "whatness" as "almost accidental" (*quasi per accidens*). For Duns, the wayfarer's concept of divinity was quidditative in the full sense of the word.[2] Like Henry, too, he specified that precisely because this knowledge was natural, the concept of God it provided had to be derived from knowledge of creatures – which was to say, it must originate in sensory cognition.[3] But surpassing Henry once more, he insisted that this meant the wayfarer's natural knowledge of God was entirely a posteriori.[4] William remained more ambiguous, holding closer to the literal formulations in Henry's work while still denying any immediate grasp of a concept of God.[5]

Due to the limitations imposed by its sensible origin, intellect's

---

primo quod non tantum haberi potest conceptus naturaliter in quo quasi per accidens concipitur Deus, puta in aliquo attributo, sed etiam aliquis conceptus in quo per se et quiditative concipiatur Deus." On Henry's view, see above, Pt. 3, ch. 10, nn. 104 and 108. Since Duns realized it might be argued God had no quiddity, in the sense of an essence capable of being represented by a definition, he took care to explain the special way he thought the notion of quiddity could be applied to God: see *Quaestiones super libros Metaphysicorum* I, q. 1 (Opera Phil., 3:24, n. 23); and for related comments on "being," pp. 40–41, n. 75. Strictly speaking, it was not "quiddity" but a "quidditative aspect" (*quid*) one identified in God, and in such general objects as "being." Olivier Boulnois, in the "Introduction" to Jean Duns Scot, *Sur la connaissance de Dieu et l'univocité de l'étant* (Paris, 1988), pp. 68–69, has taken all this as evidence Duns agreed with Henry and the authors of the Condemnation of 1277, implicitly against Thomas Aquinas, that the viator must have a positive, not just privative, concept of God. Against it, however, must be set a more cautious attitude evidenced by Duns in nn. 122 and 123 below.

[2] Duns, *Lectura* I, d. 3, p. 1, qq. 1–2 (Vatican, 16:225 and 231–32, nn. 10 and 20); and *Ordinatio* I, d. 3, p. 1, qq. 1–2 (Vatican, 3:11, n. 20, and 16–17, n. 25 – quoted above, n. 1). For an idea what the phrase "quasi per accidens" means in this context, see *Lectura* Prol., p. 3, qq. 1–3 (Vatican, 16:29 and 30, nn. 77 and 80): it implies knowledge solely by means of a property or attribute. On Henry's position, see above, Pt. 3, ch. 10, n. 107. Timotheus Barth, "De univocationis entis scotisticae intentione principali necnon valore critico," *Antonianum* 28 (1953): 95–97, concludes from this that Scotus believed Henry allowed no natural quidditative notion of God. It is interesting that in *Quaestiones quodlibetales*, q. 14, n. 2 (Vivès, 26:3a), Duns himself used the phrase "per accidens" loosely in association with knowledge in line with the way he claimed mind knew God *in via* – that is, in a common, confused concept.

[3] Duns, *Reportatio parisiensis* Prol., q. 1, n. 16 (Vivès, 22:16a); and less explicitly, *Collationes* 13, n. 2 (Vivès, 5:200b).

[4] Duns, *Quaestiones super libros Metaphysicorum* I, q. 1 (Opera Phil., 3:24, n. 24) ". . . sicut prius de 'si est' [Deus] . . . ita de quid est. Potest tamen utrumque a posteriori in hac scientia [metaphysicali] manifestari. . . ." Henry had insisted the wayfarer's natural knowledge of God was a priori: see above, pt. 3, ch. 10, n. 21.

[5] William, *Quaestiones*, q. 21 (ed. Daniels, in *Quellenbeiträge und Untersuchungen*, p. 102).

natural knowledge of God was, though quidditative, never perfect
under conditions of sin. While William tried to explain by saying
that divinity could never be known faultlessly by means of its effects,
since nothing other than God himself was really, and pari passu epis-
temically, commensurate with him, Duns was satisfied with the simple assertion that imperfect understanding of the term "God" was
the best mind could attain by natural means in its present state
(*naturaliter nunc*).[6] For him, such imperfection came down to the fact
that the knowledge in question was confused rather than distinct: it
was simple knowledge which had not been reduced to a clear
definition.[7] William, too, took "imperfect" and "indistinct" to be
equivalent descriptions in this regard.[8] Both conceded one could
make the same point by noting that mind's natural knowledge of
God *in via* was not under the formal aspect of divinity itself (*sub
ratione Dei*) or the Godhead's particular essence (*sub ratione huius essentiae ut haec*), reservations reflective of Henry's insistence that God did
not intervene in humankind's natural cognition as object in his own
essence.[9] They were aware, moreover, that separating perfect from

---

[6] William, *Quaestiones*, q. 2 (MS Vat., Chigi. B. VIII. 135, f. 2rb): ". . . causa
nunquam per effectum cognoscitur perfecte, nisi effectus adequet suam causam.
Cum igitur nullus effectus adequetur ipsi Deo, ipse perfecte cognosci non potest per
effectus naturales." Duns, *Ordinatio* Prol., p. 1, q. un. (Vatican, 1:29–30, n. 48); and
Quaestiones quodlibetales, q. 14, n. 3 (Vivès, 26:5b).

[7] *Quaestiones quodlibetales*, q. 14, n. 2 (Vivès, 26:3a), cited above, n. 2. Duns
confirmed such language, stating that intellect could form no distinct and fully quidditative concept of God by natural means in the world of sin, in *Quaestiones quodlibetales*, q. 7, n. 11 (Vivès, 25:293a–b). On distinct and confused knowledge according
to Duns, see above, Pt. 4, ch. 13, nn. 160–61.

[8] William, *Quaestiones*, q. 2 (MS Vat., Chigi. B. VIII. 135, f. 2rb): "Ad primum
pro opinione [MS Vat., Chigi. B. VII. 114, f. 2vb, adds: contraria secundo adduc-
tum] dicendum quod ad illam connexionem cognoscendam aliquo modo se extendit scientia que oritur a sensu, et tantum possumus scire de ea et de extremis
naturaliter, ad quantum se extendit ista scientia. Et hoc non est nisi sub ratione
entis et esse uniuersalis, non ad perfectam et distinctam cognitionem."

[9] William, *Quaestiones*, q. 2 (MS Vat., Chigi. B. VIII. 135, f. 2rb): "Sed nulla scientia acquisita determinat de Deo sub ratione Dei. Quia si aliqua esset, hec esset
methaphysica, sed hec non, quia de Deo determinat sub ratione cause et sub ratione
entis communissimi." Duns, *Ordinatio* I, d. 3, p. 1, qq. 1–2 (Vatican, 3:39, n. 57),
and especially (Vatican, 3:38, n. 56): "Tertio dico quod Deus non cognoscitur naturaliter a viatore in particulari et proprie, hoc est sub ratione huius essentiae ut
haec et in se." See also Duns, *Lectura* I, d. 3, p. 1, qq. 1–2 (Vatican, 16:238 and
247, nn. 35 and 57); and *Reportatio parisiensis (examinata)* IA, d. 2, qq. 1–3 (ed. Wolter
and Adams, in "Parisian Proof," p. 254): ". . . quia medium ad esse est nobis igno-
tum, scilicet essentia Dei ut haec vel deitas sub ratione deitatis." On Henry, see
above, Pt. 3, ch. 10, nn. 7, 8, and 38.

imperfect cognition of divinity in this way mirrored Henry's distinction between knowing God in particular (*in particulari* or *in speciali*) and knowing him in general (*in universali* or *in generali*), a division commensurate with the difference between human knowledge of God in beatitude and in the world of sin.[10]

On this last point, Duns added that Henry's description "in universali" did not refer to the strict universality of categorical predication but rather, as Henry had made plain, to the fact that God was known in a general nature (*communis ratio*) loosely shared with creatures.[11] Furthermore, in accord with Henry, both he and William were prepared to link up with the hybrid of Augustine and Avicenna that had become increasingly entrenched over the course of the thirteenth century, declaring that the general nature in which divinity was known was "being" itself. William accepted Henry's reasoning on the matter without hesitation, and from his earliest references to knowledge of God in the *Questions on the Metaphysics* Duns seems to have done the same.[12] As with Henry, and the classic Augustinians before him, the two theologians defended their views by referring to the famous text from Avicenna on "being" as among the first ideas impressed on mind, a passage liberally quoted throughout their works.[13] Duns read Avicenna as arguing, moreover, that "being" was

---

[10] On Henry, see above, Pt. 3, ch. 10, nn. 9 and 36–38. Richard of Conington, like Duns and William, characterized the difference as between "perfect" and "imperfect" knowledge – see the same chapter, n. 40. William referred to Henry's distinction in *Quaestiones*, q. 2 (MS Vat., Chigi. B. VIII. 135, f. 2rb), in a passage immediately preceding that quoted above, n. 9: "Item, omnis scientia acquisita uel est uniuersalis, uel particularis. Si particularis, sic est de aliquo subiecto sub ratione particulari, et si sit uniuersalis, de aliquo erit sub ratione uniuersali et communi." Duns explicitly recognized the parallel between his perfect versus imperfect and Henry's special versus general knowledge in *Ordinatio* Prol., p. 1, q. un. (Vatican, 1:29–30, n. 48 – cited above, n. 6); while in *Lectura* I, d. 3, p. 1, qq. 1–2 (Vatican, 16:226, n. 11); and *Ordinatio* I, d. 3, p. 1, qq. 1–2 (Vatican, 3:12, n. 20), he referred to Henry's division "in universali" as opposed to "in particulari." In *Lectura* I, d. 3, p. 1, qq. 1–2 (Vatican, 16:238 and 241, nn. 35–36 and 44); and *Ordinatio* I, d. 3, p. 1, qq. 1–2 (Vatican, 3:38–39, nn. 56–57 – partly quoted above, n. 9), he said he agreed with Henry that humankind's natural knowledge of God was universal and not particular, but not for the same reasons.

[11] Duns, *Ordinatio* I, d. 3, p. 1, qq. 1–2 (Vatican, 3:12, n. 20); and for the term "communis ratio," *Lectura* I, d. 3, p. 1, qq. 1–2 (Vatican, 16:226, n. 11).

[12] See the passages from William's *Quaestiones*, q. 2, quoted above, nn. 8 and 9; and the implication of the same in q. 21 (ed. Daniels, in *Quellenbeiträge und Untersuchungen*, p. 102 [Ad illud Augustini]); and Duns, *Quaestiones super libros Metaphysicorum* II, qq. 2–3 (Opera Phil., 3:233–34, nn. 115–16).

[13] William, *Quaestiones*, q. 2 (MS Vat., Chigi. B. VIII. 135, f. 2ra): ". . . primum

absolutely first of all precisely because "being" qua "being" (*ens inquan-tum ens*) was most common or inclusive, from which it followed that positively every other concept, including that of God, was ultimately known in and through it.[14] While recognizing that Henry had referred to the primitive common concepts as "first intentions," Duns chose to call them "transcendental universals" (*universalia transcendentia*) or just "transcendentals" (*transcendentia, rationes transcendentes*).[15]

Plainly both William and Duns were not just well acquainted with their predecessor's position on natural knowledge of God and God as first object of intellect but also inclined to draw on it for their own work. Again it was Duns who went the extra mile to lay out Henry's views in detail, and as before with the metaphysics of essence, here, too, he revealed himself a perceptive reader.[16] Especially impressive is his sketch of Henry's three levels of the sinner's knowledge of divinity and, within the most general, three sublevels comprising mind's very first steps to God.[17] Careful to reproduce the description

---

principium incomplexum est ens secundum Auicennam . . ."; and also q. 19 (ed. Daniels, in "Wilhelm von Ware," p. 214) – neither passage, however, arguing specifically about knowledge of God. For Duns, see *Quaestiones super libros Metaphysicorum* Prol.; I, q. 10; and VI, q. 3 (Opera Phil., 3:8, n. 17; and 182, n. 6; and 4:63, n. 20); *Lectura* Prol., p. 1, q. un. (Vatican, 16:1, n. 1); *Ordinatio* Prol., p. 1, q. un. (Vatican, 1:2, n. 1); *Lectura* I, d. 3, p. 1, qq. 1–2 (Vatican, 16:270, n. 120); and *Ordinatio* I, d. 8, p. 1, q. 3 (Vatican, 4:215, n. 125) – all of the latter referring to the problem of knowing divinity. On Henry and the reference to Avicenna, see above, Pt. 3, ch. 10, n. 13.

[14] Duns, *Collationes* 19, n. 2 (Vivès, 5:222a); and *Quaestiones super libros Metaphysicorum* Prol.; and I, q. 10 (Opera Phil., 3:8, n. 17; and 182, n. 6). *Quaestiones super libros Metaphysicorum* I, q. 1 (Opera Phil., 3:38–39, nn. 68 and 70) makes the point that "ens inquantum ens" is "communissimum;" while the same question, p. 71, n. 161, advances the claim for "ens in communi." William of Ware had already noted that the "being" in which God was known was "communissimum": see above, n. 9. For Henry and Vital du Four on "ens in quantum ens" as a primary concept, see above, Pt. 3, ch. 10, nn. 30–31.

[15] Duns, *Quaestiones super libros Metaphysicorum* Prol.; I, q. 1; IV, q. 1; and VI, q. 3 (Opera Phil., 3:9, n. 18; 15, ll. 5–6; and 308, n. 51; and 4:63, n. 20); *Lectura* I, d. 3, p. 1, qq. 1–2 (Vatican, 16:263, n. 103); and d. 8, p. 1, q. 3 (Vatican, 17:37, n. 107). His definition of the transcendentals was specifically devised so as to include more than just the traditional "first intentions": *Lectura* I, d. 8, p. 1, q. 3 (Vatican, 17:37–38, n. 110); and *Ordinatio* I, d. 8, p. 1, q. 3 (Vatican, 4:206, n. 114).

[16] Duns examined Henry's ideas about knowing God most extensively in his commentaries on the *Sentences*, at distinction three of the first book: *Lectura* I, d. 3, p. 1, qq. 1–2 (Vatican, 16:225–30, nn. 10–17); and *Ordinatio* I, d. 3, p. 1, qq. 1–2 (Vatican, 3:11–15, nn. 20–23).

[17] Duns, *Lectura* I, d. 3, p. 1, qq. 1–2 (Vatican, 16:227–28, n. 12); and *Ordinatio* I, d. 3, p. 1, qq. 1–2 (Vatican, 3:12–13, n. 21. On Henry, see above, Pt. 3, ch. 10, pp. 309 and 311–12.

of the second of the three sublevels as involving abstraction of an all-inclusive notion of being and the third the quite different extraction of a notion of being applicable solely to the perfectly subsistent form of God, he repeated Henry's observation that the former notion signified "being" in general as privatively indeterminate while the latter extrapolated still further to the stage of negative indetermination. In his uncompromisingly logical way, he even eliminated the ambiguity in the second stage as Henry had presented it, stipulating that "being" at this level referred to both creatures and God.[18]

He then went on to explain how for Henry all the levels, from most general to general, could be distributed between two basic ways of knowing God in the world: naturally and rationally. So far as divinity was known "naturally" in the first two sublevels of most general knowledge, it constituted mind's very first object, while known "rationally" in the last sublevel of most general and the two somewhat narrower levels that followed, it was among the last objects of mind, coming well after knowledge of most creatures.[19] He even pointed out that Henry had been forced to concede that God as known first in natural knowledge was not consciously perceived by intellect and how he had turned by way of explanation first to the extraordinary simplicity of the concept of being in which God was initially conceived, second to the fact that the manner in which mind grasped its first two sublevels of most general knowledge was not, in Henry's words, according to any formal characteristic by which God's being could be distinguished from that of creatures.[20] The *Lectura* added Henry's conclusion that since God was truly first known, though unperceived, the concept of God was "means of knowing" (*ratio cognoscendi*) all else.[21]

Finally, Duns recognized that for Henry and his followers the unity

---

[18] On this second stage, see especially Duns, *Ordinatio* I, d. 3, p. 1, qq. 1–2 (Vatican, 3:15, n. 22); and *Lectura* I, d. 8, p. 1, q. 3 (Vatican, 17:20, n. 59). For the ambiguity in Henry, see above, Pt. 3, ch. 10, nn. 61–62.

[19] Duns, *Lectura* I, d. 3, p. 1, qq. 1–2 (Vatican, 16:228–30, nn. 14 and 16); and *Ordinatio* I, d. 3, p. 1, qq. 1–2 (Vatican, 3:14–15, n. 22). On Henry, see above, Pt. 3, ch. 10, nn. 49, 50, 52 and 54.

[20] Duns, *Lectura* I, d. 3, p. 1, qq. 1–2 (Vatican, 16:229, n. 15); and *Ordinatio* I, d. 3, p. 1, qq. 1–2 (Vatican, 3:15, n. 23). For Henry on mind's failure to perceive God as object, see above, Pt. 3, ch. 10, n. 63; on the lack of distinction and the extreme simplicity of the primitive idea of being, the same chapter, nn. 91–92.

[21] Duns, *Lectura* I, d. 3, p. 1, qq. 1–2 (Vatican, 16:230–31 and 258, nn. 17 and 88); merely implied in *Ordinatio* I, d. 3, p. 1, q. 3 (Vatican, 3:78, n. 125). On Henry, see Pt. 3, ch. 10, nn. 11, 33 and 34.

attributable to the primitive notion of being mind retrieved from the
depths of sensory cognition was no more than analogical, spanning
two similar but still divergent concepts. He realized Henry had tried
to account for intellect's impression that at the level of "natural"
knowledge of God it was directed to a single common concept by
fixing the blame on mental error, a predictable conceptual confusion resulting from the fact that the two authentic concepts of being
were formally so close (*propinqui, proximi*).[22] Even more astutely, he
understood that Henry's insistence that there was no single concept
truly common to God and creatures – "being" in absolutely every
case signifying, strictly speaking, either one or the other class of
object but not both – meant not only that all the wayfarer's natural
ideas of God were proper, picking out God as object and nothing
else, but also that, in light of "being"'s radical conceptual simplicity no matter how construed, as referred to God the concept was at
the same time proper and absolutely simple (*simpliciter simplex*). Here
he brought to the surface more of the philosophical implications of
Henry's system than Henry had himself, almost surely providing the
inspiration for Conington's similar conclusions about Henry's ideas
on "being" signifying God.[23]

Yet if Duns was a keen reader of Henry, ready to adopt a good
part of the latter's theory of the wayfarer's natural knowledge of
divinity, he was ruthless in expunging logical confusion as well as
anything he thought savored of either ontologism or suspension of

---

[22] On the analogical nature of "being" and mind's error, see Duns, *Lectura* I,
d. 3, p. 1, qq. 1–2 (Vatican, 16:226, n. 11); d. 8, p. 1, q. 3 (Vatican, 17:17 and
26, nn. 53 and 77); and *Ordinatio* I, d. 8, p. 1, q. 3 (Vatican, 4:171, n. 44); and
d. 22, q. un. (Vatican, 5:341–42, n. 2); on the closeness of the two concepts, *Lectura*
I, d. 3, p. 1, qq. 1–2 (Vatican, 16:226, n. 11); *Ordinatio* I, d. 3, p. 1, qq. 1–2
(Vatican, 3:12 and 20, nn. 20 and 30); and d. 8, p. 1, q. 3 (Vatican, 4:179, n. 59).
For Henry's views, see above, Pt. 3, ch. 10, nn. 68, 85, 86 (on knowledge of being
most generally as a "modus confusus"), 90 and 91. It is interesting to note that in
Collationes 3 (ed. Harris, in *Duns Scotus*, 2:371), or 24 (ed. Balić, in "De collationibus," pp. 212–13), Duns described the pertinent position as holding that the most
general concept of being was "unus secundum quid," a characterization appearing
not in Henry but rather in Richard of Conington – see above, Pt. 3, ch. 10, n. 76.
[23] Duns, *Lectura* I, d. 8, p. 1, q. 3 (Vatican, 17:26, n. 77), on all Henry's concepts of God as proper; and *Ordinatio* I, d. 2, p. 1, qq. 1–2 (Vatican, 2:141, ll.
15–17); and d. 3, p. 1, qq. 1–2 (Vatican, 3:10 and 20, nn. 18 and 31), on "being"
applied to God as both proper and absolutely simple. On the general idea of
absolute simplicity, see Wolter, *The Transcendentals*, pp. 81–82. For Henry's confirmation
that all concepts referred strictly either to God or to creatures, see above, Pt. 3,
ch. 10, n. 75; for Conington's conclusions, the same chapter, nn. 84 and 93; and
below, n. 87.

the order of nature. And evidently he believed there was a great deal to be expunged. In sharp contrast to William of Ware, he was convinced that Henry's theory, at least according to the precise terms in which Henry had presented it, would not suffice to account for knowledge of God, or if it did, accounted for knowledge of the wrong kind.

So far as concerns the latter charge, he argued that if Henry really meant for mind to know divinity across an analogical divide, and thus by means of creaturely imitation of the divine, then the principles of his own philosophy made it more reasonable to suppose that God was grasped as ideal exemplar than as simple being, for it was as idea that God was most closely imitated by his effects. But in that case, since Henry held that God served as idea in his particular, or "bare," essence, it followed that intellect should know God naturally in particular (*in particulari* or *ut haec*), which both Henry and Duns vigorously denied.[24] In fact, the rejection by Henry of knowledge of divinity in any concept common to it and creatures immediately implied the same. As indicated just above, Duns took such rejection as requiring that the concept mind formed of God as "being" be proper and absolutely simple, and this, to his view, necessitated that it represent divine essence *ut haec*.[25]

Surely more weighty, however, was the claim that, questions of particularity or generality aside, Henry had failed to provide a plausible explanation for how sinful intellect working by natural means obtained whatever general knowledge of God he claimed it did. If creatures and divinity had nothing really in common, as all scholastics agreed, then despite what Henry said, there was simply no way mind, beginning solely with information provided by sensation, could pierce through to (*suffodere*) a concept of God – or more precisely, a concept of God's being – formally divergent, as Henry insisted, from any concept legitimately applied to creatures. To Duns's way of seeing things, an object just could not provide material for

---

[24] See Duns's argument, *Ordinatio* I, d. 3, p. 1, qq. 1–2 (Vatican, 3:38–39, n. 56). For Henry on God as creative ideal in his own particular essence, see above, Pt. 3, ch. 10, n. 7; on Henry and Duns against natural knowledge of God *ut haec*, see above, this chapter, n. 9.

[25] Duns, *Ordinatio* I, d. 8, p. 1, q. 3 (Vatican, 4:177, n. 55); q. 4 (Vatican, 4:257–58, n. 188); and d. 22, q. un. (Vatican, 5:342–43, n. 31). The reading chosen by the editors for Vatican, 4:177, l. 9 – "non" – should surely be replaced by the variant: "enim." For the argument about "being" signifying God as proper and absolutely simple concept, see above, n. 23.

a cognitive representation formally unlike (*omnino alterius rationis*) every concept by which the object itself was naturally known.[26]

Of course it could hardly be said that Henry's philosophy was devoid of resources to deflect criticism of this sort. Having begun the revisionism of Augustinian epistemology by taking serious steps away from a doctrine of divine illumination, and having sought support for his notion of natural knowledge of divinity exclusively in the theory of cognition of all things in "being," he at least intuitively sensed that he was putting at risk the ideal of the wayfarer's special access to God. Absent divine illumination, he needed new corroboration for the claim that mind could span the gap between the being of creatures and the merely analogous being of divinity so as to move to a knowledge of the latter sufficiently dense to be characterized as quidditative.[27] Deliverance for him lay with his views on essence – or more precisely, because of them he felt free to regard neither the distance between creature and divinity nor the solely analogical unity of "being" as destructive of his espousal of a natural, quidditative knowledge of God.[28]

Duns was acutely aware of the crucial role Henry's vision of essence played, and despite the fact that its function was never expressly acknowledged by Henry himself, he made a special point of airing his own dissatisfaction with any attempt to redeem Henry's account of natural knowledge of divinity by relying on metaphysics of so unusual a sort. He particularly targeted the efforts advanced in Henry's name to use the idea of essence as founded on a relation to God, or perhaps even equivalent to such a relation. Of course Richard of Conington had been one of those proposing just such a defense; Matthew of Aquasparta seems to have been another. Duns had already criticized Conington's view of essence, or *ens ratum*, on its own terms. He now made clear he believed that even if such a view

---

[26] Duns gave Henry's view in *Lectura* I, d. 3, p. 1, qq. 1–2 (Vatican, 16:228, n. 13); offering his own counterargument in the same question (Vatican, 16:245, n. 54); and in *Ordinatio* I, d. 3, p. 1, qq. 1–2 (Vatican, 3:43, n. 62).

[27] On this problem, see Marrone, "Knowledge of Being," pp. 31, 51 and 52; and above, Pt. 3, ch. 11, n. 7. Robert P. Prentice, *The Basic Quidditative Metaphysics of Duns Scotus as Seen in his De primo principio*, Spicilegium Pontificii Athenaei Antoniani, 16 (Rome, 1970), p. 22, affirms the not uncommon view that it was allegiance to a theory of illumination which allowed Henry to tolerate the analogical character of "being."

[28] See above, Pt. 3, ch. 11, pp. 337–38; and Marrone, "Knowledge of Being," pp. 35 and 39.

could be upheld, it would do nothing to salvage the account of the wayfarer's knowledge of God.[29]

Both *Lectura* and *Ordinatio* laid out the basics of Conington's argument: that knowledge of a created essence, because it necessarily entailed perception of the relation to God by which all essence was constituted, sufficed to explain knowledge of the divine correlative making the object what it was. In other words, the relational character of essence itself ensured that immanent in cognition of any created thing lay knowledge of a formally distinct divine being.[30] Duns responded that this turned the process of intellection on its head. To his eyes, one could know the relation Henry and Conington had in mind only if one already knew both correlatives upon which it was based, so that knowledge of essence as they conceived of it, rather than accounting for knowledge of God, was instead attainable only after God was already known.[31] Yet even if one conceded that a relation might be perceived before the correlative extremes were known, and thus that Henry and Richard were correct about mind's initial grasp of essence as relative, this still would not serve to explain the knowledge of God they had in mind. The relation of creatures to divine ideal was merely conceptual, therefore woefully inadequate for generating understanding of a divine correlative which was in fact God's absolute essence or perfection.[32]

But criticizing Henry brought Duns only halfway. Indeed, the very sharpness of his criticism intensified the urgency to devise his own explanation for humankind's natural knowledge of God. Along with

---

[29] On Duns's critique of this application of Henry's theory of essence, see Marrone, "Knowledge of Being," p. 35. For the attack on Conington's metaphysics of essence in itself, see above, Pt. 4, ch. 14, nn. 89 and 90; on Matthew in this regard, Pt. 3, ch. 11, n. 87; and Pt. 2, ch. 7, nn. 52–53.

[30] Duns, *Lectura* I, d. 8, p. 1, q. 3 (Vatican, 17:21, n. 63); and *Ordinatio* I, d. 8, p. 1, q. 3 (Vatican, 4:174–75, n. 52) – both cited above, Pt. 4, ch. 14, n. 86. See a quick statement of the same in *Collationes* 3 (ed. Harris, in *Duns Scotus*, 2:374); or 24 (ed. Balić, in "De collationibus," p. 216). For Conington on his own position, see above, Pt. 3, ch. 11, n. 81.

[31] Duns, *Lectura* I, d. 8, p. 1, q. 3 (Vatican, 17:21, n. 64); and as an aside in *Ordinatio* I, d. 8, p. 1, q. 3 (Vatican, 4:176, n. 54 [p. 176, ll. 1–3]).

[32] Duns, *Lectura* I, d. 8, p. 1, q. 3 (Vatican, 17:22–23, nn. 67–68); and *Ordinatio* I, d. 8, p. 1, q. 3 (Vatican, 4:175–76, nn. 53–54), the later version homing in precisely on the inadequacy of a conceptual relation to generate absolute knowledge of an exalted extreme. For a short version of the more general argument given in the *Lectura* (Vatican, 17:22–23, n. 68), see *Collationes* 3 (ed. Harris, in *Duns Scotus*, 2:375); or (with a better variant of the text) 24 (ed. Balić, in "De collationibus," p. 217).

William of Ware, he had modeled his general approach to the problem on Henry's, yet after careful scrutiny of the details, he himself had been led to reject several critical assumptions Henry brought to bear. How could he make good on the Augustinian promise of intimate knowledge of divinity while repudiating so much of his predecessor's account of the way it was to be achieved? His problem was potentially even more intractable than that Henry had faced after moving away from divine illumination, a dilemma of a philosophical order unmatched in the thought of any Augustinian examined so far. Could Duns, without the classic doctrine of divine illumination, without Henry's conviction that knowledge of essence directed mind to God, without even his vision of the constitution of essence itself, explain the natural origin of a quidditative concept of God? Could he, equipped with so few of the tools the Augustinian current had traditionally employed, span the chasm the analogical nature of "being" set before the wayfarer's inquiring mind?

Duns appears to have been aware of the precariousness of his plight. His hope for natural theology – what he called metaphysics – as well as positive theology – plain "theology" in his lexicon – among believers in the world depended on a successful resolution. At stake, in short, lay his aspirations for defending meaningful discourse about God *in via* – meaningful for anyone, that is, but those to whom a vision had been granted in which the significance of the term "God" or its equivalent was revealed. If there was no explanation for natural knowledge of divinity other than Henry's, then one would have to count on a miracle for sinful humanity to form a serviceable concept of its God.[33]

So serious a challenge demanded a radical response. First among all scholastics, Duns moved beyond the analogical unity of "being" to claim that the concept was, in its absolute simplicity, fully univocal. At a stroke he thereby eliminated the noetic discord between knowing creatures and knowing the divine and made it easy to explain how, starting with only knowledge drawn from and legitimately referring to created objects, one could work by natural means to meaningful, indeed quidditative, cognition of God. The maneuver

---

[33] On Duns's hope for positive theology, see *Lectura* I, d. 3, p. 1, qq. 1–2 (Vatican, 16:266–67, n. 113); on the more general need to resolve his problem in order to defend discourse about God, *Lectura* I, d. 8, p. 1, q. 3 (Vatican, 17:20–21, nn. 61–62), partially quoted below, n. 56.

was undeniably bold. The history of the concept of being as well as of the notion of univocity had seen little change since Aristotle's day. Overnight, discourse on both topics was transformed, as if Duns alone realized the extent of the noetic problem first evident in Henry's search for an alternative to the classic Augustinian route to God and dared opt for a solution resolving all the philosophical difficulties simultaneously. With his audacity, he reaped the harvest of what Henry had sown.[34]

There is, of course, nothing new about calling attention to the revolutionary nature of the espousal of univocity of "being," nor is it novel to suggest that Duns's motive was to facilitate explanation of natural knowledge of God. Both claims have a venerable past, harking back among medievalists to Gilson and Bettoni.[35] But the

---

[34] On the problem of univocity of "being" introduced by Henry but not fully plumbed or resolved by him, see above, Pt. 3, ch. 10, pp. 316–17. Just prior to Duns, Matthew of Aquasparta put into words the theoretical dilemma facing Augustinians on this score: how to explain knowledge of God in a world where all cognition began with created objects if there was nothing common between the concepts of created and divine being – see *Quaestiones de anima beata*, q. 1, arg. 11 (ed. Emmen, BFS 18:182). He chose to resolve the matter by having recourse to Henry's noetics – see above, Pt. 2, ch. 8, nn. 125 and 128. Having rejected this route, Duns was forced to mount a more audacious attack on the character of "being." For a discussion of Duns's metaphysics of being, see Hadrianus Borak, "Metaphysischer Aufbau des Seinsbegriffes bei Duns Scotus," WuW 28 (1965): 39–54.

[35] See Etienne Gilson, "Avicenne et le point de départ de Duns Scot," AHDLMA 2 (1927): 116–17; and Efrem Bettoni, *Duns Scotus: The Basic Principles of His Philosophy*, pp. 16–17, 43, 46; *Il problema della conoscibilità di Dio*, esp. pp. 254, 354–55, and 387–90; "Punti di contatto," pp. 520–25 and 529–30; "De argumentatione Doctoris Subtilis quoad existentiam Dei," *Antonianum* 28 (1953): 55; "The Originality of the Scotistic Synthesis," in *John Duns Scotus, 1265–1965*, ed. John K. Ryan and Bernardino M. Bonansea (Washington, D.C., 1965), pp. 41–44; and "Duns Scoto nella scolastica del secolo XIII," in *De doctrina Ioannis Duns Scoti*, Acta Congressus Scotistici Internationalis, 1, Oxford and Edinburgh, 11–17 September 1966 (Rome, 1968), vol. I, p. 111. One of the earliest modern statements of this position is Séraphin Belmond, *Etudes sur la philosophie de Duns Scot*, 1: *Dieu: Existence et cognoscibilité* (Paris, 1913), pp. 164–65. On its appearance among other scholars, see the other listings in Marrone, "Knowledge of Being," nn. 2 and 3, especially the references to Wolter, *The Transcendentals*, p. 32; and "The 'Theologism' of Duns Scotus," FrS 7 (1947): 398. To the citations made there to Timotheus Barth must be added "Zur univocatio entis bei Johannes Duns Scotus," WuW 21 (1958): 95–108; and "De fundamento univocationis apud Ioannem Duns Scotum," *Antonianum* 14 (1939): 181–206, 277–98 and 373–92 – this latter work not so reliable as Barth's other studies. See also Parthenius Minges, "Beitrag zur Lehre des Duns Scotus über die Univokation des Seinsbegriffes," *Philosophisches Jahrbuch (der Görresgesellschaft)* 20 (1907): 307; Franz Paul Fackler, *Der Seinsbegriff in seiner Bedeutung für die Gottes-Erkenntnis bei Duns Scotus* (Augsburg, 1933), p. 16 (imprecise on the exact meaning of univocity for Duns);

standard account contends that prompting the move was rejection of the Augustinian theory of divine illumination. The point here is instead that Henry had already taken this step, at least to the extent of removing illumination as a factor in knowledge of God. What led Duns to go further and embrace the idea of univocity was an additional, and for him more immediate, stimulus: resistance to Henry's theory of essence and the noetics it implied.

Before showing how univocity of "being" worked to make natural knowledge of God in the world of sin plausible even within the constraints Duns placed on Augustinian noetics and Henry's metaphysics, it is necessary briefly to examine the theory itself and Duns's defense of it. In his early, logical works he had opted for the stance on both univocity and "being" that had prevailed for centuries, holding, like all thinkers since Boethius, to an expanded version of Aristotle's position: that univocity entailed commonness of both concept and reality and pertained exclusively to the five predicables of Porphyry: genus, difference, species, accident and property. The concept of being, an intention transcending genera, was consequently not a candidate for univocity, a prohibition so generally agreed upon that Duns characterized it as the common opinion.[36]

<hr>

André Marc, *L'idée de l'être chez saint Thomas et dans la Scolastique postérieure*, Archives de Philosophie, 10, 1 (Paris, 1933); Cyril L. Shircel, "Analogy and Univocity in the Philosophy of Duns Scotus," *Proceedings of the American Catholic Philosophical Association* 18 (1942): 143–64; Michael Schmaus, *Zur Diskussion über das Problem der Univozität im Umkreis des Johannes Duns Skotus*, Sitzungsberichte der bayerischen Akademie der Wissenschaften, Philosophisch-historische Klasse (1957), n. 4 (Munich, 1957); Gonsalvus Scheltens, "Die thomistische Analogielehre und die Univozitätslehre des J. Duns Scotus," FS 47 (1965): 315–38 – to be read with caution; Ludger Honnefelder, "Die Lehre von der doppelten ratitudo entis," p. 671; and *Ens inquantum ens. Der Begriff des Seienden als solchen als Gegenstand der Metaphysik nach der Lehre des Johannes Duns Scotus*, Beiträge, N.F. 16 (Münster, 1979), p. 305 – this latter one of the very best analyses of the basis of Duns's metaphysics; Douglas C. Langston, "Scotus and Ockham on the Univocal Concept of Being," FrS 39 (1979): 105–29; and Bernardino M. Bonansea, *Man and his Approach to God in John Duns Scotus* (Lanham, Md., 1983), pp. 118–19, which explicitly echoes Bettoni's view on the role of both univocity and first object of mind.
[36] For closer examination of Duns's early views, see Marrone, "The Notion of Univocity," pp. 349–58. On Duns and the "common opinion," see, for instance, *Quaestiones super libros Metaphysicorum* I, q. 1 (Opera Phil., 3:58, n. 125): and from near the end of his career, *Ordinatio* II, d. 24, q. un., n. 8 (Vivès, 13:184a) – also cited below, n. 82. Parthenius Minges, "Beitrag zur Lehre des Duns Scotus," pp. 315–17, was a strong early voice arguing that Duns already held to the univocity of "being" in his early works, while Raymond de Courcerault, "L'ontologie de Duns Scot et le principe du panthéisme," EF 24 (1910): 138 and 154n, perceptively opposed him. De Courcerault's position has been upheld by S.Y. Watson, "Univocity

Along with his contemporaries, the early Duns naturally conceded a degree of unity to "being," not the strong unity of univocity but rather the weaker one of analogy. William of Ware had couched his own defense of the analogical unity of "being" in the traditional Boethian language of attribution, whereby "being" of the highest sort was "attributed" to other types of being, each of which in some way approached it.[37] Duns agreed but took greater pains to be precise, following Henry's example by saying that, strictly speaking, "being" according to its broadest usage constituted a unity only in word (*vox*).[38] Even here, where loyal to convention, he added a special touch. The analogical unity of "being," Duns said, held only for the metaphysician and the natural philosopher; for the logician "being" was purely equivocal. The reason was that both metaphysics and natural philosophy looked beyond language to reality, to the real *significanda* where the attribution at the heart of analogy of "being" was located. Logic, on the other hand, attended just to terms and the way they signified. Since the word "being" referred to any one of its *significanda* no more immediately than to another, here there was no order of attribution and only equivocation among the differing applications.[39]

---

and Analogy of Being in the Philosophy of Duns Scotus," *Proceedings of the American Catholic Philosophical Association* 32 (1958): 189–206; Robert P. Prentice, "Univocity and Analogy according to Scotus's *Super libros Elenchorum Aristotelis*," AHDLMA 35 (1968): 39–64; and *An Anonymous Question on the Unity of the Concept of Being (Attributed to Scotus)* (Rome, 1972), p. 11; and Honnefelder, *Ens inquantum ens*, pp. 274–75.

[37] William, *Quaestiones*, q. 15 (ad 2.) (ed. Muscat, in "Guillelmi de Ware quaestio inedita," p. 348). In q. 85 (ed. Schmaus, in *Der Liber propugnatorius*, pp. 268*–69*), William commented that the unity of "being" was something like that of a genus, but there is no reason to believe he meant this to contradict his other statements limiting "being" to strictly analogical unity. For Henry on analogy and attribution, see above, Pt. 3, ch. 10, n. 71.

[38] On attribution, consult the text cited below, n. 39; on the unity of a word, Duns, *In librum Praedicamentorum*, q. 4, n. 9 (Vivès, 1:448b). For Henry, see above, Pt. 3, ch. 10, n. 83.

[39] See the classic passage in *Quaestiones super libros Metaphysicorum* IV, q. 1 (Opera Phil., 3:315–16, n. 70) – translated in Marrone, "The Notion of Univocity," p. 352. On challenges to the authority of this passage, which I regard as excessively sceptical, see the same article, p. 352, especially the reference in n. 18 to Wolter, *The Transcendentals*, p. 46n. It should also be noted that the new edition of the *Questions on the Metaphysics* deletes from the first sentence of this passage the explicit denial of univocity to "being" that is present in six of the eleven manuscripts collated as a basis for the edited text. As Pini points out, "Duns Scotus's Metaphysics," p. 364, the editors have not provided sufficient justification for this inherently controversial decision. But the matter is, in the end, less significant than even Pini believes, for what remains in the newly edited text can still not be seen as avoiding explicit

In his later works, however, Duns unambiguously rejected this original position on "being," and on univocity, too. The first signs of a change of heart appear in the *Questions on the Metaphysics*, where alongside the prevailing wisdom can occasionally be found arguments for greater unity to "being" than that of analogy alone. The two views sit side by side, no attempt made to reconcile them or even confront the contradiction. Either Duns began revising the *Questions* without finishing the job, or he simply composed them at a transitional moment, unable to make up his mind at the time and never bothering subsequently to tidy up the text.[40] But the commentaries on the *Sentences*, starting with the *Lectura*, embrace a fully new perspective, one plainly at odds with Duns's stand in the logical works and radically opposed to the centuries-old tradition to which all his contemporaries subscribed.

Here for the first time was offered a definition of univocity looking exclusively to the conceptual side of philosophical discourse. Continuing, in Henry's wake, to link univocity with isolation of a single concept, or even a single formal aspect (*ratio*), for all legitimate referents, Duns now explicitly put aside consideration of objective realities and their degree of commonness.[41] For a term to be considered univocal, it was sufficient that it entail contradiction when affirmed and denied of the same subject, no further extra-logical conditions needing to be taken into consideration.[42] In line with this

contradiction with Duns's later views on "being." In the rest of the passage from the *Questions on the Metaphysics* IV, q. 1, Duns stipulates that "being" is equivocal for the logician, though that is exactly the point at which he later introduces univocity, holding that for the logician, in contrast to the metaphysician or natural philosopher, "being" is univocal. On this change, see below, n. 45, and the comments in Marrone, "The Notion of Univocity," pp. 378–84. It is furthermore of interest that in the passage under discussion here Duns says that "being" is considered by the metaphysician to be analogical by attribution, thus linking up with Henry's view that the analogy of "being" is a case of Boethius's *aequivocatio a consilio* (see again above, Pt. 3, ch. 10, n. 71; and Marrone, "The Notion of Univocity," pp. 352–53), while in *In librum Praedicamentorum*, q. 4, nn. 4–7 (Vivès, 1:446a–47b), he takes pains to show "being" constitutes for the logician a simple instance of *aequivocatio a casu*. See the same idea in Duns, *In libros Elenchorum*, q. 15, nn. 3 and 6 (Vivès, 2:20b and 22a).

[40] See Marrone, "The Notion of Univocity," p. 391, and for discussion of evidence concerning Duns's opinion in the *Questions*, pp. 385–91.

[41] On univocity as synonymous with unicity of concept, see Duns, *Lectura* I, d. 3, p. 1, qq. 1–2 (Vatican, 16:235–36, n. 30). For Henry, see above, Pt. 3, ch. 10, n. 73.

[42] Duns, *Ordinatio* I, d. 3, p. 1, qq. 1–2 (Vatican, 3:18, n. 26): ". . . univocum

dramatic shift, moreover, he further insisted that univocity, previously limited to the five predicables, applied to "being" as well.[43] In fact, for the later Duns, univocity attached to all the first intentions, or in his words, transcendentals.[44]

Indeed, Duns even corrected his own previous comments on the different sciences, still affirming that "being" was only analogical to the eyes of the metaphysician or natural philosopher but contending, in sharp contrast to the *Questions on the Metaphysics*, that the logician, taking heed of the fact that despite real divergence among objects the concept of being was itself unitary, could legitimately treat it as univocal.[45] Here the consequences of defining univocity so as to play down real differences and focus instead on unity or diversity at the conceptual level emerged in highest relief. Duns could now defend univocity of "being" without in any way narrowing the real – both physical and metaphysical – gap between creatures and God, so important for preserving divine transcendence.[46]

---

conceptum dico, qui ita est unus quod eius unitas sufficit ad contradictionem, affirmando et negando ipsum de eodum. . . ."

[43] Duns, *Lectura* I, d. 3, p. 1, qq. 1–2 (Vatican, 16:232, n. 21): ". . . non concipitur Deus in conceptu communi analogo sibi et creaturae, sed in conceptu communi univovco sibi et creaturae, ita quod ens et bonum et sapientia dicta de Deo et creatura univoce dicuntur de eis . . ."; and *Ordinatio* I, d. 3, p. 1, qq. 1–2 (Vatican, 3:18, n. 26), the latter passage not explicit but still intended as referring to a univocal concept of being. See also *Lectura* I, d. 8, p. 1, q. 3 (Vatican, 17:17 and 33, nn. 53 and 99); and *Ordinatio* I, d. 8, p. 1, q. 3 (Vatican, 4:198, n. 95). This view was confirmed in *Ordinatio* III, d. 24, q. un, n. 22 (Vivès, 15:53b); and *Collationes* 3 (ad 2.) (ed. Harris, in *Duns Scotus*, 2:371); or 24 (ed. Balić, in "De collationibus," p. 213, where "maior" must be changed to read "minor"). In the latter text Duns confessed less than absolute confidence in his position. See also below, n. 91.

[44] For example, *Lectura* I, d. 3, p. 1, qq. 1–2 (Vatican, 16:232, n. 21 – quoted just above, n. 43); and also *Lectura* I, d. 8, p. 1, q. 3 (Vatican, 17:37, n. 107).

[45] Duns, *Lectura* I, d. 3, p. 1, qq. 1–2 (Vatican, 16:268–69, nn. 117–18 – partly translated in Marrone, "The Notion of Univocity," p. 379); and a bit less clearly in *Ordinatio* I, d. 3, p. 1, q. 3 (Vatican, 3:100–101, nn. 162–63). See also *Collationes* 3 (ad Porphyrium) (ed. Harris, in *Duns Scotus*, 2:371 and 373), or 24 (ed. Balić, in "De collationibus," pp. 213 and 214). For Duns's position in his work on the *Metaphysics*, see above, n. 39.

[46] For the new emphasis on conceptual over real unity, see the references given above, n. 45, as well as *Lectura* I, d. 8, p. 1, q. 3 (Vatican, 17:46–47, n. 129); *Ordinatio* I, d. 8, p. 1, q. 3 (Vatican, 4:190, n. 82; and 221, ll. 19–21); and *Collationes* 3 (ed. Harris, in *Duns Scotus*, 2:374), or 24 (ed. Balić, in "De collationibus," p. 215). The point is perhaps made best in *Lectura* I, d. 8, p. 1, q. 3 (Vatican, 17:29, n. 84): "Nunc autem creatura et Deus conveniunt in uno conceptu absque unitate in aliqua realitate, sicut post dicetur; sunt igitur primo diversa in realitate, sed non in conceptu." *Ordinatio* I, d. 8, p. 1, q. 3 (Vatican, 4:195, n. 88) shows clearly how for the later Duns precise conditions of reality were relatively unimportant in

In support of his claim of conceptual unity, Duns furthermore drew on an idea introduced in his logical works about the exceptional formal simplicity of "being," its purity as a *ratio*, regardless of the reality it signified. The early works had maintained that such extreme simplicity accounted for mind's curious proclivity for grasping a concept of being without knowing which genus it fell into, although in every instance the concept, since not absolutely all-inclusive, in fact pointed to just one genus or another. He now returned to the idea of simplicity to propose that the concept of being was in every case so all-embracing, thus so empty of formal content, as to be among the very simplest concepts of all. It was indeed so simple that it could not be further analyzed, which was to say that it was absolutely simple (*simpliciter simplex*).[47] Such radical simplicity furnished yet another reason for concluding that all concepts of being were actually identical, a single intentional form applicable to all objects, and thus "being," in light of the new standards for univocity, a univocal term.

In all this, of course, univocity was for the first time in philoso-

---

determining univocity, but it should be noted that in *Collationes* 3 (Responsio) (ed. Harris, in *Duns Scotus*, 2:374), or 24 (ed. Balić, in "De collationibus," p. 216 – a somewhat less satisfactory reading), he admitted that at least analogical unity at the level of reality was necessary for univocity at the conceptual level.

[47] For Duns's early views, see Marrone, "The Notion of Univocity," pp. 367–71, especially n. 56, quoting from *In librum Praedicamentorum*, q. 4, n. 13 (Vivès, 1:449b), and the comments on p. 371. On his later understanding of "being" as absolutely simple, see *Ordinatio* I, d. 8, p. 1, q. 3 (Vatican, 4:222, n. 138), where the idea is implied; and *Ordinatio* I, d. 3, p. 1, qq. 1–2 (Vatican, 3:9, n. 17), where it is explicitly set forth; as well as the same question (Vatican, 3:54–55, n. 80): "Ens autem non potest concipi nisi distincte, quia habet conceptum simpliciter simplicem." Duns had come to this position already by *Lectura* I, d. 2, p. 1, qq. 1–2 (Vatican, 16:118, n. 24), where he mentioned it almost casually, as if expecting no opposition. Of course, he had always held that Henry, despite his stance on the analogical unity of "being," would have been forced to concede the absolute simplicity of the term under any one of its analogous meanings – see above, nn. 20 and 23. De Courcerault, "L'ontologie de Duns Scot," pp. 423–25 and 430; Séraphin Belmond, "Duns Scot métaphysicien," *Revue de Philosophie* 36 (1929): 422–23; Timotheus Barth, "Die Stellung der univocatio im Verlauf der Gotteserkenntnis nach der Lehre des Duns Skotus," WuW 5 (1938): 240 and 246; and Prentice, *The Basic Quidditative Metaphysics*, p. 24, have all emphasized the importance of the simplicity and intentional emptiness of "being" for Duns's thought. For Duns's definition of an absolutely simple concept as not reducible to prior or simpler concepts, in contrast to simple concepts that could be further analyzed into subjective or essential parts, see *Lectura* I, d. 2, p. 1, qq. 1–2 (Vatican, 16:118–19, n. 24 – cited just above); *Ordinatio* I, d. 2, p. 1, qq. 1–2 (Vatican, 2:142–43, n. 31); *Lectura* I, d. 3, p. 1, qq. 1–2 (Vatican, 16:250, n. 68); and *Ordinatio* I, d. 3, p. 1, qq. 1–2 (Vatican, 3:49, n. 71).

phy's history being held to extend above Aristotle's ten categories, thus above all genera. That was what positing the transcendental univocity of "being" entailed.[48] So novel an idea raised the question of how such super-generic unity descended to the separate genuses without addition of specific differences, something which could not be allowed short of conceding that the genuses themselves fell within a genus. Here, too, Duns came up with an innovative response. On the conceptual level, the move from "being" pure and simple to a more determinate class – "substantial being," for example – involved the addition of an intrinsic mode (*modus intrinsecus entitatis* or *entis*) – in the example just offered, "substantial" or "per se" – which unlike a specific difference supposited for nothing really distinct from the more general referent but nonetheless could be, indeed had to be, separated off when conceptualizing the absolutely simple general term. It constituted a kind of marker for the grade of perfection attained by the referent in a specific case, much like the varying grades of whiteness possessed by objects all of which fell without difference under the univocal term "white."[49] In this way, the concept of being descended to "divine being" or "created being" by mind's recognition of the mode of existence a specific instance of being actually possessed, but not by means of any real, or really different, addition.

A second question that needed answering as well was: How could "being" be predicable of all reality, as would seem to be demanded of a true transcendental, when by Duns's own argument it could not be predicated "in quid" of a range of special terms, including the intrinsic modes of being? The answer was crucial for Duns's philosophy, and controversial even among his followers, but not especially relevant to the matters at issue here. Suffice it to say that he posited a distinction between primacy of commonness, which permitted truly quidditative predication, and primacy of virtuality, allowing

---

[48] Duns, *Lectura* I, d. 3, p. 1, qq. 1–2 (Vatican, 16:267–68, n. 115); and *Ordinatio* I, d. 8, p. 1, q. 3 (Vatican, 4:198, n. 95); as well as note 44, above.

[49] Duns, *Lectura* I, d. 3, p. 1, qq. 1–2 (Vatican, 16:271–72, n. 122); *Ordinatio* I, d. 3, p. 1, qq. 1–2 (Vatican, 3:40, n. 58); *Lectura* I, d. 8, p. 1, q. 3 (Vatican, 17:43–44, n. 123); and *Ordinatio* I, d. 8, p. 1, q. 3 (Vatican, 4:202–3, 221 and 222–23, nn. 108, 136 and 139). Duns included this idea of modality among the arguments of his opponents in the early *In libros Elenchorum*, q. 15, n. 4 (Vivès, 2:21a), making it likely, therefore, that he did not invent it himself but borrowed it from an earlier source.

predication only denominatively, and then claimed that the absolute transcendence of "being" could be adequately defended by showing how it was prior to and predicable of all other concepts in one or the other of these two ways.[50]

Armed with responses to these two questions, Duns was ultimately satisfied he could put forth a theory of univocity of "being" both plausible and equal to the philosophical tasks expected of it. One can scarcely imagine a more dramatic deviation from intellectual traditions or clearer instance of a thinker proposing radical ideological revision entirely on his own. Yet the core issue, at present, is why he made this break with the past, specifically whether it was, as argued above, to save for the wayfarer a natural, quidditative knowledge of God in face of the ideological abandonment of divine illumination and rejection of Henry's views on essence. Fortunately, a resolution can in great measure be obtained simply by looking to the reasons Duns himself gave for taking the stand he did.

Duns focused on the univocity of "being" at two places in his lectures on the *Sentences*, as evidenced by both the *Lectura* and *Ordinatio*. The first was in Book I, distinction 3, where he posed the questions, greatly inspired by Henry of Ghent, whether the wayfarer had natural knowledge of God and, if so, whether God was first object known. The second came in distinction 8 of the same book, on the question of whether any predicate legitimately applicable to God placed him within a genus.[51] In both cases, Duns's reply drew on

---

[50] Duns, *Ordinatio* I, d. 3, p. 1, q. 3 (Vatican, 3:85, n. 137): "... dico quod primum obiectum intellectus nostri est ens, quia in ipso concurrit duplex primitas, scilicet communitatis et virtualitatis, nam omne per se intelligibile aut includit essentialiter rationem entis, vel continetur virtualiter vel essentialiter in includente essentialiter rationem entis...." See also, *Lectura* I, d. 3, p. 1, qq. 1–2 (Vatican, 16:261–62, n. 99), with an exemplifying application (Vatican, 16:263, n. 104); and *Ordinatio* I, d. 3, p. 1, q. 3 (Vatican, 3:93, n. 151). This theory, like that of modes of being, was foreshadowed by comments in the early Duns, but this time in passages he may have at least partially intended to endorse – see the discussion of *Quaestiones super libros Metaphysicorum* IV, q. 1 (Opera Phil., 3:310–13, nn. 58 and 60–61), in Marrone, "The Notion of Univocity," pp. 386–89. The same language appears in *Collationes* 3 (ed. Harris, in *Duns Scotus*, 2:373), or 24 (ed. Balić, in "De collationibus," p. 215). For full exposition of Duns's ideas on the matter, see Wolter, *The Transcendentals*, pp. 77–98, and the chart epitomizing his views, p. 99.

[51] See, for example, *Lectura* I, d. 3, p. 1, qq. 1–2 (Vatican, 16:223 and 224, nn. 1 and 6): "... utrum Deus sit naturaliter cognoscibilis a nobis pro statu isto.... [U]trum Deus sit primum cognitum a nobis..."; and d. 8, p. 1, q. 3 (Vatican, 17:16, n. 48): "Utrum cum simplicitate Dei stet quod sit in genere, vel quod aliquid formaliter dictum de Deo sit in genere."

his new theory of univocity, and each time he gave considerable attention to the reasons he felt justified his unprecedented views, distinction 8 presenting largely a recapitulation of those already aired in distinction 3.

The Oxford lectures, known through the *Lectura*, list three principal grounds for holding to univocity of "being" besides the testimony of "authorities." First was an argument Duns habitually referred to as "de conceptu certo et dubio," which ran that if one were certain about the meaning or reference of one term but doubtful about that of two others, then the three must correspond to completely different concepts. Even his opponents recognized that everyone confidently used the term "being" while many were not clear about what was meant by "divine being" or "created being." Thus "being" by itself must stand for a concept prior to and discrete from those represented by the latter two phrases, making it a candidate for univocity.[52] Duns was, of course, taking aim here at Henry, whose defense of analogy claimed that the notion of being mind began with, and which it could not specify as either "created" or "divine," was not a single concept but rather a confused amalgam of two, disjunctively referring properly to creatures and to God. His point was that Henry drew the wrong conclusion from the right set of facts.[53] Mind's original, unqualified notion of being was not a sign of confusion but rather of the existence of a unique and univocal general term. Such reasoning may have been prompted by Avicenna, whose *Metaphysics* had argued for "being" as among the most fundamental objects of mind by remarking how intellect grasped it before any of the other general constructions of reality – for instance, the division into agent and patient.[54]

---

[52] Duns, *Lectura* I, d. 3, p. 1, qq. 1–2 (Vatican, 16:232–33, n. 22); and d. 8, p. 1, q. 3 (Vatican, 17:23, n. 69).

[53] For Henry, see above, Pt. 3, ch. 10, nn. 86, 90 and 91. The form of the argument "de certo" Duns gives in *Collationes* 3 (ad 1.) (ed. Harris, in *Duns Scotus*, 2:372), or 24 (ed. Balić, in "De collationibus," pp. 213–14), appears expressly tailored to refute Henry, as in the passage in his *Summa*, a. 75, cited above, Pt. 3, ch. 10, n. 84. That in *Collationes* 3 (si respondeatur) (ed. Harris, in *Duns Scotus*, 2:371), or 24 (ed. Balić, in "De collationibus," pp. 212–13), targets instead Conington, in whose words analogical "being" was one concept "secundum quid." On the latter view, see above, n. 22; and Pt. 3, ch. 10, n. 76.

[54] Avicenna, *Liber de philosophia prima* I, 5 (ed. Van Riet, 1:33–34 [esp. p. 33, ll. 32–34]), a reference suggested by Olivier Boulnois in his introduction to John Duns Scotus, *Sur la connaissance de Dieu*, p. 30, n. 52. Henry of Ghent presents his own argument "de conceptu certo et dubio," applied to a different issue, in *Summa*,

The second argument for univocity of "being" claimed that otherwise the wayfarer would by natural means know nothing of God –
or more precisely, would be unable to fashion a concept designating
divinity.[55] Since all natural knowledge depended on phantasms drawn
from sensation, the only concepts naturally generable were those of
sensible objects and general qualities essentially or virtually contained
in them. But no idea of being merely analogically related to the
being of sensible things met this criterion. If God could not therefore be known as "being" according to the sense of the term univocally signifying creatures as well, he would have to be perceived
by some other, necessarily supernatural, procedure or not at all.
Lectura I, distinction 8, made the case vividly and to the point: Unless
"being" was univocal to God and creatures, only a miracle would
allow the wayfarer knowledge of God.[56]

Third came the argument that theologians had always actually
relied on the univocity of "being" to devise a concept of God, regardless of attempts to deny such univocity in theory. For the truth was
that all had agreed one should work to knowledge of divinity by
selecting the noblest attributes of creatures, removing whatever there
was of imperfection from the concepts by which they were perceived,
then attributing the residue to God.[57] One might, for instance, identify wisdom in humankind, clear away any implication of limitation
or blemish, and predicate of God the perfect wisdom that remained.
This would be impossible, Duns insisted, unless the "wisdom" of the
perfection one ended up with was formally the same (*eiusdem rationis*)
as, thus univocal with, that of the imperfect attribute with which
one began. One might otherwise just as well turn to any creaturely

---

a. 21, q. 3, arg. 1 (1:125vA), thus indicating that the general topos was known in
scholastic circles before Duns. What would appear to be an early version of it as
applied to the univocity of "being" appears in passages in Duns's *Quaestiones super
libros Metaphysicorum* that may have been added to an earlier redaction of the work:
see *Quaestiones* II, qq. 2–3; and IV, q. 1 (Opera Phil., 3:230, n. 106; 306–7, n. 46;
and 320, n. 91).

[55] Duns, *Lectura* I, d. 3, p. 1, qq. 1–2 (Vatican, 16:233–35, nn. 25–28). Note the
general statement (Vatican, 16:233, n. 25): "Praeterea, si conceptus dictus de Deo et
creatura sit analogus et realiter duo conceptus omnino nihil congosceremus de Deo."

[56] Duns, *Lectura* I, d. 8, p. 1, q. 3 (Vatican, 17:20–21, nn. 61–62), especially the
conclusion, p. 21, n. 62: "Igitur si nihil sit commune Deo et creaturae, numquam
proprium conceptum de Deo habebimus nec aliquam cognitionem omnino, nisi ille
conceptus imprimatur per miraculum."

[57] Duns, *Lectura* I, d. 3, p. 1, qq. 1–2 (Vatican, 16:235–36, nn. 29–30); and
d. 8, p. 1, q. 3 (Vatican, 17:26–27, n. 79).

attribute to construct a description of the divinity, for everything about a creature was at least analogously related to an exemplary ideal, in which case describing God as a "rock" should be regarded as of equal insight to calling him "wise."[58] What could be said of "wisdom," moreover, held even truer where "being" was concerned. Duns was in fact so convinced that this was how theological discourse functioned that he insisted the process of winnowing down to a univocal concept lay at the heart even of the Dionysian negative way, which consequently should not be seen as ultimately negative but instead reliant on a positive core.[59]

In the *Ordinatio*, the same three reasons reappear. There, Duns drew the argument "de conceptu certo et dubio" even more clearly than before. With regard to the unqualified notion of "being," mind was either certain about predicating it as a single, univocal term or completely at sea, in which case its very use of the word was open to doubt.[60] He added that the attempt to circumvent such reasoning by resorting to Henry's claim that there were two primary analogical concepts of being so close (*propinqui*) that mind could not initially distinguish them would destroy all confidence in philosophical speech, leaving any appeal to univocity vulnerable to the identical rejoinder that intellect was merely confused.[61] The argument from the impossibility of natural knowledge of God *in via* without univocity of "being" remained essentially unchanged, though aired at greater length.[62] As for the invocation of the way theologians

---

[58] See especially *Lectura* I, d. 3, p. 1, qq. 1–2 (Vatican, 16:235–36, n. 30).

[59] Duns, *Lectura* I, d. 8, p. 1, q. 3 (Vatican, 17:27, n. 80); repeated in *Ordinatio* I, d. 8, p. 1, q. 3 (Vatican, 4:186 and 193, nn. 73 and 85). *Ordinatio* I, d. 3, p. 1, qq. 1–2 (Vatican, 3:4, n. 10), laid down Duns's "positive" approach to the negative way, the heart of which he summed up nicely in the phrase (p. 5, n. 10): "Negationes etiam non summe amamus."

[60] Duns, *Ordinatio* I, d. 3, p. 1, qq. 1–2 (Vatican, 3:18, nn. 27–28); with another version of the same in q. 3 (Vatican, 3:86, n. 138). *Ordinatio* I, d. 8, p. 1, q. 3 (Vatican, 4:178, n. 56) simply refers back to the text of *Ordinatio* I, d. 3, p. 1, qq. 1–2.

[61] Duns, *Ordinatio* I, d. 3, p. 1, qq. 1–2 (Vatican, 3:20, n. 30): "Quod si . . . dicas quod quilibet [philosophans] habet duos conceptus in intellectu suo, propinquos, qui propter propinquitatem analogiae videntur esse unus conceptus, – contra hoc videtur esse quod tunc ex ista evasione videretur destructa omnis via probandi unitatem alicuius conceptus univocam. . . ." A longer refutation of the argument from propinquity appears in *Ordinatio* I, d. 8, p. 1, q. 3 (Vatican, 4:179–82, nn. 59–64). On Henry and the two close concepts, see above, n. 22.

[62] Duns, *Ordinatio* I, d. 3, p. 1, qq. 1–2 (Vatican, 3:21–24, n. 35); and d. 8,

historically worked their way to knowledge of God, this, too, was recapitulated in slightly expanded form, with the eventual addition of a more technical version of the argument analyzing what it meant for a perfection to be attributed to God.[63]

All this in what must have been an early redaction of the *Ordinatio*. A later reworking of the text afforded the opportunity to add two other reasons Duns had not thought of before, both specifically tailored to Henry's views. Duns invariably held that the argument for the analogical nature of the wayfarer's primitive knowledge of God implied that the only concepts of divinity intellect could generate were proper concepts. He now observed that if this were true, then sinful mind should be naturally able to know every necessary proposition affirmable of God. As that was obviously not the case, Henry must be wrong, even about the analogical nature of "being."[64] Next came a complicated argument that if Henry were again correct about the analogical nature of the primitive grasp of God in "being," then created objects at different levels of perfection should yield more or less perfect notions of divinity. Given the whole range of creation, it should theoretically be possible for the wayfarer to come up with concept of God equivalent to the face-to-face vision of beatitude. Once more, the conclusion was unacceptable. Clearly preferable was the assumption that each grasp of a created object produced the same, univocal notion of being, upon which knowledge of God was built.[65]

---

p. 1, q. 3 (Vatican, 4:173–74, n. 51). The argument is mentioned in *Ordinatio* I, d. 3, p. 1, q. 3 (Vatican, 3:86–87, n. 139).

[63] See Duns, *Ordinatio* I, d, 3, p. 1. qq. 1–2 (Vatican, 3:26–27, nn. 39–40), with the addition inserted in a revision (Vatican, 3:25–26, n. 38). *Ordinatio* I, d. 8, p. 1, q. 3 (Vatican, 4:184–85, n. 70) refers back to just the original argument of Vatican, 3:26–27.

[64] Duns, *Ordinatio* I, d. 3, p. 1, qq. 1–2 (Vatican, 3:24–25, nn. 36–37). On his view of Henry and proper concepts, see above, n. 23. Of course, Duns himself did not deny to the wayfarer a proper concept of God – see below, nn. 88–90. He must therefore have composed this additional argument hastily, for in this form it applied as much to himself as to Henry, and in an even later interpolation he summarily dismissed it – see *Ordinatio* I, d. 3, p. 1, qq. 1–2 (Vatican, 3:29, l. 15–30, l. 3). On the other hand, he continued to maintain that a proper concept of God that was also absolutely simple would necessarily reveal everything about the divinity, meaning that any such concept could be known only to the blessed – see above, n. 25, and below, nn. 87 and 115. Surely it was the latter understanding of the matter that lay at the heart of Duns's argument here against analogical "being."

[65] Duns, *Ordinatio* I, d. 3, p. 1, qq. 1–2 (Vatican, 3:27–28, nn. 41–43). No effort is made to justify the sweeping minor premise of this argument.

Looking back over all five arguments, it is plain they each hinge on explaining natural knowledge of God in the world of sin. Considering the context, this comes as no surprise, but the fact is significant nonetheless. While there might be other grounds for affirming univocity of "being," these five were, by Duns's testimony, the reasons convincing him.[66] To be sure, they do not all introduce the fact of knowledge of divinity at precisely the same turning in their logical structure. The first and third in the order given above argue from the actual way God has been known after the Fall – the first drawing more on the experience of mankind in general, the third on that of intellectuals speculating on divinity. The second argues more ambitiously that there could be no other means short of miraculous intervention for the wayfarer to arrive at a meaningful concept of God. This puts analogy's alleged noetic inadequacy to safeguard discourse about the divine in sharpest relief. The two added later are similarly oriented but directed more to Henry alone, and to showing that positing analogy of "being" was not a viable alternative. All point to the conclusion, however, that Duns was led to espouse univocity of "being" precisely in order to save the wayfarer's natural knowledge of God – to solve, in short, the very noetic difficulty his criticism of classic Augustinianism and Henry's metaphysics confronted him with.

Admittedly, none of this technically constitutes more than circumstantial evidence. In fact there is no way to prove beyond a doubt that the claim advanced here is true. But built on circumstance or not, the argument in its favor is strong. It was, after all, just when Duns came to examine issues concerning the wayfarer's natural knowledge of God and the foundation for discourse in the sinful world about divinity – that is, when he began lecturing on

---

[66] It must be noted that Duns did, on occasion, mention two other reasons. His first was that if "being" were not univocal, then there would be no first or adequate object of intellect – see *Lectura* I, d. 3, p. 1, qq. 1–2 (Vatican, 16:261, nn. 97–98); and *Ordinatio* I, d. 3, p. 1, qq. 1–2 (Vatican, 3:16, ll. 20–23); and q. 3 (Vatican, 3:80–81, n. 129). This issue will be dealt with below, pp. 518–20; and also in Pt. 4, ch. 16, pp. 542–43. The second additional reason was that if "being" were not univocal, then in the state of sin there would be no knowledge of substance: see *Lectura* I, d. 3, p. 1, qq. 1–2 (Vatican, 16:265–66, nn. 110–11); and *Ordinatio* I, d. 3, p. 1, q. 3 (Vatican, 86–87, n. 139). On this matter Duns's thinking mirrored his approach to the second of his five main reasons, to which indeed he always subordinated the arguments concerning knowledge of substance, as can be seen in the citation to the *Ordinatio* given just above. For present purposes, therefore, the second additional reason need not be taken as going beyond the original five.

the *Sentences* – that he set out his new theory. In his earlier works, where he had scrutinized "being" and univocity with only logical considerations in mind, he had been content with tradition. It is hard not to believe that change of venue related to change of mind as cause to effect.[67]

Only two major objections can be raised against such an interpretation. One has to do with scattered statements by Duns indicating uncertainty about the ability of his theory of "being" to solve the aforementioned problems surrounding natural knowledge of God; the other with entirely divergent grounds for supporting univocity. Regarding the former, the Vatican edition of the *Ordinatio* reveals a lengthy passage inserted into the text of questions 1–2 of Book I, distinction 3, part 1, revising the original redaction of the work.[68] It is conceivable Duns made the insertion the same time he introduced his additional fourth and fifth arguments for univocity mentioned above, and in it he turned to consider a number of counterarguments to reasons he had initially adduced in his favor, perhaps criticisms encountered in debate. The counterarguments were aimed at the first two of his three original rationales – that is, at the argument "de conceptu certo et dubio" and that from the impossibility by any other means of natural knowledge of God *in via*.

The attack on the argument "de conceptu certo et dubio" Duns eventually succeeded in turning aside. In the insertion to distinction 3 he referred his reader to *Ordinatio* I, distinction 8, where three specific counterarguments to his own original reasoning had already been laid out in full. There he had dealt with the first two easily enough, dismissing them with what he thought were incontrovertible rebuttals in his own behalf.[69] The third, the only one explicitly taken up in the distinction 3 insert, proved more intractable. This counterargument, referred to as "de toto disiuncto," proposed that it was not a single concept about which intellect was certain in its very first apprehension of "being" but rather two concepts in disjunction: "either divine or created being." Duns's revision to distinction 3 conceded he had not effectively opposed this counterargument

---

[67] See similar comments in Marrone, "The Notion of Univocity," pp. 392–94; and "Knowledge of Being," p. 54.

[68] Duns, *Ordinatio* I, d. 3, p. 1, qq. 1–2 (Vatican, 3:31–38, nn. 46–55).

[69] Duns, *Ordinatio* I, d. 8, p. 1, q. 3 (Vatican, 4:178–83, nn. 57–67). The second of these counterarguments, depending on Henry's notion of the propinquity of analogical concepts of being, and Duns's rebuttal of it are also mentioned above, n. 61.

in distinction 8, where indeed no response in support of Duns's view is to be found in what appears to be the first redaction of the text. A rebuttal to his opponents does, however, appear in a reworking of distinction 8 probably postdating the insertion in distinction 3. It is therefore likely, or at any rate possible, Duns was in the end at least minimally satisfied that on this point he had successfully defended his original ideas.[70]

The counterarguments against the second original reason for univocity constituted a more serious threat. Here, where the general possibility of natural knowledge of God in the world of sin was at issue, Duns had to grant that his opponents managed to make a serious case for sticking with the analogical nature of "being," even absent the theoretical support of divine illumination and Henry's view of essence. Following the trace of an analogy from created to divine being might not yield a perfect idea of God, they conceded, but then that was not what one was after, and it was reasonable to presume that analogical thinking generated a concept of divinity adequate to the less stringent demands of theology as actually practiced by the wayfarer.[71] Duns responded that generating a concept of God based on analogy would render that *concept* less perfect than any proper concept referring to creatures themselves. How then could intellect be considered blessed by theological knowledge, even if one meant by this only a natural beatitude, when the operative idea of God was in itself inferior to the notion of something so lowly, for example, as a stone?[72]

What is important is that, having said this, Duns then went on to list further defenses of the counterargument, holding that the theory of univocity of "being" raised comparable difficulties concerning the wayfarer's theology, especially in light of what will later be shown to be Duns's insistence on the specifically constructed nature of a natural, proper concept of God, and that technical adjustments made to circumvent these difficulties with regard to univocity worked equally

---

[70] Duns, *Ordinatio* I, d. 3, p. 1, qq. 1–2 (Vatican, 3:31, n. 46); and d. 8, p. 1, q. 3 (Vatican, 4:184, nn. 68 [the counterargument] and 69 [Duns's eventual rebuttal]). The editors of the Vatican edition (3:184) note that a version of this third counterargument can be found in Thomas of Sutton.

[71] Duns, *Ordinatio* I, d. 3, p. 1, qq. 1–2 (Vatican, 3:31, n. 47).

[72] Refer to Duns, *Ordinatio* I, d. 3, p. 1, qq. 1–2 (Vatican, 3:32–33, nn. 48–49). On p. 33, it would seem that in lines 7 and 8, the reading "concepto" would be preferable to the editors' choice, "conceptu."

well for analogy. And this time his response was reduced to the
retort that his opponents defended analogical unity of "being" no
better than he defended univocity. Thus if their counterarguments
provided no compelling reason to abandon univocity in favor of analogy, he was nonetheless forced to admit he could neither advance
an absolute imperative for his own side nor put to rest all doubts
about his second main reason.[73]

That Duns was ultimately left with nagging doubts about his theory of univocity is confirmed by an authorial annotation to distinction 3, part 1, qq. 1–2, composed most likely after the inserted
discussion of counterarguments just reviewed. The note lists ten arguments regarding univocal versus analogical unity of "being," six exclusively in favor of univocity. These six consisted of the five main
reasons presented in the expanded redaction of the body of the question, the last one duplicated by being offered in two slightly different
forms – that is, they were the arguments "de conceptu certo et
dubio," on the impossibility otherwise of knowing God *in via*, on
knowledge otherwise of all necessary propositions about God, on theologians' attribution of perfection to the divinity, and two on the
multitude of grades of cognition that would otherwise be involved,
leading perhaps to perfect cognition.[74] After setting them quickly
before the reader, Duns returned to each one, showing what counterarguments his opponents made and indicating where, or if, in his
works – especially distinctions 3 and 8 of the *Ordinatio*, Book I – he
had responded.[75]

As the text shows, Duns's own reservations about arguments in

---

[73] Duns, *Ordinatio* I, d. 3, p. 1, qq. 1–2 (Vatican, 33–37, nn. 50–54), especially
the concluding remarks in n. 54: "Non ergo propter istam rationem [contra uni-
vocationem] dimittatur opinio [de univocatione], quia est communis difficultas utrique,
et aeque, si analogia conceptuum exponatur de conceptis."

[74] See the marginal note, Duns, *Ordinatio* I, d. 3, p. 1, qq. 1–2 (Vatican, 3:29,
ll. 3–10). The order of arguments in the note differs slightly from that given above
in the exposition of *Ordinatio* I, d. 3 (see above, nn. 60, 62–65), with three and four
reversed. The note, not the exposition, is true to the actual order in which they
appeared in the revised body of the *Ordinatio* text.

[75] Duns, *Ordinatio* I, d. 3, p. 1, qq. 1–2 (Vatican, 3:29, l. 11–31, l. 13). The
examination of the first two reasons in the note refers the reader to the passages
cited above, nn. 69–73. As for the fourth – on arguing to God from the perfection of creaturely attributes – the note produces an argument against, a rebuttal
referring to the practice of the saints and most theologians, and then alludes to
another counterargument and rebuttal added as an insertion into *Ordinatio* I, d. 8,
p. 1, q. 3 (Vatican, 4:187, nn. 75–77).

his favor now extended to three more of his main reasons – the third, fifth and sixth of the annotation's listing, corresponding effectively to the two added to the body of the *Ordinatio*, distinction 3, in the first reworking.[76] Apparently he had come to believe that these arguments raised difficulties just as vexing to those positing univocity of "being" as to those holding for analogy. His conclusion was that his opponents need worry seriously only about the first and fourth reasons listed in the note – that is, the argument "de conceptu certo et dubio" and that from the theological practice of attributing all perfection to God. These, he had now come to think, were the only ones not generating equally weighty problems for both sides or perhaps rendering the defense of natural knowledge of God impossible under any terms.[77]

By the end, therefore, Duns admitted that the reason he might have been expected to emphasize most – his argument that otherwise the wayfarer would have absolutely no natural knowledge of God – perhaps worked to sustain his position on "being" no better than that of his opponents, or at least raised comparable obstacles to both. Still, he continued to promote two arguments, each dealing, if less categorically, with natural knowledge of divinity, one by appealing to how the wayfarer normally understood God, the other by considering the way theologians constructed their idea of the divine. Even after sober reflection, he could thus honestly maintain that univocity of "being" fit better than analogy with the most prominent – maybe the sole – two ways humans *in via* actually came to know God. He had been forced to draw in his horns, tempering his confidence that only univocity of "being" preserved the promise of knowing and talking about God in this life.[78] But the fact remains that a powerful original impulse for turning to univocity was the desire to expound a noetics successfully compensating for his criticism of Henry and classical Augustinian ideas about knowing God. This

---

[76] See above, nn. 64 and 65.

[77] Duns, *Ordinatio* I, d. 3, p. 1, qq. 1–2 (Vatican, 3:31, ll. 14–17): "Itaque de sola prima ratione et quarta cures, tum quia non sunt 'aeque difficiles' utrique parti, tum quia non concludunt nimis ultra propositum. Non enim concludunt quod nullus conceptus potest haberi proprius Deo, sed quod aliquis communis."

[78] It should be remembered that, as mentioned above, n. 43, in *Collationes* 3 (ed. Harris, in *Duns Scotus*, 2:371), or 24 (ed. Balić, in "De collationibus," p. 213), Duns conceded that he could not be absolutely certain of his position on univocity. Barth, "De argumentis et univocationis entis natura apud Joannem Duns Scotum," CF 14 (1944): 35, concluded that Duns was never sure "being" was univocal.

is what the initial recensions of the *Ordinatio* declare, and what no later reconsiderations can put in doubt.

There is, however, still the second possible objection to the interpretation offered here of Duns's philosophical motivation for positing univocity of "being." For one can point to a rationale Duns put forth entirely different from any mentioned so far. At times he contended that a first or adequate object of intellect had to be a common concept univocally predicable of all knowable objects. Since everyone conceded that mind could know things in each of the ten categories, and theologians agreed that eventually it would know both creatures and God, it followed that only "being" was broad enough to serve as this common term. In short, the very notion of a first object of intellect was reliant on the theory of univocity of "being."[79] From this it could be argued further – though the argument was never explicitly advanced by Duns – that if a first object of intellect was a requirement for cognition, then the very possibility of knowledge entailed univocal "being." Or one might assert even more poignantly that, given the fact of the wayfarer's knowledge of created things, upon Duns's theory of "being" as univocal to creatures and divinity rested the hope that humanity might also know God, not only in sin but also in beatitude.[80] Here was thus a second motive, independent of any reason examined above, for Duns to espouse his new views.

But if this was a fundamental concern driving him to promote univocity of "being," it is odd that in neither of two annotations to the *Ordinatio* where he listed arguments for univocity is it so much as mentioned.[81] And well might he have left it out, since apparently

---

[79] See the references given above, n. 66.

[80] An argument coming close to this does appear in Duns, *Collationes* 11, n. 8 (Vivès, 5:191a): that if intellect's first object was not all-inclusive "being," then mind could never know God. Yet it is not claimed there that a first object has to be univocal, and *Reportatio parisiensis (examinata)* Prol., q. 3 (cited below, n. 83), shows Duns making a related argument about first object of intellect but willing to concede, at least for the sake of debate, that it could be either univocal or equivocal.

[81] See *Ordinatio* I, d. 3, p. 1, qq. 1–2 (Vatican, 3:29, ll. 3–10) – cited above, n. 74 – and d. 8, p. 1, q. 3 (Vatican, 4:173, ll. 13–18) – the latter passage adding nothing to the former but a few citations to authorities. Note that Stephen F. Brown, "Scotus' Univocity in the Early Fourteenth Century," in *De doctrina Ioannis Duns Scoti*, Acta Congressus Scotistici Internationalis, Oxford and Edinburgh, 11–17 September 1966 (Rome, 1968), vol. 4, p. 38, counts the need for a single formal object of intellect as a major reason impelling Duns to advocate univocity of "being." Simo Knuuttila, "Being *qua* Being in Thomas Aquinas and John Duns Scotus," in *The*

he was not at all sure of two crucial premises: either that a first adequate object of intellect was required for cognition or that univocity of predication was necessary for an object to be considered first and adequate.

In two versions of his commentary on Book II of the *Sentences*, both composed toward the end of his career, Duns took the position that if "being" were not univocal to creatures and divinity, then there could be no first adequate object of intellect, since it was certain that at least the blessed knew both God and creation. Here was a perfect opportunity to make the argument for univocity. Rather than do so, he backed off instead from his insistence that there be a first object. Admitting that he would prefer not to dispense with the requirement himself, he confessed nevertheless that since common opinion regarded all-inclusive "being" as not univocal, most theologians would have no choice but to accommodate themselves to such a loss. He even offered a possible rationale, claiming that it spoke to the perfection of humankind's intellect for it to be capable of seizing disparate objects without having to reduce them to a common core.[82]

In the *Quodlibetal Questions*, when faced with a similar dilemma, he took the opposite tack. There, in what is surely among his last writings, he said that so far as first object of intellect was concerned, he did not care whether one held it to be by univocity or by analogy that "being" was common to all particular objects. In either case, "being" was obviously the sole term uniting all things to which mind was directed.[83] This time, in other words, it was the notion of a

---

Logic of Being. Historical Studies, ed. Simo Knuuttila and Jaakko Hintikka (Dordrecht, 1986), pp. 201–22, argues that Duns's novel intensional notion of modality was a motivating factor, admittedly one he might not be expected to have reflected upon himself.

[82] Duns, *Ordinatio* II, d. 24, q. un., n. 8 (Vivès, 13:183b-84a); and *Reportatio parisiensis* II, d. 24, q. un., n. 12 (Vivès, 23:115b), which is even clearer on the last point.

[83] Duns, *Quaestiones quodlibetales*, q. 3, n. 2 (Vivès, 25:114b): ". . . et isto intellectu communissimo, prout res vel ens dicitur quodlibet conceptibile . . . sive illa communitas sit analogiae, sive univocationis, de qua non curo modo, posset poni ens primum objectum intellectus. . . ." He made the same point in *Quaestiones quodlibetales*, q. 14, n. 11 (Vivès, 26:40a), adding that "being" at its broadest was only potentially first object to which the mind of the wayfarer was inclined. See below, Pt. 4, ch. 16, pp. 539–48, for Duns's theory of the adequate object of mind. In *Reportatio parisiensis (examinata)* Prol., q. 3 (ed. Bérubé, in "De l'être à Dieu," p. 57, n. 25), one finds the same indifference concerning univocity or analogy in face of the question of first object of intellect. See also a similar attitude in *Quaestiones super*

necessary connection between univocity and first object from which he opted to retreat.

No matter how he resolved the issue, all these late passages reveal Duns as convinced, in short, that the question of first object of intellect was not the appropriate venue for determining whether "being" was univocal. The plain philosophical plausibility of knowledge of God – whether natural or supernatural, in beatitude or *in via* – viewed apart from the question of how such knowledge might be generated, simply did not depend on one's views about the nature of the concept of being.

In the final analysis, therefore, neither objection holds, and the most convincing argument remains that Duns came to espouse univocity of "being" in order to insure natural knowledge of God for intellect in the world of sin. If early on he realized that the theory of univocal "being" could also be applied to other problems, like the matter of first object of intellect, his eventual appreciation of the complexity of such issues and the awkwardness of using them to decide about univocity dampened his initial enthusiasm. By career's end, the only defense of univocity of "being" he regarded as valid appealed, as at the beginning, to the wayfarer's knowledge of God. The difference was that he now inclined towards retracting a number of the specific ways he had mounted this defense at the start.

Of course, having made his dramatic break with the past on the issue of univocity, Duns could then proceed to tap into the Augustinian tradition of intimate natural knowledge of God so fully exploited by Henry, but without recourse to what he saw as the illogical maneuverings of the latter's metaphysics and the implicit ontologism of his noetics. Like Henry he started with the conviction that the wayfarer in the world of sin, working only with knowledge made available through the processes of sensation, could come to know God, which, he explained, meant fashioning a concept or idea of divinity.[84] Like Henry he also thought that such fashioning began

---

libros Metaphysicorum II, qq. 2–3; and IV, q. 1 (Opera Phil., 3:228–29, nn. 94–95 and 100–104; and 319–20, nn. 86–88). Note the dramatic contrast between this stance and that Duns assumed on the choice between not positing a first object and conceding that univocity was not critical in the passage from *Reportatio parisiensis* cited above, n. 82.

[84] This is exactly how Duns framed the issue in *Ordinatio* I, d. 3, p. 1, qq. 1–2 (Vatican, 3:11, n. 19): "Est ergo mens quaestionis ista, utrum aliquem conceptum simplicem possit intellectus viatoris naturaliter habere, in quo conceptu simplici concipiatur Deus." See also above, n. 1, and on Henry, Pt. 3, ch. 10, n. 17.

with intellect's primitive grasp of "being." Since "being" was a concept immediately predicable of God, in knowing "being" mind at least inchoately and incompletely conceived of the divine.

Yet the theory of univocity lent a wholly different coloring to Duns's understanding of what the doctrine of a primitive knowledge of God in "being" implied. In sharp contrast to Henry, he insisted that the "being" mind grasped at every stage of cognition was the same concept, undivided and indivisible. And unlike Henry he also held that this single concept was univocally predicable of all its referents. In this assertion of conceptual unity and commonness of predication lay all that was new about Duns's approach. It was unity and commonness that allowed "being," discovered in the business of knowing creation, to serve as foundation for knowledge of a reality so elevated as God. But it was the same unity and commonness which signaled that the wayfarer's intellect had no a priori – or to be fair to Henry, quasi a priori – route straight to divinity. There was nothing in mind's primitive cognition of "being" that was not both derivative from and legitimately predicable of created, even sensible, things.[85]

Since for Duns "being" was absolutely simple, it was perforce represented by a concept itself irreducible into further subjective or essential parts.[86] The all-inclusive univocity of this concept meant, however, that the primitive knowledge of God it provided could not be proper – that is, knowledge exclusively predicable of divinity. Duns's ideas were thereby shielded from what he saw as the intolerable implications of Henry's theory: that because initial knowledge of "being" encompassed two analogical concepts, the wayfarer's primary knowledge of the divine was already proper, making it naturally possible *in via* to have proper and absolutely simple knowledge of God.[87] In lieu of such a vision, he came to the inevitable conclusion

---

[85] See Duns, *Lectura* I, d. 3, p. 2, q. un. (Vatican, 16:314, n. 220): "Item, omnes creaturae repraesentant Deum sub ratione generali tantum, quod probatum est supra in ista distinctione quod ex creaturis tantum cognoscimus Deum in conceptu communi entis...." The reference "supra" is to *Lectura* I, d. 3, p. 1, qq. 1–2: see Vatican, 16:232, n. 21, quoted below, n. 91. For Henry's view, see above, Pt. 3, ch. 10, nn. 19–21.

[86] See above, n. 47.

[87] On these implications, see above, n. 23; on the results of conceding them to be true, nn. 25 and 64. Richard of Conington accepted Duns's reading of the implications of Henry's theory (see above, n. 23; also Pt. 3, ch. 10, n. 93) and to avoid the undesirable results commented that although God was first known in a proper,

that all proper knowledge of God would have to be constructed on the initial common concept through a process of modification and restriction of its referential sweep. A proper concept of divinity devised by the wayfarer would therefore be more complicated than the initial knowledge in "being" and necessarily fall short of absolute simplicity.[88]

Because the proper knowledge in question was naturally attained *in via*, all the building blocks for fashioning it would be concepts derived from knowledge of creatures and legitimately predicable of them. Since the goal was knowledge of God, the same building blocks had likewise to be predicable of divinity. The upshot was that for Duns proper but natural knowledge of God was fabricated exclusively out of common terms: univocal general terms like "being," most fundamental of them all. In short, the wayfarer had to bring together or "compound" absolutely simple terms, none of which referred exclusively to God, until it reached an aggregate concept, no longer absolutely simple, that pointed to divinity and nothing else. It was thus aggregation alone that worked to restrict the referential domain to divinity, not the addition of a specifically divine signifier. As examples of constructs intellect might end up with Duns listed the compound concepts "highest being" or "highest good," also "highest and most actualized good." He even noted that their gen-

---

absolutely simple concept, mind did not really "perceive" that it possessed the concept and therefore could not draw from it any conclusions about the divine nature (see Richard of Conington, *Quaest. ord.*, q. 1, ad 2. and ad 3. [ed. Doucet, p. 438], cited above, Pt. 3, ch. 10, n. 84). These comments were given in answer to an initial argument that sounds as if it came from Duns, or was at least inspired by him – see Conington, *Quaest. ord.*, q. 1, arg. 2 (ed. Doucet, p. 430). Richard was plainly taking refuge in Henry's idea of mental confusion of concepts in primary knowledge of "being," a notion Duns likewise considered philosophically reprehensible and that he had combated with his argument "de conceptu certo et dubio" – see above, n. 53. Richard knew Duns's argument "de conceptu certo et dubio" and believed he could refute it – see his *Quodlibet* 1, q. 2, "Sed contra . . . Primo"; and ad 1. (ed. Brown, pp. 303 and 306–7). For his part, Duns realized his opponents would take – or had taken – Richard's route in defense of Henry's view, and when not arguing specifically about the way mind formed its natural knowledge of God he was willing to lay out the defense and even concede it for the sake of argument – see *Ordinatio* I, d. 2, p. 1, qq. 1–2 (Vatican, 2:141, ll. 14–21).

[88] Duns, *Lectura* I, d. 2, p. 1, qq. 1–2 (Vatican, 16:119, n. 25): ". . . omnis conceptus proprius, quem nos concipimus de Deo, est non simpliciter simplex . . ."; and his argument for this conclusion, taking as a premise the univocity of concepts like "being," in the same question (Vatican, 16:120, n. 27). Both argument and conclusion are repeated in *Ordinatio* I, d. 2, p. 1, qq. 1–2 (Vatican, 2:140–41 and 142, nn. 29 and 31). See also *Ordinatio* I, d. 3, p. 1, qq. 1–2 (Vatican, 3:9, n. 17): ". . . nulla ratio simpliciter simplex habetur de Deo quae distinguit ipsum ab aliis. . . ."

eration was by the same operation as that by which mind contrived fictions like "golden mountain," the difference being that in the case of the divinity there was a real referent, though one that had not been directly perceived.[89]

From all this it is clear that there were for Duns two basic ways the wayfarer could naturally conceive of God: either in a common concept that was absolutely simple and univocally applicable to both God and creatures – for instance, "being" or "good" – or in a proper concept compounded of conceptual parts themselves univocally applicable to all reality – "highest good" or "infinite being."[90] He once even offered a summary of how these two ways fit into the broader debate over analogy and univocity. In *Lectura*, Book I, distinction 3, he had attacked Henry's position on the analogical nature of mind's primitive notion of being by insisting that God was never known in a common concept analogically signifying divinity and creatures but only in one that was univocal to the two.[91] When this statement was reworked for the *Ordinatio*, he took pains to make the still more

[89] Duns, *Lectura* I, d. 3, p. 1, qq. 1–2 (Vatican, 16:246, n. 56), especially the last sentence: "Sic igitur, abstrahendo a creaturis intentiones communes et coniungendo eas, possumus cognoscere Deum in universali, et etiam illum conceptum dictum de Deo qui maxime sibi convenit prout a nobis congnoscitur." The same question (Vatican, 16:247, n. 57) also uses the term "componendo" to describe the process. Duns's account of the procedure is repeated in *Ordinatio* I, d. 3, p. 1, qq. 1–2 (Vatican, 3:42, n. 61); and again in the late *Quaestiones quodlibetales*, q. 14, n. 3 (Vivès, 26:5b–6a). A more subtle description can be found in the intermediate *Reportatio parisiensis*, Prol., q. 1, n. 16 (Vivès, 22:16a). The clearest statement that the parts of such a compound concept would be common, only the aggregate proper to God, can be found in *Collationes* 3 (ad aliud) (ed. Harris, in *Duns Scotus*, 2:375); or 24 (ed. Balić, in "De collationibus," p. 217) – a combination of which readings gives the most plausible text. As noted in *Collationes* 3 (ad 3.) (ed. Harris, in *Duns Scotus*, 2:372–73); or 24 (ed. Balić, in "De collationibus," p. 214), all this meant that the proper concept of God was "composite." For mention of "golden mountain," see the passages from *Lectura* I, d. 3; and *Ordinatio* I, d. 3, cited just above; on other fictions, see above, Pt. 4, ch. 14, n. 125.
[90] See Duns, *Collationes* 13, n. 4 (Vivès, 5:202a–b): "Dico quod conceptus conclusi per modum complexionis conveniunt Deo, nec conveniunt creaturae – hujusmodi sunt conceptus compositi – non autem simplices conceptus – cujusmodi sunt conceptus entis, boni, etc. – nam tales conceptus dicuntur univoce de Deo et creatura." The punctuation here is mine.
[91] Duns, *Lectura* I, d. 3, p. 1, qq. 1–2 (Vatican, 16:232, n. 21): "De secundo articulo est dicendum, in quo expresse sibi [i.e. Henrico] contradico, quod non concipitur Deus in conceptu communi analogo sibi et creaturae, sed in conceptu communi univoco sibi et creaturae, ita quod ens et bonum et sapientia dicta de Deo et creatura univoce dicuntur de eis, et non dicunt duos conceptus." See also the reference to this passage in n. 85, above.

revealing assertion that intellect formed concepts of God both univocally and analogically applicable to creation.[92] Univocity characterized the common concepts like "being," analogy the proper concepts
like "highest being," analogically related to terms for created objects
such as "this sensible being" or "that sensible being" from which its
conceptual ingredients were drawn.

There are scholars to be sure, Allan Wolter most prominent among
them, who have taken Duns's words in the *Ordinatio* to mean that
he posited not only a common, univocal concept of being *tout court*
but also at least two more proper ones, related by analogy. Using
the former concept mind would comprehend God and all creatures
at once, while calling upon one of the latter it would be directed
exclusively either to "being" that was divine or "being" that was created. I have argued elsewhere that Wolter is wrong to say Duns's
early works posit a concept of being univocally predicable of all
things, and I must now add that I find it equally incorrect to claim
his later writings hold that the term "being" alone might be employed
according to several proper, analogous meanings.[93] In short, at no
time in his career did Duns believe that "being" was both univocal
and analogical. It is true that Henry's viewpoint approached the
position Wolter attributes to Duns.[94] But such an attitude was just
what the latter was careful to avoid, and, in his maturity, to expunge
wherever it threatened to take hold. The argument "de conceptu
certo et dubio" plainly demands that there be only one concept of
being and one term, "being," univocally predicable of everything.[95]

---

[92] Duns, *Ordinatio* I, d. 3, p. 1, qq. 1–2 (Vatican, 3:18, n. 26): "Secundo dico
quod non tantum in conceptu analogo conceptui creaturae concipitur Deus, scilicet
qui omnino sit alius ab illo qui de creatura dicitur, sed in conceptu aliquo univoco
sibi et creaturae."

[93] See Wolter, *The Transcendentals*, pp. 46–48, n. 35, and 55–56; and my contrasting argument in Marrone, "Notion of Univocity," pp. 372–76. Cyril L. Shircel,
The Univocity of the Concept of Being in the Philosophy of John Duns Scotus (Washington,
D.C., 1942), p. 164, has also maintained that the later Duns denied that the term
"being" alone should ever be taken as analogical.

[94] Most clearly in Henry, *Summa*, a. 26, q. 2, ad 1. (1:159rT) – quoted above,
Pt. 3, ch. 10, n. 78 – and a. 75, q. 6, ad 3. (2:311rY) – cited in the same chapter,
n. 84. The view is also implied in other passages referred to in that chapter, n. 81.

[95] Manifest most clearly in Duns's argument against Henry's more pliant use of
"being" from *Lectura* I, d. 3, p. 1, qq. 1–2 (Vatican, 16:233, n. 24): "Praeterea,
quilibet experitur in se ipso quod potest concipere ens non descendendo ad ens
participatum vel non participatum. Si fiat descensus ad utrumque conceptum, quaero
an stet conceptus entis, aut non? Si sic, habetur propositum; si autem indeterminate importat quasi unum, et quando fit descensus, est duo conceptus, tunc impos-

So far as concerns proper knowledge by itself, Duns proposed that the "most perfect" – that is, simplest and most precise – concept of God the wayfarer could naturally construct was the notion of "infinite being."[96] In taking this stand he put himself in opposition to Henry, who had said that the best way rational mind could know God naturally was by reducing all divine attributes to simplicity.[97] Duns added that the distinction between knowing God as "being" and knowing him as "infinite being" was equivalent to the difference between cognition in imperfect and perfect concepts. Only the latter seized the reality with its intrinsic mode of existence, and thus only the latter truly described what it was to be God.[98] It should be remembered that perfect knowledge of God in this sense was not yet the authentically perfect cognition intellect would attain in beatitude, when it saw God face-to-face in his full particularity, *ut haec*. In that case, mind would conceive of "being" and its intrinsic divine mode at a single stroke, without need for even the minimal conceptual composition manifest in a term like "infinite being."[99]

Equipped with these convictions about the differing ways intellect conceived a notion of God, Duns managed to elude the ambiguity regarding order of concepts that had plagued Henry's account of natural knowledge of divinity.[100] Along the way, he criticized his

sibile esset probare aliquid esse univocum. . . ." See also *Ordinatio* I, d. 2, p. 1, qq. 1–2 (Vatican, 2:142, n. 31).

[96] Duns, *Lectura* I, d. 3, p. 1, qq. 1–2 (Vatican, 16:244, n. 50); and *Ordinatio* I, d. 3, p. 1, qq. 1–2 (Vatican, 3:40, n. 58 – with an argument for why p. 41, n. 60). See also *Ordinatio* I, d. 2, p. 1, qq. 1–2 (Vatican, 2:215, n. 147), referring to the passage in distinction 3. Note, however, that in *Ordinatio* I, d. 8, p. 1, q. 3 (Vatican, 4:194, n. 86), Duns said "bonum per se" was the most perfect concept. In a similar vein, Augustinus Daniels, "Zu den Beziehungun," pp. 226 and 228, remarks that William held at one point that God "sub ratione bonitatis sue" was the object of theology, at another point that it was God under the aspect of infinite.
[97] Duns, *Ordinatio* I, d. 3, p. 1, qq. 1–2 (Vatican, 3:41–42, n. 60). Henry's view is referred to above, Pt. 3, ch. 10, n. 46. It must be admitted that in the passage from the *Reportatio parisiensis* cited above, n. 89, Duns comes strikingly close to Henry's view.
[98] Duns, *Ordinatio* I, d. 8, p. 1, q. 3 (Vatican, 4:222, n. 138). On "being" and its intrinsic modes, see above, n. 49.
[99] On knowing God in particular, see above, n. 9, and also *Lectura* I, d. 22, q. un. (Vatican, 17:301–2, n. 4); on particular knowledge of God as "perfect," above, n. 6. In *Ordinatio* I, d. 8, p. 1, q. 3 (Vatican, 4:224, n. 142), Duns explained how perfect knowledge of God – this time in the sense of beatific knowledge – would seize object and intrinsic mode without any distinction of formalities. Compare *Lectura* I, d. 8, p. 1, q. 3 (Vatican, 17:44–45, n. 125).
[100] For the ambiguity in Henry, see above, Pt. 3, ch. 10, nn. 61–62; as well as this chapter, nn. 18 and 20. In *Ordinatio* I, d. 3, p. 1, qq. 1–2 (Vatican, 3:67–68,

predecessor for alleging that God was first object naturally known, even if unperceived, reasoning that if all natural cognition derived from knowledge of creatures, as both thinkers agreed, then it made no sense to say God was apprehended before anything else.[101] He also reproached him for holding on principle that the more indeterminate the object, the earlier it was known. Henry's "more indeterminate" was translatable into Duns's lexicon as "more confused," and it was at the very opposite end of the conceptual spectrum, with "most distinct," that Duns believed the order of intellection began. For him it was not what was most general or confused but rather particulars available to mind through sensation that constituted, absolutely speaking, its first cognitive objects.[102]

Yet he still found a way to preserve the core Augustinian vision of a knowledge of God, in "being," somehow primary and implicated in knowledge of all else. To remove all doubt about precisely where this cognition was situated in the natural conceptual order, he simply appealed to his pair of distinctions: knowing a confused versus knowing a distinct object and knowing confusedly versus knowing distinctly.[103] Directly contradicting Henry, for whom primitive knowledge of God in "being" was confused cognition (*modus confusus* or *intelligere confuse*), he insisted that although "being" was a general or "confused" term (*confusum*), the fact that it was absolutely simple meant it could not be known confusedly (*confuse*). With no simpler conceptual parts into which it might be resolved, it had to be known distinctly (*distincte*) or not at all.[104] Since for Duns the order of know-

n. 107), Duns accused Henry of contradicting himself on primary knowledge of God. Taking a page from Matthew of Aquasparta, he suggested that the best Henry might manage would be to maintain that although divinity was not for human intellect "first known" (*primum cognitum*), it was in itself "first knowable" (*primum cognoscibile*) – *Ordinatio* I, d. 3, p. 1, qq. 1–2 (Vatican, 3:63–64, n. 100); on Matthew, see above, Pt. 2, ch. 8, nn. 130–31. What for Matthew had been a mark of some sympathy with Henry was thereby reduced, in Duns's hands, to a sign of exasperation.

[101] Duns, *Lectura* I, d. 3, p. 1, qq. 1–2 (Vatican, 16:257–58, nn. 85–86).

[102] In *Ordinatio* I, d. 3, p. 1, qq. 1–2 (Vatican, 3:66, n. 104), Duns expressly announced that his position on the order of intellection was diametrically opposed to Henry's, referring readers back to the account of his own views earlier in the same question (Vatican, 3:56 and 50, nn. 82 and 73). See also above, Pt. 4, ch. 13, n. 164.

[103] For Duns's pair of distinctions, see above, Pt. 4, ch. 13, nn. 160–61.

[104] Duns, *Lectura* I, d. 3, p. 1, qq. 1–2 (Vatican, 16:250, n. 69) "Et sic ens, licet sit confusum cognitum, non tamen confuse cosgnoscitur, quia non habet per quod potest distingui in plura aut priora . . ."; and also *Ordinatio* I, d. 3, p. 1, qq. 1–2 (Vatican, 3:54–55, n. 80): "Ens autem non potest concipi nisi distincte, quia habet

ing confusedly preceded that of knowing distinctly, it followed that "being" was not a candidate for mind's very first object.[105] Looking to the order of distinct cognition alone, however, a different picture emerged. Here, where clear articulation of conceptual parts was key, it was the simpler concept that was more easily grasped and thus known first. "Being" was not just absolutely simple; it was, as most general term of all, the absolute simplest. In the line of knowing distinctly, "being" was thus first concept known. In fact, since "being" was part of the definition of everything else, all other distinct cognition was ultimately built upon knowledge of it.[106]

Translated into Henry's terminology, to which Duns temporarily reverted, this meant that "being" as privatively indeterminate (*indeterminatum privative*) – that is, as a universal term – was "being" as mind knew it first. It constituted indeed first concept distinctly known. Only after grasping this common concept could intellect go on to construct a notion of "negatively indeterminate being" – that is, "being per se," or God himself.[107] For Duns, therefore, Augustinianism had to be tempered so as to eliminate a priori knowledge of God. Yet because "being," first concept distinctly known, applied univocally to both creatures and God, the wayfarer's distinct natural knowledge of God was directly derived from the most primitive concept it distinctly perceived in attending to created things. With only slight strain to his philosophical lexicon, Duns could even say that God was known confusedly (*quasi confuse*) in the primitive perception of "being" as an absolutely simple common term.[108] It was in this

---

conceptum simpliciter simplicem." On Duns, see also above, n. 53; for Henry's views, Pt. 3, ch. 10, nn. 36 and 86.

[105] On priority among the two orders of knowing, see again above, n. 102; and Pt. 4, ch. 13, n. 164.

[106] Duns, *Lectura* I, d. 3, p. 1, qq. 1–2 (Vatican, 16:252–53, nn. 75 and 77); and *Ordinatio* I, d. 3, p. 1, qq. 1–2 (Vatican, 3:55, n. 80). For Duns on priority in distinct cognition, see above, Pt. 4, ch. 13, n. 163. There was a way Duns saw the most confused or general term as absolutely first known, and this was in habitual or virtual cognition. He thus saved Avicenna's famous pronouncement on "being" by reading it to mean that "being" was very first object habitually or virtually conceived – see *Lectura* I, d. 3, p. 1, qq. 1–2 (Vatican, 16:255, n. 81); and *Ordinatio* I, d. 3, p. 1, qq. 1–2 (Vatican, 3:60–61, n. 93). For other references to Avicenna on "being," see *Quaestiones super libros Metaphysicorum* I, q. 10 (Opera Phil., 3:182, n. 6; 185, n. 21; and 301–2, nn. 31–32).

[107] In *Lectura* I, d. 8, p. 1, q. 3 (Vatican, 17:30, n. 87), Duns expressly used Henry's language of privitive and negative indetermination. By *Ordinatio* I, d. 8, p. 1, q. 3 (Vatican, 4:193–94, n. 86), he had cast the argument in more general terms.

[108] See Duns, *Quaestiones quodlibetales*, q. 14, n. 3 (Vivès, 26:5b–6a): "Breviter dico,

restricted, but still precious, sense that he was able to redeem the frequently quoted phrase from John of Damascus, that knowledge of God had been inserted into all human minds.[109]

On such foundations he erected his theory of the wayfarer's access to theology. Duns agreed with William of Ware that metaphysics, if not exclusively about God, at least dealt with him extensively, drawing out all that could be known about divinity simply as perceived in the term "infinite being."[110] To this degree metaphysics constituted a naturally constructed science of God, or what could be referred to as natural theology.[111] But what today might be called positive theology – and which Duns spoke of as "our" theology, in opposition to God's – looking to divinity's precise attributes, like "trine," and manifesting its hidden truths, was also in Duns's opinion elaborated on the basis of natural understanding of God as "infinite being." Although the particular propositions Christian theology held as true were divinely revealed, the intentional content of

---

quod quodcumque transcendens per abstractionem a creatura cognita [for: cognitum?], potest in sua indifferentia intelligi, et tunc concipitur Deus quasi confuse, sicut animali intellecto, homo intelligitur."

[109] Duns, *Lectura* I, d. 2, p. 1, qq. 1–2 (Vatican, 16:122–23, n. 34); and *Ordinatio* I, d. 2, p. 1, qq. 1–2 (Vatican, 2:145, n. 34): "Ad argumentum principale Damasceni: potest exponi de potentia cognitiva naturaliter nobis data per quam ex creaturis possumus cognoscere Deum esse, saltem in rationibus generalibus . . . vel de cognitione Dei sub rationibus communibus convenientibus sibi et creaturae. . . ." Bettoni took such passages in Duns as evidence of a theory of virtual innatism of knowledge of God in humankind, a version of what he called *apriorismo*: see his comments in "Oggetto e soggetto nell'atto intellettivo secondo Duns Scoto," SF 39 (1942): 31; "Rapporti dottrinali," p. 130; *Duns Scoto filosofo* (Milan, 1966), p. 61; "Punti di contatto," pp. 528–31; and "Il fondamento della conoscenza umana secondo Duns Scoto," FS 47 (1965): 300–314. Barth, "Duns Scotus und die ontologische Grundlage unserer Verstandeserkenntnis," FS 33 (1951): 348–84; and "De univocationis entis," pp. 106–7; and Bérubé, in "Jean Duns Scot: Critique," pp. 208, 235–36 and 243; and "De l'être à Dieu chez Jean Duns Scot," pp. 50–53, have rightfully contested the presence of innatism in Duns's thought, whether virtual or not. However, Bérubé, in "Dynamisme psychologique et existence de Dieu," pp. 18–19; and "De l'être," pp. 56–59, posits – wrongly, I believe – for Duns's early work the same virtual innatism Bettoni claims to have found throughout.

[110] William, *Quaestiones*, q. 2 (MS Vat., Chigi. B. VIII. 135, f. 2rb): ". . . sed hec [scientia metaphysica] . . . de deo determinat sub ratione cause, et sub ratione entis communissimi." Duns, *Quaestiones quodlibetales*, q. 7, n. 11 (Vatican, 25:293b): "Viator habens conceptum simplicem et perfectissimum ad quem attingit homo ex naturalibus, non transcendit cognitionem perfectissimam simplicem de Deo possibilem metaphysico." On Duns and the wayfarer's most perfect concept of God, see above, n. 96.

[111] Duns, *Reportatio parisiensis* Prol., q. 3 (quaestiuncula 1), n. 11 (Vatican, 22:51a); and *Quaestiones quodlibetales*, q. 17, n. 10 (Vivès, 26:219b), which refers to metaphysics as a "cognitio naturalis scientifica de Deo."

the term "God" contained in them did not exceed the concept compounded naturally by the wayfarer's intellect. It was, in fact, the very
referential limitation of positive theology to concepts that could be
devised naturally by intellect which opened it up to general discussion, exposition as well as debate, even among non-believers.[112]
Thus, faith did not render the naturally constructed concept of God
otiose, for though divine inspiration was the motor driving mind to
assent to positive theological truths, understanding their meaning
remained the job of the wayfarer's natural intellectual powers.[113]

Of course all this entailed equally well, both Duns and William
conceded, that there was in the world of sin no naturally acquired
science of God as trine – in other words, that for the wayfarer positive theology was not a demonstrative discipline.[114] Only if God were
known in his essence *ut haec* would it be evident to mind, either
immediately or by demonstration, what his proper attributes were
and thus whether or not the specific propositions of Christian theology

---

[112] On the meaning of "God" as well as other terms in "our" theology, see *Lectura*
Prol., p. 2, qq. 1–3 (Vatican, 16:32, n. 88); *Ordinatio* III, d. 23, q. un., n. 9 (Vivès,
15:15b); and d. 24, q. un., n. 22 (Vivès, 15:53b). On the possibility of theological
discussion between Christians and non-Christians, see *Ordinatio* III, d. 24, q. un.,
n. 11 (Vivès, 15:42b); *Quaestiones quodlibetales*, q. 14, n. 4 (Vivès, 26:6a); and *Reportatio
parisiensis* III, d. 24, q. un., n. 12 (Vatican, 23:452b): ". . . illum conceptum quem
habet theologus de Deo trino et uno, habet haereticus, quia idem post negat quod
prius affirmavit. . . ."

[113] Duns, *Reportatio parisiensis* Prol., q. 2 (ad 3.), n. 21 (Vivès, 22:45b); and *Quaestiones
quodlibetales*, q. 14, n. 3 (Vivès, 26:6a); and q. 7, n. 11 (Vivès, 25:293b): "Cognitio
enim fidei non tribuit conceptum simplicem de Deo, sed tantummodo inclinat ad
assentiendum quibusdam incomplexis [for: complexis!], quae non habent evidentiam ex terminis simplicibus apprehensis, et per consequens per fidem non habetur
conceptio simplex transcendens omnem conceptum simplicem apud metaphysicum."
On the importance to Duns of univocity of "being" for founding both metaphysics
and positive theology, see the comments of Belmond, *Etudes sur la philosophie de Duns
Scot.* Vol. 1: *Dieu. Existence et cognoscibilité,* pp. 162–64 and 354; Wolter, *The Transcendentals,*
p. 31; Stephen Brown, "Scotus' Univocity," p. 38; and "Avicenna and the Unity
of the Concept of Being," pp. 130–31; Robert P. Prentice, "The Fundamental
Metaphysics of Scotus Presumed by the *De primo principio,*" *Antonianum* 44 (1969):
227–308; Ivo Zielinski, "Möglichkeit und Grenzen der natürlichen Erkenntnis Gottes
bei Johannes Duns Scotus," WuW 48 (1985): 17–32; and Boulnois, "Introduction"
to Jean Duns Scot, *Sur la connaissance de Dieu,* pp. 11, 12, 30, 34, 43 and 45.

[114] William, *Quaestiones,* q. 2 (MS Vat., Chigi. B. VIII. 135, f. 2rb): "Et si con-
cedatur quod de quocumque potest esse scientia naturaliter acquisita, non tamen
de quocumque et qualitercumque consideretur, quia non de deo ut est trinus et
unus." See also his q. 21 (ad illud Augustini) (ed. Daniels, in *Quellenbeiträge und
Untersuchungen,* p. 102). For Duns, see *Ordinatio* III, d. 23, q. un., n. 9 (Vivès, 15:15b);
and *Quaestiones quodlibetales,* q. 14, n. 9 (Vivès, 25:14b–15a), which specified that theology was demonstrative neither "quia" nor "propter quid."

were true, a circumstance far surpassing natural understanding of divinity in a concept compounded from universal terms (*in universali*).[115] It is worth noting, however, that in further inquiry into why intellect's natural concepts of God did not suffice for evident knowledge of his proper attributes, Duns explicitly rejected Henry's argument that such concepts always retained the flavor, or limitations, of their roots in sensible cognition. With his theory of univocity of "being," he wanted no part of an explanation that might limit the referential reach of transcendental terms. His reasoning was instead that because natural concepts of divinity were constructed out of universal terms, they could lead to knowledge of nothing more than attributes common to God and creatures, not the proper divine attributes of positive theological discourse.[116]

From Duns's perspective, even natural theology – metaphysics with respect to God – was not a science "propter quid," though since it investigated common rather than proper attributes of divinity, attributes like "being" and "wisdom," concerning which intellect could learn something from nature, it was "quia" or a posteriori.[117] The limitation here, too, was imposed by the generality of human knowledge of God *in via*. Not about divine essence in particular or *ut haec*, such knowledge provided no middle terms or true definitions by

---

[115] Duns, *Lectura* Prol., p. 1, q. un. (Vatican, 16:14, n. 33); and p. 2, qq. 1–3 (Vatican, 16:32, n. 88–cited above, n. 112); *Ordinatio* Prol., p. 1, q. un. (Vatican, 1:38, n. 62); III, d. 23, q. un., n. 9 (Vivès, 15:15b); and d. 24, q. un., n. 22 (Vivès, 15:53a); *Reportatio parisiensis* III, d. 24, q. un., n. 23 (Vivès, 23:459b); and *Quaestiones quodlibetales*, q. 14, n. 9 (Vivès, 15:15a); and also above, nn. 25 and 64. Positive theology as a true science – that is, theology as known by God – had, quite exceptionally, a singular subject, since God in himself fell under no genus or species: see *Reportatio parisiensis* Prol., q. 3 (quaestiuncula 2), n. 12 (Vivès, 22:51b).

[116] See *Lectura* Prol., p. 1, q. un. (Vatican, 16:18–19, nn. 44–45) for Duns's rejection of Henry's ideas, and (Vatican, 16:19–20, n. 46) for his own view; and the same in *Ordinatio* Prol., p. 1, q. un. (Vatican, 1:50–51, nn. 83–84 and 86). In contrast, William of Ware seems to have been satisfied with Henry's account, or at least not so bothered by the implication that the sensory origin of natural knowledge limited reference to material things: see William, *Quaestiones*, q. 2 (MS Vat., Chigi. B. VIII. 135, f. 2rb): "... postquam cognitio istorum principiorum non aduenit homini nisi amminiculo sensus uel sensuum, non possunt ducere naturaliter nisi in cognitionem eorum que aliquo modo cadunt sub sensu cum sunt materialia." On Henry and "savoring of roots," see above, Pt. 3, ch. 11, n. 3.

[117] Duns, *Ordinatio* I, d. 2, p. 1, qq. 1–2 (Vatican, 2:148, n. 39); *Reportatio parisiensis* Prol., q. 3 (quaestiuncula 1), n. 11 (Vivès, 22:51a) – cited above, n. 111; *Reportatio parisiensis (examinata)* IA, d. 2, qq. 1–3 (ed. Wolter and Adams, in "Parisian Proof," pp. 254–56); and *Quaestiones quodlibetales*, q. 7, n. 12 (Vivès, 25:294a). The idea appears in Duns as early as *Quaestiones super libros Metaphysicorum* I, q. 1 (Opera Phil., 3:22, n. 19).

which even common properties could be demonstrated of God a priori.[118] Such a position entailed diminution of Augustinian claims about the wayfarer's knowledge of God, forcing Duns to take issue with William of Ware himself, for whom propositions such as "God exists" could be known as true *per se* – immediately evident, like principles of science – by those who did the hard work of searching the recesses of mind.[119] He nevertheless hastened to point out that a posteriori reasoning sufficed to make natural theology authentically scientific or minimally demonstrative. Though the existence of God was not grasped by the wayfarer as an immediate, *per se* truth, it could still be proven by indubitable argument from his effects in the world.[120]

More than any of his fellow Augustinians, Duns thus succeeded in laying out a fully naturalizing explanation for simple knowledge of God, on the basis of which could be established the framework for a natural theology as well as the linguistic substratum for a positive theology open to rational examination even outside Christian circles. All the while, he made good on Augustinian presumptions of the centrality of "being" for understanding theology and the possibility of natural concepts capturing something of God's essence and referring directly to it. It was as if he brought to completion the efforts of Henry of Ghent and Matthew of Aquasparta to set mind and its activity entirely in the world while not forgetting its natural orientation towards God. Here was an Aristotelianizing noetics and epistemology effectively harnessed to the aspirations of an Augustinian cast of mind.[121]

---

[118] Duns, *Reportatio parisiensis (examinata)* IA, d. 2, qq. 1–3 (ed. Wolter and Adams, in "Parisian Proof," p. 254), cited just above, n. 117; and *Quaestiones quodlibetales*, q. 7, n. 11 (Vivès, 25:293a–b).

[119] See William, *Quaestiones*, q. 21 (ad illud Augustini) (ed. Daniels, in *Quellenbeiträge und Untersuchungen*, p. 102): ". . . in quantum . . . est unum et primum ens et causa omnium, potest esse per se notum, modo supradicto, Deus est." Duns argued vigorously against the *per se* character of the wayfarer's knowledge of such propositions: see *Lectura* I, d. 2, p. 1, qq. 1–2 (Vatican, 16:117, 120 and 122, nn. 22, 25 and 33); *Ordinatio* I, d. 2, p. 1, qq. 1–2 (Vatican, 2:138–39 and 141, nn. 26 and 29); and *Reportatio parisiensis (examinata)* IA, d. 2, qq. 1–3 (ed. Wolter and Adams, in "Parisian Proof," p. 254), cited above, n. 117.

[120] On demonstration of the fact of God's existence, see Duns's *Ordinatio* I, d. 2, p. 1, qq. 1–2 (Vatican, 2:161–62, n. 56). In *Reportatio parisiensis* Prol., q. 2, n. 19; and q. 3 (Vivès, 22:44a and 47b), he noted that although such propositions were not grasped as true *per se* in metaphysics, they could still be naturally proven to be true.

[121] See above, Pt. 2, ch. 8, pp. 243–45, on Pecham's and Matthew's steps away from a Bonaventuran dynamic of mind; Pt. 3, ch. 10, p. 330, on the more formidable effort of Henry. Gilson remarked, in *Jean Duns Scot. Introduction à ses positions*

To the end, Duns retained some doubt, perhaps a healthy scepticism, about the extent of his achievement. In his *Collationes* he admitted that it was only loosely one could claim to devise an idea of God's quiddity from what could be known of creatures. Indeed, looking disjunctively at the separate parts of a natural concept of God, the common notions compounded by aggregation, one could well appreciate how profoundly creature-oriented the cognitive object remained, so that even the fully constructed proper concept could hardly be held to say much positively about the divine. The Dionysian negative way, with its imputation of real ignorance, best expressed the character of human knowledge of God in the world of sin.[122] And here in the *Collationes*, in contrast to the commentaries on the *Sentences*, it was clearly the "negative" in the *via negativa* Duns wanted to emphasize. Reminding his readers that God's essence was in itself most suited to being seized in an absolutely simple concept, he explained that when in the world of sin the wayfarer managed to put together a compound proper concept referring to divinity, it was still the elusive absolutely simple concept to which it intentionally aspired.[123] Natural knowledge of God *in via* was at bottom an ersatz cognition, inclining intellect towards an object that could not truly be naturally known.

Sober thoughts like these surely explain Duns's willingness to concede to the wayfarer, in exceptional cases, knowledge of divinity vastly superior to naturally attained cognition if still short of rapturous or beatific vision. God could, he confessed, grant more perfect than usual understanding of himself without lifting intellect out of the wayfaring state. He was aware that Henry had posited a kind of knowledge available to theologians surpassing natural comprehension and constituting a true science of Christian theology *in via*:

---

fondamentales (Paris, 1952), p. 573, that Scotus transformed Augustinian metaphysics – to Gilson's mind, by laying out a program of theological certitude or science – but still managed to retain a place for Franciscan emphasis on affect or love.

[122] Consider the pointed remarks in Duns, *Collationes* 13, n. 4 (ad quaestionem) (Vivès, 5:202a). Barth, "De univocationis entis," pp. 102–5, comments on Duns's realization of the limits to natural knowledge of God.

[123] The same *collatio*, n. 5 (Vivès, 5:202b): "Ideo licet in altissimo conceptu [quem habemus de Deo in via] nihil concipimus, nisi modo composito, tamen intendimus conceptum simpliciter simplicem, quia illum habemus in communi tantum, et confusissimum, et communem Deo et creaturae." On Duns more typically about the Dionysian way, see above, n. 59.

the knowledge made possible by Henry's *lumen medium*.[124] Special theological understanding in precisely this form was not, however, a
proposal he could underwrite. In an argument reminiscent of his
opposition to traditional doctrines of divine illumination, he observed
that no matter what extraordinary light of intellectual operation was
provided to mind, the fact remained that the terms of simple cognition garnered naturally in the world imposed limitations on the
semantic value of theological propositions. Any such proposition composed of naturally constructed terms was simply incapable, no matter
what the conditions, of revealing truths beyond those already plain
in the glow of mind's natural light. Under no circumstances could
the wayfarer's positive theology attain to the level of true science.[125]

What Duns was prepared to allow for was a different sort of positive theology, short of strict science but more far-reaching than natural theology or metaphysics, manifesting the truths of faith with
greater clarity than faith by itself. There were, he explained, three
ways other than by rapture to know about divinity *in via*: by faith,
by the exegetical and, from a scientific point of view, dialectical arguments of most theologians, and by the kind of extraordinary insight –
the vision from the mountaintop – God vouchsafed to the Apostles
and prophets.[126] In virtue of his omnipotence, God could bestow the
gift of this third type of knowledge upon the wayfarer without revealing himself openly and thus without canceling the terms of mind's
sinful exile from the divine presence. Indeed, he had often opted to
do so in order to steel his chosen earthly emissaries against the tri-
als and tribulations they faced in building his church, for anyone

---

[124] Henry's ideas are referred to above, Pt. 4, ch. 13, n. 147. For Duns's presentation of them, see *Ordinatio* III, d. 24, q. un, n. 5 (Vivès, 15:39a); *Reportatio parisiensis* Prol., q. 2, n. 6 (Vivès, 22:36a); and III, d. 24, q. un., n. 7 (Vivès, 23:449b–50a).

[125] For Duns's argument against the cognitive effects Henry attributed to a *lumen
medium*, see *Ordinatio* III, d. 24, q. un., n. 11 (Vivès, 15:42a–b); *Reportatio parisiensis*
Prol., q. 2, n. 14 (Vivès, 22:40b–41a); and III, d. 24, q. un., n. 13 (Vivès, 23:452a–b);
on the impossibility of a scientific theology for the wayfarer, *Ordinatio* III, d. 24,
q. un., nn. 13 and 17 (Vivès, 15:44b and 48a); and *Reportatio parisiensis* III, d. 24,
q. un., nn. 16 and 22 (Vivès, 23:454b and 457a). In the Prologue to *Reportatio
parisiensis*, Duns surprisingly defended the contrary position, that there could be a
demonstrative theology *in via*: see below, n. 129.

[126] Duns, *Ordinatio* III, d. 24, q. un., n. 14 (Vivès, 15:45a); *Reportatio parisiensis* III,
d. 24, q. un., n. 17 (Vivès, 23:454b–55a); and most fully in *Reportatio parisiensis* Prol.,
q. 2, n. 17 (Vivès, 22:42b–43a), where two still higher kinds of knowledge are
added: knowing God face-to-face and knowing him in a species.

receiving understanding of this sort would cling to the truths of faith
with a certitude equivalent to that of science itself. Although lacking the evidence for true belief that strict scientific knowledge could
have provided, the strength of such an individual's intellectual adherence would permit characterizing his or her knowledge as something
like science, loosely construed.[127] To this degree, Henry was on the
right track, and to this extent Duns was prepared to admit supernaturalism into his otherwise rigorously naturalizing account of the
wayfarer's knowledge of God.

On rare occasions – just two, in fact – he dared suggest even
more. The Prologue to the *Reportatio parisiensis* and question 7 of the
Quodlibetal Questions reveal a step further in Henry's direction. First
hint of the move comes in the *Reportatio*, where Duns took note of
attacks that had been made on Henry regarding the *lumen medium*,
commenting that he thought they went too far. From his point of
view, Henry's opponents risked giving too little credit to Christian
theology and theologians, thereby fueling the efforts of Christianity's
adversaries, inspired by the example of Averroes, to poke fun at
Christian speculation.[128] Then, in both *Reportatio* and *Quodlibetal Questions*,
he went on to make clear he thought it possible for the wayfarer to
receive from God simple knowledge, in the form of a concept of
divinity, that would contain evidence for many of the hidden propositions of theology and thereby permit demonstration of most such
truths. God could moreover grant this simple knowledge without
needing to reveal himself face-to-face, as entailed in either rapture
or beatific vision. Here was Duns positing for the wayfarer just the
kind of scientific theology he had twice rejected elsewhere in the
commentaries on the *Sentences*.[129]

---

[127] Duns, *Ordinatio* III, d. 24, q. un., n. 17 (Vivès, 15:47b–48a); and *Reportatio parisiensis* III, d. 24, q. un., n. 21 (Vivès, 23:456b–57a). On certitude as one of two perfections of science in the strict sense of the word, and thus as worthy of special emphasis, see above, Pt. 4, ch. 13, n. 146.

[128] Duns, *Reportatio parisiensis* Prol., q. 2, n. 8 (Vivès, 22:38a): "Sed isti nimis parum attribuunt theologo et theologiae. . . . Sed quod aliquis doctor propter auctoritatem Averrois, qua deridet Christianos, dimittat opinionem aliquam, videtur potius deri-dendus, quam tenens priorem opinionem propter auctoritates sanctorum plurimas." This is, of course, the text of what is actually the *Additiones magnae*. For a slightly variant version, as given in the *Reportatio examinata*, see Dumont, "Theology as a Science," p. 590, n. 49, which article, pp. 589–91, offers an excellent synopsis of Duns's extreme position in the Prologue and the *Quodlibetal Questions*, q. 7.

[129] Duns, *Reportatio parisiensis* Prol., q. 2, n, 15 (Vivès, 22:41b), quoted in Dumont,

The way the requisite simple cognition was produced, Duns explained, was by God furnishing mind with an intelligible species representing himself distinctly. The wayfarer would then have access to perfect abstractive knowledge of divinity *ut haec*, though not the intuitive knowledge of direct mental vision. Abstractive understanding of this sort fully sufficed for science, strictly construed, and Duns insisted that any theologian receiving it would be able to theologize "perfectly scientifically" (*perfecte scientifice*).[130] He even added that if such intellection in a species was what Henry had had in mind with his theory of a *lumen medium*, as unlikely as he thought this to be, then Henry's ideas could be nearly totally vindicated.[131] One had only to be cautioned that where Henry believed such special knowledge was available to all hard-working theologians, he was sure God granted it in just the most extraordinary circumstances. The Apostles and prophets might have theologized scientifically; in his own day theology was routinely a less strictly demonstrative business.[132]

Hedged about with qualifications, Duns's admission that Henry was close to being right on this issue is remarkable nonetheless. His readiness to follow his predecessor on so controversial a matter, even during his years at the University of Paris, where Henry's ideas were coming under attack, speaks eloquently of his intellectual debt to the

---

"Theology as a Science," n. 50; and *Quaestiones quodlibetales*, q. 7, n. 7 (Vivès, 25:289a). On his previous denial of anything approaching this position, see above, n. 125. The fact that the contradictory views both appear in *Reportatio parisiensis* complicates understanding the history of this text's composition.

[130] See *Reportatio parisiensis* Prol., q. 2, n. 15 (Vivès, 22:42a); and *Quaestiones quodlibetales*, q. 7, n. 8 (Vivès, 25:290a), for confirmation of such abstractive knowledge; and the quodlibetal question, n. 10 (Vivès, 25:290b–91a) for discussion of its scientific value, ending with the remarkable assertion: "Esset ergo viator perfecte scientifice theologus, qui per conceptum distinctissimum divinitatis possibilem haberi, citra cognitionem intuitivam, cognosceret ordinate veritates omnes necessarias. . . ." There is further evidence from his treatment of other issues, such as angelic cognition, that Duns accepted the idea God could be known by means of a proper intelligible species: see *Lectura* II, d. 3, p. 2, q. 2 (Vatican, 18:323–24, n. 292); and *Ordinatio* II, d. 3, p. 2, q. 2 (Vatican, 7:554–55, n. 324). This was, of course, one of the two additional ways of knowing God Duns had listed in the passage from the Prologue to the *Reportatio parisiensis* cited above, n. 126. Alluntis and Wolter, in John Duns Scotus, *God and Creatures. The Quodlibetal Questions*, p. 163, nn. 10 and 11, comment on this late position of Duns concerning the possibility of an abstractive concept of God.

[131] Duns, *Reportatio parisiensis* Prol., q. 2, n. 17 (Vivès, 22:43a b); and *Quaestiones quodlibetales*, q. 7, n. 10 (Vivès, 25:291a), where he revealed his doubts about Henry's real intentions.

[132] Duns, *Reportatio parisiensis* Prol., q. 2, n. 17 (Vivès, 22:43b).

theologian whose theories he commonly took as a foil to his own. That he would find a way of defending Henry on a point which did so little to promote his own assiduous efforts to institute a more natural and worldly vision of the workings of mind testifies to a deep loyalty to the Augustinian current to which they both belonged.[133]

---

[133] William of Ware considered the notion that God could be known by the wayfarer in a species representing his nature, and rejected it: see William, *Quaestiones*, q. 20 (in Gál, "Guilielmi de Ware doctrina," p. 174; a longer, less reliable version of which can be found in Doyle, "The Disintegration," p. 326, nn. 101 and 102). Perhaps William felt no pressure to make room for Henry's views on a *lumen medium* because he had already accepted so much of what Henry posited about natural a priori knowledge of divine things.

CHAPTER SIXTEEN

WHAT ABOUT AUGUSTINE?

Scotus's fully developed noetics, along with his semantics of "being," made it possible to account for entirely natural knowledge of divinity that was, in keeping with the tradition on which he had been nourished, at least minimally quidditative. Even more than William of Ware he thus managed to preserve a sense of intimacy between mind and God, so important in earlier Augustinian circles, despite the eclipse of classic Augustinian ideas about processes of intellection and the nature of the cognitive object. No one since Matthew of Aquasparta had gone so far towards meeting the philosophical demands of high-scholastic naturalism while simultaneously reaffirming the affective core of Augustinian thought, and unlike Matthew, Duns accomplished the task alongside definitive abandonment of the notion of special illumination. Here was a scientific Augustinianism set to compete with the efforts of Aristotelianizing purists in staying resolutely in the world.

But still a classic Augustinian looking at Duns's noetics and epistemology, as well as his ontology, might have wondered whether his efforts were sufficient. There were limitations to the intimacy with God Duns allowed intellect in the world of sin that would surely have disappointed traditionalists of radically Augustinian hue. The problem emerges in sharpest relief in connection with the notion of first object of intellect, an issue briefly described above as providing a subsidiary reason for positing univocity of "being."[1] Not surprisingly, Duns's thoughts on the matter were deeply influenced by Henry of Ghent, for whom mind's first object was God, and through him by the general ideological drift of Augustinians throughout the century. As usual, however, he took issue with the particulars of his predecessors' ideas, ending up by recasting the question in a fashion at once technically more precise and philosophically more subtle.

As early as the *Questions on the Metaphysics* Duns defined the first object of intellect as a single element or attribute included essentially

---

[1] See above, Pt. 4, Ch. 15, n. 66 and pp. 518–20.

in everything that was properly and in itself intelligible.[2] Conversely, all things embraced by mind's first object as logically inferior to it were themselves properly and naturally objects of intellection.[3] The implication was that the first object was a common property distributed among the class of all knowables, but Duns hastened to explain that technically speaking it could also be a thing virtually containing all other objects – that is, one object having the power, once known, to generate knowledge of all others.[4] To express the commensurability of the relation between first object and intellect he said that the former was adequated (*adaequatum*) to the latter, by which he meant that it was operatively exactly proportional to it.[5] The first object constituted, in short, the "precise cause" of cognition on the part of what was known, a single ingredient necessary and sufficient to account for intelligibility.[6] Putting all this together he came up with the phrase "first adequate object," highlighting the peculiarly epistemic character of the priority he was thinking of,

---

[2] *Quaestiones super libros Metaphysicorum* VI, q. 3 (Opera Phil., 4:63, n. 20): "... primum objectum intellectus non potest esse aliquid nisi quod essentialiter includitur in quolibet per se intelligibili."

[3] Duns, *Lectura* Prol., p. 2, qq. 1–3 (Vatican, 16:27, n. 69); and *Quaestiones quodlibetales*, q. 14, n. 11 (Vivès, 26:40a): "... quidquid per se continetur sub primo objecto naturali alicujus potentiae, ad illud potentia potest naturaliter attingere, alioquin objectum primum non esset adaequatum potentiae, sed transcendens in ratione objecti. ..."

[4] On a common property as first object, see the first passage cited in the preceding note as well as *Ordinatio* Prol., p. 3, qq. 1–3 (Vatican, 1:100, n. 146): "... primum obiectum potentiae est aliquid commune ad omnia per se obiecta illius potentiae." For first object as virtually containing the rest, *Lectura* I, d. 3, p. 1, qq. 1–2 (Vatican, 16:259, n. 90): "Alio modo dicitur esse obiectum adaequatum potentiae quia movet potentiam ad actum circa alia, quae virtualiter continentur in ipso. ..." On virtuality see also, *Ordinatio* I, d. 3, p. 1, q. 3 (Vatican, 3:79, n. 127). Duns sometimes distinguished the two ways of being first object as serving "secundum praedicationem" (for something common) in contrast to "secundum virtualitatem" (for something by reason of which all other things are known) – see *Collationes* 12, n. 10 (Vivès, 5:199a); and *Reportatio parisiensis* Prol., q. 1, n. 7(!) (Vivès, 22:11b).

[5] Duns, *Lectura* Prol., p. 1, q. un. (Vatican, 16:1, n. 1); and *Ordinatio* Prol., p. 1, q. un. (Vatican, 1:2, n. 1): "... primum obiectum dicitur quod est adaequatum cum potentia. ..." See also the references to *Lectura* I, d. 3; *Collationes*; *Reportatio parisiensis*; and *Quaestiones quodlibetales* given above in nn. 3 and 4. For the term "proportional," see *Lectura* I, d. 3, p. 1, qq. 1–2 (Vatican, 16:260, n. 94). A clear statement of how adaequation between first object and power typically fell to a common element comes in *Ordinatio* Prol., p. 3, qq. 1–3 (Vatican, 1:100–101, n. 148).

[6] See *Ordinatio* I, d. 3, p. 1, qq. 1–2 (Vatican, 3:48, n. 69), where in speaking of intelligibility Duns used the term "adaequatio" interchangeably with "causalitas praecisa."

different from that of objects first according to either order of cognition or perfection of intelligibility.[7]

He knew that a common opinion among thinkers of his day was that the quiddity of material things comprised first adequate object of human mind.[8] This was the view associated with Aristotle, in whose words, he said, first object was simply "quiddity of sensibles" – that is, whatever quidditative content could be abstracted from sensible things or derived from knowledge of them – and it was also the position taken by Thomas Aquinas, whom Duns referred to by name in a late note added to the *Ordinatio*'s discussion of Aristotle's stand on the matter.[9] A second, conflicting opinion asserted that intellect's first object was God. This was Henry of Ghent's contention, which Duns correctly characterized as applying only to what Henry called the power of mind to know naturally, not to its rational processes of cogitation.[10]

Rejecting both of these prominent views, Duns maintained humankind's first adequate intellectual object to be, as indicated in the previous chapter, none other than "being" itself.[11] This had not been

---

[7] For example, *Ordinatio* I, d. 3, p. 1, q. 3 (Vatican, 3:68): "Utrum Deus sit primum obiectum naturale adaequatum respectu intellectus viatoris"; or *Lectura* I, d. 3, p. 1, qq. 1–2 (Vatican, 16:261, n. 98): "obiectum primum adaequatum." On priority of order (*primitas originis et generationis*) and priority of perfection (*primitas perfectionis*), see *Lectura* I, d. 3, p. 1, qq. 1–2 (Vatican, 16:249, n. 66); and *Ordinatio* I, d. 3, p. 1, qq. 1–2 (Vatican, 3:48, n. 69).

[8] *Lectura* I, d. 3, p. 1, qq. 1–2 (Vatican, 16:259, n. 92); and *Ordinatio* I, d. 3, p. 1, q. 3 (Vatican, 3:69, n. 110). In *Quaestiones super libros Metaphysicorum* II, qq. 2–3 (Opera Phil., 3:207, n. 25), Duns called this the "proper" object of intellect.

[9] On Aristotle, see Duns, *Ordinatio* Prol., p. 1, q. un. (Vatican, 1:20, n. 33); and for Aquinas, *Ordinatio* I, d. 3, p. 1, q. 3 (Vatican, 3:76, n. 124 [quoted below, n. 37]), which refers back to an exposition (Vatican, 3:70, nn. 111–12) of Thomas's three kinds of intellective power, among which was human intellect, directed to the quiddity of material things. The latter exposition is repeated nearly verbatim in Duns, *Quaestiones quodlibetales*, q. 14, n. 11 (Vivès, 26:40a–b).

[10] Duns, *Lectura* I, d. 3, p. 1, qq. 1–2 (Vatican, 16:258, n. 88); and *Ordinatio* I, d. 3, p. 1, q. 3 (Vatican, 3:78, n. 125). On the distinction between natural and rational cognition, see *Lectura* I, d. 3, p. 1, qq. 1–2 (Vatican, 16:228–29, n. 14); and *Ordinatio* I, d. 3, p. 1, qq. 1–2 (Vatican, 3:14–15, n. 22). For Henry's views on first object of mind, see above, Pt. 3, Ch. 10, nn. 52, 54, 94 and 96.

[11] Refer to n. 1, above. Duns presented the arguments in favor of "being" as early as *Quaestiones super libros Metaphysicorum* VI, q. 3 (Opera Phil., 4:63, n. 20), but definitively supported this view only in *Lectura* I, d. 3, p. 1, qq. 1–2 (Vatican, 16:261–62 and 264, nn. 99 and 104; and especially 16:277, n. 133): "Sic igitur dictum est quod ens est primum obiectum adaequatum intellectui nostro, et non Deus, nec 'quod quid' substantiae materialis, nec alia passio entis, ut verum aut bonum aut unum." See the same in *Ordinatio* I, d. 3, p. 1, q. 3 (Vatican, 3:80–81, n. 129).

his posture at the beginning of his career, when he defended substance as intellect's first object, nor was it unambiguously his stance as late as early sections of the *Questions on the Metaphysics*.[12] Yet by the time of the commentaries on the *Sentences* he had come to accepting it fully, explaining that he got the idea from Avicenna, especially the famous comments in the *Philosophia prima* concerning first impressions on mind.[13]

As for Duns's reasons, they were varied and complicated. A quick look was taken above at his arguments against Henry on God as first object.[14] Only for divine mind itself was God first object of intellection, in which it saw not merely its own essence but also all other things as virtually contained in its perfection.[15] With regard to quiddity of material things, it seems that when Duns initially inclined towards positing "being" as first object he felt he could disprove the Aristotelianizing position with a host of philosophical rationales as well, clear to anyone of sound and open mind.[16] In his *Sentences* commentaries, however, he carefully segregated philosophical grounds for rejecting Aristotle from theological ones, convincing only to those accepting the tenets of faith, and in the process substantially reduced the number and range of arguments to be regarded as authentically philosophical.

Theology, of course, promised believers the intellectual vision of God, at least in beatitude. Unless one were to suppose that the blessed intellect constituted an entirely different cognitive power from intellect in this world, a supposition severely compromising to the

[12] Duns, *In librum Praedicamentorum*, q. 4, n. 12 (Vivès, 1:449a–b); and *Quaestiones super libros Metaphysicorum* IV, q. 1 (Opera Phil., 3:319, nn. 86–87), which should be contrasted to the reference to the same work cited above, n. 11. Later, in *Lectura* I, d. 3, p. 1, qq. 1–2 (Vatican, 16:260–61, n. 95); and *Ordinatio* I, d. 3, p. 1, q. 3 (Vatican, 3:80, n. 128), Duns categorically rejected his earlier view.
[13] *Ordinatio* Prol., p. 1, q. un. (Vatican, 1:15, n. 24); and the reference to Avicenna's *Philosophia prima* (*Metaphysics*) in *Quaestiones super libros Metaphysicorum* VI, q. 3 (cited above, n. 11); and *Ordinatio* Prol., p. 1, q. un. (Vatican, 1:2, n. 1). For the Avicenna text, see above, Pt. 2, ch. 8, n. 52.
[14] See above, Pt. 4, ch. 15, nn. 100–102.
[15] Duns, *Lectura* I, d. 3, p. 1, qq. 1–2 (Vatican, 16:259, n. 90); *Ordinatio* I, d. 3, p. 1, q. 3 (Vatican, 3:80, n. 127); and *Reportatio parisiensis* Prol., q. 1, n. 7 (Vivès, 22:10b–11a). By God as object Duns did not here mean a confused knowledge of God, which he saw in some way as primary to human mind in the confused concept of being – see above, Pt. 4, ch. 15, n. 108.
[16] Duns, *Quaestiones super libros Metaphysicorum* II, qq. 2–3 (specifically Opera Phil., 3:221–23, nn. 67–75, but also pp. 208–12, nn. 27–37; and pp. 215–21, nn. 51–66, against the corollary that separate substances were not naturally known).

Christian message of personal salvation, it was necessary to infer that immaterial things were among the proper objects of mind and consequently that intellect's first object was not so narrow as Thomas and Aristotle had proposed.[17] Against the counterargument that God could raise intellect in glory to see beyond its natural first object by granting it an extraordinary light or cognitive *habitus*, one could simply respond that this retort itself confirmed the weakness of the case. For such a gift to work and expand the domain of objects of mind, after all, it would have effectively to obliterate the original power by turning it into something else. Again all hope for personal salvation would disappear.[18]

On the other hand, philosophy, as Duns now saw it in the *Sentences* commentaries, offered just two, or maybe three arguments.[19] Both *Lectura* and *Ordinatio* invoked the Aristotelian principle that a natural desire could not exist in vain to conclude that, since human intellect plainly longed to grasp its immaterial cause in particular, not just general, terms, it must possess the natural power to acquire distinct knowledge of more than material objects. Duns likewise pointed in both works to the evident feasibility of a science of metaphysics as grounds for taking intellect's object to be other than Aristotle had supposed. Metaphysics, after all, considered things under the universal category of "being," which stretched far beyond material quiddity. To limit mind's first object to material quiddity alone would put such a science completely out of reach. Finally, the *Ordinatio* added a third reason, which Duns admitted came very close to the second. It, too, appealed to the existence of metaphysics, claiming that if the latter were to be different from physics it must have "being" qua "being" as its subject. The inescapable conclusion was again that nothing more restricted than "being" qua "being" was suited to serve as intellect's first object.

---

[17] See the argument in *Lectura* I, d. 3, p. 1, qq. 1–2 (Vatican, 16:240 and 241–42, nn. 40 and 44), and the reminder (Vatican, 16:259, n. 92) that it would work only among believers (*catholici*), since it depended on faith in the beatific vision. In *Ordinatio* I, d. 3, p. 1, q. 3 (Vatican, 3:70, n. 113) Duns explicitly presented the argument as exclusively theological. It is reproduced without comment about its theoretical coloration in *Collationes* 11, n. 8 (Vivès, 5:191a).

[18] See above, Pt. 4, Ch. 13, n. 49; also the comments in the same note on how William of Ware was willing to concede more here on God's ability to extend the reach of a power than was Duns.

[19] Duns, *Lectura* I, d. 3, p. 1, qq. 1–2 (Vatican, 16:241 and 259–60, nn. 42 and 92–93); and *Ordinatio* I, d. 3, p. 1, q. 3 (Vatican, 3:72–73, nn. 116–18).

Important to note is that the arguments against Aristotle, especially the last two philosophical ones, appear to rest on the notion of first adequate intellectual object as an element common to all things known, though Duns had already conceded in theory that an object might also be first and adequate because it "virtually contained" knowledge of all others.[20] In fact the restriction of intellect's first object to a common property was a relic of Duns's early thoughts on the matter, and when it came to affirmative arguments for "being" as first object, this narrow approach was dominant no later than among passages in the *Questions on the Metaphysics*.[21] The idea was most likely inherited from William of Ware, though William would never have supported the univocal commonness of object promoted by the mature Duns.[22] In any case, by the time of the commentaries on the *Sentences*, Duns had switched to defending "being" as first object on the basis of his broader understanding of what a first object entailed. It was, after all, in the *Sentences* commentaries that he elaborated his famous doctrine of the double primacy of "being." Henceforth, "being" was for him first object *both* by commonness, because it was essentially included in most specific objects of intellection, *and* by virtuality, because it virtually included a few specific objects while others were virtually or essentially included in an object essentially including "being."[23]

Of course, while Duns originally concluded that "being" could serve in this way as first object only if it were univocal – indeed the need for a first object afforded an argument in favor of univocity of "being" – he later reconsidered and decided maybe not. As a result, in his final works he felt free to call upon the idea of "being" as first object in the debate about knowledge of God without having

---

[20] See above, n. 4.

[21] See Duns, *Quaestiones super libros Metaphysicorum* II, qq. 2–3 (Opera Phil., 3:228, n. 94). The same idea did carry over vestigially into *Lectura* I, d. 3, p. 1, qq. 1–2 (Vatican, 16:261, n. 98); and *Ordinatio* I, d. 3, p. 1, q. 3 (Vatican, 3:80, n. 129). The constraints this assumption placed on the nature of human intellect's first object were what prompted Duns in *Ordinatio* II, d. 24, q. un., n. 6 (Vivès, 13:183a–b), to say that only God's mind had a first adequate object which was not an abstracted quality (*abstractum*).

[22] Consult William's comments on the nature (*ratio*) of mind's object in his *Quaestiones*, q. 85 (ed. Schmaus, in *Der Liber propugnatorius*, p. 269*).

[23] Duns, *Lectura* I, d. 3, p. 1, qq. 1–2 (Vatican, 16: 261–64, nn. 99 and 104); and *Ordinatio* I, d. 3, p. 1, q. 3 (Vatican, 3:85 and 93, nn. 137 and 151) – all referred to above, Pt. 4, Ch. 15, n. 50. The point is made most succinctly in a note Duns added to *Ordinatio* I, d. 3, p. 1, qq. 1–2 (Vatican, 3:16, ll. 20–23).

simultaneously to resolve the question of "being"'s univocity. Even Henry's theory of analogy of "being" would, for Duns in his Parisian years, suffice to sustain the assertion that "being" was mind's first object and thus that God could, at least in beatitude, be directly known.[24] Such an attitude about the nature of first object appears to have been adopted as well by William of Ware, for whom "being" was intellect's "formal object," though not univocal.[25] Admittedly, the late Duns remained somewhat tentative in this regard, for on occasion in his Parisian works he volunteered for argument's sake to forego the requirement of a first object for human cognition in order to save the necessary connection between univocity and an adequate object of mind.[26]

More significant, as this wavering on the tie between univocity and first object suggests, the commitment to "being" as first object of mind laid out in the early avatars of Duns's *Sentences* commentaries turns out itself not to have been the last word. On the contrary, his ideas about "being" as first adequate object of intellect continued to evolve even in his maturity. He had recognized from the start that despite his rejection of the quiddity of material things as first object, only material things were directly known by intellect in the world of sin.[27] Duns was always enough of an Aristotelianizer to insist that the wayfarer's knowledge begin with sensibles, having

---

[24] On the demand for univocal "being," see the discussion above, Pt. 4, ch. 15, p. 518, and the citations given in n. 66 of that chapter. Duns made the point clearly in *Lectura* I, d. 3, p. 1, qq. 1–2 (Vatican, 16:261, n. 97): "Ideo concludo quod vel nullum obiectum erit primum intellectus nostri, vel oportet ponere univocationem entis, modo praedicto." For his later change of mind, see Pt. 4, ch. 15, pp. 518–20, and the citations to *Reportatio parisiensis* and *Quaestiones quodlibetales*, qq. 3 and 14, given there in n. 83. In a late addition to *Ordinatio* Prol., p. 1, q. un. (Vatican, 1:29–30, n. 48), Duns applied his realization that the questions of univocity of "being" and mind's first object were separable to consideration of the necessity for revealed knowledge in salvation. Curiously, these final views of Duns on univocity and first object brought him back full circle to precisely his position in *Quaestiones super libros Metaphysicorum* II, qq. 2–3 (Opera Phil., 3:228–29, nn. 94–95 and 100–101).

[25] William, *Quaestiones*, q. 85 (ed. Schmaus, in *Der Liber propugnatorius*, p. 268*).

[26] See the references to Book II, d. 24 of the *Ordinatio* and *Reportatio parisiensis* given above, Pt. 4, ch. 15, n. 82. Since these works predate the *Quaestiones quodlibetales*, it is possible that the position taken in these two passages represents a penultimate view, superseded by a real last stand, that of the citations of n. 24, above.

[27] *Lectura* I, d. 3, p. 1, qq. 1–2 (Vatican, 16:244, n. 49): ". . . licet pro statu viae ex statuto divino non possumus de facto intelligere nisi ista materialia, non tamen ipsum materiale est primum obiectum intellectus nostri." On quiddity of material things as object of sinful mind, see also above, Pt. 4, ch. 14, nn. 53–54.

taken the injunction so strictly after all as to rule out Henry's noetics of essence, whereby normal cognition was grounded in a primitive perception of the being of God.[28] And like all thirteenth-century
scholastics, he held that special revelation alone would permit human
mind to know the Godhead precisely in its own particular essence.[29]
Knowledge of that sort was the privilege of the blessed in heaven
and perhaps a select number of souls on earth, among them the
apostle Paul.[30] Only the exotic idea, repudiated even by William of
Ware, that God might in extraordinary circumstances grant the wayfarer an intelligible species furnishing distinct knowledge of himself
outside the state of rapture licensed the slightest deviation in Duns's
later thought from Aristotle's vision of the origin and range of knowledge in the world.[31]

   To accommodate this understanding of the limits of cognition in
the world with affirmation of universal "being" as properly first object
of intellect, the mature Duns moreover gradually devised a language
distinguishing that which mind was ultimately created to know from
effective cognitive capacity at any given time. Already in the *Lectura*
he explained that one could speak of mind's natural object as that
either towards which it was naturally inclined or by which it was
naturally moved. In the first instance, the object was "being" in its
totality, but in the second it was something much less.[32] Distinction
3 of Book I of the *Ordinatio* advanced an even more rigorous formulation, in which Duns specified that by nature of the pure power of
cognition (*ex ratione potentiae*) "being" in all its commonness was intellect's adequate first object, although in the present state of sin (*pro*

   [28] On origin of knowledge in sensation, see above, Pt. 4, ch. 13, p. 419; and ch.
14, nn. 10–11. For explicit indication that non-material things, including God, were
not known by the wayfarer except in a general concept of being, see *Ordinatio* I,
d. 3, p. 1, q. 3 (Vatican, 3:112, n. 185).
   [29] See above, Pt. 4, ch. 15, nn. 9 and 10.
   [30] On knowledge of the blessed (or "sancti"), see the preceding n. 29; and also
Ordinatio I, d. 22, q. un. (Vatican, 5:341, ll. 9–12). On Paul's special vision, see
Lectura Prol., p. 1, q. un. (Vatican, 16:14, n. 33); and I, d. 3, p. 1, qq. 1–2 (Vatican,
16:243, n. 47). Duns held that even the contemplative in the world of sin did not
see God in his essence: *Lectura* I, d. 3, p. 1, qq. 1–2 (Vatican, 16:249, n. 65); and
Ordinatio I, d. 3, p. 1, qq. 1–2 (Vatican, 3:47, n. 66).
   [31] See above, Pt. 4, ch. 15, nn. 130, 132 and 133.
   [32] Duns, *Lectura* Prol., p. 1, q. un. (Vatican, 16:21, n. 49). The general idea is
not far from Matthew's distinction between *apprehensum* and *apprehensibile*: see above,
Part 2, ch. 8, n. 130.

statu isto) the quiddity of sensible things was adequate object actually moving it to know (*in ratione motivi, in movendo*).[33]

A still more exacting version of this analytical scheme had, in fact, already appeared in the Prologue to the *Ordinatio*. There Duns noted that the notion of a natural object could be taken to mean either that towards which a perceptive power was by nature inclined, whether it could naturally attain knowledge of it at any moment or not, or that knowledge of which the power could in a specific instance, by solely natural means, attain.[34] He then continued that an object, most especially a common property, would qualify as a naturally attainable *first* object (*primum obiectum naturaliter attingibile*) only if all objects logically inferior to it – that is, all particular instances – were also naturally attainable. This was what it should mean, after all, for the first object to be adequated to the power, and to hold otherwise would deprive the notion of its philosophical utility.[35] Applying these ideas to the question of first object of human intellect, one had to conclude that "being" at its broadest was not the naturally attainable first object for every state in which mind might find itself, most especially not for the state of sin. In the sinful condition, "being" qualified merely as first object to which mind was by nature inclined.[36] As Duns had come to realize, and as he confessed in a very late addition to the *Ordinatio*, he ultimately agreed with Aristotle, and Thomas, that for the wayfarer mind's first adequate object was just the quiddity of material things. He differed with them only in insisting that absolutely speaking – considering intellect without reference to limitations imposed by any particular state (*ex natura potentiae*) – the first object was nothing less than "being" in general.[37]

---

[33] Duns, *Ordinatio* I, d. 3, p. 1, q. 3 (Vatican, 3:112–14, nn. 186 and 187).

[34] Duns, *Ordinatio* Prol., p. 1, q. un. (Vatican, 1:54, n. 90): ". . . distinguo de obiecto naturali. Potest enim accipi obiectum naturale vel pro illo ad quod naturaliter sive ex actione causarum naturaliter activarum potest potentia attingere, vel pro illo ad quod naturaliter inclinatur potentia, sive possit attingere naturaliter illud obiectum sive non." The same idea was touched on above with regard to Duns's views on "naturalism" in a power (see Part 4, ch. 13, nn. 48–50, and esp. n. 51). He felt that a power must be naturally inclined to any object it could ever be expected to reach, although it might not actually be able to grasp every such object on its own.

[35] Duns, *Ordinatio* Prol., p. 1, q. un. (Vatican, 1:55, n. 91), especially the passage quoted below, n. 40; as well as *Ordinatio* I, d. 3, p. 1, q. 3 (Vatican, 3:77, n. 124), also quoted in the same note.

[36] Duns, *Ordinatio* Prol., p. 1, q. un. (Vatican, 1:56, n. 92); and more dramatically, *Quaestiones quodlibetales*, q. 14, n. 11 (Vivès, 26:40a).

[37] Duns, *Ordinatio* I, d. 3, p. 1, q. 3 (Vatican, 3:76, nn. 123–24: "Concordant

In light of these considerations it should already be clear how
widely disparate were the epistemic overtones of Duns's views about
first object of intellect and those of his theory of univocity of "being,"
and, when all is said and done, how modest the claims of his theory of univocity for saving fully Augustinian intimacy of God to
mind. Having conceded to human intellect a concept of being univocal to God and creatures, he could easily explain how, though all
sinful cognition derived from sensible things, the wayfarer's intellect
was able naturally to know objects beyond those sensation could
grasp and denominate them by compounding general terms extrapolated from sensory cognition.[38] For this reason he had rejected
Henry's claim that the wayfarer's knowledge retained the flavor or
limitation of sensible cognition, laying out his own quite contrary
exposition of the possibility, in sin, of a natural, proper, and quidditative conception of God.[39] Yet the wayfarer's knowledge of "being"
in a single concept, as "hoc intelligibile" known "uno actu," though
univocal and not limited in reference to any particular class of objects

hic Aristoteles et 'articulus' [i. e. Duns's view], quod quiditas rei sensibilis est nunc
obiectum adaequatum, intelligendo 'sensibilis' proprie, vel inclusi essentialiter vel
virtualiter in sensibili. . . . Discordat: – obiectum adaequatum 'intellectui ex natura
potentiae' nihil sub ente. Hoc 'articulus' contra Aristotelem, et bene contra Thomam
hic prima ratio." Duns returned to this point in *Quaestiones quodlibetales*, q. 14, nn.
12 and 16–20 (Vivès, 26:46b–47a, 54a and 62b–65b), not only to confirm it but
also to emphasize that "being" was, in fact, naturally mind's first object, if in this
life only that to which it was naturally inclined or directed. Thus God, too, was a
natural object, and the reason he could not be seen by the wayfarer was due not
to the constraints of nature but rather to the artifical limitations imposed by God's
will. See also *Ordinatio* I, d. 3, p. 1, q. 3 (Vatican, 3:113–14, n. 187). It should be
noted that Boulnois, claiming support from both Giuseppina Cannizzo and Vladimir
Richter, takes the word "articulus" in the passage quoted above from *Ordinatio* I,
d. 3, as more properly to be read "Harcley" – that is, as referring to the views of
Duns's contemporary and sometime disciple, Henry of Harcley. He thus takes issue
with the editors of the Vatican edition on what is admittedly an arguable point of
interpretation. (See Boulnois, *Sur la connaissance de Dieu*, p. 135; and the discussion
on pp. 7; 447–48, n. 1 to para. 184; and 451, n. 4 to para. 185.) Whether Boulnois
or the editors are right has little bearing on the point made here. Even if Duns's
special reference was to Harcley, he still wanted to indicate his own partial agreement and partial disagreement with Aristotle and Thomas. Boulnois himself takes
the discussion in question as referring as much to Duns's own views as to Harcley's –
see Boulnois, p. 360, n. 1 to para. 123, and n. 1 to para. 124.

[38] Duns, *Ordinatio* 1, d. 3, p. 1, q. 3 (Vatican, 3:76, n. 123): "Non igitur nunc
est adaequatum obiectum eius [i.e. intellectus] quod supremae sensitivae, quia intelligit omne inclusum in sensibili essentialiter, usque ad ens, sub qua indifferentia
nullo modo sensus cognoscit, – et etiam inclusum virtualiter, ut relationes, quod
non sensus."

[39] See above, Pt. 4, ch. 15, n. 116.

such as material things, still did not imply direct cognitive access to all the particulars falling under it, most importantly not to divinity itself. For this to be so, "being" would have had to constitute the actually attainable first object of mind, which in the present state it most certainly did not.[40] Simply knowing "being" as univocal did not, therefore, chip away much at the need for a special, revealed knowledge of God. In Duns's eyes even his opponents' theory of the analogical nature of "being" contributed little towards that.[41] The wayfarer's natural knowledge of God was in either case like knowing the first figure of plane geometry merely by abstracting the term "figure" from a quadrangle, the term "first" from random first things, and then combining the two into the proper term "first figure," without ever coming to perceive a triangle, the first figure itself. Minus immediate grasp of "triangle," knowledge of "first figure" remained forever vague and imprecise.[42] In similar fashion, knowledge of the divinity as "infinite being" did not remotely approach the cognitive amplitude of beatitude or salvation.

By the end in fact, Duns actually came to believe that to remain true to his own principles he must admit that the confidence intellect would ultimately be capable of immediate proper knowledge of God, which underlay his claim that considered as a power without regard to any particular state mind was inclined into "being" as first adequate object, was not justifiable by reason on its own.[43] Thus in

---

[40] This is the combined meaning of Duns, *Ordinatio* I, d. 3, p. 1, q. 3 (Vatican, 3:77, n. 124): "Ens enim in quantum ens, communius est quocumque alio conceptu primae intentionis . . . et sic intelligitur nulla contractione omnino cointellecta – nec habitudine ad sensibile, nec quacumque"; and *Ordinatio* Prol., p. 1, q. un. (Vatican, 1:55, n. 91): "Licet enim ens ut est quid intelligibile uno actu (sicut homo est intelligibilis una intellectione) sit naturaliter intelligibile (illa enim unica intellectio entis ut unius obiecti est naturalis), non tamen potest ens poni primum obiectum naturaliter attingibile, quia est primum obiectum ut includitur in omnibus per se obiectis, et ut sic non est naturaliter attingibile nisi quodlibet illorum sit naturaliter attingibile." For the phrase "hoc intelligibile" referring to a single concept, see *Ordinatio* I, d. 3, p. 1, q. 3 (Vatican, 3:77, n. 124): ". . . ens ut 'hoc intelligibile' intelligitur a nobis, sed si esset primum obiectum, hoc esset secundum totam indifferentiam ad omnia in quibus salvatur, non ut aliquod unum intelligibile in se, – et quidlibet illius indifferentiae posset intelligi. Ideo non est obiectum adaequatum pro nunc."

[41] Duns, *Ordinatio* Prol., p. 1, q. un. (Vatican, 1:29–30, n. 48).

[42] Duns, *Ordinatio* Prol., p. 1, q. un. (Vatican, 1:27–28, n. 46).

[43] See the addition to *Ordinatio* I, d. 3, p. 1, q. 3 (Vatican, 3:76–77, n. 124), where Duns betrayed ambivalence about whether his view on "being" as ultimate first object of the mind was rationally demonstrable or not; and the categorical admission that it was not in *Ordinatio* Prol., p. 1, q. un. (Vatican, 1:19, n. 33): "Ad aliud negandum est illud quod assumitur, quod scilicet naturaliter cognoscitur ens

a dramatic late addition to the *Ordinatio*'s Prologue he confessed that all his arguments, and not just some as he had previously maintained, about ultimate first object of intellect and the beatific requirement for special revelation were not philosophical but strictly theological, and therefore technically "persuasions" rather than proofs. Philosophically speaking, Aristotle had the best of the debate on both counts: the quiddity of material things was first object, both now and forever, and special revelation did not factor into mind's attainment of perfection.[44] Moreover, the appeal to Avicenna and his remarks on first impressions was not philosophically compelling. Avicenna had said what he did about "being" and mind because as a Muslim he took on faith that ultimately intellect would know God and other immaterial substances directly and in particular, not because reason had convinced him this was true.[45]

When, on top of this final admission, one adds Duns's denial of Henry's metaphysics of essence and all which that denial entailed, the lament of the Augustinian imagined at the outset of this chapter that the theory of univocity of "being" and Scotistic ideas about first object of intellect retained little of the fullness of the classic understanding of mind's road to God begins to reverberate with ever

---

esse primum obiectum intellectus nostri. . . ." Consult Boulnois, *Sur la connaissance de Dieu*, pp. 360–61, n. 2 to para. 124, on Duns's ambivalence in *Ordinatio* I, d. 3, and his firmness in the Prologue. This important aspect of Duns's theory of first object of intellect has been noted by Wolter, "The 'Theologism' of Duns Scotus," pp. 382–83; Balić, "Circa positiones fundamentales I. Duns Scoti," *Antonianum* 28 (1953): 268–69 and 278; and most recently, Honnefelder, *Ens inquantum ens*, pp. 84–85 and 88–89, all of which are excellent on the more general aspects of the theory. Other pieces dealing with the first object are Minges, "Zur Erkenntnislehre des Duns Scotus," *Philosophisches Jahrbuch (der Görres-Gesellschaft)* 31 (1918): 52–74; and Colman Ó Huallacháin, "On Recent Studies of the Opening Question in Scotus's *Ordinatio*," FrS 15 (1955): 1–29. Not so reliable are Paul Tochowicz, *Joannis Duns Scoti de cognitionis doctrina* (Fribourg, 1926); and Basil Heiser, "The *Primum Cognitum* according to Duns Scotus," FrS 2 (1942): 193–216.

[44] Duns, *Ordinatio* Prol., p. 1, q. un. (Vatican, 1:9, n. 12): "Nota, nullum supernaturale potest ratione naturali ostendi inesse viatori, nec necessario requiri ad perfectionem eius; nec etiam habens potest cognoscere illud sibi inesse. Igitur impossibile est hic contra Aristotelem uti ratione naturali; si arguatur ex creditis, non est ratio contra philosophum, quia praemissam creditam non concedet. Unde istae rationes hic factae contra ipsum alteram praemissam habent creditam vel probatam ex credito; ideo non sunt nisi persuasiones theologicae, ex creditis ad creditum." For Duns's earlier claim that some of his arguments were authentically philosophical, see above, pp. 439–43, and also nn. 17 and 19.

[45] Duns, *Ordinatio* Prol., p. 1, q. un. (Vatican, 1:19–20, n. 33), referring back to Vatican, 1:15, n. 24. On the appeal to Avicenna, see above, n. 13.

greater force. One is tempted to regard the assertion made in the preceding chapter that Duns's achievement was to naturalize Augustinianism and purge it of the quasi-mystical dynamic that had animated it for over seventy years as something of an understatement.[46] For all the arguments of this final section that he kept alive the flame of Augustinian intimacy between mind and God, it would appear that the fire had grown frightfully cold.

No doubt there is value in this perspective and profit to be gained from the reminder that despite his debt to Henry and the many Augustinian resonances of language and metaphor, Duns had strayed far from what the classic Augustinians had had in mind. Yet this should not be taken to mean he had turned his back on the current of thought with which the present study has been concerned. Above all, it must not be forgotten how important it was for him to retain an authentic place in his thought for Augustine's own words, and for the images commonly employed by his Augustinian predecessors in the schools. Indeed, even given the philosophical ground covered so far, there remains in Duns's thought a residue still of something more, a kind of persistence of intention that transcends doctrinal content, sometimes flies in the face of it, and stands as confirmation of the historical reality of intellectual currents in the thirteenth century.

One last time, therefore, it is instructive to return to the theme of truth. Despite his naturalizing and demystifying, on which score he surpassed all others examined above, including Matthew and William of Ware, Duns insisted on going beyond the "common opinion" that Augustinian references to "pure truth" in human cognition evoked merely God's role as remote general cause of all things, beyond even the view associated with John of La Rochelle that they pointed to divinity as efficient cause of soul's inherent agent intellect and thus in its own way a kind of agent itself.[47] The latter was all William of Ware would concede in his attempt to validate the language of seeing truth in the divine light.[48] Duns demanded something

---

[46] See above, Pt. 4, ch. 15, p. 490.

[47] See the discussion of both views above, Pt. 4, ch. 13, pp. 415–18; and ch. 14, pp. 451–52.

[48] William of Ware, *Quaestiones*, q. 19 (ed. Daniels, in "Wilhelm von Ware," p. 318). In the same question (p. 317), William made it clear he did not see God's action in this case as in any way that of a formal principle – that is, something contributing to the substantial content of knowledge.

further, with greater capacity to elicit the special timbre of Augustine's authentic modes of speech and thought.

There are two places where he made clearest this determination to remain loyal to Augustine. They are the parallel sections in Book I, distinction 3, of the *Lectura* and *Ordinatio* where he posed the question inspired by Henry of Ghent, whether intellect could know pure truth (*sincera veritas*) without a special divine influence or illumination.[49] Notwithstanding his explicit repudiation there of the answer typically attributed to Henry, when it came to the texts of Augustine so often cited in defense of the cognitive role of divine light Duns offered an interpretation surprisingly evocative of Henry's ideas. It is as if having rejected his predecessor's earliest thoughts on the process of knowing pure truth, implicating God literally in a comparison of images or exemplars, he then took uncharacteristic strides towards accepting the more mature account, dependent on the conviction that precise grasp of essence somehow opened directly onto God. He managed this feat, moreover, in spite of, sometimes even in virtual contradiction to, his own quite un-Henrican ontology of essence.

Since his views on the matter were, as so often, marked by a pattern of development, they are best approached by examining the two instances in turn. In the *Lectura* he first commented that one could affirm Augustinian language about knowing pure truth in divine light by reading it along the lines mentioned just above, echoing John of La Rochelle. According to this view, God's cognitive light, his Truth, was implicated in normal human cognition precisely at the level of efficient causality (*effective*). After all, divine truth stood as ultimate efficient cause of mind's intrinsic agent, which was in turn proximate efficient cause of true knowledge. The image of divine illumination was intended to signify just this efficient causal nexus.[50]

Against such reasoning the objection might be raised, however, that if God's truth or cognitive light was responsible for true knowledge in its role as cause of agent intellect, much more so was God's will, efficient cause of creation in the most proper sense of the word. Taking efficient causality as litmus test for illumination, therefore,

---

[49] Duns, *Lectura* I, d. 3, p. 1, q. 3 (Vatican, 16:281, ll. 18–20); and *Ordinatio* I, d. 3, p. 1, q. 4 (Vatican, 3:123, ll. 14–16).

[50] See above, n. 47, and the relevant passage in *Lectura* I, d. 3, p. 1, q. 3 (Vatican, 16:301–2, n. 189).

would lead one to regard God's will as an even more prominent factor in knowledge of truth. The result was a reading of illumination invoking a voluntarism any theologian would be forced to disavow.[51]

Duns believed the objection would not hold, and to show why he returned to a theory of creation examined above. In so doing he exhibited an analysis of the function of God's light significantly different from what he had laid out just before. The retort rested on his conviction that God produced all things other than himself in cognitive or conceptual being (*esse intelligible*) by the primitive act of knowing all possible objects in his own essence. Only then, in a secondary act, did he choose by his will to create some of them in actual existence. The order of the two acts was crucial. Since the initial production into cognitive being preceded the operation of will, it had to be a purely natural act. Thus God was natural, not voluntary, cause of things in their cognitive being, and he served this function as light or intellect.[52] The idea was akin to Henry's earlier insistence that being of essence arose eternally and directly from divine mind, being of existence only later from the act of divine will.[53]

Having established the character of causality exercised by God's light, Duns then responded to the objection. If divinity as truth or light was natural cause of all things in cognitive being, then whatever pertained to things precisely because of such being was due to God's action as intellective light (*convenit eis naturaliter respectu lucis increatae*). Yet things were understood by human intellect – that is, they were constituted as intelligible objects – just insofar as they inclined mind into their cognitive being. Inescapable was the conclusion that objects were intelligible, and thus understood, precisely with respect to God's action on them as light of truth. It was God's intellective light, not his will, that accounted for cognition and thus knowledge of truth.[54]

---

[51] Duns, *Lectura* I, d. 3, p. 1, q. 3 (Vatican, 16:302, n. 190).

[52] Duns, *Lectura* I, d. 3, p. 1, q. 3 (Vatican, 16:302, n. 191), concluding with the phrase: "... igitur Deus est causa naturalis aliorum a se secundum esse intelligibile." For Duns's more extensive presentation of his views on creation, see above, Pt. 4, ch. 14, nn. 138–39.

[53] See above, Pt. 3, ch. 11, nn. 49–50.

[54] Duns, *Lectura* I, d. 3, p. 1, q. 3 (Vatican, 16:302–3, n. 191), especially: "Quidquid igitur convenit rebus secundum esse intelligibile, convenit eis naturaliter respectu lucis increatae; sed res ut obiecta intellectui, inclinant intellectum naturaliter in esse intelligibile; et sic inclinare intellectum convenit essentiae lapidis vel aliorum in quantum sunt a Deo ut est lux quaedam, a qua prius sunt secundum esse intelligibile quam a voluntate. Et ideo dicimur intelligere in luce increata, et non in voluntate increata."

For present purposes there is not much of interest here in Duns's conclusion that divine will was not a primary factor in knowledge of truth. Important, instead, is how close his argument brought him to the noetics and metaphysics of Henry of Ghent and Richard of Conington. By Duns's own words, it was now "with respect to divine light" that things were constituted as objects of intellect. It was "with respect to divine light" that they inclined mind into knowledge of truth. Gone was the emphasis on God as efficient cause of agent intellect; in its place the telltale notion of a relation to God as constitutive of and fundamentally implicated in things' knowability. All that separated Duns from Conington was the latter's admission that in knowing things with respect to God, mind somehow perceived the relation itself, and thus both extremes. Even Henry, in his theory of natural knowledge of God, had avoided explicitly requiring intellect to register the relation underlying its knowledge of truth.[55] On the surface, Duns and Henry look much the same.

It is a sign of the harmony between the two thinkers' ideas that at this point in the *Lectura* Duns expressly shifted attention to examining the role of God's light as not efficient (*effective*) but rather objective (*obiective* or *sicut in obiecto*) – today one might say "formal" or perhaps "material" – cause of knowledge of truth. Henry had always insisted on God's illuminative role as due to formal, not efficient, causality. And of course Duns was already considering God's light more under the guise of formal than efficient causation ever since he introduced the factor of cognitive being. As if to underline the importance of the objective or formal construction of God's role, he even added the claim that this was how Augustine himself understood the business of seeing truth in God's light.[56]

According to Duns, there were three ways God's light might intervene objectively in the wayfarer's normal cognition – that is to say, as a sort of object in or by virtue of which mind grasped pure truth.[57]

---

[55] On Henry and Richard, see above, Pt. 3, ch. 11, pp. 353–56. Admittedly, Duns's express denial of mind's knowledge of the relation might be seen as significantly separating him from Henry of Ghent – see Duns, *Lectura* I, d. 3, p. 1, q. 3 (Vatican, 16:303, n. 192 [ll. 26–30]).

[56] Duns, *Lectura* I, d. 3, p. 1, q. 3 (Vatican, 16:303, n. 192) for the switch to God's objective role; the same (Vatican, 16:305, n. 196), for the comments on Augustine. On Henry's views, see above, Pt. 3, ch. 10, n. 7; and ch. 11, nn. 48 and 50.

[57] Duns, *Lectura* I, d. 3, p. 1, q. 3 (Vatican, 16:303, n. 192).

The first way, God acted formally as object known (*obiective formaliter*), so that strictly speaking intellect saw the divine light and in it truth.[58] Here Duns simply picked up where he had left off with his preceding analysis of knowing cognitive being. As he explained, it was in the very same way and according to the very same conditions by which things were objects for divine intellection that they were subsequently objects for human knowledge. This was so because the essences of things were seized by intellect insofar as they had cognitive being (*esse intelligibile*), which being they originally and eternally received from God's intellective act and which remained objectively (*obiective*) – perhaps one could say, so far as content was concerned – identical and undivided in all instances in which they were known.[59] By virtue of the formal process of knowing things, therefore, mind was thrown back on a cognitive field ontologically constituted by God's own light.

The second way, God acted as that which contained the known object but was itself not seen. Presumably the metaphysical grounds for this way were the same as for the first, with the difference that the focus now lay not on formal conditions of intellection but on the end or goal: the truth of the created thing known. Set in these terms, God's noetic role was much reduced. The third way, divinity reappeared again authentically as object known. Here mind actually saw truth in divine light as in its cognitive goal (*sicut in obiecto cognito*), or in other words not because God was formal cause of intelligibility, as in the first way, but rather because mind consciously extrapolated from its cognition an awareness of the original principle from which all things were derived. This was the only way in which mind was fully cognizant of God's light as cause of true knowledge.

---

[58] Duns, *Lectura* I, d. 3, p. 1, q. 3 (Vatican, 1:304, n. 193): "Sic . . . intellectus noster potest in via videre sinceram veritatem in luce aeterna obiective formaliter, ita quod lux aeterna formaliter videatur. . . ."

[59] Duns, *Lectura* I, d. 3, p. 1, q. 3 (Vatican, 16:303, n. 192): ". . . illud idem et sub eadem ratione obiectiva quod est secundarium obiectum intellectus divini, est obiectum viatoris. Et . . . ideo secundum hoc dici potest quod viator videt veritatem in luce aeterna, quia videt essentiam lapidis vel alterius rei, quae secundum esse intelligibile semper fuit et aeterna. . . ." It is striking how greatly this language recalls that of Henry of Ghent in *Quod.* IX, q. 15 (ed. Macken, p. 262), quoted also above, Pt. 3, ch. 12, n. 90: "Sunt enim eadem cognita et praedicta intellecta in phantasmatibus, et ipsae incorporeae rationes in ipsa veritate aeterna: non sunt enim aliud quam ipsae naturae et essentiae rerum."

It was also much less what the classic Augustinian model of illumination was meant to entail.[60]

Historically interesting as they may be, the second and third of these "objective" ways of interpreting illumination hardly constitute significant indicators of traditionalist leanings. The same cannot be said about the first. Duns's analysis of God as formal object in normal knowledge of truth represented a step well outside the usual ambit of his mature approach to human cognition in the world of sin. Working with ideas he had begun to articulate in the reply to the objection about God's will as efficient cause of truth, he had effectively displaced his theory of knowledge in the semi-ontologist direction associated with Henry of Ghent. And while technically not violating his mature rejection of Henry's contention that the immediate object of all intellection possessed in itself being of essence, he nonetheless managed momentarily to project onto his own version of the intellective object as an entity in cognitive being alone practically the same divine-oriented metaphysical configuration that had characterized his predecessor's view.[61] One is reminded of similarly suggestive echoes of Henry in Duns's discussion of possibles, where for all his insistence that possibility rested exclusively on logical coherence he still managed to speak of the divine mind as principiant cause whereby possibles were produced.[62] Such turns of phrase, innocuous in isolation, loom large in their cumulative effect. When it came to glossing Augustine, Duns could evidently be as radically illuminationist as Henry himself.

Had he paused at this point to attend carefully to what he was saying, perhaps he would have been forced to agree, and maybe he would have been prompted to modify his language. It would seem, at any rate, that when he later re-examined the matter – that is, when he came to composing the parallel section of the *Ordinatio* – he entertained second thoughts about some of the claims made in

---

[60] For the second and third ways, see Duns, *Lectura* I, d. 3, p. 1, q. 3 (Vatican, 16:304, nn. 194–95).

[61] For Duns's evolving views on the correct ontological characterization of the cognitive object, see above, Pt. 4, ch. 14, nn. 71, 107, 111 and 146. It must be remembered that despite the fact that by the *Lectura* Duns had expressly severed the connection between cognitive object and being of essence (or quidditative being), his language still sometimes betrayed the lingering influence of Henry's ideas: see Pt. 4, ch. 14, nn. 107, 114 and 140.

[62] See above, Pt. 4, ch. 14, nn. 139, 140 and 142.

the *Lectura*. The *Ordinatio* submits a more cautiously nuanced interpretation of the illuminative role of divine light. Not only did Duns
no longer accept efficient causality as an apt description of any of
the functions he had in mind for God's illumination, dropping it
from his explicit analytical scheme and incorporating whatever could
be salvaged from the *Lectura* analysis of God's light as efficient cause,
including his response to the objection about voluntarism, into
another – the third by his new numbering – of the ways God acted
as "objective" cause of knowledge of truth.[63] He also trod more carefully over the ontologizing topography of his previous views, taking
pains to specify the exact mechanism by which God's light worked
in each of the ways it served as illuminator for human mind. Yet
in the end, the impression of his words upon the reader is much
the same.

According to the *Ordinatio* there were four legitimate readings of
Augustine's language about seeing "infallible truths" in the "eternal
reasons," and in all of them God's light acted as objective cause
(*obiective*).[64] The first reading took up the analysis of the first of the
three "objective" ways presented in the *Lectura*, by which divine light
had acted formally as object known (*obiective formaliter*). Abandoning
that earlier terminology, Duns now explained that God's radiance
functioned as illuminator in this instance because it was specifically
proximate – that is, immediate or direct – object of intellection (*sicut
in obiecto proximo*), the reason being, as previously indicated in the
Lectura, that all objects were intelligible only insofar as they received
cognitive being (*esse intelligibile*) from the intellective act of God's mind.
Since every truth predicable of intelligibles was potentially contained
in them as they were constituted in cognitive being, human intellect
could be said to know such truths precisely by virtue of its knowing the objects themselves, and thus by virtue of grasping them as
they were rendered intelligible by God.[65]

To guarantee his readers understood why the image of light was
appropriate, Duns actually drew upon traditional figures of speech
absent in the passage from the *Lectura*. The very same act of divine

---

[63] For the new version of Duns's arguments against voluntarism and for God as
"natural" cause of objects' intelligibility, see *Ordinatio* I, d. 3, p. 1, q. 4 (Vatican,
3:163–64, n. 268).
[64] Duns, *Ordinatio* I, d. 3, p. 1, q. 4 (Vatican, 3:160, n. 261).
[65] Duns, *Ordinatio* I, d. 3, p. 1, q. 4 (Vatican, 3:160, nn. 261–62).

intellection that constituted cognitive objects in intelligible being also
made them "truths," since it established them in conformity to the
divine exemplar. It made them "light" as well, since it gave them
the power of manifesting truth by becoming known.[66] Here was language harking back to Robert Grosseteste and William of Auvergne.[67]
The maxims of Augustinian epistemology were evidently as valid as
ever: knowing truth entailed knowing intelligible objects as they were
grasped by God's mind, and that meant knowing them as conforming
to divine exemplars, by which conformity they were both truth and
eternal light.[68]

The second reading offered in the *Ordinatio* echoed the second of
the "objective" ways of the *Lectura*. In fact the exposition here was
literally a reprise of the earlier analysis, identifying God's light as a
kind of vessel containing the object (*continens obiectum*), in which truth
was seen without the vessel itself being perceived. As before, Duns
explicitly tied this interpretation to Augustine's reference to God's
light as a book in which all truths had been inscribed.[69]

Both of these first two readings plainly validated Augustinian illumination and maintained a place for classic descriptions of divine
radiance as revealer of truth, yet neither fully satisfied Duns. The
first, in particular, fell short. By its terms, intellect saw truth "in the
eternal light" because whatever it knew had been constituted in cognitive being by God and thereby rendered "truth" and "light" to
mind. But as Duns already admitted in the *Lectura*, unlike divinity
itself such truth or light was not authentically eternal. In fact, it did
not fully exist. Grasped by mind in cognitive being, it possessed existence only in a manner of speaking (*secundum quid*).[70] Should one thus

---

[66] For the foregoing description, see Duns, *Ordinatio* I, d. 3, p. 1, q. 4 (Vatican,
3:160, n. 262).

[67] See above, Pt. 1, ch. 1, nn. 3 and 8, on truth as conformity; nn. 38, 43 and
50, on truth as manifest in the manner of light.

[68] Duns concluded the passage cited in n. 66 as follows: "Sic igitur . . . possumus
dici 'videre in luce aeterna,' hoc est in obiecto secundario intellectus divini, quod
est veritas et lux aeterna. . . ."

[69] Duns, *Ordinatio* I, d. 3, p. 1, q. 4 (Vatican, 3:160–61, n. 263), making explicit
mention of Augustine's *De Trinitate* XIV, 15 (eds. Mountain and Glorie, 2, 451).
Notable is how Duns's words recall those of William of Auvergne, who spoke in
more authentically Neoplatonic terms of God the illuminator as a "living book" of
forms – see above, Pt. 1, ch. 2, n. 64.

[70] See Duns's *Ordinatio* I, d. 3, p. 1, q. 4 (Vatican, 3:160, n. 262): "Sed [illa
obiecta in quantum sunt veritates,] aeternae sunt secundum quid, quia 'aeternitas'
est condicio exsistentis, et illa non habent exsistentiam nisi secundum quid." He

take Augustine to have been saying that intellect saw infallible truth in a light that was eternal, and thus divine, only in a manner of speaking as well?[71]

To meet this deficiency Duns introduced his third interpretation. Here is where he now situated what remained of the ideas inspired by John of La Rochelle, taken in the *Lectura* as implicating divine light in efficient causality of knowledge of truth but regarded this time as indicative of yet another of God's "objective" roles, specifically as cognitive light by virtue of which the direct or proximate object moved mind to know.[72] This constituted, for the later Duns, the principal way to read the Augustinian image of illumination.

The argument in the *Ordinatio*, like the response to the objection from its counterpart in the *Lectura*, started with the principle that things were objects for mind only insofar as they possessed cognitive being, which they originally received by virtue of God's knowledge of them. Now, however, Duns added a line of reasoning initially absent in the earlier work.[73] He reminded his readers that, as he had just remarked with reference to his first reading of illumination, cognitive being was being, or existence, improperly and in a manner of speaking (*secundum quid*), thus not real being (*esse simpliciter*) at all. Since what did not really exist was incapable of real operation, if intelligible objects were to move mind to intellection, they had to do so in virtue of something else which was existent and could therefore lend them the power to act. This "something else" must be

had made the same point in his description of the first "objective" way in *Lectura* I, d. 3, p. 1, q. 3 (Vatican, 16:303, n. 192).

[71] Duns, *Ordinatio* I, d. 3, p. 1, q. 4 (Vatican, 3:161–62, n. 264): ". . . quomodo dicemur 'videre in luce increata' ex hoc quod videmus in tali 'luce aeterna secundum quid'? . . ." Duns's ideas here are reminiscent of comments of Bonaventure and Matthew of Aquasparta on immutability of truth *ex suppositione* as opposed to immutability *simpliciter*, the latter tied to absolute certitude but the former to certitude *secundum quid*: see above, Pt. 2, ch. 7, nn. 21, 23 and 25.

[72] See Duns, *Ordinatio* I, d. 3, p. 1, q. 4 (Vatican, 3:160, n. 261), characterizing God's light in this way as "[id] virtute cuius obiectum proximum movet."

[73] Duns, *Ordinatio* I, d. 3, p. 1, q. 4 (Vatican, 3:162, n. 265). Similar reasoning was inserted into the text of the *Lectura* as a late addition: see *Lectura* I, d. 3, p. 1, q. 3 (Vatican, 16:305–6, n. 198). In both cases, the argument relied on the notion Duns was to defend in *Ordinatio* I, d. 36, whereby the "being in a manner of speaking" of an object of divine intellection could be reduced to the "being pure and simple" of God, which as being pure and simple did not actually belong to the object but was properly attributable only to divinity – see above, Pt. 4, ch. 14, n. 146. In fact, just following the passage quoted in that note, Duns referred back to the discussion from *Ordinatio* I, d. 3, of God as source for the force of intelligibility: see *Ordinatio* I, d. 36, q. un. (Vatican, 6:289–90, n. 47).

divine intellect, which indisputably existed and was, after all, what produced intelligible objects in the first place and sustained them in cognitive being.

No matter, then, that the first reading, by construing Augustine's words as referring to mind's direct or proximate object, yielded a "light of truth" that existed, and a fortiori was eternal as well as divine, only in a manner of speaking. It was still correct to say that a strictly eternal light illuminated intellect, for by the Augustinian "light" one could equally well understand not the proximate object but rather the direct cause of intellection – in other words, that by virtue of whose intelligible force the object was capable of acting on mind and coming to be understood. In this case, the "light of truth" was authentically eternal and fully divine; it was, quite simply, God's intellect, cause of all intelligibility.[74]

Having laid out this new argument, Duns then returned to language more resonant of the *Lectura*. God not only provided mind's objects with their intellective force; precisely because he produced them in intelligible being he also furnished each with the essential traits characterizing it as "this" or "that" sort of thing, thus imbuing it with a determinate nature as object of intellect (*talis ratio obiecti*). Besides being cause of the power of intelligibility, God's light was thus also cause of the intelligible objects themselves and in this way, too, that by virtue of which truth was known.[75]

Combining the two accounts, Duns described them as comprising a "dual causality" by which God was light of truth. Under the guise of light, divinity was both productive cause of intelligible objects and direct source of the power by which they moved human mind to

---

[74] See from the first passage cited above, n. 73: "Sic ergo in 'luce aeterna secundum quid' sicut in obiecto proximo videmus, sed in 'luce aeterna increata' videmus secundum tertium modum, sicut in causa proxima, cuius virtute obiectum proximum movet." For similar analysis of God as cause of knowledge, see Duns, *Collationes* 13, n. 8 (Vivès, 5:204a–b).

[75] Duns, *Ordinatio* I, d. 3, p. 1, q. 4 (Vatican, 3:162, n. 266), especially: "Iuxta hoc etiam potest dici quod . . . videmus in luce aeterna sicut in causa obiecti in se." The language of this passage draws most from the sections of the *Lectura* cited above, nn. 52 and 54. It is worth noting that the same schema provided one of the ways by which Duns understood the notion of divine ideas or eternal reasons, an idea being the object of God's knowledge as produced in cognitive being: see *Ordinatio* I, d. 35, q. un. (Vatican, 6:261, n. 40); and also *Lectura* I, d. 35, q. un. (Vatican, 17:455, n. 30). Paulus, *Henri de Gand*, p. 135, commented how on this matter Duns followed, even surpassed, Henry of Ghent in identifying idea with "exemplatum," but without Henry's idealism.

cognition. The third reading of Augustine was, in sum, ultimately to be construed in complex fashion as positing two roles embedded in a single figure of speech.[76] As if to signal that he had set out on the road to these ideas by considering the role of mind's intrinsic agent intellect – here the genuine echo of John of La Rochelle – Duns even drew an analogy to the latter's operation in the cognitive process. Just like God, the agent was also a light, active cause bringing objects to intelligible actuality and endowing them with the force to set intellect in motion.[77]

For all his circumspection, once again Duns had fallen back onto the metaphysical universe of Henry of Ghent, with its ontologist implications for the noetics of truth. The discussion of the third way of affirming Augustine makes no allowance for a natural capacity of real created objects in the physical world for cognitive self-manifestation. Here mind's objects are entities in intelligible being whose power to become known arises directly from God. One might even see Duns as reaching beyond Henry to the classic Augustinians. The words about divine mind as that in virtue of which objects move intellect echo Matthew's ideas about divinity as motive object, a Godly power immanent in intelligibles and leading to truth.[78]

More precisely, Duns would appear to be moving, as suggested at the outset of this return to Augustinian motifs, into the world of Henry's late discussions of knowledge of truth. Whether God's illuminative power be traced back to his general influence (*influentia generalis*) or to the natural necessity (*necessitas naturalis*) Duns had proposed, in either case it bespoke a normally hidden but everpresent divine action in all human intellectual acts that made superfluous any special illumination (*illustratio specialis*).[79] As with the late Henry, so with the mature Duns, because God's role in the noetics of truth arose from the essential and intelligible heart of things, it did not require

---

[76] Duns, *Ordinatio* I, d. 3, p. 1, q. 4 (Vatican, 3:163, n. 267), describing the "duplex causalitas" of divine intellect, whereby it was "vera lux increata, videlicet quae producit obiecta secundaria in 'esse intelligibili'" and "illud virtute cuius secundaria etiam obiecta producta movent actualiter intellectum."

[77] Duns, *Ordinatio* I, d. 3, p. 1, q. 4 (Vatican, 3:162–63, n. 266).

[78] On Matthew's motive object, see above, Pt. 2, ch. 5, pp. 144–46. Duns's description of God as intellectual mover in the passage from *Ordinatio* I, d. 36, cited at the end of n. 73, above, is the closest he comes to Matthew's words.

[79] Duns, *Ordinatio* I, d. 3, p. 1, q. 4 (Vatican, 3:164–65, n. 269). For his analysis of God's role in natural necessity, see above, nn. 52 and 63. On Henry's late skittishness about affirming a special illustration, see above, Pt. 3, ch. 12, pp. 359–61.

a separate, supernatural intervention from above. The same perspective allowed him to show why knowledge of truth, and thus access to God's light, did not presume moral elevation. Naturally implicated in the workings of the constituent elements of cognition, the illuminative power of God's truth was available to pagan philosophers as readily as to the faithful. More ample natural gifts of mind or more diligent application to the search for truth were what provided greater access to this light, not a more religious life.[80]

Duns corroborated this approach, more tellingly still, by turning to both the Aristotelianizing vision of cognition Henry had expounded in his early writings, equating knowledge of quiddity with knowledge of truth, and that from the later works, whereby true knowledge consisted in distinct as opposed to confused cognition. These were the cardinal elements Duns had already incorporated into his own mature notion of science as dependent on grasp of quiddity, seen clearly in the definition and not confusedly in the sensible phantasm or the inchoate intellectual perception emergent immediately from it, and they constituted, in the end, the instruments whereby he made Henry's term "pure truth" his own.[81] Following much the same path as Henry at career's end, he thus blended Aristotle and Augustine into a noetic and epistemological amalgam maintaining the link to illuminationist currents of the past.[82] His efforts reaffirmed the her-

---

[80] Duns, *Ordinatio* I, d. 3, p. 1, q. 4 (Vatican, 3:166–67, nn. 273–74); and n. 276 (Vatican, 3:168), where he commented that the few who knew truth best were distinguished "non . . . propter specialem illustrationem, sed vel propter meliora naturalia (quia habent intellectum magis abstrahentem et magis perspicacem), vel propter maiorem inquisitionem. . . ." Duns inserted similar views into the *Lectura* by means of a late addition: see *Lectura* I, d. 3, p. 1, q. 3 (Vatican, 16:306–7, n. 201).

[81] Duns, *Ordinatio* I, d. 3, p. 1, q. 4 (Vatican, 3:167–68, nn. 275–76). Again, he inserted the same views in a late addition to *Lectura* I, d. 3, p. 1, q. 3 (Vatican, 16:307, n. 202). On these ideas in Duns's epistemology, see above, Pt. 4, ch. 13, pp. 439–43. On early Henry and quiddity, see above, Pt. 3, ch. 9, nn. 27 and 29; on late Henry and distinct cognition, Pt. 3, ch. 12, nn. 34–35; and Marrone, *Truth and Scientific Cognition*, pp. 78–79.

[82] General evaluations of Duns's thought are varied and numerous, but many have noted its tendency to combine two quite distinct doctrinal currents. Etienne Gilson, "Avicenne et le point de départ," pp. 146–47, saw Duns as injecting Augustinian ideas into Aristotelianism, although he often emphasized the Augustinian (and Platonic) side of the combination (see Gilson, *Jean Duns Scot*, p. 112), as did Barth, "Being, Univocity, and Analogy according to Duns Scotus," in *John duns Scotus, 1265–1965*, eds. John K. Ryan and Bernardino M. Bonansea (Washington, D.C., 1963), p. 233. Charles R.S. Harris, *Duns Scotus* (Oxford, 1927), vol. 2, p. 61; Barth, "De tribus viis diversis existentiam divinam attingendi. Disquisitio historico-collativa inter S. Thomam, Henricum Gandavensem, Duns Scotum," *Antonianum* 18

meneutic expedient Henry had grasped but more hide-bound minds like Vital du Four would not accept: that Aristotelianizing motifs did not necessarily endanger an Augustinian appreciation of the noetic role of God.[83] On the contrary, Augustine's call for recourse to divine light could well be taken as one more reason to promote the meticulous and critical standards of scientific discourse in the schools.[84]

This was as far as the late Duns would go. For his fourth and final reading of Augustinian illumination he returned to the third of the *Lectura*'s "objective" roles for God's light, by which divinity entered into the cognitive process as mind resolved separate truths into the ultimate principle of truth in divine mind. He now explicitly characterized divine light viewed from this angle as remote object of intellect, in contrast to its function as direct or proximate object in the first of his four ways, adding that this mode of understanding was peculiar to theology. It was after all theologians who considered

---

(1943): 91–117; and "Duns Scotus und die ontologische Grundlage," p. 372; and Bettoni, "Duns Scoto nella scolastica del secolo XIII," pp. 101–11, make the same point by describing Duns as occupying a middle way between Thomas Aquinas and Henry of Ghent. On the other hand, Hadrianus Borak, "Aspectus fundamentales," p. 137; and Bettoni in his earlier work, *Duns Scoto* (Brescia, 1946), pp. 200, 217–18 and 249 (English translation: *Duns Scotus. The Basic Principles*, p. 152), characterize Scotus's thought as more monolithically Augustinian; while Séraphin Belmond, "Simples remarques sur l'idéologie comparée de saint Thomas et de Duns Scot," *Revue de Philosophie* 24 (1914): 242–60; Bettoni in "La posizione storica di Duns Scoto nel problema della conoscenza," SF 39 (1942): 97–109; and Bérubé, "Pour une histoire des preuves," pp. 17–18, all describe him as Aristotelian. Léon Veuthey, "L'école franciscaine et la critique philosophique moderne," EF 48 (1936): 257–58 and 266; "Cohérence: Eclectisme ou synthèse"; and "L'esprit du concret," argued that Scotus failed in his attempt to synthesize Augustine and Aristotle, a position Belmond criticized in "Le scotisme philosophique manque-t-il de cohérence?" EF 49 (1937): 178–88. Olivier Lacombe, "La critique des théories de la connaissance chez Duns Scot," *Revue Thomiste* 35 (1930): 24–47, 144–57 and 217–35, argued that it was wrong to classify Scotus as either Thomist or Augustinian.

[83] On Henry as combining Aristotle and Augustine, see Marrone, *Truth and Scientific Knowledge*, pp. 136–7 and 140. For Vital's rejection, see above, Pt. 3, ch. 9, nn. 35–36.

[84] See, for example, Duns's Aristotelianizing reading of Augustine's famous analogy between seeing truth and gazing at the sun as one stands on the mountaintops high above the clouds (*Ordinatio* I, d. 3, p. 1, q. 4 [Vatican, 3:168–69, n. 276]). The Augustine text is *De Trinitate* IX, 6 (eds. Mountain & Glorie, 1, 302–3). This attitude explains why the late Duns took the Augustinian notion of illumination to refer only to knowledge of necessary truths: see *Ordinatio* I, d. 3, p. 1, q. 4 (Vatican, 3:164 and 166, nn. 269 and 272). A similar restriction appears in a late addition to *Lectura* I, d. 3, p. 1, q. 3 (Vatican, 16:306, n. 200).

all truths insofar as they pertained to divinity and to divine providence.[85] And in what looks to be an afterthought, he virtually admitted that full realization of this fourth sort of illumination would occur
only in revealed or supernatural cognition. God alone, who knew
things by knowing himself, knew everything invariably as "pure truth"
in this way; other minds typically followed a more mundane route
to veracity.[86]

Of all the readings of illumination in the *Ordinatio*, clearly the third
resonates most vibrantly of the tradition nourished by the classic
Augustinians. Here lies concentrated the theoretical distillate of Duns's
hopes for keeping a place in noetics and epistemology for Augustine's
vision of God's natural intimacy to the wayfarer's mind. Here, more
than at any other point in his thought, are reproduced not only the
most characteristic elements of Henry's Augustinianizing language of
knowing but also the contours of much of the special ontological
structure that gave meaning to those words.

Of course, this suggestive moment must be set beside Duns's more
characteristic efforts to construct a philosophy purified of the ontologism still suffusing the thought of Henry of Ghent. Again, central
to this endeavor was his concern to make clear that the essences of
things, the epistemic and ontological center of gravity for entities in
the objective world, were not to be identified with their cognitive
being as understood by God or any other active intellect.[87] Yet even
with this caveat, Duns's reading of Augustine on illumination works
to powerful effect. It was not philosophical necessity that drove him
to reinsinuate God's light into his account of knowing truth, for by
the terms of both his metaphysics and his noetics, objects in the
physical world had the power to move mind, and mind the capacity to know material objects. He brought God's light into play just
because he chose to do so, and this in a way that was not simply
metaphorical. The language from *Ordinatio* I, d. 3, and that of the
parallel section of the *Lectura*, is indeed so unmitigatedly Augustinian

---

[85] Duns, *Ordinatio* I, d. 3, p. 1, q. 4 (Vatican, 3:169, n. 277), especially his comment about theologians: "Et hoc modo cognitio omnium pertinet ad theologum."

[86] Duns, *Ordinatio* I, d. 3, p. 1, q. 4 (Vatican, 3:170, n. 277): "Hoc modo solus
Deus cognoscit omnia tantum sincere . . .; omnis alius intellectus moveri potest ab
obiecto alio, ad cognoscendum veritatem aliquam virtute eius."

[87] See particularly the passage quoted in Pt. 4, ch. 14, n. 146 (referred to above,
n. 73); and the discussion in the same chapter, pp. 470–75 and 483–85; as well as
the mention above at n. 61.

as to make sense more from the perspective of Henry's ontology than from the metaphysics of Duns himself. Here was an unabashed effort to replicate the Augustinian core of Henry's thought.

One could ask for no clearer sign of the continuing strength of the Augustinian current at century's end. On the periphery of an ontology, epistemology and noetics conceding so much to the increasing worldliness of high-medieval scholastic thinking, Duns reintroduced the specter of a metaphysically immanent God that he elsewhere had done so much to dispel.[88] Precisely here can be registered the impress of tradition's weighty hand, or discerned the vestiges of a past one must never lose sight of but which requires such effort to bring into view. Only when one is fully attuned to the resonances of the philosophical discourse that had gone on before and the ideological alliances worked out and renewed decade after decade is it possible truly to evaluate Duns's words. Only after taking stock of more than technical precision and logical coherence, and recognizing the sometimes unconscious, even contradictory impulses linking him to what preceded, to ways of thinking and speaking to which he felt alternatively loyal and opposed, can one begin fully to appreciate his thought. In the process, one comes to realize how the Augustinian agenda, that protean force apparent throughout thirteenth-century Scholasticism, was as much alive in Duns as it had been among his intellectual forebears eighty years before.

---

[88] Refer back to the remarkable passages cited above, Pt. 4, ch. 14, nn. 141–42; and this chapter, n. 62; where Duns seemed to sense this very tension and grapple with it.

CONCLUSION

Now that so long a story has reached its end, it is time to step back and consider once more what it all might mean. The foregoing analysis has engaged itself massively with detail. But obsession with particulars would seem in this instance to be a necessary part of the investigative apparatus. To make such sweeping assertions about events covering nearly a century of time, on the basis of interpretative models of such porousness and malleability, would hardly be credible without testing hypotheses against practically every scrap of evidence. A mountain of circumstance about other scholastics and other philosophical issues remains uninvestigated, but this study has made an attempt at comprehensiveness within the limits of its subject domain.

If meaning, not its validity, is at issue now, then it is probably best to approach this work from three perspectives. First has to do with the history of science, or at least of a scientific mentality among Europe's educated elite. It should be clear that from beginning to end the thirteenth century witnessed a progressive acceptance of what is here called an Aristotelianizing, apodictic model of scientific knowledge, closely associated with concrete explication and an appeal to worldly, naturalizing operations. Less has been said above concerning the positive promotion of new theories and methods than what one might call the negative side of the phenomenon, evaporation of opposition to them. Practically ignored have been what most modern readers would principally associate with "science," the substantive pronouncements of the natural sciences, especially those approximating what is accepted as scientifically valid today. Yet that does not mean this book is not about the development of a body of knowledge intimately linked to "science" at the beginning of the twenty-first century. It is, and to that degree it contributes to the prehistory of modern science in the late medieval West.

Important to remember above all is that substantive theories and models – such as laws of motion or an idea of atomic particles – are not the only intellectual constructs contributory to the development of scientific thought. An adequate account of the Scientific Revolution of the seventeenth century, for instance, must counterbalance the origin of specific hypotheses and arguments with transformation in methodology. And even there the story is by no means confined to the often-extolled rise of an experimental method. Ideas about how the results of investigation should be presented and what general standards should apply to qualify arguments as scientific are equally important in accounting for what went on among intellectuals in that century of change. The vast literature on rationalism and scepticism in the seventeenth century should make this plain.[1]

What the present study has emphasized on this positive score can be called a matter of organization of knowledge. For thirteenth-century thinkers the term "scientific" applied, after all, principally to the way knowledge was defended and displayed. It summarized an array of logical and discursive practices that had been introduced in Aristotle's Organon, were aimed towards achieving demonstration in the strict sense of the word, and received their first significant exposition in efforts to comment on the *Posterior Analytics*. Despite the fact that such formal considerations resonate little with modern attitudes towards science as experimental, mathematical, even statistical, it would seem that the habits of mind necessary for the practice of modern science were incubated in these early preoccupations of the medieval universities. As argued in the introduction, the transition from prescholastic literate discourse to the highly formalized procedures of the late thirteenth century constituted a gigantic step, one whose equivalent cannot be found anywhere along the line from thirteenth century to contemporary world. Classical mechanics, relativity, quantum physics all arose within a rationalist conceptual universe established, at least for Western Europe, in the twelfth- and thirteenth-century schools. They bear almost no affinity to even educated modes of thought typical of preceding medieval culture. To this extent Duhem and those who have insisted on the importance of medieval science are right in searching for the origins of modernity in the Middle Ages.

---

[1] It suffices merely to look at work on Descartes, reputed master of both sceptical and rationalist trends. The classic study tying together scepticism and rationalism in Descartes is Richard H. Popkin, *The History of Scepticism from Erasmus to Descartes*, rev. ed. (New York, 1964) – in its latest avatar, Popkin, *The History of Scepticism from Erasmus to Spinoza* (Berkeley, 1979). But the perennial interest of Descartes scholars in investigating these themes is evident in such recent introductory collections as John Cottingham, ed., *The Cambridge Companion to Descartes* (Cambridge, 1992), esp. ch. 3 and 9; or even more, Cottingham, ed., *Descartes* (Oxford, 1998), ch. 1, 11 and 12.

And while the present book has focused more on the negative side of the ledger, adding up efforts to accommodate the novel epistemic approach and clear away obstacles to its acceptance, here, too, there are lessons to learn. The new model of science generated predictable ripples in the broader expanse of thirteenth-century culture, not simply posing the question of whether such a model was consistent with discursive procedures already long ingrained but at times frontally assaulting familiar cognitive and ethical assumptions and the rationales upon which they had been built. Implications of the new attitudes for religious and devotional commitments epitomized in the notion of God's intimacy to mind constituted the primary irritant for the story told above. The fact that ways were found to adapt tradition to the demands of the new paradigm, in some instances in fact by discarding elements of traditional ideology, as with insistence on illumination for arriving at truth, stands as testimony to the power of the forces of intellectual innovation. Apparently inconceivable was any effective effort to halt their advance, so firm was their hold on the thirteenth-century imagination. Indeed, the apodictic, naturalizing paradigm for science made inroads in all philosophical and theological circles over the course of the century, with the imperative to accommodate it only growing in urgency the more the new model was elaborated and explored.

Even on this "negative" side, moreover, one can discern secondary developments feeding back into the positive efforts to establish and understand the new scientific model. Ideological operations were at work in the processes of accommodation vital for determining the shape the model would assume in the fourteenth century. In short, the very business of critically reconsidering old explanatory devices and attempting to salvage what could be retained from them set in motion mechanisms of constructive character that fed back onto the very intellectual innovations generating the critique in the first place.

The irony, therefore, is that fruitful intellectual invention occurred within circles typically regarded as conservative, associated with a defensive posture reactive to the most obviously dynamic elements in the thirteenth-century ideological mix. Prominent examples were Henry of Ghent's almost intuitive awareness that God's illuminative function in truth-finding had to be separated from the noetics of the wayfarer's grasp of divinity, as well as his speculations on being and essence and the way things' natures related eternally to divine intelligence. More significant over the long haul were the accomplishments

of Duns Scotus. For historians of philosophy, of critical importance
was his revolutionary espousal of the univocity of "being," prompted
in large part by his conviction that a way must be found to render
the "scientific" understanding of natural knowledge in the world compatible with unequivocal use of normal language by the wayfarer to
describe divinity.[2]

Most relevant to history of science were Duns's ruminations on
the foundations of cognitive certitude. His determination to make a
place for intellectual assent to statements of particular fact led him
to break free of strictly Aristotelian epistemology, most especially the
demand for universality and solely demonstrative argument, and
encouraged his predilection to appeal to experience as one among
several guides to scientific truth. And although on these matters Duns
had been anticipated by other Augustinian thinkers in the last decades
of the thirteenth century, his contributions on the question of intuitive cognition, which promised to provide for certitude about particulars a firm theoretical ground, belonged more nearly to him alone.

In all these cases, the ramifications for theories of knowledge in
the fourteenth century, and for attitudes towards scientific method
up through the modern period, were far-reaching and profound. One
need only consider the crucial question of what should count as evidence to see how this is so. Though an honest reckoning of the
significance of such instances of ideological invention is impossible
here, it is tempting nonetheless to hypothesize a fundamental connection between mental processes of reaction and critique, which
surely set a premium on the ability to reconceptualize the old at just
the spots where it is most threatened by the new, and procedures
of intellectual discovery. The idea is at least worth exploring, by
means of both historical and philosophical investigations capable of
putting it to the test.

Beyond history of science, however, lies a second approach to the
meaning of the present work. It focuses more narrowly on the philosophical fate of the notion of divine illumination throughout the thirteenth century. Since the chronicle of the figures of speech and
analytical devices associated with *in via* intellectual illumination by
God lies nearer to the surface of the narrative laid out above, there

---

[2] On what motivated Scotus to promote univocity of "being," and on potential
challenges to adopting exclusively the account presented in this book, see above,
Pt. 4, ch. 15, pp. 508–20, especially the last three pages.

is less need than in the case of the history of science to comment
on it. The story of divine illumination comprises, in the most obvious
way, the story of this book, the twists and turns of which will surely
have asserted themselves to even the least committed reader. But
still, a further word is due.

Central to all the foregoing observations about illuminationist theory and philosophical functions associated with it either occasionally
or in nearly every case resides the emphatic insistence that there was
over the course of the thirteenth century no single continuous understanding of what divine illumination entailed. Certainly there existed
no integrated doctrine of illumination for any more than a short
period of time. As an explanatory device in epistemology and noetics, illumination instead followed a more complicated course, beginning with early efforts to explore functions traditionally ascribed to
God's intelligible light and compare them to Aristotelianizing attitudes about intellection and mind, passing through attempts to construct a unified theory of divine illumination in the wayfarer's cognition
actively promoted under Augustine's name, then through a period
of crisis as inconsistencies between the classic construct and the growing consensus about natural operations and apodictic standards of
argument came to light, and culminating in an ingenious project to
salvage a devotional core from illuminationist traditions compatible
with an enlarged vision of science and invulnerable to charges of
anti-naturalism.

Less conspicuous but in the final analysis equally germane is the
contention that various positions put forth in the thirteenth century
on the wayfarer's natural ability to form a concept of divinity, some
of which had nothing explicitly to do with God's light shining on
intellect or any intellectual intervention directly from God, are fully
comprehensible only if linked historically to other positions advanced
in those same years that did in fact draw upon illuminationist language to account for the same phenomenon. Since all the positions
in question, both illuminationist and those shunning appeal to illumination in the literal sense, are found among a group of thinkers
whose theories of knowledge and mind patently echo each other at
numerous points, it seemed likely that at some level they resonated
with a common attitude toward processes of intellect. Profound structural parallels among the explanations, despite differences in receptivity to the notion of illumination, suggest that this was in fact the
case. On this issue – natural knowledge of God – all these thinkers

were bound up in a single causal nexus, wherein ideas advanced earlier to one effect inspired theoretical solutions advocated later with quite another noetic configuration in mind. That the lines of influence strayed across the illuminationist versus non-illuminationist divide, with formal structures of explanation passing as if by osmosis from one side to the other, only confirms the depth at which their community of intention lay fixed. It was, in the end, a commonality manifest in an unshakable agreement about a primitive and foundational connection between knowing being in the most abstract terms and knowing God.

Of course the active ingredient in that common resolve, as well as the source of the determination to salvage from illuminationist language an inalienable core, is here taken to consist in an attachment to generous assumptions about God's intimate presence to mind, itself sign of a yet more basic religious and devotional posture of ultimate commitment to the contemplative life.[3] Both inclinations might loosely be thought of as comprising an attitude prevalent among Franciscan thinkers in the thirteenth century though surely adopted by others as well, as shown above especially by scholars involved in their own day with Franciscan education or those whose works were assiduously mined by Franciscans following upon them. The argument for their existence is even more circumstantial than any of the arguments presented so far, but the power of their presence to explain otherwise mysterious ideological parallels and lines of continuity renders the hypothesis plausible at the very least. If there was such a shared posture, and if there were the consequent assumptions about God and intellect, two dispositions of mind typically associated with the image of divine illumination, but not necessarily dependent on it in the strict sense of the word, attach to all eleven thinkers investigated above. And that means, as in the end this study implies, that the historical reach of illuminationist ideas far exceeded actual recourse to the literal images of shining and light.

All of which calls to mind a final approach to the present work's significance. It bears upon the question of an Augustinian school of thought in the thirteenth century and, more generally, what to make

---

[3] This is "contemplative life" in the broad sense of a fundamental orientation to living in expectation of ever deepening communion with the divinity. See above, Pt. 1, ch. 4, n. 34.

of the notion of intellectual schools altogether. For the fact that one can trace the progress of an unbroken line of speculation among like-minded thinkers about the place of God in normal workings of the wayfarer's mind, a train of thought invariably characterized by the functional centrality of philosophical tropes associated with divine illumination, can be taken as evidence for the existence of a similarly continuous, but ideologically much broader intellectual current represented at least in part by the very same thinkers. And as with the narrow line of speculation, so with the broad current or school of thought subsuming it, the nature of the uniformity brought to light must necessarily be formally quite loose, as of a community of ideological inclination rather than convergence upon a crisply delineated doctrinal core. As promised, therefore, this study begins to put forth an argument reasserting the historiographical validity of talking about an Augustinian school in the thirteenth century. Though establishing full confidence in such unfashionable terms of analysis will require confirmation by more investigations than this alone, the case presented here is already substantial. It works, of course, precisely because its understanding of schools is so much less constrictive than any applied by historians in the past.

On the one hand, this looser standard for intellectual consanguinity can be thought of as a matter of cause or motivation. Making sense of a discrete line of speculation regarding the constellation of functions associated with divine illumination depended on postulating a shared religious and devotional orientation, summed up in the notion of God's intimacy to human intellect. Rendering understandable the existence of an Augustinian school will require presuming that there were many such nodes of conjoint sentiment and intellectual inclination, perhaps all related but surely not containable under a single rubric as simple as the notion of divine intimacy to mind.

On the other hand, the standard will have to be associated with an especially elastic set of formal boundaries or constraints. As proposed in the introduction to Volume 1, the concrete expression of a school in the extant philosophical and theological literature will most likely consist in a tendency to call upon a common fund of metaphors and models of analysis, ideological tools like the image of divine cognitive light in the present case or the acceptance of an almost a priori knowledge of God in being. Behind this concrete expression, and discernible in the textual evidence as well in a proclivity for using such metaphors and models in a fashion evocative of particular thinkers who have come before, will surely also lie that shared disposition to evoke a resonance of meaning and an intellectual attitude likewise pointed to in the introduction.[4]

No matter how one approaches them, commonalities of this sort have to be considered as much political as philosophical or formally intellectual. The identity of a school will subsist to that degree more in the intentions and sometimes unconscious motivations of scholastics engaged in their work, and in the reactions of readers poring over their writings, than in the actual substance of the theories or doctrines propounded. For the philosophically-minded, that might not seem like much upon which to build a school. Yet political lines of affinity are surely important factors in all cases of ideological debate, no matter how conspicuously and clearly defined the contours of doctrinal differentiation. Hardly a word spoken in defense of any idea or a criticism leveled against it does not conjure up in the mind of contemporary readers and listeners tacit sympathies with or antipathies to familiar groups of allies or opponents. One might say that the primary job of the intellectual historian is to amplify these reverberations, long-muffled with the demise of both principals and audience of the original debate, and thus render them audible to the modern ear. Nor should one presume that such subtle concomitants of political affinity, because not explicitly introduced into the argument, do not have doctrinal repercussions. Though they could hardly be expected to determine doctrine precisely, as might the kind of canonical lists this study has conceded are rarely to be found, they certainly would point the way towards a limited range of doctrinal options, the theoretical specifics likely changing with time but the cumulative degree of divergence among the currents, groups or schools remaining much the same.

Among Augustinians in the thirteenth century the lines of continuity, amorphous though they may be when measured against the expectations of historians like Mandonnet and Gilson, seem furthermore to yield a strange pattern of regularity, at least with regard to the subjects examined in this book. Twice in the course of the narrative presented here is completed a cycle of movement from a period of exploration, with little doctrinal focus or coherence, to one of synthesis, when theoretical consistency and systematic unity are

---

[4] See Introduction, pp. 15–16.

more on display. The largely tentative periods are associated with the work of William of Auvergne and Robert Grosseteste, exploratory in the truest sense of the word, and Henry of Ghent and Vital du Four, perhaps critical rather than exploratory but open to ideological reassessment and experimentation all the same. The periods of synthesis come in the mid-century offensive of Bonaventure and his followers, purveyors of practically the stereotype of Augustinian illumination, and the twenty-year inventive enterprise of William of Ware and Duns Scotus, hardly stereotypical Augustinians but ralliers to a kindred cause in what was still a philosophically Aristotelianizing world.

Of course, the theoretical confections of the moments of synthesis are the more readily reducible to philosophical schemata, and thus the more easily reproducible by medieval or modern scholars searching the past for a defining core of doctrinal orthodoxy. No wonder that both Bonaventure's and Scotus's works have been employed by historians as the basis for establishing canonical lists of teachings for a presumed Augustinian School. Equally unsurprising is the fact that reputed Augustinians from late Middle Ages to post-Neoscholastic twentieth century have looked to Bonaventure and Scotus as favorite ideological types.

Yet if the story told in this book about illumination, science and knowledge of God is true, then whatever the cycles or patterns of recurrence, there is no good reason to privilege one stage over another, times of synthesis over times of exploration or critique. For Augustinianism in the only way sense can be made of the idea for the entire span of the thirteenth century, and in all likelihood beyond, the continuing reality lies in the repeated effort from generation to generation to make contact with elements of the intellectual past and perpetuate collective propensities and disinclinations, broadly ideological but not necessarily determinate in philosophical or theological detail. No simple doctrinal list could possibly reveal such an effort. Required instead is the painstaking comparison of analytical approaches and theoretical concerns over long stretches of time. The work is arduous and the results bound to yield less than apodictic certainty. But the rewards are great for those seeking insight into processes of philosophical development and change. In such a climate, and among investigators with such goals in mind, one can begin to speak meaningfully again of the history of an Augustinian school.

BIBLIOGRAPHY OF WORKS CITED

Primary Sources

Anonymous. *De anima et de potenciis eius*. Ed. René A. Gauthier, "Le traité *De anima et de potenciis eius* d'un maître ès arts (vers 1225)," RSPT 66 (1982): 3–55.

——. *De potentiis animae et obiectis*. Ed. Daniel A. Callus, "The Powers of the Soul. An Early Unpublished Text," RTAM 19 (1952): 131–70.

Anselm. *De veritate*. In *Opera omnia*, ed. Francis S. Schmitt, 1, 173–99. Edinburgh, 1946.

Aristotle. *Analytica posteriora*. Ed. Lorenzo Minio-Paluello and Bernard G. Dod. 2nd ed. Aristoteles Latinus, 4.1–4. Bruges, 1968.

——. *Categoriae vel praedicamenta*. Ed. Lorenzo Minio-Paluello. Aristoteles Latinus, 1.1–5. Bruges, 1961.

——. *De anima*. Ed. William D. Ross. Oxford, 1956.

——. *De interpretatione*. Ed. Lorenzo Minio-Paluello and Gérard Verbeke. Aristoteles Latinus, 2.1–2. Bruges, 1968.

——. *Ethica Nicomachea*. Ed. René A. Gauthier. Aristoteles Latinus, 26.1–3. Leiden, 1972–74.

——. *Metaphysica*. Ed. Gudrun Vuillemin-Diem. Aristoteles Latinus, 25.1–3. Brussels, 1970; Leiden, 1976 and 1995.

——. *Physica*. Ed. Fernand Bossier, Josef Brams and Augustinus Mansion. Aristoteles Latinus, 7.1–2. Bruges, 1957; Leiden, 1990.

Augustine. *De civitate Dei libri XXII*. Eds. B. Dombart and A. Kalb. 2 vols. CC, 47–48. Turnhout, 1955.

——. *De diversis quaestionibus octoginta tribus*. Ed. Almut Mutzenbecher. CC, 44A. Turnhout, 1975.

——. *De Genesi ad litteram*. Ed. Joseph Zycha. CSEL, 28, 3, 2. Vienna, 1894.

——. *De libero arbitrio libri tres*. Ed. William M. Green. CSEL, 74. Vienna, 1956.

——. *De magistro*. Ed. Günther Weigel. CSEL, 77, 1. Vienna, 1961.

——. *De Trinitate libri XV*. Ed. William J. Mountain and Fr. Glorie. 2 vols. CC, 50–50A. Turnhout, 1968.

——. *In Epistolam Joannis ad Parthos tractatus decem*. PL, 35, 1977–2062.

——. *Retractationum libri II*. Ed. Almut Mutzenbecher. CC, 57. Turnhout, 1984.

——. *Soliloquia*. PL, 32, 869–904.

Averroes. *Commentaria in libros de Physico magna. Aristotelis opera cum Averrois commentariis*, 4. Venice, 1562; repr. Frankfurt am Main, 1962.

——. *Commentarium magnum in Aristotelis De anima libros*. Ed. F. Stuart Crawford. Corpus Commentariorum Averrois in Aristotelem, Versionum Latinarum, 6.1. Cambridge, Mass., 1953.

Avicenna. *Liber de anima seu sextus de naturalibus*. Ed. Simone Van Riet. 2 vols. Avicenna Latinus. Leiden, 1972 and 1968.

——. *Liber de philosophia prima sive scientia divina*. Ed. Simone Van Riet. 2 vols. Avicenna Latinus. Leiden, 1977 and 1980.

Bacon, Roger. *Opus maius*. Ed. John H. Bridges. 3 vols. Oxford, 1897, and London, 1900.

——. *Opus tertium*. In *Opera quaedam hactenus inedita*, ed. J.S. Brewer, 1, 3–310. London, 1859.

Boethius. *In Categorias Aristotelis libri quatuor*. PL, 64, 159–294.

Bonaventure. *Collationes de septem donis Spiritus Sancti.* In Opera Omnia, 5, 455–503. Quaracchi, 1981.

——. *Collationes in Hexaëmeron.* In Opera Omnia, 5, 327–449. Quaracchi, 1891.

——. *Collationes in Hexaëmeron et Bonaventuriana quaedam selecta.* Ed. Ferdinand Delorme. Quaracchi, 1934.

——. *Commentaria in quatuor libros Sententiarum.* 4 vols. Opera Omnia, 1–4. Quaracchi, 1882, 1885, 1887, 1889.

——. *Itinerarium mentis in Deum.* In Opera Omnia, 5, 293–313. Quaracchi, 1891.

——. *Quaestiones disputatae de mysterio Trinitatis.* In Opera Omnia, 5, 45–115. Quaracchi, 1891.

——. *Quaestiones disputatae de scientia Christi.* In Opera Omnia, 5, 3–43. Quaracchi, 1891.

——. "Sermo, Christus unus omnium magister." In Opera Omnia, 5, 567–74. Quaracchi, 1891.

——. *Sermones de tempore, de sanctis, de B. Virgine Maria et de diversis.* Opera Omnia, 9. Quaracchi, 1901.

——. "Unus est magister vester Christus." Ed. Renato Russo, in *La metodologia del sapere nel sermone di S. Bonaventura "Unus est magister vester Christus"*, 100–132. Grottaferrata, 1982.

Conington, Richard of. *Quaestiones ordinariae*, q. 1. Ed. Victorin Doucet, "L'oeuvre scolastique de Richard de Conington, O.F.M.," AFH 29 (1936): 430–38.

——. *Quodlibet I*, q. 2. Ed. Stephen F. Brown, "Richard of Conington and the Analogy of the Concept of Being," FS 48 (1966): 300–307.

Damascene, John. *De fide orthodoxa. Versions of Burgundio and Cerbanus.* Ed. Eligius M. Buytaert. St. Bonaventure, N.Y., 1955.

Duns Scotus, John. *Collationes.* In Opera Omnia (Vivès), 5, 129–317. Paris, 1892.

——. *Collationes Parisienses et Oxonienses.* In Charles Balić, "De Collationibus Ioannis Duns Scoti doctoris subtilis ac mariani," *Bogoslovni Vestnik* 19 (1929): 201–19.

——. *Collationes Parisienses et Oxonienses.* In Charles R.S. Harris, *Duns Scotus*, 2, 361–78. Oxford, 1927.

——. *In duos libros Perihermenias, operis secundi, quaestiones octo.* In Opera Omnia (Vivès), 1, 581–601. Paris, 1891.

——. *In libros Elenchorum quaestiones.* In Opera Omnia (Vivès), 2, 1–80. Paris, 1891.

——. *In librum Praedicamentorum quaestiones.* In Opera Omnia (Vivès), 1, 437–538. Paris, 1891.

——. *In primum librum Perihermenias quaestiones.* In Opera Omnia (Vivès), 1, 539–69. Paris, 1891.

——. *Lectura in librum primum Sententiarum.* Opera Omnia (Vatican), 16–17. Vatican City, 1960 and 1966.

——. *Lectura in librum secundum Sententiarum.* Opera Omnia (Vatican), 18–19. Vatican City, 1982 and 1993.

——. *Ordinatio.* Opera Omnia (Vatican), 1–. Vatican City, 1950–.

——. *Quaestiones in quatuor libros Sententiarum (Ordinatio).* Opera Omnia (Vivès), 8–21. Paris, 1893–94.

——. *Quaestiones quodlibetales.* Opera Omnia (Vivès), 25–26. Paris, 1895.

——. *Quaestiones super libros Metaphysicorum Aristotelis.* Eds. R. Andrews et al. Opera Philosophica (Opera Phil.), 3–4. St. Bonaventure, N.Y., 1997.

——. *Reportatio examinata* (Reportatio 1A) I, dist. 2, qq. 1–4. In Allan B. Wolter and Marilyn McCord Adams, "Duns Scotus' Parisian Proof for the Existence of God," FrS 42 (1982): 252–321.

——. *Reportatio parisiensis.* Opera Omnia (Vivès), 22–24. Paris, 1894.

——. *Super Universalia Porphyrii quaestiones.* In Opera Omnia (Vivès), 1, 51–435. Paris, 1891.

Gilbert of Tournai. *Rudimentum doctrinae* (excerpts from Pars I, tr. 1). Ed. Servus

Gieben, "Four Chapters on Philosophical Errors from the Rudimentum Doctrinae of Gilbert of Tournai O. Min. (died 1284)," *Vivarium* 1 (1963): 148–64.

———. *Rudimentum doctrinae* (excerpts from Pars I, tr. 2–3). Ed. Servus Gieben, "Guibert de Tournai et Robert Grosseteste. Sources inconnues de la doctrine de l'illumination suivi de l'Edition critique de trois chapitres du Rudimentum Doctrinae de Guibert de Tournai," in *S. Bonaventura, 1274–1974*, 2, 643–54. Grottaferrata, 1973.

Giles of Rome. *Questiones de cognitione angelorum*. In *De esse et essentia, De mensura angelorum, et De cognitione angelorum*, ff. 76b–119b. Venice, 1503; repr. Frankfurt am Main, 1968.

———. *Questiones de esse et essentia*. In *De esse et essentia, De mensura angelorum, et De cognitione angelorum*, ff. 2a–35d. Venice, 1503; repr. Frankfurt am Main, 1968.

Grosseteste, Robert. *Commentarius in Posteriorum analyticorum libros (Comm. Post. an.)*. Ed. Pietro B. Rossi. Corpus Philosophorum Medii Aevi, Testi e Studi, 2. Florence, 1981.

———. *Commentary on De divinis nominibus* (c. 1 and excerpt from c. 5); and *Commentary on Angelica hierarchia* (excerpt from c. 2). Ed. Francis Ruello, "La *divinorum nominum reseratio* selon Robert Grossetête et Albert le Grand," AHDLMA 25 (1959): 134–71, 177–78, 194–97.

———. "Ecclesia sancta celebrat." Ed. James McEvoy, "Robert Grosseteste's Theory of Human Nature," RTAM 47 (1980): 169–87.

———. *Epistolae*. Ed. Henry R. Luard. London, 1861.

———. "Ex rerum initiarum." Ed. Servus Gieben, "Robert Grosseteste on Preaching," CF 37 (1967): 120–41.

———. *Hexaëmeron*. Ed. Richard C. Dales and Servus Gieben. Auctores Britannici Medii Aevi, 6. London, 1982.

———. *Die philosophischen Werke des Robert Grosseteste, Bischofs von Lincoln (Phil. Werke)*. Ed. Ludwig Baur. Beiträge, 9. Münster, 1912.

———. *Quaestiones theologicae*. Ed. Daniel A. Callus, "The *summa theologiae* of Robert Grosseteste," in *Studies in Medieval History Presented to Frederick Maurice Powicke*, 180–208. Oxford, 1948.

———. *Super Dionysium De caelesti hierarchia* (excerpt from c. 4). Ed. Hyacinthe-François Dondaine, "L'objet et le 'medium' de la vision béatifique chez les théologiens du XIIIe siècle," RTAM 19 (1952): 124–25.

Henry of Ghent. *Quodlibet I*. Ed. Raymond Macken. Henrici Opera, 5. Leuven, 1979.

———. *Quodlibet II*. Ed. Robert Wielockx. Henrici Opera, 6. Leuven, 1983.

———. *Quodlibet VI*. Ed. Gordon A. Wilson. Henrici Opera, 10. Leuven, 1987.

———. *Quodlibet VII*. Ed. Gordon A. Wilson. Henrici Opera, 11. Leuven, 1991.

———. *Quodlibet IX*. Ed. Raymond Macken. Henrici Opera, 13. Leuven, 1983.

———. *Quodlibet X*. Ed. Raymond Macken. Henrici Opera, 14. Leuven, 1981.

———. *Quodlibet XII*. Ed. Jos Decorte. Henrici Opera, 16. Leuven, 1987.

———. *Quodlibet XIII*. Ed. Jos Decorte. Henrici Opera, 18. Leuven, 1985.

———. *Quodlibeta (Quod.)*. 2 vols. Paris, 1518; repr. Leuven, 1961.

———. *Summa (Quaestiones ordinariae), art. XXXI–XXXIV*. Ed. Raymond Macken. Henrici Opera, 27. Leuven, 1991.

———. *Summa quaestionum ordinariarum (Summa)*. 2 vols. Paris, 1520; repr. St. Bonaventure, N.Y., 1953.

———. *Tractatus super facto praelatorum et fratrum*. Ed. Ludwig Hödl and Marcel Haverals. Henrici Opera, 17. Leuven, 1989.

John of La Rochelle. *Summa de anima*. Ed. Jacques Guy Bougerol. Paris, 1995.

———. *Summa de anima*. Ed. Teofilo Domenichelli. Prato, 1882.

———. *Tractatus de divisione multiplici potentiarum animae*. Ed. Pierre Michaud-Quantin. Paris, 1964.

Liber de causis. Ed. Adriaan Pattin. Leuven, 1966.

Marston, Roger. *Quaestiones de anima*. In Roger Marston, *Quaestiones disputatae de emanatione aeterna, de statu naturae lapsae et de anima*, 201–454. BFS, 7. Quaracchi, 1932.

Matthew of Aquasparta. *Animadversiones ad libr. I Sententiarum*. In Matthew of Aquasparta, *Quaestiones disputatae de gratia*, ed. Victorin Doucet, LXXXV–LXXXVII. BFS, 11. Quaracchi, 1935.

——. *Commentarius in librum I. Sententiarum*. Ms. Todi, Bibl. com. 122 (ff. 3r–165r).

——. *Commentarius in librum II. Sententiarum*. Ms. Assisi, Bibl. com. 132 (ff. 1r–225v).

——. *Quaestiones de anima beata*. Ed. Aquilinus Emmen. In Matthew of Aquasparta, *Quaestiones disputatae de anima separata, de anima beata, de ieiunio et de legibus*, ed. Gedeon Gàl et al. BFS, 18. Quaracchi, 1959.

——. *Quaestiones de cognitione*. In *Quaestiones disputatae de fide et de cognitione*, 199–406. 2nd ed. BFS, 1. Quaracchi, 1957.

——. *Quaestiones de fide*. In *Quaestiones disputatae de fide et de cognitione*, 35–198. 2nd ed. BFS, 1. Quaracchi, 1957.

——. *Quaestiones de productione rerum*. In Matthew of Aquasparta, *Quaestiones disputatae de productione rerum et de providentia*, ed. Gedeon Gál, 1–227. BFS, 17. Quaracchi, 1956.

——. *Quaestiones disputatae de gratia*. Ed. Victorin Doucet. BFS, 11. Quaracchi, 1935.

——. *Quodlibet IV*. Ms. Todi, Bibl. com. 44 (ff. 213v–223r).

Mediavilla, Richard of. *Super quatuor libros Sententiarum quaestiones subtilissimae*. 4 vols. Brescia, 1591; repr. Frankfurt, 1963.

Olivi, Petrus Ioannis. *Quaestiones in secundum librum Sententiarum*. Ed. Bernhard Jansen. 3 vols. BFS, 4–6. Quaracchi, 1922, 1924 and 1926.

Pecham, John. *In I. Sententiarum*, d. 2, qq. 1a and 1aa. Ed. Augustinus Daniels, *Quellenbeiträge und Untersuchungen zur Geschichte der Gottesbeweise im dreizehnten Jahrhundert*, 41–50. Beiträge, 8.1–2. Münster, 1909.

——. *In I. Sententiarum*, d. 3, qq. 3 and 3a. In John Pecham, *Tractatus de anima*, ed. Gaudenzio Melani, 131–38. Florence, 1948.

——. *In I. Sententiarum*, quaestiones selectae. In John Pecham, *Quaestiones tractantes de anima*, ed. Hieronymus Spettmann, 183–221. Beiträge, 19.5–6. Münster, 1918.

——. *Quaestiones de anima*. In John Pecham *Quaestiones tractantes de anima*, ed. Hieronymus Spettmann, 1–104. Beiträge, 19.5–6. Münster, 1918.

——. *Quaestiones de beatitudine corporis et animae*. In John Pecham *Quaestiones tractantes de anima*, ed. Hieronymus Spettmann, 107–80. Beiträge, 19.5–6. Münster, 1918.

——. *Quodlibet Romanum*. Ed. Ferdinand M. Delorme. Rome, 1938.

——. *Quodlibeta quatuor*. Eds. Girard J. Etzkorn and Ferdinand Delorme. BFS, 25. Grottaferrata, 1989.

——. *Registrum epistolarum*. Ed. C. Trice Martin. 3 vols. London, 1882, 1884, 1885.

——. *Tractatus de anima*. Ed. Gaudenzio Melani. Florence, 1948.

Thomas Aquinas. *Commentarium in libros Posteriorum analyticorum*. Opera Omnia (Leonine edition), 1. Rome, 1882.

Vital du Four. *Quaestiones 8 de cognitione*. Ed. Ferdinand M. Delorme, "Le Cardinal Vital du Four. Huit questions disputées sur le problème de la connaissance," AHDLMA 2 (1927): 156–336.

——. *Quodlibeta tria*. Ed. Ferdinand M. Delorme. Spicilegium Pontificii Athenaei Antoniani, 5. Rome, 1947.

William of Auvergne. *De anima*. Mag. div., 2, supp., 65–228.

——. *De bono et malo (Tractatus primus)*. Ed. J. Reginald O'Donnell. In MS 8 (1946): 245–99.

——. *De retributionibus sanctorum*. Mag. div., 1, 315–28.

——. *De Trinitate*. Ed. Bruno Switalski. Toronto, 1976.

——. *De universo*. Mag. div., 1, 593–1074.

———. *De virtutibus. Mag. div.*, 1, 102–91.

William of Ware. *In primum librum Sententiarum*, dd. 26, qq. 2–3; 27, qq. 1 and 3; 28, qq. 1–3. Ed. Michael Schmaus, *Der Liber propugnatorius des Thomas Anglicus und die Lehrunterschiede zwischen Thomas von Aquin und Duns Scotus*, Vol. 2, *Die Trinitarischen Lehrdifferenzen*, 234*–85*. Beiträge, 29. Münster, 1930.

———. *Quaestiones super quatuor libros Sententiarum*, qq. 14 and 21. Ed. Augustinus Daniels, *Quellenbeiträge und Untersuchungen zur Geschichte der Gottesbeweise im dreizehnten Jahrhundert*, 89–104. Beiträge, 8.1–2. Münster, 1909.

———. *Quaestiones super quatuor libros Sententiarum*, q. 15. Ed. Pierre Muscat, "Guillelmi de Ware quaestio inedita de unitate Dei," *Antonianum* 2 (1927): 344–50.

———. *Quaestiones super quatuor libros Sententiarum*, q. 19. Ed. Augustinus Daniels, "Wilhelm von Ware über das menschliche Erkennen," *Festgabe zum 60. Geburtstag Clemens Baeumker*, 311–18. Beiträge, Supplementband, 1. Münster, 1913.

———. *Quaestiones super quatuor libros Sententiarum*. Ms. Bibl. Vat., Chigi. B.VIII.135 (ff. 1r–160v).

———. *Quaestiones super quatuor libros Sententiarum*. Ms. Bibl. Vat., Chigi. B.VII.114 (ff. 1r–204r).

Secondary Works

Adams, Marilyn McCord. *William Ockham*. 2 vols. Notre Dame, Ind., 1987.

"Adnotationes." In John Duns Scotus, *Ordinatio*, Opera Omnia (Vatican), 7, 1*–10*. Rome, 1973.

Alluntis, Felix, and Wolter, Allan B. "Introduction." In John Duns Scotus, *God and Creatures. The Quodlibetal Questions*, xvii–xxxiv. Princeton, 1975.

Baeumker, Clemens. "Jahresbericht über die abendländische Philosophie im Mittelalter. 1890." *Archiv für Geschichte der Philosophie* 5 (1892): 113–38.

Balić, Charles. "Circa positiones fundamentales I. Duns Scoti." *Antonianum* 28 (1953): 261–306.

———. "De Collationibus Ioannis Duns Scoti doctoris subtilis ac mariani." *Bogoslovni Vestnik* 19 (1929): 185–219.

———. "The Life and Works of John Duns Scotus." In *John Duns Scotus, 1265–1965*, ed. John K. Ryan and Bernardine M. Bonansea, 1–27. Washington, D.C., 1965.

———. "Quelques précisions fournies par la tradition manuscrite sur la vie, les oeuvres et l'attitude doctrinale de Jean Duns Scot." *Revue d'Histoire Ecclésiastique* 22 (1926): 551–66.

Barth, Timotheus. "Being, Univocity, and Analogy according to Duns Scotus." In *John Duns Scotus, 1265–1965*, eds. John K. Ryan and Bernardine M. Bonansea, 210–62. Washington, D.C., 1965.

———. "De argumentis et univocationis entis natura apud Joannem Duns Scotum." *CF* 14 (1944): 5–56.

———. "De fundamento univocationis apud Ioannem Duns Scotum." *Antonianum* 14 (1938): 181–206, 277–98 and 373–92.

———. "De tribus viis diversis existentiam divinam attingendi. Disquisitio historico-collativa inter S. Thomam, Henricum Gandavensem, Duns Scotum." *Antonianum* 18 (1943): 91–117.

———. "De univocationis entis scotisticae intentione principali necnon valore critico." *Antonianum* 28 (1953): 72–110.

———. "Duns Scotus und die ontologische Grundlage unserer Verstandeserkenntnis." *FS* 33 (1951): 348–84.

———. "Die Stellung der unovicatio im Verlauf der Gotteserkenntnis nach der lehre des Duns Skotus." *WuW* 5 (1938): 235–54.

——. "Zum Problem der Eindeutigkeit." *Philosophisches Jahrbuch* 55 (1942): 300–321.

——. "Zur univocatio entis bei Johannes Duns Scotus." WuW 21 (1958): 95–108.

Baudry, L. "Wibert de Tournai." *Revue d'Histoire Franciscaine* 5 (1928): 23–61.

Baumgartner, Matthias. *Die Erkenntnislehre des Wilhelm von Auvergne.* Beiträge 2.1. Münster, 1893.

Baur, Ludwig. *Die Philosophie des Robert Grosseteste, Bischofs von Lincoln.* Beiträge 18.4–6. Münster, 1917.

Bayersmidt, Paul. *Die Seins- und Formmetaphysik des Heinrich von Gent in ihrer Anwendung auf die Christologie.* Beiträge, 36.3–4. Münster, 1941.

Beha, Helen Marie. "Matthew of Aquaspart's Theory of Cognition." FrS 20 (1960): 161–204; 21 (1961): 1–79 and 383–465.

Bellofiore, Luigi. "La dottrina dell'illuminzione dell'intelletto in S. Bonaventura." *Sophia* 6 (1938): 535–37: 7 (1939): 172–87.

Belmond, Séraphin. "Duns Scot métaphysicien." *Revue de Philosophie* 36 (1929): 405–23.

——. *Etudes sur la philosophie de Duns Scot.* Vol. 1, *Dieu: Existence et cognoscibilité.* Paris, 1913.

——. "Le scotisme philosophique manque-t-il de cohérence?" EF 49 (1937): 178–88.

——. "Simples remarques sur l'idéologie comparée de saint Thomas et de Duns Scot." *Revue de Philosophie* 24 (1914): 242–60.

Bérubé, Camille. "De l'être à Dieu chez Jean Duns Scot." In *Regnum hominis et Regnum Dei,* ed. Camille Bérubé, I, 47–70. Acta Quarti Congressus Scotistici Internationalis. Rome, 1978. (Also in *De l'homme à Dieu,* 291–310.)

——. *De l'homme à Dieu selon Duns Scot, Henri de Gand et Olivi.* Bibliotheca Seraphico-Cappuccina, 27. Rome, 1983.

——. *De la philosophie à la sagesse chez saint Bonaventure et Roger Bacon.* Bibliotheca Seraphico-Cappuccina, 26. Rome, 1976.

——. "De la théologie de l'image à la philosophie de l'objet de l'intelligence chez saint Bonaventure." In *S. Bonaventura 1274–1974,* 3, 161–200. Grottaferrata, 1973. (Also in *De la philosphie à la sagesse,* 163–900.)

——. "Dynamisme psychologique et existence de Dieu chez Jean Duns Scot, J. Maréchal et B. Lonergan." *Antonianum* 48 (1973): 5–45. (Also in *De l'homme à Dieu,* 185–223.)

——. "Henri de Gand et Mathieu d'Aquasparta interprètes de saint Bonaventure." *Naturaleza y Gracia* 21 (1974): 131–72.

——. "Jean Duns Scot: Critique de l'"avicennisme augustinisant.'" In *De doctrina Ioannis Duns Scoti,* I, 207–43. Acta Congressus Scotistici Internationalis, Oxford/Edinburgh, 11–17 September 1966. Rome, 1968. (Also in *De l'homme à Dieu,* 113–46.)

——. "Olivi, critique de Bonaventure et d'Henri de Gand." In *Studies Honoring Ignatius Charles Brady Friar Minor,* ed. Romano S. Almagno and Conrad L. Harkins, 57–121. St. Bonaventure, N.Y., 1976. (Also in *De l'homme à Dieu,* 19–79.)

——. "Olivi, interprète de saint Anselme." In *Die Wirkungsgeschichte Anselms von Canterbury,* 147–58. Akten des ersten internationalen Anselmus-Tagung, 13–16 September 1970. (Also in *De l'homme à Dieu,* pp. 225–39.)

——. "Pour une histoire des preuves de l'existence de Dieu chez Duns Scot." In *Deus et homo ad mentem I. Duns Scoti,* 17–46. Acta Tertii Congressus Scotistici Internationalis, Vienna, 28 September-2 October 1970. (Also in *De l'homme à Dieu,* 241–79.) Rome, 1972.

Bérubé, Camille, and Gieben, Servus. "Guibert de Tournai et Robert Grosseteste. Sources inconnues de la doctrine de l'illumination suivi de l'Edition critique de trois chapitres du Rudimentum Doctrinae de Guibert de Tournai" In *S. Bonaventura, 1274–1974,* 2, 626–54. Grottaferrata, 1973.

Bettoni, Efrem. "De argumentatione Doctoris Subtilis quoad existentiam Dei." *Antonianum* 28 (1953): 39–58.

——. "La dottrina bonaventuriana dell'illuminazione intellettuale." RFN 36 (1944): 139–58.

——. *Le dottrine filosofiche di Pier di Giovanni Olivi*. Milan, 1959.

——. *Duns Scoto*. Brescia, 1946.

——. *Duns Scoto filosofo*. Milan, 1966.

——. "Duns Scoto nella scolastica del secolo XIII." In *De doctrina Ioannis Duns Scoti*, 1, 101–11. Acta Congressus Scotistici Internationalis, Oxford/Edinburgh, 11–17 September 1966. Rome, 1968.

——. *Duns Scotus. The Basic Principles of his Philosophy*. Trans. Bernardino M. Bonansea. Washington, D.C., 1961.

——. "Il fondamento della conoscenza umana secondo Duns Scoto." FS 47 (1965): 300–314.

——. "Introduzione." In Bonaventure, *L'ascesa a Dio*, ed. Efrem Bettoni, vii–xxxi. Milan, 1974.

——. "Matteo d'Acquasparta e il suo posto nella scolastica post-tomistica." *Filosofia e cultura in Umbria tra Medioevo e Rinascimento*, 231–48. Atti del IV Convegno di Studi Umbri, Gubbio, 22–26 May 1996. Perugia, 1967.

——. "Oggetto e soggetto nell'atto intellettivo secondo Duns Scoto." SF 39 (1942): 3–31.

——. "The Originality of the Scotistic Synthesis." In *John Duns Scotus, 1265–1965*, ed. John K. Ryan and Bernardino M. Bonansea, 28–44. Washington, D.C., 1965.

——. "La posizione storica di Duns Scoto nel problema della conoscenza." SF 39 (1942): 97–109.

——. "Il problema degli universali in Duns Scoto." SF 38 (1941): 37–63.

——. *Il problema della conoscibilità di Dio nella Scuola Francescana*. Padua, 1950.

——. *Il processo astrattivo nella concezione di Enrico di Gand*. Milan, 1954.

——. "Punti di contatto fra la dottrina bonaventuriana dell'illuminazione e la dottrina scotista dell'univocità." In SRHCI, 519–32.

——. "Rapporti dottrinali fra Matteo d'Acquasparta e Giovanni Duns Scoto." SF Ser. 3, 15 (1943): 113–30.

——. *S. Bonaventura da Bagnoregio. Gli aspetti filosofici del suo pensiero*. Milan, 1973.

——. *S. Bonaventura*. Brescia, 1945.

——. *Saint Bonaventure*. Trans. Angelus Gambatese. Notre Dame, 1964; repr. Westport, Conn., 1981.

——. *Vent'anni di studi scotisti (1920–1940)*. Milan, 1943.

Beumer, Johannes. "Robert Grosseteste von Lincoln der angebliche Begründer der Franziskanerschule." FS 57 (1975): 183–95.

Bianchi, Luca. "1277. A Turning Point in Medieval Philosophy?" In *Was ist Philosophie im Mittelalter?* eds. Jan A. Aertsen and Andreas Speer, 90–110. Akten des X. Internationalen Kongresses für mittelalterliche Philosophie. Miscellanea Mediaevalia, 26. Berlin, 1998.

Boehner, Philotheus. *The History of the Franciscan School*. 2 vols. Typescript, St. Bonaventure, N.Y., 1943.

——. "The Spirit of Franciscan Philosophy." FrS 2 (1942): 217–37.

Bonafede, Giulio. "La gnoseologia di Matteo d'Acquasparta." In *Filosofia e cultura in Umbria tra Medioevo e Rinascimento*, 249–69. Atti del IV Convegno di Studi Umbri, Gubbio, 22–26 May 1966. Perugia, 1967.

——. *Il pensiero francescano nel secolo XIII*. Palermo, 1952.

——. "Il problema dell'illuminazione in S. Bonaventura." *Sophia* 4 (1936): 78–82; 5 (1937): 48–55.

Bonansea, Bernardino M. *Man and his Approach to God in John Duns Scotus*. Lanham, Md., 1983.

Borak, Hadrianus. "Aspectus fundamentales platonismi in doctrina Duns Scoti." In

De doctrina Ioannis Duns Scoti, 1, 113–38. Acta Congressus Scotistici Internationalis, Oxford/Edinburgh, 11–17 September 1966. Rome, 1968.

——. "De radice ontologica contingentiae." *Laurentianum* 2 (1969): 122–45.

——. "Metaphysischer Aufbau des Seinsbegriffes bei Duns Scotus." WuW 28 (1965): 39–54.

Borok, Helmut. *Der Tugendbegriff des Wilhelm von Auvergne (1180–1249). Eine moralhistorische Untersuchung zur ideengeschichtlichen Rezeption der aristotelischen Ethik.* Düsseldorf, 1979.

Bougerol, Jacques Guy. "Introduction." In John of La Rochelle, *Summa de anima*, ed. Jacques G. Bougerol, 7–43. Paris, 1995.

——. *Introduction a l'étude de Saint Bonaventure.* Tournai, 1961.

——. "Jean de La Rochelle. Les oeuvres et les manuscrits." AFH 87 (1994): 205–15.

Boulnois, Olivier, intr., trans. and comm. for Jean Duns Scot, *Sur la connaissance de Dieu et l'univocité de l'étant.* Paris, 1988.

Bourgeois, Robert. "La théorie de la connaissance intellectuelle chez Henri de Gand." *Revue de Philosophie* n.s. 6 (1936): 238–59.

Brady, Ignatius C. "Questions at Paris c. 1260–1270 (cod. Flor. Bibl. Naz. Conv. sopp. B.6.912)." AFH 61 (1968): 434–61; 62 (1969): 357–76 and 678–92.

——. "St. Bonaventure's Doctrine of Illumination: Reactions Medieval and Modern." In *Bonaventure and Aquinas. Enduring Philosophers*, ed. Robert W. Shahan and Francis J. Kovach, 57–67. Norman, Oklahoma, 1976.

Brampton, C.K. "Duns Scotus at Oxford, 1288–1301." FrS 24 (1964): 5–20.

Braun, Raphael. *Die Erkenntnislehre des Heinrich von Gent.* Fribourg, 1916.

Brown, Jerome V. "Abstraction and the Object of the Human Intellect according to Henry of Ghent." *Vivarium* 11 (1973): 80–104.

——. "Duns Scotus on the Possibility of Knowing Genuine Truth: The Reply to Henry of Ghent in the 'Lectura Prima' and in the 'Ordinatio.'" RTAM 51 (1984): 136–82.

——. "Henry of Ghent on Internal Sensation." *Journal of the History of Philosophy* 10 (1972): 15–28.

——. "John Duns Scotus on Henry of Ghent's Arguments for Divine Illumination: The Statement of the Case." *Vivarium* 14 (1976): 94–113.

——. "John Duns Scotus on Henry of Ghent's Theory of Knowledge." *The Modern Schoolman* 56 (1978–79): 1–29.

——. "Sensation in Henry of Ghent: A Late Medieval Aristotelian-Augustinian Synthesis." *Archiv für Geschichte der Philosophie* 53 (1971): 238–66.

Brown, Stephen F. "Avicenna and the Unity of the Concept of Being. The Interpretations of Henry of Ghent, Duns Scotus, Gerard of Bologna and Peter Aureoli." FrS 25 (1965): 117–50.

——. "Richard of Conington and the Analogy of the Concept of Being." FS 48 (1966): 297–307.

——. "Scotus' Univocity in the Early Fourteenth Century." In *De doctrina Ioannis Duns Scoti*, 4, 35–41. Acta Congressus Scotistici Internationalis, Oxford/Edinburgh, 11–17 September 1966. Rome, 1968.

——. "Sources for Ockham's Prologue to the Sentences." FrS 26 (1966): 36–65.

Burr, David. *The Persecution of Peter Olivi.* Transactions of the American Philosophical Society, n.s. 66, 5. Philadelphia, 1976.

Butterfield, Herbert. *The Origins of Modern Science, 1300–1800.* London, 1949.

Callebaut, André. "Le B. Jean Duns Scot étudiant à Paris vers 1293–96." AFH 17 (1947): 3–12.

Callus, Daniel A. "The Date of Grosseteste's Translations and Commentaries on Pseudo-Dionysius and the Nichomachean Ethics," RTAM 14 (1947): 186–210.

——. "The Powers of the Soul. An Early Unpublished Text." RTAM 19 (1952): 131–70.

——. "The *summa theologiae* of Robert Grosseteste." In *Studies in Medieval History Presented to Frederick Maurice Powicke*, 180–208. Oxford, 1948.

Cannizzo, Giuseppina. "La dottrina del 'verbum mentis' in Enrico di Gand." RFN 54 (1962): 243–66.

Catto, J. I. "Theology and Theologians 1220–1320." In *The History of the University of Oxford*, vol. 1, *The Early Oxford Schools*, ed. J.I. Catto, 471–517. Oxford, 1984.

Châtillon, Jean. "Saint Bonaventure et la philosophie." In *San Bonaventura maestro di vita francescana e di sapienza cristiana*, ed. Alfonso Pompei, I, 429–46. Atti del Congresso Internazionale, Rome, 19–26 September 1974. Rome, 1976.

Chenu, Marie-Dominique. *Nature, Man, and Society in the Twelfth Century*. Chicago, 1968.

——. *La théologie au douzième siècle*. 2nd ed. Paris, 1966.

"Conington, Richard de." In *A Biographical Register of the University of Oxford to A.D. 1500*, ed. A.B. Emden, 1, 447. Oxford, 1957.

Copleston, Frederick C. *A History of Philosophy*. Vol. 2, *Medieval Philosophy*. Westminster, Maryland, 1950.

Corti, Guglielmo. "Le sette parti del *Magisterium divinale ac sapientiale* di Guglielmo di Auvergne." *Studi e ricerche di scienze religiose*, 289–307. Rome 1968.

Corvino, Francesco. *Bonaventura da Bagnoregio francescano e pensatore*. Bari, 1980.

Cottingham, John, ed. *The Cambridge Companion to Descartes*. Cambridge, 1992.

——. *Descartes*. Oxford, 1998.

Courtenay, William J. "Scotus at Paris." In *Via Scoti. Methodologica ad mentem Joannis Duns Scoti*, ed. Leonardo Sileo, 1, 149–63. Atti del Congresso Scotistico Internationale, Rome, 9–11 March 1993. Rome, 1995.

——. "Theology and Theologians from Ockham to Wyclif." In *The History of the University of Oxford*, Vol. 1, *Late Medieval Oxford*, eds. J.I. Catto and Ralph Evans, 1–34. Oxford, 1992.

——. "Was There an Ockhamist School?" In *Philosophy and Learning. Universities in the Middle Ages*, eds. Maarten J.F.M. Hoenen, J.H. Josef Schneider and Georg Wieland, 263–92. Leiden, 1995.

Cousins, Ewert H. "St. Bonaventure, St. Thomas, and the Movement of Thought in the 13th Century." *In Bonaventure and Aquinas. Enduring Philosophers*, eds. Robert W. Shahan and Francis J. Kovach, 5–23. Norman, Okla., 1976.

Crombie, Alistair C. *Robert Grosseteste and the Origins of Experimental Science, 1100–1700*. Oxford, 1953.

Crowley, Theodore. "St. Bonaventure Chronology Reappraised." FS 56 (1974): 310–22.

Daniels, Augustinus. "Zu den Beziehungen zwischen Wilhelm von Ware und Johannes Duns Skotus." FS 4 (1917): 221–38.

Day, Sebastian J. *Intuitive Cognition. A Key to the Significance of the Later Scholastics*. St. Bonaventure, N.Y., 1947.

de Basly, Déodat. "L'intuition de l'extramental matériel." EF 48 (1936): 267–79.

de Courcerault, Raymond. "L'ontologie de Duns Scot et le principe du panthéisme." EF 24 (1910): 141–49 and 423–39.

Delehaye, Hippolyte. "Notes sur Henri de Gand." *Messager des Sciences Historiques ou Archives des Arts et de la Bibliographie de Belgique* (1888): 421–56.

——. "Nouvelles recherches sur Henri de Gand." *Messager des Sciences Historiques ou Archives des Arts et de la Bibliographie de Belgique* (1886): 328–55 and 438–55; (1887): 59–85.

de Libera, Alain. *Penser au moyen âge*. Paris, 1991.

Delisle, Léopold. "Das Pariser Nationalkonzil vom Jahre 1290." *Journal des Savants* (1895): 240–44.

Delorme, Ferdinand M. "Le Cardinal Vital du Four. Huit questions disputées sur le problème de la connaissance." AHDLMA 2 (1927): 151–337.

——. "Introductio." In John Pecham, *Quodlibet Romanum*, ed. Ferdinand M. Delorme, XVIII–LI. Rome, 1938.

——. "L'oeuvre scolastique de maître Vital du Four d'après le MS. 95 de Todi." *La France Franciscaine* 9 (1926): 421–71.

——. "Praefatio." In Vital du Four, *Quodlibeta tria*, ed. Ferdinand M. Delorme, V–XXII. Spicilegium Pontificii Athenaei Antoniani, 5. Rome, 1947.

——. "Les questions brèves 'De rerum principio' du Cardinal Vital du Four." *Sophia* 10 (1942): 290–327.

——. "Le Quodlibet I du Cardinal Vital du Four." *La France Franciscaine* 18 (1935): 105–44.

——. "Quodlibets et questions disputées de Raymond Rigaut, maître franciscain de Paris, d'après le Ms. 98 de la Bibl. Comm. de Todi." In *Aus der Geisteswelt des Mittelalters. Studien und Texte Martin Grabmann . . . gewidmet*, ed. Albert Lang et al., 2, 826–41. Beiträge, Supplementband 3.2. Münster, 1935.

"De ordinatione I. Duns Scoti disquisitio historico-critica." In John Duns Scotus, *Ordinatio*, Opera Omnia (Vatican), 1, 1*–329*. Rome, 1950.

De Pauw, Napoléon. "Dernières découvertes concernant le Docteur solennel Henri de Gand, fils de Jean le Tailleur (Formator ou de Sceppere)." *Bulletin de la Commision Royale d'Histoire* (Brussels) 4th ser., 16 (1889): 27–138.

——. "Note sur le vrai nom du Docteur solennel Henri de Gand." *Bulletin de la Commision Royale d'Histoire* (Brussels) 4th ser., 15 (1888): 135–45.

De Wulf, Maurice. "L'augustinisme 'avicennisant." RNS 33 (1931): 11–39.

——. "Augustinisme et aristotélisme au XIIIᵉ siècle." RNS 8 (1901): 151–66.

——. "Courants doctrinaux dans la philosophie européenne du XIIIᵉ siècle." RNS 34 (1932): 5–20.

——. "L'exemplarisme et la théorie de l'illumination spéciale dans la philosophie de Henri de Gand." RNS 1 (1894): 53–75.

——. *Histoire de la philosophie en Belgique*. Brussels, 1910.

——. *Histoire de la philosophie scolastique dans les Pays-Bas et la Principauté de Liège jusqu'à la Révolution Française*. Mémoires Couronnés et Autres Mémoires publiés par l'Académie Royale des Sciences, des Lettres et des Beaux-Arts de Belgique, 51. Brussels, 1894–95.

——. *Medieval Philosophy. Illustrated from the System of Thomas Aquinas*. Cambridge, Mass., 1922.

——. *Philosophy and Civilization in the Middle Ages*. Princeton, 1922.

——. "Qu'est-ce que la philosophie scolastique?" RNS 5 (1898): 141–53, 282–96.

Distelbrink, Balduinus. *Bonaventurae scripta authenticia dubia vel spuria critice recensita*. Rome, 1975.

Dobbs, Betty Jo Teeter. *The Janus Faces of Genius. The Role of Alchemy in Newton's Thought*. Cambridge, 1991.

Dondaine, Antoine. "Le 'Quodlibet' de Jean Pecham 'De natali' dans la tradition manuscrite thomiste." In *Studies Honoring Ignatius Charles Brady Friar Minor*, eds. Romano S. Almagno and Conrad L. Harkins, 199–218. St. Bonaventure, N.Y., 1976.

Dondaine, Hyacinthe-François. "L'objet et le 'medium' de la vision béatifique chez les théologiens du XIIIᵉ siècle." RTAM 19 (1952): 60–130.

Doucet, Victorin. "L'enseignement Parisien de Mathieu d'Aquasparta (1278–79)." AFH 28 (1935): 568–70.

——. "Introductio critica." In Matthew of Aquasparta, *Quaestiones disputatae de gratia*, ed. Victorin Doucet, XI–CLXIII. BFS, 11. Quaracchi, 1935.

——. "Maîtres franciscains de Paris. Supplément au 'Répertoire des maîtres en théologie de Paris au XIIIᵉ siècle' d M. le chan. P. Glorieux." AFH 27 (1934): 531–64.

——. "Notulae bibliographicae de quibusdam operibus Fr. Ioannis Pecham, O.F.M." *Antonianum* 8 (1953): 307–28 and 425–59.

———. "L'oeuvre scolastique de Richard de Conington, O.F.M." AFH 29 (1936): 396–442.

Douie, Decima L. *Archbishop Pecham*. Oxford, 1952.

Dowd, John D. "Matthew of Aquasparta's *De Productione Rerum* and its Relation to St. Thomas and St. Bonaventure." FrS 34 (1974): 34–73.

Doyle, Patrick J. *The Disintegration of Divine Illumination Theory in the Franciscan School, 1285–1300: Peter of Trabes, Richard of Middleton, William of Ware*. Ph.D. diss., Marquette University 1983; Ann Arbor (University Microfilms), 1984.

Duhem, Pierre. *Etudes sur Léonard de Vinci*. 3 vols. Paris, 1906–13.

———. *Le système du monde*. 10 vols. Paris, 1913–59.

Dumont, Richard E. "Scotus's Intuition Viewed in the Light of the Intellect's Present State." In *De doctrina Ioannis Duns Scoti*, 2, 47–64. Acta Congressus Scotistici Internationalis, Oxford/Edinburgh, 11–17 September 1966. Rome, 1968.

Dumont, Stephen D. "Giles of Rome and the 'De rerum principio' Attributed to Vital du Four." AFH 77 (1984): 81–109.

———. "The quaestio si est and the Metaphysical Proof for the Existence of God according to Henry of Ghent and John Duns Scotus." FS 66 (1984): 335–67.

———. "Theology as a Science and Duns Scotus's Distinction between Intuitive and Abstractive Cognition." *Speculum* 64 (1989): 579–99.

———. "The Univocity of the Concept of Being in the Fourteenth Century: John Duns Scotus and William of Alnwick." MS 49 (1987): 1–75.

Dwyer, Edward. *Die Wissenschaftslehre Heinrichs von Gent*. Würzburg, 1933.

Eastwood, Bruce S. Review of Southern, *Robert Grosseteste*. *Speculum* 63 (1988): 233–37.

Ehrle, Franz. "L'Agostinismo e l'Aristotelismo nella Scolastica del secolo XIII." *Xenia Thomistica* 3:517–88. Rome, 1925.

———. "Der Augustinismus und der Aristotelismus in der Scholastik." *Archiv für Litteratur- und Kirchengeschichte des Mittelalters* 5 (1889): 603–35.

———. "Beiträge zu den Biographen berühmter Scholastiker: Heinrich von Gent." *Archiv für Litteratur- und Kirchengeschichte des Mittelalters* 1 (1885): 360–401 and 507–8.

———. "John Peckham über den Kampf des Augustinismus und Aristotelismus in der zweiten Hälfte des 13. Jahrhunderts." *Zeitschrift für katholische Theologie* 13 (1889): 172–93.

———. "Recherches critiques sur la biographie de Henri de Gand dit le Docteur Solennel." Trans. J. Raskop. *Bulletins de la Société Historique et Littéraire de Tournai* 21, supp. (1887): 7–51.

———. "Das Studium der Handschriften der mittelalterlichen Scholastik mit besonderer Berücksichtigung der Schule des hl. Bonaventura." *Zeitschrift für katholische Theologie* 7 (1883): 1–51.

Emmen, Aquilinus. "Wilhelm v. Ware." In *Lexikon für Theologie und Kirche*, ed. Josef Höfer and Karl Rahner, 10:1154–56. 2nd ed., fully revised. Freiburg im Br., 1965.

Epping, Adelhard. "Seraphische Weisheit." FS 56 (1974): 221–48.

Etzkorn, Girard J. "Révision dans l'ordre des Quodlibets de Jean Pecham." *Bulletin de Philosophie Médiévale* 19 (1977): 65.

Fackler, Franz Paul. *Der Seinsbegriff in seiner Bedeutung für die Gottes-Erkenntnis bei Duns Scotus*. Augsburg, 1933.

Finke, Heinrich. "Das Pariser Nationalkonzil vom Jahre 1290." *Römische Quartalschrift* 9 (1895): 171–82.

Forest, Aimé. "Guillaume d'Auvergne, critique d'Aristote." In *Etudes médiévales offertes à Augustin Fliche*, 67–79. Vendôme, 1953.

Funkenstein, Amos. *Theology and the Scientific Imagination from the Middle Ages to the Seventeenth Century*. Princeton, 1986.

Gál, Gedeon. "Gulielmi de Ware, O.F.M. Doctrina philosophica per summa capita proposita." FrS 14 (1954): 155–80 and 265–92.

——. "Preface." In Matthew of Aquasparta, *Quaestiones disputatae de productione rerum et de providentia*, ed. Gedeon Gál, 5*–10*. BFS, 17. Quaracchi, 1956.

Gauthier, René A. "Notes sur les débuts (1225–1240) du premier 'averroïsme.'" RSPT 66 (1982): 322–73.

——. "Notes sur Siger de Brabant." RSPT 67 (1983): 201–32.

——. "Le traité *De anima et de potenciis eius* d'un maître ès arts (vers 1225)." RSPT 66 (1982): 3–55.

Gieben, Servus. "Four Chapters on Philosophical Errors from the Rudimentum Doctrinae of Gilbert of Tournai O. Min. (died 1284)." *Vivarium* 1 (1963): 141–64.

——. "Robert Grosseteste on Preaching." CF 37 (1967): 100–41.

Gilson, Etienne. "Avicenne et le point de départ de Duns Scot." AHDLMA 2 (1927): 89–149.

——. *History of Christian Philosophy in the Middle Ages*. New York, 1955.

——. *Jean Duns Scot. Introduction à ses positions fondamentales*. Paris, 1952.

——. *La philosophie de saint Bonaventure*. 2nd ed. Paris, 1943.

——. "La philosophie franciscaine." In *Saint François d'Assise*, 148–75. Paris, 1927.

——. *The Philosophy of Saint Bonaventure*. Trans. Illtyd Trethowan and Frank J. Sheed. London, 1938.

——. "Pourquoi saint Thomas a critiqué saint Augustin." AHDLMA 1 (1926–27): 5–127.

——. "Roger Marston: Un cas d'augustinisme avicennisant." AHDLMA 8 (1933): 37–42.

——. "Les sources gréco-arabes de l'augustinisme avicennisant." AHDLMA 4 (1929): 5–149.

——. "Sur quelques difficultés de l'illumination augustinienne." RNS 36 (1934): 321–31.

Glorieux, Palémon. "Autour de Raymond Rigauld, O.F.M., et de ses Quodlibets." AFH 31 (1938): 528–33.

——. *Aux origines de la Sorbonne*. Vol. 1, *Robert de Sorbon*. Paris, 1966.

——. "D'Alexandre de Halès à Pierre Auriole. La suite des maîtres franciscains de Paris au XIIIᵉ siècle." AFH 26 (1933): 257–81.

——. *La Faculté des arts et ses maîtres au XIIIᵉ siècle*. Paris, 1971.

——. *La littérature quodlibétique*. 2 vols. Bibliothèque Thomiste, 5 and 21. Le Saulchoir, 1925, and Paris, 1935.

——. "Maîtres franciscains régents à Paris. Mise au point." RTAM 18 (1951): 324–32.

——. "Pour en finir avec le 'De rerum principio.'" AFH 31 (1938): 225–34.

——. "Prélats français contre religieux mendiants. Autour de la Bulle 'Ad fructus uberes.'" *Revue d'Histoire de l'Eglise de France* 11 (1925): 309–31 and 471–95.

——. *Répertoire des maîtres en théologie au XIIIᵉ siècle*. 2 vols. Paris, 1933–34.

Godefroy, P. "Vital du Four." In *Dictionnaire de Théologie Catholique* 15, 2, 3102–3115. Paris, 1950.

Goering, Joseph. "When and Where Did Grosseteste Study Theology?" In *Robert Grosseteste. New Perspectives on his Thought and Scholarship*, ed. James McEvoy, 17–51. Instrumenta Patristica, 27. Turnhout, 1995.

Gogacz, Mieczysław. "Czy według Henryka z Gandawy jest możliwe poznanie czystej prawdy bez pomocy oświecenia" ("La connaissance de la vérité pure selon Henri de Gand"). *Roczniki Filozoficzne* 8, n. 1 (1960): 161–71.

——. *Problem istnienia boga u Anselma z Canterbury i problem prawdy u Henryka z Gandawy*. Lublin, 1961.

Gómez Caffarena, José. "Cronología de la 'Suma' de Enrique de Gante por relación a sus 'Quodlibetos.'" *Gregorianum* 38 (1957): 116–33.

——. *Ser participado y ser subsistente en la metafísica de Enrique de Gante*. Analecta Gregoriana, 93. Rome, 1958.

Gondras, Alexandre-Jean. "Un commentaire avignonnais sur le *Liber de sex principiis*, attribué à 'Maître Vital.'" AHDLMA 42 (1975): 183–317.

———. "Les *Quaestiones de Anima VI*, manuscrit de la Bibliothèque communale d'Assise n° 159, attribuées à Matthieu d'Aquasparta." AHDLMA 24 (1957): 203–352.

Grabmann, Martin. *Der göttliche Grund menschlicher Wahrheitserkenntnis nach Augustinus und Thomas von Aquin*. Münster, 1924.

———. *Mittelalterliche lateinische Aristotelesübersetzungen und Aristoteleskommentare in Handschriften spanischer Bibliotheken*. Sitzungsberichte der Bayerischen Akademie der Wissenschaften, Philosophisch-philologische und historische Klasse, 1928, 5. Abhandlung. Munich, 1928.

———. *Die philosophische und theologische Erkenntnislehre des Kardinals Matthaeus von Aquasparta*. Theologische Studien der Leo-Gesellschaft, 14. Vienna, 1906.

Grajewski, Maurice. "Duns Scotus in the Light of Modern Research." *Proceedings of the American Catholic Philosophical Association* 18 (1942): 168–85.

Guimaraens, Francisco de. "La doctrine des théologiens sur l'Immaculée Conception de 1250 à 1350." EF n.s. 9 (1952): 181–203; 10 (1953): 23–51 and 167–87.

Gutting, Gary, ed. *Paradigms and Revolutions. Appraisals and Applications of Thomas Kuhn's Philosophy of Science*. Notre Dame, 1980.

Hackett, M. B. "The University as Corporate Body." In *The History of the University of Oxford*, vol. 1, *The Early Oxford Schools*, ed. J. I. Catto, 37–95. Oxford, 1984.

Hacking, Ian, ed. *Scientific Revolutions*. Oxford, 1981.

Hagemann, "De Henrici Gandavensis quem vocant ontologismo." *Index lectionum quae auspiciis augustissimi ac potentissimi Imperatoris Regis Guilelmi II in Academia Theologica et Philosophica Monasteriensi . . . publice privatimque habebuntur*. Summer, 1898 (pp. 3–12) and Winter, 1898/99 (pp. 3–13). Münster, 1898.

Haren, Michael. *Medieval Thought. The Western Intellectual Tradition from Antiquity to the Thirteenth Century*. 2nd ed. Toronto, 1992.

Harris, Charles R.S. *Duns Scotus*. 2 vols. Oxford, 1927.

Haskins, Charles H. *The Renaissance of the Twelfth Century*. Cambridge, Mass., 1927.

Hauréau, Barthélemy. *Histoire de la philosophie scolastique*. 3 vols. Paris, 1872 and 1880.

Heer, Friedrich. *The Medieval World*. London, 1962.

———. *Mittelalter*. Zurich, 1961.

Heinzmann, Richard. "Wilhelm von Auvergne." In *Lexikon für Theologie und Kirche*, 2nd ed., 10, 1127–28. Freiburg im B., 1965.

Heiser, Basil. "The *Primum Cognitum* according to Duns Scotus." FrS 2 (1942): 193–216.

Henquinet, François-Marie. "Un recueil de questions annoté par S. Bonaventure." AFH 25 (1932): 553–55.

Heynck, Valens. "Vitalis de Furno." In *Lexikon für Theologie und Kirche*, 2nd ed., ed. Josef Höfer and Karl Rahner, 10, 819–20. Freiburg im Br., 1965.

———. "Zur Busslehre des Vitalis de Furno." FS 41 (1959): 163–212.

Hissette, Roland. *Enquête sur les 219 articles condamnés à Paris le 7 mars 1277*. Leuven, 1977.

———. "L'implication de Thomas d'Aquin dans les censures parisiennes de 1277." *Recherches de Théologie et Philosophie Médiévales* 64 (1997): 3–31.

Hocedez, Edgar. "Gilles de Rome et Henri de Gand sur la distinction réelle (1276–1287)." *Gregorianum* 8 (1927): 358–84.

———. "Le premier Quodlibet d'Henri de Gand (1276)." *Gregorianum* 9 (1928): 92–117.

———. *Richard de Middleton. Sa vie, ses oeuvres, sa doctrine*. Leuven, 1925.

Hödl, Ludwig. "Introduction." In Henry of Ghent, *Summa (Quaestiones ordinariae) art. XXXI–XXXIV*, ed. Raymond Macken, XI–XXIV. Henrici Opera, 27. Leuven, 1991.

———. "Literar- und Problemgeschichtliches zur neuen kritischen Edition der Opera omnia des Heinrich von Gent." *Freiburger Zeitschrift für Philosophie und Theologie* 32 (1985): 295–322.

———. "Neue Begriffe und neue Wege der Seinserkenntnis im Schul- und Einflussbereich des Heinrich von Gent." In *Die Metaphysik im Mittelalter*, ed. Paul Wilpert,
607–15. Miscellanea Midiaevalia, 2. Berlin, 1963.

———. "Neue Nachrichten über die Pariser Verurteilungen der thomasischen
Formlehre." *Scholastik* 39 (1964): 178–96.

———. "Der Projektband der kritischen Edition der Summa des Heinrich von Gent."
Ephemerides Theologicae Lovanienses 64 (1988): 225–28.

———. "Theologiegeschichtliche Einführung." In Henry of Ghent, *Tractatus super facto
praelatorum et fratrum*, ed. Ludwig Hödl and Marcel Haverals, vii–xcvii. Henrici
Opera, 17. Leuven, 1989.

———. "Die Zeichen-Gegenwart Gottes und das Gott-Ebenbild-Sein des Menschen
in des hl. Bonaventura 'Itinerarium mentis in Deum' c. 1–3." In *Der Begriff der
Repraesentatio im Mittelalter*, ed. Albert Zimmermann, Miscellanea Mediaevalia 8,
94–112. Berlin, 1971.

Hoenen, Maarten J.F.M. "Late Medieval Schools of Thought in the Mirror of
University Textbooks. The *Promptuarium argumentorum* (Cologne 1492)." In *Philosophy
and Learning. Universities in the Middle Ages*, eds. Maarten J.F.M. Hoenen, J.H. Josef
Schneider and Georg Wieland, 329–69. Leiden, 1995.

Hoeres, Walter. "Wesen und Dasein bei Heinrich von Gent und Duns Scotus." FS
47 (1965): 121–86.

Honnefelder, Ludger. *Ens inquantum ens. Der Begriff des Seienden als solchen als Gegenstand
der Metaphysik nach der Lehre des Johannes Duns Scotus*. Beiträge, N.F. 16. Münster,
1979.

———. "Die Lehre von der doppelten ratitudo entis und ihre Bedeutung für die
Metaphysik des Johannes Duns Scotus." In *Deus et homo ad mentem I. Duns Scoti*,
661–71. Acta Tertii Congressus Scotistici Internationalis, Vienna, 28 September-
2 October 1970. Rome, 1972.

Huet, François. *Recherches historiques et critiques sur la vie, les ouvrages et la doctrine de
Henri de Gand*. Ghent, 1838.

Hurley, M. "Illumination according to S. Bonaventure." *Gregorianum* 32 (1951):
388–404.

Hyman, Arthur. "Aristotle's Theory of the Intellect and its Interpretation by Averroes."
In *Studies in Aristotle*, ed. Dominic J. O'Meara, 161–91. Washington, D.C., 1981.

Jacob, Margaret C. *The Cultural Meaning of the Scientific Revolution*. New York, 1988.

———. *The Newtonians and the English Revolution, 1689–1720*. Ithaca, N.Y., 1976.

Jüssen, Gabriel. "Idee" (II, B, 6: Bonaventura). In *Historisches Wörterbuch der Philosophie*,
ed. Joachim Ritter and Karlfried Gründer, 4, 87–90. Basel/Stuttgart, 1976.

———. "Wilhelm von Auvergne und die Entwicklung der Philosophie im Übergang
zur Hochscholastik." In *Thomas von Aquin im philosophischen Gespräch*, ed. Wolfgang
Kluxen, 185–203. Freiburg/Munich, 1975.

———. "Wilhelm von Auvergne und die Transformation der scholastischen Philosophie
im 13. Jahrhundert." In *Philosophie im Mittelalter*, ed. Jan P. Beckmann et al.,
141–64. Hamburg, 1987.

Kaluza, Zénon. "La crise des années 1472–1482: L'interdiction du Nominalisme
par Louis XI." In *Philosophy and Learning. Universities in the Middle Ages*, eds. Maarten
J.F.M. Hoenen, J.H. Josef Schneider and Georg Wieland, 293–327. Leiden, 1995.

———. *Les querelles doctrinales à Paris. Nominalistes et réalistes aux confins du XIVe et du XVe
siècles*. Bergamo, 1988.

Klug, Hubert. "Zur Biographie der Minderbrüder Johannes Duns Skotus und
Wilhelm von Ware." FS 2 (1915): 377–85.

Knowles, David. *The Evolution of Medieval Thought*. London, 1962.

———. "Some Aspects of the Career of Archbishop Pecham." *English Historical Review*
57 (1942): 1–18, 178–201.

Knuuttila, Simo. "Being *qua* Being in Thomas Aquinas and John Duns Scotus." In

The Logic of Being. Historical Studies, ed. Simo Knuuttila and Jaakko Hintikka, 201–22. Dordrecht, 1986.

Koyré, Alexandre. *Etudes galiléennes*. 3 vols. Paris, 1939.

———. *From the Closed World to the Infinite Universe*. Baltimore, 1957.

———. "Le vide et l'espace infinie au XIVe siècle." AHDLMA 17 (1949): 45–91.

Kramp, Josef. "Des Wilhelm von Auvergne 'Magisterium divinale.'" *Gregorianum* 1 (1920): 538–616; and 2 (1921): 42–103, 174–95.

Kuhn, Thomas S. *The Copernican Revolution*. Cambridge, Mass., 1957.

———. *The Structure of Scientific Revolutions*. 2nd ed. Chicago, 1970.

Lacombe, Olivier. "La critique des théories de la connaissance chez Duns Scot." *Revue Thomiste* 35 (1930): 24–47, 144–57 and 217–35.

Lakatos, Imre, and Musgrave, Alan, eds. *Criticism and the Growth of Knowledge*. Cambridge, 1970.

Lampen, Willibrord. "Jean Pecham, O.F.M., et son office de la S. Trinité." *La France Franciscaine* 11 (1928): 211–29.

Landry, Bernard. "L'originalité de Guillaume d'Auvergne" *Revue d'Histoire de la Philosophie* 3 (1929): 441–63.

Langlois, Charles-Victor. "Vidal du Four, Frère Mineur." In *Histoire Littéraire de la France*, 36, 295–305 and 647–52. Paris, 1924 and 1927.

Langston, Douglas C. "Scotus and Ockham on the Univocal Concept of Being." FrS 39 (1979): 105–29.

Lawn, Brian. *The Rise and Decline of the Scholastic "Quaestio disputata." With Special Emphasis on its Use in the Teaching of Medicine and Science*. Leiden, 1993.

Lazzarini, Renato. *S. Bonaventura. Filosofo e mistico del Cristianesimo*. Milan, 1946.

Lechner, Josef. "Beiträge zum mittelalterlichen Franziskanerschrifttum, vornehmlich der Oxforder Schule des 13./14. Jahrhunderts, auf Grund einer Florentiner Wilhelm von Ware-Hs." FS 19 (1932): 99–127.

———. "Die mehrfachen Fassungen des Sentenzenkommentars des Wilhelm von Ware O.F.M." FS 31 (1949): 14–31.

———. "Wilhelm von Ware." In *Lexikon für Theologie und Kirche*, ed. Michael Buchberger, 10:910–11. 2nd. ed. Freiburg im Br., 1938.

Leclercq, Jean. *Etudes sur le vocabulaire monastique du moyen âge*. Rome, 1961.

Ledoux, Athanasius. "De gratia creata et increata iuxta quaestionem ineditam Guillelmi de Ware." *Antonianum* 5 (1930): 137–56.

Leff, Gordon. *Medieval Thought. St. Augustine to Ockham*. Harmondsworth, England, 1958.

Lindberg, David C. *Theories of Vision from Al-Kindi to Kepler*. Chicago, 1976.

Lindberg, David C., ed. *John Pecham and the Science of Optics. Perspectiva communis*. Madison, Wis., 1970.

Little, Andrew G. "The Franciscan School at Oxford in the Thirteenth Century." AFH 19 (1926): 803–74.

———. "Was St. Bonaventure a Student in Oxford? His Visit to England in 1259." AFH 19 (1926): 289–91.

Longpré, Ephrem. "Le Commentaire sur les Sentences de Guillaume de Nottingham." AFH 22 (1929): 232–33.

———. "Le courant franciscain d'Alexandre de Halès à Duns Scot." *Revue des Questions Historiques* 3rd. ser., 18 (1938): 387–95.

———. "Guillaume d'Auvergne et l'Ecole Franciscaine de Paris." *La France Franciscaine* 5 (1922): 426–29.

———. "Guillaume de Ware O.F.M." *La France Franciscaine* 5 (1922): 71–82.

———. "Matthieu d'Aquasparta." In *Dictionnaire de théologie catholique*, 10.1, coll. 375–89. Paris, 1928.

———. "Pour la défense de Duns Scot." RFN 18 (1926): 32–42.

———. "S. Augustin et la pensée franciscaine." *La France Franciscaine* 15 (1932).

Lottin, Odon. "L''Ordinatio' de Jean Duns Scot sur le livre III des Sentences."
    RTAM 20 (1953): 102–19.
——. "Les traités sur l'âme et les vertus de Jean de la Rochelle." RNS 32 (1930):
    5–32.
Luyckx, Bonifaz A. *Die Erkenntnislehre Bonaventuras*. Beiträge 23.3–4. Münster, 1923.
Lynch, John E. *The Theory of Knowledge of Vital du Four*. St. Bonaventure, N.Y.,
    1972.
Lynch, Lawrence E. "The Doctrine of Divine Ideas and Illumination in Robert
    Grosseteste, Bishop of Lincoln." MS 3 (1941): 161–73.
Macken, Raymond. *Bibliotheca manuscripta Henrici de Gandavo*. 2 vols. Henrici Opera,
    1–2. Leuven, 1979.
——. "Les diverses applications de la distinction intentionelle chez Henri de Gand."
    In *Sprache und Erkenntnis im Mittelalter*, 2, 769–76. Akten des VI. internationalen
    Kongresses für mittelalterliche Philosophie, 29 August–3 September 1977. Miscellanea
    Mediaevalia, 13. Berlin, 1981.
——. "Die Editionstechnik der 'Opera Omnia' des Heinrich von Gent." FS 63
    (1981): 227–39.
——. "Hendrik van Gent (Henricus de Gandavo), wijsgeer en theoloog." In *Nationaal
    biografisch woordenboek*, 8, 377–95. Brussels, 1979.
——. "Introduction." In Henry of Ghent, *Quodlibet I*, ed. Raymond Macken,
    VII–XXIV. Henrici Opera, 5. Leuven, 1979.
——. "The Metaphysical Proof for the Existence of God in the Philosophy of Henry
    of Ghent." FS 68 (1986): 247–60.
——. "La théorie de l'illumination divine dans la philosophie d'Henri de Gand."
    RTAM 39 (1972): 82–112.
——. "Ein wichtiges Ineditum zum Kampf über das Beichtprivilegium des Bettelorden:
    der 'Tractatus super facto praelatorum et fratrum' des Heinrich von Gent." FeS
    60 (1978): 301–10.
Madec, Goulven. "La notion d'augustinisme philosophique." In *Jean Duns Scot et ses
    auteurs*, 147–61. Paris, 1988.
Magrini, Elia. "La produzione letteraria di Guglielmo di Ware." *Miscellanea Francescana*
    36 (1936): 312–32; 38 (1938): 411–29.
Mandonnet, Pierre. "L'augustinisme Bonaventurien." *Bulletin Thomiste* 3 (1926): 48–54.
——. *Siger de Brabant et l'averroïsme latin au XIIIe siècle*. Fribourg, 1899; 2nd ed., 2
    vols. Les Philosophes Belges 6–7, Leuven, 1911 & 1908.
Manser, G. "M. Johann von Rupella +1245. Ein Beitrag zu seiner Charakteristik
    mit besonderer Berücksichtigung seiner Erkenntnislehre." *Jahrbuch für Philosophie
    und spekulative Theologie* 26 (1912): 290–324.
Marc, André. *L'idée de l'être chez saint Thomas et dans la Scolastique postérieure*. Archives
    de Philosophie, 10, 1. Paris, 1933.
Marrone, Steven P. "Concepts of Science among Parisian Theologians in the
    Thirteenth Century." In *Knowledge and the Sciences in Medieval Philosophy*, eds. Reijo
    Työrinoja et al., 3, 124–33. Proceedings of the Eighth International Congress of
    Medieval Philosophy. Helsinki, 1990.
——. "Duns Scotus on Metaphysical Potency and Possibility." In *Essays in Honor
    of Dr. Girard Etzkorn*, eds. Gordon A. Wilson and Timothy B. Noone, 265–89
    (FrS 56 [1998]). St. Bonaventure, N.Y., 1998.
——. "Henry of Ghent and Duns Scotus on the Knowledge of Being." *Speculum*
    63 (1988): 22–57.
——. "Henry of Ghent in Mid-Career as Interpreter of Aristotle and Thomas
    Aquinas." In *Henry of Ghent. Proceedings of the International Colloquium on the Occasion
    of the 700th Anniversary of his Death (1293)*, ed. Willy Vanhamel, 193–209. Leuven,
    1996.

——. "Matthew of Aquasparta, Henry of Ghent and Augustinian Epistemology after Bonaventure." FS 65 (1983): 252–90.

——. "The Notion of Univocity in Duns Scotus's Early Works." FrS 43 (1983): 347–95.

——. "Revisiting Duns Scotus and Henry of Ghent on Modality." In *John Duns Scotus: Metaphysics and Ethics*, eds. Ludger Honnefelder, Rega Wood and Mechthild Dreyer, 175–89. Leiden, 1996.

——. "Robert Grosseteste on the Certitude of Induction." In *L'homme et son univers au moyen âge*, ed. Christian Wénin, 2, 481–88. Actes du Septième Congrès International de Philosophie Médiévale, 30 August–4 September 1982. Louvain-la-Neuve, 1986.

——. *Truth and Scientific Knowledge in the Thought of Henry of Ghent*. Cambridge, Mass., 1985.

——. *William of Auvergne and Robert Grosseteste. New Ideas of Truth in the Early Thirteenth Century*. Princeton, 1983.

Martel, Benoît. *La psychologie de Gonsalve d'Espagne*. Montreal, 1968.

Martin, Julian. *Francis Bacon, the State, and the Reform of Natural Philosophy*. Cambridge, 1992.

Masnovo, Amato. *Da Guglielmo d'Auvergne a s. Tommaso d'Aquino*. 2nd ed. 3 vols. Milan, 1945–46.

——. "Guglielmo d'Auvergne." RFN 19 (1927): 132–45.

Mathias, Thomas R. "Bonaventuran Ways to God through Reason." FrS 36 (1976): 192–232; 37 (1977): 153–206.

Maurer, Armand. "*Ens Diminutum*: A Note on its Origin and Meaning." MS 12 (1950): 216–22.

——. *Medieval Philosophy*. 1st ed. New York, 1962.

Mazzarella, Pasquale. *La dottrina dell'anima e della conoscenza in Matteo d'Acquasparta*. Padua, 1969.

McAndrew, P.J. "The Theory of Divine Illumination in St. Bonaventure." *The New Scholasticism* 6 (1932): 32–50.

McEvoy, James. "The Chronology of Robert Grosseteste's Writings on Nature and Natural Philosophy." *Speculum* 58 (1983): 614–55.

——. "La connaissance intellectuelle selon Robert Grosseteste." *Revue Philosophique de Louvain* 75 (1977): 5–48.

——. *The Philosophy of Robert Grosseteste*. Oxford, 1982.

——. Review of Southern, *Robert Grosseteste. Bulletin de Théologie Ancienne et Médiévale* 14 (1987): 353–58.

——. "Robert Grosseteste's Theory of Human Nature. With the Text of his Conference 'Ecclesia Sancta Celebrat.'" RTAM 47 (1980): 131–87.

McKeon, Charles K. *A Study of the Summa philosophiae of the Pseudo-Grosseteste*. New York, 1948.

Merton, Robert K. *Science, Technology and Society in Seventeenth-Century England*. Bruges, 1938.

Michaud-Quantin, Pierre. "Introduction." In John of La Rochelle, *Tractatus de divisione multiplici potentiarum animae*, ed. Pierre Michaud-Quantin, 7–38. Paris, 1964.

Minges, Parthenius. "Beitrag zur Lehre des Duns Scotus über die Univokation des Seinsbegriffes." *Philosophisches Jahrbuch (der Görresgesellschaft)* 20 (1907): 306–23.

——. "Zur Erkenntnislehre des Duns Scotus." *Philosophisches Jahrbuch (der Görresgesellschaft)* 31 (1918): 52–74.

——. "Zur Erkenntnislehre des Franziskaners Johannes von Rupella." *Philosophisches Jahrbuch der Görresgesellschaft* 27 (1914): 461–77.

Modrić, Luka. "Osservazioni su una recente critica all'edizione Vaticana dell'*Opera omnia* di Giovanni Duns Scoto." *Antonianum* 58 (1983): 336–57.

———. "Rapporto tra la 'Lectura' II e la 'Metaphysica' di G. Duns Scoto." *Antonianum* 62 (1987): 504–9.

Moody, Ernest A. "Empiricism and Metaphysics in Medieval Philosophy." *The Philosophical Review* 67 (1958): 145–63.

———. "William of Auvergne and his Treatise *De anima*." In *Studies in Medieval Philosophy, Science, and Logic*, 1–109. Berkeley, 1975.

Muckle, J. T. "The Hexameron of Robert Grosseteste. The First Twelve Chapters of Part Seven." MS 6 (1944): 151–74.

Murdoch, John E. "The Analytic Character of Late Medieval Learning: Natural Philosophy without Nature." In *Approaches to Nature in the Middle Ages*, ed. Lawrence D. Roberts, 171–213. Binghamton, N.Y., 1982.

———. "The Development of a Critical Temper: New Approaches and Modes of Analysis in Fourteenth-Century Philosophy, Science, and Theology." In *Medieval and Renaissance Studies*, ed. Siegfried Wenzel, Proceedings of the Southeastern Institute of Medieval and Renaissance Studies, Summer 1975, 51–79. Chapel Hill, 1978.

———. "From Social into Intellectual Factors: An Aspect of the Unitary Character of Late Medieval Learning." In *The Cultural Context of Medieval Learning*, eds. John E. Murdoch and Edith C. Sylla, 271–348. Boston, 1975.

———. "The Involvement of Logic in Late Medieval Natural Philosophy." In *Studies in Medieval Natural Philosophy*, ed. Stefano Caroti, 3–28. Florence, 1989.

———. "Philosophy and the Enterprise of Science in the Later Middle Ages." In *The Interaction between Science and Philosophy*, ed. Yehuda Elkana, 51–74. Atlantic Highlands, N.J., 1974.

———. "Pierre Duhem and the History of Late Medieval Science and Philosophy in the Latin West." In *Gli studi di filosofia medievale fra otto e novecento*, 253–301. Rome, 1991.

Muscat, Pierre. "Guillelmi de Ware quaestio inedita de unitate Dei." *Antonianum* 2 (1927): 335–50.

Nuchelmans, Gabriel. *Theories of the Proposition. Ancient and Medieval Conceptions of the Bearers of Truth and Falsity*. Amsterdam, 1973.

Nys, Theophiel V. *De psychologia cognitionis humanae secundum Henricum Gandavensem*. Excerpta ex dissertatione Pontificiae Universitatis Gregorianae. Rome, 1949.

———. *De werking van het menselijk verstand volgens Hendrik van Gent*. Leuven, 1949.

Ó Huallacháin, Colman. "On Recent Studies of the Opening Question in Scotus's *Ordinatio*." FrS 15 (1955): 1–29.

Palhoriès, Fortuné. *Saint Bonaventure*. Paris, 1913.

———. "La théorie de l'intelligence chez saint Bonaventure." *Revue des Sciences Philosophiques et Théologiques* 6 (1912): 465–89.

Pasnau, Robert. "Henry of Ghent and the Twilight of Divine Illumination." *The Review of Metaphysics* 49 (1995): 49–75.

Pattin, Adriaan. "Pour l'histoire du sens agent au moyen âge." *Bulletin de Philosophie Médiévale* 16–17 (1974–75): 100–113.

Paulus, Jean. "A propos de la théorie de la connaissance d'Henri de Gand." *Revue Philosophique de Louvain* 47 (1949): 493–96.

———. "Les disputes d'Henri de Gand et de Gilles de Rome sur la distinction de l'essence et de l'existence." AHDLMA 13 (1940–42): 323–58.

———. *Henri de Gand. Essai sur les tendances de sa métaphysique*. Paris, 1938.

———. "Henri de Gand et l'argument ontologique." AHDLMA 10–11 (1935–36): 265–323.

Pegis, Anton C. "Henry of Ghent and the New Way to God (III)." MS 33 (1971): 158–79.

———. "Matthew of Aquasparta and the Cognition of Non-Being." In SRHCI, 463–80.

———. "The Mind of Augustine." MS 6 (1944): 1–61.

——. "A New Way to God: Henry of Ghent (II)." MS 31 (1969): 93–116.

——. "St. Bonaventure Revisited." In *S. Bonaventura, 1274–1974*, 4, 21–44. Grotta-ferrata, 1973.

——. "Toward a New Way to God: Henry of Ghent." MS 30 (1968): 226–47.

Pelster, Franz. "Franziskanerlehrer um die Wende des 13. und zu Anfang des 14. Jahrhunderts in zwei ehemaligen Turiner Hss." *Gregorianum* 18 (1937): 291–317.

——. "Handschriftliches zu Skotus mit neuen Angaben über sein Leben." FS 10 (1923): 1–32.

——. "Die Kommentare zum vierten Buch der Sentenzen von Wilhelm von Ware, zum ersten Buch von einem Unbekannten und von Martin von Alnwick im Cod. 501 Troyes." *Scholastik* 27 (1952): 344–67.

——. "Neue Textausgaben von Werken des hl. Thomas, des Johannes Pecham und Vitalis de Furno." *Gregorianum* 31 (1950): 284–303.

Pinborg, Jan. "Diskussionen um die Wissenschaftstheorie an der Artistenfakultät." In *Die Auseinandersetzungen an der Pariser Universität im XIII. Jahrhundert*, ed. Albert Zimmermann, Miscellanea Mediaevalia 10, 240–68. Berlin, 1976.

Pini, Georgio. "Duns Scotus's Metaphysics: The Critical Edition of his *Quaestiones super libros Metaphysicorum Aristotelis*." RTAM 65 (1998): 353–68.

Popkin, Richard H. *The History of Scepticism from Erasmus to Descartes*. Rev. ed. New York, 1964.

——. *The History of Scepticism from Erasmus to Spinoza*. Berkeley, 1979.

Porro, Pasquale. *Enrico di Gand. La via delle proposizioni universali*. Bari, 1990.

Prentice, Robert P. *An Anonymous Question on the Unity of the Concept of Being (Attributed to Scotus)*. Rome, 1972.

——. *The Basic Quidditative Metaphysics of Duns Scotus as Seen in his De primo principio*. Spicilegium Pontificii Athenaei Antoniani, 16. Rome, 1970.

——. "The Fundamental Metaphysics of Scotus Presumed by the *De primo principio*." *Antonianum* 44 (1969): 40–92 and 227–308.

——. "Univocity and Analogy according to Scotus's *Super libros Elenchorum Aristotelis*." AHDLMA 35 (1968): 39–64.

Prezioso, Faustino A. "L'attività del soggetto pensante nella gnoseologia di Matteo d'Acquasparta e di Ruggiero Marston." *Antonianum* 25 (1950): 259–326.

——. *La critica di Duns Scoto all'ontologismo di Enrico di Gand*. Padua, 1961.

"Prolegomena." In John Duns Scotus, *Lectura in librum primum Sententiarum*, Opera Omnia (Vatican), 17, 2*–19*. Rome, 1966.

Putallaz, François-Xavier. *La connaissance de soi au XIIIe siècle de Matthieu d'Aquasparta à Thierry de Freiberg*. Paris, 1991.

Quinn, John F. "Chronology of Bonaventure's Sermons." AFH 67 (1974): 145–84.

——. "Chronology of St. Bonaventure (1217–1257)." FrS 32 (1972): 168–86.

Richter, Vladimir. *Studien zum literarischen Werk von Johannes Duns Scotus*. Munich, 1988.

Robert, Patrice. "Le problème de la philosophie bonaventurienne." *Laval Théologique et Philosophique* 6 (1950): 145–63; 7 (1951): 9–58.

Rohls, Jan. *Wilhelm von Auvergne und der mittelalterliche Aristotelismus. Gottesbegriff und aris-totelische Philosophie zwischen Augustin und Thomas von Aquin*. Munich, 1980.

Rosenmöller, Bernhard. *Religiöse Erkenntnis nach Bonaventura*. Beiträge, 25.3–4. Münster, 1925.

Rosini, Ruggero. "Gli 'intelligibili' nella dottrina di Geiovanni Duns Scoto." In *Deus et homo ad mentem I. Duns Scoti*, 673–91. Acta Tertii Congressus Scotistici Internationalis, Vienna, 28 September–2 October 1970. Rome, 1972.

Rossi, Pietro B. "Robert Grosseteste and the Object of Scientific Knowledge." In *Robert Grosseteste. New Perspectives on his Thought and Scholarship*, ed. James McEvoy, 53–75. Instrumenta Patristica, 27. Turnhout, 1995.

Rudavsky, Tamar M. "The Doctrine of Individuation in Duns Scotus." FS 59 (1977): 320–77; 62 (1980): 62–83.

Ruello, Francis. "La *divinorum nominum reseratio* selon Robert Grossetête et Albert le Grand." AHDLMA 25 (1959): 99–197.

Rüssmann, Heinrich. *Zur Ideenlehre der Hochscholastik unter besonderer Berücksichtigung des Heinrich von Gent, Gottfried von Fontaines und Jakob von Viterbo.* Würzburg, [1937].

Russell, Josiah Cox. "Some Notes Upon the Career of Robert Grosseteste." *Harvard Theological Review* 48 (1955): 197–211.

Salman, Dominique. "Note sur la première influence d'Averroès." RNS 40 (1937): 203–12.

Scheltens, Gonsalvus. "De bonaventuriaanse illuminatieleer." *Tijdschrift voor Philosophie* 17 (1955): 383–408.

——. "Die thomistische Analogielehre und die Univozitätslehre des J. Duns Scotus." FS 47 (1965): 315–38.

Schindele, Stephan. *Beiträge zur Metaphysik des Wilhelm von Auvergne.* Munich, 1900.

Schmaus, Michael. *Zur Diskussion über das Problem der Univozität im Umkreis des Johannes Duns Skotus.* Sitzungsberichte der bayerischen Akademi der Wissenschaften, Philosophisch-historische Klasse (1957), n. 4. Munich, 1957.

Schneider, Artur. *Die abendländische Spekulation des zwölften Jahrhunderts in ihrem Verhältnis zur aristotelischen und jüdisch-arabischen Philosophie*, Beiträge 17.4 (Münster, 1915).

Schulman, N.M. "Husband, Father, Bishop? Grosseteste in Paris." *Speculum* 72 (1997): 330–46.

Shapin, Steven, and Schaffer, Simon. *Leviathan and the Air-Pump. Hobbes, Boyle and the Experimental Life.* Princeton, 1985.

Shapiro, Barbara J. *Probability and Certainty in Seventeenth-Century England. A Study of the Relationships between Natural Science, Religion, History, Law, and Literature.* Princeton, 1983.

Sharp, Dorothea E. *Franciscan Philosophy at Oxford in the Thirteenth Century.* Oxford, 1930.

Shircel, Cyril L. "Analogy and Univocity in the Philosophy of Duns Scotus." *Proceedings of the American Catholic Philosophical Association* 18 (1942): 143–64.

——. *The Univocity of the Concept of Being in the Philosophy of John Duns Scotus.* Washington, D.C., 1942.

Siemianowski, Antoni. "Teoria istnienia realnego i tzw. sposoby istnienia u Henryka z Gandawy" ("La théorie de l'existence réelle et les 'modes d'existence' chez Henri de Gand"). *Roczniki filozoficzne* 13, n. 1 (1965): 33–41.

Southern, Richard W. "From Schools to University." In *The History of the University of Oxford*, vol. 1, *The Early Oxford Schools*, ed. J.I. Catto, 1–36. Oxford, 1984.

——. "Intellectual Development and Local Environment: The Case of Robert Grosseteste." In *Essays in Honor of Edward B. King*, eds. Robert G. Benson and Eric W. Naylor, 1–22. Sewanee, Tenn., 1991.

——. "Medieval Humanism." In *Medieval Humanism and other Studies*, 29–60. New York, 1970.

——. *Robert Grosseteste. The Growth of an English Mind in Medieval Europe.* Oxford, 1986; 2nd ed. Oxford, 1992.

——. *Scholastic Humanism and the Unification of Europe.* Vol. 1, *Foundations.* Oxford, 1995.

Speer, Andreas. "The Discovery of Nature: The Contribution of the Chartrians to Twelfth-Century Attempts to Found a *Scientia Naturalis*." *Traditio* 52 (1997): 137.

——. *Die entdeckte Natur.* Leiden, 1995.

——. "Wissenschaft und Erkenntnis. Zur Wissenschaftslehre Bonaventuras." WuW 49 (1986): 168–98.

Spettmann, Hieronymus, ed. and trans. *Die Erkenntnislehre der mittelalterlichen Franziskanerschulen von Bonaventura bis Skotus.* Paderborn, 1925.

——. "Die philosophiegeschichtliche Stellung des Wilhelm von Ware." *Philosophisches Jahrbuch der Görres-Gesellschaft* 40 (1927): 410–13; 41 (1928): 42–49.

——. *Die Psychologie des Johannes Pecham.* Beiträge, 20.6. Münster, 1919.

———. "Der Sentenzenkommentar des Franziskanererzbischofs Johannes Pecham (+1292)." *Divus Thomas* (Fribourg) 3rd ser., 5 (1927): 327–45.

Stegmüller, Friedrich. *Repertorium commentariorum in Sententias Petri Lombardi.* 2 vols. Würzburg, 1947.

———. "Vitalis de Furno." In *Repertorium biblicum medii aevi*, 5, 424–25. Madrid, 1955.

Stella, Prospero. "La prima critica di Herveus Natalis O.P. alla noetica di Enrico di Gand: Il 'De intellectu et specie' del cosiddetto 'De quatuor materiis.'" *Salesianum* 21 (1959): 125–70.

Tachau, Katherine H. Review of Marrone, *William of Auvergne and Robert Grosseteste. Isis* 75 (1984): 755–56.

———. *Vision and Certitude in the Age of Ockham. Optics, Epistemology and the Foundations of Semantics 1250–1345.* Leiden, 1988.

Teske, Roland J. "William of Auvergne on Philosophy as *divinalis* and *sapientialis*." In *Was ist Philosophie im Mittelalter?* eds. Jan A. Aertsen and Andreas Speer, 475–81. Akten des X. Internationalen Kongresses für mittelalterliche Philosophie. Miscellanea Mediaevalia, 26. Berlin, 1998.

Thijssen, Johannes M.M.H. *Censure and Heresy at the University of Paris 1200–1400.* Philadelphia, 1998.

Tochowicz, Paul. *Joannis Duns Scoti de cognitionis doctrina.* Fribourg, 1926.

Tugwell, Simon. "Thomas Aquinas: Introduction." In *Albert and Thomas. Selected Writings*, ed. Simon Tugwell, 201–351. New York, 1988.

Van de Woestyne, Zacharias. "Augustinismus in gnoseologia S. Bonaventurae et S. Thomae." *Antonianum* 8 (1933): 281–306; 9 (1934): 383–404 and 475–504.

Van Steenberghen, Fernand. *Aristote en Occident.* Leuven, 1946.

———. *Aristotle in the West.* Leuven, 1955; 2nd ed., Leuven, 1970.

———. *The Philosophical Movement in the Thirteenth Century.* Edinburgh, 1955.

———. *La philosophie au XIIIᵉ siècle.* Leuven, 1966.

———. *Siger de Brabant d'après ses oeuvres inédites.* Vol. 2, *Siger dans l'histoire de l'aristotélisme.* Les Philosophes Belges 13. Leuven, 1942.

Verbeke, Gérard. "Aristotle's Metaphysics Viewed by the Ancient Greek Commentators." In *Studies in Aristotle*, ed. Dominic J. O'Meara, 107–27. Washington, D.C., 1981.

Veuthey, Léon. "Cohérence: Eclectisme ou sythèse." EF 49 (1937): 324–32.

———. "Les divers courants de la philosophie augustino-franciscaine au moyen âge." In SRHCI, 627–52.

———. "L'école franciscaine et la critique philosophique moderne." EF 48 (1936): 129–43 and 257–66.

———. "L'esprit du concret." RFN 29 (1937): 44–58.

———. "L'intuition scotiste et le sens du concret." EF 49 (1937): 76–91.

———. "Johannes Pecham." *Miscellanea Francescana* 39 (1939): 678–81.

———. "Le problème de l'existence de Dieu chez S. Bonaventure." *Antonianum* 28 (1953): 19–38.

———. *S. Bonaventurae philosophia christiana.* Rome, 1943.

Vier, Peter C. *Evidence and its Function according to John Duns Scotus.* St. Bonaventure, N.Y., 1951.

Vogt, Berard. "The Origin and Development of the Franciscan School." FrS 3 (1925): 5–23.

———. "Der Ursprung und die Entwicklung der Franziskanerschule." FS 9 (1922): 137–57.

von Untervintl, Leo. "Die Intuitionslehre bei Vitalis de Furno. O. Min. (+1327)." CF 25 (1955): 53–113 and 225–58.

Wanke, Otto. *Die Kritik Wilhelms von Alnwick an der Ideenlehre des Johannes Duns Scotus.* Bonn, 1965.

Watson, S. Y. "Univocity and Analogy of Being in the Philosophy of Duns Scotus." *Proceedings of the American Catholic Philosophical Association* 32 (1958): 189–206.

Wauters, Alphonse. "Le mot latin *Formator*, au moyen âge, avait la signfication de Professeur." *Bulletin de la Commision Royale d'Histoire* (Brussels) 4th ser., 16 (1889): 400–410.

———. "Sur la signification du mot latin *Formator*, à propos de Henri de Gand." *Bulletin de la Commision Royale d'Histoire* (Brussels) 4th ser., 16 (1889): 12–15.

———. "Sur les documents apocryphes qui concerneraient Henri de Gand, le docteur solennel, et qui le rattachent à la famille Goethals." *Bulletin de la Commision Royale d'Histoire* (Brussels) 4th ser., 14 (1887): 179–90.

Wéber, Edouard-Henri. *Dialogue et dissensions entre saint Bonaventure et saint Thomas d'Aquin à Paris (1252–73)*. Bibliothèque Thomiste, 41. Paris, 1974.

Weinberg, Julius R. *A Short History of Medieval Philosophy*. Princeton, 1964.

Werner, Karl. "Heinrich von Gent als Repräsentant des christlichen Platonismus im dreizehnten Jahrhundert." *Denkschriften der kaiserlichen Akademie der Wissenschaften*. Philosophisch-historische Classe, 28, 97–154. Vienna, 1878.

———. *Die Psychologie des Wilhelm von Auvergne*. Vienna, 1873.

———. *Die Psychologie und Erkennntnislehre des Johannes Bonaventura*. Vienna, 1876; repr. New York, 1973.

———. *Die Scholastik des späteren Mittelalters*. Vol. 3, *Der Augustinismus in der Scholastik des späteren Mittelalters*. Vienna, 1883.

———. *Wilhelms von Auvergne Verhältniss zu den Platonikern des XII. Jahrhunderts*. Vienna, 1873.

Wieland, Georg. "Der Mendikantenstreit und die Grenzen von Theologie und Philosophie. In *Philosophy and Learning. Universities in the Middle Ages*, eds. Maarten J. F. M. Hoenen, J. H. Josef Schneider and Georg Wieland, 17–28. Leiden, 1995.

———. "Plato or Aristotle—a Real Alternative in Medieval Philosophy? In *Studies in Medieval Philosophy*, ed. John F. Wippel, 63–83. Washington, D.C., 1987.

Wielockx, Robert. "Autour du procès de Thomas d'Aquin." In *Thomas von Aquin. Werk und Wirkung im Licht neuerer Forschungen*, ed. Albert Zimmermann, 413–38. Miscellanea Mediaevalia, 19. Berlin, 1988.

———. "Commentaire." In Giles of Rome, *Apologia*, ed. Robert Wielockx, 67–225. Aegidii Romani Opera Omnia, 3, 1. Unione Accademica Nazionale, Corpus Philosophorum Medii Aevi, Testi e Studi, 4. Florence, 1985.

Wippel, John F. "Bishop Stephen Tempier and Thomas Aquinas. A Separate Process Against Aquinas?" *Freiburger Zeitschrift für Philosophie und Theologie* 44 (1997): 117–36.

———. "The Condemnations of 1270 and 1277 at Paris." *The Journal of Medieval and Renaissance Studies* 7 (1977): 169–201.

———. "Godfrey of Fontaines and Henry of Ghent's Theory of Intentional Distinction between Essence and Existence." In *Sapientiae procerum amore. Mélanges médiévistes offertes à Dom Jean-Pierre Müller O.S.B.*, ed. Theodor W. Köhler, 289–321. Rome, 1974.

———. *The Metaphysical Thought of Godfrey of Fontaines*. Washington, D.C., 1981.

———. "The Relationship between Essence and Existence in Late-Thirteenth-Century Thought: Giles of Rome, Henry of Ghent, Godfrey of Fontaines, and James of Viterbo." In *Philosophies of Existence. Ancient and Medieval*, ed. Parviz Morewedge, 131–64. New York, 1982.

———. "Thomas Aquinas and the Condemnaton of 1277." *The Modern Schoolman* 72 (1995): 233–72.

Wolter, Allan B. "Duns Scotus at Oxford." In *Via Scoti. Methodologica ad mentem Joannis Duns Scoti*, ed. Leonardo Sileo, 1, 183–92. Atti del Congresso Scotistico Internationale, Rome, 9–11 March 1993. Rome, 1995.

———. "Duns Scotus on Intuition, Memory and Our Knowledge of Individuals."

In *History of Philosophy in the Making. A Symposium of Essays to Honor Professor James D. Collins on his 65th Birthday*, ed. Linus J. Thro, 81–104. Washington, D.C., 1982.
——. "The 'Theologism' of Duns Scotus." FrS 7 (1947): 257–73 and 367–98.
——. *The Transcendentals and their Function in the Metaphysics of Duns Scotus*. St. Bonaventure, N.Y., 1946.
Zielinski, Ivo. "Möglichkeit und Grenzen der natürlichen Erkenntnis Gottes bei Johannes Duns Scotus." WuW 48 (1985): 17–32.
Zigrossi, Antonio. *Saggio sul Neoplatonismo di S. Bonaventura. Il concetto di unità e la struttura del reale come problema teologicao*. Florence, 1954.

INDEX OF NAMES

(The names of the 11 scholastics focused on in this book (see above, p. 23) are not included in the following list. To locate references to them the reader should begin with the table of Contents.)

INDEX OF PLACES

INDEX OF SUBJECTS

176, 189, 190n, 286, 366, 375, 439,
448–55, 457n, 510, 560
Physics 56
Platonism 3, 8, 29n, 152, 353n,
401n, 470
Possibility 195, 341–42, 356, 463–64,
469–70, 474–84, 554; logical
464–65, 476–80, 483; metaphysical
464–66, 476–80; objective 476
Potency 450–52, 455–56, 464
Powers of mind 173, 175, 177, 374.
See also Forces of mind
Premises of demonstration 142–43
Primacy of commonness or virtuality
507–8, 542
Principle, as God 163
Principles of science 48–49, 52–54,
64, 73–76, 79, 84, 93, 191, 209,
281, 287, 327–28, 331–34, 422–24,
433, 440, 487, 531; common
54–55, 57–58, 77–79, 81, 87, 164,
167–68, 198, 202, 331–32, 424
(*see also* Axiom; Common
conceptions of mind; First
impressions; Principles of science,
first); first 54, 78, 153, 157, 173,
188, 229, 287, 311, 332–34, 420,
423, 425–27, 428, 430, 431, 434;
proper 55, 79, 93, 424, 427–33
Privation 90, 215
Production 483. *See also* Creation
Professionalism 18n
Prophecy 106n
Prophets 210, 535
Proposition 50–51, 54–55, 57–58,
72, 84–91, 95, 149–51, 178,
188–90, 191–93, 306, 363–64, 378,
403, 406–7, 421, 424–25, 427, 455,
478. *See also Enuntiabile*; Logical
object
Providence 141, 147, 275, 287, 417
Psalm 4, 7 22, 115, 116n, 173, 207n,
208–9, 212, 214n, 415
Psychology 56
Pure truth (*sincera veritas*) 132, 185,
288, 294, 297, 362, 365, 379,
382–84, 408–10, 410n, 412, 414,
416n, 417–19, 549–50, 560

Quantum mechanics 566
Quidditative knowledge 276–78, 281,
305–6, 308, 329–30, 336–38,
366–68, 370, 442, 443n, 490–92,
498, 500, 508, 532, 534, 537, 560

Quiddity 44, 311, 339–41, 353–54,
363–65, 382, 446, 458–59, 469n,
475, 481, 539–41, 543, 544–45, 548
(*see also* Essence; *Quod quid est*);
absolute 194, 199, 356 (*see also*
Essence, absolute)
Quod quid erat esse 440
Quod quid est 122, 194, 281, 366–67,
371, 380, 440, 459–60

Rapture 45, 210, 244–45, 308, 328,
532, 534
Rational knowledge of God 219,
311–12, 314–16, 333, 495
Rationalism 4–5, 8, 9n, 566
Ratum quid or *ens ratum* 341, 355–56,
463, 467–69, 481n, 498
Reasons: causal 64, 95; eternal 40,
49, 61, 64, 127, 130–31, 137, 139,
142, 147, 149, 154, 156–57, 188–91,
193, 198–99, 209, 224, 273, 282,
341, 348, 383, 439, 445, 555, 558n
(*see also* Exemplar, divine; Idea,
divine); seminal 159–60
Rectitude 39, 44, 60, 127, 130, 149,
403
Reflexive act 364, 406
Relative orientation (*respectus*) 349–50,
355n, 381, 403n, 467
Relation 354–56, 498–99; conceptual
196; passive 85–86, 89–91; real
196
Relativity, theory of 566
Reminiscence, theory of 68, 416n,
447
Resurrection 107
Revelation 101, 112, 148, 316, 412,
416n, 544, 548, 562
Rose 477n, 481n
Roots, flavor of 336–37, 530, 546
Rules of truth 75–76, 164. *See also*
Principles of science, common; first

Sapientia. See Wisdom
Scepticism 411, 566
Science: apodictic 12, 17–18, 53–54,
64, 111, 114, 128–29, 130, 133,
187–88, 247–48, 251, 281, 360, 369,
378, 380–82, 422, 433–34, 439–43,
561, 565–67; beyond apodictic
423n, 434–38; "perfect" 287, 372,
525
Scientific Revolution of 17th century
10, 13, 17n, 565–66

Studies in the History
of Christian Thought

EDITED BY HEIKO A. OBERMAN

46. GARSTEIN, O. *Rome and the Counter-Reformation in Scandinavia.* 1553-1622. 1992
47. GARSTEIN, O. *Rome and the Counter-Reformation in Scandinavia.* 1622-1656. 1992
48. PERRONE COMPAGNI, V. (ed.). *Cornelius Agrippa, De occulta philosophia Libri tres.* 1992
49. MARTIN, D. D. *Fifteenth-Century Carthusian Reform.* The World of Nicholas Kempf. 1992
50. HOENEN, M. J. F. M. *Marsilius of Inghen.* Divine Knowledge in Late Medieval Thought. 1993
51. O'MALLEY, J. W., IZBICKI, T. M. and CHRISTIANSON, G. (eds.). *Humanity and Divinity in Renaissance and Reformation.* Essays in Honor of Charles Trinkaus. 1993
52. REEVE, A. (ed.) and SCREECH, M. A. (introd.). *Erasmus' Annotations on the New Testament.* Galatians to the Apocalypse. 1993
53. STUMP, Ph. H. *The Reforms of the Council of Constance (1414-1418).* 1994
54. GIAKALIS, A. *Images of the Divine.* The Theology of Icons at the Seventh Ecumenical Council. With a Foreword by Henry Chadwick. 1994
55. NELLEN, H. J. M. and RABBIE, E. (eds.). *Hugo Grotius – Theologian.* Essays in Honour of G. H. M. Posthumus Meyjes. 1994
56. TRIGG, J. D. *Baptism in the Theology of Martin Luther.* 1994
57. JANSE, W. *Albert Hardenberg als Theologe.* Profil eines Bucer-Schülers. 1994
59. SCHOOR, R.J.M. VAN DE. *The Irenical Theology of Théophile Brachet de La Milletière (1588-1665).* 1995
60. STREHLE, S. *The Catholic Roots of the Protestant Gospel.* Encounter between the Middle Ages and the Reformation. 1995
61. BROWN, M.L. *Donne and the Politics of Conscience in Early Modern England.* 1995
62. SCREECH, M.A. (ed.). *Richard Mocket, Warden of All Souls College, Oxford, Doctrina et Politia Ecclesiae Anglicanae.* An Anglican Summa. Facsimile with Variants of the Text of 1617. Edited with an Introduction. 1995
63. SNOEK, G.J.C. *Medieval Piety from Relics to the Eucharist.* A Process of Mutual Inter-action. 1995
64. PIXTON, P.B. *The German Episcopacy and the Implementation of the Decrees of the Fourth Lateran Council, 1216-1245.* Watchmen on the Tower. 1995
65. DOLNIKOWSKI, E.W. *Thomas Bradwardine: A View of Time and a Vision of Eternity in Fourteenth-Century Thought.* 1995
66. RABBIE, E. (ed.). *Hugo Grotius, Ordinum Hollandiae ac Westfrisiae Pietas (1613).* Critical Edition with Translation and Commentary. 1995
67. HIRSH, J.C. *The Boundaries of Faith.* The Development and Transmission of Medieval Spirituality. 1996
68. BURNETT, S.G. *From Christian Hebraism to Jewish Studies.* Johannes Buxtorf (1564-1629) and Hebrew Learning in the Seventeenth Century. 1996
69. BOLAND O.P., V. *Ideas in God according to Saint Thomas Aquinas.* Sources and Synthesis. 1996
70. LANGE, M.E. *Telling Tears in the English Renaissance.* 1996
71. CHRISTIANSON, G. and T.M. IZBICKI (eds.). *Nicholas of Cusa on Christ and the Church.* Essays in Memory of Chandler McCuskey Brooks for the American Cusanus Society. 1996
72. MALI, A. *Mystic in the New World.* Marie de l'Incarnation (1599-1672). 1996
73. VISSER, D. *Apocalypse as Utopian Expectation (800-1500).* The Apocalypse Commentary of Berengaudus of Ferrières and the Relationship between Exegesis, Liturgy and Iconography. 1996
74. O'ROURKE BOYLE, M. *Divine Domesticity.* Augustine of Thagaste to Teresa of Avila. 1997
75. PFIZENMAIER, T.C. *The Trinitarian Theology of Dr. Samuel Clarke (1675-1729).* Context, Sources, and Controversy. 1997
76. BERKVENS-STEVELINCK, C., J. ISRAEL and G.H.M. POSTHUMUS MEYJES (eds.). *The Emergence of Tolerance in the Dutch Republic.* 1997
77. HAYKIN, M.A.G. (ed.). *The Life and Thought of John Gill (1697-1771).* A Tercentennial Appreciation. 1997
78. KAISER, C.B. *Creational Theology and the History of Physical Science.* The Creationist Tradition from Basil to Bohr. 1997
79. LEES, J.T. *Anselm of Havelberg.* Deeds into Words in the Twelfth Century. 1997
80. WINTER, J.M. VAN. *Sources Concerning the Hospitallers of St John in the Netherlands, 14th-18th Centuries.* 1998

81. TIERNEY, B. *Foundations of the Conciliar Theory.* The Contribution of the Medieval Canonists from Gratian to the Great Schism. Enlarged New Edition. 1998
82. MIERNOWSKI, J. *Le Dieu Néant.* Théologies négatives à l'aube des temps modernes. 1998
83. HALVERSON, J.L. *Peter Aureol on Predestination.* A Challenge to Late Medieval Thought. 1998.
84. HOULISTON, V. (ed.). *Robert Persons, S.J.: The Christian Directory (1582).* The First Booke of the Christian Exercise, appertayning to Resolution. 1998
85. GRELL, O.P. (ed.). *Paracelsus.* The Man and His Reputation, His Ideas and Their Transformation. 1998
86. MAZZOLA, E. *The Pathology of the English Renaissance.* Sacred Remains and Holy Ghosts. 1998.
87. 88. MARSILIUS VON INGHEN. *Quaestiones super quattuor libros sententiarum.* Super Primum. Bearbeitet von M. Santos Noya. 2 Bände. I. Quaestiones 1-7. II. Quaestiones 8-21. 2000
89. FAUPEL-DREVS, K. *Vom rechten Gebrauch der Bilder im liturgischen Raum.* Mittelalterliche Funktions-bestimmungen bildender Kunst im *Rationale divinorum officiorum* des Durandus von Mende (1230/1-1296). 1999
90. KREY, P.D.W. and SMITH, L. (eds.). *Nicholas of Lyra.* the Senses of Scripture. 2000
92. OAKLEY, F. *Politics and Eternity.* Studies in the History of Medieval and Early-Modern Political Thought. 1999
93. PRYDS, D. *The Politics of Preaching.* Robert of Naples (1309-1343) and his Sermons. 2000
94. POSTHUMUS MEYJES, G.H.M. *Jean Gerson – Apostle of Unity.* His Church Politics and Ecclesiology. Translated by J.C. Grayson. 1999
95. BERG, J. VAN DEN. *Religious Currents and Cross-Currents.* Essays on Early Modern Protestantism and the Protestant Enlightenment. Edited by J. de Bruijn, P. Holtrop, and E. van der Wall. 1999
96. IZBICKI, T.M. and BELLITTO, C.M. (eds.). *Reform and Renewal in the Middle Ages and the Renaissance.* Studies in Honor of Louis Pascoe, S.J. 2000
97. KELLY, D. *The Conspiracy of Allusion.* Description, Rewriting, and Authorship from Macrobius to Medieval Romance. 1999
98. Marrone, S.P. *The Light of Thy Countenance.* Science and Knowledge of God in the Thirteenth Century. 2 volumes. 1. A Doctrine of Divine Illumination. 2. God at the Core of Cognition. 2001